INTERNATIONAL C(LIBRARY • FT MYERS

P9-DHA-238

Duane Champagne has been teaching at the University of California, Los Angeles, since 1984. In 1986, he became editor of the *American Indian Culture and Research Journal* and went on to be named associate professor in 1992.

Dr. Champagne is also the director of the UCLA American Indian Studies Center, which carries out research, conducts a master's degree program in American Indian studies, and publishes books for both academic and Indian communities.

Dr. Champagne received a postdoctoral award from the Rockefeller Foundation in 1982–83 and, during this time, completed fieldwork trips to the Tlingit of southeast Alaska and to the Northern Cheyenne in Montana.

Most of Dr. Champagne's writings focus on issues of social, cultural, and political change in American Indian societies as they adapted to European political, cultural, and economic incorporation. He has published in both the sociology and American Indian studies fields, including his books *The Native North American Almanac* (1993), *American Indian Societies: Strategies and Conditions of Political and Cultural Survival* (1989) and *Social Order and Political Change: Constitutional Governments Among the Cherokee, the Choctaw, the Chickasaw, and the Creek* (1992).

Dennis Banks, a Native leader, teacher, lecturer, activist, and author, is co-founder of the American Indian Movement (AIM). In addition to leading and organizing sacred runs, he stays involved in American Indian issues and travels around the world lecturing, teaching Native American traditions, and sharing his experiences.

Native America

Portrait of the Peoples

Brother,

    When you first came to this island

    you were as children, in need of food and shelter,

    and we, a great and mighty nation.

    But we took you by the hand

    and we planted you and watered you

    and you grew to be a great oak,

    we a mere sapling in comparison.

    Now we are the children

    (in need of food and shelter).

An opening speech often used by Northeastern Indian leaders at conferences with Europeans during the early colonial period.

INTERNATIONAL COLLEGE
LIBRARY • FT MYERS

Native America

Portrait of the Peoples

Duane Champagne

Foreword by
Dennis Banks

VISIBLE INK PRESS

DETROIT • LONDON • WASHINGTON, D.C.

Native America: *Portrait of the Peoples*

Duane Champagne, Editor
Troy Johnson, Associate Editor
Judith St. George, Production Editor
Stephen Lehmer, Photography Editor
Viviana Quintero, Assistant Editor
Roselle Kipp, Production Assistant

Copyright © 1994 by Visible Ink Press

Cover painting "Sunset in Memoriam" by Woodrow (Woody) Wilson Crumbo:
  The Philbrook Museum of Art, Tulsa, Oklahoma
Back cover painting "The Blessing of the Deer Dancer" by Gilbert Benjamin Atencio:
  The Philbrook Museum of Art, Tulsa, Oklahoma

Native America: Portrait of the Peoples is a creative work fully protected by all applicable copyright laws, as well as by misappropriation, trade secret, unfair competition, and other applicable laws. The editors of this work have added value to the underlying factual information herein through one or more of the following: unique and original selection, coordination, expression, arrangement, and classification of the information.

No part of this book may be reproduced in any form without permission in writing from the publisher, except by a reviewer who wishes to quote brief passages in connection with a review written for inclusion in a magazine or newspaper.

All rights to this publication will be vigorously defended.

Published by Visible Ink Press™
a division of Gale Research Inc.
835 Penobscot Building
Detroit, MI 48226-4094

Visible Ink Press is a trademark of Gale Research Inc.

Most Visible Ink Press books are available at special quantity discounts when purchased in bulk by corporations, organizations, or groups. Customized printings, special imprints, messages, and excerpts can be produced to meet your needs. For more information, contact Special Markets Manager, Gale Research Inc., 835 Penobscot Bldg., Detroit, MI 48226. Or call 1-800-877-4253, extension 1033.

ISBN 0-8103-9452-9
Printed in the United States of America
All rights reserved

10 9 8 7 6 5 4 3 2 1

CONTENTS

Foreword
by Dennis Banks,
Native Activist
xi

Introduction
xv

Board of Advisors
xvii

Contributors
xix

♦ *Native Nations of the United States and Canada*

Major Native Nations
xxvii

♦ *U.S. Indian Activist Movements*   ♦ *Canadian Native Activist Movements*   ♦ *Biographies*

Activism
1

♦ *Introduction to Chapters 1–10*

Major Culture Areas
51

♦ *The Iroquoian Peoples*   ♦ *Contemporary Haudenosaunee Cultural Restoration*   ♦ *Chippewa Fishing and Treaty Rights in Michigan, Wisconsin, and Minnesota*   ♦ *Termination and the Menominee Nation of Wisconsin*   ♦ *Maine Indian Claims*   ♦ *Contemporary Connecticut Indian Land Claims*   ♦ *Claims by Massachusetts Indians in the Last Generation*   ♦ *Recent New York Indian Land Claims* ♦ *Current Narragansett Indian Claims*   ♦ *Analysis of Intercourse Act Claims in the Northeast*   ♦ *Conclusion*   ♦ *Biographies*

Native Peoples of
the Northeast
55

Native Peoples of the Southeast
93

♦ *The Catawba* ♦ *The Cherokee* ♦ *The Creek* ♦ *The Seminole* ♦ *The Choctaw* ♦ *The Chickasaw* ♦ *Conclusion* ♦ *Biographies*

Native Peoples of the Southwest
129

♦ *The Apache* ♦ *The Navajo Nation* ♦ *The Hopi* ♦ *The Pueblo Villages of New Mexico* ♦ *The Future* ♦ *Biographies*

Native Peoples of the Northern Plains
161

♦ *The Sioux* ♦ *The Cheyenne* ♦ *The Blackfeet* ♦ *The Crow* ♦ *The Pawnee* ♦ *The Ponca* ♦ *The Shoshoni* ♦ *The Arapaho* ♦ *The Cree* ♦ *The Omaha* ♦ *Historical Precedents* ♦ *Early Reservation Economic Pursuits* ♦ *Land Allotment* ♦ *The Reservation New Deal* ♦ *The Post-War Experience* ♦ *Biographies*

Native Peoples of the Northwest Coast
195

♦ *Tribal Distribution* ♦ *The Tlingit* ♦ *The Haida* ♦ *The Tsimshian* ♦ *The Haisla* ♦ *The Haihais* ♦ *The Bella Bella* ♦ *The Owekeeno* ♦ *The Kwakiutl* ♦ *The Nuu-Chah-Nulth* ♦ *The Coast Salish* ♦ *The Chinook* ♦ *The Makah* ♦ *The Annual Cycle of Economic Subsistence* ♦ *Housing* ♦ *Food Resources* ♦ *Culture* ♦ *European Contact* ♦ *Contemporary Life* ♦ *Biographies*

Native Peoples of Alaska
215

♦ *Traditional Life among the Aleut, Yupik, Inuit, Tlingit, Haida, and Athapascan* ♦ *Russian Colonialism* ♦ *American Colonialism* ♦ *The Land Claims Movement* ♦ *Social and Economic Profile of Alaska Natives* ♦ *Subsistence* ♦ *Economic Development* ♦ *Tribal Sovereignty* ♦ *Biographies*

Native Peoples of Oklahoma
237

♦ *The Choctaw* ♦ *The Chickasaw* ♦ *The Creek* ♦ *The Cherokee* ♦ *The Seminole* ♦ *The Quapaw* ♦ *The Seneca* ♦ *The Shawnee* ♦ *The Comanche* ♦ *The Kiowa* ♦ *The Cheyenne* ♦ *The Caddo* ♦ *The Ponca* ♦ *The Apache* ♦ *The Peoria* ♦ *The Modoc* ♦ *The Ottawa* ♦ *The Wyandot* ♦ *The Osage* ♦ *The Kaw* ♦ *The Pawnee* ♦ *The Tonkawa* ♦ *The Oto* ♦ *The Missouri* ♦ *The Sac and Fox* ♦ *The Iowa* ♦ *The Kickapoo* ♦ *The Potawatomi* ♦ *The Wichita* ♦ *Biographies*

♦ *The Bannock* ♦ *The Shoshoni* ♦ *The Flathead* ♦ *The Spokane* ♦ *The Wishram* ♦ *The Yakima* ♦ *The Nez Percé* ♦ *The Cayuse* ♦ *The Okanogan* ♦ *The Wanapum* ♦ *The Walla Walla* ♦ *The Wasco* ♦ *The Clackamus* ♦ *The Tenino* ♦ *The Skin* ♦ *The Cathlapotle* ♦ *The Wah Kla Kum* ♦ *The Cathlamet* ♦ *The Clatsop* ♦ *The Sanpoil* ♦ *The Nespelem* ♦ *The Colville* ♦ *The Umatilla* ♦ *The Palouse* ♦ *Biographies*

Native Peoples of the Plateau, Great Basin, and Rocky Mountains
273

♦ *The Yuman* ♦ *The Yokut* ♦ *The Miwok* ♦ *Chumash* ♦ *The Pomo* ♦ *The Cahuilla* ♦ *The Mohave* ♦ *The Gabrielino* ♦ *The Kumeyaay* ♦ *The Hupa* ♦ *The Modoc* ♦ *The Patwin* ♦ *European Contact* ♦ *Spanish Colonization* ♦ *Termination* ♦ *Cultural Revitalization* ♦ *Tribal Recognition* ♦ *Biographies*

Native Peoples of California
301

♦ *Aboriginal Peoples: A Profile* ♦ *The Indians* ♦ *The Inuit* ♦ *The Métis* ♦ *The Changing Status of Canada's Aboriginal Peoples* ♦ *Aboriginal Peoples in the Constitutional Forum* ♦ *Aboriginal Peoples in the Legislative, Administrative, and Judicial Arenas* ♦ *Toward the Future* ♦ *Biographies*

The Canadian Natives
331

♦ *Classification* ♦ *Phyla and Families* ♦ *Language Contact* ♦ *Types of Language Structure* ♦ *Geographical Areas and Language Areas* ♦ *Language and Culture* ♦ *Traditional Literature* ♦ *Writing Systems* ♦ *Language Maintenance*

Native North American Languages
397

♦ *Native American Religions: Creating through Cosmic Give and Take* ♦ *Pluralistic Religious Beliefs* ♦ *Biographies*

Religion
441

♦ *Traditional Indian Health Practices and Cultural Views*

Health
525

♦ *Native Art in North America* ♦ *Traditional and Contemporary Ceremonies, Rituals, Festivals, Music, and Dance* ♦ *Native North American Visual Arts* ♦ *Biographies* ♦ *Exhibitors of Contemporary Native Arts* ♦ *American Indian Cultural Events* ♦ *American Indian Art Markets and Fairs*

Arts
549

Literature
665
♦ *Oral Literature*   ♦ *Life Histories and Autobiographies*   ♦ *Fiction and Poetry*   ♦ *Biographies*

Media
701
♦ *American Indian Tribes in the Media Age*   ♦ *Indians in Film and Theater*   ♦ *Biographies*   ♦ *U.S. and Canada Press*   ♦ *Radio, Television, and Theater Organizations*

Index
759

Illustrations
775

Afterword by Suzan Shown Harjo, Native Activist
784

Foreword

Dennis Banks, also known as **Nowa-cumig**

Although almanacs exist for many many subjects, until now none have really come close to providing any meaningful information about Native People. *Native America: Portrait of the Peoples* has involved Native writers and photographers in working towards the compilation of Native facts, figures, names, and events that constitute an American Indian Almanac.

I am grateful that Native people have been contributors to this project. No longer will we have to sift through non-Indian writings looking for shreds of the truth. Why we took so long to do this, I don't know, but I welcome the effort. Non-Indian writers tend to insert their versions of what they perceive to be the truth. Sadly, we Native People let them roll along without challenge, until the non-Indians writing about Native People now number in the thousands. And they seem to want to romanticize how we rode into history.

Too much writing about Native People has been like the Hollywood movies, with epilogues that conclude, "and so the Indian wars ended, and the Indians would never again return to their position of power," as if we Indian People only did war. But some efforts to correct the stereotype are finally beginning to bear fruit. We do see Native People, both in television and movies, who have roles with character. Floyd "Red Crow" Westerman has not only been educating the public for several decades through his album *Custer Died for Your Sins,* but he recently moved into Hollywood with performances in many films, including *Dances with Wolves.* That Kevin Costner production won seven Academy Awards, including Best Picture of 1990. Red Crow recently signed to appear in a weekly television series, *Walker, Texas Ranger,* with Chuck Norris. What we can't forget is that Hollywood doesn't have a conscience about history, nor does it care who it defames along the way. We Native People therefore must always be on the alert for a return of the old-style westerns that helped promote the silver-screen stereotypes of the marauding Indian. It is now on our shoulders to assume a more active role in film production, direction, and script writing. We must tell our own stories.

In 1970 when the movie *A Man Called Horse* was being released around the country, the American Indian Movement (AIM) called for a national boycott against the film, protesting the degradation of our culture through Hollywood and its films. After twelve weeks, *Horse* ended its public showings. But AIM was formed to do more than protest cultural stereotyping.

When AIM was founded on July 28, 1968, in Minneapolis, Minnesota, the living conditions we found ourselves in were deplorable. It wasn't that we didn't know there was racism in the cities. It was how racism forced us into squalid slum tenement buildings, closed doors to job opportunities, and fostered racist laws, jails, courts, and prisons. Beginning with our founding meeting, we immediately set out to bring about change in those institutions of public concern: housing, education, employment, welfare, and the courts.

Because we took to the streets and began demonstrating with signs, placards, and bullhorns, the media termed us militants, activists, and outsiders. Not once did they admit to the many wrongs we faced daily. Not once did the Minneapolis and St. Paul papers run editorials agreeing with our positions. But this negative reporting didn't stop our campaign to challenge the employment picture of Native People nor to attack the slum housing conditions, the de-humanizing handling of Native People on welfare, the racist and discriminatory practices in the police department, sheriff's department, courts, and prison system. Fifty percent of the 1,000 inmates in Minnesota prisons were Native People, yet the ratio of Native People living in Minnesota was (like now) only one percent. It was shameful.

In 1971 we opened our first Native Peoples' survival school in Minneapolis. That same year we founded—with joint efforts of the black community—the Legal Rights Center. A welfare rights and reform committee was established, as well as a jobs and jobs-training task force. We began monitoring the police arrests through our AIM Patrol and assigned observers to the city, county, and state courts. We notified prison officials of our campaign and formed a Prison Watch to notify us of Native inmate traffic. We began to move and results began to emerge. AIM never let up. Never will.

Today, because of AIM, more than 20,000 Native People have received legal assistance through the Legal Rights Center. The job training turned into the Indian Industrialization Center, which has trained more than 5,000 Native People and has placed over 8,000 people into jobs still being held. Native People are employed by the courts and the police. The prisons are no longer disproportionately crowded with Native People. Yes, we still have many social problems like alcoholism, drug abuse, and gang violence. And like the 1960s, we as Native People must band together, as parents, grandparents, and teachers, to provide solutions to these problems and provide direction for the future. This I see is the most pressing issue of our time: the social destruction of our community. Family strength is giving way to street values, community gatherings are now either funerals or wakes, and parental guidance is being replaced by police counselors. Is this our future? No, it isn't. And I know you will join me as I say *never* to that way of life.

AIM has worked night and day to bring about much-needed change. In order to bring about meaningful change, we also have to educate and re-educate ourselves. That's why I call upon Native People to share their information with each other. This

Portrait will certainly be one of many ways to do that. After all, isn't that what we Native People are about? And isn't that a purpose in our activities? I believe sharing is perhaps the last real action we have to help each other. When our children are becoming parents as children; when our children start roaming in gangs or packs; when our children challenge the very foundation of what being Indian is; then I believe we must not only share each other's cries for help but we must rush to defend that heritage that was handed down to us. Seven generations ago our ancestors believed in and thought about us. It is in these beliefs that we find our spiritual foundation. And that foundation must never be attacked.

An eagle is an eagle, still practicing the ways of its ancestors, long since gone. The beaver still makes its home along the streams and creeks of our land. The buffalo still teaches its young and the salmon still travels the thousands of miles to spawn its future generations. If we Native People are to survive as a cultural species, then we must follow the way of our ancestors. We must continue to sing the songs and have ceremonies to welcome each day. Like the eagle and buffalo, we must never abandon our old ways. Those ways have been good to us and they will provide us with direction for our future generations. Like an eagle flying high, we are who we are. Still strong!

Our land struggle will always be going on, and we must always support those issues related to our lands. If, however, we cannot rise to the occasion of developing ourselves for the land, then perhaps we must back up and face the struggle of social behavior head on. In the end that's what we must ultimately do. Face the Struggle and Accept the Challenge.

Once we do that, who cares what they call us?

INTRODUCTION

Native America: Portrait of the Peoples is an abridged version of the massive *Native North American Almanac*, published in 1994. It captures the scope and Native voice of the *Almanac* and carries forward nearly two hundred inspiring illustrations and photographs, many of which were taken by Native photographers. Like its source, *Native America* presents an overview of the history of Native peoples in North America and provides new and probing perspectives not found elsewhere.

Many books on Native Americans provide little information about contemporary life, leaving Native peoples stranded in the nineteenth century. Consequently, accurate, accessible, and systematic information about contemporary Native cultures and issues is hard to come by. *Portrait of the Peoples* is both a wide-ranging historical reference and a concise portrait of Native America today, reflecting cultural aspirations and identities. *Portrait of the Peoples,* with its emphasis on Native peoples as communities or nations, also includes extensive information on Canadian Natives, who often play a greater role in Canadian constitutional issues and politics than do Native peoples in the United States.

Each chapter within *Native America* is composed of pieces written by experts engaged in Native life and issues. An effort has been made to include a diversity of points of view, and as many Native voices as possible. Seventeen chapters cover current and historical issues surrounding Native history and culture, protest movements, language, religion, health practices, art, literature, and media. Biographies of prominent historical figures and today's leaders are included in fifteen chapters. An extensive index provides access to the people, places, and events significant in Native North America.

With energy, range, and a clear, detailed vision of Native cultures, issues, and history, *Portrait of the Peoples* captures the epic story of Native America yesterday and today. It carefully articulates the values, struggles, triumphs, and spirit of Native communities, creating a powerful, fact-based portrait of the peoples.

Acknowledgments   The editor gratefully acknowledges the contributions of the advisors, associate and assistant editors, writers, copy editors, and designers who assisted in developing and producing *Native America*. This edition was developed for Visible Ink Press by Martin Connors and Julie Winklepleck. Art Chartow designed the cover and Mark Howell the pages. Keith Reed sought permissions. Typesetting was managed by Judith St. George, and Stephen Lehmer served as photography editor; they both deserve special thanks for their conscientious efforts. A note of appreciation, as well, to Dennis Banks for his foreword and to the Philbrook Museum of Art for their fine images.

Duane Champagne

BOARD OF ADVISORS

John Aubrey
Librarian, The Newberry Library, Chicago, Illinois

Cheryl Metoyer-Duran
Assistant Professor, Graduate School of Library and
Information Science, University of California, Los Angeles

G. Edward Evans
University Librarian, Loyola Marymount University, Los
Angeles

Hanay Geiogamah
Adjunct Professor of Theater, University of California, Los
Angeles

Carole Goldberg-Ambrose
Professor of Law, University of California, Los Angeles

Vee Salabiye
Librarian, American Indian Studies Center, University of
California, Los Angeles

CONTRIBUTORS

Frances Abele
School of Public Administration, Carleton University, Ottawa, Ontario, Canada

Angela Aleiss
American Indian Studies Center, University of California, Los Angeles

Robert Appleford
Graduate Centre for the Study of Drama, University of Toronto, Toronto, Ontario, Canada

Janet Berlo
Department of Art History, Washington University, St. Louis, Missouri

Daniel Boxberger
Department of Anthropology, Western Washington University, Bellingham, Washington

William Bright
Department of Linguistics, University of Colorado, Boulder

Paola Carini
English Department, University of California, Los Angeles

Edward Castillo
Native American Studies, Sonoma State University, Rohnert Park, California

Katherine Beaty Chiste
Department of Social Sciences, University of Lethbridge, Lethbridge, Alberta, Canada

Richmond Clow
Native American Studies, University of Montana, Missoula

James Coulon
Coulon, Ink., San Diego, California

Hanay Geiogamah
Theater Department, University of California, Los Angeles

Donald Grinde
History Department, California Polytechnic State University, San Luis Obispo

Charlotte Heth
Department of Ethnomusicology, University of California, Los Angeles

Jennie Joe
Native American Research and Training Center, University of Arizona, Tucson

Richard Keeling
Ethnomusicology Department, University of California, Los Angeles

J. Anthony Long
Department of Political Science, University of Lethbridge, Lethbridge, Alberta, Canada

David C. Maas
Department of Political Science, University of Alaska, Anchorage

Patrick Macklem
Assistant Professor, Faculty of Law, University of Toronto, Toronto, Ontario, Canada

Kenneth M. Morrison
Religious Studies, Arizona State University, Tempe

James O'Donnell III
Department of History, Marietta College, Marietta, Ohio

Roxanne Dunbar Ortiz
Department of History, California State University, Hayward

Kathryn W. Shanley
Department of English, Cornell University, Ithaca, New York

Rennard Strickland
School of Law, University of Oklahoma, Norman

Steve Talbot
Department of Sociology and Anthropology, San Joaquin College, Stockton, California

Clifford Trafzer
Department of Ethnic Studies, University of California, Riverside

Joan Vastokas
Department of Anthropology, Trent University, Peterborough, Ontario, Canada

Native America

America

Portrait of the Peoples

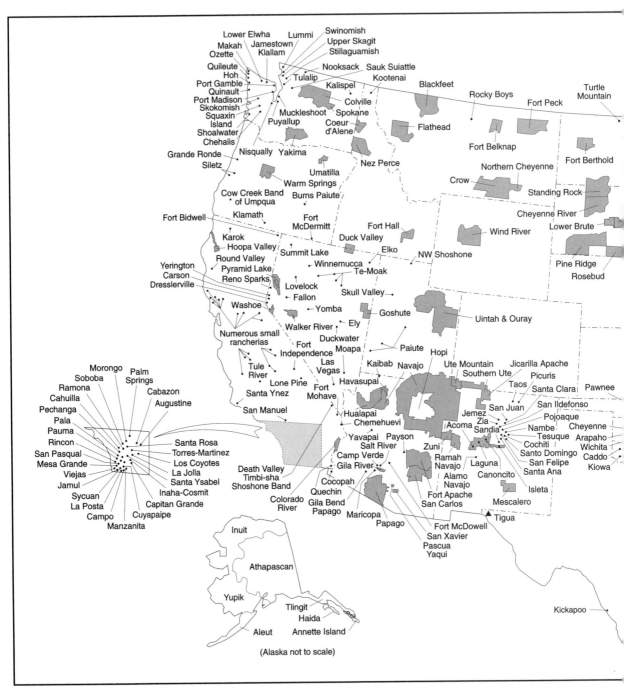

State and Federally Recognized

Federal Indian Reservations
• Federal Indian Reservations
▲ State Indian Reservations

Micmac
Houlton Maliseet
Indian Township
Bois Forte
Deer Creek
Vermillion
Lake
Pennocook
Pleasant Point
Red Lake
Red Cliff
Bad River
Grand
Portage
Ganienkeh
Penobscot
Devils
Lake
L'Anse
Lac Vieux
Desert
Hannahville
St. Regis
Nipmuk-
Hassanamisko
White Earth
Leech Lake
Bay Mills
Abnaki
Sisseton
Fond
du Lac
Sault Ste Marie
Oneida
Ontonagon
Grand Traverse
Onondaga
Wampanoag
Sandy Lake
Mille Lacs
Lac du
Flambeau
Sokaogan Chippewa
Tonawanda
Shagticoke
Crow
Creek
St. Croix
Lac Courte-Oreilles
Potawatomi
Tuscarora
Paugusett
Narragansett
Upper Sioux
andreau
Shakopee
Prairie
Island
Oneida
Oil Springs
Mashantucket
Pequot
Lower Sioux
Menominee
Allegheny
Paucatuck
Pequot
Yankton
Winnebago
Stockbridge-
Munsee
Cattaraugus
Shinnecock
Santee
Sioux
Winnebago
Isabella
Poosepatuck
Omaha
Potawatomi
Sac and Fox
Iowa
Mattaponi
Pamunkey
Kickapoo
otawatomi
Peoria
Quapaw
onkawa
Shawnee
Ottawa
onca
Kaw
Wyandot
oe
Osage
Seneca Cayuga
Cherokee
E. Shawnee
Miami
Modoc
Catawba
Cherokee
Creek
Seminole
owa
Choctaw
Chickasaw
Shawnee
Mississippi
Choctaw
Potawatomi
Sac and Fox
Coushatta
Poarch Creek
Kickapoo
Alabama-Coushatta
Tunica-Biloxi
Chitimacha
Brighton
Seminole
Big Cypress
Seminole
Dania
Miccosukee

U.S. Indian Reservations

Canadian Native

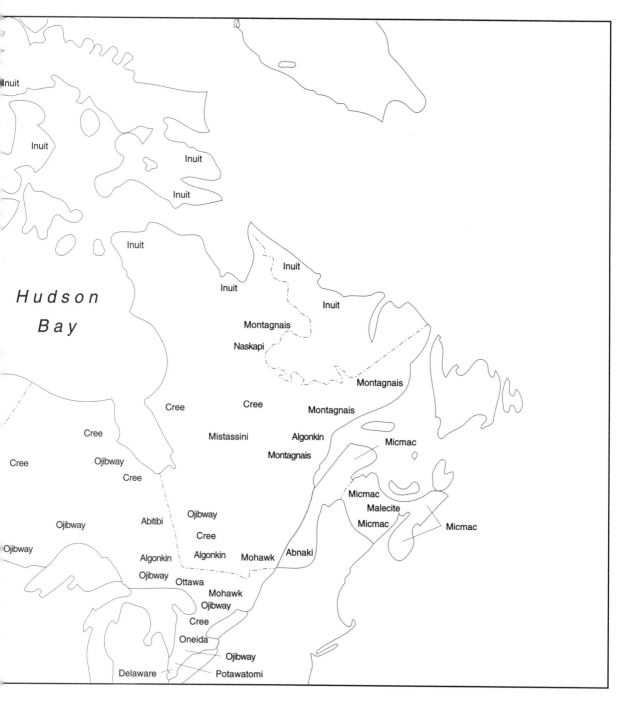

Inuit

Inuit

Inuit

Inuit

Inuit

Inuit

Inuit

Inuit

Inuit

Inuit

Hudson Bay

Montagnais

Naskapi

Montagnais

Cree

Cree

Montagnais

Cree

Cree

Mistassini

Algonkin

Micmac

Cree

Montagnais

Ojibway

Cree

Micmac

Malecite

Ojibway

Abitibi

Ojibway

Micmac

Micmac

Cree

Ojibway

Algonkin

Algonkin

Mohawk

Abnaki

Ojibway

Algonkin

Ojibway

Ottawa

Mohawk

Ojibway

Cree

Oneida

Ojibway

Delaware

Potawatomi

Culture Groups

*M*ajor Native Nations

Northeast

Abenaki
Brotherton
Cayuga
Chickahominy
Chippewa (Ojibway)
Fox
Huron
Maliseet
Mattaponi
Menominee
Miami
Mohawk
Mohegan
Montauk
Nanticoke
Narragansett
Nipmuc-Hassanamisco
Oneida
Onondaga
Ottawa

Pamunkey
Passamaquoddy
Paugusset
Penobscot
Pequot
Piscataway
Poosepatuck
Potawatomi
Rappahanock
Sauk
Schaghticoke
Seneca
Shawnee
Shinnecock
Sioux
Stockbridge-Munsee
Tuscarora
Wampanoag
Winnebago

Southeast

Alabama
Biloxi

Catawba
Cherokee (Eastern)

Chitimacha
Choctaw (Mississippi)
Coharie
Coushatta
Creek
Edisto
Haliwa
Houma

Lumbee
Miccosukee
Santee
Saponi
Seminole
Texas Kickapoo
Tunica
Waccamaw

Oklahoma

Apache
Caddo
Cherokee
Cheyenne-Arapaho
Chickasaw
Choctaw
Comanche
Creek
Delaware
Iowa
Kaw
Kickapoo
Kiowa
Miami
Modoc

Osage
Otoe-Missouri
Ottawa
Pawnee
Peoria
Ponca
Potawatomi
Quapaw
Sac and Fox
Seminole
Seneca-Cayuga
Shawnee
Tonkawa
Wichita
Wyandotte

Plains

Arikara
Assiniboine
Blackfeet
Cheyenne
Chippewa
Crow
Delaware
Gros Ventre
Hidatsa
Iowa

Kickapoo
Mandan
Omaha
Plains Ojibwa
Potawatomi
Sac and Fox
Sioux
Winnebago
Wyandotte

Rocky Mountain Area

Arapaho
Bannock
Cayuse
Coeur d'Alene
Confederated Tribes of Colville

Flathead
Gosiute
Kalispel
Klamath
Kootenai

Nespelem
Nez Percé
Paiute (Northern)
Sanpoil
Shoshoni (Northern)
Spokane
Umatilla

Ute
Walla Walla
Warm Springs
Wasco
Washo
Yakima

Apache
Chemehuevi
Havasupai
Hopi
Hualapai
Mohave
Maricopa
Navajo

Paiute
Pima
Pueblo
Tohono O'Odham (Papago)
Yaqui
Yavapai
Yuma
Zuni

Southwest

Achumawi
Atsugewi
Cahuilla
Cupeño
Diegueño
Gabrieliño
Hupa
Karok
Luiseño
Maidu
Miwok
Mohave
Mono
Ohlone

Paiute
Patwin
Pomo
Serrano
Shasta
Shoshoni (Western)
Tolowa
Washo
Wintu
Wiyot
Yana
Yokuts
Yuki
Yurok

California

Bella Bella
Bella Coola
Chehalis
Chinook
Clallam
Coos
Coquille
Gitksan
Haida

Heiltsuk
Hoh
Kalapuya
Kwakiutl
Lillooet
Lummi
Makah
Molala
Muckleshoot

Northwest Coast

Nisgha
Nisqually
Nooksack
Nootka
Puyallup
Quileute
Quinault
Rogue River
Sauk-Suiattle
Shasta
Siletz
Siuslaw
Skagit

Skokomish
Snohomish
Squaxin Island
Stillaguamish
Suquamish
Swinomish
Tillamook
Tlingit
Tsimshian
Tulalip
Twana
Umpqua
Wishram

Alaska

Ahtena
Aleut
Athapascan
Eyak
Haida

Inuit
Tlingit
Tsimshian
Yupik

CANADA ✦ ✦ ✦ ✦ ✦ ✦ ✦ ✦ ✦ ✦ ✦ ✦ ✦ ✦ ✦ ✦ ✦

Abenaki
Algonquin
Assiniboine
Beaver
Bella Bella
Bella Coola
Blackfoot
Blood
Carrier
Chilcotin
Chipewyan
Chippewa (Ojibway)
Comox
Cowichan
Cree
Dakota
Dogrib

Gitksan
Gros Ventre
Haida
Haisla
Hare
Heiltsuk
Huron
Inuit
Kootenay
Kutchin
Kwakiutl
Lillooet
Loucheux
Maliseet
Micmac
Mohawk
Montagnais

Nahani
Naskapi
Nisgha
Nootka
Ntlakyapamuk
Okanagon
Potawatomi
Sarsi

Sekani
Shuswap
Slave
Songhees
Squamish
Tagish
Tahltan
Tsimshian

Activism

U.S. INDIAN ACTIVIST MOVEMENTS ♦ ♦ ♦ ♦ ♦ ♦ ♦ ♦ ♦ ♦ ♦

In the centuries since European contact American Indians have been engaged in a struggle to survive as distinct social and cultural communities with political and economic rights within American society. They have engaged in the fight for tribal rights and survival rights on many fronts: legally, in the courtrooms and chambers of government throughout American history; militarily, on eighteenth and nineteenth century battlefields; and more recently, politically, in the streets of cities and on reservations. These battles have met with great resistance as American political and military might was directed against Indian efforts to resist forced removal, secure treaty rights, and enforce tribal rights and sovereignty.

Unlike other minority groups in the United States, American Indians have a special legal relationship with the federal government by virtue of more than 400 treaties and agreements between the United States government and hundreds of Indian societies. As a result of this treaty relationship, American Indian struggles for survival and equality have taken place in two legal forums, one of which—the domain of federal Indian law—is unique to Native Americans and the other of which—local, state, and federal law—is shared by all other Americans.

Since the activities of American Indian advocacy groups have been played out in both of these arenas, their struggles for survival and equality are complex. For instance, under treaties and federal Indian law, Native American communities have the right to maintain law and order on reservations. However, these federally-based tribal rights often conflict with local, state, and other federal laws. Thus tribal law and jurisdiction on reservations can be overridden in the case of "major" crimes (such as arson, burglary, or murder) or if non-Indians or Indians from other tribes are involved. Similarly, many reservation community development projects face regulations and restrictions from various levels of government, and suffer delays resulting from jurisdictional disputes involving tribal, state, and federal governments. For instance, legal confusion about bingo and casino gambling enterprises on reservations required the passage of federal legislation in 1988 (the Indian Gaming Regulatory Act) in order to clarify Indian tribes' rights to pursue these development projects. Despite this legislation, sovereign reservation communities must still negotiate with state governments.

Native Americans have had to travel a varied legal and political terrain in their quest for tribal survival. Their strategies for action reflect the diversity of this legal landscape. Thus, American Indians and their supporters have responded in many ways to frequent and diverse historical and contemporary challenges to Indian rights. During the twentieth century, the two major strategies to secure and protect Native American rights have centered on organization and activism.

American Indian Political Advocacy Organizations

Early Indian Rights Organizations

The importance of law in American society and the complexity of American Indian legal affairs, have placed organizations concerned with matters of law in a prominent role in the struggle for Indian legal rights in the United States. Among the earliest organizations dedicated to protect and further the rights and interests of Native Americans, were the Women's National Indian Association, founded in 1879, and the Indian

Rights Association, founded in 1882. The Indian Rights Association remains as the oldest still-active organization of its kind in the United States. Founded in Philadelphia by Quakers and other Christian reformers, the Indian Rights Association was followed by a number of early Indian rights organizations, such as the Lake Mohonk Conference of the Friends of the Indian, founded in 1883, the Society of American Indians, founded by six Native Americans in 1911, and the American Indian Defense Association, founded by John Collier in 1923. While these early organizations varied in their goals and their emphasis on preserving indigenous cultures and institutions, their agendas for reform tended to combine concern for the rights of tribes with an orientation toward assimilating American Indians into the larger Euro-American culture. Their tactics were moderate: they employed lobbying, education, social programs, and legal defense.

The Quaker City banquet of the Society of American Indians. Hotel Walton, February 14, 1914.

Indian Advocacy after World War II

The post-Second World War period witnessed a transformation in the composition and focus of American Indian political advocacy organizations. Beginning with the establishment of the National Congress of American Indians (NCAI) in 1944, the membership of advocacy organizations tended to be exclusively or primarily Indian, and the focus shifted from assimilation to tribal sovereignty and self-determination. One reason for this shift toward indigenous membership and tribal rights was the Second World War. Native American veterans returning from World War II battlefields and American Indian workers returning from labor force participation in wartime industries returned to the reservation with a new view of the place of the Indian in American society. This view was based on Native American contributions to the war effort. Furthermore, the American Indian urban population was growing, providing an increasingly educated, intertribal point of view on Indian affairs.

These more activist groups spoke in a strong voice for Indian rights and tribal sovereignty. For instance, the NCAI was founded by representatives from Indian tribes—many of whom were World War II veterans—with the goal of representing tribal interests, especially before Congress and the Bureau of Indian Affairs. Similarly, another important pan-Indian organization, the National Indian Youth Council (NIYC), which was established following the NCAI-University of Chicago-sponsored Chicago Indian Conference in 1961, had a membership composed mainly of urban Indians concerned with issues involving both reservation and non-reservation groups.

While the National Indian Youth Council shared the NCAI's goals of defending and representing the interests of the Indian community, it was different from the NCAI in two ways: it had a younger membership and employed a more activist repertoire of tactics to achieve its goals. The NIYC was a reflection of its time. That time was the Civil Rights era in American history, an era of protest and activism. The political times were also reflected in another influential urban Indian activist organization, the American Indian

Movement (AIM), founded in Minneapolis in 1968. The NIYC and AIM formed the organizational backbone of the period of greatest Indian activism in the twentieth century. Their combined activities along with those of other American Indian protesters came to be known as the Red Power Movement (discussed below).

Native American Organizational Growth During the 1960s

The 1960s reform era in American politics was sparked by the Civil Rights movement, and saw a widespread organizational and activist response in American Indian communities. The National Indian Youth Council and the American Indian Movement were part of a great proliferation of organizations on reservations and in cities. Dozens of American Indian newspapers and periodicals were established during the late 1960s and 1970s, including the American Indian Historical Society's *The Indian Historian* and *Wassaja*, the National Indian Youth Council's *ABC: Americans Before Columbus*, and the influential *Akwesasne Notes*, published by the Mohawk Nation. These periodicals joined the ranks of older, more established newspapers and journals such as the *Navajo Times* and the *Indian Leader*, published by Haskell Indian Junior College in Kansas.

In addition to the growth in publications, Native American history and culture became a topic of serious study during the 1960s, and this new academic focus was reflected in educational institutions. American Indian Studies centers were established at a number of universities around the United States, and, in the decade following the 1968 founding of Navajo Community College, the first tribally controlled institution, nearly two dozen reservation community colleges were established.

A number of important legal, political, and economic national organizations were also established during this period. In addition to the National Indian Youth Council (founded in 1961) and the American Indian Movement (founded in 1968), were the National Indian Education Association (founded in 1969), the Native American Rights Fund (founded in 1970), the National Tribal

Chairman's Association (founded in 1971), and the Council of Energy Resource Tribes (founded in 1975).

These organizations provided lines of communication among American Indian communities and represented Indian interests at various levels of government. National organizations with members from different Indian tribes and communities contributed to a growing awareness of common problems and interests shared by many tribes as well as by the growing urban Indian population. By 1960, 28 percent of American Indians lived in urban areas. This figure rose to 44 percent in 1970, reached 50 percent in 1980, and by 1990 more than half of American Indians lived in cities. The growth of the urban Indian population, particularly during the period from 1960 to 1980, contributed to the emergence of a national Indian protest movement during the late 1960s: the Red Power Movement.

American Indian
Activist Movements

Early Indian Movements

Despite the prominence of Red Power activism during the 1960s and 1970s, American Indian protest activity and collective action stretches back to the point of European contact. Despite similarities to later movements, early Indian collective action was likely not to be seen as protest, but rather, tended to be defined as "war." One important type of historical tribal collective action took the form of "revitalization" movements. These were movements that looked toward an end to white rule and a return to pre-Columbian Indian life. Revitalization movements tended to have an important religious or spiritual dimension, and were often inspired or led by prophets, such as Handsome Lake of the Seneca, Tenskwatawa of the Shawnee, Smohalla of the Columbia River Shahaptan, Kenekuk of the Kickapoo, or Wodziwob and Wovoka of the Paiute.

Perhaps the best known of the primarily nineteenth century movements were the Handsome Lake movement, which actually began in 1799, and the two waves of the Ghost Dance movement, which began in 1869 and continued in 1889. While the Handsome Lake movement was limited mainly to the Seneca and other Iroquois tribes, the first Ghost Dance movement involved a number of

Great Basin and West Coast tribes, and the second, larger Ghost Dance movement spread east to include many Plains tribes as well.

The Handsome Lake movement emphasized the importance of maintaining strong traditional families, tribal structures, and land, and it permitted some accommodation to U.S. culture and government. The Ghost Dance movements, on the other hand, took a much more critical stance toward whites, blaming the European invasion and the Americans for the miserable state of affairs on Indian reservations and for the destruction of traditional Indian ways of life. Further, Ghost Dance teachings predicted the disappearance of non-Indian settlers and a return to life as it had been before the Europeans came.

Unfortunately, the Ghost Dance movement also differed from the Handsome Lake movement in the response it received from the American government. The most infamous instance was the massacre of 146 Indian men, women, and children by U.S. Seventh Cavalry troops at Wounded Knee, South Dakota, in December, 1890. The Ghost Dance indictment of Euro-American rule had been interpreted as a threat by the American military. The movement ended in the early 1890s with the American Indian population confined to the reservations.

Twentieth Century American Indian Protest before Red Power

The first decades of the twentieth century saw little Indian protest as the tribes languished on reservations, far removed from centers of power, their energies focused on day-to-day survival. There was, however, some activism particularly that organized by the Indian Defense League of America (IDLA), which protested the lack of recognition of Indian treaty rights by the American and Canadian governments, mainly involving Eastern tribes. Beginning in the 1920s, IDLA protests of governmental noncompliance with the Jay Treaty and the Treaty of Ghent took the form of refusals to pay customs duties or to possess or surrender passports, resistance against restrictions on passage across the American-Canadian border, and annual protests staging reenactments of the Jay Treaty signing.

The New Deal era of the 1930s and the Indian Reorganization Act of 1934 (IRA) provided resources and impetus to reservation political life, and increased activism resulted. For instance, the decision whether or not to adopt IRA constitutions rallied both support and opposition forces on many reservations and animated reservation political action. The Bureau of Indian Affairs began a long career as the target of tribal protests during this period. Particularly notable was the Navajo response to BIA livestock reduction programs during the 1930s and 1940s, which took the form of a prolonged conflict on the reservation, as did the Navajo-Hopi land dispute, whose resolution dragged on for the rest of the century.

Tuscarora protest against the New York State Power Authority's condemnation of their lands for a reservoir, 1958. Photograph courtesy of the Buffalo and Erie County Historical Society.

The post-Second World War period saw an increase in Indian activism, again organized mainly at the tribal level, often directed against U.S. government public works projects which threatened Indian land holdings and sacred areas. Federal water and power projects were among the most common targets of Indian protest. The various nations of the Iroquois Confederacy, for example, resisted several water projects affecting Iroquois land: these included Seneca legal challenges and protests against the Kinzua Dam project in Pennsylvania during the 1940s and 1950s; Mohawk and Tuscarora legal and activist resistance to the St. Lawrence Seaway project in New York in the 1950s and 1960s; and Tuscarora armed resistance to the seizure of tribal land for a reservoir associated with the Niagara Power Plant project in New York in the 1950s.

American Indian protest activity often accompanied legal actions. Many twentieth century "Indian Wars" have been fought inside closed doors, where the battleground was the courtroom, where the combatants are attorneys, and where the weapons were the rules and precedents of law. In a number of cases, these legal battles took place against a backdrop of protest activism. That backdrop often drew its symbolic vitality from the ironies and contradictions of American-Indian relations, particularly the tensions between Indians as sovereign "dependent" nations on the one hand, and as American citizens (after the 1924 Indian Citizenship Act) on the other.

The use of dramatic symbolism in Indian protest was especially characteristic of the Red Power movement, but could be seen in many earlier protests. For example, Iroquois protesters during the 1950s and 1960s led annual delegations to the United Nations in New York to report American and Canadian violations of various treaties. Delegates wore traditional ceremonial clothing and used their visits, which captured media attention, to spotlight their grievances. Protesters were often sensitive to the nuances of international politics in staging these events. For example, two Iroquois delegations arrived at the U.N. in May and September, 1950, at the height of the Cold War, and the second delegation met with Soviet foreign minister Andrei Y. Vishinski.

Indian protesters also drew protest themes and tactics from American political culture. For instance, in December 1960, a group of Ute Indians in Utah captured national attention with a strategy that resonated with American domestic history—the True Ute seceded from the United States in order to protest the Bureau of Indian Affairs' control over funds paid by the federal government for mineral and land holdings. Still other tribes employed protest tactics from their own cultural repertoire. In September 1953, a group of Cheyenne and Arapaho Indians protested the draining of water from their hunting and fishing grounds at Canton Lake in Oklahoma, by breaking a peace pipe and invoking a curse in a drum-beating ceremony.

The 1960s saw an increase in the amount of protest activity by American Indians. While issues tended to center on problems confronting reservation tribes, and activists tended to be tribe members, urban Indian activist groups were becoming increasingly involved, and acted in concert with tribal protesters. The most dramatic and widespread of the early to mid-1960s protests occurred in the Northwest and involved the struggle over fishing rights.

Tuscarora protesting reservoir. Photograph courtesy of the Buffalo and Erie County Historical Society.

The Fish-ins of the 1960s

The term *fish-in* reveals a powerful marriage of protest cultures in the United States: the Civil Rights movement and Native American activism, which came to be known as "Red Power." The lunch counter desegregation sit-in tactic of the Civil Rights movement found its rhetorical counterpart in the

American Indian fish-ins in the Pacific Northwest during the mid-1960s. The issue that launched the fish-in movement, however, was not desegregation; at issue were court and law enforcement restrictions on Northwest tribes' access to fishing, an access which the tribes asserted, and the courts later found to be guaranteed by treaty.

While tension between Indians and non-Indians over hunting and fishing rights stretched back into American history, the fish-in campaign of the 1960s had its contemporary origins in a 1957 Washington Supreme Court case, in which the court split 4-4 over the case of Robert Satiacum, a Puyallup and Yakima, who had been arrested for fishing steelhead out of season with fixed gill nets. On the basis of this ambiguous decision, law enforcement efforts to restrict tribal fishing activities escalated in the 1960s, and as Indian fishermen continued to cast their nets, the fish-in movement took off. Fish-in activity was centered mainly in the states of Washington and Oregon, but drew support from groups outside the region, most notably the National Indian Youth Council. The involvement of the NIYC together with the organization's recruitment of national entertainment figures (e.g., Dick Gregory and Marlon Brando) as sympathizers with the Northwest tribes' cause, brought national media attention to the region. This tactic presaged Red Power's unprecedented use of the national news media as an instrument of Indian protest. In 1974, Federal District Judge George H. Boldt interpreted the 1855 Camp Stevens treaty to mean that Indians and whites were to share equally all fishing rights. The decision, while extremely unpopular with whites, reaffirmed tribal rights, and the fish-in movement subsided.

In addition to forcing an eventual legal victory for Native American fishing rights in the Northwest, the fish-in movement provided a training ground for future Red Power activists in other parts of the United States. With the founding of the American Indian Movement in 1968, coupled with the spread of activism out of the Northwest, Native American protesters became a part of the momentum of the Civil Rights era by the end of the decade.

The Occupation of Alcatraz Island, 1969–71

In the early morning hours of November 20, 1969, eighty-nine "Indians of All Tribes" landed on Alcatraz Island, the former site of the famous U.S. federal penitentiary, in San Francisco Bay. The group claimed the island, by the "right of discovery," and by the terms of an 1868 Sioux treaty that permitted Indians the right to unused federal property on Indian land. In a press statement, Indians of All Tribes set the tone of the occupation:

> We, the native Americans, re-claim the land known as Alcatraz Island in the name of all American Indians by right of discovery . . . . We will purchase said Alcatraz for twenty-four dollars in glass beads and red cloth . . . . Our offer of $1.24 per acre is greater than the 47 cents per acre the white men are now paying the California Indians for their land.

Indian children playing on Alcatraz Island during the 1969–71 occupation. Note burnt-out structure (previously warden's house). Photographer unknown.

During the next nineteen months, the estimated number of Alcatraz occupiers ranged from close to one thousand in June 1970 to the fifteen Indians removed by federal marshals on June 11, 1971. The Indian occupiers and visitors to the island represented many different Indian tribes; among them were Sioux, Navajo, Cherokee, Mohawk, Puyallup, Yakima, Hoopa, and Omaha. The months of occupation were marked by proclamations, news conferences, powwows, celebrations, skirmishes, and negotiations with federal officials. In the early months of the occupation, food and supplies were gathered on the mainland, partly by the San Francisco Indian Center. Over time, however, the occupying force, which generally numbered around one hundred, had to contend with increasing hardships as federal officials interfered with delivery boats and cut off the supply of water and electricity to the island.

The federal government never embraced Indians of All Tribes' plans for an American Indian cultural, educational, and spiritual center to be located on Alcatraz Island, although federal response was not uniformly negative. On December 23, 1969, for example, House Joint Resolution 1042 was passed directing President Richard Nixon "to initiate immediate negotiations with delegated representatives of . . . the Indian community with the objective of transferring unencumbered title in fee of Alcatraz Island . . . to any . . . designated organization of the American Indian Community."

Red Power

While the negotiations did not result in any plan for the future of Alcatraz Island that was acceptable to the Indian protesters, the occupation itself represented a turning point in patterns of Ameri-

During the 1969–71 Indian occupation of Alcatraz Island, Indian men and women learned beadwork and other cultural skills. Photographer unknown.

can Indian protest. Alcatraz heralded the beginning of the Red Power movement, a period of greatly increased levels of American Indian activism in urban centers as well as on reservations. Red Power activists took their tactical cue, in part, from the Alcatraz occupation. After federal officials retook the Island, Indians of All Tribes moved their protest to an abandoned Nike missile base in the Beverly Hills, overlooking San Francisco Bay. While this occupation lasted only three days, it set in motion a pattern of similar occupations during the next several years—many of which involved unused or abandoned federal property—at government buildings, or at sites in national parks. Members of the American Indian Movement often led these protest events.

Occupations represented a tactic designed to draw attention to American Indian historical and contemporary grievances: unsettled land claims, conditions on reservations, recognition of cultural and social rights, and tribal self-determination. Most occupations were short-lived, lasting only a few days or weeks, such as the occupations that took place during 1970–71 at Fort Lawton and Fort Lewis in Washington; at Ellis Island in New York; at an unused army communications center and at former Nike Missile sites in Davis, California; at the Twin Cities Naval Air Station in Minneapolis; on Lake Michigan near Chicago; at Argonne, Illinois; and at an abandoned Coast Guard lifeboat station in Milwaukee.

A number of protest camps were also established during the early 1970s, including those at Mount Rushmore and the Badlands National Monument. During the same years, government buildings also became the sites of protests, including regional Bureau of Indian Affairs offices in Cleveland and Denver, as well as the main headquarters of the BIA in Washington, D.C. Many of these occupations took on a festive air, as celebrations of Indian culture and ethnic renewal, while others represented efforts to provide educational or social services to urban Indians.

As the 1970s proceeded, American Indian protest occupations lasted longer, and some took on a more serious, sometimes violent tone, revealing the depth of grievances and the difficulty of creating solutions to the problems that confronted Native Americans after nearly five centuries of Euro-American contact. The November 1972 week-long occupation of the Bureau of Indian Affairs in Washington, D.C. was one such example. The unplanned occupation of BIA headquarters occurred at the end of "The Trail of Broken Treaties," a protest event involving caravans that traveled across the United States to convene in Washington at a large camp-in, in order to dramatize and present Indian concerns at the national BIA offices. As a result of the breakdown of accommodations arrangements protesters occupied BIA offices and seized BIA files; the protest ended a week later, after a series of negotiations with federal officials.

Red Power protest activity shifted after the late-1972 BIA occupation, from mainly symbolic, short-term actions, to longer, more violent events, often on or near reservations. While these reservation-based protest actions further dramatized Indian grievances, they also revealed tensions within Indian communities, tensions between urban and reservation Indians, and tensions that reflected political divisions on reservations. No single event of the Red Power era more clearly illustrated the combination of Indian grievances and community tensions than the events on the Pine Ridge reservation in the spring of 1973, a ten-week long siege which came to be known as "Wounded Knee II."

Wounded Knee II involved a dispute within the Oglala Sioux tribe over the controversial tribal chairman, Richard Wilson. Some members of the tribe—including those associated with AIM—viewed Wilson as a corrupt puppet of the BIA. An effort to impeach Wilson resulted in a division of the tribe into opposing camps that eventually armed themselves and entered into a two and one-half month-long siege involving federal law enforcement officials, the BIA, local citizens, nationally prominent entertainment figures, and the national news media.

Just as Red Power tactics in the early 1970s followed the pattern set by the Alcatraz occupation, Wounded Knee II reshaped Red Power protest in the mid-1970s in the direction of longer, reservation-based protest actions. These included a six-month occupation of a former girls' camp in Moss Lake, New York beginning in 1974; the five-week occupation of a vacant Alexian Brothers noviciary by the Menominee Warrior Society in Wisconsin in 1975; the eight-day takeover of a tribally owned Fairchild electronics assembly plant on the Navajo reservation in New Mexico in 1975; and the week-long occupation of a juvenile detention center by members of the Puyallup tribe in Washington State in 1976.

The last major event of the Red Power era occurred in July 1978, as several hundred Native Americans marched into Washington, D.C., at the end of the "Longest Walk," a protest march that had begun five months earlier in San Francisco. The Longest Walk was intended to symbolize the forced removal of Native Americans from their aboriginal homelands in order to draw attention to the continuing problems faced by Native Americans. The event was also intended to expose and challenge the backlash movement against Indian treaty rights which was gaining strength. This backlash was represented by a growing number of bills before Congress to abrogate Indian treaties and restrict Indian rights. Unlike the events of the mid-1970s, the Longest Walk was seen as a peaceful and spiritual event which ended without violence. Red Power had come full circle, from the festive Alcatraz days, through a cycle of violent confrontation, to the spiritual unity which marked the end of the Longest Walk.

The Legacy of Red Power: Indian Self-Determination

The decline of the Red Power movement corresponded to a renaissance in federal Indian policy. From 1975 to 1977, the American Indian Policy Review Commission traveled around the United States holding the first extensive hearings in half a century on the conditions confronting American Indians on reservations and in cities. In the 1970s, a number of pieces of federal legislation were passed denouncing the "termination" policies of the 1950s and reaffirming Indian tribal self-determination. Among these important legislative acts were the 1971 Alaska Native Claims Settlement Act (ANCSA), which recognized the land rights of Alaska Natives, and provided for mineral royalties payments, land payments, and land transfers; the 1974 Indian Financing Act, which established a revolving loan fund to facilitate reservation economic development; the 1975 Indian Self-Determination and Education Assistance Act which remanded to the tribes many of the decision-making and contracting rights formerly held by the BIA; and the 1978 Rhode Island Indian Claims Settlement Act, which was fashioned after the 1971 ANCSA.

It is difficult to prove whether the protest activism of the 1960s and 1970s was responsible for this new era in federal Indian policy: much of this legislation was underway early during the period of protest. However it is difficult to imagine that Congressional deliberations on these bills occurred without knowledge of what was happening outside the Capitol building: the occupation of Alcatraz Island, the Trail of Broken Treaties, the occupation of BIA headquarters, the sieges at Wounded Knee, Moss Lake, and on the Menominee reservation, the Longest Walk, and the dozens of collective action events all served as a foil against which federal Indian policy was judged.

American Indian Activism after Red Power

During the 1980s, Indian activism shifted to more legal forums. America's courtrooms became the contended terrain in American Indian affairs. The numbers of American Indian attorneys increased greatly and Indian communities became increasingly sophisticated at negotiating the legal complexities of Indian resource rights, land claims, and sovereignty issues. The law became a double-edged sword, to be wielded by Indian tribes and organizations, not only against them. American Indian protest energies were more and more spent in these legal arenas.

Legal activism on behalf of Indian tribes during the 1980s focused on several issues: unsettled land claims, repatriation of Indian remains and artifacts, and self-determination rights, including the right to regulate and develop reservation resources.

Land Claims

In 1946, Congress established the Indian Claims Commission (ICC), as part of a program to terminate American Indian treaty rights. Indian tribes had five years to file land claims before the ICC. Once these claims were settled, the U.S. obligation to the tribes was to end. However, the goal of termination was abandoned by the time the ICC ceased its operations in 1978, after which the remaining unsettled claims were transferred to the U.S. Court of Claims. While land claims awards varied in amount and in the extent to which they were judged to be fair, the ICC served as a mechanism of mobilization for Indian communities as they researched their histories and organized their cases for litigation. A number of successful claimants were able to reestablish and revitalize community life. The Passamaquoddy of Maine, for instance, invested a portion of the proceeds from their multi-million dollar settlement in a variety of community enterprises, including a housing manufacturing firm and timber mill, as well as in educational programs in Passamaquoddy language and culture.

Not all land disputes were settled by the ICC and the U.S. Court of Claims. Many areas sacred to Native Americans remained the subjects of controversy as American Indian groups sought to reclaim the land or stop development projects seen as despoiling these religious sites. The Black Hills in South Dakota was one such disputed sacred area. Several groups of American Indian protesters occupied a portion of the Black Hills, establishing Yellow Thunder Camp. While the U.S. government acknowledged that the Black Hills land was illegally seized, it made no provision to return the land to the Sioux. Instead, the government offered a monetary settlement, which the Sioux refused. In the 1990s, Yellow Thunder Camp remained a symbol of unresolved land disputes between Indian tribes and the United States.

Repatriation of Remains and Artifacts

The 1980s witnessed a shift in the definition of acceptable treatment of American Indian burial remains and cultural artifacts. Throughout the period since European contact, explorers and settlers engaged in the excavation of ancient (such as the Anasazi) and contemporary Indian gravesites and the acquisition of Native American artwork, sacred objects, and cultural artifacts. While there is a lengthy history of Indian efforts to force the return of these remains and artifacts, successful reacquisition by Indian tribes only occurred in the 1980s. The reaffirmation of Native American tribal sovereignty by the self-determination legislation and programs of the 1970s is in part responsible. Perhaps most symbolic of the shift in acceptable practices was the 1989 decision by the Smithsonian Institution, after several years of negotiation, to return the skeletal remains and burial artifacts of hundreds of Indians to their modern descendants. Fast on the heels of this decision, the state of New York agreed to return twelve wampum belts, some of which had been in the state's possession since the late 1800s, to the Onondaga Nation, which had actively sought their return since the 1950s. The following year, 1990, saw the successful negotiation for the return of rare wooden statues of Zuni war gods from museums around to country to their New Mexico homeland so that Zuni priests could expose them to weather to facilitate their rightful decay into dust.

Tribal Self-Determination Rights

American Indian efforts to bring reservation resources under tribal control comprised another important set of legal actions during the 1980s. Battles for control of tribal water rights, mineral and resource development rights, and the right to develop reservation enterprises such as manufacturing, tourism, and recreation, were fought in courtrooms and on reservations around the country. Other campaigns involved the protection of Native American religious rights, the protection of Indian children from adoption by non-Indians, and the continuing struggle to preserve Indian hunting and fishing rights. One of the most controversial outgrowths of the legal reaffirmation of tribal sovereignty involved gambling on Indian reservations. This potentially lucrative source of reservation income sparked disputes within tribes and between the tribes and local and state governments. Similarly controversial was the right of tribal governments to tax reservation residents and enterprises. The limits of tribal sovereignty continue to be tested in the courts.

Joane Nagel
University of Kansas

CANADIAN NATIVE ACTIVIST MOVEMENTS ✦ ✦ ✦ ✦ ✦ ✦ ✦

Over the last three decades, aboriginal peoples in Canada have formed a number of political advocacy organizations to represent their interests to the federal government, and to Canadians in general. They have also created organizations that focus on the local, regional, provincial and international level. Some organizations are of general scope, while others pursue a particular interest or point of view, such as women's rights or protection of the fur harvest. A third type of organization formed by aboriginal peoples exists to provide particular services, such as policing or child protection.

The Principal Pan-Canadian Organizations

Well over one million people in Canada identify themselves as aboriginal. They are represented by four political organizations of general scope, and at least three Canada-wide aboriginal women's organizations.

Federal government statutes and federal funding practices have affected the number and type of aboriginal organizations. The federal law and practices, and the organizations themselves, to some extent reflect the colonial past and the history of relations between aboriginal peoples and those who have come from other continents over the last five hundred years. The organizations are also shaped, of course, by the heritage and the living traditions of the aboriginal peoples whose interests they represent.

The Assembly of First Nations is a federation representing almost all status Indians in Canada. A 'status Indian' is someone who is registered under the Indian Act, a statute of the federal

Parliament, in recognition of that person's entitlement to certain rights and benefits. People in this category are usually descendants of those who signed treaties with the British Crown or the Canadian government. In some cases, though, the ancestors of status Indians are not treaty-signatories; these Indians are simply groups of aboriginal people to whom the Canadian government has extended status. (Such is the case, for example, with some of the aboriginal people in the province of British Columbia; many have status although no treaties have been signed in this province.)

The Assembly of First Nations represents approximately 700,000 people, about two-thirds of whom live on Indian reserves. The local level of First Nations' government is the band; all 596 Canadian bands are part of regional organizations, and in federation comprise the Assembly of First Nations, which is led by a Grand Chief and Council of Chiefs. Although for many First Nations in Canada the band or local government is the most important political body, it is the Assembly of First Nations to which federal policy-makers and others most often turn when status Indians in Canada must be consulted.

The Native Council of Canada (NCC) was originally formed to include all aboriginal people who did not have status under the Indian Act, and who were not Inuit. This group was potentially very large, and was probably larger than the status Indian population, since many Canadian Indians are descended from people who were not included in the treaty-making process, or who forfeited their status for various reasons. The interests of the people who formed the Native Council of Canada were quite different from the interests of status Indians, since they lacked a land base (since status is required for the creation of reserves) and they often lived in urban settings, unorganized by bands or other forms of First Nation affiliation.

In 1983, a portion of the NCC membership left the organization to form the Métis National Council. This group, based in the western Canadian provinces of Alberta, Saskatchewan, Manitoba, and the Northwest Territories, trace their lineage from the "Red River

Métis." The Red River Métis are a distinct culture of aboriginal people originating in the Red River Valley of western Canada (in what is now Manitoba). During the late eighteenth and early nineteenth centuries, marriages between prairie aboriginal people and French and Scottish fur traders created a Creole society with its own language, traditions, and a sense of collective identity. Led by Louis Riel and Gabriel Dumont (see their biographies), among others, in the late nineteenth century, the Red River Métis campaigned for political self-determination and rights against the colonial rulers in central Canada. Although the so-called Riel Rebellion was not immediately successful in forging a new democratic polity on the Canadian prairies, it did begin a tradition of democratic and populist movements in western Canada, and it forms the touchstone of Métis unity to the present day.

The fourth nationwide aboriginal organization in Canada is the Inuit Tapirisat of Canada. This body represents the Canadian Inuit (formerly known as Eskimos), whose traditional homeland is the vast Arctic region of Canada, which represents about one-third of Canadian territory. Inuit now share their homeland with a small number of migrants from southern Canada, but in most places where they live, they are still the large majority of the population.

The Inuit Tapirisat of Canada represents all Inuit in Canada, whether they live in Labrador, northern Quebec, the Northwest Territories, or in other parts of Canada to which Inuit have migrated in small numbers in recent times. There are also numerous other Inuit organizations, such as the Tungavik Federation of Nunavut (formed to negotiate a comprehensive claims agreement) and many smaller, region-specific bodies. Inuit have a distinctive economic base in the difficult conditions of the Far North, and they have had a relatively short history of contact with non-aboriginal peoples. These factors have given rise to a pragmatic, constructive, and very successful political style, which has been rewarded with completed comprehensive claims agreements as well as some progress in gaining increased political autonomy.

There are Canada-wide national organizations for aboriginal women as well, formed out of the recognition that the special needs and circumstances of women did not always receive the emphasis they deserved by the older national aboriginal organizations. Inuit women formed Pauktuutit, a body representing all Inuit women in Canada. The Native Women's Association of Canada represents mainly Status Indian women across the country, while Métis women have formed the Women of the Métis Nation.

The history of treaty-making, diplomatic relations, and military conflict between the indigenous nations of Canada and migrants from other continents is at least 450 years old, yet the existing political organizations of aboriginal peoples in Canada were all formed during the late 1960s and early 1970s.

Historical Background

There are many reasons for this. First, until 1953, it was illegal for status Indians in Canada to raise funds to form political organizations. Until 1959, status Indians did not have the right to vote in the Canadian federal Parliament. These circumstances, and the close administration of Indian bands by federal officials called Indian agents, inhibited political organization. Compounding these obstacles was the simple poverty of many aboriginal people in Canada, who did not have the resources to mount political campaigns over large geographical areas for sustained periods of time. In yet others cases, as for Inuit and some northern Indians and Métis, people lived in areas relatively undisturbed by the migration of non-aboriginal people or by industrial activity. They were able to live their lives with limited contact with outside forces, and thus perhaps did not see a need for political organizing.

Changes that took place in post-war Canada eliminated or ameliorated many of the obstacles outlined above, and also provided the impetus for vigorous efforts to form political organizations in addition to the state-sanctioned and contained community-level organizations. The sources of change are numerous and are interrelated in complex ways, but it is possible to sketch the major changes in relations between aboriginal and nonaboriginal Canadians as a means of indicating the general dynamic.

Relations between the societies indigenous to northern North America and those which began to be established here with European and Asian migration may be divided into three broad periods. The Royal Proclamation of 1763 (a proclamation of the British Crown which recognizes the rights of the societies indigenous to North America) and the signing of the last Treaty in 1921, mark a period in which the British Crown and then the Canadian federal government recognized the rights of aboriginal peoples to their territories by making treaties concerning joint use and occupancy of Indian lands, among other more specific matters.

For more than fifty years there were no more treaties, even though the treaty-making process was far from complete. Large parts of Canada were not covered by treaty, including British Columbia, both northern territories, and parts of northern Quebec and Labrador. Then, in the mid-1970s, the treaty-making process resumed. The new generation of treaties were called "comprehensive claims agreements" by the Canadian government, which indicated its willingness to negotiate these agreements with those First Nations whose territories were not yet covered by treaty.

Indigenous Rights and Modern Treaties

The comprehensive claims process, and the new national political organizations, were launched by a number of changes in post-war Canada. First, a growing consciousness of civil rights, and the strength of progressive movements in Canada after the Second World War, led to many political movements to enfranchise the disenfranchised. In Canada, these movements were often state-funded, or at least were encouraged through state policies. Thus aboriginal peoples' demands for political rights, and for recognition of treaty rights found resonance in the broader movements for a more democratic society, and the new aboriginal organizations eventually received public funding to represent the interests of their constituencies .

A second political impetus came from the economic changes that followed the Second World War. The war had knit the Canadian and United States economies more closely together than ever, and in particular had established markets for Canadian natural resources in the burgeoning U.S. economy of the post-war period. This in turn led to the opening of mines, to hydroelectric projects, and to oil and gas exploration in the Canadian North and mid-North, and to competition for land use with the indigenous peoples who were harvesting food and fur from the same areas.

Finally, and perhaps ironically, a policy reversal occasioned by a new, liberal Canadian government in the late 1960s galvanized status Indians across Canada into a most vigorous period of political activity. The pivotal document was the White Paper on Indian Policy, released by the federal government in 1969. This document contradicted the findings of a federal royal commission of inquiry (a process of research and public hearings, named the Hawthorn Inquiry after its chairman), which was formed in response to protests and political advocacy by Indian rights activists across Canada. The 1966 report of the Hawthorn Inquiry had responded to the arguments of status Indians across Canada by acknowledging that their treaty rights gave them special status within Canada, in addition to the range of citizen rights enjoyed by all other people living in Canada.

Soon after Hawthorn reported, however, a new government was elected in Canada. The Liberal Party of Pierre Trudeau entered Canadian politics in a fashion somewhat analogous to the Kennedy administration in the United States a few years earlier. Many felt that the new Trudeau government represented the forces of democratization and progressive change then surging through Canada as through most western nations. Yet it was the new Trudeau government that released the 1969 White Paper on Indian Policy. A White Paper is a government discussion paper, meant to engage public debate about a proposed policy change. The White Paper on Indian Policy proposed the abolition of special rights for Indians in Canada, recommending instead strong measures leading to their incorporation into the mainstream of Canadian economic, cultural, and political life. It is a measure of the ignorance then prevalent in nonaboriginal Canadian society that a putatively progressive new government could so misunderstand broad currents in aboriginal peoples' political life.

The 1969 White Paper led immediately to protests from treaty Indians across Canada, and eventually to their organization at the provincial, territorial, and national level. The federal government provided funding for these organizations, and retreated in short order from the assimilationist vision presented in the White Paper.

The new aboriginal organizations did not only oppose the White Paper policy; they began to struggle for Indian land rights and against involuntary expropriation in those large parts of Canada where joint use and occupancy was still unregulated by Treaty. This resistance prompted the federal government to establish a comprehensive claims process and policy. Under this policy, the parties negotiate specific land entitlements, compensation money, and a package of benefits, in exchange for which the First Nation signatories cede aboriginal rights and title to their original territories, in perpetuity.

Outstanding Issues   The comprehensive claims negotiation process in all parts of Canada has been long and expensive. By 1993, four comprehensive claims negotiations had been completed, or nearly completed, by the Council for Yukon Indians (in Canada's northwesternmost territory), the Inuvialuit (Inuit) of the Mackenzie River Delta area, the Gwi'chin (Indians) neighbors of the Inuvialuit, the Inuit of the northern eastern half of the Northwest Territories, and by the Cree and Inuit of the James Bay area in northern Quebec. Many agreements are still in negotiation, and more First Nations are lined up to enter the process.

Only four agreements were completed in twenty years in part because the starting points and priorities of the negotiating parties were very different. Federal politicians and lawyers have been most concerned with "closure"—with ending the dispute over land for all time. They have understood this to require that aboriginal signatories of the agreements agree to extinguish their aboriginal rights in the land, absolutely and for all time. The aboriginal negotiators, on the other hand, sought agreements that entrenched their aboriginal rights, recognized these for all time. They saw extinguishment of aboriginal rights

as an incomprehensible step, akin to voluntary relinquishment of someone's human rights.

A second sticking point has been the reluctance of the federal government to negotiate political or constitutional rights at the comprehensive claims table. Aboriginal peoples see recognition of their political rights as essential to meaningful comprehensive claims agreements, since it is only through political power that they can be self-determining and self-governing.

Over the last twenty years, a variety of means have been used to moderate the conflicting objectives of aboriginal peoples in Canada and the federal government. One product of the struggle has been the implementation of a process separate from

Canadian Natives protesting before Parliament for land rights and aboriginal rights within the Canadian Constitution.

comprehensive claims negotiations to secure the entrenchment in the Canadian Constitution of "the existing aboriginal and treaty rights of Indians, Inuit and Métis in Canada." Most aboriginal people feel that further constitutional specificity would be desirable—in the identification of these rights—but recognize that they have achieved a measure of constitutional security not available to them before.

Another development has been the formation of a new territory in Canada, to be called Nunavut. Neither a reserve or reservation, Nunavut will be a new territory (and perhaps eventually a province) in which Inuit are likely to form the large majority of the population for many years. The formation of Nunavut has been accompanied by the conclusion of the Inuit land claim, so Canadian Inuit in Nunavut will have exclusive rights to relatively small plots of land in the larger territory that they will share with non-Inuit. This "public government" model of aboriginal self-determination is available to some few other aboriginal peoples in Canada, where they live in sufficient numbers to exercise political power. In most cases, however, it is likely that "self-government," or ethnically exclusive governments such as those on reserves, will be preferred.

An enduring feature of the political landscape in Canada has been the creation of aboriginal political organizations which now exercise many governmental responsibilities. Moreover, there is a growing acceptance among the Canadian population of the need for the provision of aboriginal services and political organizations. The new organizations at least provide a means for aboriginal people to struggle against poverty and racism, and for a better future. Battles will continue over hunting and fishing rights (to which aboriginal people have special access under Canadian law and in conformance with the treaties), and the protection of the ecosystems upon which these activities depend.

Frances Abele
Carleton University

◆ **BIOGRAPHIES**

Hank Adams was born on the Fort Peck Indian Reservation in Montana at a place known as Wolf Point, but more commonly referred to as Poverty Flats. He graduated from Moclips High School in 1961, where he was student-body president, editor of the school newspaper and annual, and a starting football and basketball player. Following graduation he developed an interest in politics and moved to California where he was a staunch supporter of President John F. Kennedy and a campaign worker for the president's brother, Robert F. Kennedy, in the 1968 Democratic primary.

Hank Adams

1944–

Assiniboine/Sioux activist

In 1964, Adams played a behind-the-scenes role when actor Marlon Brando and a thousand Indians marched on the Washington State capitol in Olympia to protest state policies toward Indian fishing rights. Indians reserved the right to take fish in "the usual and accustomed places" in numerous treaties negotiated in the 1850s. State officials, commercial, and sports fisherman tried to restrict the amount, time, and places where Indian people could fish, thus prompting the treaty-fishing rights battles.

Adams began his activist career in April 1964 when he refused induction into the U.S. Army until Indian treaty rights were recognized. His attempt failed and he ultimately served in the U.S. Army.

In 1968, Adams became the director of the Survival of American Indians Association, a group of 150 to 200 active members primarily dedicated to the Indian treaty-fishing rights battle. Late in 1968, he actively campaigned against state regulation of Indian net fishing on the Nisqually River near Franks Landing, Washington. For this and his role in the fishing-rights battles, Adams was regularly arrested and jailed from 1968 to 1971. In January 1971, on the banks of the Puyallup River near Tacoma, Washington, Adams was shot in the stomach by an unknown assailant. He and a companion, Michael Hunt, had set a fish trap about midnight and remained to watch it. That section of the Puyallup River had been the scene of recent altercations as Indian people claimed fishing rights guaranteed by treaties, despite state laws to the contrary. Adams recovered from the gunshot wound and continued to fight for Indian fishing rights in the state of Washington into the mid-1970s.

Anna Mae Aquash
1945–76

Micmac activist

Anna Mae Aquash, née Pictou, a Micmac Indian from Nova Scotia, Canada, was active in the American Indian Movement. AIM is an organization aimed at advancing the rights of Indian people in North America. Originally formed in 1968 to address the problems of Indian people living in urban areas, it quickly expanded to address issues surrounding housing, education, and treaty rights. In the early 1970s, AIM became involved in events on the Pine Ridge Reservation in South Dakota, home to approximately fourteen thousand Oglala Sioux and mixed-blood Indians. Charges of corruption had been leveled against the Pine Ridge Tribal Council, and AIM members, together with members of the reservation committed to the impeachment of the tribal chairman Richard Wilson, occupied the town of Wounded Knee, located within the Pine Ridge Reservation. Wounded Knee is identified in American Indian history as the site at which, in the 1890s, an estimated three hundred Indian men, women, and children were massacred by federal calvary as they were surrendering their arms. Although the 1973 siege resulted in a negotiated settlement, AIM's occupation of the town also ended in tragedy. Two Indians were killed by government fire.

Anna Mae Aquash was born and raised by her mother, Mary Ellen Pictou, on a Micmac Reserve five miles outside the town of Shubenacadie, Nova Scotia. The Micmac people traditionally have occupied lands located in eastern Canada. After attending school in Nova Scotia, Aquash left her reserve and lived in Boston for several years, where she had two children, became involved in political causes aimed at improving the life of urban Indians, and worked at a low-income day care center. In Boston, she met Nogeeshik Aquash, a Chippewa artist from Ontario, and in 1973, they traveled to Wounded Knee to show solidarity with AIM. They married in Wounded Knee in April 1973 in a traditional Sioux ceremony. Their marriage lasted little more than a year, and Anna Mae became increasingly involved in AIM's activities.

In 1975, the Pine Ridge Reservation again was the site of a confrontation between AIM and federal authorities. Two FBI agents were killed. Anna Mae was found dead five months later, her body abandoned in a field on the Pine Ridge Reservation. According to autopsy reports, she died from a bullet wound to the head. This homicide has not been solved.

Dennis J. Banks (Nowacumig) 1932–

Anishinabe activist

Dennis Banks—Native American leader, teacher, lecturer, activist, and author—was born on the Leech Lake Indian Reservation in northern Minnesota. In 1968, he was a co-founder of the American Indian Movement (AIM), which was established to protect the traditional ways of Indian people and to engage in legal cases protecting treaty rights of Natives, such as treaty and aboriginal rights to hunting and fishing, trapping, and gathering wild rice.

AIM has been quite successful in bringing Native American issues to the public. Among other activities, AIM members participated in the occupation of Alcatraz Island, where demands were made that all federal surplus property be returned to Indian control. In 1972, AIM organized and led the Trail of Broken Treaties Caravan across the United States to Washington, D.C., calling attention to the plight of Native Americans. The refusal of congressional leaders to meet with the Trail of Broken Treaties delegation led to the 1972 takeover of the Bureau of Indian Affairs offices in Washington, D.C.

Under the leadership of Banks, AIM led a protest in Custer, South Dakota, in 1973 against the judicial process that found a non-Indian innocent of murdering an Indian. As a result of his activities at Custer, Banks and three hundred others were arrested. Banks was convicted of riot and assault stemming from the confrontation at Custer. Refusing to serve time in prison, Banks went underground but later received amnesty from Governor Jerry Brown of California.

Between 1976 and 1983, Banks earned an associate of arts degree at the University of California, Davis, and taught at Deganawidah-Quetzecoatl (DQ) University (an all-Indian controlled institution), where he became the first American Indian university chancellor. In the spring of 1979, he taught at Stanford University in Palo Alto, California.

After Governor Brown left office, Banks received sanctuary on the Onondaga Reservation in upstate New York in 1984. While living there, Banks organized the Great Jim Thorpe Run from New York City to Los Angeles, California. A spiritual run, this event ended in Los Angeles, where the Jim Thorpe Memorial Games were held and where the gold medals that Thorpe had previously won in the 1912 Olympic games were restored to the Thorpe family.

In 1985, Banks left the Onondaga Reservation to surrender to law enforcement officials in South Dakota and served eighteen months in prison. When released, he worked as a drug and alcohol counselor on the Pine Ridge Reservation in South Dakota.

In 1987, Banks was active in convincing the states of Kentucky and Indiana to pass laws against desecration of Indian graves and human remains. He organized reburial ceremonies for over 1,200 Indian grave sites that were disturbed by graverobbers in Uniontown, Kentucky.

In 1988, Banks organized and led a Sacred Run from New York to San Francisco, and then across Japan from Hiroshima to Hakkaido. These runs have continued each year. Also in 1988, his autobiography *Sacred Soul* was published in Japan and won the 1988 Nonfiction Book of the Year Award.

In addition to leading and organizing sacred runs, Banks stays involved in American Indian issues, including AIM, and travels the globe lecturing, teaching Native American traditions, and sharing his experiences. He had key roles in the films *War Party*, *The Last of the Mohicans* (1992), and *Thunderheart* (1992). In 1994, he led a Walk for Justice from California to Washington, D.C. to bring public attention to Native issues and to collect signatures requesting executive clemency for Leonard Peltier.

Born on the White Earth Reservation in Minnesota in 1939, Clyde Bellecourt was one of the founders of a national activist organization called the American Indian Movement (AIM) and a powerful force in major activist struggles of the early 1970s. AIM was founded by Dennis Banks, George Mitchell, and Bellecourt, all Ojibwa, in 1968. On February 27, 1973, they and other leaders led an armed occupation of Wounded Knee, South Dakota, after Dee Brown's book *Bury My Heart at Wounded Knee* (1971) had established the site as a nationally recognized symbol.

Bellecourt also helped draft twenty demands that were put before the government during the Indian occupation of a Bureau of Indian Affairs building in 1972. Among other things, the protestors demanded a separate government for Indians, the restoration of Indian lands, the renegotiation of all treaties, and a special agency in Washington, D.C., for the reconstruction of Indian communities. Although the White House did not meet these demands, the government established a task force to meet with the protest leaders and promised to make no arrests for the occupation.

Smokey Bruyere was raised in bush camps in northwestern Ontario. He attended school until the age of 18 and then worked with a mining company for a year and in the lumber industry in the bush camps for more than ten years. During this time, Bruyere helped establish the Ontario Métis and Non-Status Indian Association, an organization geared to the advancement of the Métis people. The Métis are persons of mixed Indian-European heritage who forged a common identity on the plains of Western Canada in the nineteenth century; non-status Indians are aboriginal people not legally recognized by Canadian authorities as Indians. Bruyere served as president of the association for two years and was involved in constitutional reform and dealings with the provincial government of Ontario, trying to secure better housing and employment services for his people.

In 1979, Bruyere turned his attention to the Native Council of Canada, a national organization representing Métis and non-status Indians. He was subsequently elected president of the council

Clyde Bellecourt
1939–

Ojibway activist

Louis (Smokey)
Bruyere
1948–

Ojibway activist

in 1981 and served in this capacity until 1988. During this time, aboriginal issues were attracting greater attention on the national stage, and Bruyere and the council advocated stronger constitutional guarantees to protect aboriginal people. He also was at the forefront of a movement to amend federal law so that Indian women no longer were treated as non-Indians at law when they married non-Indian men. In March 1991, Bruyere was hired by the federal Department of Indian and Northern Affairs as a spokesperson for aboriginal trappers.

Bruyere has long been a domestic and international advocate of aboriginal people. He has traveled with the World Council of Indigenous Peoples to the United States, Central and South America, and Europe, assisted in the drafting of a United Nations Declaration of Indigenous Peoples, and lectured in many universities throughout the world on indigenous peoples and the law. Bruyere is married and has four children.

Frank Arthur Calder
1915–

Nisga'a tribal leader

Frank Calder was the first Indian member of a Canadian legislature, serving as a member of the National Assembly of British Columbia for twenty-six years and as a provincial Cabinet Minister for a short time in the 1970s. His people, the Nisga'a, occupy the Nass River valley and adjacent lands of the British Columbia coastline. Calder was adopted by his aunt and uncle, whose own son had died in childhood. In accordance with Nisga'a custom, they adopted him, in order to pass family rank onto a son. His adoptive mother, Louisa, was the eldest of six sisters in a leading Nisga'a family. His adoptive father, Arthur Calder, himself played a leading role in the political life of the Nisga'a Nation. Calder attended a Methodist residential school far from home, which was established to inculcate Anglo-Canadian values in First Nation children. Much of his tribal cultural learning occurred during summers when, home from school, he went fishing with his father and other elders, who instructed him on his future responsibilities as a Nisga'a leader.

Calder has been an important political leader of the Nisga'a Nation. He was the founder and president of the Nisga'a Tribal Council, which united four diverse clans (Eagle, Wolf, Raven, and Killer Whale) located in four communities in northwestern British Columbia (Kincolith, Greenville, Canyon City, and Aiyansh). He is also widely known as a result of the landmark decision of the Supreme Court of Canada in *Calder v. The Queen* (1973), where the Court held that aboriginal people located in British Columbia possessed special rights to their ancestral lands that survived the establishment of the province. Calder currently lives in Greenville, British Columbia.

Ada Deer, a Menominee, is a social worker and political organizer involved in restoring federal recognition to her tribe in the 1970s. The Menominee (whose name means Wild Rice People in Ojibway) are located along the Menominee River in Wisconsin and Michigan.

Ada Deer

1935–

Menominee educator and activist

Born at Keshena, Wisconsin, on August 7, 1935, Deer received her bachelor's degree in education from the University of Wisconsin–Madison (1957) and went on to complete her master's degree in social welfare at Columbia University (1961).

In the 1970s, Deer played a major role in the social and political development of her tribe. During 1972 and 1973, she was vice-president and Washington lobbyist of an organization called National Committee to Save the Menominee People and Forest, Inc. From 1973 until 1976, she was the chair of the Menominee Restoration Committee. This group was largely responsible for the congressional action to restore Menominee to tribal status following the termination of the tribe in 1954. The Menominee were one of the major tribes whose reservation was dissolved by federal policies of the 1950s, and since 1977 several other terminated tribes have been restored to federal recognition, all following the Menominee example.

Since 1977, Deer has been a faculty member in the School of Social Work and Native American Studies at the University of Wisconsin–Madison. She has won many awards and honors over the years, including honorary doctorates from Northland College in Wisconsin (1974) and the University of Wisconsin–Madison (1974).

**Alexander General
(Deskahe)
1889–1965**

Cayuga and Oneida
tribal leader and activist

Alexander General was a tribal leader and intellectual figure of Cayuga and Oneida descent. The Cayuga and Oneida are both tribes of the Iroquois Confederacy; the Cayuga were located along the shores of Cayuga Lake in New York State, and the Oneida are also located in New York, though some now also live in Wisconsin and Ontario, Canada.

Born on the Six Nations Reserve in Ontario, Canada, in 1889, General was the youngest of eight children. His family lived in poverty as marginal subsistence farmers, a situation that worsened after the accidental death of his father when General was only ten years old.

After his father's death, General went to work to help support his mother and therefore never went beyond the fourth or fifth grade in school. He later said that he learned more English through working than in school, holding jobs on the railroad and in foundries. Through diligence and good fortune he gradually saved enough money to go into farming with his brother and became a very successful farmer by reservation standards.

Alexander belonged to a chiefly lineage of the Iroquois Confederacy, and, at the age of eighteen, he began memorizing the ritual speeches of the Iroquois longhouse, the meeting place of confederate council. He gradually became known as the major speaker and ritualist of his community, and later, at the age of thirty-six, General was elected by his lineage to represent their views and took the chiefly title Deskahe.

Because of his cultural knowledge and his ability to explain Longhouse ceremonials and religious concepts in an intellectual manner, Deskahe became an important figure in anthropology. Frank Speck's book *The Midwinter Rites of the Cayuga Longhouse* (1949) was written as a collaboration with Deskahe and includes his name on the title page, but Speck was only one of many scholars who worked with this extraordinary leader and ritualist during the years between 1932 and 1959.

Most importantly, Deskahe was a political activist who once even traveled to England (in 1930) to argue that Canada had no jurisdiction over the Iroquois. He felt that tribal sovereignty could only be guaranteed by retaining the hereditary Iroquois council, and he also fought to re-establish the position of traditional Iroquois chiefs and to broaden their authority. He argued to anthropologists, in the news media, and to anyone who would listen, that his people had been robbed of their birthright. He also organized groups such as the Indian Defense League and the Mohawk Workers to help the Iroquois resist Canadian government authority.

LaDonna Harris
1931–

Comanche activist

LaDonna Harris is a Comanche woman who has promoted equal opportunity for Indian people on a nationwide level and has accomplished much in helping to strengthen self-government and economic self-sufficiency among Native Americans throughout the United States. Born in Temple, Oklahoma, on February 15, 1931, Harris was raised in a conservative household and spoke only the Comanche language before attending public school. Her work in the public eye began during the 1960s, when she was thrust onto the national political scene as the wife of Fred Harris, the Democratic Senator from Oklahoma. In 1965 she founded Oklahomans for Indian Opportunity, a nationally known Indian self-help organization, and since then she has been active as chair or board member of groups such as the Women's National Advisory Council on Poverty, the National Rural Housing Conference, the National Association of Mental Health, and the Joint Commission on Mental Health of Children. In 1970, Harris founded and is president of Americans for Indian Opportunity, a national advocacy group dedicated to helping Indian tribal groups achieve self-determined political, economic, and social goals.

A strong activist for world peace, Harris has participated in several international conferences on peace since 1968. She has traveled in the (then) Soviet Union, Mali, Senegal, and various South American countries as a representative of the Inter-American Indigenous Institute, an agency of the Organization of American States. Harris has received many awards, including an honorary doctorate in law from Dartmouth University.

**Susette La Flesche
1854–1903**

Omaha activist

Susette La Flesche devoted much of her life to working for women's and Indian rights. Her father was Chief Joseph La Flesche, and she was a stepsister of Francis La Flesche, the famous Omaha anthropologist. La Flesche was also known by her translated Omaha name, Bright Eyes (Inshata Theumba).

Like her sister, Susan La Flesche, Susette was educated by Christian missionaries and later studied art at the University of Nebraska. From 1877 to 1879, she was a teacher and conducted a Sunday school for Omaha children. During that time, La Flesche became involved in the plight of the Ponca and the controversy over their removal. In 1877, the Ponca were forced by the U.S. government to leave northern Nebraska and move to Indian Territory, present-day Oklahoma, and settle on a 101,000-acre reservation. The Ponca were greatly dissatisfied with the forced removal and petitioned Congress for permission to return to their homeland in Nebraska. They were eventually granted a 10,000-acre reservation in Nebraska but lost their Oklahoma lands to U.S. settlers. In 1879 and 1880, La Flesche made a speaking tour of the eastern United States, with her brother Francis and Ponca chief Standing Bear on behalf of the Ponca. La Flesche was called "Bright Eyes" on the tour. The purpose of the tour was to publicize the conditions and plight of Standing Bear and his people. La Flesche continued to tour the United States, speaking on Indian affairs. In 1881, she met and married philanthropist and journalist Thomas H. Tibbles. Throughout the late 1880s, La Flesche and her husband made numerous public appearances, including trips to England and Scotland, where they made pleas for improving the condition of the Omaha and Ponca. In 1894, La Flesche and her husband were supervising editors of *The Weekly Independent*, a Populist newspaper in Lincoln, Nebraska. With Standing Bear, La Flesche coauthored *Ploughed Under: The Story of an Indian Chief.*

**Russell Means
1940–**

Oglala-Yankton Sioux
activist

Russell Means led the American Indian Movement (AIM) in a 1973 armed seizure of Wounded Knee, South Dakota, site of the previous massacre of Sioux by Seventh U.S. Cavalry troops on December 29, 1890. With co-leaders Dennis Banks and Leonard Peltier, Means and AIM held off hundreds of federal agents on the Pine Ridge Reservation for seventy-one days before their surrender.

Means was born at Porcupine, South Dakota, on the Pine Ridge Reservation, but was raised around the Oakland, California, area. His father was part Oglala, part Irish, and his mother was Yankton Sioux. He was a rodeo rider, Indian dancer, ballroom dance instructor, and public accountant before returning to South Dakota to work in the Rosebud Agency's tribal office. He moved to Cleveland, Ohio, and became director of the Cleveland Indian Center, which later changed its name to Cleveland AIM. Means was aggressive and outspoken regarding pan-Indian religious, territorial, cultural, and social rights.

In February 1972, an Oglala man, Raymond Yellow Thunder, was beaten, publicly humiliated, and died after being locked in a car trunk in Gordon, Nebraska. Means led a caravan of two hundred cars filled with AIM-supporters across the state line to demand the arrest of the two brothers who perpetrated the crime. Means and AIM were successful in dismissing the local Gordon police chief and initiating dialogue regarding racial grievances between Indians and local Nebraskans.

In January 1973, after Wesley Bad Heart Bull had been killed by a South Dakota businessman, a subsequent altercation between AIM and police at the Custer, South Dakota, courthouse exploded into a riot. Thirty people were arrested, and this incident prompted the Federal Bureau of Investigation (FBI) to assign sixty-five U.S. marshals to Pine Ridge to enforce security, protect mining interests, and conduct surveillance. Fed up with government intervention, Means, along with several hundred people, traveled to the small community of Wounded Knee and demanded recognition as a sovereign nation on February 28, 1973. They were quickly surrounded by the FBI and other government agents. What began as a two-day protest became a prolonged siege. When it was over, two Indians were dead and a federal marshal was permanently paralyzed. Means and Banks were prominent within the international media as spokesmen for the Sioux. Both were arraigned on ten felony counts in a trial that lasted eight months.

The federal judge, Frederick Nichol, finally threw the case out of court on the grounds of prosecutorial misconduct.

In February 1974, in a hotly contested and rigged election, Dick Wilson barely defeated Means as tribal chairman. AIM was pitted against non-AIM factions. Tensions increased dramatically when Wilson's supporters ordered all those who voted for Means off the reservation and terrorized AIM members. Means was shot in the kidney by a Bureau of Indian Affairs officer and, along with six other pending charges against him, was arraigned for assault.

Between 1973 and 1980, Means was tried in four separate cases, spent one year in state prison in Sioux Falls, South Dakota, was stabbed there, and survived four other shootings. In April 1981, Means and a caravan of twenty cars journeyed to Victoria Creek Canyon in the Black Hills and established Camp Yellow Thunder, with the intent to build eighty permanent structures. Claims against the U.S. Forest Service were filed for 800 acres of surrounding forest, and the issue became embroiled in legal proceedings.

Since then, Means has traveled extensively and adopted many causes, including the Miskito Indians of Nicaragua. As of 1984, he had been married four times and fathered eight children. He left the American Indian Movement in January 1988, stating that it "had accomplished the impossible." In 1992, he played the role of Chingachgook in the movie *The Last of the Mohicans* and, while on the set, served as liaison between Indian extras and the movie producers.

Richard Oakes
1942–72

Mohawk activist

Richard Oakes was born on the St. Regis Reservation in New York, near the Canadian border. He attended school until he was sixteen years old and quit during the eleventh grade because he felt the U.S. school system "never offered me anything." Oakes then began a brief career in the iron work industry, working both on and off reservation. The early years of his life were spent in New York, Massachusetts, and Rhode Island before he moved to California. During that time, he attended Adirondack Community College in Glen Falls, New York, and Syracuse University. While traveling cross-country to San Francisco, California, Oakes visited several Indian reservations and became aware of their political and economic situations.

Oakes worked at several jobs in San Francisco until he had an opportunity to enroll in San Francisco State College in February 1969. During this time, he married Annie Marufo, a Kashia Pomo Indian from northern California, and adopted her five children.

Oakes was a leader in the November 1969 occupation of Alcatraz Island, an event that became the catalyst for the emerging Indian activism that continued into the 1970s. The occupation of Alcatraz Island was an attempt by urban Indians to attract national attention to the failure of U.S. government policy toward American Indians. The press and many of the Indian occupiers recognized Oakes as the "Indian leader" at Alcatraz. He left Alcatraz Island in January 1970 after his stepdaughter, Yvonne Oakes, died from a head injury after falling down a stairwell. After leaving Alcatraz Island, Oakes remained active in Indian social issues and was particularly instrumental in the Pit River Indian movement to regain ancestral lands in northern California.

On September 21, 1972, Oakes was shot and killed by a YMCA camp employee in Sonoma County, California. He had gone to the camp to find a youth who was staying with the Oakes family. The camp employee was charged with involuntary manslaughter, but charges were later dropped on the grounds that Oakes had come "menacingly toward" him.

Richard Oakes still lives in the memory of thousands of Indian people who remember the rise of Indian activism and the effort to regain traditional Indian lands in the Bay Area. Most particularly, Oakes is remembered for his leadership during the Alcatraz Island occupation.

William Lewis Paul was born in southeast Alaska, and as a young man was sent to the Carlisle Boarding School in Pennsylvania. He went on to complete a law degree, which he used to campaign against discrimination and to fight for labor rights and Tlingit land rights. The Tlingit are a Northwest Coast people, organized

William Lewis Paul, Sr.
1885–1977

Tlingit lawyer and activist

into Raven and Eagle moieties (half divisions), which are further subdivided into clans and houses.

After finishing his education, Paul became an active leader within the Alaska Native Brotherhood (ANB), which was formed in 1912 by one Tsimpshian and eleven Tlingit Indians, as an organization to fight for Tlingit, and more generally Indian, civil rights and economic development. During the 1920s and 1930s, Paul became one of the main leaders of the ANB, and the organization made considerable progress in increasing membership and in pursuing its organizational goals. From 1923 to 1932, Paul edited *The Alaska Fisherman*, a newspaper devoted to Indian issues and especially fishing rights issues. In *The Alaska Fisherman*, Paul criticized non-Indian use of fish nets that took too much fish and threatened to destroy the salmon supplies. He also took on civil rights issues and advocated the boycotting of theaters that forced Natives to sit in special sections of the theater. Paul used his legal background to gain the right of Natives to vote in Alaska Territory elections, for Native children to attend public schools, and to form a union for Alaska Natives who worked in the cannery industry.

Paul was a central figure in the Tlingit and Haida land claim case between 1929 and 1965. The Haida are another Northwest Coast people who live at the southern tip of the Alaska panhandle and are organized by moieties and clans like the Tlingit. In 1929, the ANB initiated a land claim suit against the United States for the loss of most of the land in the panhandle of Alaska, which the U.S. government in 1912 made into the Tongass National Forest. After gaining a waiver from the U.S. government in the 1930s, the Tlingit and Haida were allowed to sue for their lost land. Nevertheless, the Tlingit and Haida claim was not settled until the late 1950s, and in 1965 Tlingit and Haida Indians were paid $7.5 million. Paul devoted much of his time to seeing through the successful resolution of the Tlingit and Haida land claims case.

For his work and dedication for the Indian community, the Tlingit and Haida people greatly revere Paul's name and memory. His papers (1915–70) are deposited at the University of Washington archive in Seattle.

Andrew Paull was born at the Mission Reserve of the Squamish Nation in southwestern British Columbia. He worked as a longshoreman until the age of twenty-one, when he quit his job to become an interpreter for the McKenna-McBride Commission, established by the federal and British Columbia governments to address issues surrounding Indian reserves in the province. Paull interpreted and translated the Salish language, the language of the Squamish people and other aboriginal groups in southwestern British Columbia. His participation brought him prominence and introduced him to many different indigenous peoples of the province.

In June 1916, Paull, with Peter Kelly of the Haida Nation, organized a conference in Vancouver to address tribal rights to land. Sixteen tribal groups from across the province were represented, and the conference formed itself into the Allied Indian Tribes of British Columbia. In 1919, the Allied Tribes, after extensive consultation, prepared a statement of Indian rights to ancestral land in British Columbia that many viewed as the authoritative statement of British Columbia Indian claims. In 1927, Paull advocated the recognition of Indian lands before a special parliamentary committee struck in Ottawa to address Indian issues. The committee refused to recognize aboriginal rights to land and recommended the prohibition of any transaction designed to assist the bringing of Indian land claims to court. When the committee's recommendation became law, the Allied Tribes ceased to exist, and Paull turned to other activities. He became a sportswriter for a Vancouver daily and promoted Indian social events ranging from lacrosse games to beauty pageants. He re-entered political life in 1944 when he served as president of the North American Indian Brotherhood for three years before quitting amid charges of financial mismanagement. Paull then spent the next decade as a spokesperson for Salish people in the British Columbia interior.

Leonard Peltier figured prominently in the American Indian Movement (AIM), an activist organization working for Indian treaty and civil rights. He is now serving two consecutive life sentences in prison, after a controversial conviction for killing two Federal Bureau of Investigation (FBI) agents.

Andrew Paull
1892–1959

Squamish activist

Leonard Peltier
1944–

Ojibway activist

Born on September 12, 1944, in Grand Forks, North Dakota, Peltier spent a difficult childhood, moving with his family from copper mines to logging camps. When his parents separated, he was placed in Wahpeton Indian School in North Dakota, where he encountered strict disciplinary treatment. He returned to live with his mother in Grand Forks, but at fourteen he left home to find work, and by the age of twenty, he was part owner of an auto body shop in Seattle, Washington.

Peltier first became involved with AIM in 1970 and was soon he a member of AIM's inner circle, traveling with Dennis Banks, a major AIM leader, to raise financial support for the group. Peltier participated in many AIM activities, including the takeover of the Bureau of Indian Affairs offices in the early 1970s.

In August 1973, Peltier undertook a Sun Dance, a sacred vision-seeking ceremony practiced by members of many Plains Indian nations. To induce pain in order to obtain a vision, his chest was pierced with bone thongs tied to a sacred stick, and he stood before the sacred center pole for four days and nights.

In October 1973, Peltier returned to Seattle but spent the next year-and-a-half traveling about the country. In the summer of 1975, he was living on the Pine Ridge Reservation in South Dakota.

There are many conflicting stories regarding the events of June 26, 1975, which ultimately led to Peltier's conviction and jail sentence. Nevertheless, this much is clear: FBI agents Jack Coler and Ronald Williams and Pine Ridge resident Joe Killsright were killed in a shootout near Oglala, South Dakota, on the Pine Ridge Reservation. Leonard Peltier was among a group of Lakota engaged in a shooting exchange with the FBI agents. FBI and Indian police reinforcements soon arrived and returned fire, killing Killsright. Peltier and others hid out in homes of relatives or friends in Pine Ridge; Peltier then slipped into Canada, where he was arrested in early 1976.

In a controversial and disputed trial at Fargo, North Dakota, from which 80 percent of the defense testimony was excluded, Peltier was convicted of the murder of the two FBI agents. Peltier was sentenced to two consecutive life terms in prison and transferred to the high-security penitentiary at Marion, Illinois. After a brief transfer to a prison in California, Peltier was returned to the Marion prison.

In many foreign nations, especially in the former socialist countries, Peltier is considered a political prisoner of the United States. New evidence regarding the Pine Ridge shootout has been presented by Peter Matthiessen in the *Nation*, disputing Peltier's involvement in the murder of the FBI agents.

Redbird Smith was an advocate for the restoration of cultural traditions among his people and led a resistance movement against policies of the U.S. government to redistribute Indian lands. He and a number of colleagues revived the Keetoowah Society to protect Indian sovereignty.

Redbird Smith
1850–1918

Cherokee tribal leader and activist

Redbird Smith was born near Fort Smith, Arkansas. His father was Cherokee and his mother, part-Cherokee. By the late 1890s, the U.S. government's land allotment policies were finally reaching the so-called "Five Civilized Tribes" in present-day Oklahoma. The Choctaw, Chickasaw, Cherokee, Creek, and Seminole were called the Five Civilized Tribes because they had formed constitutional governments, many had accepted Christianity, and they had organized school systems. For most Indians, allotment was tantamount to cultural and political extinction. In 1898, Congress passed the Curtis Act, which abolished most operations of the governments among the Five Civilized Tribes. For land to be allotted, however, the government still sought some degree of Indian acceptance. This approval was usually obtained through rather unscrupulous methods. In response to these events, some members of the Cherokee Nation revived the Nighthawk Keetoowah society, an old religious group with a strong interest in perpetuating Cherokee culture and religion. Redbird Smith was one of the primary leaders in the revival movement.

The Nighthawk Keetoowah was a conservative wing of the original Keetoowah society that had been reorganized in the late 1850s before the U.S. Civil War in order to promote political unity among the Cherokee. Smith and the Nighthawks claimed that their society was a religious organization and refused to recognize the right of the U.S. government to disperse tribal lands. Smith led a passive resistance movement that used civil disobedience tactics to disrupt enrollments for distribution of allotted land, which was usually about 160 acres for a male head of household. In 1902, Smith was arrested by federal marshals and forced to sign the enrollment. Under unrelenting federal pressure, the allotment agreements were eventually signed.

In 1907, the Indian Territory became the state of Oklahoma. Smith himself was elected principal chief of the Cherokee in 1908. His activism did not end however. In 1912, he co-founded the Four Mothers Society, dedicated to preserving and advocating for the political and legal rights of Indian tribes. The Keetoowah society continues to exist today, including the Nighthawk segment revived by Smith's activities in the middle 1890s.

John Baptiste Tootoosis, Jr.
1899–1989

Cree activist

The grandson of Poundmaker, the famous Cree chief who fought for better treaty terms from Canadian authorities for his people, John Tootoosis was an important political organizer and leader of the Plains Cree people, a tribe that had moved west from central Canada to the Canadian plains with the expansion of the fur trade in the seventeenth century. He was born on his grandfather's reserve, the Poundmaker Indian Reserve in Saskatchewan, and was one of eleven children. When he was young, Tootoosis tended to his father's sheep. At the urging of Canadian authorities, he was sent by his parents to a residential school. At the age of sixteen, John worked for a farmer in Saskatchewan to contribute to the family expenses. In his late teens, he nearly died of an unknown disease, and while he was ill, he vowed that he would devote his life to his people if he were to recover.

Upon his recovery, Tootoosis was chosen chief of his people at the tender age of twenty, only to be informed by Canadian authorities that Canadian law prohibited the selection of a chief under twenty-one years of age. In the same year, Tootoosis demonstrated his rebellious and proud nature by fencing in land on his reserve to prevent Canadian authorities from leasing it to third parties against his people's will. Tootoosis spoke out often against the failure of Canadian authorities to permit Indian people to participate in decisions that affect their lives. He fought for better health care and educational facilities for his people. Tootoosis was instrumental in organizing Native people throughout the province of Saskatchewan and indeed across the country. He was a founding member of the League of Indians of Canada in 1919, the National American Indian Brotherhood in 1943, and the Union of Saskatchewan Indians in 1946. Later in life, Tootoosis worked as a teacher and an authority on the Cree language.

John Trudell was an active participant in many Native American protests of the 1960s and 1970s.

John Trudell
1947–

Santee Sioux activist and musician

He participated in the 1969 occupation of Alcatraz Island by Indians of All Tribes, Inc., an organization that symbolized participation of all Native American Indians. He joined the Alcatraz occupation ten days after the November 20, 1969, landing and remained on the island until U.S. officials removed the last fifteen occupiers on June 11, 1971. The occupation of Alcatraz Island was an attempt by urban Indians to attract national attention to the failure of U.S. government policy toward American Indians. Trudell became the occupation's voice through Radio Free Alcatraz, a radio station set up on the island which broadcast from Berkeley, Los Angeles, and New York City, thus bringing the occupation and the concerns of Indian people before a national audience. During the occupation period, Trudell traveled throughout the nation, speaking to Indian and non-Indian groups regarding the occupation and raising support for the return of Alcatraz Island to Indian people. Alcatraz Island, however, later became a national park. The occupation of Alcatraz Island is seen by many as an early catalyst to the rising Red Power movement which continued into the mid-1970s.

Trudell joined the American Indian Movement (AIM) in the spring of 1970 and became a national spokesman for AIM soon thereafter. Although much of its inspiration derived from Indian fishing-rights battles during the 1960s and 1970s in the states of Washington and Oregon, AIM's initial concerns were jobs, housing, education, and the protection of Indians from police abuse and violence. In 1970, AIM started a program to assist juvenile offenders as an alternative to reform school.

Trudell participated in the 1972 Trail of Broken Treaties, a national car-caravan bringing together urban and reservation Indians from across the nation designed to culminate in the presentation of a formal list of demands on the federal government by Indian people. Failure of communication between leaders of the caravan and federal officials resulted in an impasse and a seventy-one hour occupation of the Bureau of Indian Affairs office in Washington, D.C., where thousands of dollars worth of damage to the building and office equipment occurred.

Trudell was elected co-chair of AIM in 1973, and he participated in the 1973 armed seizure of Wounded Knee, a small town in the heart of the Pine Ridge Sioux Reservation in South Dakota. Wounded Knee is the site of the 1890 massacre by the Seventh Calvary of Sioux Chief Big Foot and two hundred or more Sioux men, women, and children.

In 1976, he coordinated the AIM support for the defense of Leonard Peltier, who was convicted of murdering two FBI agents in June 1975 on the Pine Ridge Reservation. Trudell's wife Tina, her mother, and the three Trudell children were burned to death in a mysterious fire on February 11, 1979, twelve hours after Trudell, during a demonstration in support of Leonard Peltier, burned an upside-down American flag on the steps of the FBI building in Washington, D.C.

John Trudell now resides in Los Angeles. He served as a consultant for the documentary film, *Incident at Oglala*, and worked as an actor in the film *Thunderheart*. In 1992, he released his debut album *AKA Graffiti Man,* in which he reads his poetry backed by rock and Indian musical styles. Trudell toured with his Graffiti Man Band in the fall of 1992.

Sarah Winnemucca was active as a peacemaker, teacher, and defender of her people's rights. She was born near the Humboldt River in western Nevada, the fourth of nine children. When she was ten, she and her family moved to where her grandfather, Truckee, lived near San Jose, California. When she was fourteen, she moved in with the family of a stagecoach agent, Major William Ormsby, where she learned English. She returned to San Jose in 1860 at her grandfather's dying request. Winnemucca was able to study at a convent school only one month before several non-Indian parents objected to the presence of Paiute girls. Thereafter, she found work as a servant and spent much of her salary on books.

The Paiute War began in 1860 and was led by Winnemucca's cousin, Numaga. She and many non-hostile Paiute were moved to a reservation near Reno, Nevada. During the Snake War in 1866, the military requested that she and her brother, Naches, act as intermediaries. Winnemucca became the official interpreter in the military's negotiations with the Paiute and Shoshoni. She was convinced that the army could be trusted more than the Indian agents, and she voiced her concerns to U.S. Senator John Jones about mistreatment of Indians by Indian service employees.

Some northern Paiute, including Winnemucca, were relocated to the Malheur Reservation in Oregon in 1872. While there, she met and became friends with reservation agent Samuel Parrish. She assisted with his agricultural program, served as interpreter, and taught school. Agent William Rinehart replaced Parrish, and his failure to pay the Paiute for their agricultural labors led to the Bannock War of 1878. General Oliver Howard used Winnemucca as a peacemaker and interpreter. The Paiute were forced to leave the Malheur Reservation and relocate to the Yakima Reservation in present-day Washington State.

Winnemucca went to San Francisco and Sacramento in 1879; in lectures to sympathetic audiences, she discussed the treatment of Indians by Indian service employees. Despite widespread public support for the Paiute's right to return to Malheur, no funding

Sarah Winnemucca
1844–91

Northern Paiute
activist and educator

Major Culture Areas

Culture areas, such as Southwestern or Northeastern Woodlands, are used to describe geographical areas in which several Native American nations lived and shared a similar ecological environment, and hence similar methods of food production, such as hunting and gathering or horticulture. Nevertheless, within a specific culture area, there may be several very different cultures and a multiplicity of languages and dialects, such as the Southeast, where the Cherokee speak an Iroquoian language, while the Choctaw speak a Muskogean language. Anthropologists have used culture areas extensively, and they have been primarily interested in reconstructing how Indian peoples lived prior to extensive Western contact after 1500. This chapter presents a series of culture areas, however, that differs from the usual culture areas used by anthropologists, since our primary concern is for presenting contemporary Native North American life. The way that Native North Americans live today is more determined by political and economic relations with U.S. or Canadian society than by the ecological environments of the pre-

contact period. For example, Oklahoma is a culture area on our list, and not on the traditional anthropologist lists, because during the nineteenth century, many Indian nations from the East, Plains, and other places, such as the Delaware, Shawnee, Cherokee, Choctaw, Modoc, and many others, were moved by the U.S. government to Indian Territory (present-day Oklahoma). While in Oklahoma, these nations were relegated to similar relations with the state of Oklahoma and the federal government, and were greatly affected by the changing national market economy, as were all U.S. citizens. These many immigrant tribes are now known as Oklahoman Indians, and they themselves identify as Oklahoman Indians. Similarly, we have used Canada as a culture area, rather than Arctic and sub-Arctic, and list Alaska and California as culture areas, because of their unique histories and relations with non-Indians.

Consequently, the ecological models of the anthropologists do not suit the purposes of portraying contemporary Native life. The following list of culture areas draws on the basic culture areas of anthropology, but our concerns are focused on providing an overview of the peoples who live in the culture area, their cultural, social, and political history, and major contemporary issues. Most culture areas have far too many tribes to discuss individually, so a regional map for each culture area is provided for the reader to note the range of contemporary Native peoples living in the culture area. Since there are too many communities to describe within the space allowed, the authors selected specific Indian communities for short descriptions, and gave general overviews of the history and significant contemporary issues of the culture areas.

*N*ative Peoples of *the Northeast*

It is often asserted that the Northeast is not a single culture area but is a region that has significant ecological diversity while maintaining a nominal degree of cultural cohesiveness. During the period from 1000 B.C. to A.D. 200, the Adena Culture, a variety of mound building sites and cultures, was spread across the present-day Ohio Valley and extended east to sites in present-day western New York and western Pennsylvania. The Hopewell Culture, another mound building culture stretching across the southern Great Lakes and the Mississippi and Ohio valleys, followed from A.D. 300 to A.D. 700. Both the Hopewell and Adena people lived in villages, and corn was a staple part of their diet. The mounds of this period, often built as burial memorials, were cone-shaped. The Mississippian Culture, A.D. 800 to A.D. 1600, had influence only in the southern portion of the northeast coast, and here the mounds became temples for an aristocratic priesthood. When the earliest Europeans visited the northeast area in the early 1500s, they did not find stratified societies with temples built on mounds, but found fortified sedentary towns, with houses organized according to clan and lineage groups, as were found among the Iroquois along the St. Lawrence River. In the early 1500s, the peoples of the northeast had hunting cultures; horticulture (farming with hand implements) increased in the south. During the latter part of the sixteenth century, Algonkian-speaking hunting nations, like

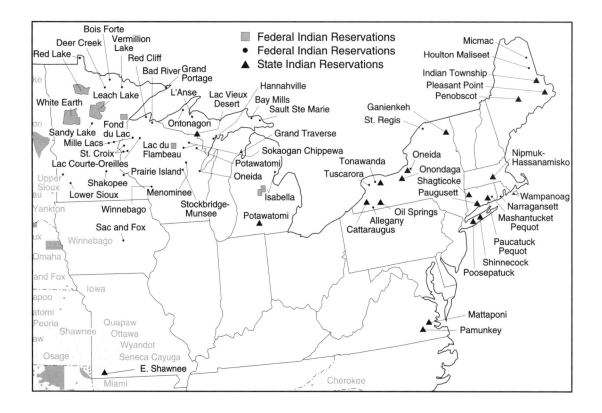

Federal Indian Reservations
Federal Indian Reservations
State Indian Reservations

Bois Forte
Deer Creek
Vermillion Lake
Red Lake
Red Cliff
Bad River
Grand Portage
White Earth
Leach Lake
L'Anse
Hannahville
Lac Vieux Desert
Bay Mills
Sault Ste Marie
Fond du Lac
Ontonagon
Sandy Lake
Mille Lacs
Lac du Flambeau
St. Croix
Lac Courte-Oreilles
Prairie Island
Potawatomi
Sokaogon Chippewa
Grand Traverse
Oneida
Upper Sioux
Shakopee
Lower Sioux
Menominee
Winnebago
Stockbridge-Munsee
Isabella
Sac and Fox
Potawatomi
Winnebago
Omaha
and Fox
Iowa
apoo
atomi
Peoria
Shawnee
Quapaw
Ottawa
Wyandot
Seneca Cayuga
Osage
E. Shawnee
Miami
Cherokee

Micmac
Houlton Maliseet
Indian Township
Pleasant Point
Penobscot
Ganienkeh
St. Regis
Oneida
Nipmuk-Hassanamisko
Tonawanda
Onondaga
Tuscarora
Shagticoke
Paugusett
Wampanoag
Narragansett
Oil Springs
Mashantucket Pequot
Allegany
Cattaraugus
Paucatuck Pequot
Shinnecock
Poosepatuck
Mattaponi
Pamunkey

Contemporary Indian tribes of the northeastern United States.

the Ottawa and Ojibway, were migrating into the northeast area and started pushing sedentary Iroquoian people further west and south. Many Algonkian-speaking nations, such as the Lenape (or Delaware) and Wampanoag, occupied the coastal regions of present-day New England, and they lived by hunting, fishing and planting corn, beans, pumpkins and other vegetables. Iroquoian peoples occupied present-day upstate New York and sites along the lower Great Lakes. It appears that during the 1500s, the Iroquoian peoples were already subject to Algonkian invasion, and the arrival of the Europeans tended to intensify the struggle. By the 1700s, these invasions induced many Algonkian nations to move further west into the Great Lakes region, where they often displaced the Natives of the region. Riding the wave of colonial expansion, the Ojibway, Potawatomi, and Ottawa all migrated into the upper Great Lakes area and displaced the peoples of the Illinois Confederacy, who moved from Wisconsin into

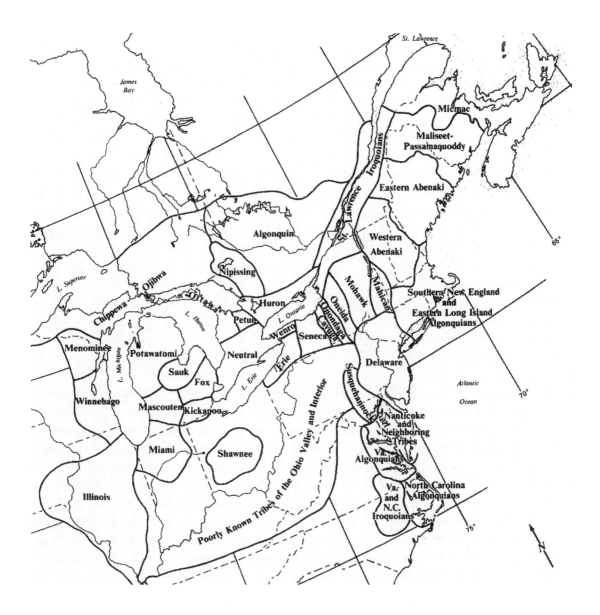

present-day Illinois. During the 1700s, the Ojibway moved into the Minnesota region and began to contest hunting, trapping, and wild rice resources. American Indians in the Northeast region sustained almost continual contact with European explorers from about 1497 onward. Native American contact with Europeans was particularly prolonged and intense along the eastern seaboard of

Key to Tribal Territories.

Courtesy of the

Government Printing Office,

Washington, D.C.

the Atlantic Ocean. Many coastal American Indian groups in the Northeast consequently did not have the liberty or the time to bounce back from the onslaught of European diseases, military aggression, land cessions, and political demands. Thus, these coastal groups were often dispersed into other tribes or decimated, often before Europeans were able to record information about them.

The coastal peoples of present-day New England were rapidly brought under colonial law by the end of King Philip's War (1675–76), and most Indians who stayed in the English New England colony were left to small towns, and adopted Christian religion and town government. Many of the New England Indians, most of whom were Algonkian speakers, lived on the margins of New England society and became "praying Indians." A similar fate awaited the Indians of Virginia: By 1675, the Powhatan Confederacy was demolished by Virginia settlers, and the Indians were forced to live under Virginia law and custom. As in New England, these Indians lived in obscurity until this century.

However, a surprising amount of their culture survives in coastal northeastern Indian oral traditions. The Penobscot and Passamaquoddy of Maine and several other groups (mostly of the Algonkian linguistic group) survive in their original homeland largely because white settler pressure was less severe in the northern coastal part of the region. The Algonkian-speaking peoples of the southern coastal part of the region (the Powhatan, Nanticoke, Delaware, Pequot, Abenaki, and others) bore the full brunt of European settler pressure and thus had a great deal more difficulty maintaining their land base and traditions.

In the end, the Indian nations of the Great Lakes did not fare much better than the coastal peoples did. The Great Lakes region was inhabited by Central Algonkian- and Siouan-speaking groups (such as the Shawnee, Fox, Sauk, Kickapoo, Winnebago, Menominee, Potawatomi, Chippewa, Ottawa and others), who engaged in horticulture and hunting. Except for a few isolated examples, these groups did not come in contact with French traders until the latter part of the seventeenth century. Until well into the eighteenth century, the French used the Iroquois as middlemen in the fur trade, or they had to use devious routes to overcome the economic and military control of the Iroquois. In 1763, Pontiac, an Ottawa chief, and in 1805–12, Tecumseh, a Shawnee warrior, organized alliances of tribal groups and made political and military efforts to slow down European encroachment in the Great Lakes region. These efforts demonstrated the resolve of the Great Lakes Native peoples to resist European domination.

By the late 1790s, however, the once powerful Iroquois nations were scattered and living on small reservations of land in present-day New York and southern Canada. By the 1860s, the Algonkian speakers of the Great Lakes regions were also relegated to small reservations. These Indians suffered the fate of most northern Indian nations following the decline of the fur trade market: Many Indians no longer had the means to trade for the manufactured goods—such as guns, metal tools, and textiles—that had become necessities during the 1700 and 1800s. Consequently, the impoverished Indians sold land and, in return, lived on small reservations. However, in some cases, such as the Chippewa (Ojibway), the Indians retained treaty rights to hunt and fish in their accustomed places. These treaty rights to land and hunting and fishing places, negotiated in the 1850s, later became major points of controversy in the 1970s and 1980s.

While some important groups in the Great Lakes—such as the Shawnee, Delaware, Potawatomi, and others—yielded to settler pressure and were dispersed to Oklahoma and other areas, many of today's indigenous groups along the Great Lakes live on reservations. Throughout much of this century, most Indians of the Great Lakes region lived in poverty and in social and political marginality. Only after the 1960s were there greater efforts at community organization to assert treaty rights, land claims, and tribal and cultural identities.

THE IROQUOIAN PEOPLES ✦ ✦ ✦ ✦ ✦ ✦ ✦ ✦ ✦ ✦ ✦ ✦ ✦ ✦ ✦ ✦ ✦ ✦ ✦

Iroquoian is a term used to identify several indigenous nations that shared a similar language and culture. The major Iroquoian nations included the Mohawk, Seneca, Cayuga, Onondaga, Oneida, Susquehannock, Erie, Huron, and others. The Iroquoian peoples shared a similar way of life, usually based on intensive horticulture, fishing, and hunting. Their villages were often palisaded and organized according to clans, which were kinship groups reckoned through mothers.

At the time of European contact in the early 1500s, the Iroquoian peoples lived along the St. Lawrence River (in upper New York State), along the lower Great Lakes, and in the Susquehanna River Valley (in present-day Pennsylvania). Because of their inland location, they were relatively unaffected, compared to Native coastal peoples, by early European trade and settler expansion. Thus, we know more about the pre-colonial life-styles of the Iroquoian nations than we know about cultures and histories of the indigenous coastal nations.

One of the most well-known Iroquoian groups was the Five Nations of the Haudenosaunee, which means People of the Longhouse. Sometime between A.D.1000 and 1350, the Mohawk, Oneida, Onondaga, Cayuga, and Seneca formed a confederation consisting of their five nations, with chiefs drawn from forty-nine families, who were present at the origin of the confederacy. The origin story of the Iroquois Confederacy holds that a Peacemaker, Deganawidah, and his spokesman, Hiawatha, planted a Great Tree of Peace at the Onondaga Nation (near Syracuse, New York) to resolve the blood feuds that had been dividing the Haudenosaunee people. Through the symbolic tree planting, the Haudenosaunee Peacemaker instituted peace, unity, and clear thinking among the Haudenosaunee people. Deganawidah passed on the Great Law, which is the constitution of the Iroquois Confederacy.

During the colonial period, this structure enabled them to take advantage of their political, economic, and geographic position in the northeast. By adopting members of other Iroquoian groups, such as the Huron and Tuscarora, the Haudenosaunee maintained their historically strategic position in the Northeast, between the colonies of New France and New York, in the fur trade, and during the diplomatic rivalries between England and France in the seventeenth and eighteenth centuries. At the height of their influence, from about 1650–1777, the Haudenosaunee heartland extended from Albany, New York to Niagara Falls, with its outermost borders stretching to southeastern Ontario, New England, northern Pennsylvania, and northeastern Ohio.

The Iroquois played an important role in the birth of the United States. Even before the advent of the American Revolution, the Haudenosaunee had counseled American leaders on the virtues of Iroquois-style unity, democracy, and liberty. From the writing of the Albany Plan of Union, a 1755 plan to unite the colonies, to the creation of the United States Constitution, the Iroquois were present in body and/or spirit as Americans sought to create a democratic alternative to the British monarchy. At the request of the Founders, Iroquois chiefs were present at the debates on the Declaration of Independence in Philadelphia in May and June of 1776.

On June 11, 1776, an Onondaga sachem gave John Hancock an Iroquois name at Independence Hall. Drawing by John Kahionhes Fadden.

Over the course of several weeks, the Iroquois observed the new American nation emerging and gave the president, John Hancock, an Iroquois name, "Karanduawn," which means "the Great Tree." Indeed, some Americans, such as Thomas Jefferson, believed that American governments were very similar to American Indian governments

like that of the Iroquois; Jefferson stated in 1787 that the "only condition on earth to be compared to [our government] . . . is that of the Indians, where they still have less government than we." On the eve of the Constitutional Convention, John Adams admonished the delegates to the convention to conduct "an accurate investigation of the form of government of the . . . Indians," since the separation of powers in American Indian governments [like the Iroquois] is "marked with a precision that excludes all controversy." During the Constitutional Convention, delegates such as James Wilson of Pennsylvania clearly stated that the "British government cannot be our model." In 1790, Thomas Jefferson and others toasted the U.S. Constitution as an [Iroquois] "tree of peace" that sheltered the Americans "with its branches of union." Thus, American Indian ideas associated with groups like the Iroquois of the Northeast had a decided impact on the development of American democracy.

Even though the Founders respected the Iroquois for their wisdom in governmental organization, between 1777 and 1800, the U.S. government allowed various land companies to buy virtually all Iroquois lands. By 1880, the Iroquois either left to live in Canada or were relegated to several small reservations in upper New York State. The remaining Iroquois lands and disputed territories were guaranteed by contract with the land companies and by treaties with the United States and New York State.

CONTEMPORARY HAUDENOSAUNEE
CULTURAL RESTORATION ◆

The Haudenosaunee of the twentieth century saw the traditionalist Longhouse religion of the prophet, Handsome Lake, revived on the Caughnawaga and St. Regis Mohawk reservations. Handsome Lake was a Seneca prophet whose ministry extended from 1799 to 1815. His message urged accommodation to the presence of the white people while maintaining many of the important traditional ways of the Haudenosaunee. In the 1830s, Iroquois traditionalists and the followers of Handsome Lake formed a church and resurrected the traditional Iroquois chief system in opposition to the "elected" chief system that currently asserts power on their reservations. Today, the Iroquois traditional chieftainship system is present on three reservations in New York (Onondaga, Tuscarora, and Tonawanda Seneca). There, the clan mothers still nominate the chiefs of their clans, and the chiefs are brought into office through an ancient condolence ceremony.

The Iroquois have survived, and they have struggled to maintain their ancient traditions. Various Iroquois languages are still spoken and are being taught to Indian and non-Indian students alike. But the Iroquois culture has also changed, as it must if the people are to endure. Today, the Iroquois work in many of the same professions as the dominant society. They are ironworkers, steel workers, teachers, businesspersons, and artists. However, many still maintain the traditional culture in the modern setting. At the Onondaga Reservation, the Great Law is still recited as it was in precolonial times, and such meetings are well attended by reservation and urban Iroquois. The great festivals and thanksgivings continue as a part of their lives. They are forging a life-style that includes the wisdom of their ancestors and the benefits of modern technology, to create a culture in which they can live comfortably and in peace.

Contemporary Iroquois are insisting on their treaty rights. For example, since the 1920s, Iroquois stage annual "border crossings" into Canada in the summer to assert their right, through the Jay's Treaty (1794), to uninhibited passage across the U.S. and Canadian border. The Iroquois have also filed claims against the U.S. government relating to fraudulent loss of land. The results of these claims have been uneven; many Iroquois believe that the only real settlement of land claims can come through some form of land restoration.

Recently, after a generation of struggle, the Iroquois were also able to repatriate, or reclaim, wampum belts that had been held in the New York State Museum. Wampum belts are diplomatic and ceremonial records made from shells and fastened into a string or chain of several rows. Symbols were embroidered into the belts as documents and historical records of diplomatic agreements, treaties, records of important historical events, and records of sacred and ceremonial law. The Iroquois wanted the wampum belts returned so that they could be used and cared for by people who can read and interpret these important documents. Today, as in the past, the Haudenosaunee use the wampum belts as a record of their laws, treaties, and other important events of the past. Wampum belts are analogous in importance to U.S. government documents, such as the Declaration of Independence and the United States Constitution.

Recently, Iroquois leaders have also been active in numerous international treaty forums relating to indigenous people's rights. Since the early 1900s, the Iroquois Confederacy has issued its own passports, which are recognized for travel purposes by many nations.

The Iroquois continue to have a strong affinity for their homeland. Their reservations are parcels of land that they have held on to through hundreds of years of settler pressure. Maintaining and preserving contemporary landholdings is crucial to the continuance of their communities, culture, and identity. The reservation is a place where the Iroquois practice their customs and rituals. Many urban Iroquois return to these homelands to be culturally and spiritually refreshed among their friends and kin. The Iroquois strive to retain their sovereignty, independence, and culture in their reservation communities.

CHIPPEWA FISHING AND TREATY RIGHTS IN MICHIGAN, WISCONSIN, AND MINNESOTA ♦ ♦ ♦ ♦ ♦ ♦ ♦ ♦ ♦ ♦

Many tribes in the northeast continue to struggle to gain national recognition, to maintain cultural communities, and to assert treaty rights. One of the most prominent examples of Native assertion

of treaty rights involves the retention of fishing and hunting privileges among the Chippewa (Anishnabe) of Wisconsin and Minnesota.

The Chippewa in the upper Great Lakes region retained the right to hunt, fish, and gather on lands they sold through treaties to the United States government in the mid-1800s. The United States Constitution states that "treaties are the supreme law of the land"; states may not interfere with such treaties, since they are based on the notion that Indian nations are sovereign and thus have rights to self-determination and self-government. In the early 1980s, the Chippewa began to reassert their aboriginal rights to hunt, fish, and gather in areas specified in treaties that were negotiated in the nineteenth century. This reassertion of treaty rights resulted in legal disputes. On January 25, 1983, a federal court agreed with the Lake Superior Chippewa that hunting, fishing and gathering rights still were reserved and protected in Chippewa treaties. This decision is known as the Voight Decision. Later, the United States Supreme Court refused to hear an appeal of the Voight Decision. Subsequently, federal judges returned the case to district court to "determine the scope of state regulation." Recent court decisions have defined the scope of Chippewa hunting, fishing, and gathering rights in Wisconsin so that they have a right:

(1) to harvest and sell hunting, fishing, and gathering products,
(2) to exercise these rights on private land if necessary to produce a modest living, and
(3) to harvest a quantity sufficient to produce a modest living.

In addition, portions of the game and forest products (excluding commercial timber) available to the Chippewa through their treaty rights have been quantified in court rulings since the Voight Decision. In 1991, the rulings in the Federal District Court implementing the Voight Decision were allowed to stand, since neither the Chippewa nor the state of Wisconsin appealed them by the deadline of May 1991. On May 20, 1991, the Chippewa announced their decision not to appeal, with the following message:

Anishnabe man and woman gather wild rice from canoe in Minnesota. Courtesy of the Minnesota Historical Society.

The . . . Lake Superior Chippewa . . . have preserved . . . [their hunting, fishing and gathering] rights for generations to come, [and they] . . . have this day foregone their right to further appeal . . . . They do this as a gesture of peace and friendship towards the people of Wisconsin, in a spirit they hope may be reciprocated on the part of the general citizenry and officials of this state.

The path to resolving Chippewa fishing rights was littered with racial conflict. During the Indian spearfishing seasons in the late 1980s, Chippewa were subjected to violent harassment by non-Indians while attempting to exercise their treaty rights. They were also subject to numerous racial slurs by non-Indians. Anti-spearfishing slogans included "Save a Walleye; spear a squaw" and "Custer had the right idea." A suit filed by the American Civil Liberties Union on behalf of the Chippewa served to deter some of the more ardent anti-Indian violent protests by the 1990 fishing season. Recently, the Chippewa have exercised their sovereignty by establishing gambling halls on their reservations.

TERMINATION AND THE
MENOMINEE NATION OF WISCONSIN ✦ ✦ ✦ ✦ ✦ ✦ ✦ ✦ ✦ ✦ ✦ ✦ ✦

In the 1950s, the U.S. government embarked on a policy to terminate the treaties and reservations of American Indian nations. The Menominee, a northeast Indian nation, was the first to be

stripped of treaty rights under this policy. Although they were one of the most self-sufficient Indian nations, the Menominee were not prepared to cope with the withdrawal of federal services and trust responsibilities by the time their termination became final in 1961. Although criticism of the termination policy was rapidly mounting in Congress from 1958–60, the Menominee were unsuccessful in having their termination decision reevaluated.

Menominee Enterprises, Inc. (MEI) was set up to manage the tribe's forests, lumber mill, land, and other assets after termination, but it gave too much power to non-Menominee individuals over Menominee affairs. While the Menominee were made shareholders in the new corporation, a Milwaukee trust company controlled a block vote of minors and incompetents (almost 50 percent of the shareholder votes). When the Menominee Reservation became Menominee county, taxes became unrealistically high, unemployment rose, medical care deteriorated and a large part of the housing stock became substandard. In 1967, MEI contracted with a land developer to subdivide lakefront property for sale to vacationers so that the tax base could be broadened. This decision outraged almost every Menominee, leading to the creation of DRUMS (Determination of Rights and Unity for Menominee Shareholders), which filed suit against MEI. The group also protested land sales to outsiders and advocated the restoration of federal jurisdiction on the Menominee Reservation. In 1975, Congressional legislation was finally passed to restore the Menominee treaty rights and federal trust status.

♦ **MAINE INDIAN CLAIMS**

Other Northeastern Indian groups have struggled to keep their land base and identity as the Iroquois have. In 1777, the U.S. government negotiated a treaty with the Maine Indians. In exchange for their assistance in the American Revolution, the government promised to protect the Maine Indians (this treaty, however, was never ratified and the U.S. government did not provide protection). In 1791, the Passamaquoddy Nation of

Maine ceded all but 23,000 of its acres to the Commonwealth of Massachusetts (at this time, Massachusetts had jurisdiction over what is now the State of Maine). Another Maine Indian nation, the Penobscot, ceded almost all of its land through treaties in 1796 and 1818 and a land sale in 1833. The validity of these agreements was not questioned until 1972, when the Passamaquoddy Tribe asked the United States government to sue the State of Maine, arguing that the treaties and agreements had never been approved by the U.S. government. The attorney for the Passamaquoddy stated that the lack of approval of the agreements by the federal government rendered Massachusetts, and later Maine, in violation of the Indian Trade and Intercourse Act of 1790, which required the approval of the U.S. government for any transfer of lands from Indian ownership. The Secretary of the Interior, however, did not agree with the Maine Indians (the Interior Department held that the Maine Indians were not a federally recognized tribe) and did not sue; the Maine Indians went to court to claim approximately two thirds of the state of Maine. Basically, the following were the legal issues involved:

> (1) ascertaining the legality of applying the Indian Trade and Intercourse Act to the Passamaquoddy Indians;
> (2) resolving whether the Act instituted a trust relationship between the United States and the tribe;
> (3) determining whether the U.S. could deny the tribe's request to sue on the basis that there was no trust relationship.

Subsequently, the federal district court held in favor of the tribe on all points, stating that the language of the Act protected the lands of "any . . . tribe of Indians," and that the Passamaquoddy were, indeed, a tribe. The case was appealed to the circuit court and it reaffirmed the rulings of the lower court. However, its ruling narrowly defined the case, holding that the U.S. government had never sufficiently severed the trust relationship with the Maine Indians. The court also stated that it did not foreclose later consideration of whether Congress or the tribe should be deemed in some manner to have acquiesced in, or Congress to have ratified, the tribe's land transactions with Maine.

The state of Maine argued in this case that (1) the Intercourse Acts were never intended to apply to the thirteen original colonies after they became states; (2) the Indians transferred the lands before the Intercourse Act of 1790; and (3) in ratifying the process by which Maine was separated from Massachusetts and admitted as a state in 1820, Congress approved implicitly "all treaties concluded by Massachusetts up to that time."

This decision forced the federal government to act since the president, the Congress, the state, and the tribe all wanted a speedy and less costly solution to the case than continued adjudication. Negotiations began in earnest in 1977 when a report to President Jimmy Carter recommended: (1) the appropriation of $25 million for the Passamaquoddy and Penobscot tribes; (2) requiring the state of Maine to convey a 100,000-acre tract of land to the U.S. government,which would act as a trustee for the tribes; (3) giving assurances to the tribes that U. S. Bureau of Indian Affairs benefits would be accorded them in the future; (4) asking the state of Maine to continue state benefits to the tribes at current fiscal levels; (5) requiring the secretary of the interior to obtain 400,000 additional acres in the claims area for Maine Indians to purchase at fair market value, if so desired by them; (6) that, having received the consent of the state of Maine that it will accomplish the items in points 2 and 4 above, Congress, with tribal consent, shall extinguish all remaining aboriginal title to all lands in Maine; (7) that if tribal consent cannot be obtained, Congress will extinguish all aboriginal title, and the tribes' cases would then proceed through the judicial system to recover or not recover state owned land; (8) that if the consent of the state of Maine cannot be obtained, Congress will appropriate 25 million dollars for the use and benefit of the tribes and will extinguish all aboriginal title whereupon tribes' cases would proceed through the courts against the state-owned land in Maine.

In 1980, after protracted negotiation, the Maine Indians finally reached a settlement that implemented many of the above points while avoiding the pitfalls of numbers 7 and 8. At the signing of the Maine Indian Claims Settlement Act of 1980, President Carter asserted:

> This should be a proud day for . . . the tribes who placed their trust in
> the system that has not always treated them fairly, the leaders of the
> state of Maine who came openly to the bargaining table, the land-
> owners who helped to make the settlement a reality by offering land
> for sale that they might not otherwise have wanted to sell, the mem-
> bers of Congress who realize the necessity of acting and all the citi-
> zens of Maine who have worked together to resolve this problem of
> land title.

If the president had not taken the lead in seeking a consensus, a
long and costly court process or unilateral act by Congress might
have resulted. But Carter seized the initiative by developing a
reasonable set of recommendations and appointing a team to represent the U.S. government in negotiations with the Indians and
Maine. In effect, Carter forced both the state of Maine and the
Indians to negotiate an equitable solution to the Maine Indians'
Claims case.

CONTEMPORARY CONNECTICUT
INDIAN LAND CLAIMS ✦

Other cases involving the land claims of Indians of the Northeast have been working their way through the courts, but Congress and the courts have been slow to act on such suits in the
1980s. In the late 1970s, suits—filed in Connecticut by the
Schaghticoke tribe, the Western Pequot tribe, and the Mohegan tribe—seeking lands allegedly alienated in violation of the
Indian Trade and Intercourse Act of 1790, met with varying
results. The Western Pequot obtained a settlement of their
claims during the Reagan administration. A federal district
court also held that the Mohegan were a tribe and thus had
been violated under the Intercourse Act; the Supreme Court
upheld this decision by refusing to review the lower court's
decision. The Schaghticoke case remains unresolved, but the
Schaghticoke Reservation of 400 acres of allotted land in Connecticut remains secure as a basis for rebuilding the
Schaghticoke Nation.

♦ ♦ ♦ ♦ ♦ ♦ ♦ ♦ ♦ ♦ ♦ ♦ CLAIMS BY MASSACHUSETTS INDIANS IN THE LAST GENERATION

In 1974, the Wampanoag tribe of Gay Head sought recovery of 5,000 acres of land, and in 1976, the town of Gay Head, Massachusetts, voted to deed certain lands to the Indians. While some Indians have agreed to this proposal, others opposed, and final action had to be approved by the state of Massachusetts. The Wampanoag claims were further clouded in 1976, when the Mashpee tribe (Wampanoag) filed suit in federal court to recover 17,000 acres allegedly alienated in violation of the Intercourse Act by the state of Massachusetts. The federal courts subsequently held that the Mashpee were not a tribe and were therefore not subject to the act. The defense questioned the Mashpee's identity as Native Americans, alleging that the Mashpee had American Indian, Caucasian, and African-American blood. It is significant that Native Americans are the only American ethnic group that must legally "prove" their identity by blood quantum and that such exclusive and unequal standards were entertained in the U.S. court system. Contradictions in the court's decisions in these claims matters awaited further clarification. Finally, in 1987, the U.S. government formally recognized the Wampanoag Council of Gay Head, Massachusetts.

♦ ♦ ♦ ♦ ♦ ♦ ♦ ♦ ♦ ♦ RECENT NEW YORK INDIAN LAND CLAIMS

In New York, the Oneida, Cayuga, and St. Regis Mohawk also filed claims under the Intercourse Act. In 1970, the Oneida (New York, Wisconsin, and the Thomas Band Council of Ontario) filed suit for damages for the use of 100,000 acres obtained by New York without the approval of the U.S. government. Although the court ruled that the lands were illegally taken and that damages are in order, there has been little progress in finalizing an agreement. In 1979, the Oneida filed another claim for five million acres, but to date there has been no final resolution of this case.

The Cayuga laid claim to 64,000 acres in New York and got a negotiated settlement that included a $4 million trust fund and a 5,481 acre reservation in return for the extinguishment of the 64,000 acre claim. The land for the settlement was to come from a national forest land and a state park. However, the House of Representatives in 1980 failed to pass legislation to implement the negotiated settlement, and the Cayuga sought the return of the 64,000 acres and damages. The final resolution of this suit is still pending.

The St. Regis Mohawk filed land claims in upper New York State. A proposed settlement in 1980 would have granted them a $7.5 million federal trust fund and 9,750 acres of state land. The case is still under negotiation.

The land claims of the Oneida, Cayuga, and Mohawk nations are among the most difficult claims cases of the twentieth century, and it will take years to settle and fully implement the negotiated agreements. However, these cases received a boost in 1985 when the Supreme Court held in County of Oneida v. Oneida Indian Nation that Oneida lands transferred over 175 years earlier had violated the Indian Intercourse Act. In a landmark decision in American Indian law, the court's opinion found no applicable statute of limitations and no legal basis to deny the Oneida's land claim. The Oneida case established important legal principles that apply to all pending and future Eastern Indian land claims.

CURRENT NARRAGANSETT INDIAN CLAIMS ♦ ♦ ♦ ♦ ♦ ♦ ♦ ♦ ♦ ♦ ♦

In Rhode Island, the Narragansett Indians negotiated a claim with private landholders, the state of Rhode Island, representatives from the Carter Administration, and the town of Charlestown, where the claim was located. The agreement hammered out by the above parties provided the basis for state legislation and a federal statute that provided for the extinguishment of all Narragansett land claims in exchange for 900 acres from the state and another 900 acres to be purchased at federal expense. Subsequently, the Narragansett chartered a state corporation to manage the 1,800 acres of land. To implement the act, the U.S. government established a $3.5 million settlement fund.

ANALYSIS OF INTERCOURSE ACT CLAIMS IN THE NORTHEAST ♦

The court decision that resulted in the Maine Indians obtaining resources and a larger land base clearly makes it easier for them to maintain their communities in the contemporary world. Other Indian groups in the Northeast that filed subsequent claims have had some successes and some failures. The most successful solutions to these claims issues come when tribal governments, Indian interest groups, Indian individuals and the federal and state governments are involved in the formulation and implementation of claims settlements. The most important case to date has been County of Oneida v. Oneida Indian Nation, since it upheld the American Indian argument that there is no applicable statute of limitations on the claims of Eastern Indians based on the Indian Intercourse Act. In 1985, another important administrative decision made by the Federal Internal Revenue Service helped the cause of American Indian recognition among Eastern Indians. When the IRS recognized the Pamunkey tribe of Virginia as a state (a bona fide governmental entity within the United States) for purposes of the Tribal Government Tax Status Act, the IRS, and by implication the U.S. government, asserted that the Pamunkey Nation of Virginia could exercise government functions under existing American Indian legislation. Eastern American Indian tribes have struggled to maintain their identity and land base in spite of overwhelming demographic pressures, obstacles, and land disputes; the legal ambiguities relating to the recognition or non-recognition of the Mashpee

Indians of Massachusetts and other groups in the East also demonstrated the devastating results of non-recognition. (See also the subsection on nonrecognized tribes in Chapter 9.)

Ultimately, responsibility for changing American Indian policies rests with all of American society since the limits of such settlements are determined by the parameters of public opinion. If there is to be an equitable settlement of American Indians claims and issues in the Northeast, the general public and the Indian participants must both have a concept of the larger American Indian policy that squarely recognizes Native American and U.S. sovereignty and seeks to develop a plan of action that appreciates the complex forces, existing governmental entities, and special interests.

CONCLUSION ✦

While Indian groups in the Northeast have won important precedent-setting cases in the last generation, it is important to note that the Iroquois and others have also been active in the international arena in presenting their claims over the taking of Indian lands, unfair leases, and restrictions on tribal religious practices. There is a growing body of international human rights law that recognizes that Native Americans are entitled to political and economic self-determination as well as religious freedom. Although the early European colonists who came to the Northeast did not appreciate the sovereignty of American Indians, contemporary federal and international law is paving the way for American Indians of the Northeast and elsewhere to survive as distinct communities with well-defined sovereign rights and powers.

Donald A. Grinde, Jr.
California Polytechnic State University,
San Luis Obispo

♦ **BIOGRAPHIES**

During his lifetime Black Hawk resisted the expansion of U.S. settlement into his homeland, located near the Rock River in present-day Illinois. As a young man, Black Hawk showed interest in forming a confederation of Indian tribes to protest the many dubious treaties that were the basis of U.S. settlement in the region. In 1832, he fought a series of ill-fated engagements with U.S. forces, known as Black Hawk's War.

In 1829, when Black Hawk and his followers returned to their homeland in the Rock River country from a hunting trip, they found it occupied by white squatters. Some settlers had even moved into Indian dwellings. For the next few years Black Hawk and his people lived an uneasy coexistence with the U.S. intruders. In June 1831, the U.S. Army tried to dislodge Black Hawk from his village. Black Hawk and his people escaped by crossing the Mississippi River.

Black Hawk and about two thousand followers remained on the western side of the Mississippi River until April 5, 1832. As he crossed the Mississippi, U.S. Army troops were hurriedly deployed to meet him. On May 14, the two forces met and Black Hawk's men won the first battle with U.S. forces.

For the next few months, Black Hawk and his followers moved northward into Wisconsin. Meanwhile, the U.S. troops were put under the command of General Winfield Scott who organized a large army in Chicago. Two U.S. military forces caught up with Black Hawk and his followers after months of traveling and subsistence living. On July 21, 1832, at the battle of Wisconsin Heights, a number of Black Hawk's people were killed. Black Hawk hoped to escape via the Mississippi. His path was blocked on August 1, 1832, by the cannon-laden steamship Warrior. With reinforcements of thirteen hundred U.S. regular troops, on August 3, the U.S. forces attacked and killed about three hundred of Black Hawk's people. Black Hawk and a few followers escaped to northern Wisconsin.

Black Hawk

1767–1838

Sac (Sauk) tribal leader

On August 27, Black Hawk and about fifty companions were persuaded to surrender. Black Hawk was imprisoned at Fort Monroe, Virginia. In 1833, the defeated leader was taken to Washington, D.C., where he met President Jackson. In the ensuing years, Black Hawk became something of a media celebrity. Many authors vied to write his biography, which he dictated in 1833. In 1837, Charles Bird King painted his now-famous portrait of Black Hawk. Black Hawk died in 1838 in a land that was not his own and among people he barely knew.

Joseph Brant (Thayendanegea) 1742–1807

Mohawk tribal leader

Joseph Brant (Thayendanegea) was a British army officer and a Mohawk tribal leader. The Mohawk were the easternmost tribe of the Iroquois Confederacy (a group of six nations), and their native territory is located along the Hudson and Mohawk River valleys in New York State and Canada.

He was the son of a full-blooded Mohawk chief, but there are claims that his mother was half European. After the death of the father, his mother remarried a man named Brant; thus he became known as Joseph Brant among the colonists. His sister Molly married Sir William Johnson, a British official who was superintendent in charge of Indians north of the Ohio from 1755 until 1774, and the young Brant went to live in their home as a child.

He attended a Christian school in Connecticut and mastered spoken and written English. In the early 1760s and 1770s, as a translator and diplomat, he helped the English to negotiate with Iroquois tribes. When the American Revolution broke out, Brant aligned himself with the Loyalist cause and traveled to England in 1775. He was quickly commissioned a colonel in the British army and put his diplomacy skills to work enlisting Iroquois allies for the Loyalist cause.

Brant participated in a number of battles directly, and insisted on using his own military tactics and stratagems. In 1777 and 1778, the persistent raids by Indians and British soldiers against settlements in the Ohio Valley convinced General George Washington, the future U.S. president, to send an army into Iroquois country. The Americans succeeded in destroying a number of Iroquois villages, but Brant did not sanction the subsequent American-Iroquois peace treaty and continued to launch raids against American forces.

In appreciation of his military services the English gave him a retirement pension and a large tract of land along the Grand River in Ontario, Canada. Like many others, Brant was an Indian who lived between two worlds. He is credited with having translated the Bible into the Mohawk language and died near his estate near Brantford, Ontario, on November 24, 1807.

Cornplanter was a leading warrior and village leader among the Seneca, one of six nations of the Iroquois Confederacy, who lived in present upstate New York. The Iroquois Confederacy consisted of forty-nine chiefs, or sachems, whose families attended the first meeting of the Iroquois Confederacy some few hundred years before Europeans arrived in North America. Cornplanter belonged to the Seneca Turtle clan, whose sachem held the title of Handsome Lake. Cornplanter, however, was not elected sachem. He earned his role as leader largely through military command and personal influence, which attracted friends and relatives to live on his reserved lands, which by 1800 totaled 1300 acres in northern Pennsylvania.

Cornplanter

d. 1836

Seneca tribal leader

Cornplanter's father was a trader named John O'Bail, who, during the 1730s, lived among the Seneca and traded manufactured goods for furs and skins. O'Bail chose not to live among the Iroquois and left his Seneca wife and child in care of her clan. Cornplanter grew to be a warrior leader. He fought with the French during the French and Indian War (1755–59) and with the British during the American Revolutionary War (1775–83).

After the Revolutionary War, Cornplanter argued that the Iroquois would not survive unless they adopted agriculture and U.S. forms of government. He was opposed by the nationalistic Seneca leader, Red Jacket, who thought the Iroquois would lose their identity if they adopted American life-styles. Between 1799 and 1815, however, Cornplanter's half-brother, Handsome Lake, led a religious and social movement that reorganized much of Iroquois culture.

Cornplanter supported this movement, which led to adoption of agriculture, small farms, and new emphases on moral and religious order within Iroquois communities. Late in life, Cornplanter emphasized the need to retain Iroquois culture and ways.

Keokuk

1783–1848

Sac (Sauk) tribal leader

Keokuk was born around 1783 in the village of Saukenuk in present-day Illinois. He obtained a position of power among his people by demonstrating bravery against the Sioux, although he was not a hereditary chief.

By the early 1800s, the official policy of the U.S. government had become one of forced treaties and acquisition of Indian land. Keokuk, though not recognized as a chief among his own people, was selected by the U.S. government as the official representative of the Sauk because of his refusal to support the British in 1812 and his friendly overtures to the United States. During this era, the government used bribery to bring Keokuk into line with federal land policies. Keokuk signed a number of treaties that included an exchange of Sauk land in the Rock River country for a tract located westward and an annual cash compensation, which was to be administered by Keokuk.

In the 1830s, Keokuk redeemed himself in the eyes of some Sauk by his skillful defense of Sauk land interests against Sioux territorial claims in Washington, D.C. In 1845, Keokuk ceded Iowa lands in exchange for a reservation in Kansas. He died three years later, amid reports that followers of Black Hawk had killed him. Though it is believed Keokuk actually died of dysentery, the rumors of murder were not surprising since in the eyes of many, Keokuk, unlike his peer Black Hawk, did not represent his people in the most loyal fashion.

Little Turtle

(Michikinikwa)

1752–1812

Miami-Mahican tribal leader

Little Turtle was the leader of a Miami Band located near present-day Fort Wayne, Indiana. He was principal war chief of his people during the 1780s and 1790s.

After the American Revolution, a number of wars broke out in the Old Northwest between the Indians living in this region and the growing number of white settlers. Between 1783 and

1790 ongoing skirmishes and attacks made the region a flash point for Indian relations. In 1790, President George Washington ordered federal troops into the region to quell the attacks. Their staunchest opponent was Little Turtle, principal war chief of the regional tribes. During his initial encounters with the federal troops, Little Turtle perfected military tactics, making the best use of concealment, and quick, short, attacks. The methods were devastingly effective in two major encounters against Generals Josiah Harmar and Arthur St. Clair. On November 3, 1791, Little Turtle and his forces surprised St. Clair leaving behind over 600 dead, and almost 300 wounded. It was the worst defeat suffered by U.S. forces against Indians.

Washington's response was to field a third army, this time under the leadership of a seasoned revolutionary war veteran, General Anthony Wayne. Wayne planned his attack carefully and cautiously. Little Turtle's warriors with the encouragement of British officials were confident of victory. Little Turtle himself, however counseled peace in the face of Wayne's well organized campaign. The attack came in an area known as Fallen Timbers. Wayne's forces took so long to get to the battle, that many of Little Turtle's troops had left the battle site. Though the Battle of Fallen Timbers was short, with only few casualties, it was a disheartening defeat for Little Turtle and his followers, who realized that their British supporters were not going to come to their aid. After the battle, Wayne proceeded to destroy Indian villages and farmlands.

The defeat changed Little Turtle's outlook. A year later Wayne dictated the terms of the Treaty of Greenville, in which Little Turtle ceded large sections of Ohio and parts of Indiana. Little Turtle also signed a number of treaties in Fort Wayne in 1803 and 1809, and put his signature on the Treaty of Vincennes in 1805. Little Turtle spent the later part of his life traveling to eastern cities, where he met some of his former adversaries, including George Washington. The former U.S. adversary was granted an annual pension by the government and returned to his homeland on the Maumee River. Even the pleas of Tecumseh to join his cause could not persuade Little Turtle to take up arms again. The former war chief was committed to peace, and encouraged his people to take up farming and abstain from alcohol. He died in 1812 while at Fort Wayne.

John Logan (Tachnechdorus) 1725–80

Mingo (Cayuga) tribal leader

John Logan was a Mingo leader during the Lord Dunmore's War of 1774, when the Mingo and Shawnee Nations tried to block Virginia settlers from crossing the line set by the Proclamation of 1763, which forbade colonial settlement beyond the crest of the Appalachian mountains. Despite the proclamation, settlers and merchants continued to swarm into the Mississippi and Ohio valleys. During this era a number of Shawnee and Mingo allies attempted to withstand the onrush. The Mingo were a group of Iroquois who moved to live and trap in the Ohio Valley and left their homeland in present-day upstate New York.

Logan (Tachnechdorus) was the leader of the bands of Iroquois-speaking Mingo who lived near the headwaters of the Ohio River in western Pennsylvania. He was born a Cayuga, an Iroquois nation, near the Susquehanna River. Over the years Tachnechdorus was given the name Mingo or The Great Mingo. Mingo is the tribal name given to Iroquois living in Pennsylvania and Ohio. After moving to the Ohio region, Logan became a strong supporter of peaceful relations with the colonists. However, when members of his family were massacred for no apparent reason by settlers in 1774, Logan adopted a militant stance and began a series of raids against settlers throughout the trans-Appalachian region. His actions were abetted by British allies and the Shawnee leader, Cornstalk. Logan and Cornstalk fought together in what is known as Lord Dunmore's War. After their defeat in 1774, at the Battle of Point Pleasant, Pennsylvania, Logan refused to attend a peace conference at Scioto, Ohio. It is believed (though some doubt its authenticity) that he delivered an eloquent letter much admired at the time and later cited by Thomas Jefferson. Logan continued his attacks during the American War for Independence. He was killed while returning from Detroit in 1780.

Massasoit was a principal leader of the Wampanoag people in the early 1600s who encouraged friendship with English settlers. As leader of the Wampanoag, Massasoit exercised control over a number of Indian groups that occupied lands from Narragansett Bay to Cape Cod in present-day Massachusetts. Massasoit negotiated friendly relations with the recently arrived Puritan settlers. As early as 1621, with the aid of Squanto, a Wampanoag who spoke English, Massasoit opened communications with the Pilgrims at their Plymouth settlement. He established trading relationships with the settlers, exchanging food for firearms, tools, and other sought-after European products.

Massasoit helped the Puritan settlers in a number of ways including donations of land and advice on farming and hunting. Massasoit also offered the settlers important council on how to protect themselves from other tribes. In 1623, he warned them of an impending attack by hostile Indians. Massasoit's alliance with the settlers created divisions among the region's Indian nations and problems for the Wampanoag who were loyal to Massasoit. Consequently, Massasoit's warriors were forced to wage frequent attacks against hostile Indian groups less inclined to welcome the English settlers.

The Wampanoag chief became close friends with the progressive-minded theologian, Roger Williams, and according to many accounts influenced Williams's relative understanding and favorable view of New England Indians' lives and right to territory. In 1636, when Williams was threatened with imprisonment for heresy by the Massachusetts colonial government, he fled to Massasoit's home. Despite the efforts of Williams to maintain peace, Massasoit eventually came to resent the growing encroachment of English settlers. It would be his son Philip, however, who would turn this resentment into war in 1675–76.

Though the exact details of the event have become clouded in secular mythology, it is believed that Massasoit participated in what has come to be called the first Thanksgiving. Around 1621, Massasoit traveled to Plymouth with a number of followers where they took part in a meal with the colonists. Judging by the inabil-

**Massasoit
1580–1661**

Wampanoag tribal leader

ity of the colonists to provide for themselves at this time, it is most likely that Massasoit and his people provided the food for the "historic" meal.

Samson Occum
1723–92

Mohegan minister

Samson Occum became a Christian convert at the age of eighteen. As a minister and educator, he devoted his life to teaching and converting Indians to Christianity. He was the first Indian to preach in England.

Occum was born in New London, Connecticut. He was the first student of Eleazor Wheelock, a Christian missionary who had been teaching Indians since about 1743 in his church-sponsored Indian Charity School. Wheelock's goal was to train his students to become Christian ministers. When Occum finished his studies, he was a school teacher for a short while at which time he married Mary Montauk. In 1759, he was ordained by the Presbyterian Church. Occum's parish was among the Montauk Indians, and among his duties was the recruitment of Indian youths for Wheelock's school.

In 1765, Occum traveled to England as Wheelock's representative. He stayed in England for two years, preaching and fund raising. It was during this trip that Occum obtained the funds to establish a new school for Indian children. While Occum was in England, Wheelock's Indian school was moved to New Hampshire and, in 1769, became Dartmouth College.

When he returned to New England, Occum left Wheelock's organization over differences on the emphasis and focus of their mission. Wheelock was interested mainly in training non-Indian missionaries. Occum wanted to teach and minister to the Indians directly. As a result, Occum became a minister and teacher in an Algonkian-speaking community of Indian people in eastern New York called Brotherton. Brotherton was composed of several Indian tribes that accepted Christianity, and Occum welcomed them all to his church and school. Because of encroachment by New York settlers, Occum spent many of his later years working to relocate his followers further west on Oneida territory in central New York. The Oneida, one nation of the Iroquois Confederacy, welcomed the Brotherton community and allowed them to live on their land. The resettlement to Oneida territory was completed in 1786 with the establishment of a town named New Stockbridge. Occum died six years later.

Ely S. Parker was the first Indian commissioner of Indian affairs. During the Civil War, Parker, a close friend and colleague of General Ulysses S. Grant, served the Union cause and penned the final copy of the Confederate army's surrender terms at the Appomattox Courthouse in 1865.

Ely S. Parker
1828–95

Seneca tribal leader, commissioner of Indian affairs, and engineer

Ely Parker was educated at Yates Academy in Yates, New York, and Cayuga Academy in Aurora, New York. In 1852, he became a chief among the Seneca Indians and helped the Tonawanda Seneca secure land rights to their reservation in western New York State. Parker hoped to become a lawyer, but because he was an Indian, he was denied entry to the bar. Undaunted, Parker studied engineering at Rensselaer Polytechnic Institute instead.

With the outbreak of the Civil War, Parker tried to serve the Union by enlisting in the Army Corps of Engineers but was refused again because of racial prejudice. He eventually received a commission in May 1863 as captain of engineers in the Seventh Corps. This was due in part to his friendship with General Ulysses S. Grant, whom he had met by chance before the war and with whom he later served during the Vicksburg campaign. When Grant became president in 1868, he appointed Parker his commissioner of Indian affairs. It was the first time an Indian had held the post. As commissioner, Parker worked to rid the bureau of corruption and fraud. He was an advocate for western Indian tribes and gained a reputation for fairness and progressive thinking. In 1871, Parker was falsely accused of fraud. Although he was acquitted of all charges, Parker resigned and moved to New York City, where he lived and worked until his death in 1895.

Philip (Metacom)
1639–76

Wampanoag tribal
leader

From 1675 to 1676, Philip planned and carried out an unsuccessful attempt to oust English settlers from New England. The conflict has come to be known as King Philip's War. It was one of the most destructive Indian wars in New England's history.

Like his father Massasoit, Philip (among the English colonists, he was called King Philip) was the grand sachem of the Wampanoag Confederacy, an alliance of Algonkian-speaking peoples living in present-day New England. Unlike his father, however, Philip found peace with the New England colonists impossible, and he led a revolt against them. The seeds of revolt were laid before Philip became grand sachem. Although Massasoit had worked successfully with the progressive-minded New England minister, Roger Williams, to maintain peaceful relations between Indians and the English, when Philip came to power the mood of his people was more militant. There were several reasons for the change: Colonists now outnumbered Indians in the region two to one, and English farms, animals, and villages were overtaking Indian land. Puritans subjected Philip's people to unfair laws, taxes, and jurisdictions. Alcohol and disease were also taking their toll. It was against this backdrop that Philip planned for war against the English.

Fighting erupted in 1675, at the frontier settlement of Swansea on June 16. The conflict quickly escalated across southern New England, involving the colonies of Plymouth, Massachusetts, Connecticut, and, to a limited extent, Rhode Island. Some tribes, including the Narragansett and Nipmuck, supported Philip; others gave valuable assistance to the English. Losses on both sides were brutal. (Puritans recorded with relish the massacre of noncombatants.) Villages, farms, and animals were destroyed. The colonists had underrated Philip's talents as a military strategist and leader. Wampanoag and Narragansett warriors fought with a deep courage fostered by equal doses of optimism and desperation. Although for the first few months of the war the outcome was in doubt, the English eventually were victorious. On December 19, 1675, a decisive battle in southern Rhode Island resulted in the deaths of as many six hundred Indians and four hundred captured. In August 1676,

Philip himself was killed after being betrayed by his own warriors. His body was mutilated and displayed publicly.

It is believed that Pontiac was born along the Maumee River, in present-day northern Ohio. By 1755, he was chief and probably participated in the French and Indian War of 1754–63 as a French ally. Pontiac had built up a profitable trading partnership with the French, so it was with dismay that he watched the British gradually gain control of French land and trade relationships. Besides the less-favorable trading policies of the British, Pontiac also was apprehensive over the British propensity for settling on Indian lands. For these reasons, in 1763, Pontiac led a military campaign against the British, who were occupying the old French forts, such as Detroit, in the Great Lakes region.

Pontiac

1720–69

Ottawa tribal leader

Pontiac's plan was founded on the belief that he could unite diverse Indian nations against the British and that the French would follow through on their promises of support. Pontiac's efforts to forge an anti-British alliance were fairly successful. The Ottawa leader was a skillful orator, and he spread his message of resistance effectively throughout the Old Northwest tribes of the Great Lakes area. He was aided in this cause by the Delaware prophet, whose anti-British teachings and spiritual visions provided Pontiac's crusade with a spiritual foundation. Though Pontiac and the Delaware Prophet disagreed on the use of guns (Pontiac advocated their use), the two leaders were a potent organizing force that united many diverse Indian nations.

Traders in the region spread the news of Pontiac's alliance and eventually alerted the British, who sent reinforcements into the Detroit region. In April 1763, Pontiac made final plans for a coordinated siege carried out by separate Indian bands throughout the Great Lakes region. On May 5, he visited Fort Detroit probably for reconnaissance purposes. The fort's leader, Major Henry Gladwin, knew of the planned surprise attack and prevented Pontiac from bringing in any large numbers of his warriors. Finally on May 9, Pontiac, under pressure from restless warriors, attacked the fort. Simultaneously, he ordered a siege of the entire region, by alerting his network of sympathetic bands.

Many tribes answered Pontiac's call for attack, including Chippewa, Delaware, Huron, Illinois, Kickapoo, Miami, Potawatomi, Seneca, and Shawnee. In the ensuing attacks, about two thousand settlers were killed and a number of British posts and forts fell. In October 1763, the British government issued a Royal Proclamation that forbade English settlement on land west of the Appalachians. Pontiac, meanwhile, persisted in his siege of Fort Detroit. When French support failed to materialize, however, Pontiac's warriors began to question the wisdom of continuing the siege with winter approaching and food supplies dwindling. A letter from a French commander finally persuaded Pontiac to call off the siege. Although he continued to believe in his resistance movement, he signed a peace pact in 1765 and a peace treaty in 1766. He was pardoned by the British and returned to his village on the Maumee River.

Despite the 1763 proclamation forbidding it, English settlers continued to settle on Indian lands west of the Appalachians. However, Pontiac counseled peace. In 1769, the Ottawa leader was killed by an Indian who had probably been paid by the British. The alliances that Pontiac forged among diverse Indian groups set a precedent for future resistance efforts among Indian leaders of this region, who like Pontiac, sought ways to halt settler encroachment on their lands.

Powhatan
1550?–1618

Powhatan tribal
leader

In the late 1500s and early 1600s, the Indian chief Wahunsonacock presided over the Powhatan Confederacy, an alliance of Indian tribes and villages stretching from the Potomac River to the Tidewater region of present-day Virginia. The English called Wahunsonacock Powhatan (Falls of the River), after the village where the Indian leader dwelled. (Today this village is Richmond, Virginia.) As ruler of this region, Powhatan played a pivotal role in relations with early English colonists in Virginia. One colonist described Powhatan as regal and majestic: "No king, but a kingly figure." Powhatan's daughter, Pocahontas, married John Rolfe, the Englishman who developed tobacco farming in Virginia. Powhatan's brother, Opechancanough, led the Powhatan uprisings against English settlers in 1622 and 1644.

Powhatan inherited from his father a confederacy of six tribes, but the ambitious leader quickly expanded his domain. Estimates of the Powhatan Confederacy range from 128 to 200 villages consisting of eight to nine thousand inhabitants and encompassing up to thirty different tribes. It is believed that Powhatan built the confederacy using a combination of incentives and coercion.

Communities under Powhatan's jurisdiction received military protection and adhered to the confederacy's well-organized system of hunting and trading boundaries. In return, subjects paid a tax to Powhatan in the form of food, pelts, copper, and pearls. Europeans who visited Powhatan in the 1600s have described a large structure filled with "treasures," probably Powhatan's storehouse and revenue collection center.

Powhatan was an important figure in the opening stages of English efforts to settle in the Tidewater region, in particular the Jamestown expedition of 1607. Setting foot on the shores of Powhatan's domain the English were unaware that they were trespassing on a land ruled by a shrewd and well-organized head of state. Powhatan, approximately sixty years old at the time, could easily have demolished the faltering community, but instead chose to tolerate the English for a time—one reason being his desire to develop trade with them. Metal tools and weaponry were of special interest to Powhatan. Despite a mutual desire for trade, relations between Powhatan and the Virginia settlers were rocky—attacks and counterattacks were common.

The English government in the early 1600s knew that maintaining friendly relations with the Powhatan people was a key to establishing a foothold in the region. For this reason, Powhatan was courted by several colonial leaders. In 1609, he was offered a crown from the King of England and reluctantly agreed to have it placed ceremoniously on his head. In return, Powhatan sent the King of England his old moccasins and a mantle.

In 1614, a degree of harmony was eventually achieved after the marriage of Pocahontas (who, in 1613, was kidnapped by the Virginia settlers) to John Rolfe, a leading citizen of Jamestown Colony. After the marriage of his daughter, Powhatan negotiated a peace settlement that produced generally friendly relations with the English until a few years after Powhatan's death in 1618.

Red Jacket

1758–1830

Seneca tribal leader

Red Jacket supported the British during the American Revolution (1777–83) and later became a spokesman for his people in negotiations with the U.S. government. Red Jacket was also a staunch opponent of Christianity and worked to prevent Iroquois conversions to Christianity.

Although Red Jacket eventually allied himself with other Indian nations in support of the British during the American Revolution, he was originally hesitant about the affiliation. This ambivalence perhaps explains why he did little fighting during the conflict. According to a number of accounts, Red Jacket's reluctance to fight was perceived as cowardice by some Iroquois war leaders such as Cornplanter and Joseph Brant.

After the war, Red Jacket became a principal spokesman for the Seneca people. He was present at treaty negotiations in 1794 and 1797 in which major portions of Seneca land in upstate New York were ceded or partitioned into smaller reservations. During this era, Red Jacket also became an outspoken opponent of Christianity and an advocate for preserving traditional Iroquois beliefs. His efforts to protect traditional beliefs culminated in the temporary expulsion of all Christian missionaries from Seneca territory in 1824. Red Jacket and the so-called Pagan Party were undermined in the ensuing years, however, by accusations of witchcraft and Red Jacket's own problems with alcohol. In 1827, Red Jacket was deposed as a Seneca chief. He died three years later, after his own family had converted to Christianity.

Red Jacket is immortalized in a now-famous painting by Charles Bird King. In this historical painting, Red Jacket is depicted with a large, silver medal that was given to him in 1792 by President

George Washington during a diplomatic visit to the then-U.S. capital at New York City.

In 1605, Tasquantum, also known as Squanto, was abducted in present-day Massachusetts by Europeans and sold into slavery in Malaga, an island off the Mediterranean coast of Spain. He eventually escaped to England where he enlisted in the Newfoundland Company. After sailing to America and back again, Squanto finally returned to his homeland in 1619 to find his people wiped out by disease. Squanto took up life with the Pilgrims at Plymouth and provided invaluable instruction on farming, hunting, fishing, and geography. According to one colonial historian: "He directed them how to set their corne, when to take fish, and to procure other commodities, and was also their pilott to bring them to unknowne places for their profitt." It is also believed that Squanto helped the Pilgrims maintain friendly relations with neighboring tribes.

In 1622, Squanto died of disease while helping the Pilgrims negotiate trade agreements with the Narragansett Indians. In recent history the story of Squanto and the Pilgrims has become an oft-repeated, frequently distorted tale for young people as an example of friendly relations between Indians and the early colonists.

Squanto (Tasquantum) 1580–1622

Wampanoag interpreter and cultural mediator

In the early 1800s, Tecumseh and his brother Tenskwatawa organized Indian resistance to U.S. territorial expansion along the Mississippi Valley. Tecumseh was born in a Shawnee settlement known as Old Piqua (near the present-day city of Springfield, Ohio) in the Ohio Valley. Tecumseh, (which means "goes through one place to another") learned warfare early in life. In his early teens Tecumseh took part in the American Revolution on the side of the British.

After the revolution, the Shawnee regularly took up arms to defend their Ohio land against U.S. settlers. In 1795, many of the Indian leaders living in the Ohio region gathered at Greenville, Ohio, to negotiate sale of land to the United States. When the land exchange was formalized in the Treaty of Greenville, Tecumseh re-

Tecumseh 1768–1813

Shawnee tribal leader

fused to recognize it. Upon hearing of U.S. intentions to buy Indian land, Tecumseh is said to have replied, "Sell the land? Why not sell the air, the clouds, the great sea?" This belief in an Indian land with no tribal borders would become the foundation for Tecumseh's Indian confederation in the years to follow.

Tecumseh soon emerged as a spokesman for the Midwest Indians. He attended councils, studied treaties, and learned all that he could about the historical and legal status of American Indians. It was during this time that Tecumseh conceived a new mission for his life, a destiny linked to the growing restlessness among the Indians of the Old Northwest Territory (present-day Great Lakes area). This restlessness was caused in part by the preachings of a new Indian leader spreading a message of religious rebirth and resistance. Tecumseh knew this emerging leader very well for he was Laulewasika, his younger brother who had changed his name to Tenskwatawa (which means "open door") but was generally known as the Shawnee Prophet.

The two brothers united to forge an intertribal confederacy, which they hoped would contain U.S. territorial expansion into Indian lands. Tecumseh and his brother urged their people to forgo the sale of Indian land, to reject European ways, and to renew Indian traditions. In particular, the brothers warned against the use of alcohol, which was devastating many Indian communities.

Within a few years, the brothers had assembled a growing community of believers in Prophetstown, located at the junction of the Wabash River and Tippecanoe Creek in present-day Indiana. Tensions between the growing Indian community and the U.S. government were high, however, because of Indian resentment over recent treaties ceding about 110 million acres to the United States. At the Battle of Tippecanoe in November 1811, the Prophet and his followers fought U.S. Army units. The Prophet proclaimed that his spiritual power would protect the Indians from army bullets, but when the Indians suffered significant casualties in the battle, the Prophet lost prestige and his followers abandoned him. Many members of Tecumseh's alliance dispersed, and Tenskwatawa himself fled to Canada.

Tecumseh joined the British to fight against the Americans in the War of 1812. He played a decisive role in the British capture of Detroit. In the months to follow, Tecumseh rallied other Indians to the British effort and continued to lead them into battle. On October 5, 1813, however, he was killed at the Battle of the Thames, in southern Ontario.

Native Peoples of the Southeast

When Europeans reached the southeastern United States, they encountered Native peoples who were the predecessors of tribes known today as the Catawba, the Cherokee, the Creek, the Chickasaw, the Choctaw, and the Seminole. Some of these peoples were emerging from the decline of the once widespread culture identified as Mississippian, a term referring to practices associated with the construction of ceremonial mounds central to a village and its cultivated fields of corn, beans, and squash. Although the earthen mounds were passing into disuse, the lives of the succeeding Native peoples still were town centered. In the sixteenth century the villages of the southeastern peoples were distributed across a territory bounded by the Atlantic Ocean, the Gulf of Mexico, the Trinity River in present Texas, and the Ohio River.

Central to the ritual life of these peoples was the Green Corn Ceremony, an elaborate thanksgiving and renewal festival usually observed in mid-summer. The occasion was significant because the maturation of new corn promised food for winter and seeds for spring; crop failures threatened immediate hunger and long-term famine. The anthropologist Charles Hudson believes "we would have something approaching the Green Corn Ceremony if we combined Thanksgiving, New Year's festivities, Yom Kippur, Lent, and Mardi Gras."

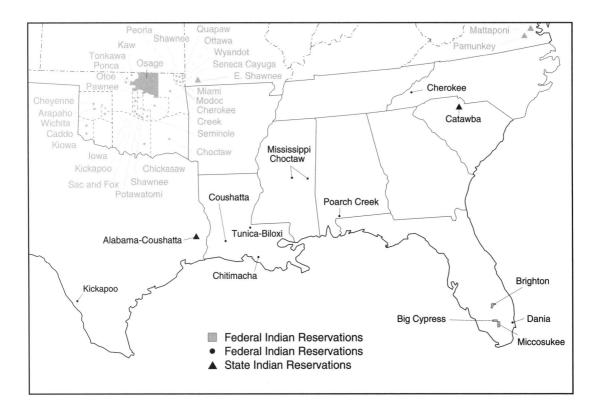

Contemporary southeastern tribes.

The successful farming reflected in the Green Corn celebration was only part of the economy of the Southeastern Indians. Hunting also provided important dietary ingredients. Like farming, hunting was interconnected with spiritual beliefs. Hunters prayed to the spirits of the game before they went hunting, since offending the animal spirits would mean no game for the next hunt. Likewise, once on the hunt the hunter killed no more than needed, since useless slaughter also might anger the spirits of the game.

Even as the Southeastern peoples shared common practices in farming, hunting, and spiritual belief, they also shared games. One of the most widely played was the ball game, vividly captured by the American painter George Catlin in his 1834 portrayals of a Choctaw ball play in Oklahoma. So great was Catlin's fascination that he depicted not only two scenes from a match, one with the ball in the air and the other with it on the ground, but also left a portrait of the Choctaw ball player named He-Who-Drinks-the-Juice-of-Stone. The contest was played by teams from competing villages on a level field perhaps 200 yards long. The object was for a team to throw a deerskin ball (stuffed with deer or squirrel hair) past the opposition's goal post at the other end of the field. In the southeastern versions of the game, the players carried two ball play sticks, which could be used to scoop up the ball and forward it.

Two other rituals common to the Southeastern cultures were the use of sacred tobacco and the black drink. The black drink, as the Europeans called it, was a tea brewed from the roasted leaves of the yaupon holly, a shrub which contained caffeine. Because the black drink ceremony was often a preliminary to any major decision or celebration, the participants were left highly stimulated. So important was this shrub to ceremonial life that it was cultivated in small patches far outside its normal range.

A second plant-oriented ritual involved the use of tobacco in a pipe, a ceremony associated with welcome and with diplomacy. The sacred or so-called white tobacco was put in a pipe and passed around the circle of participants, a practice which nauseated English Lieutenant Henry Timberlake on his visit to the Cherokee villages in the 1760s.

Another similarity for these southeastern peoples was their life in villages, often bound together by common practices and language into a tribe. Most villages were governed by a council of elders and warriors presided over by a chief, who usually came to power through a combination of talent, accomplishment, and membership in an influential family or clan. In most southeastern societies, descent was traced through the mother's line.

Beyond the family, clan membership was extremely important, since clans transcended village boundaries, thus affording the individual a social and political connection throughout the tribe. The mixed-blood Creek leader Alexander McGillivray, for example, had the advantages of bilinguality, basic education, service as a British trading agent, and opportunity through the death of the Upper Creek principal warrior in 1782; but it was his mother's influential Wind clan that provided him a Creek political power base from 1783 to 1793, when he was a primary Creek leader.

Tribes were loose associations of villages bound together by language, heritage, custom, and proximity of location. None were tightly structured by modern standards; the Creek, for example, more appropriately might be called a confederation, since they were formed as much by outside pressure as by powerful cultural bonds. Certain villages in a tribal grouping sometimes were more influential or sacred than others, such as the Cherokee beloved town of Chota on the Little Tennessee River in present-day Tennessee; yet even the leader of a prominent town really had no more power than persuasion could provide. Efforts by European colonial powers to designate emperors for particular tribes were largely empty gestures. In most instances, if all the tribal villages or a percentage of them voted for war or approved a treaty, that decision prevailed only while those villages continued their support. Withdrawal of any village's support freed its people from obligations, a practice that frustrated Europeans, who professed to operate in terms of permanent treaties, boundaries, and alliances. Native peoples, however, were more attuned to political flexibility, social harmony, and spiritual significance than to contractual agreements.

Indeed the religious values of the southeastern peoples might be expressed best in terms of balance or harmony of human beings with one another, as well as with the natural and spiritual worlds in which they saw themselves. All things had spirits, either good or evil; success in life depended on the careful cultivation of these spirits by the proper behaviors or the appropriate remedy if you were guilty of an act of disharmony. Even so grave an act as murder might be compensated for if the proper remedies were taken.

The old harmonies were shattered forever when the Europeans arrived. The first visitation for which there is substantial historical evidence was led by the Spanish adventurer Hernando de Soto. During 1540–41, de Soto led his expedition from Tampa Bay into

Georgia and then to the Mississippi River. From these newcomers the Southeastern peoples learned of a foreign culture, and, unfortunately, of fatal European diseases, against which the Native peoples carried no inherited resistance; they died by the thousands. Continued Spanish exploration brought settlements along the Gulf and Atlantic borders from St. Augustine to Pensacola in present-day Florida.

Ultimately, European imperial rivalry brought French and English adventurers to the southeastern region. By the early seventeenth century, Spain, England, and France expanded their global territories by establishing outposts, subjugating Native peoples, and developing an economic exchange. Although all three promoted conversion of the Native peoples to Christianity, only the Spanish achieved limited and temporary success.

For the Native peoples, the exchange of furs and skins for European manufactures created a major alteration in the balance of their lives. Previously hunters had pursued the white-tailed deer only as need dictated. Because deer range only a five-square-mile area during their lifetimes, only careful avoidance of overhunting and controlled burning of forest underbrush (which renewed the vegetation) had maintained the deer herds. The new trade changed the balance, as European market demands for leather enticed the hunters to kill more than they needed. By the 1730s, there was a noticeable decline in the Southeastern deerskin trade.

At the same time, the trade goods impacted cultural patterns. The attraction of finished cloth and clothing items persuaded villagers that bartering was far easier than tanning deerskins. Desirable luxury items also could be obtained in the trade, which provided mirrors, knives, awls, scissors, and Jew's harps. As a result, certain handicrafts disappeared, displaced by European weapons, tools, cloth, and decorative goods. Other dramatic trade-induced changes also altered Native societies as alcohol was introduced, gender roles were realigned, and towns became more non-Indian. Beverage alcohol quickly became a curse, as alcoholism and excessive drinking undermined village stability. Alcohol was used by unscrupulous colonials to influence the Native peoples into disadvantageous agreements.

Gender roles, too, were modified by the trade. Formerly these matrilineal, agricultural societies defined roles for males and females in relatively clear, yet balanced terms. Females were important because they bore the children, provided food from the fields, and transformed raw materials into usable products. The trade, however, gave a place of greater importance to the hunters, since commercial hunting brought both staples and luxury goods to the villages. Trading activities also ignored women, since the male-oriented Europeans sought to bargain with the hunters.

Still further social changes took place as traders took up residence in the villages. The households that they developed were patterned after the male-dominated European families. The children of these unions adopted their fathers' entrepreneurial lifestyles, thus diluting traditional social practices and increasing the number of mixed bloods. As a result many tribes became economically dominated by mixed-blood trader families toward the end of the eighteenth century.

The emergence of these trader-originated families also helped intensify tribal divisions. The mixed-blood peoples often were among the first to adopt life-styles similar to their neighbors who were U.S. citizens. Among the Cherokee, the Choctaw, the Chickasaw, and the Creek, the new European cultural orientations were reflected in economic terms, as the mixed bloods used their linguistic, educational, and political advantages to prosper. Ferries, inns, trading posts, and farms most often were owned or controlled by those of mixed ancestry. In the 1830s, when the U.S. government sought to relocate the Southeastern peoples west of the Mississippi River, antagonism between conservatives and mixed blood entrepreneurs heightened arguments over whether or not the tribes should move. After removal, even though they may have lost more both in quality and quantity of life, the mixed bloods were better equipped to start again. Once relocated, they contended for political leadership and held economic control of mills, ferries, inns, stores, and ranching operations.

In the three centuries before their forced move westward, Southeastern tribal governments underwent evolution and transformation. From the earliest contacts, Europeans sought to impose their own governmental views on their new neighbors by designating Indian nations, kings, princesses, and emperors. Such titles had little meaning for the Native peoples, who continued their tribal associations until early in the nineteenth century. Only as their populations became more and more mixed blood and as their U.S. neighbors greedily eyed their lands and pressured for removal did the villages and tribal councils seek more formally structured governments, modeled for practical diplomatic purposes after the government of the United States. In the decades just before the tribes were forced westward, they adopted constitutions and created governing bodies that were then transferred west. The Cherokee adopted a constitutional government in 1828, while the Choctaw constitution of 1826–30 proved unstable but was revived again in 1834. The more conservative Creek and Chickasaw retained their traditional government with little change until after removal to Indian Territory, where they adopted constitutional governments in the 1850s and 1860s. Originally they hoped such nation building would help them resist pressure from the United States. However, both before removal and during the period of so-called detribalization in the years between 1880 and 1934, much of this structure was destroyed. In the last fifty years, however, some tribes have reconstituted their governments into the leadership that serves them today.

During the era of removal, because of the continued focus of basic power at the village level, not every individual tribal member, family, or village participated in the move west. The Native peoples living east of the Mississippi River today testify powerfully to the persistence and cultural tenacity of these peoples against overwhelming odds. Today's descendants of the Southeastern tribal peoples proudly continue to claim the heritage of their ancestors, in most cases virtually undistinguishable from their non-Indian neighbors. In 1990 there were 211,000 persons of Native American descent living in the ten states (North Carolina, South Carolina, Georgia, Florida, Kentucky, Tennessee, Alabama, Mississippi,

Arkansas, and Louisiana) considered within the southeastern United States. In addition, Oklahoma has a Native American population of 252,000, many descended from Southeastern peoples. A century and a half after most of the Southeastern peoples were forced to move west, the Catawba, the Cherokee, the Creek, the Seminole, and the Choctaw continue to live in South Carolina, Mississippi, Alabama, North Carolina, and Florida.

THE CATAWBA ♦ ♦ ♦ ♦ ♦ ♦ ♦ ♦ ♦ ♦ ♦ ♦ ♦ ♦ ♦ ♦ ♦ ♦ ♦

Today most Catawba live in the vicinity of Rock Hill, South Carolina, either on a small state-owned reservation or in nearby communities; unlike many Native peoples, all live relatively close to their eighteenth-century homelands. Because they are few in number and lack a large land base or potentially profitable natural resource, they are not well known. Their mere existence testifies powerfully to their persistence, resilience, and flexibility. Time after time observers predicted the end of the Catawba, yet they still survive.

As the British colonies emerged in the late seventeenth century, Indians settled along the upper Wateree River in South Carolina were identified as the Catawba nation. From the outset of Catawba-South Carolina relations, the Catawba followed a policy of friendly cooperation. During the American Revolution they served as scouts for the South Carolinians. They paid dearly for this when a British raiding force destroyed their settlements. In the years after the revolution, however, the Catawba wrapped themselves in the flag of patriotism shared with other revolutionary veterans, thus making it difficult for South Carolina to ignore them. Because they could claim no ancestral homeland for time immemorial, and because of colonial South Carolina's rapid expansion, the Catawba had sought and received a 144,000 acre reservation in 1763. For the next forty years they persisted by leasing their land, selling pottery and skins, practicing subsistence farming, and serving as slave catchers for tidewater slave owners. After 1800, the equation changed, when slavery and upland cotton marched into the Piedmont, the region of rolling hills between the level coastal plain of the Atlantic Ocean and the rugged mountains of the southern Appalachians. At that point Catawba land became more valuable than tribal slave catching. Reduced in population to no more than thirty families and under unrelenting pressure to sell their land, the Catawba signed a treaty with South Carolina in 1840 exchanging their 144,000 acres for $5,000 and promises of assistance in relocation. Many moved to North Carolina in a fruitless attempt to live with the Cherokee. Within twelve years they returned to South Carolina, where they were given 630 acres of their old land.

After the Civil War, their survival faced another threat in the rise of Jim Crow legislation; in 1879 South Carolina law forbade interracial marriage. Freedom to move back and forth socially and economically became further restricted. Consequently the Catawba either had to cling to the security of Indianness or face an insurmountable color barrier that placed them in the "black" category. The Catawba responded by asserting their Indianness through speaking Catawba and expanding the production and sale of Indian crafts. Then, in a departure from their traditional resistance toward converting to Christianity, they welcomed Mormon missionaries in 1883. Over time the Mormons assisted the Catawba in building community cohesion and gaining education through the establishment of Catawba schools, a necessity in South Carolina, where the only schools for non-whites were for blacks. In the last fifty years, however, a modified racial climate has eliminated the need for separate Catawba schools; there are none listed in the 1990 report of the National Advisory Council on Indian Education.

In 1943, the Catawba became legal citizens of South Carolina and federally recognized Indians, which means they were acknowledged as a tribe and eligible for the governmental benefits available to existing tribes. The next year an additional 3,400 acres of land were purchased for them. Although this step was intended to allow the Catawba to become small farmers, that option proved unprofitable. By 1959, consequently, they voted to terminate their tribal status and sell most of their lands. Under the plan, any tribal member could choose land from the reservation tract or a cash settlement from the sale of unclaimed portions of the reservation. On July 2, 1960, the final tribal roll listed 631 Catawba; termination came on July 1, 1962.

Despite their vote to terminate and to sell the reservation, the Catawba persist, which is an astonishing testimony to their survival in the face of adversity. Some still have ties to the existing Old Reservation, others make and sell Catawba pottery, and a few have participated in the Indian awareness movements. In these modern Catawba still survive the spirits of ancestral heroes many decades after the predicted demise of the tribe.

THE CHEROKEE ✦ ✦ ✦ ✦ ✦ ✦ ✦ ✦ ✦ ✦ ✦ ✦ ✦ ✦ ✦ ✦ ✦ ✦

The Cherokee Indians who once inhabited the southern Appalachian Mountains live today in widely separated areas. Those of the Eastern Band live in western North Carolina on or near the Qualla Boundary, as the Eastern Reservation is called; those who claim membership in the Western Band live in Oklahoma. There are many from both bands who live and work as Cherokee Americans throughout the United States. Those who keep their language alive speak an Iroquoian language with some regional variations.

According to archaeological evidence, the Cherokee and their ancestors lived in the southern Appalachians for several hundred years before the Europeans arrived. Seventeenth-century visitors to the Cherokee villages found them located in mountain river valleys where there was adequate space for dwellings, council houses, and agricultural fields. Because the Cherokee were a matrilineal society, their fields were controlled by the Cherokee women. Women of great influence became known as Beloved Women, often working behind the scenes in shaping decisions. A woman who had taken her husband's place in war might be awarded the title War Woman. That the role of women still has a powerful effect today is reflected in Wilma

Mankiller's elections as tribal chair of the Western Cherokee (1987 and 1991).

In the late seventeenth century, there were approximately 30,000 Cherokee living in about sixty settlements. Within one hundred years, smallpox, other epidemics, and warfare had reduced their population to only 7,500.

From the early seventeenth through twentieth centuries, the major point of contention between the Cherokee and the Europeans was land. As the venerable chief Old Tassel bluntly put it in 1777: "Brothers . . . the issue is about our land." From 1783 to 1835 the Cherokee fought a losing battle in defense of their lands. After the revolution, land-hungry settlers crossed the mountains in search of homesteads; then came eager planters seeking new soil for upland cotton cultivation. By 1825, some Cherokee had relocated voluntarily to Arkansas and Texas, hoping to escape the encroaching Americans. Those still in the east were divided between the highly acculturated mixed bloods and the more conservative, traditionalist full bloods.

In 1835, a minority of the tribal leaders, primarily mixed bloods, signed the controversial Treaty of New Echota, which led to the eviction of those Cherokee living in South Carolina, Georgia, Tennessee, and Alabama. In North Carolina, however, about 1,000 Cherokee managed to escape removal with the cooperation of sympathetic state officials. According to their understanding of the treaties of 1817, 1819, and 1835, the Cherokee claimed North Carolina citizenship. One North Carolinian, William H. Thomas (or Wil-Usdi, as the Cherokee called him) bought land in his name for the Cherokee, went to court in their defense, and visited Washington on behalf of the Eastern Band's share in any general settlement with all Cherokee.

When the majority of the Cherokee moved to the Indian Territory (present-day Oklahoma), the tribe's internal problems were not solved. Hatred deepened after the political murders on June 22, 1839, of John Ridge, Major Ridge, and Elias Boudinot, three Cherokee leaders who had signed the despised removal agreement.

During the early years west of the Mississippi, the Cherokee sought to survive economically, establish a workable government acceptable to all, reduce tribal factionalism, avoid rivalries with traditional tribal enemies, and maintain relations with the federal bureaucracy. Even in the west the Cherokee could not escape demands on their land base. Ranchers desired the Cherokee Outlet, a sixty-mile-wide strip running west from the 96th to the 100th meridians. After the Civil War, the federal government demanded land as compensation because the Cherokee Nation officially joined the South; this action ignored the loyal Union service of several hundred non-slaveowners. Then promoters of all stripes began eyeing the unused or unassigned Cherokee lands. Even after the Cherokee ceded their unassigned lands to the federal government in 1891, speculators schemed to divide the tribal land into individual allotments. Land interests ultimately prevailed with the passage of the Dawes Act (1887) and the Curtis Act (1898); the first divided the lands and the second eliminated tribal governments. The Curtis Act, however, led to wholesale fraud. After Oklahoma statehood in 1907 almost every species of trickery imaginable was practiced; the Cherokee were bribed, threatened, cajoled, bought out, and generally manipulated. With few exceptions all the mineral rich or arable lands fell into the hands of non-Cherokee.

Today, the Western Cherokee number more than 175,000, many of whom live in northeastern Oklahoma. Despite the frequent assertions of some non-Indians that there are fewer Indians, the opposite is true. There are more numerically, and, of those, an increasing number are proud to identify themselves as such.

During the 1980s and 1990s, the Western Cherokee have reasserted themselves under the leadership of Principal Chief Wilma Mankiller. An inspirational leader who empowers people to independence, Mankiller was re-elected with more than 83 percent of the vote. Community rebuilding and building since the early 1980s has resulted in tribally owned businesses, including defense subcontracting plants and horticultural operations. The annual budget for the tribe is $54 million. Whether the accomplishment is as basic as the men, women, and children of the tiny village of Bell laying sixteen miles of pipe for running water, or as venturesome as the construction of a hydroelectric facility worth millions, power is returning to these Western Cherokee peoples at every level. The key to their success, says Mankiller, is that Cherokee never give up.

During the first three decades of the twentieth century, the Eastern Band wrestled with the related difficulties of tribal membership, enrollment, and allotment. When a tribal roll was opened, more than 12,000 people applied to be included; tribal leaders protested that no more than 2,000 could possibly be eligible. The long disagreement over this matter delayed any action of dividing the land until the Indian Reorganization Act of 1934 ended allotment of Indian land. There was a further economic decline in the 1930s when a chestnut blight destroyed more than 60 percent of the timber on the tribal lands. After World War II some economic recovery came to the Eastern Cherokee in the form of highways, a national park, and a historical drama. The roads needed for modern automobile travel were developed by those seeking creation of the Great Smoky Mountains National Park, whose lands lay adjacent to the Cherokee homeland. If visitors who came to the park in search of natural splendor could be tempted to stay overnight, an income-producing tourist industry might develop. By the early 1950s the Cherokee Historical Association had commissioned and then produced "Unto These Hills," an emotional drama based on the Cherokee experience. Regardless of its historical accuracy, it attracts many visitors, as do Oconoluftee Village and the Museum of the Cherokee Indian. All are aimed at affording a glimpse of Cherokee culture, distinct from the trinket businesses, where a few Cherokee pose for tourists in Plains Indian costumes. Even this prosperity, however, has had its problems, since much of the money and influence tends to be controlled by a relatively few Cherokee.

A cross-section of Eastern Cherokee society includes tribal members with relatively stable incomes as well as many living near or below the poverty level. The relative isolation of many tribal members plus the seasonal nature of the tourist industry continues to work to the economic disadvantage of many

Cherokee. One unusual bright spot on the economic horizon has been the development of an enormous bingo parlor, where almost 4,000 people can play for prizes worth thousands of dollars.

Today, there are more than 9,500 Eastern Cherokee who share an abiding sense of place and kinship, as well as an egalitarianism that makes tribal politics both interesting and fractious. Most of those who live on the Qualla Boundary, as the reservation for the Eastern Band of Cherokee is known, work in Waynesville or Sylva, North Carolina, while those from the outlying conservative Cherokee village known as Snowbird work for the National Forest Service, the Tennessee Valley Authority, or the Stanley Furniture plant in nearby Robbinsville, North Carolina. In an attempt to guarantee employment for their children, the Eastern Cherokee paid $28.8 million for the Carolina Mirror Company in 1986; as the tribal council leader has indicated, there is no future without jobs. Jobs will mean the Cherokee can continue their tradition of mixed dependency on both non-Indian economic culture and personal self-reliance that has allowed them to face the twenty-first century as both Cherokee and Americans.

THE CREEK ✦

At the end of the twentieth century, the Creek, like their former adversaries the Cherokee, live in widely separated areas. Before the Civil War, the majority of the Creek moved to Indian Territory, but a remnant remained in Alabama. Today their descendants live in Alabama, Oklahoma, and across the United States.

After the arrival of the Europeans, the Muskogee peoples moved inland away from the expanding newcomers. Clustering on Ochese Creek as well as on the Chattahoochee River, the villagers were labeled Creek by British traders from Charleston, South Carolina. Those nearest to Charleston were called the Lower Creek, those farther away the Upper Creek. Expansion of Georgia after

1733 pushed these peoples deeper into the interior, eventually into present Alabama. From their towns they attempted to play off the European powers seeking dominance in eastern North America.

Wherever they located, Creek lands lay in the path of the westward expanding United States. Creek defensive actions brought repeated invasions until 1814, when forces under General Andrew Jackson defeated them at the Battle of Horseshoe Bend. In the minds of Jackson and his fellow expansionists, Creek resistance legitimized removal beyond the Mississippi River. Although the Creek ceded 20 million acres of southern Georgia and central Alabama lands at the Treaty of Fort Jackson, the Jacksonians would

Christy Godwin O'Barr,

Poarch Creek Indian Princess

in 1987, sings at a 1987

Thanksgiving powwow.

not be satisfied until all Native Americans east of the Mississippi had been relocated. The Creek War provided a convenient excuse for Tennessee to demand the removal of the Creek, the Cherokee, and the Chickasaw. Georgia politicians, moreover, were eager to manipulate the Creek agency for purposes of profit and land speculation. When Georgia succeeded in expelling the Creek, her neighbor Alabama acted to keep the refugees moving west. First, Alabama extended her laws over all the Indian lands in the state. Then, under the Treaty of 1832, the Creek Nation in the east was no longer recognized by the federal or state governments. Creeks who wished to claim allotments and stay in the east were soon subjected to constant harassment, as their white neighbors sought to drive them away. From 1820 to 1840, by one

means or another, the Creek were forced to move to Indian Territory. They were exposed to a foreign climate, often without the barest of necessities, despite promised aid from the U.S. government. Dispossessed and abandoned, many died, yet others survived, intent on rebuilding the Creek Nation in the west. Those who remained behind in Alabama eked out a marginal existence, while resisting pressure to move. They insisted that according to the Treaty of Fort Jackson (1814) they could claim a section of land. Despite the pressures against them, a few held on; land belonging to the McGhee family was reaffirmed in 1836. Lynn McGhee's 240-acre claim at the headwaters of Perdido Creek became the center for three nearby settlements that came to be known as the Poarch Band of Creek. In 1975, the Poarch Band of Creek petitioned the U.S. government for recognition and were acknowledged as a federally recognized tribe in 1984. Today these Poarch Creek peoples number more than four hundred; in 1990, their tribal chairman was Eddie L. Tullis, who was also chairperson of the National Advisory Council on Indian Education.

THE SEMINOLE ✦ ✦ ✦ ✦ ✦ ✦ ✦ ✦ ✦ ✦ ✦ ✦ ✦ ✦ ✦ ✦ ✦ ✦

During the years of Creek withdrawal westward, a number of Lower Creek migrated intro present Florida. In order to distinguish them from their kinsmen, British officials called these separatists the Seminole Creek, or Seminole, a corruption of the Spanish *cimarrone*. Quickly adapting to their new environment, they became skillful herders, raising sleek ponies and fat cattle on the grassy savannas. So complete was their cultural adjustment that one of their leading chiefs was named Cowkeeper, who was vividly described in the prose of William Bartram, a Philadelphia botanist who visited the Seminole in the 1770s.

When Georgia frontiersmen expanded farther south, the Seminole retreated again. They continued their adaptation, adopting lighter dress and modifying the Creek cabin so that it became an open-sided dwelling, called a *chiki*, with raised floor and thatched roof. Changes in agricultural patterns followed, since Florida soils differed from those to the north. Ultimately the pressure of expanding plantations and farms pushed the Seminole so far south they had little land.

During the period that these former Creek were becoming Seminole, they attracted the attention of both the neighboring states and the national government. Officials in Georgia, Alabama, and Florida became unhappy because the Seminole would not agree to join the exodus westward by southeastern tribes. Their presence threatened Florida's claim to all the state's lands. At the same time, the Seminole were regarded as dangerous to peace and stability, because they harbored runaway slaves. As long as the Seminole camps remained in Florida, their camps a refuge for runaways, no slave-owning planter could feel secure. For the slaves captured by the Seminole, however, slavery was a much less rigorous institution. Several former slaves rose to positions of influence through their ability as interpreters and their familiarity with plantation lifeways. In the 1830s, the increasingly racist and xenophobic society in the southern United States denounced Seminole toleration of African-Americans. Outside the South, ironically, courageous Seminole resistance attracted some public sympathy.

No amount of sympathy, however, changed the federal government's demand that the Seminole move. By force and by forced treaty, the Seminole were transported west. By 1842, there were 2,833 Seminole survivors in Oklahoma. The Oklahoma Seminole of today are the descendants of these refugee peoples.

While many Seminole moved west, small bands in Florida remained hidden deep in Big Cypress Swamp, in the Everglades, and in other isolated areas. During the second half of the nineteenth century and the first decade of the next, these survivors existed by hunting, trapping, and fishing. The fashion industry's demand for bird feathers and animal skins offered them a means to trade for the basic necessities unavailable in nature. Most of their food came from subsistence farming of small patches.

Their fragile lifesystem began to collapse, however, early in the twentieth century. In 1906, Florida began to drain the Everglades in hope of producing more agricultural land for commercial purposes; more people began coming to Florida via the ever expanding railroad system; and both federal and state laws outlawed the use of bird plumes.

In the 1890s, however, Florida officials began buying land as a place for the Seminole to locate. The greatest difficulty arose in trying to persuade these fiercely independent people that they should live on these reservations. By 1932, less than 20 percent of the 562 Florida Seminole had relocated. The spirit of resistance and self-reliance built from years of avoiding the federal government was unlikely to disappear overnight. Living in remote, self-sufficient camps, they supplied their basic needs, but needed cash to buy coffee, salt, sugar, rifles, ammunition, and the seemingly ever-present sewing machine. With the decline of the trade in plumes and hides, seasonal agricultural labor became a source of cash. A few families became part of the growing tourist industry by establishing "commercial villages" where they put on public displays of "Seminole life."

During the 1930s, however, in response both to federal Indian policy and activities by tribal leaders and pro-tribal Florida interest groups, Seminole life patterns began to change. Tracts of land were obtained through purchase and exchange that resulted in the creation of several reservations, two of which were developed into cattle-raising operations. The success of the cattle ranches enticed some Seminole to abandon isolated settlements and relocate on the reservations. A new and more dependable economic base likewise meant an improved quality of life for the Seminole. At the same time the creation of federal agencies for the Seminole increased the tribe's exposure to and cooperation with federal officials. Also during the 1930s and 1940s came the first major success in converting the Seminole to Christianity. All of these changes went a long way toward forming the lives of the twentieth-century Seminole. Indeed the adaptability they have displayed since the seventeenth century has assisted them over and over again. Thereby they were able to deal with the termination policies of the 1950s as well as the creation and federal recognition in 1957 of the Seminole Tribe of Florida, Inc., followed in 1962 by the separation of a group who wished to be recognized as the Miccosukee Tribe of Indians.

Today, both the Seminole and the Miccosukee survive in heavily populated, non-Indian Florida. Beginning in 1979, the Seminole began operating a bingo parlor offering 1,700 seats and $10,000 jackpots. Since that time, more parlors have been opened, generating enough revenue to endow tribal scholarships, establish a credit union, and expand the tribal cattle herds. Despite this success, the tribe must be aware that they receive only 50 percent of the income and that organized crime is always ready to move in. On the environmental front, too, some difficulties may arise, as developers seek far and wide for new sources of natural resources, such as those in the Big Cypress area.

♦ **THE CHOCTAW**

Before the majority of the Choctaw were forced west in the nineteenth century, their settlements were located in present day central and southern Mississippi, as well as southwestern Alabama. During the seventeenth and eighteenth centuries, their lives were impacted by European newcomers. Although the French (and the Spanish after 1763) at New Orleans were the closest in proximity, enterprising English traders also reached their villages; the traders introduced cloth, firearms, tools, and alcohol. During the late seventeenth and early eighteenth centuries, there was also traffic in Indian slaves, an exchange that intensified rivalries with the Chickasaw, the Creek, and other nearby peoples. Trade generated rivalries, since some villages supported the most generous provider of quality goods at the lowest prices, whether France, Spain, or Great Britain. Included in the trade-induced stress were the resident traders, whose mixed-blood families later rose to positions of prominence in the tribe.

After the emergence of the United States, Choctaw lands became the stumbling block in Choctaw relations with the new country. Eager land developers paid little attention to Choctaw claims as

Evajean Felihkatubbee,
Choctaw Indian woman,
cleaning a basket.

they laid off lines across maps of the Mississippi Territory. So great was the demand for new acreage that the federal government pressured for rights of way to allow the construction of roads through the Choctaw homeland. Nothing seemed an obstacle to the settlers. From the time the Mississippi Territory was organized in 1798 until removal, politicians repeated their demands for the relocation of the tribes and the distribution of their lands. The cooperation of some Choctaw leaders was bought with cash and other gifts. Choctaw tribal integrity also was undermined by the efforts of missionaries to convert them into Christian farmers, who could practice a market agriculture.

In 1801, the Choctaw signed the Treaty of Fort Adams, hoping a definition of tribal boundaries would satisfy the demands of the United States. No treaty was ever enough, not even the combined results of Fort Adams, Mount Dexter (1805), and Doak's Stand

(1820), the latter of which exchanged 9 million acres of Choctaw homelands for 13 million unfamiliar western acres. Although a few moved voluntarily, most wished to stay. Yet even loyal service as allies during the Creek War of 1813–14 did not protect them, for the determined state of Mississippi moved to terminate all their rights in 1830. By the notorious Dancing Rabbit Creek Treaty in September 1830, the Choctaw signed over their homelands and agreed to emigrate; this was accomplished through a combination of threatened force and the bribery of certain chiefs.

The Choctaw movement west was as painful as those of their southeastern neighbors. Fraud, mismanagement, and corruption marked those in charge of the move, while disease and death stalked the Choctaw each mile. The combined deaths from the journey's difficulties plus subsequent cholera and smallpox outbreaks reduced the tribal population from 18,963 in 1830 to 13,666 by 1860.

Once in the West, the Choctaw tended to follow divisional lines between mixed bloods and full bloods, with the former following the market agricultural economy they had practiced in Mississippi and the latter retreating to subsistence agriculture. Despite privation, drought, and floods, the Choctaw rebuilt their government, their towns, and their farms. By the 1850s their economy had recovered sufficiently to allow them to market cotton, cattle, and timber.

When they moved west, the Choctaw took along their slaves. Because of their close proximity to the Confederate states of Arkansas and Texas, the tribe almost unanimously sided with the Confederacy in 1861. At war's end, however, the Choctaw were forced to abolish slavery and to cede the western portion of their territory, for which they were compensated $300,000.

Yet even as they tried to rebuild once more , the U.S. Government pressured the Choctaw to abandon tribal control in favor of private land ownership. Railroad expansionists clamored for rights-of-way and land grants, while coal developers pressured for mineral rights and access. The end of the Choctaw Nationwas assured by the Curtis Act of 1898, under which the remaining tribal lands in Indian Territory were divided into individual private allotments. The process required the creation of a tribal roll listing 18,981 Oklahoma Choctaw, 5,994 freedmen and their descendants, and 1,639 Choctaw who had moved west from Mississippi after the Civil War. Approximately 1,000 Choctaw still lived in the east. After 1906 there was no tribal government, a status in effect until 1934 when the Indian Reorganization Act allowed a return toward tribal governments; the Choctaw first formed an Advisory Council, but did not elect a tribal chief until 1948.

In Oklahoma today, the tribal government promotes programs aimed at improving the quality of life among the Choctaw people. There is a Choctaw Housing Authority in Hugo, an Indian Hospital in Tallahina, three Indian health clinics, five community centers, and ten Headstart centers. Several businesses also are operated by the Choctaw, including a bingo parlor, a resort complex, and a travel center. Profits from these along with federal funds then can be directed toward projects needed by the tribe.

Those who remained behind in Mississippi were driven into the depths of poverty by the new landowners. Yet the Mississippi Choctaw persisted. After the passage of the Indian Reorganization Act, they moved slowly toward recognition as a separate entity; their cause was helped in 1944 by the creation of a land base, a 16,000 acre reservation. The federal government also sanctioned the Mississippi Choctaw Agency, which assists the seven Choctaw settlements with education and general welfare. With their tribal headquarters at Philadelphia, Mississippi, they have established a development company and created an industrial park, which houses plants producing not only greeting cards but also wiring harnesses and radio speakers for automobiles.

Despite some economic progress, the Mississippi Choctaw lag behind their neighbors in income, employment, education, health care, and housing. Nevertheless, more than 6,000 Choctaw live in Mississippi today, with approximately 4,400 living on the reservation itself. The majority speak both Choctaw and English, but there are continuing adult education efforts aimed at improving language skills and educational attainment. According to the revised tribal constitution of 1975, the Mississippi Choctaw govern themselves under the protection of the federal government. Together with their Oklahoma kin and those living elsewhere, the Choctaw number more than 45,000. Many travel each year to the Choctaw Indian Fair at Pearl River, Mississippi, or to the Tuskahoma, Oklahoma, Labor Day festival to celebrate and preserve their Choctaw heritage.

◆ ◆ ◆ ◆ ◆ ◆ ◆ ◆ ◆ ◆ ◆ ◆ ◆ ◆ ◆ ◆ ◆ ◆ ◆ **THE CHICKASAW**

The Chickasaw, kinsmen of the Choctaw with whom they share the Muskogean language and a migration story, lived in present extreme northwestern Alabama, northern Mississippi, western Tennessee, and western Kentucky. Although relatively few in number, the 3,500 to 4,500 Chickasaw gained wide respect for courageously defending their homelands. Their success in defeating French invaders on three different occasions attracted the attention of the British, who won the Chickasaw as allies through exploiting their trade advantage. However, this involved the Chickasaw in an almost unending series of wars against France and her Indian allies. As a result many Chickasaw lives were lost; some losses were replaced, however, by the Chickasaw practice of adoption and absorption of remnant tribes.

After the defeat of France in 1763, the Chickasaw lived in relative peace for more than twenty years under the leadership of Payamataha and Piomingo. Both these leaders tried to stem the tide of European influences, but pressure to accommodate came from increasing numbers of mixed-blood families, whose success in trade, agriculture, and slavery created a life-style different from the traditional Chickasaw way. During the Revolution, Chickasaw service as British allies brought more outsiders when Loyalists sought refuge in the Chickasaw towns. After the Revolution, the Chickasaw signed a treaty with the United States at Hopewell, South Carolina, in January 1786. The treaty guaranteed the Chickasaw their lands, territories, and the right to manage their own affairs.

Initial U.S. relations with the Chickasaw were ineffective, because the Spanish at New Orleans wooed the Chickasaw. Consequently Chickasaw politics were complicated by rivalries among a Spanish allied party, an American allied party, those who vacillated, and the self-serving mixed bloods. Pressure from the pro-Spanish Creek under Alexander McGillivray added to Chickasaw woes. McGillivray's death in 1793 and the signing of the Treaty of San Lorenzo (1798) reduced Chickasaw difficulties slightly.

Despite internal political rivalries, the Chickasaw became increasingly tied to the United States. After 1802 a government trading post operated at Chickasaw Bluffs (present-day Memphis) to trade for the skins and furs brought in by the still successful Chickasaw hunters. The tribe supported the United States by rejecting Tecumseh's appeals in 1811 and aiding Jackson's forces against the Redstick Creek at Horseshoe Bend in 1814. Their loyalty, however, did not protect them when U.S. commissioners stripped them in 1818 of their Tennessee and Kentucky lands, leaving only their territory in northern Mississippi and northwestern Alabama.

Although political rivalries prevailed within the nation, all agreed in their opposition to removal. Under constant pressure from both federal and state governments, a few Chickasaw leaders were persuaded to look at a proposed western territory in 1828, but they returned to report they found nothing suitable. Despite their persistence, their resistance was undermined by the passage of the Indian Removal Act (1830)and the impact of Mississippi and Alabama state laws, especially the statutes that abolished tribal law and forbade the functioning of tribal government.

In 1830, at Franklin, Tennessee, the Chickasaw finally agreed to exchange their eastern territory for suitable western lands. The new stumbling block was suitability, which delayed migration for another seven years. When no acceptable land was found, the treaty of Pontotoc Creek (1832) was forced on them to increase the pressure. By then most Chickasaw regarded removal as inevitable. Ultimately, the Chickasaw were permitted to buy land in Indian Territory from their former neighbors the Choctaw. This arrangement was to be temporary, but after their migrations began in 1837, many Chickasaw preferred the security of Choctaw lands. They were persuaded to relocate only after the federal government had built Forts Washita and Arbuckle to protect them from the Plains peoples.

By the 1850s, the beginnings of Chickasaw recovery were apparent in the farms, ferries, mills, gins, and mercantile establishments appearing in the Chickasaw District. Prosperity especially was obvious among the mixed bloods; a Colbert family member operated a Red River ferry at an annual profit of $1,000. One promising development was in stock raising, a natural step for the well-known breeders of the Chickasaw horse. During the 1850s a tribal constitution and government were put in place and efforts undertaken to establish schools.

Much of their recovery was undermined, however, by the Civil War. Although the Chickasaw had little affection for the South, their location near the southern states of Arkansas and Texas prompted them to join the Confederacy. Tragedy came in the destruction and dislocation caused by the war, as once again they underwent economic decline and loss of land. A particularly thorny problem was the place of the Chickasaw freedmen, the former slaves of the Chickasaw who became free at the end of the Civil War. From 1866 to 1906, the Chickasaw resisted pressure to incorporate the freedmen into the tribe. Final settlement of the matter came only when the names of 4,670 Chickasaw freedmen were listed on the tribal rolls in 1906. Pressure for more land cessions after the war disturbed the Chickasaw even as it did their neighbors. Some Chickasaw favored allotment as a means of ending the ongoing disputes with the federal and state governments and to satisfy individuals and businesses clamoring for land. Under the stipulations of the Dawes Commission, the Chickasaw began enrollment and allotment. The Chickasaw list included the names of 1,538 full bloods, 4,146 mixed bloods, 635 intermarried whites, and 4,670 Chickasaw freedmen. The result of this procedure ultimately was the loss of most Chickasaw lands and mineral developments. Even the tribal leadership became a shadow.

Within the last three decades, there has been an attempt to re-establish a Chickasaw presence in Oklahoma. One of the obstacles in the path is the fractional number of those who can claim to be Chickasaw. Practically speaking the Chickasaw, never numerous to begin with, are perhaps the most intermarried of those who once lived in the southeast. Nevertheless there are more than 8,000 persons today who identify themselves as Chickasaw. In recent years, the governor and council of the Chickasaw Nation have worked to re-awaken a sense of pride. Several local councils have been organized in Oklahoma counties and an annual gathering called at Byng, Oklahoma. A Chickasaw Housing Authority worked tirelessly in the 1970s to improve the quality of housing, especially for those living at the poverty level. Arts and crafts outlets, a motel owned by the tribe, and several educational programs have been pushed, all of which offer economic opportunities and encouragement to the people who proudly carry their Chickasaw heritage into the twenty-first century.

CONCLUSION ✦ ✦ ✦ ✦ ✦ ✦ ✦ ✦ ✦ ✦ ✦ ✦ ✦ ✦ ✦ ✦ ✦ ✦ ✦

For many of the Native peoples living in the Southeast today, the past twenty years have been a period of marked population growth. Those who reported their Indian heritage to the census questions in 1970 numbered nearly 70,000, while in 1990 the total had risen to more than 211,000. Included in this total are persons living as independent citizens in urban centers as well as those living as members of organized groups on or near reservations, such as the Eastern Cherokee, the Mississippi Choctaw, the Poarch Creek, the Seminole, and the Miccosukee. There are others closely attached to tribal remnants, some of whom wish federal recognition, and others of whom have abandoned it, such as the Catawba.

Attempts to retain identity through practicing culture and language are difficult as well as painstakingly slow. For those who speak no Cherokee, the learning process is a difficult one. Attending tribal gatherings, participating in attempts at intertribal cooperation, and taking steps toward recognition are all steps that may be taken. Many Southeastern peoples, however, face the twenty-first century with pride and expectation. The Seminole, the Eastern Cherokee, the Miccosukee, the Mississippi Choctaw, and the Poarch Creek enjoy the benefits of tribal organization and federal status. They anticipate continued economic opportunity and improvement. Their success, moreover, may encourage some of the smaller groups to press for federal recognition in hope of improving their situation.

James O'Donnell III
Marietta College

Dedication of new Poarch Creek Tribal Center, April 1987. Poarch Creek elder gives an opening blessing at the ceremony.

BIOGRAPHIES ✦ ✦ ✦ ✦ ✦ ✦ ✦ ✦ ✦ ✦ ✦ ✦ ✦ ✦ ✦ ✦ ✦ ✦ ✦

Hagler

1690–1763

Catawba tribal leader

It is believed that Hagler was born along the Catawba River in northern South Carolina and became principal chief of the Catawba about 1748. By this time the Catawba had been greatly reduced in numbers as the result of warfare with their traditional enemies, the Shawnee, Cherokee, and Iroquois, as well as from European-introduced diseases such as smallpox.

Hagler developed friendly relations with the British colonists, meeting with them on numerous occasions for negotiations, and thus helped ensure his people's survival and maintenance of their traditional ways. In 1751, he attended a peace conference in Albany, New York. In a meeting with North Carolina officials in 1754 and in a letter to the chief justice in 1756, he argued against the sale of liquor to the Catawba. In 1758, during the French and Indian War, Hagler and his warriors sided with the English in an attack on the French garrison at Fort Duquesne (present-day Pittsburgh, Pennsylvania). In 1759, Hagler assisted the English in battle against Cherokee militants. Because of his support, the English built forts along the Catawba River to prevent attacks on the Catawba by other tribes. They also granted a reservation to the Catawba in 1792, near present-day Rock Hill, South Carolina.

Hagler was killed by a party of Shawnee in 1763. In 1826, South Carolina erected a statue of Hagler at Camden, considered to be the first such memorial to an American Indian in the United States.

Hancock

fl. early 1700s

Tuscarora tribal leader

From 1711 to 1713, the Iroquoian-speaking Tuscarora, living in present-day North and South Carolina, fought a series of battles to protect their lands against English settlers. Hancock, who some colonists called "King Hancock," was a Tuscarora leader in these wars.

The open conflict between the Tuscarora and English settlers began in 1711. Swiss settler Christoph Von Graffenried forced a group of Tuscarora families off their land. When Von Graffenried refused to pay for the land he seized, Tuscarora warriors retaliated with raids against settlements between Pamlic Sound and the Neuse River. A series of attacks and counterattacks ensued. In 1712, leaders in North and South Carolina sent a large military brigade led by Colonel John Barnwell to quell the Tuscarora. The first battle took place in Cotechney, Hancock's home village. After the English attackers were repulsed, a temporary truce was struck between Hancock and Barnwell. North Carolina officials, however, ordered Barnwell back into the field. In the face of another battle, Hancock agreed to a lasting truce, which was quickly violated by Barnwell's men, who captured Tuscarora for slaves. (During the late 1600s and early 1700s, many Indians were sold to work on plantations or shipped for sale in the Caribbean Islands off the southern coast of the present-day United States.)

In 1713, the colonists amassed a final assault on the Tuscarora. Under the command of Colonel James Moore, the colonial army and 1,000 Indian allies defeated Hancock and his followers. Hundreds of Tuscarora were killed, and hundreds more sold into slavery. Many Tuscarora survivors fled northward to New York colony.

When they arrived in New York, the Tuscarora found that they spoke a language closely related to the Iroquois of the Iroquois Confederacy, composed of the Seneca, Oneida, Mohawk, Cayuga, and Onondaga Nations. The Tuscarora were not allowed to place their leaders among the forty-nine chiefs of the Iroquois Confederate Council, but Tuscarora interests were represented by the Oneida chiefs. The Tuscarora took up residence near Oneida villages and have ever since maintained close alliance with the Oneida. Before the arrival of the Tuscarora in the 1710s, the Iroquois Confederacy was often called the Five Nations, but after the Tuscarora arrival the confederacy was often referred to as the Six Nations.

Alexander McGillivray 1759–93

Creek tribal leader

Alexander McGillivray's father was a Scottish trader who married a woman of Creek and French ancestry and who belonged to the prominent Creek Wind clan. McGillivray was born near the upper town village, Little Talisee, which was a "daughter village" or related village to Coosa, a traditional leading white, or peace, village among the upper Creek towns, located in present-day Alabama. He was sent to school in Charleston, in present-day South Carolina, and received additional private tutoring from a relative. The American Revolutionary War disrupted his studies, and he returned to the Creek Nation, where the upper towns generally favored British alliance. In late 1778, the upper town chief, Emisteseguo, also chief of Little Talisee, transferred political leadership to McGillivray, who was then only about eighteen years old. Emisteseguo, who belonged to a lowly ranked clan, feared assassination from pro-American villages and told McGillivray that his membership in the sacred Wind clan would protect him. This plan seemed to work as McGillivray was not troubled with assassination. The choice of McGillivray as upper town principal chief was unusual, since Creek leaders were generally older men who had acquired considerable training in ritual and religious knowledge. McGillivray, however, spoke English and knew colonial institutions, which were great advantages in treaty and diplomatic negotiations.

After the war, McGillivray entered into a business partnership with the British trading firm, Panton, Leslie & Company. He worked a plantation at Hickory Ground, a sacred white village in the upper town region. As chief, McGillivray tried to protect Creek lands from U.S. settlers, and tried to reorganize the Creek National Council by replacing the elderly town chiefs with the village head warriors. In 1790, he negotiated a treaty with George Washington in New York City. He died in 1793 of natural causes at a young age.

William McIntosh
(1775–1825)

Creek tribal leader

William McIntosh, a mixed-blood, became a successful entrepreneur, owning an inn, two plantations, and slaves. In addition, he rose to political influence as head warrior of Coweta. Coweta was the central red or war village among the Creek lower towns, located in present-day western Georgia. McIntosh came to prominence during the Red Stick War (1813–14), when mainly upper town Creek villages, those in present-day Alabama, rebelled against U.S. influence over the leaders of the Creek Council. During the war, McIntosh zealously led the lower towns and cooperated with U.S. forces to secure the Red Stick defeat in 1814. In 1814 at Fort

Jackson, present-day Jackson, Mississippi, General Andrew Jackson (future U.S. president) demanded 22 million acres of Creek national territory. The Creek, staggered at the demand, thereafter resolved not to cede land again to the U.S., and to punish with death any persons who sold land without national council authorization.

Nevertheless, in 1818 and 1821, McIntosh led Creek delegations that ceded more land to the U.S. After the second treaty, McIntosh was warned by the council that further unauthorized treaty cessions would result in his trial for treason. In the Treaty of Indian Springs of 1825, McIntosh and a dozen other chiefs ceded the last Creek holdings in western Georgia. For this act, McIntosh was condemned and executed by the Creek council. While McIntosh gained private advantages from the treaty negotiations, he argued that the Creek could not remain in their homeland, present-day Georgia and Alabama, because of U.S. settler expansion. Thus, he argued, it was better to sell the land and migrate west of the Mississippi River. Most of the Creek, however, disagreed and preferred to remain in their sacred homeland by resisting land cessions.

In the early 1820s, Opothleyoholo was speaker for Tuckabatchee, the leading red town among the Creek upper towns, located in present-day Alabama; the lower towns were located in present-day western Georgia. The Creek were divided into red and white towns; white towns led during times of peace and red towns led during times of war. Between 1810 and 1862, Tuckabatchee, with U.S. political support, led the upper towns. Talisee (present Tulsa), the leading white upper town, led the opposition and favored British alliance between 1790 and 1820. In the Red Stick War or Creek War (1813–14), most upper town Creek villages rebelled against the U.S.-supported villages, which consisted mostly of lower towns, with some exceptions like Tuckabatchee. The Red Sticks lost the war in 1814.

Opothleyoholo played an increasingly important role in Creek leadership. By the middle 1830s, he was the leading upper town

**Opothleyoholo
d. 1862**

Creek tribal leader

chief. He led delegations to negotiate the treaty of 1826, which ceded most of western Georgia, and the treaty of 1832, which provided the Creek villages with small reservations within the state of Alabama. By 1836, the Creek reservations were overrun by settlers. A brief insurgency by several lower town villages was put down by U.S. and upper town forces. Creek leaders felt compelled to migrate west to present-day Oklahoma. While retaining upper town leadership, Opothleyoholo emphasized retention of Creek culture and political institutions, but favored adoption of agriculture. The U.S. Civil War split the Creek Nation, largely between upper and lower town factions. In 1862, while Opothleyoholo led his people north toward Union alliance and protection, he was killed by Confederate forces.

Osceola
1803–42

Seminole tribal leader

In the 1830s, Osceola led a resistance movement to prevent the relocation of his people from their homeland in Florida to Indian reservations west of the Mississippi in present-day Oklahoma.

It is believed that Osceola was born near the Talapoosa River along the border between present-day Georgia and Alabama. As a boy, he and his mother moved to Florida, where they first settled along the Apalachicola River and in 1815 moved to St. Marks, a trading post in northern Florida. During this time, the Seminole Indians were caught up in the general removal of Indians from the southwest United States that affected, among others, the Cherokee and Creek. When he was still a teenager, Osceola fought in the First Seminole War of 1817–18. Seven years later, Osceola would fight in a Second Seminole War for his people, but this time in the role of leader.

A number of agreements and laws in the 1820s and 1830s led to the Third Seminole War. In 1823, an agreement at Camp Moultrie, Florida, was signed by a single tribe of Seminole in which they agreed to live on a reservation in exchange for annual payments of food and money. Passed by the U.S. Congress in 1830, the Indian Removal Act authorized the removal of all Indians in Florida within three years. In 1832, a treaty signed by a minority of Seminole at Payne's Landing required them to move to lands west of the Mississippi in exchange for food and money. By 1835, many Seminole had not complied with the removal treaty. Osceola traveled from band to band, urging his people to remain in their homelands. On December 28, 1835, Osceola led a party that ambushed Wiley Thompson, an Indian agent who was working to gain Seminole compliance with the removal treaty. (This marked the beginning of the Third Seminole War, within which fighting continued long after its recorded ending date of 1842.) Three days after the ambush of Thompson, Osceola and his warriors met and defeated General Duncan Clinch and a force of eight hundred troops.

For the next two years, Osceola spearheaded a relocation resistance movement. The Seminole warriors made good use of the Florida Everglades, a swampy region, to wage a successful hit-and-run campaign. Although many of the Indian chiefs fighting with Osceola surrendered during the war, Osceola continued to fight until his capture in 1842 by General T. S. Jesup, who captured him by deceiving him into attending a "peace council." As Osceola met with Jesup's envoy several miles outside of St. Augustine, Florida, troops secretly surrounded the Seminole leader, eventually swooping in to take him and his followers prisoner. The U.S. military often used such deception to capture and control Indian leaders. Osceola died in prison three months after his capture.

The capture of Osceola marked the official end of the Third Seminole War, although many Seminole continued to resist U.S. removal efforts by retreating to the isolated swampy regions of Florida. It is estimated that the war resulted in the deaths of fifteen hundred American troops and cost the U.S. government $20 million. Although many of the Seminole eventually relocated to Indian Territory in present-day Oklahoma, a number remained behind, clinging to their strongholds in the Everglades. To this day, their descendants can be found in southern Florida, where they live on state- and federally recognized reservations.

Pushmataha
1764–1824

Choctaw tribal leader

Choctaw legend says that Pushmataha was an orphan, and he himself maintained that he was born of a splinter from an oak tree. Such a story was unusual in Choctaw society where everyone was conscious of his or her Native iksa (local matrilineal family). At a young age, Pushmataha was recognized as a great warrior and hunter. He participated in many Choctaw hunting forays across the Mississippi River into the Osage and Caddo country, since by the early 1800s, fur-bearing animals suitable for trade were already significantly depleted in Choctaw country. These hunting trips led to war with the Caddo and Osage, who protected their land from the Choctaw intruders.

In 1805, Pushmataha was elected chief of the southern or Six Towns district of the Choctaw Nation. The Choctaw government was divided into three politically independent districts, each with a chief and council. From 1805 to 1824, Pushmataha led the southern district, which was the most conservative district, and, before 1760, allied to the French Louisiana Colony. In the early 1800s, Pushmataha owned a small farm, had two wives, which was possible under Choctaw custom, and owned several slaves. Pushmataha favored friendly relations with the U.S., siding with the U.S. against the British, Tecumseh (the Shawnee war leader), and the Red Stick Creek during the War of 1812. For his services, he earned the rank of U.S. brigadier general. The Choctaw, including Pushmataha, signed treaties of land cession in 1805, 1816, and 1820. In 1824, Pushmataha died from an infection while in Washington negotiating yet another treaty. He was buried with full U.S. military honors.

Major Ridge
1771–1839

Cherokee tribal leader

In his younger days, Major Ridge went by his Cherokee name, Nunna Hidihi (He Who Stands on the Mountaintop and Sees Clearly), a name of great respect for a man who showed wisdom and understanding in the Cherokee councils. As a young man, Ridge fought as a warrior in the numerous border wars with U.S. settlers until the peace emerged about 1795. Thereafter, Ridge and a small group of Cherokee leaders decided that agriculture and political change were the only means of ensuring Cherokee national survival from U.S. pressures for land cessions. Between

1797 and 1810, Ridge was a leading advocate for abolishment of the law of blood, the rule that clans exacted a death for a death in cases of murder. During the Creek War of 1813–14, many Cherokee fought with the U.S. Army and lower town Creek villages. Ridge rose to the rank of major, and thereafter was called Major Ridge.

Between 1810 and 1828, the Cherokee incrementally formed a constitutional government, modeled after the U.S. government. The new Cherokee government instigated strong efforts by surrounding state governments to resettle the Cherokee west of the Mississippi River, because they feared the Cherokee might remain permanently in their eastern homeland. In 1835, Ridge and a minority group of Cherokee planters signed the Treaty of New Echota, thereby agreeing to migrate to present-day Oklahoma. The treaty signers feared that remaining in the east was impossible because American settlers were confiscating Cherokee property and the Cherokee government was outlawed. Many conservative Cherokee considered Major Ridge and the others traitors for signing the treaty and were embittered by the significant loss of life during the ensuing forced removal, the Trail of Tears, during the winter of 1838–39. Major Ridge and several others were assassinated in 1839.

Native Peoples of the Southwest

Before European colonization, the area of the world that now comprises the U.S. Southwest and northern Mexican states was called Aztlán by the Aztecs, who built a powerful empire in central Mexico. Aztlán remained a coherent cultural and geopolitical region under Spanish rule until 1820 and under independent Mexican rule until 1848, when the United States annexed the northern part of Aztlán after the Mexican-American War (1846–48). Mostly a desert and alpine arid and semi-arid region, the Southwest has a fragile land base. Water is a scarce commodity, and drought easily brings starvation to the inhabitants.

The pre-colonized Southwest saw the gradual development of many agricultural communities, which by A.D. 900 consisted of multistory buildings and large ceremonial centers. These buildings very much resemble the round underground kiva ceremonial rooms found among the present-day Hopi in northern Arizona and the Pueblo villages in eastern New Mexico. First on the Colorado Plateau (Mesa Verde) in present-day Colorado were the Anasazi, or "Ancient Ones," who lived in multistoried cliff dwellings. Between A.D. 900 and 1200, many major trade and ceremonial towns emerged at places known today as Canyon de Chelly and Chaco Canyon, where archaeologists have been studying the ruins of these relatively large prehistoric towns. Some one hundred to two hundred towns developed and were interconnected

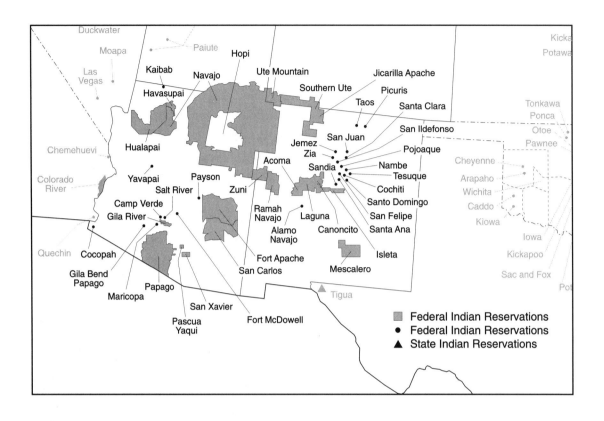

Map legend:

- ◼ Federal Indian Reservations
- ● Federal Indian Reservations
- ▲ State Indian Reservations

Contemporary southwestern tribes.

by walkways and trade relations. The large cities of Central America appear to have carried on trade with towns as far north as the U.S. Southwest, and objects have been found to indicate that significant trade also took place with the Indian peoples living as far west as the Pacific Coast.

An extreme drought between 1275 and 1300 caused the Southwestern peoples to abandon their towns and move closer to fresh water sources. The Hopi moved to live in villages along the Colorado River, while most others moved to present-day eastern New Mexico and constructed villages along the Rio Grande River and its tributaries. In 1540, on the eve of Spanish exploration of northern Mexico, the village-dwelling agriculturalists numbered around 200,000. Other peoples, including many Hohokam speakers, such as the Tohono O'Odham, were previously living by irrigation and farming but were forced to rely more and more on hunting and gathering in the harsh desert area of the Southwest, and to live near major water sources such as the Colorado River.

Besides the Pueblo, the other major people in the Southwest were the Athapascan-speaking Navajo and Apache, who migrated south from the sub-Arctic around the thirteenth century. A hunting and gathering people, the Athapascan traded and intermarried with the village peoples and also became involved in the intervillage conflicts and wars engendered by disputes over water usage and territory. Navajo and Apache groups allied with one or another of the villages. Both the Navajo and western Apache bands absorbed significant aspects of Pueblo culture and world view. The Navajo creation history of early prehuman beings struggling to gain greater moral balance by moving from three dark worlds beneath the earth to the present fourth world par-

Hopi child clown.

allels Hopi and other Pueblo creation stories. Similarly, some Apache groups adopted the ceremonies and dance costumes of the village farming peoples in the form of kachina dancers, which for the Pueblo were ancestral spirit beings who, if properly placated, granted sufficient rain for the growing of crops. While the Navajo and Apache borrowed some elements of Pueblo culture and world view, the Athapascan combined the new elements with their own cultural themes and created complex and powerful creation histories and pantheons of spirit beings (see the Navajo creation history in the section on traditional Indian religions).

When Spanish colonization began in the early 1600s, the village peoples were controlled strictly and their ceremonies and rituals suppressed. The Spanish authorities gave land grants to military officers for past service, and also granted the officers the right to command Indian labor. Many Pueblos were annually forced to perform work on the ranches and farms of the Spanish officers and upper class. Furthermore, by 1628, Spanish missionaries were establishing churches among the Pueblos and increasingly demanding conversion to Christianity and abandonment of traditional Indian religious views. Young Pueblos were forced into the Spanish military, which existed principally to make slave raids into areas peripheral to the New Mexico colony. For two centuries, the Navajo, the Apache, and the Ute, a hunting and gathering people who lived in present-day southern Colorado, defended themselves ferociously from these raids.

In 1682, the Pueblo spiritual leader, Popé, led a rebellion that forced the Spanish and allied Indians to retreat to present-day El Paso (Texas). Spanish military forces again regained control of the Pueblo villages in the Rio Grande Valley, by 1696, and many Pueblos left their villages to join the Navajo bands, which were hunting and migrating in the north. Thereafter many Navajo bands raided Spanish farms and the Pueblos for horses, manufactured goods, cattle, and sheep. Eventually, during the 1700s, many Navajo relied less on hunting and adopted the pastoral life of herding sheep. Eating mutton and sheep herding became the preferred way of life for many Navajo, and a large number of conservative Navajo continue to this day to herd sheep and cattle primarily for subsistence, while small numbers are sold and traded.

During the early eighteenth century, the Comanche, who emigrated from their Shoshoni homeland in present-day Wyoming, moved into the northern Spanish colony of New Mexico. The Comanche set out to control the horse trade on the southern Plains. By the mid-eighteenth century, the Comanche were the dominant bison-hunting people of the southern Plains and the Southwest. Their trade dominance grew to the point that they controlled the horse and gun trade, selling even to the Spanish themselves. By the late 1700s, there were 2,000 Comanche living east of the Rio Grande River and 4,000 living on the west side. Using war and bribery, the Spanish reached peace and trade agreements with a large number of Comanche, who, with many Ute and Pueblo, fought as allies in Spanish campaigns against the Apache and the Navajo, who often raided the Spanish and Pueblo towns for horses, sheep, and trade goods. The raids and antagonism between the Athapascan Southwestern Indians and the Mexicans did not entirely diminish during the period of rule by the Mexican Republic (1820–48).

The U.S. military and traders entered the Southwest in full force in 1848 after the Mexican-American War. They met strong opposition from the Indian people, particularly the Apache.

THE APACHE

The Apache migrated into the Southwest until around the eleventh century. They formed a small part of a large migration of Athapascan peoples from the north and are closely related to the Navajo. They divided into small bands that spread over a 700-square-mile territory, *Gran Apacheria,* as the Spaniards called it, including all of present-day New Mexico and Arizona. According to differences in language or dialect, the Apache formed into two major groups: the Jicarilla, Lipan, and Kiowa (Apache) living on the southern Plains and the Chiricahua, Mescalero, and Western Apache, who in the 1800s were migrating westward into present-day New Mexico and Arizona.

The Apache lived by hunting big game, gathering wild plants, and some farming. Their main shelter was a circular brush lodge with a fire in the center. Each Apachean group was composed of clans: basic social, economic, and political units based on female inherited leadership. From their entrance into the Southwest, the Apache groups were in conflict with the Plains peoples in the east and with the Pima, Papago (now called Tohono O'Odham), and Pueblo, then living in what is now eastern New Mexico. They did not enjoy a close relationship with the agricultural peoples, the Pueblo, as did their relatives the Navajo, and less is known about the Apache in early times.

After the Apache were hunted down and captured by the U.S. military in the 1870s and 1880s, Apache survivors were herded into desolate reservations in present-day Arizona and New Mexico. Geronimo, a Chiricahua Apache medicine man, is best known among the Apache leaders who resisted settlement onto reservations. Their resistance assured Apache survival and reservation land bases in Arizona and New Mexico (see the biographies of Geronimo, Cochise, Natchez, and other Apache leaders).

Some of the contemporary Apache reservations have been leaders in economic development of reservation resources. The White Mountain Apache in Arizona manage with considerable success Sunrise Park Ski Resort and Fort Apache Timber Company. The lumber company employs about 300 Apache residents, and grosses about $20 million in annual income. The ski resort is also a major contributor to Fort Apache Reservation economy and is one of the most successful resort ventures in Indian Country. Other Apache reservations have also invested in tourism by opening cultural centers and annual festivals to the public. In addition, some reservation lands and lakes are open for public fishing and outdoor recreation. The Apache people retain strong ties to their culture, language, dances, and other traditions. Powwows are held each year, and often many Indian people from other reservations attend.

THE NAVAJO NATION ✦ ✦ ✦ ✦ ✦ ✦ ✦ ✦ ✦ ✦ ✦ ✦ ✦ ✦ ✦ ✦ ✦

The Navajo Nation is the largest Native nation in the United States, both in territory and population. With 17 million acres, the Navajo Reservation in Arizona and New Mexico is approximately the size of the state of West Virginia or the independent country of Belize in Central America. The population is at least 160,000, and some estimates project a quarter million Navajo by the year 2000. The present-day Navajo territory is located in the Four Corners region of Arizona, New Mexico, Utah, and Colorado, with land in all but the latter. Between 1820 and 1848, the Navajo land was claimed by the Mexican

Republic, although the Navajo never submitted to Mexican authority. The United States annexed Navajo territory under the 1848 Treaty of Guadalupe Hidalgo, which ended the Mexican-American War.

Unlike the Mexican government, however, the United States was willing to adopt extreme military measures to subdue the Indians and control their land base. The Navajo successfully resisted U.S. control for seventeen years, until the U.S. Civil War (1861–65), when the U.S. Army and irregulars launched expeditions to search out the Navajo and destroy their economic livelihood. Many Navajo cornfields were burned, communities pillaged, fruit trees destroyed, and many sheep slaughtered, until the Navajo, facing starvation during 1863 and 1864, finally surrendered. The New Mexico trader Kit Carson was commissioned into the army with the rank of colonel and led irregular troops to capture and pacify numerous Navajo bands.

Eight thousand Navajo were rounded up and driven to a military-administered camp in the barren area of Bosque Redondo in eastern New Mexico, far from their high desert and alpine homeland. While there, a quarter of the Navajo died from starvation and exposure. In 1868, a treaty was negotiated with Navajo headmen, and the Navajo were allowed to settle on the present-day Navajo Reservation (see the biographies of Ganado Mucho, Manuelito, Barboncito, and other Navajo leaders).

From 1868 to 1922, when oil was discovered in Navajo territory, the Navajo were virtually ignored by the federal government. The land itself had been judged to be worthless, even for Texas longhorn cattle production. The presence of oil, however, led to intense intervention into Navajo affairs. In 1922, the Navajo Business Council was created by the U.S. agent, who needed a centralized authority to grant oil and mineral leases in the name of the entire Navajo Nation. Most Navajo were led by local headmen, who generally did not recognize a central Navajo government and often ignored the Navajo Business Council until its demise in 1936.

The Navajo firmly rejected the Indian Reorganization Act of 1934, federal legislation which sought to structure official tribal governments with constitutions. Instead the federal government allowed the Navajo to hold a constitutional convention, which proposed a government independent from the bureaucratic power of the Office of Indians Affairs (the Bureau of Indian Affairs, BIA, in the 1940s). The secretary of the interior rejected the Navajo constitution, which was a bold plan for greater Navajo political freedom. Instead, in 1938 the Department of the Interior created a new Navajo Business Council, composed of 74 elected Navajo members and generally elected chairman and vice-chairman. This government, known as the "Rules of 1938," provide the basis for the present Navajo Tribal Council.

During the late 1930s and 1940s, the Navajo became embroiled in a political and bureaucratic conflict with the BIA and U.S. government over the issues of grazing sheep and cattle on the Navajo Reservation. Most Navajo made their living from livestock—mainly sheep herding—but Navajo herds were generally small and designed mainly for supplying family food, although some mutton and wool was traded at local stores for necessary manufactured goods. During the 1930s dust bowl period, government officials decided that the Navajo were raising too many sheep for the amount of grasslands and that the overgrazing would lead to ecological ruin of Navajo lands through erosion. Beginning with a massive stock reduction program, agents of the Agricultural Department slaughtered tens of thousands of Navajo sheep to prevent overgrazing and desertification. This conflict soured Navajo and government relations for several decades.

Although the Navajo Nation possesses water rights sufficient to irrigate and farm five million acres of their land, fewer than 100,000 acres are under cultivation. Most of the land is used for grazing 500,000 sheep, 50,000 cattle, and 30,000 goats. Much of the agricultural production is animal food grain. There exists a potential basis for a successful agricultural and pastoral economy, something much desired by Navajo traditionalists struggling to maintain their subsistence economy, as well as by some economic experts.

Nevertheless, the Navajo pastoral economy often is eschewed by Navajo modernizers, who favor development of Navajo natural

resources such as oil, gas, coal, and uranium. Much Navajo land was leased by the federal government during the 1920s and 1930s, so that the main income generated from the land is from mineral and mining leases and royalties. The territory is rich in reserve subsurface minerals and resources: 100 million barrels of oil; 25 billion cubic feet of natural gas; five billion tons of surface coal; and 80 million pounds of uranium. The major companies operating in the Navajo Nation are AMOCO, Exxon, Kerr-McGee, Gulf, and Texaco. There are 500,000 acres of commercial forest on Navajo territory, which yield millions of dollars in annual stumpage payments. The forest enterprise is controlled by the Navajo government under its Navajo Forest Products Industry.

There is a wide gap between the wealth of Navajo territory and the overwhelming poverty of its residents. Unemployment hov-

A middle-aged Navajo woman stands next to her traditional hogan in Tuba City, Arizona.

ers around 50 percent. Most of those who are unemployed are unskilled and lacking in formal American education, many speaking little English. Few are familiar with the modern market economy. Support services, such as day care centers, are few. Early education is poor. The majority—some 75 percent—of employed Navajo work in the public sector, made possible by U.S. government funding amounting to hundreds of millions of dollars annually. The remaining workers on the reservation are employed in commercial agriculture, mining, forestry, wholesale and retail trade, and construction. Around 5 percent are employed in transportation, communications and utilities, all of which are Navajo-owned and -operated.

About 20 percent of the Navajo people live off the Navajo Reservation, and many have migrated to southwestern cities, as well as to San Francisco and Los Angeles, for jobs. Under the federal government's Indian Relocation Program of the 1950s, most Navajo who relocated chose California, since a large number were already living there, many having been rail workers for the Santa Fe Railroad since the 1920s. Due mainly to economic necessity, migration to and from the Navajo homeland is constant.

The influx of federal funds has not increased Navajo incomes even to national poverty levels. Navajo per capita income is around $1,000 a year. Federal funds are generally earmarked to relieve symptoms of poverty, not for capital development. The chief beneficiaries are the thousands of Navajo employees running the federal bureaucracy on the reservation; they make up a privileged group with a vested interest in maintaining and enlarging the tribal government bureaucracy.

The 1970s saw a rise in industrial activity, with the Navajo Nation taking remarkable initiatives. During the construction of the off-reservation Salt River power plant project at Page, Arizona, Navajo workers experienced blatant racial discrimination in pay and duties. They organized and pressed the Navajo Nation to support their demands, and newly elected Navajo Chairman Peter MacDonald, took up the challenge (see the biography of Peter MacDonald). Trade unions, until then banned on the reservation, were legalized and supported. The actions taken by Navajo workers and the Navajo Nation awakened workers throughout the Southwest, where the combined Mexican and Indian labor force had long been oppressed by ruling Anglo-Americans. Both New Mexico and Arizona were traditionally antiunion, with less than 5 percent of their work forces organized into trade unions. The Office of Navajo Labor Relations was established to mandate standards for Navajo workers' wages for jobs in or near the reservation. These standards required major construction projects to hire Navajo on a percentage or quota basis in specific numbers of skilled positions.

Trade unions are now an accepted part of the Navajo social structure, but are far more democratic than their typical U.S. counterparts. The Office of Navajo Labor Relations supports local workers' associations within the reservation, based in the communities where the workers live. By the late 1970s, practically all Navajo workers in the private sector were members of labor unions.

Some observers have expressed concern at the successful unionization of Navajo workers, who receive nationally mandated union wages. They fear that the high income of Navajo industrial workers will encourage unbridled industrialization as well as an economic elite. However, traditional practices of Navajo family and clan sharing and generosity actually tend to equalize incomes in the reservation, through redistribution by means of gifts of money and goods from the highly paid workers to their less fortunate relatives and neighbors. It also appears that highly paid Navajo workers tend to invest surplus funds in the traditional pastoral economy by purchasing stock, feed, equipment, and trucks.

In 1971, the Navajo Nation supported the formation of Navajo Community College (NCC) at Tsaile, Arizona, on the Navajo Reservation. The locally controlled Indian community college was the first of its kind, and many Navajo, who otherwise did not want to leave the reservation to take college credit courses, enrolled at NCC. The college was so successful that within a few years other reservations were starting colleges and having con-

Navajo medicine man Albert Yazzie chats with Navajo Education Center staff after performing a Navajo Protection Way ceremony for Navajo servicemen and women who were involved in the Persian Gulf war with Iraq.

siderable success training reservation people. Meanwhile, U.S. college institutions were showing extremely poor results retaining and graduating Indian college students. Indian-controlled community colleges have been built on about thirty Indian reservations, and many more Indian reservations are contemplating building community colleges for their people and for surrounding non-Indian students. The community college movement has become one of the most significant events on many Indian reservations during the 1970s and 1980s. The movement to build Indian-controlled community colleges was greatly inspired by the ground-breaking work of the Navajo community and the pioneers who built Navajo Community College (see the section on Indian higher education).

In November 1982, young activist lawyer Peterson Zah won election as Navajo chairman. He was defeated four years later by

MacDonald, but won again in 1990. About 35,000 Navajo vote in the Navajo tribal government elections, and over the years the Navajo government has evolved by borrowing both Western and traditional Navajo government institutions. The Navajo adopted a court system modeled after the U.S. legal system in 1959 in order to prevent the states of Arizona and New Mexico from extending their courts onto the Navajo Reservation. The Navajo prefer to manage their own courts and use their own ideas of justice, rather than submit to the U.S. court system. During the 1970s, the Navajo court system gained in power and respect, and many local courts managed disputes in the traditional manner of trying to reconcile contentious parties, according to Navajo cultural views of resolving conflict more so than U.S. legal views. Until the 1950s, the Navajo government suffered from lack of local support, but since then it has tried to directly incorporate local political communities, often called chapters, into the government and electoral process, and in this way gain the support of the Navajo communities, which still tend toward local groupings and local leaders. The Navajo government has made considerable strides in attempting to provide a truly representative government, based to some extent on traditional principles, and has developed the largest tribal government organization in Native North America.

◆ **THE HOPI**

The Hopi are descendants of the earliest inhabitants of the Southwest and for centuries occupied a large part of present-day northern Arizona. In their oral history they recount the arrival of the Paiute and the Ute, the Navajo, the Spanish, and then the Americans.

The Hopi elders tell of a time long ago, before people were really human beings, when they lived underground; this was the period of the Third World. Before the early beings lived in the Third World, they had to flee two other worlds farther underground because of their immoral behavior and disruption of the

"Lynn," a Hopi woman.

social harmony of the First and Second Worlds. For some time these early people lived in peace with all the animals and there were no problems. But then, the people began to have disputes. A council was held, with animal representatives participating in the discussions. They agreed that the Third World had become morally corrupted and out of balance, and they had to seek peace by migrating from the underworld to a Fourth World above. The Hopi arrived in the Fourth World and encountered a frightening yet attractive spirit being, Masau-u, who asked them what they sought. Masau-u told the Hopi they could live on the land of the Fourth World provided that they followed sacred rules. The Hopi would have to perform rituals to provide water for the desert land, and they would have to accept Masau-u's teachings, abiding by his/her social and religious rules. The Hopi agreed and made a covenant to obey Masau-u and serve as caretakers of the land. The Hopi attempt to keep this sacred covenant to this day.

Each Hopi clan retells a variation of the creation story, but they all share the same emergence story and consider the land they occupy as sacred. The Hopi believe they must fulfill particular sacred and ceremonial responsibilities. Creating rain for the dry land is essential and is accomplished through prayers and ceremonies held annually in the Hopi villages.

The Hopi live in northeastern Arizona, where their reservation is entirely surrounded by the large Navajo Reservation. Hopi society is divided into twelve phratries, or collections of clans, with numerous clans within each phratry. Children always belong to the clan of their mother. Like other Pueblo, Hopi honor kachinas, or rain spirits, and clan ancestors. Clans are extremely important for social and religious relations, and each clan has its own special sacred objects and ceremonies. Clan and ceremonial leaders continue to play major roles in Hopi ceremonial and social life. Many Hopi, as well as Pueblo, ceremonies are concerned with creating community harmony and appeasing the kachina spirits to bring rain for the Hopi crops. The Hopi were a horticultural people who grew several varieties of corn, beans, squash, and other plants. Men hunted animals such as deer and elk, and the women gathered nuts, fruits, and roots.

In the middle and late 1500s, there may have been as many as a dozen Hopi villages along the Colorado River, but they were quickly decimated by early diseases, and by 1600, most Hopi retreated to their present villages in northern Arizona. There they were found by the Spanish, and starting in 1628 Spanish Catholic missions were established in several Hopi villages. The Hopi helped the Pueblos in the 1680 rebellion, and even after Spanish reconquest, the Hopi strongly resisted Spanish rule and Catholic religion.

The Hopi occupy about a dozen villages on the Hopi Reservation. They still maintain many of their ceremonies and beliefs, and many still live in multistoried buildings that the Spanish called pueblos. Many within the Hopi community continue to uphold the traditional ways and actively resist U.S. cultural influences in religion, education, and government. During the 1930s, a small number of Hopi voted for adopting a constitutional government under the provisions of the Indian Reorganization Act (IRA) of 1934. The IRA was designed by the U.S. government to give Indian communities more control over their own affairs, by organizing Western-style governments among them. Many Indian nations, especially among the religiously conservative Pueblo and Hopi, rejected the IRA constitutional governments, because they were modeled after secular Western views of political organization and had little precedent or congruence with Indian political traditions and political governments. The Hopi community became divided between those willing to live under the IRA government and those who wanted to retain Hopi political institutions, which incorporated a considerable degree of traditional Hopi customs and religious orientation.

The conservative Hopi have been some of the most active nationalist Indian groups in the United States. Together with the conservative and nationalist Iroquois people of New York and southern Canada, conservative Hopi leaders have appealed to international forums such as the United Nations in order to gain redress for broken treaty agreements and for recognition of Indian national independence. Not all Hopi share the view that the Hopi reservation should be recognized as an independent nation within the international community. But the conservative Hopi reflect the active conservatism inherent within tightly interrelated Hopi clan and religious relations, which fosters strong attachment to tradition and motivates many Hopi to actively seek preservation of Hopi community and religious institutions.

THE PUEBLO VILLAGES OF NEW MEXICO ✦ ✦ ✦ ✦ ✦ ✦ ✦ ✦ ✦

When the Spanish arrived in the 1500s, there were ninety-eight villages, called pueblos by the Spanish, along the northern Rio Grande and its tributaries; within a few decades, there were only nineteen, all of which exist today. Although all Pueblo peoples have similar economic, governmental, and religious structures, they speak four distinct languages: Zuni, Keres, Tiwa, and Tewa. The languages remain strong, although most Pueblo Indians also speak English.

Each pueblo is autonomous and fiercely independent; however, all the pueblos participate in a loose federation, the All Indian Pueblo Council, which traces its origins to the successful 1680 Pueblo Revolt against the Spanish. The leader of the rebellion was Popé, a religious leader from San Juan Pueblo.

The revolt started at Taos Pueblo and moved steadily to the southern pueblos, driving the Spanish and some Pueblo allies to El Paso in present-day Texas. For about a dozen years, the Pueblo enjoyed liberty (see the biography of Popé). The Spanish, however, reconquered the Pueblo by 1695 but thereafter refrained from tampering directly with Pueblo internal affairs, particularly religious ceremonies. Many Pueblo, especially those from Jemez Pueblo, did not want to live under Spanish rule and escaped to live among the Navajo and Apache bands, many of which were constantly raiding the Spanish and Pueblo villages for livestock and trade goods. The Pueblo had a profound effect on Navajo and Apache traditions and ceremonies, which were enriched with ideas borrowed from the Pueblo refugees. The remainder of the Pueblo lived under harsh Spanish rule, which demanded Catholic Christian conversion, and forced labor on the ranches of Spanish officers and political land grantees.

Under the rule of independent Mexico from 1821 to 1848, only the Pueblo among the Southwest Indians held full Mexican citizenship. Therefore, when the United States annexed the region, Pueblo people automatically became U.S. citizens, as did the other residents of the area. Not only was citizenship of little use to the Pueblo, but their territories did not fall under the federal government's developing reservation system, which normally put Indian lands under federal protection. Encroachment on Pueblo land, the finest farm land in the Southwest, accelerated rapidly. The Pueblo petitioned and then sued for Indian status, which they finally gained in 1916 through a U.S. Supreme Court decision. Meanwhile, they had lost some of their best lands as well as important religious sites.

A congressional investigation during the 1920s revealed that 12,000 non-Pueblo claimants were living on Pueblo lands. The All Indian Pueblo Council organized delegates from all the pueblos to regain their lands, which resulted in the 1924 Pueblo Lands Act. Assisting the Pueblo in their fight was John Collier, a young Indian rights activist on the staff of the General Federation of Women's Clubs. President Franklin D. Roosevelt later named Collier Indian commissioner, a position he held from 1933 to 1945. The Pueblo successfully mounted a campaign among non-Indians for a Native issue and set an important example for other Native peoples across the country.

Pueblo lands are secure, but land in that semi-arid region is of no use without water. The most important contemporary Pueblo Indian struggle is to maintain and to acquire water rights. Water law falls under common law in the Anglo-American legal system, and under federal law devolves to state jurisdiction. Indians fought for and won exemption to state control in the early twentieth century. The Winters Doctrine, arising from a 1909 Supreme Court case, defines Indian water rights, and is based on the theory that the federal government reserves power over federal lands, which includes the necessary water supply. The Winters Doctrine implies that Indian treaty rights include the right to adequate sup-

Christmas Day Matachine dancers at San Juan Pueblo.

plies of water necessary for the Indian reservations to carry on irrigation for agriculture and to meet their population and economic development needs. However, in a court decision in 1973, the Winters Doctrine was declared to be inapplicable to the Pueblo Indians of New Mexico, since the Pueblo were not officially Indians at the time the Winters case was adjudicated.

One the most significant events in recent Pueblo history is the return of the sacred Blue Lake and about 55,000 surrounding acres to the Taos Pueblo in 1975. Taos Pueblo had lost the land to the federal government, but after a thirty-year court and political struggle, the Taos Pueblo regained ownership of Blue Lake, a sacred site in Taos creation history, since it is considered the navel of the universe and the place where the Creator first created people. The people of Taos Pueblo held annual ceremonies at Blue Lake, many of which were crucial to the Taos Pueblo religious cycle, which, the Taos people believed, ensured the well-being and prosperity of the Taos community. The return of Blue Lake marked one of the few times that the federal government returned a major sacred site and surrounding lands to Indian control. It gave hope that in the future other Indian communities may successfully regain or protect their sacred sites, often unknown to the general public.

During the 1960s and 1970s, Zuni Pueblo became a model for the present-day U.S. government self-determination policy in Indian affairs. Like other Pueblo peoples, the Zuni have a strong tradition of religious community and strong attachments to their social and political freedom. During the 1960s, when federal funds became available through antipoverty programs like the Community Action Programs (CAP), many Indian communities, for the first time, gained access to significant funds and personnel, because of direct federal grants to local tribal governments within the CAP programs (see the chronology for the 1965 to 1970s period on antipoverty grants and tribal government revitalization). The Zuni, in the late 1960s, seized this opportunity and, armed with a little-used law that required the Bureau of Indian Affairs (BIA) to contract services to tribal governments, tried to gain control over all BIA programs in the

San Ildefonso Pueblo feast day.

Zuni community. The Zuni were able to contract many BIA programs and ran most of them much more effectively and with greater community commitment and participation. The Zuni embarked on this plan as a means to exclude unwanted BIA interference into their government and community affairs. The Zuni came to the attention of President Richard Nixon, and in 1970 he made a speech in which he announced the beginning of the Indian self-determination policy, designed to allow tribal governments and reservation communities greater local control over BIA and federal programs and over local institutions such as schools. President Nixon held up the Zuni as an example to all Indian communities who wished to take a greater role in managing their local affairs.

The nineteen New Mexico pueblos remain strongly traditional communities that continue to practice and perform the major dances and rituals of their religions. They have consistently rejected U.S. efforts to significantly alter their religious, social, and cultural orders, since they continue to live by many of the religious views and customs of their forefathers. The Pueblo have generated many well-known artists, novelists, poets, scholars, and painters among their people (see the biographies of Paula Gunn Allen, Alfonso Ortiz, Leslie Marmon Silko, and other Pueblo).

♦ **THE FUTURE**

The languages and cultures of the Native peoples of the Southwest endure, and their preservation most likely is ensured. For the Native peoples of the Southwest—the Paiute and the Ute, the Walapai and the Yavapai, the Mojave and the Tohono O'Odham, the Pima and Apache, the Navajo and the Hopi, and the Pueblo of New Mexico—the Southwest is their ancient homeland. Others have come and gone for over three centuries, and those who have stayed have had to learn the lessons of the ancients in order to survive in the vast, harsh land.

Roxanne Dunbar Ortiz
California State University, Hayward

♦ **BIOGRAPHIES**

In the 1860s, under government orders, the U.S. military tried to re-settle or exterminate the Navajo Indians. Barboncito, along with Delgadito (his brother) and Manuelito, led the Navajo resistance from 1863 to 1866.

Barboncito was born at Canyon de Chelly in present-day Arizona. He was both a military and religious Navajo leader. In 1846, Barboncito signed a treaty pledging friendship with the United States. Peace would soon become impossible. In the early 1860s, the U.S. military waged an ongoing mixed campaign of warfare

Barboncito

1820–71

Navajo tribal leader

and negotiation to halt Apache and Navajo raids on U.S. settlements in the Southwest. The raids were a response to settler encroachment on Indian land. One important area of contention was the grazing lands around Fort Defiance located in present-day eastern Arizona. In 1860, after soldiers shot a number of Navajo horses, Barboncito and Manuelito led Navajo warriors in retaliation against the soldiers at Fort Defiance. After nearly taking the fort, the Indians were pushed back into their mountain strongholds. Stalemated, U.S. military leaders and Indians agreed to a short-lived peace council.

In early 1862, Barboncito made peace overtures toward General James H. Carleton. These efforts, however, were also short-lived. In 1862, the military chose a barren parcel of land located in present-day eastern New Mexico, called Bosque Redondo, as a Navajo relocation site. The relocation plans pushed Barboncito into open warfare with the United States. In 1864, at Canyon de Chelly, Barboncito was taken prisoner by soldiers commanded by Colonel Kit Carson. He was taken to the relocation camp at Bosque Redondo, where living conditions were barely survivable. In 1865, Barboncito rejoined Manuelito after escaping with about five hundred followers. He later surrendered and, in 1868, signed a treaty that established the Navajo Reservation in present-day New Mexico and Arizona. The Navajo leader died three years later.

Cochise
1812–74

Chiricahua Apache
tribal leader

In 1861, Indians in the southwest United States began an ongoing war against the U.S. settlers and army in a series of conflicts known as the Apache Wars. From 1863 to 1872, Cochise was the leader of this resistance.

The Apache Wars began when Cochise, falsely accused of abducting a rancher's child, was imprisoned by an American lieutenant. He escaped, but the ensuing years were a cycle of attack and revenge. From his stronghold in the Dragoon Mountains (located in southern Arizona), Cochise and his ally, Mangas Coloradas, led an effective guerrilla campaign against U.S. and Mexican forces. In 1863, the United States military stepped up its campaign to pacify the Apache. Although losses and atrocities occurred on both sides and the Apache were forced to return to their mountain strongholds, no Apache band was ever conquered.

In 1871, Cochise repudiated efforts to relocate his people to a reservation in New Mexico. A year later, however, the Apache leader agreed to abstain from attacks in exchange for reservation land in eastern Arizona. Consequently, peace did come to the region for the few short years before Cochise's death in 1874.

Mangas Coloradas was a member of the Mimbreno Apache, a tribe closely related to the Chiricahua Apache. Coloradas was a leader in the early years of the Apache Wars of the 1860s.

**Mangas Coloradas
1797–1863**

Mimbreno Apache
tribal leader

Coloradas fought two enemies during his lifetime. In the 1830s, there was conflict between the Apache and the Mexican government. In 1837, a number of important Mimbreno leaders were massacred by Mexican trappers who were motivated by the Mexican government's bounty on Indian scalps. Following the massacre, Coloradas united a number of tribes in present-day southern Arizona and New Mexico to rid themselves of intruding Mexican miners and trappers.

In 1846, the United States took possession of the New Mexico Territory, and Coloradas's enemy became the United States Army. In the 1850s, American miners began pouring into the region. Coloradas was captured and whipped by a group of miners, then released as a message to other Indians to stay away. Coloradas, who was probably close to sixty years old at the time of the beating, survived and stepped up his warring against U.S. and Mexican miners. In the early 1860s, when the U.S. cavalry left the southwest region to fight in the Civil War, military protection for settlers and miners was taken on by the governor of California, who dispatched around three thousand troops to the region. In 1862, Coloradas and his Apache ally, Cochise, attacked the California troops in southern Arizona at a place now known as Apache Pass. Coloradas was wounded, but continued to press his attacks. As a result, in 1863, he was invited to a peace parley by U.S.

military authorities. The peace parley was a ruse. Coloradas was murdered at Fort McLane, although U.S. authorities reported that he was killed while trying to escape. After his death, Coloradas's son, Mangus, continued his father's war to retain possession of the Apache land.

Peter MacDonald

1928–

Navajo tribal leader and businessperson

Peter MacDonald is probably best known for his tenacious and imaginative defense of Navajo land and energy resource rights. The Navajo occupy extensive parts of Arizona and New Mexico (14 million acres) and have the largest population of any tribe in the United States or Canada.

MacDonald was born on the Navajo Reservation at a place called Teec Nos Pos, and Navajo was his first language. His father died when he was only two, and MacDonald was forced to leave school after the seventh grade to herd sheep and work. Later, during World War II, he served in the marines and became one of the highly esteemed Navajo Code Talkers, whose messages in the Native language confused the Japanese military cryptographers during the Pacific campaigns. Upon being discharged, MacDonald resumed his education, getting a bachelor's degree from Bacone Junior College in Muskogee, Oklahoma, and earning a degree in electrical engineering from the University of Oklahoma in 1957.

In 1963, MacDonald returned to the Navajo Reservation, first to serve on the New Mexico Economic Development Advisory Board and later to become director of the Office of Navajo Economic Opportunity (ONEO). His aggressive management brought in more than $20 million in federal grants between the years 1965 and 1968. These successes led to his election as tribal chairman in 1970. During his three terms in office, MacDonald fought to renegotiate the leases through which outside industrial interests gained access to minerals on Navajo land and sought a more favorable policy for controlling Colorado River water rights. He also worked to keep industrial development under tribal control and tried to expand Navajo influence by encouraging the people to participate in elections.

Over the years, MacDonald has been an outspoken critic of the Bureau of Indian Affairs. His administrations faced serious issues, such as the land dispute between the Navajo and Hopi, and were subject to charges of fraud and favoritism. But his achievements in energy use management and Navajo self-determination are hard to question.

MacDonald has received numerous honorary awards and served on many advisory boards, both in his capacity as a political leader and as an engineer. A favorite target of journalists, he has been the subject of features in newspapers all over the United States.

Manuelito
1818–94

Navajo tribal leader

Manuelito was a Navajo leader during the Navajo War of 1863–66. Born in southeastern Utah, he became a powerful warrior in raids against the Mexicans, Hopi, and Zuni, and rose to prominence within his band. Unlike the peaceful Navajo leader, Ganado Mucho, Manuelito carried out a number of attacks and maintained resistance against U.S. Army troops.

Manuelito succeeded Zarcillas Largas as the head of his band in the 1850s when the latter resigned over failure to control his warriors' reprisals against U.S. soldiers. Although a major peace treaty had been ratified in 1849 by both sides, there were continuing clashes and depredations between the United States and the Navajo. The area around Fort Defiance in present-day Arizona was a major point of contention; both sides wanted the pasture land for their livestock to graze on, and both shot or stole the other's horses.

Troops destroyed Manuelito's home, crops, and livestock in 1859. The next year, he and the headman of another band led a contingent of warriors in an attack on the fort and nearly succeeded in capturing it. Colonel E.R.S. Canby (who later campaigned against the Modoc, a California Indian tribe, and was killed by the Modoc leader Captain Jack) pursued Manuelito and his followers into the Chuska Mountains near the present-day Arizona and New Mexico border. In early 1861, both sides met at Fort Fauntleroy, later renamed Fort Wingate, in present-day western New Mexico, and agreed to work toward a peaceful resolution. But in Septem-

ber 1861, hostilities again erupted after a horse race at the fort in which the Navajo claimed that Manuelito had been cheated. Artillery was fired into the crowd of Navajo to quell the ensuing riot, and ten Indians were killed. Warfare resumed between the two sides.

Troops and Ute scouts and allies, under Colonel Kit Carson, began a scorched-earth policy culminating in the Navajo War. Carson's orders were clear: Kill all hostiles and relocate all prisoners to Bosque Redondo (near Fort Sumner in present-day eastern New Mexico). Of all the resistant Navajo bands, Manuelito's held out the longest. Faced with army pursuit and starvation, Manuelito led his remaining warriors back to Fort Fauntleroy and surrendered. He joined other Navajo held in captivity at Bosque Redondo.

Along with headmen of other bands, Manuelito traveled to Washington, D.C., to petition for the return of the Navajo homelands. A peace treaty was ratified by both sides in 1868. Manuelito returned to serve as principal Navajo chief and chief of tribal police. He again traveled to Washington and met President Ulysses Grant before his death at the age of seventy-six.

Ganado Mucho
1809–93

Navajo-Hopi tribal leader

Culturally and linguistically similar to the Apache, their Athapascan neighbors, the Navajo often raided other tribes throughout the Southwest for horses, livestock, and possessions. During the eighteenth and nineteenth centuries, the Navajo acquired large amounts of land for their increasing herds of sheep and cattle. Ganado Mucho was the son of a Navajo mother and a Hopi father. He never adopted these warlike tendencies and grew up to be a successful rancher, band headman, and peacemaker in northeastern Arizona.

Ganado Mucho was a young man when the Navajo carried out particularly vehement strikes on Mexican troops in the 1830s. From 1846 to 1849, United States troops sent five expeditions in attempts to control the marauding Navajo. It seems that Ganado Mucho did not participate in any of this warfare. However, because of his large herds, in the 1850s he was accused of cattle theft, but he successfully denied the charges. In 1858, he signed an agreement with other peaceful Navajo ranchers to report any thefts of livestock and return any livestock found. Mucho became the head of his band, but since the Navajo comprised many small bands, he possessed no authority outside his own local band group, which among the Navajo was usually composed of close relatives and in-laws.

Despite the ratification of a peace treaty between some Navajo bands and the United States, other Navajo bands continued their raids and clashes with U.S. Army troops. These forays led to the outbreak of the Navajo War of 1863–66. Backed by Ute Indian scouts and allies, Colonel Kit Carson led U.S. forces through the heart of Navajo country on a search-and-destroy operation. Ganado Mucho and his followers hid from Carson, all the while encouraging peace between both sides. During the war, Mucho lost two daughters and a son to raids by the Ute and Mexicans. His band surrendered, and he led them along with others on the brutal "long walk" from Fort Defiance in Arizona to Fort Sumner at Bosque Redondo in New Mexico.

The Navajo were held as prisoners until a peace treaty was signed by Ganado Mucho and others in 1868. Until his death at age eighty-four, he lived on the Navajo Reservation, rebuilt his ranch, and continued to work for peace between the United States and the Navajo.

Natchez (Naiche)
1857–1921

Chiricahua Apache
tribal leader

Naiche was the younger son of the great Chiricahua Apache leader Cochise. When Cochise died and was secretly buried in the Dragoon Mountains of Arizona in 1874, Naiche assumed leadership of the Chiricahua. Never claiming to be equal to his father, Naiche guided the Chiricahua through their transition and surrender to General Oliver O. Howard in 1876.

The Chiricahua were moved north to the San Carlos Reservation in Arizona. In the summer of 1881, a White Mountain Apache brought news of the first Ghost Dance to the Chiricahua Apache by telling them Cochise and spirits of the great chiefs would reappear soon thereafter. At Cibecue (Arizona) in August, a num-

ber of soldiers and the Apache medicine man were murdered. When word of this spread, hundreds of U.S. troops poured into Arizona to quell what was perceived to be a Chiricahua uprising. In September 1881, Naiche and his followers fled the hot, dusty San Carlos Reservation because of the Cibecue incident.

In retaliation for the soldiers' murder, two Apache scouts were sent to Fort Alcatraz in San Francisco Bay and three others were later hanged at Camp Grant, near Bonita, Arizona, the site of the 1871 massacre of nearly one hundred Apache men, women, and children. This incident marked the beginning of four more years of bloody warfare. Naiche and the Chiricahua conducted many raids along both sides of the U.S.-Mexican border.

Naiche and his group surrendered after General Crook and his Indian scouts traced them to their Sierra Madre stronghold. They returned to the San Carlos Reservation and in May 1884 were removed to Turkey Creek in present-day Arizona. This region was more to the Apache's liking and provided cooler temperatures and more wooded terrain. It was proposed that they be given cattle and sheep to raise, but the Indian Bureau decided that the Apache should become farmers instead. Unhappy with the situation and with additional restrictions imposed upon them, Naiche, Geronimo, Nanay, and their followers again fled the reservation for Mexico in May 1885. They again raided both sides of the border for the next ten months.

Crook again met up with Naiche, Geronimo, and Nanay, and, after two days of negotiation, they agreed to surrender and move east for a period of not longer than two years. A whisky peddler sneaked into camp that night and sold liquor to the Apache. By morning, Naiche and Geronimo and their followers were again off to the mountains. As a result of this incident, General Nelson A. Miles replaced Crook. Telegraph wires, which could easily be cut down by the Chiricahua, were replaced by the heliograph, which used the sun to send Morse code messages. Five thousand troops, nearly five hundred Apache scouts, and hundreds of Mexican troops chased the small band to no avail, so Miles reduced his forces to a contingent of scouts and sent several of them to contact Naiche and Geronimo. They agreed to surrender for the final time.

By September 8, 1886, Naiche, Geronimo, and their followers were on a train bound for Florida. From there they were transferred to Mount Vernon Barracks in Alabama. The collective group of Apache were still assimilating this move, when they were transferred again to Fort Sill, Indian Territory (Oklahoma). Naiche welcomed this move, because the terrain was more similar to Arizona. His family built a house, and he became a government scout. But an attempt was made to seize even this land from them. They appealed and were finally allotted the Mescalero Reservation east of the Rio Grande in central New Mexico. Naiche and his family moved there in April 1913, and he spent the remainder of his days at peace.

Popé was an important spiritual and military leader of his people. In the 1680s, he led a successful rebellion against the Spanish in the upper Rio Grande region by uniting a number of Pueblo villages. After the rebellion, for nearly a decade, Popé was a central leader among the temporarily free Pueblo villages.

Popé
d. 1690

Tewa Pueblo tribal leader

The Spanish founded the colony of New Mexico on Indian land in 1598. The Europeans soon were using their soldiers to collect taxes and promote the Catholic religion among the Indians living in the region. Under the *repartimiento* system, Indians were forced to pay the Spanish taxes in the form of labor, crops, and cloth. Unlike British settlers in the east who chose to drive the Indians from their land, the Spanish conquerors preferred to rule over the Native inhabitants in a feudal economy. The Catholic Church, in its zeal to convert Indians, called for the expurgation of Indian religious beliefs and rituals. These efforts were enforced by the ever-present Spanish military. The Indians living under Spanish jurisdiction were forced to practice their beliefs in hiding. Among the Pueblo villages along the Rio Grande, religious ceremonies took place in semi-subterranean ceremonial chambers known as *kivas*. Many Indians gave lip service to Christian beliefs in public, but clung to their own faith in private.

Popé was an important medicine man of the San Juan Pueblo, who had resisted repeated attempts to convert him. He was captured and flogged by Spanish authorities on at least three occasions. His beatings became a symbol of resistance to his people and enhanced his efforts to gain recruits for a hoped-for uprising. In 1675, Spanish authorities arrested Popé and a number of other Pueblo medicine men. The prisoners were taken to Santa Fe where they were jailed and beaten. An Indian delegation won their release after threatening the Spanish with violence. Upon his release, Popé went to the Taos Pueblo where he began organizing a rebellion and covertly enlisting recruits. He preached that the *kachinas*, ancestral spirits, had ordered him to restore the traditional way of life for his people. A number of towns pledged allegiance to Popé's cause, and on August 10, 1675, he ordered an attack. Resistance fighters from numerous pueblos in the region moved against the Spanish. After a number of successful smaller engagements, a large Indian force moved on to Santa Fe in present-day New Mexico. A week of fighting and four hundred deaths later, the Spanish retreated south to El Paso, in present-day western Texas. About 250 Indians died in the uprising.

For the next twelve years, the Pueblo held control of their homeland. Popé oversaw the destruction of all Spanish property and cultural institutions. Indians who had been baptized by Catholic priests were washed with suds from the Yucca plant to "cleanse" their spirits. Popé chose to live in Santa Fe and used the carriage left behind by the Spanish governor. By the time of his death in 1690, the alliance of the region's Indians had dissolved in the face of drought and attacks by Apache and Ute bands. By 1692, Santa Fe was once again under Spanish control.

Peterson Zah
1928–

Navajo tribal leader

In 1992–93, Peterson Zah was the elected chairman of the Navajo Nation, which occupies extensive parts of Arizona and New Mexico (14 million acres) and has the largest population of any tribe in the United States or Canada.

As a youth, Zah was discouraged from entering college by his teachers at the Phoenix Indian School; nevertheless, he attended college on a basketball scholarship and graduated from Arizona State University with a bachelor's degree in education in 1963. On completing his education, Zah returned to Window Rock, Arizona, on the Navajo Reservation, to teach carpentry as part of a pilot program intended to develop employment skills among Navajo adults. He then served as a field coordinator at the Volunteers in Service to America (VISTA) Training Center at Arizona State University. VISTA was a federally sponsored domestic peace corps, and Zah was involved in cultural sensitivity training for VISTA volunteers in preparation for their service on Indian reservations throughout the United States.

In 1967, Zah joined DNA-People's Legal Services, Inc., a nonprofit organization chartered by the state of Arizona to help indigent and other economically disadvantaged Indian people. DNA had nine offices on the Navajo, Hopi, and Apache reservations, and in San Juan County, New Mexico. Zah later became executive director of this organization, a position he held for ten years. In this capacity he supervised thirty-three tribal court advocates, thirty-four attorneys, and a total of 120 employees. Under his direction, DNA lawyers took several landmark cases to the U.S. Supreme Court, winning cases that helped establish the rights of individual Native Americans and the sovereignty of Indian nations.

In 1982, Zah was elected chairman of the Navajo Tribal Council; in this capacity, he presided over the tribal council and served as chief executive officer of the Navajo Nation government. In 1987, he became chief fundraiser for the Navajo Education and Scholarship Foundation, a nonprofit organization that solicited funds from the private sector and provided scholarships to needy and worthy Navajo students. In 1988, he founded Native American Consulting Services, a private firm, which provided educational services to school districts on and off the reservation. As sole proprietor of the company, he developed curriculum materials on Navajo culture and history and worked with Congress on efforts to secure funds for new school construction on the Navajo and San Carlos Apache reservations.

Native Peoples of the Northern Plains

All contemporary tribal communities in the Plains north of Okla-homa possess their own distinctive qualities. Tribalism—loyalty to the group—endured despite a long history of economic and political forces designed to destroy Plains cultures. Despite U.S. attempts to end tribalism, the Indians' desire to preserve their cultural integrity, fostered changes that resulted in preservation of cultural life and heritage among contemporary northern Plains communities.

Most Indian nations identified with the High Plains Culture of horses and buffalo hunting did not live on the Plains until after 1750. Before European contact, all horses in North America died out about 8,000 to 10,000 years before the present. The horses that became part of the wild horses, or the American mustangs, were horses that escaped from early Spanish explorer expeditions. Some Indian nations lived on the Plains, but they lived in small huts and hunted the buffalo on foot. Most Indian nations, which are commonly regarded as Plains tribes, lived farther east. Most so-called Plains Indian nations migrated onto the Plains only during the colonial period, and mainly after 1650 when Euro-pean expansion forced many Indians westward. Before moving onto the Plains, many so-called Plains Indian nations, such as the Sioux and Blackfeet, lived by hunting, growing corn, and gath-ering wild foods. During the 1650s and early 1700s the Iroquois,

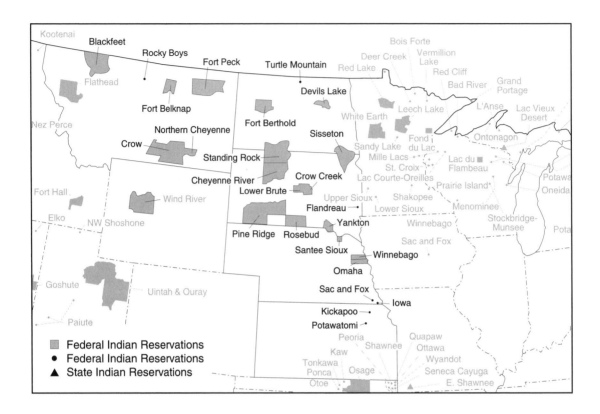

Contemporary Plains Indian tribes.

an upstate New York nation, started an expansionist trade and military campaign to control and maintain access to lands with fur bearing animals, necessary for trade with the Europeans. The Iroquois expansion pushed many Algonkian-speaking nations, such as the Chippewa and Ottawa, farther west into the upper Great Lakes area. The Chippewa, for example, migrated into present-day Minnesota and, armed with guns from their European trade allies, began pushing the Sioux Indians onto the Plains by the latter half of the 1700s. By the early 1800s, many Sioux bands moved onto the Plains from their original woodland homes in Minnesota and adopted the horse, buffalo hunting, and the sacred ceremony of the Sun Dance. They also began raiding the more sedentary farming peoples, such as the Mandan, Arikara, and Hidatsa, who were living along the Missouri River. The Sioux eventually settled in present-day central North Dakota.

The experience of Cheyenne, an Algonkian-speaking nation, is typical for the peoples who migrated onto the Plains. In the early 1600s, the Cheyenne were located in present-day southern Canada and made their livelihood by hunting, farming, and gathering wild plants. The Iroquois expansion after 1650 pushed the Cheyenne farther west and, in the 1700s, early French explorers reported that the Cheyenne people were living in present-day Minnesota. By the late 1700s, the Cheyenne were living in eastern North Dakota, and while still growing corn, were increasingly adopting the use of the horse and the hunting of buffalo. The Sheyenne River in eastern North Dakota is named after them. By the middle 1800s, the Cheyenne had moved to the western Plains and had fully adopted Plains culture, including the Sun Dance—an annual renewal ceremony, military societies of young men, portable teepees, annual gatherings in the summer for religious ceremonies, and collective buffalo hunting. In the winter, the Cheyenne, as other Plains nations like the Sioux, Blackfeet, and Crow, broke into small bands and endured the cold winter months in separate locations.

The most common image non-Indians have of Indian people is that of the Plains culture, with fierce warriors, sacred Sun Dance ceremonies, and buffalo hunting. Nonetheless the Plains culture was a relatively new mode of life for Indians and was an adaptation to the rapid expansion of colonial settlements and the extension of the colonial sphere of political influence. The Plains culture lasted only about two centuries and does not characterize the way Indians lived for centuries before its emergence in the late 1700s. Before then, most Indians in the East were farmers who lived without horses, and many of the Plains nations such as the Sioux belonged to cultures that were related to the farming and mound-building communities of the Mississippi Culture (A.D..800 to 1500). Nevertheless, the Plains cultures flourished during the 1700s and during much of the 1800s and lasted until U.S. authorities pacified the Plains Indians and placed them on reservations. By the late 1870s, U.S. hunters had virtually slaughtered the large herds of buffalo, and, without adequate buffalo supplies as a major food source, the Indian Plains culture was no longer possible.

HISTORICAL PRECEDENTS ✦ ✦ ✦ ✦ ✦ ✦ ✦ ✦ ✦ ✦ ✦ ✦ ✦ ✦ ✦ ✦ ✦ ✦ ✦

Two centuries ago, French, Scot, English, and Spanish traders moved onto the northern Plains, and their continual presence altered the demography and material culture of many Plains tribes. Traders, who were looking to exchange buffalo hides for guns, pots and pans, cloth, and other goods, preceded the more intensive settlements in the late 1880s. Diseases preceded and accompanied the European newcomers and caused many epidemics among the Plains nations. Smallpox, cholera, and whooping cough epidemics were responsible for dramatic declines in Plains Indian populations during the nineteenth and twentieth centuries. In 1837, a major smallpox epidemic dramatically reduced Mandan, Arikara, and Hidatsa numbers and forced them to combine clans and mix family lines; ultimately the three tribes coalesced and moved to a location near present-day Fort Berthold Reservation in North Dakota. Other Indian nations living on the Plains, such as the Sioux and Pawnee, suffered similar catastrophic population losses, though their exact numbers are hard to document.

The United States further displaced Plains Indian peoples by moving eastern Indian tribes to lands west of the Mississippi River. Starting in 1830, U.S. government policy authorized movement of most Indian nations east of the Mississippi River to new homelands west of the river. Most eastern Indian nations were moved to present-day Kansas and Oklahoma (See the Oklahoma section of this chapter, and see the Nineteenth Century section in Chapter 2). In the 1830s, groups from the Iowa, Kickapoo, Potawatomi, Chippewa, and Munsee Delaware, all eastern nations, migrated to Indian Territory in present-day Kansas. After agreeing to treaties with the U.S. government in 1865 and 1874, part of the Winnebago Nation, formerly located in Wisconsin, settled on a reservation in Nebraska. Frequently the indigenous Indian peoples considered the Indian newcomers as hostile intruders on their lands and hunting territories. Warfare ensued as the eastern Indians tried to re-create their communities in the west, and the Plains Indians, like the Pawnee and the Ponca of present-day Kansas, tried to defend their hunting territories. In the 1880s and 1890s, the United States relocated the Pawnee and Ponca to Indian Territory in present-day Oklahoma.

Hostility on the Plains escalated when the U.S. government assigned territorial boundaries for the Plains peoples in the 1851 Fort Laramie Treaty. Over the next thirty years, the United States redefined reservation boundaries by creating smaller reservations, sometimes forcing several tribes to live on the same reservation. The Shoshoni and Arapaho, once enemy nations, now coexist on the Wind River Reservation in Wyoming. A band of Assiniboine and a branch of the Yankton, both Siouan-speaking peoples, inhabit the Fort Peck Reservation in Montana. The Assiniboine and Gros Ventre, an Algonkian-speaking people, occupy the Fort Belknap Reservation in Montana.

Many Plains nations, however, resented U.S. restrictions on their freedom to move about the Plains, which had been their former tradition. The Lakota (the name some Sioux have for themselves), the Cheyenne, and the Blackfeet fought the United States and tried to keep U. S. settlers and miners from staying permanently in the area. Symbolizing their resistance to U.S. encroachments are such battles as the 1864 Sand Creek Battle in present-day Colorado, the 1866–68 Bozeman Trail War in Wyoming, and the defeat of U.S. troops led by Colonel George Custer at the 1876 Battle of the Little Big Horn in eastern Montana (see the biographies of Gall, Sitting Bull, Black Kettle, Crazy Horse, Lone Wolf, and other Plains Indian leaders).

By 1880, settlement on a reservation became the only political and economic option available, and the Plains Indians reluctantly moved to U.S. government controlled reservations. After resisting removal to Oklahoma in the late 1870s, the Northern Cheyenne settled onto the Tongue River Reservation in eastern Montana by the early 1880s. In 1916, a group of Plains Chippewa and Cree, both Algonkian-speaking peoples, found refuge on the Rocky Boy Reservation in Montana. However, in 1892, Chippewa leader Little Shell and his followers left the Turtle Mountain Reservation in northern North Dakota and joined the

Cree and Métis (mixed-blood people) in a non-federally recognized community that survives at Great Falls, Montana.

Eventually, the U.S. government settled most Plains Indians on reservations. The people often gathered to live near relatives, and these hamlets became the present-day reservation communities. Indian agents had near total control over reservation Indian communities, and between 1887 and 1934, official U.S. policies discouraged the exercise of traditional Indian government. Many ceremonies were banned and forced underground, and Indian cultural expression was generally discouraged in favor of Christianity and U.S. social life-styles. During this period Native languages were discouraged, and Native spiritual leaders continued their ceremonies out of the sight of U.S. officials. As a result, on many Plains reservations, traditional ceremonies like the Sun Dance were not actively revived for public consumption until the 1970s. Schools and mission churches were often constructed near reservation villages and missionaries, and school teachers and farmers introduced U.S. modes of life. Many Plains Indians continued to challenge U.S. control, however, by keeping children from attending schools. Despite initial hostility and resistance to settlement on reservations, most contemporary Plains Indians consider their reservations home.

After 1880, reservation poverty forced many Plains Indians to seek clothing from mission charities and from government distributions. These clothes were then altered by tribal artisans to suit Plains Indian tastes. The ribbon shirt is one example of tribal modification, in which colored ribbons are sewn on a "cowboy" shirt in order to make a distinct article of Indian clothing. Quilts followed a similar pattern, and northern Plainswomen are famous for their star quilts, which are richly designed blankets that many non-Indians buy as art pieces. Missionaries instructed women to quilt and introduced the eight-point star pattern found on many quilt patterns. Today the star quilt has become a distinctive Plains design. Used as gifts, the quilts help perpetuate the Plains tradition of giveaways at powwows and at some ceremonial occasions, such as funerals among the Northern Cheyenne.

♦ ♦ ♦ ♦ ♦ ♦ ♦ ♦ ♦ ♦ EARLY RESERVATION ECONOMIC PURSUITS

U.S. reservation policy limited trade and forced reservation Plains Indians to pursue a narrower range of economic activities. The upper Missouri River Fort Berthold Reservation, where the Mandan, Hidatsa, and Arikara settled, continued pre-reservation farming by planting crops. Downstream on the Missouri River, the Omaha and Winnebago also maintained farming pursuits. Other Plains peoples adopted farming. In North and South Dakota, the Sioux on the Sisseton Reservation, the Fort Totten Reservation, and the Yankton Reservation developed subsistence agricultural economies but were unable to purchase equipment necessary to farm large operations, because they lacked access to credit. On the other hand, in the western Plains reservations in Montana, many reservation Indians attempted to farm but were unable to harvest enough crops for subsistence purposes. The absence of fertile reservation land for adequate farming forced many reservation Indians to subsist on government rations or to sell reservation lands and use the money to purchase cattle.

Limited farming success on the semi-arid prairie encouraged the Office of Indians Affairs (later the Bureau of Indian Affairs, or BIA) to plan reservation irrigation projects, which began in the 1890s on the Blackfeet, the Crow, the Fort Belknap, and the Fort Peck reservations in Montana. The tribes paid the costs of the irrigation projects, which changed the reservation landscape as canals crisscrossed reservation farmland.

U.S. government agents encouraged cattle ranching as an alternative to irrigation agriculture. Ranching required less capital than farming, but even after reservation Indians began stockraising, their ranches remained small. Size, however, did not dictate success. By the turn of the century, Blackfeet ranchers registered over 400 cattle brands. Both the Blackfeet and the Northern Cheyenne ranchers produced quality stock, and cattle buyers from Chicago purchased animals from these reservations.

The Sioux Indians on the Standing Rock Reservation in North Dakota and the Cheyenne River, Pine Ridge, Lower Brulé, Crow

Creek, and Rosebud reservations in South Dakota had less success. Unable to stock their ranges with cattle, the Standing Rock, the Cheyenne River, and the Rosebud Sioux leased portions of their reservations to cattle companies at the turn of the century. A disadvantage to leasing was that the tribes lost short-term control over the land; however, they did retain ownership.

Pine Ridge and Rosebud cattle operations declined further during World War I (1914–18), when government officials encouraged Indian cattlemen to liquidate their small herds. This forced them either to lease or to sell land. Despite obstacles and hardships, many Plains Indians considered the early twentieth century cattle operations as the zenith of their reservation economic experience, because stock provided stable subsistence. More importantly, many western Plains reservations never recovered from the loss of their cattle operations, and today only a small percentage of reservation residents manage profitable stock operations. On the Northern Cheyenne reservation, for example, only 10 percent of the families make a living by cattle ranching.

LAND ALLOTMENT ✦

Beginning with the 1854 Omaha Treaty, land allotment—dividing tribal common lands into small individual tracts—became standard provision in Plains treaties and agreements. The General Allotment Act of 1887 applied the land allotment policy to all Plains reservations and also provided a mechanism for granting citizenship to the allotees. The legislation authorized the president to order the division of reservation lands into individual tracts. Allotting agents issued 40 acre to 640 acre tracts to individual tribal members. After twenty-five years, the allotted land converted to fee simple title (meaning the owner could sell whenever they wished), and U.S. citizenship was granted with the change in land status. Congressmen hoped that division and privatization of the Indian land base would eliminate Indian reservations and give individual Indians full status as citizens, which would protect their rights.

Allotment failed for many reasons. Dividing semiarid lands was ecologically unsound. Economically, reservation Indians lack access to credit, making it virtually impossible to farm profitably. Land allotment citizenship provisions failed politically because local communities refused to accept reservation Indians as social or political equals.

Irrigation projects also hastened the loss of allotted land. Congress authorized allottees to take a small irrigable allotment on a project and a larger non-irrigable tract of grazing land. Many reservation Plains Indians sold their irrigated properties, because they were unable to build improvements necessary to farm. The United States also encouraged tribes to sell non-allotted tribal lands to repay the costs of constructing the irrigation projects, further reducing the reservation resource base. Last of all, irrigation projects never recovered operation and maintenance costs forcing tribes to operate projects for non-Indians who purchased irrigable allotted lands.

After allotment, entire sections of unallotted reservation lands were sold. U.S. homesteaders purchased these non-allotted surveyed tracts and lived in the midst of the reservation. Portions of reservations never opened to homesteading were called "closed" lands. Many individual Indians sold allotments when leasing became unprofitable, and the Office of Indian Affairs sold land when the agency declared an Indian allottee incompetent.

Allotment also created heirship lands, when an allottee died without a will. In such cases, the United States granted the estate jointly to all heirs. In many cases when there was a relatively large number of heirs, shares in the deceased's allotted land were very small. Continuing the joint heirship practice beyond the first generation usually rendered the jointly owned allotments too small for economic purposes and forced the heirs either to sell or to lease the land. Today, if heirs lease the land, all receive smaller and smaller rent receipts as new heirs are added; and if they sell, the land is lost. Administering heirship lands remains a common problem on all Plains reservations and makes resource management decisions difficult.

Allotting land on Plains reservations increased the federal government's role in reservation affairs, since more staff were employed to handle additional work loads. For example, the Indian Service established a government banking system known as the Individual Indian Monies (IIM), where the reservation superintendent deposited monies gained from rent and sale of allotted lands. Consequently, allotees had to trust the BIA to properly manage their money.

THE RESERVATION NEW DEAL ✦ ✦ ✦ ✦ ✦ ✦ ✦ ✦ ✦ ✦ ✦ ✦ ✦ ✦ ✦ ✦

Allotment reduced the ability of reservation communities to participate in the prairie agricultural markets and made any downturn in the economy particularly hard-felt on the reservations. After World War I, Plains communities experienced an agricultural depression that drove lessees off the land and deprived many reservations of income. By 1930, private relief organizations were dispensing assistance to several reservation communities, because many were unable to provide for themselves.

Seeking to relieve suffering throughout the nation, Congress created a direct work relief program in 1933 known as the Civilian Conservation Corps (CCC) to employ the jobless in conservation projects. Initially reservations were excluded from this program, but Department of the Interior officials transferred the CCC concept to reservations, where unemployment was higher than among non-tribal populations. To direct this effort, Interior officials created the Indian Emergency Conservation Work (IECW), more commonly known as the Civilian Conservation Corps-Indian Division (CCC-ID), which provided employment for reservation irrigation, forestry, and grazing projects.

For many reservation Indians, this was the first time they had ever worked for wages, and the program provided relief income. Collectively, all New Deal reservation programs were crucial to reduce suffering. For example, nearly 95 percent of the Rosebud Reservation's working population found employment in New Deal direct relief reservation programs during the Depression.

Coinciding with reservation work programs, Commissioner of Indian Affairs John Collier advocated the creation of tribal economic corporations to manage tribal resources. Collier's plan became partially embodied in the Indian Reorganization Act (IRA) of 1934, which allowed reservation communities to vote to reorganize their governments along the U.S. democratic model and to create tribal economic corporations. Although Collier's proposal focused on reservation economic self-sufficiency, his proposition spawned bitter partisan battles as reservation residents discussed the strengths and weaknesses of the IRA.

These disputes contributed to the evolution of contemporary reservation political culture. Despite compelling reasons to support the IRA, many conservative Plains reservation communities would not support this legislation. The Yankton, the Standing Rock, the Crow, the Wind River, and the Fort Peck reservation communities rejected the IRA at tribal elections. Other reservations, such as Pine Ridge, approved the IRA by voting to accept the Act, then drafting new constitutions, and last of all, but more infrequently approving corporate tribal charters. Out of a total of over 500 recognized U.S. Indian tribes, only ninety-two accepted the IRA, and only about half that number went on to create tribal economic corporations. Nevertheless, while most reservation communities did not adopt the IRA, the BIA required that all tribal governments draft bylaws that in practical effect operated much like constitutional governments.

Tribal support for the IRA decreased by the end of the decade because the act failed to increase reservation self-rule. One reason for this dwindling support was that the BIA increased the number of Indian Service employees to administer Indian New Deal programs, instead of reducing government employees and turning reservation operations over to tribal governments. This trend was especially aggravating to Indians, who witnessed funding increases for the BIA. On the other hand, the passage of the Social Security Act in 1935 enabled many reservation Indians to obtain relief assistance from federal agencies.

WORLD WAR II ♦

America's entrance into World War II (1939–45) ended congressional appropriations for direct work relief programs. Jobless workers either entered the armed services or found employment in war-related industries. Plains climatic conditions also improved in the early 1940s, advancing agricultural prospects, but most reservation Indians did not participate in this prosperity. With a diminishing land base and an increasing population that had limited access to credit, most reservation Indians only marginally participated in the rural recovery either as field hands in labor intensive production or as sellers and lessors of land.

Since there were few reservation alternatives for employment, military service became an opportunity for young Indian people, and, as a result, many enlisted in the U.S. armed services. Many Indian soldiers sent money home to relatives who remained on reservations. For others, there were limited work opportunities in war-related industries such as urban munitions plants, and some Sioux found work closer to home at the ammunition ordnance storage facility at Igloo, South Dakota, near the Pine Ridge Reservation.

THE POST-WAR EXPERIENCE ♦ ♦ ♦ ♦ ♦ ♦ ♦ ♦ ♦ ♦ ♦ ♦ ♦ ♦ ♦ ♦

World War II changed Plains reservation life. Men and women left the reservations and either went to war or found work at war industries located in urban areas. After the war, many returned to their respective reservations, determined to improve their communities' economic, health, and housing conditions.

Wartime experiences made the post-war Plains reservation leaders more vocal and more aggressive than their predecessors. These pacesetters wanted greater self-rule to control reservation resources and institutions. Post-World War II Indian reservation leaders asserted that economic development was a tribal right and prepared reservation economic planning documents urging greater exploitation of tribal resources and labor to improve reservation economic welfare. These leaders also demanded equal rights with other citizens, and, to achieve equality, they demanded that Congress repeal discriminatory legislation, especially the restrictive liquor laws prohibiting the sale of alcohol to Indians. In 1952, the Indian alcohol prohibition was lifted, and now reservation governments have the right to decide whether or not to allow sale of alcohol on their reservations.

To improve economic conditions, tribal leaders needed to build infrastructures, such as roads, economic development parks, and telephone services that would facilitate economic commerce. Building economic infrastructure, however, was an imposing task, because most Plains reservations had few resources and little capital to pay for such improvements. Economically disadvantaged,

Blackfeet residence with sweat lodge and canvas lodge in foreground, Blackfeet Reservation, Montana.

the Plains peoples were distant from markets and possessed neither investment income nor access to credit, which made economic improvement difficult.

Reservation people wanted to end that pattern of economic dependency and develop their own ranching operations. They wanted to remain on the reservations, but many factors worked against them. The inability to find credit and an inadequate land base prohibited individuals from beginning ranching operations. In addition, the technological evolution decreased the demand for manual labor, reducing such employment opportunities as temporary agricultural laborers during the annual fall harvest. After World War II, new mechanized combines and other harvesting equipment rapidly spread throughout the Plains, and, for crops like wheat, oats, and other grains, the new equipment was more efficient and cheaper than traditional harvesting by seasonal labor. Consequently, in the postwar period, mechanization took away a major source of seasonal farm labor income from many Plains Indian communities, causing them to slide further into poverty.

Unable to increase their participation in the local economy, many reservation residents turned to wage work. Ideally, tribal leaders wanted labor intensive industries to locate either on or near reservations. A benefit to potential employers was that reservations contained a skilled or semiskilled work force trained during military service or at defense plants. For Indian community members, reservation-based industries would minimize family disruptions and the necessity of leaving their cultural communities, with its social and ceremonial events, for the oftentimes alien environments of cities or nearby towns.

However, industrial leaders were reluctant to establish plants near or on northern Plains reservations because of the distance from both suppliers and distributors. An alternative was to encourage Indian families to resettle in urban centers where jobs could be found. In the early 1950s, the U.S. government sponsored a program to assist rural reservation people to migrate to cities and to find jobs. Many Blackfeet moved to Seattle and New Hampshire, while many Oglala and Brule relocated to Chicago, Dallas, and Oakland. After obtaining employment, often in construction, many lost their jobs during the 1957 recession, and many returned jobless to their reservations. Others, however, remained in urban areas such as Los Angeles, Chicago, and Minneapolis, where significant urban Indian communities are present today.

Relocation pulled many Indian people away from the reservation's cultural environment and family activities. In order to maintain reservation ties, many tribal people preferred to work at jobs that were near the reservation. Others preferred to work seasonally in urban areas, usually in the winter, and then returned to the reservation during the summers, in time to participate in tribal ceremonies and powwows. The automobile encouraged migration from reservations and enabled many reservation people to work greater distances from their homes, while maintaining contact with their rural tribal communities.

Nearby reservation communities often provided temporary employment, usually seasonal construction work. That forced individuals to rely on local and state social services during periods of unemployment. Under these conditions the emigrants' economic livelihood did not improve, especially when an entire family depended on intermittent income. Even more important, the limited opportunities available in off-reservation communities made the plight of most reservation Indians more visible and encouraged discrimination.

Some Omaha and Winnebago left their reservations and assumed residence in Omaha, Nebraska, and Sioux City, Iowa. Many Crow moved to Billings, Montana, and a few Blackfeet found limited employment in Great Falls, Montana. Kansas City, due to its proximity to several reservations, became a common location for Kansas Indians who were looking for work. Rapid City and Sioux Falls, South Dakota, and Bismarck, North Dakota, became favorite Lakota destinations.

Many times, Indians seeking off-reservation work selected locales because of their proximity to reservations and familiarity with the city, or because friends and relatives were already there. The cities, with associated pressures and distractions, strained the ability of many Indians to preserve tribal identity, because of the need to adjust to the urban environment. Regardless of destination, relocation changed Plains demography and scattered tribal populations across the country. These migrations made it more difficult to maintain family relations and ceremonial ties. The reservations remained important cultural homelands for those living off the reservation.

The departure for urban environments did not improve reservation conditions for those who remained. Throughout the upper Missouri drainage, the U.S. Army Corps of Engineers completed one dam after another in the 1950s and 1960s and changed the living and subsistence patterns of several reservation communities. Tribal communities along the Missouri River lost to flooding valuable land that provided many reservation residents with fuel and food. The Fort Berthold, Cheyenne River, Standing Rock, Yankton, Lower Brule, Crow Creek, and Fort Peck reservations lost entire communities, as rising water forced reservation residents either to relocate in new communities (New Town, North Dakota, in the case of the Fort Berthold Reservation) or move to existing communities (Eagle Butte, South Dakota, in the case of the Cheyenne River Sioux Reservation). Damming prairie rivers did not stop with the Missouri River but expanded as tributaries were dammed, including the Big Horn River on the Crow Reservation. This hydraulic destruction continued the pattern of reservations supplying resources to non-tribal consumers and increased reservation poverty.

Plains reservations did not experience postwar prosperity; instead, reservation poverty increased. Plains Indian poverty excluded them from the 1950s termination legislation, which was designed to turn over tribal affairs to local state governments. Eventually, however, the Plains state governments refused to assume responsibilities over terminated Indian people, since the gains in tax revenues would have been far outweighed by the social welfare costs of supporting the impoverished Indian Plains communities.

The nation's war on poverty, initiated in the early 1960s, provided the rural Plains reservations with hope for economic progress. In 1964, Congress extended the Office of Economic Opportunity (OEO) programs to reservations and enabled tribal governments and tribal communities to write and administer Indian Community Action Program (ICAP) development grants. This provided tribal organizations an opportunity to improve reservation standards of living by building homes, constructing sanitary systems, and enhancing education. Like previous New Deal direct relief programs of the late 1930s, the 1960s enterprises provided short-term employment but did not build reservation infrastructures, and government dollars continued to pass from the reservation to non-tribal communities.

OEO and associated programs encouraged reservation communities to take control of reservation programs extending beyond

Kicking Women Singers at the North American Indian Days, Browning, Montana.

economic projects. The Crow tribe initiated a language program for young children in the Head Start Program, thereby providing a language foundation that strengthened cultural bonds. Even more important, the 1960s political climate, which favored civil rights and greater cultural awareness, increased tribal activism. The Plains reservations served as focal points for the American Indian Movement (AIM), an Indian Red Power organization, resulting in a seventy-three-day siege at Wounded Knee, South Dakota, in early 1973. In 1890, Wounded Knee was the site of the Seventh Cavalry massacre of more than two hundred Sioux men, women, and children.

Self-determination—permitting tribes to manage tribal operations—became U.S. policy in 1971 after a speech by President Richard Nixon (1969–74). Nevertheless, over the next two decades, the U.S. government, through the BIA, maintained control over tribal government budgets and law-making, thus making the trend toward tribal government self-determination a hollow victory.

Neither political activism nor government programs addressed major economic problems when government funds declined during the administrations of presidents Ronald Reagan and George Bush (1981–93). In order to generate income, some resource-rich tribes began to investigate the selling of coal and oil. As energy resources increased in value in the 1970s, companies pursued coal and oil contracts with several Plains reservations. The international energy crisis became a blessing and a curse to these reservations. Tribal leaders hoped energy leases would provide jobs and increase tribal government budgets. On the other hand, there was not universal support in the reservations on the issue of coal sales because of the long-range environmental and cultural effects. In the late 1970s, the Northern Cheyenne voted to reject massive coal sales and potentially millions of dollars of royalty income, because strip mining threatened to destroy nearly half of the Northern Cheyenne's Tongue River Reservation land base.

Different energy programs characterized each reservation, but the desire to control individual reservation energy development remained a common theme. The Crow entered into coal-mining contracts, the Blackfeet entered into oil exploration contracts, and the Fort Peck leadership opened the reservation to oil exploration, but oil companies paid Fort Peck prices.

Erratic energy markets encouraged tribes to pursue more stable economic projects. The Fort Peck (Montana) and Fort Totten (North Dakota) reservations built manufacturing plants that relied on government defense contracts. The Turtle Mountain Reservation, North Dakota, also sought contract work with the U.S. Defense Department for manufacturing trailers to haul heavy military equipment. These were successful reservation industries, but they employed only a small percentage of the people and forced most residents either to seek employment off the reservation or to remain unemployed or underemployed on the reservation.

Mosquito Run, Milk River Indian Days, August 1986, Fort Belknap Agency, Montana.

Nevertheless, after decades of economic development effort, Plains reservations are still some of the most impoverished places in the United States. Regardless of the standard applied, Plains Indians are

among the poorest of the poor (for example, real unemployment reached 80 percent on the Northern Cheyenne Reservation). High unemployment creates low reservation standards of living and results in malnutrition, poor health, and sub-standard housing.

Many Indian reservation communities adopted and modified U.S. institutions as a means to maintain their identity and traditions. Initially, tribal contact with U.S. schools produced negative experiences, as teachers tried to remove children from their culture, family, and heritage. Instead of fighting the schools, tribal leaders demanded change and assumed greater control over their children's education. Reservation parents and leaders insisted that school curricula become more relevant to reservation needs and values. Now many elementary and secondary reservation schools emphasize study of Indian cultures and help prepare children to participate in the reservation cultural community.

This concept has been carried into higher education. On the Plains, tribes have been leaders in community education, establishing a large number of tribally controlled community colleges. These institutions satisfy local needs to educate individuals, providing a mechanism for high school dropouts to complete graduation requirements, and providing college students with skills essential for employment (see the section on Indian Higher Education).

Improving each reservation's education system is essential, because residents need specific skills before they can even work for their own tribal governments. For example, tribal governments today administer multi-million dollar budgets, providing funds for a wide array of services from education to economic development. To accomplish these services, tribal leaders require that employees have expertise in accounting, administration, and environmental issues.

Contemporary reservation life is the result of change and continuity reflecting the ability of Plains Indians to accommodate outsiders without surrendering their cultural heritage. As a result, Plains cultures endure, because many tribal members continue to attend powwows, tribal fairs, Sun Dances, sweat ceremonies, and naming ceremonies. Powwows are held annually in most

Plains reservations, and many powwows still retain sacred dances as well as more social and public dances. Since the 1970s, many Plains tribes have revived public enactment of the traditional Sun Dance or adopted new versions of the Sun Dance, as with the Crow, who in the 1940s accepted a Sun Dance ceremony from the Shoshoni on the Wind River Reservation in Wyoming. On the Northern Cheyenne reservation, each of the four major reservation communities holds a powwow, during which a major Sun Dance is held in early July at Lame Deer, Montana, where the tribal government buildings are located. Traditional giveaway ceremonies are carried out at many Plains powwows. The purpose of the giveaways is to cement ties of friendship with members of other tribal communities. The peyote religion, or Native American Church, finds many converts among the Plains peoples (see the sections on Indian religions). Urban Indians maintain their cultural ties by either returning to their reservations to take part in the annual ceremonies and powwows or by participating in tribal social activities at urban Indian centers. Many sacred ceremonies and significant aspects of Plains culture remain strongly supported by Plains reservation communities. Despite poverty and isolation, Plains Indian culture is alive and well.

Richmond Clow
University of Montana, Missoula

◆ **BIOGRAPHIES**

In the 1860s and 1870s, American Horse was a Sioux leader in Red Cloud's War, which was fought for control of the Bozeman Trail, a major passage through the present states of Wyoming and Montana. He was a cousin of Red Cloud, another major Sioux leader and, until his death, remained a militant opponent to U.S. settlement of the western Plains.

In the mid-1860s, U.S. settlers and military attempted to build a string of forts along the Bozeman Trail. Settlers and miners had traveled the important passageway illegally since its discovery by

American Horse
1840–76

Oglala Sioux tribal leader

John Bozeman in 1863. Much of the trail crossed land that was reserved by treaty for the Sioux and Cheyenne, and from 1866 to 1888, the Sioux and Cheyenne tried to maintain control of the region. American Horse, the son of Smoke, participated in many of the skirmishes and battles of Red Cloud's War.

Despite the temporary land concessions made to Red Cloud in the Fort Laramie Treaty of 1868 and the momentary peace that agreement procured, American Horse remained contentious and militant. In 1870, he accompanied Red Cloud to Washington, D.C., for a meeting with government officials, but diplomatic relations were short-lived. In 1874, after the discovery of gold in the Black Hills, an area sacred to the Sioux located in present-day South Dakota, U.S. miners and speculators streamed to the Black Hills. In 1876, American Horse once again took up arms in the fight for the Black Hills and was present at the Battle of the Little Bighorn in 1876.

In September 1876, American Horse took a band of Oglala and Minniconjous southward to present-day South Dakota. Their encampment was attacked by General George Crook. The ensuing Battle of Slim Buttes resulted in the capture of American Horse. Alerted to American Horse's capture, the prominent Sioux leaders Sitting Bull and Gall gathered a rescue party to secure American Horse's release. Although he had been badly wounded from a shot to the abdomen, American Horse refused help from army surgeons. His rescuers were unable to come to his aid or negotiate his release, and American Horse died.

The capture and death of American Horse was one in a series of defeats for the Sioux after the Battle of the Little Bighorn and foreshadowed the Sioux surrender in 1877.

Gertrude Simmons Bonnin (Zitkala-Sa) 1876–1938

Sioux author and activist

Gertrude Simmons Bonnin, also known as Zitkala-Sa, or Red Bird, was born at the Yankton Sioux Agency in South Dakota on February 22, 1876, the third child of Ellen Simmons, a full-blood Sioux. Sioux agency land allotment applications indicate that her father was white. She was reared as Sioux until she was eight years old, at which time she left the reservation to attend a Quaker missionary school for Indians, White's Indiana Manual Labor Institute in Wabash, Indiana. She received her high school diploma and at the age of nineteen went on to Earlham College in Richmond, Indiana, where she received recognition and prizes for her oratorical skills. Following graduation Bonnin taught for two years at Carlisle Indian School in Carlisle, Pennsylvania. She then left to study at the Boston Conservatory of Music. In 1900, she accompanied the Carlisle Indian Band to the Paris Exposition where she performed as a violin soloist. During this period she also wrote three autobiographical essays, which were published in the *Atlantic Monthly* and two stories based on Indian legends for *Harper's Monthly*. Her book *Old Indian Legends* was published in 1901.

She returned to Sioux country and in 1902 married Raymond Talesfase Bonnin, a Sioux employee of the Indian Service. In 1902, they transferred to the Uintah and Ouray Reservation in Utah, where she was employed as a clerk and briefly as a teacher. She organized a brass band among the children of the reservation and undertook home demonstration work among the women. During this period, she also became a correspondent of the Society of American Indians, entering into what would become a life work in Indian reform. The society, organized at Ohio State University in 1911, was the first Indian reform organization to be managed exclusively by Indians and to require that active members be of Indian blood. Its aims included not only governmental reforms, but also the employment of Indians in the Indian Service, the opening of the Court of Claims to all equitable claims of Indian tribes against the United States, and also the preservation of the accurate Indian history and its records. Essentially, the society's aims were assimilationist: citizenship for all Indians, abolition of the office of Indian affairs (after 1940s called the Bureau of Indian Affairs), and termination of communal property holdings.

Bonnin was elected secretary of the society in 1916 and moved to Washington, D.C., which remained her home until her death in 1938. She carried on the society's correspondence with the Office of Indian Affairs, lectured from coast to coast as its representative, and acted as editor of its periodical, the *American Indian*

Magazine. After the demise of the society in 1929, Bonnin organized the National Council of American Indians. She remained its president until her death, lobbying in Washington on behalf of Indian legislation.

Bonnin's activities as author slackened after she abandoned the editorship of the *American Indian Magazine.* Her second book, *American Indian Stories* (1921), reprinted stories written at the beginning of the century. She retained her interest in music, and one of her last undertakings was the composition, with William F. Hanson, of an Indian opera, *Sun Dance.* She died in Washington, D.C., in 1938, at the age of sixty-one.

Crazy Horse
1842–77

Oglala-Brulé Sioux
tribal leader

Crazy Horse was a war leader of the Oglala subgroup of the Teton Sioux. He was born to the east of the sacred Black Hills near present-day Rapid City. As a boy, he was called Curly. Since his mother was a Brulé Sioux, he spent time in the camps of the Oglala and the Brulé. By the time he was twelve, he had killed a buffalo and received his own horse. His father, a holy man, changed Curly's name to the same as his own, Crazy Horse, after watching his son's exploits in battle against another tribe. While still a young man, Crazy Horse had a vivid dream of a rider on horseback in a storm, which his father interpreted as a sign of future greatness in battle.

In the 1866–68 war over the Bozeman Trail, Crazy Horse joined the Oglala chief Red Cloud in raids against U.S. settlements and forts in Wyoming. In these forays, Crazy Horse became adept in the art of decoying tactics. With the 1868 treaty at Fort Laramie, the U.S. Army agreed to abandon its posts along the Bozeman Trail. Crazy Horse became war chief of the Oglala and married a Cheyenne woman. He later took a second Oglala wife.

The Black Hills Gold Rush in 1876 brought more conflict to the region when miners and speculators began indiscriminately exploring the Sioux's sacred territory. Crazy Horse's camp became a rallying point for many warriors eager to drive the intruders away. On the upper Rosebud Creek in present-day southern Montana, in the spring of 1876, General George Crook's army of thirteen hundred attacked Crazy Horse's force of twelve hundred. Crazy Horse's feinting and assault techniques baffled Crook, who withdrew after heavy losses. Crazy Horse then moved his camp to the Bighorn River in Montana and joined Sitting Bull and Gall. U.S. Army troops, including a force led by Colonel George Armstrong Custer, set out to find and pacify the Sioux and Cheyenne, who were gathering at the Bighorn River.

On June 25, 1876, the famous Battle of the Little Bighorn commenced. In a masterful series of decoys and feints by the Sioux, aided by Colonel Custer's poor military judgment, Crazy Horse and his predominantly Cheyenne warriors attacked Custer's men from the north and west. Gall, after routing Major Marcus Reno's forces, charged Custer from the south and east. The U.S. troops were surrounded and completely annihilated.

Despite several other brilliant campaigns against U.S. troops, the Sioux were starving and weary of battle. On May 6, 1877, Crazy Horse reluctantly surrendered with eight hundred followers at Fort Robinson in northwestern Nebraska. However, the promises of a reservation for the Sioux were not kept. Crazy Horse was bayoneted at Fort Robinson during an attempt to confine him to a guardhouse on September 5, 1877. According to legend, he is buried in his homeland near Wounded Knee, South Dakota.

Dull Knife
1810–83

Northern Cheyenne tribal leader

Dull Knife and his warriors were active in the Cheyenne-Arapaho War in Colorado in 1864–65, the Sioux Wars for the Northern Plains in 1866–67 (including the Fetterman Fight), and also joined the Sioux under Sitting Bull and Crazy Horse in the War for the Black Hills of 1876–77. Many of his warriors participated in the battle of the Rosebud and the Little Bighorn in June 1876, where Colonel Custer and over two hundred soldiers met their death in present-day southern Montana.

Dull Knife and Little Wolf, another Cheyenne war chief, proved difficult to capture, even during the massive government retaliation for the Little Bighorn defeat. On November 25, 1876, General George Crook attacked Dull Knife's camp in the battle of Dull Knife on the Red Fork of the Powder River in Wyoming. The

Indians suffered twenty-five deaths and 173 tipis destroyed, along with food and clothing, plus five hundred ponies captured. In May 1877, Dull Knife and his followers surrendered at Fort Robinson in Nebraska, and were relocated to a reservation in Indian Territory (present-day Oklahoma).

The Northern Cheyenne were not happy living in Indian Territory, far from their traditional lands on the northern plains. The government had provided few supplies, little food, and malaria was rampant. Dull Knife and Little Wolf led an escape of nearly three hundred people from the assigned reservation in September 1878. They set out for their Tongue River homeland in northern Wyoming and southern Montana.

In a six-week, 1,500-mile flight, Dull Knife and his followers eluded some ten thousand pursuing soldiers and an additional three thousand civilians until many became too sick or exhausted to continue the flight. Dull Knife's group was captured on October 23, 1878, and taken back to Fort Robinson. Upon learning that they were once again in route to Fort Robinson, Dull Knife led his followers on another breakout on January 9, 1879, in the dead of winter. Only Dull Knife, his wife, son, daughter-in-law, grandchild, and another boy escaped capture and completed the trip to Chief Red Cloud's Pine Ridge Reservation in present-day South Dakota. Dull Knife and his small party were allowed to remain at Pine Ridge until, finally, in 1884, the Northern Cheyenne were officially granted the Tongue River Reservation in Montana. Dull Knife had died the year before, however, and was buried on a high butte near the Rosebud River in present-day South Dakota.

Gall (Pizi)
1840–94

Hunkpapa Sioux tribal leader

In the 1860s and 1870s, Gall was a leader in the wars for the Bozeman Trail and the Black Hills in present-day Wyoming, Montana and South Dakota. He was one of the principal strategists in the Battle of Little Bighorn, where in June 1876 Colonel George Custer and some two hundred U.S. soldiers were badly defeated. Gall is credited with developing the successful tactics that led to Custer's defeat.

Raised as an orphan until his adoption by Sitting Bull, a major Sioux leader, Gall proved his abilities as a warrior early in life. During the skirmishes for control of the Bozeman Trail in 1866 and 1867, Gall established and honed the guerrilla techniques and decoy tactics he used later in the struggle for control of the Black Hills. During the war for the Black Hills, he was Sitting Bull's chief military strategist. In the now-famous Battle at Little Bighorn, Gall's military prowess gained its greatest notoriety, and his tactics played a major role in the victory.

After the Indian defeats following Little Bighorn, Gall left for Canada with Sitting Bull. In 1881, he returned to the United States with about three hundred people and surrendered at the Poplar Agency in present-day eastern Montana. He was relocated on the Standing Rock Reservation in North Dakota. There, Gall became friends with Indian agent James McLaughlin and adopted a way of life more European than Indian. Gall negotiated a number of treaties that divided Sioux lands, and he did not take a stance in the Ghost Dance Uprising of 1890. His relationship with the U.S. government was not well perceived by other Indians, including those who had fought with him years earlier. In a gesture of rejection by another veteran of the Little Bighorn Battle, Kicking Bear left out Gall's portrait from a famous pictographic version of Custer's defeat.

Little Wolf was a chief of the Cheyenne military society known as the Bowstring Soldiers and, along with Dull Knife, was a war leader of the Northern Cheyenne. Little Wolf established his reputation as a war chief in his battles against the Comanche and Kiowa.

Little Wolf
c. 1820–1904

Northern Cheyenne tribal leader

During the 1866–68 war for the Bozeman Trail, Little Wolf fought alongside the Sioux leaders Crazy Horse and Gall in an attempt to protect Sioux lands in present-day Montana and Wyoming. In May 1868, Little Wolf was one of the signers of the Fort Laramie Treaty, which obligated the U.S. government to vacate the forts along the Bozeman Trail. In July 1868, after the Indians had driven the soldiers from the Powder River country, Little Wolf and his followers occupied Fort Phil Kearny (one of the Bozeman Trail Forts in present-day northern Wyoming), abandoning and burning it one month later.

When the Southern Cheyenne surrendered in 1875, however, the government concentrated on uniting the two Indian tribes onto one Indian reservation, primarily because gold was discovered in the Northern Cheyenne area of the Black Hills in present-day South Dakota. Little Wolf was one of the most active war chiefs in the War for the Black Hills of 1876–77. He was shot seven times during the Battle of Dull Knife (in present-day Wyoming) in November 1876 but survived the wounds.

The Northern Cheyenne were not willing to live in Indian Territory (Oklahoma) and repeatedly tried to return to their homeland in present-day Wyoming and Montana. Little Wolf joined Dull Knife, the Cheyenne chief, in the flight of the Northern Cheyenne from their assigned reservation in Indian Territory and proved difficult to capture. Dull Knife surrendered in October 1878, but Little Wolf successfully evaded government troops until March 1879, when he surrendered. The soldiers forced Little Crow and his remaining warriors to march from North Dakota south to Indian Territory. Though Little Wolf and Dull Knife escaped during the forced march, they finally surrendered in 1879.

Little Wolf became an army scout for General Nelson Miles and was allowed to remain in the Tongue River country of Montana. In 1880, he killed a fellow Cheyenne and lost his standing as chief. As was the Cheyenne tradition, he went into voluntary exile until his death in 1904.

Red Cloud

1822–1909

Oglala Sioux tribal leader

Red Cloud was a war chief and leader of the Oglala subdivision of the Teton Sioux. He was born in present-day north-central Nebraska near the forks of the Platte River. His father was Lone Man and his mother was Walks as She Thinks. Lone Man died soon after the birth of his son, and Red Cloud was raised by an Oglala headman, Smoke, his mother's uncle. Red Cloud quickly gained a reputation for bravery and cunning in raids against the Pawnee and Crow. When he was about nineteen, Red Cloud shot his uncle's rival, the most powerful Oglala chief, Bull Bear, at Fort Laramie, located in present-day eastern Wyoming. Because of these exploits, he was chosen to be leader of the Iteshicha (Bad Face) band over Man Afraid of His Horses, the hereditary leader.

Tensions dramatically increased between the Plains tribes and the United States with the advent of the Bozeman Trail, which passed through the present-day states of Wyoming and Montana, and its connection to the Oregon Trail, which provided passage to the Northwest Coast. Immigrants, miners, wagon trains, and U.S. troops began entering the area that was a prime resource to the Indians for bison hunting. The Oglala and Hunkpapa Sioux, Northern Cheyenne, and Northern Arapaho were enraged by these transgressions. Revenge for the murders of about 150 Cheyenne people at the 1864 Sand Creek Massacre, in present-day Colorado, may also have played a role. At Fort Laramie in 1866, Red Cloud, along with Man Afraid of His Horses, refused to sign a non-aggression treaty and declared war on all non-Indians entering the region.

Red Cloud was the architect of a number of attacks against U.S. settlers and miners who were traveling the Bozeman and Oregon trails. The Sioux employed guerrilla-like tactics to harry soldiers and would-be settlers. In December 1866, Captain William Fetterman led a relief party of eighty-one men to their deaths after supposedly boasting, "Give me eighty men and I'll ride through the whole Sioux nation." Subsequent battles, including the Wagon Box Fight and the Hayfield Fight, led the army to evacuate the region in 1868 and then agree in the Treaty of Fort Laramie to relinquish the Bozeman Trail in exchange for the cessation of further Indian raids. The Sioux celebrated this announcement by burning down every abandoned fort along the trail.

In 1870, Red Cloud traveled to Washington, D.C., to meet with President Ulysses Grant and then went on to New York City, where he gave a public speech. A Sioux agency bearing his name was established in present-day southern South Dakota, and Red Cloud spent the remainder of his life seeking to mediate peaceful relations between the Sioux and the United States. After government officials accused him of secretly aiding the Sioux and Cheyenne bands that defeated Colonel George Custer at the Little Bighorn in June 1876, the Red Cloud Reservation was renamed Pine Ridge, which name the reservation still bears.

Few on either side trusted Red Cloud's willingness to compromise, although he maintained that he supported peace, even during the Ghost Dance Uprising in 1890, when many Sioux sought religious solutions to reservation poverty and political confinement. During his later years, Red Cloud lost his sight, and he was baptized in the Catholic Church. He died in his home on the Pine Ridge Reservation.

Sacajawea 1784?–?

Shoshoni guide

In the early 1800s, Sacajawea accompanied Meriwether Lewis and William Clark on their historical expedition from St. Louis, Missouri, to the Pacific Ocean. Sacajawea is responsible in large part for the success of the expedition, due to her navigational, diplomatic, and translating skills.

Although Sacajawea's exact date of birth is unknown, the best estimates are 1784 or 1787. She was born among the Lemhi Shoshoni who lived in present-day Idaho. When she was only ten years old, a group of Hidatsa Indians kidnapped her during a raid and took her to a village near present-day Mandan, North Dakota. In 1804, she was purchased, or won, by French-Canadian fur trader Toussaint Charbonneau. When Charbonneau was hired by Lewis and Clark in 1804, he insisted that Sacajawea accompany the expedition. Sacajawea herself entertained hopes that she would be reunited with the Shoshoni Nation during the trip.

Sacajawea proved to be a valuable liaison for the U.S. explorers, since she spoke a number of languages, including Shoshoni and Siouan. Sacajawea translated Shoshoni into Hidatsa for her husband, who would then translate again into English for the leaders of the expedition. When language barriers were insurmountable, Sacajawea communicated with others by sign language. During the expedition Sacajawea revealed to Lewis and Clark important passageways through the wilderness. She also provided the expedition with valuable information about edible plants. Besides these duties, Sacajawea performed countless services during the trip, like the time she saved the expedition's records when her boat capsized. One of the most amazing incidents during the trip was the almost miraculous reunion of Sacajawea with her brother Cameahwait in August 1805. They met at the Three Forks of the Missouri River in present-day Montana. Cameahwait was then chief of his band. He gave the expedition horses and the use of an elderly Shoshoni guide. The expedition reached the Pacific Ocean in 1805.

The strength and endurance of this amazing woman cannot be exaggerated. Just two months before the expedition left Mandan in 1805, Sacajawea gave birth to Charbonneau's child. The journals of the trip show there was no hesitation over a teenage Sacajawea carrying an infant on her back at least as far as the Rocky Mountains. Throughout the trip she carried the infant (known as Little Pomp to those on the expedition) in a cradleboard strapped to her back. Sacajawea continued to travel despite a debilitating illness that struck her midway through the trip. Besides her duties as guide and interpreter, Sacajawea was responsible for housekeeping and food preparation. However, her husband was the only one Lewis and Clark paid.

Sitting Bull was a major military, spiritual, and political leader of his people in the 1800s. He was an important figure in the war for the Black Hills from 1876 to 1877 and helped to engineer the Indian victory at Little Bighorn.

Sitting Bull
1831–90

Hunkpapa Sioux tribal leader

Sitting Bull's military and leadership abilities became evident at an early age. At age twenty-two, he was leader of a warrior society known as the "Strong Hearts." It was probably not a coincidence that a warrior society would come into existence in the 1850s. It was during this time that U.S. settlers were sowing the seeds for a larger conflict that would force Sioux warriors like Sitting Bull into a major military confrontation.

The Hunkpapa Sioux were able to avoid the early confrontations in the 1860s. However, when Red Cloud, a major Hunkpapa Sioux leader, negotiated the Fort Laramie Treaty of 1868, Sitting Bull chose not to abide by its territorial provisions, which would have restricted his ability to hunt and travel. Sitting Bull's adherence to traditional ways of life had made him a spiritual as well as military leader among his people. In 1874, gold was discovered in the Black Hills, and the subsequent illegal incursions by U.S. miners created tension with Sitting Bull and the Sioux bands. After a number of limited skirmishes with the U.S. military, matters came to a head in 1876. It was in this year that the U.S. government ordered all hunting bands to report to U.S. government agencies attached to reservations. It was an impossible situation for Sitting Bull who now prepared for all-out battle with U.S. forces. As it turned out, the confrontation would be a historical one.

To enforce the U.S. order to have all Indian bands report to agencies by the January 1876 deadline, a number of military divisions were sent. A three-pronged military attack had been planned by U.S. forces to pin down the Indians in the Bighorn Valley in present-day eastern Montana. Unbeknownst to U.S. forces, one of the largest concentrations of Plains Indians ever assembled had gathered in response to the U.S. presence. Due in large part to Sitting Bull's influence, a village of between twelve and fifteen thousand Indians gathered along the Little Bighorn River. Sitting Bull engaged forces under General George Crook in the Battle of the Rosebud on June 17 and sent the U.S. Army into retreat. Eight days later, the U.S. troops led by Colonel George A. Custer attacked several points along the Indian encampment and were soundly defeated. Custer's forces were annihilated. The Battle of Little Bighorn is recorded as a signal Indian victory.

The Indian successes at Rosebud and at Little Bighorn were the last major Indian victories of the campaign. As was the custom, the large Indian encampment dispersed into small bands, since there was not enough food and grazing land to sustain such a large population for long at one place. The U.S. increased its military presence and forced many of the Sioux into surrender. Instead of capitulation, Sitting Bull and a number of his followers escaped to Canada. The Canadian government, however, offered no refuge, and the emigrant Sioux led by Sitting Bull were near starvation. Sitting Bull and most of his camp surrendered to U.S.

authorities on July 19, 1881, at Fort Buford, North Dakota. For nearly two years, Sitting Bull was held prisoner; in 1883, he was allowed to settle on the Standing Rock Reservation, which straddles the border of present-day North and South Dakota.

From 1885 to 1886, Sitting Bull joined William Cody's Wild West Show, a traveling exhibition of "Indian fighters" and "Indian War Chiefs." In 1886, Sitting Bull left the Wild West Show and returned to Standing Rock Reservation.

In his remaining years, he continued to oppose assimilation into U.S. culture and the seemingly inevitable breakup of Sioux land. Sitting Bull was killed by government-paid Indian police in October 1890 over a dispute that erupted during a Ghost Dance ceremony at Standing Rock. Government officials were extremely nervous about Sioux participation in the Ghost Dance, because they thought it might lead to the organization of militant resistance to U.S. authority.

Native Peoples of the Northwest Coast

The cultures of the Northwest Coast have long fascinated scholars because of the region's unique life-styles, sophisticated art, and flamboyant ceremonies. These cultures underwent dramatic changes beginning in the late eighteenth century when Europeans came into the area. Nevertheless, Northwest Coast Indians persist today as distinct cultures within the ever-expanding Canadian and American societies, largely because of their tenacity, but also because of the leading role they have taken in exerting their aboriginal rights to land and resources. A reliance on two Northwest Coast resources, salmon and cedar, was a characteristic of almost all of the diverse peoples of the area at the time of European contact and, to a certain extent, still is today.

To discuss the nature of the Northwest Coast culture prior to European contact, we have to be largely speculative. By basing our discussion on archaeological, historical, and ethnographic information, we can satisfactorily reconstruct the traditional lifeways of the Northwest Coast people. As today, aboriginally a great deal of variation was evident along the coast. The Indians spoke a variety of languages and represented an assortment of cultural adaptations to the coastal environment. Some groups relied more heavily on salmon than others. Some were whalers or deep-sea fishers. Some lived inland and relied more heavily on the fruits of the forest and on big game. Some traded extensively, while others stayed close to home and let traders come to them. Some warred on their neighbors, while others were the prey. Despite these differences, the Northwest Coast culture area can be discussed in general terms, as a way of laying a foundation upon which to explore the post-contact history of the various tribes.

TRIBAL DISTRIBUTION ♦ ♦ ♦ ♦ ♦ ♦ ♦ ♦ ♦ ♦ ♦ ♦ ♦ ♦ ♦ ♦ ♦ ♦ ♦

The Northwest Coast culture area is generally considered to be the part of North America that lies along the Pacific Ocean from roughly 42 north latitude (the California-Oregon border) to 60 north latitude. This includes southeast Alaska and western portions of British Columbia, Washington, and Oregon. To introduce the various Northwest Coast tribes, we will begin at the north end of the culture area and work southward. Present-day place names are used in this discussion.

The Tlingit inhabited the area that is now southeast Alaska, from Yakutat Bay to Portland Canal. The Tlingit fished salmon in kin-owned areas and also depended upon other resources of the sea, especially halibut and seal. Clinging to the mountainous shores and rugged offshore islands, Tlingit villages were usually large in comparison to other Northwest Coast tribes. The total Tlingit population at the time of European contact is estimated to have been 15,000.

Immediately to the south of the Tlingit, the Haida inhabited the southern portion of Prince of Wales Island in southeast Alaska and the Queen Charlotte Islands in British Columbia. Well known along the coast for their woodworking creations, especially large totem poles and huge seaworthy canoes, the several bands of Haida probably numbered about 14,000 when first contacted in the late 1700s.

The Tlingit, the Haida, and a third group, the Tsimshian, are sometimes collectively known as the "northern matrilineal tribes" because of their distinctive form of social organization. The Tsimshian, who resided on the north-central coast of British Co-

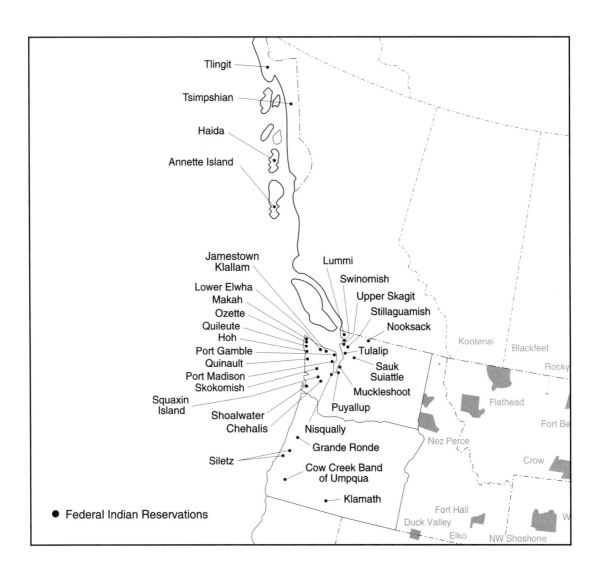

Tlingit

Tsimpshian

Haida

Annette Island

Jamestown
Klallam

Lower Elwha
Makah

Ozette

Quileute

Hoh

Port Gamble

Quinault

Port Madison

Skokomish

Squaxin
Island

Shoalwater

Chehalis

Siletz

Lummi

Swinomish

Upper Skagit

Stillaguamish

Nooksack

Tulalip

Sauk
Suiattle

Muckleshoot

Puyallup

Nisqually

Grande Ronde

Cow Creek Band
of Umpqua

Klamath

Kootenai

Blackfeet

Rocky

Flathead

Fort Be

Nez Perce

Crow

Fort Hall

Duck Valley

Elko

NW Shoshone

● Federal Indian Reservations

lumbia and inland in the Nass and Skeena River valleys, numbered approximately 14,500 at the time of first contact.

Various bands of Kwakwala speakers lived along the south-central British Columbia coast and adjacent eastern shores of Vancouver Island. These bands can be broadly divided into the northern groups and the southern groups. The northern groups include the Haisla, Haihais, Bella Bella, and Owekeeno; the southern groups are known collectively as the Kwakiutl, or

Contemporary Northwest Coast Indian tribes.

Kwakwaka'wakw. The Kwakiutl are famous in anthropological literature for their extravagant ceremonies known as "potlatches" (discussed later in this entry), and also for the other types of religious and secular ceremonies that permeated every aspect of their lives. At the time of contact, these groups numbered approximately 7,500 for the northern groups and 19,000 for the southern.

Facing the Pacific Ocean, the west coast of Vancouver Island was home to the Nuu-Chah-Nulth (formerly known as Nootka). They and the Makah (a closely related group who lived across the Strait of Juan de Fuca in present-day Washington State) were famous for their skills as whalers and deep-sea navigators. One of the Nuu-Chah-Nulth bands was host to the first European settlement on the Northwest Coast. The bands totaled about 10,000 at the time of contact.

The Coast Salish, consisting of more than three dozen distinct tribes and bands, resided in southwest mainland British Columbia, southeast Vancouver Island, and much of western Washington. Two linguistically related groups, the Bella Coola of the central coast of British Columbia and the Tillamook of the north-central Oregon coast, make up the largest number of Salish speakers in the Northwest Coast culture area. The Bella Coola numbered about 3,000; the Tillamook about 4,000. The rest of the Coast Salish, which for linguistic and cultural reasons are perhaps better broken down into four groupings, numbered 4,000 for the Northern Coast Salish, 20,000 for the Central Coast Salish, 12,500 for the Southern Coast Salish, and 12,000 for the Southwestern Coast Salish.

The Chinook inhabited the lower Columbia River from the Cascade Mountains to the Pacific Ocean. The Chinook—perhaps the Native group most written about in Northwest Coast history—are renowned in history and legend as traders extraordinaire. Because they controlled the waterways into the interior, the Chinook were masters over trade north and south along the coast and inland to the Columbia Plateau and beyond. In addition to their prowess as traders, the Chinook also realized the potential of the enormous Columbia River salmon runs. Numbering perhaps 10,500 in the mid-1700s, the Chinook population had dwindled to just a few hundred by 1850.

Numerous bands of linguistically diverse tribes resided along the Oregon coast and inland in the Willamette River valley. These groups spoke a number of languages from unrelated linguistic stocks, such as Athapascan and Penutian. Culturally, these tribes were transitional between the Northwest Coast and California culture areas and shared many traits in common with both. In all, they numbered as many as 30,000 people when first contacted by Europeans.

♦ ♦ ♦ ♦ ♦ THE ANNUAL CYCLE OF ECONOMIC SUBSISTENCE

While the most striking thing about the Northwest Coast culture area may be the linguistic and cultural diversity evident from north to south, we nevertheless can identify some general characteristics. Let us explore a "yearly round" of social and economic activities as a means of identifying some of the culture traits common to the Northwest Coast.

♦ HOUSING

The typical habitation of the Northwest Coast Indians was the longhouse. The structure was large, capable of sheltering several families. Generally, the families who inhabited a longhouse were related to one another in some way: among the northern matrilineal groups, they were related through the female lineage; among the other tribes, the relation was through either the house owner or his spouse.

Inside the longhouse, each family had its own area, usually partitioned off. Central fires burned for heat and light, but each family cooked its own meals and ate separately. Families could change houses if they wished, or the house might break up in the summer months while individual families pursued subsistence activities. In the winter, the longhouse served as a ceremonial center; the partitions were taken down to make room for dances and for guests.

FOOD RESOURCES ✦ ✦ ✦ ✦ ✦ ✦ ✦ ✦ ✦ ✦ ✦ ✦ ✦ ✦ ✦ ✦ ✦

The inside of a house at Nootka Sound, from the Cook Expedition, 1778. Courtesy of Special Collections Division, University of Washington Libraries.

Certainly the most prolific and dependable resource throughout the Northwest Coast was the abundant runs of salmon. Five species of salmon inhabit the Pacific Coast, spending their adult life in the offshore waters and traveling up freshwater streams to spawn. Native people caught some salmon by trolling in the saltwater, but large numbers of fish taken for preservation were captured in or near the freshwater streams with traps, weirs, and nets. Typically, salmon enter freshwater in the spring; subsequent runs may occur throughout the summer and into the fall. Because not every stream supports all five species nor successive

runs, some Northwest Coast groups focused their attention on specific runs of fish to take in abundance for drying or smoking as a means of preservation. Preserved salmon provided a dietary staple which was supplemented with other locally available food resources, such as shellfish, plant foods, marine mammals, land mammals, and waterfowl.

Although some salmon fishing took place throughout the year, the bulk of the fish were taken in the spring and fall at specific locations where the family groups tended to resort year after year. Probably the most widely employed fishing device at such locations was the weir, a barricade placed across a stream to divert the runs of fish into a trap. While the men worked the traps, the women cut the fish along the back, removing the bone and internal organs. The filleted fish were then hung on a rack to be preserved by drying winds, or in the rafters of the longhouse where the slow-burning fires would dry them. Some groups preserved as much as five hundred pounds of fish per person through the year. Even to this day, many Native people feel a meal is incomplete without at least a little salmon.

Not all of the summer was spent salmon fishing. For many groups, shellfish—especially clams, mussels, and oysters—provided important food. Shellfish could be taken anytime of year, although in some areas the flesh might be poisonous in the summer months. Usually the "spring tides," when the lowest tides of the year occurred during the daylight hours, were the important shellfish gathering times. Like salmon, shellfish were dried in abundance, providing not only sustenance, but also an important item to trade with groups farther inland.

In late spring, many other types of fish were utilized, depending on local availability. For example, the Tsimshian harvested tons of a small fish known as oolichan, which they rendered into oil. Oolichan was an important addition to the diet, as well as a trade item. Other Northwest Coast groups harvested herring (both the fish and the spawn), halibut, rockfish, and other deep-sea fish. Marine mammals—seals, porpoises, and whales—were also harvested. Whales, especially gray whales, were taken during their migratory pass in the spring. The Nuu-Chah-Nulth, Makah, and Quileute, who were all expert whalers, hunted these large animals from dugout canoes, using hand-thrown spears. Other Northwest Coast tribes might have used a whale that had beached or drifted ashore, but the Nuu-Chah-Nulth, Makah, and Quileute pursued the migrating whales far out at sea. Many miles from shore, for days on end, these Native whalers would pursue their quarry in hopes of not only obtaining an important source of food, but also the prestige that came with being a successful whaler.

The land mammals most frequently hunted by the Northwest Coast Indians were deer, elk, bear, and mountain goat. Either solitary hunters would hunt the animals, or groups would drive them into nets or ambushes. Typically, the inland groups were more involved in hunting land mammals. Mountain goats were most particularly hunted for their horns, which could be fashioned into implements, usually spoons, and for their wool, which was spun into yarn and then woven into blankets for ceremonial garb and day-to-day use. In addition to mountain goats, some women kept a type of small dog which could be shorn like a sheep; its woolly fur was then spun into yarn.

The time of gathering plant foods began in the spring, but was more intensive in the late summer and early fall. Starchy tubers, such as camas and wapato, and broken fern roots were taken in abundance, in some cases from kin-controlled plots. Berries and other fruits were also abundant; they were dried as well as eaten fresh.

CULTURE ✦

Of course, the Northwest Coast people did not spend their time just pursuing food. Artisans, such as weavers, basket makers, wood carvers, and stone workers, spent many hours crafting their handiwork. Winter months were busy with ceremonial activities such as spirit dances, ceremonial performances, the demonstration of inherited privileges like masked dances, and the most famous ceremony of all, the potlatch. Potlatches, the ceremonial distribution of wealth goods, could actually take place any time of year, to commemorate a naming, wedding, or funeral. Potlatching was a way for an individual to express his social standing in the community, and to reinforce that position through the giving away of wealth and feasting with the guests. Numerous other ceremonies also were held, but certainly the potlatch is the most widely known. Some evidence suggests that potlatching may have increased in the 1800s because of the influx of wealth items through the fur trade and subsequent interactions with Europeans, but that was only one of the dramatic changes to occur during the contact period.

◆ ◆ ◆ ◆ ◆ ◆ ◆ ◆ ◆ ◆ ◆ ◆ ◆ ◆ ◆ ◆ EUROPEAN CONTACT

Many of the earliest explorers of northern North America, such as John Cabot, who sailed from England in 1497, were searching for a direct passage from Europe to China by way of an open sea passage across North America. Such an ocean route would have allowed Europeans an efficient means of carrying on trade with the Far Eastern empires. In the end, no such passage existed, but considerable European effort was expended before the twentieth century in search of the fabled Northwest Passage. In their continuing search for wealth and for the Northwest Passage, Europeans eventually reached the Northwest Coast during the latter part of the eighteenth century. Initially, the Spanish explored northward from their settlements in Mexico. Shortly afterward, the Russians reached southeast Alaska from Siberia. At first, the Europeans found little to compel them to stay. Some shipboard trade took place, but the Northwest Coast was not particularly rich in furs, and the Natives were hard bargainers. Soon, however, sea otter pelts began to bring phenomenal prices in China, and a lively trade quickly developed.

In 1789, the Spanish established a post at Nootka Sound on Vancouver Island, and the struggle for control of trade began. The trade eventually included the Russians, Spanish, British, and Americans. The Native people were unconcerned with European

Cedar house, Dundas Island, British Columbia.

political struggles, so long as they gained access to manufactured goods. Such items greatly increased the Natives' efficiency and economic well-being. The initial changes brought by the fur trade were primarily in material goods; little change was evident in social or religious life.

In 1795, the Spanish relinquished claim to the area north of 42 latitude, and the Russians held southeast Alaska. In 1818, the British and Americans agreed to joint occupation of the area in between. The establishment of land-based trading operations began in 1811, with the building of the American Fur Company's post at the mouth of the Columbia River. Lost during the War of 1812, the post eventually fell into the hands of the Hudson's Bay Company, which came to dominate the fur trade of the Northwest. The Hudson's Bay Company expanded operations to Fort Vancouver in 1824, Fort Langley in 1827, Fort Nisqually and Fort

McLoughlin in 1833, Cowlitz Station in 1838, Fort Victoria in 1843, and, by agreement with the Russians, Fort Stikine and Fort Taku in 1840. The economic control of the Northwest Coast was in the hands of the Hudson's Bay Company until the 1840s, when American settlers began moving into the joint-occupied area. In 1846, the British and Americans negotiated the Treaty of Oregon, establishing the boundary at the 49th parallel between the United States and Canada.

Through the late 1800s, non-Native settlement of the Northwest Coast progressed at a staggering rate. The settlement period was marked by the negotiation of treaties in the United States, by the establishment of reservation communities in British Columbia, and by the contraction of villages into a few Native communities in Alaska. During the same time, the Native population rapidly declined because of European diseases for which the Indians had no resistance. By 1900, non-Natives outnumbered Natives in most areas and the Native societies were quickly engulfed by the growing dominant society.

New religious expressions among the Indians became evident early in the settlement period. Considerable evidence shows that syncretic movements occurred, as well as strong efforts to continue the practice of traditional religious expression of shamanism and spirit quests. Christianity attracted many converts as well, especially among those communities in close proximity to non-Native communities. Today, in any given Native community, there are a number of Christians, as well as followers of Shakerism, a religious movement stemming from the experience of a Coast Salish prophet in the 1880s. Still other Northwest Coast Indians are practitioners of the traditional forms of spiritualism.

As the non-Native population became more dominant, the Northwest Coast people found it increasingly difficult to continue to fish, hunt, and gather as they had before. Fishing, logging, and farming became the area's principle economic activities. Conflicts over non-Native and Native uses of the land and resources were inevitable. As Native societies became more restricted in their traditional activities, they sought wage labor in nearby non-Native communities, or became entangled in the growing poverty and political domination of the reservation communities. Many Native people chose to leave the reservations during this time, an act encouraged by government policy.

CONTEMPORARY LIFE ✦ ✦ ✦ ✦ ✦ ✦ ✦ ✦ ✦ ✦ ✦ ✦ ✦ ✦ ✦

The Northwest Coast culture of the twentieth century is a complex combination of traditional values and political-economic factors that emerged from interaction with the dominant society. Modern Northwest Coast Natives—now minorities in their own land—are citizens of either Canada or the United States. They also have the rights and privileges that go with being a member of a tribe or band.

While the multi-family longhouses were abandoned in most areas by 1900, the strong kin ties that were a part of the longhouse living situation have endured. Extended family groups depend upon one another for help in times of need, for assistance in sponsoring feasts or potlatches, and for support in the attempt to gain political power. Many Native communities may at first appear indistinguishable from their non-Native neighbors, but behind the familiar housing, clothing, and jobs is an undercurrent of Native life that has persisted and adapted to the modern context.

To understand the changes that have occurred over the past 100 years, we must look at some important political events that have had lasting impacts on the Northwest Coast people. Because the Native people have lived under different polities, their situations have all been different. Historical changes in the Northwest Coast can best be studied by looking individually at three main areas within the region: Alaska, British Columbia, and western Washington and Oregon.

Alaska   Until 1867, the Tlingit and some of the Haida lived in an area of North America claimed by Russia. While southeast Alaska was part of Russian America, the impact on the Native people was minimal. Even after the United States acquired Alaska, its isolation meant the Native people were left to themselves. In the 1890s, however, the situation began to change rapidly. With the Alaskan gold rush, followed by the influx of settlers, the Native people rapidly found themselves part of a larger political reality. They participated in the growing economy as fishers and loggers, and in other occupations. Many adopted Christianity in the late 1800s and early 1900s. Formal education became a priority for many Tlingit and Haida families.

Soon after Alaska became a state in 1959, interest in its resources grew, especially when oil was discovered in the North Slope. It became clear that some settlement had to be reached between the United States government and the Native people. In 1971, the Alaska Native Claims Settlement Act terminated Native title to land in Alaska. In return, Alaska Natives were to select certain lands that they would retain. They received federal funds to establish Native-controlled share-holding corporations to be operated as profit-making operations. The Native people of southeast Alaska were formed into one of thirteen corporations that have since become the primary political bodies of the Native people. Although the Native villages have elected their own political bodies, and other forms of Native political expression are available, the Native corporations wield the most power and influence.

Since its inception, the Alaska Native Claims Settlement Act has been the primary political influence in Native Alaska. Unencumbered by a reservation system, the Tlingit and Haida have prospered. As they begin to exert their Native rights over land and resources, they will likely continue to be a dominant force in the state of Alaska.

British Columbia

The Native people of British Columbia have had a somewhat different experience. Many of the Native people live in remote areas and have participated in the principle economic activities of the province, especially logging and commercial fishing. Unlike most Native people of Canada, the Natives of British Columbia never signed treaties with the federal government (although the Hudson's Bay Company negotiated a few legally valid treaties with Native people on Vancouver Island). Instead of treaties, British Columbia instituted a system of reserves, setting aside Natives' lands until they became assimilated into the dominant society.

Native policy in Canada primarily stems from the Indian Act, an all-encompassing piece of legislation first passed in 1884 and revised several times since (the last in 1985). With special attention to the Northwest Coast, the Indian Act specifically outlawed the potlatch. British Columbia officials were incapable of enforcing this policy until the 1920s, when concerted efforts were made to abolish the ceremony. While potlatching never completely disappeared, it did go underground for many years. When the potlatch law was abolished in 1951, potlatching was publicly revived.

Beginning in the 1880s, Native leaders in British Columbia sought to affirm Native rights to land and resources. Forming a province-wide organization in 1916, the tribes have actively pursued recognition of their claims. Although seeking reprieve in the courts as early as the 1920s, it was not until the 1970s that the tribes began to make some important progress. With the provision in the Canadian Constitution of 1982 that "existing aboriginal and treaty rights of the aboriginal peoples of Canada are . . . recognized and affirmed," the British Columbia Natives finally had a firm commitment on the part of the federal government to support their claims. Nevertheless, the outcomes of land and resource claims have been varied. Perhaps the most famous case was one in which the Gitskan (Tsimshian) were involved. This claim attempted to assert Native sovereignty over a large portion of west-central British Columbia. Dragging through the courts for several years, the case was decided against the Gitskan in 1991. The case is currently under appeal. Simultaneously, a case involving Coast Salish fishing on the Fraser River was decided in favor of the Native claim to aboriginal rights to the resources. Since there is no clear agenda for the recognition of Native rights in British Columbia, their future prospects remain unclear.

The Native people of western Washington and Oregon represent the third set of circumstances of historical change in the Northwest Coast. In the mid-1850s, these tribes entered into treaties with the United States government, forming the basis of interaction for the last 135 years. Most important among the treaty provisions was the establishment of reservations and the protection of certain aboriginal rights, especially fishing. From the treaty era to the present, various federal policies have been enacted which have had lasting impacts on the Native people of the northwest United States. Beginning with "assimilationist" policy in the late 1800s and continuing into the present era of "self-determination," the federal policies that have marked the relationship between Native people and the federal government can be used as a means of discussing social changes in this region.

Western Washington and Oregon

Native fashion show, Prince George, British Columbia.

Assimilation refers to the social, cultural, and political incorporation of a person or group into the mainstream national culture and society. From the 1880s to 1934, the U.S. government actively sought to convince Indians to abandon their traditional cultures and join U.S. society and culture. Perhaps the most influential policy of the assimilationist period was the General Allotment Act of 1887. This policy allowed for the allotment of reservation lands. Allotting parcels of land to individuals had two dramatic impacts on the Native people. First, it was designed to instill a Western notion of private property in the form of alienable land. Second, it served to break up the multi-family units and encouraged individual activities, especially farming. The long-lasting effect of allotment was that since the land was individually owned, the tribe had no means to keep reservation land in the control of the tribe. Consequently, much land was sold to non-tribal members. From the implementation of the General Allotment Act, until the 1930s, the design of federal policy was to break up the tribal units and encourage the assimilation of Native people into the dominant society. This was reinforced by the schooling of Native children in off-reservation boarding schools that taught them trades and required that they speak English. A famous saying of boarding school administrators succinctly sums up their educational philosophy: "Kill the Indian but save the person." Children from the Northwest Coast went to many different boarding schools, but the most common was Chemawa, near Salem, Oregon.

In 1924, all Native people of the United States were granted citizenship. Instead of marking the desired results of forced assimilation, it marked the end of an era of policy. In the 1930s, Congress passed a series of new legislative acts that were designed to strengthen the tribal units and encourage independent tribal economic development. Under the Indian Reorganization Act of 1934, tribes in the Northwest were assisted in developing tribal governments based on a constitution and were governed by elected bodies of officials. Rather than encouraging independent development, however, the Indian Reorganization Act actually strengthened the power that the Bureau of Indian Affairs had over the

Native people's lives. For example, now the Bureau of Indian Affairs had the power to override decisions made by tribal governments even though tribes were considered sovereigns within the United States. The bold new plans of the federal government during the 1930s were to be short-lived after World War II, when the United States began a series of policies designed to terminate the special relationship Native people had with the federal government. Many powers, such as law enforcement, were turned over to the states; individual Indians were encouraged to leave the reservations for urban areas; and some tribes were actually terminated—formal ties with the federal government ended and tribal resources divided among the individuals, who collectively ceased being a federally recognized Indian tribe with legal protections for land and tribal rights.

Termination policies were enacted in two important ways. First, the relocation policies, described as "termination by attrition," encouraged reservation residents to move to urban areas where they were to find jobs. However, since the reservation populations were generally undereducated and unskilled, the types of jobs they found were usually menial. Making minimum wage, they were forced to live in the least desirable parts of the cities, and, as a result, urban Indian ghettos were created in cities like Portland and Seattle. Some reservations estimate that as many as one-third of their entire populations were relocated during the 1950s, an action that not only created a drain on the reservation community, but also created an intertribal urban population. Today, approximately 20,000 Native people live in Seattle, where they are represented by such groups as the United Indians of All Tribes Foundation.

The second action was the actual termination of some tribes. While many tribes throughout the United States were scheduled for termination, in actuality most were not. Three Oregon tribes were terminated: the Klamath of southeast Oregon and the Siletz and Grande Ronde of the Oregon coast. Siletz and Grande Ronde were the reservation homes of the Oregon coast tribes, and because of their economic success, they were considered likely candidates for termination of their relationship with the federal government. It soon became clear that without their special status as a federally recognized tribe, the Siletz and Grand Ronde had little power to hold their lands together and continue to promote economic well-being. Almost as soon as they were terminated, both tribes sought to be reinstated as federally recognized tribes, an act that was finally granted after nearly thirty years.

The prospects for the future are promising. As Native communities in Alaska, British Columbia, Washington, and Oregon begin to assert their sovereignty as a means to develop economically and politically, they will continue to bring about positive change in a culturally sensitive manner. The present era of "self-determination" is marked by Indian tribes successfully exerting their legal rights to land and resources and the strengthening of tribal self-governance to promote development. The self-determination policy recognizes tribal interests in regaining greater control over reservation institutions, such as education and local administration, and over tribal economic resources such as land, minerals, and hunting and fishing. Perhaps the most well-known example of this is the 1974 Boldt Decision, which resulted from the court case *United States v. Washington,* brought by the treaty tribes of western Washington. This case determined that Native people retained certain rights to fisheries and other resource-gathering activities that included the right to commercial use of the salmon resource. Consequently, the Native people now harvest 50 percent of the commercial salmon resource as well as significant numbers of other fisheries such as herring, halibut, and crab. This treaty-assured right has formed a base upon which other economic activities, such as processing and marketing, have been built. Additionally, Native people operate hatcheries that release millions of salmon fry into the public waters every year.

Although Natives participate in American and Canadian society, this does not mean that they have "assimilated" or "acculturated," or any of the other terms that suggest they are no longer Indian. Speaking English, fishing with modern power boats and synthetic nets, or even carving a dug-out canoe with a chain saw does not mean that the Northwest Coast Natives are any less Indian. White Americans, after all, are not expected to cook in the fireplace or support themselves by hitching the horse to the plow. Being a

Northwest Coast Indian today means participating in the modern political and economic structures of North American society while maintaining a distinct ethnic identity. It is this identity that will strengthen the efforts toward tribal development—a development that will lead not only to the persistence of Native people into the twenty-first century but also to their prosperity.

Daniel Boxberger
Western Washington University

♦ ♦ ♦ ♦ ♦ ♦ ♦ ♦ ♦ ♦ ♦ ♦ ♦ ♦ ♦ ♦ ♦ ♦ ♦ **BIOGRAPHIES**

In the early 1800s, U.S. settlers poured into the Pacific Northwest region, leading to inevitable conflict with the Indians living there. During the first half of the nineteenth century, Sealth, a principal chief of the Duwamish people, encouraged friendship and commerce with the newcomers, and avoided being drawn into the ongoing regional conflicts between settlers and Indians that were permeating the Northwest during this time.

Seattle (Sealth)
1788–1866

Duwamish-Suquamish
tribal leader

As a youth, Sealth had already witnessed the growing number of U.S. settlers moving into his homeland. In the 1830s, he was influenced by French missionaries and converted to Catholicism. Throughout the gold rush era of the 1850s, he maintained peace, despite the influx of miners and settlers. Sealth fostered trading relationships with the newcomers. By 1855, tensions between settlers and the other Indians in the area were mounting, and the breaking of treaty terms finally led to the Yakima War of 1855–56. Sealth chose not to fight and signed the Fort Elliot Treaty, in which he agreed to relocate his people to a reservation. Chief Sealth and his people remained allied with American forces and withstood an attack by the neighboring Nisqually Indians. He and his people later relocated to the Port Madison Reservation, near present-day Bremerton, Washington. The city of Seattle, Washington, was named after the Duwamish chief Sealth in 1852.

David Sohappy, Sr.
1925–91

Yakima fisherman and
activist

After he was laid off from a sawmill in the 1960s, David Sohappy returned to the traditional Indian way of life, settling in a self-made wooden house on the Columbia River. From there he undertook a campaign for Indian treaty fishing rights along the rivers in Washington State. For Sohappy, there was no compromising his belief that Indians have the right to fish when and where they want, guaranteed by the Yakima Nation's Treaty of 1855. In a long-standing battle over tribal fishing rights, Sohappy was arrested numerous times and had 230 fishing nets confiscated over twenty years because of his insistence on fishing out of season on the Columbia River. He did this to assert his tribal right to take fish in the usual and accustomed places and times. The 1968 case *Sohappy v. Washington State* started a series of legal rulings and investigations, which resulted in the 1974 Boldt Decision by U.S. District Court Judge George Boldt. Boldt held that treaties negotiated in the 1850s gave many western Washington State Indian nations the right to catch half the harvestable salmon in Washington waters. The Boldt Decision was considered a great victory for Indian fishing rights and cleared the path for a resurgence of commercial and subsistence fishing activity by the western Washington State Indians.

In 1983, Sohappy was convicted of selling 317 fish out of season to undercover agents taking part in a federal sting operation. He was sent to prison and served eighteen months before being released in poor health in 1988. He died at a nursing home in Hood River, Oregon, at the age of 66. Soshappy is considered a major figure and activist within the Northwest Coast Indian fishing rights campaign, a major economic issue in the region that continues to require legal and legislative attention.

Native Peoples of Alaska

TRADITIONAL LIFE ✦ ✦ ✦ ✦ ✦ ✦ ✦ ✦ ✦ ✦ ✦ ✦ ✦ ✦ ✦ ✦ ✦

There are four major indigenous groups in Alaska: the Aleut, the Eskimo (Yupik and Inuit), the coastal Tlingit and Haida, and the Athapascan. While all have been traced to the people who crossed the Bering Land Bridge (Berengia) 25,000 to 40,000 years ago, each has occupied a different territory, spoken a distinctive language, and built a unique heritage.

The Aleut occupy the 1,400-mile-long Aleutian Chain, part of the Alaskan peninsula and the Pribilof Islands in the Bering Sea. An area rich in resources, it supported the densest aboriginal population in Alaska. At the time of the first Russian voyages in the seventeenth century, there were approximately 16,000 Aleut, most residing in the eastern region. The rich marine environment provided the Aleut with a wide variety of sea life, including sea urchins, clams, octopuses, fish, sea otters, seals, and whales, which were used for food, clothing, and homes. Birds and their eggs, berries, wild rice and celery, and plant stalks were also part of their diet. The men were skilled open sea hunters and relied on two-person skin boats (*baidarka*) for hunting seals and whales.

Aleutian villages were situated along the coast, allowing easy access to the sea. They were small, usually supporting one hundred to two hundred inhabitants. Two to five families lived in semi-subterranean houses called *barabaras*. A person's lineage followed the mother's line, and children were disciplined and trained by the mother's family. Men were responsible for hunting and the care of implements and boats. Women cared for the home and gathered food along the beaches and shallow intertidal zones. Traditional society was divided between a small group of nobles, commoners, and slaves captured in wars with other villages. Aleut chiefs were the most respected hunters with long experience and exceptional abilities. Chiefs had little power, and decisions required common agreement. Internal conflict was reduced by making war on others for retribution, the taking of slaves, or trading through intermediaries. The family served as the basis of village organization, economic exchange, warfare, and occasionally political authority.

Chief Shake's house at Wrangell, about the turn of the twentieth century.

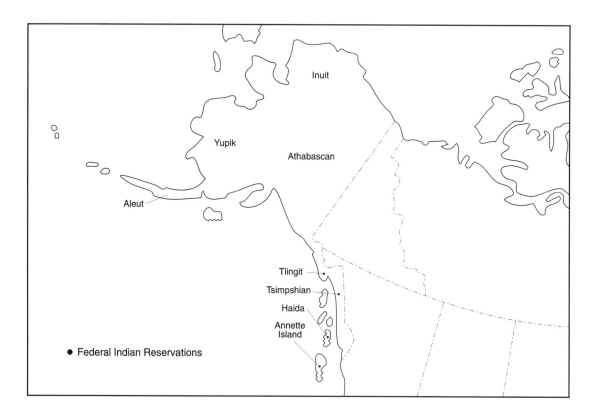

Contemporary Alaska Native tribes.

The Eskimo reside in an extensive and diverse environment from the deep fjords and mountain ranges of the south to the wind-swept mountains of the Alaskan peninsula, to the tundra and relative flat coasts and lowlands of the Arctic province. Yupik Eskimo is spoken in southwestern Alaska and Inuit to the north stretching across northern Canada to Greenland. Subsistence patterns varied from the caribou hunters of interior Alaska, to the Arctic whalers along the coasts, and the fishermen of southwestern Alaska.

Yupik and Inuit societies were geared toward the continual search for food. They are classified by anthropologists as "central-based wanderers" who spent part of the year on the move and some time at a settlement, or "central base." From a dozen to fifty people would travel together. Extended families composed of three to four generations were basic to an individual's life. Families were

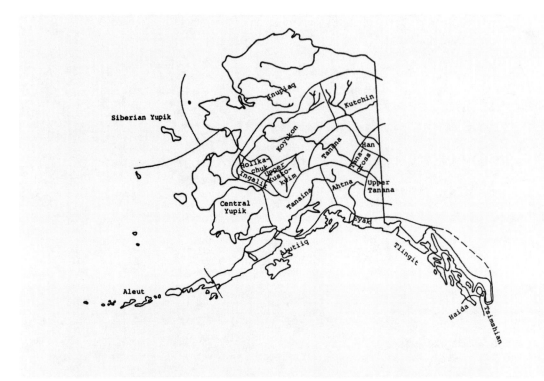

Major languages of Alaska Natives.

relatively equal and autonomous; they would often share with others, intermarry, and hunt together. There was considerable conflict, though, between different groups; strangers with no specific reasons for being in an area were in great danger.

Within each family, people were divided by age and gender. At the head was the boss, or *umialik*. Leaders were usually those who displayed exceptional skill or courage and those who were able to anticipate future problems. Shamans, or spiritual leaders, were also influential because of their familiarity with the spiritual world, their curative powers, and their prescience. Every settlement had a gathering place, or *qargi*, where men, boys, and families would meet for conversation and ritual.

Three major groups occupied southeastern Alaska: the Tlingit, the Haida, and the Tsimshian. Geographically the area is distinct. It is isolated, with high mountains and dense forest to the east and the Pacific Ocean to the west; it is interlaced by fjords and valleys on the mainland and a string of islands off the coast. It is a bountiful environment, which nurtured a formal and complex social system.

Society was divided between two major *moieties,* the Eagle and the Raven, which had their own rules and corporate functions. Within each moiety were numerous clans. The clan was the fundamental political unit; each had its own territory, history, and particular traits. The clan was responsible for settling feuds, property, and subsistence activities. The most basic unit was the house, which was run by a "master of the house," a maternal or great uncle. Houses had their own plots, name, and crest, which displayed major cultural figures in the history of the clan and house. Clans and houses had rights to specific areas for fishing, berry picking, and hunting. In practice anyone could use the sites provided they asked for permission. Areas between each territory were open to everyone for travel.

Rank and status, built on the accumulation of wealth, underlay the system of clans and houses. Possession of material goods, including slaves, crests, blankets, totems, a generous disposition, oratorical skill, and past accomplishments, determined the position of individuals, clans, and houses. The potlatch was an integral part of southeastern cultures. It involved a feast, performances, and the distribution of valuable goods. Potlatches were given to honor an individual and they served to strengthen kin relations, to display one's generosity, and to honor the memory of those who had passed away.

The northern Athapascan occupied a vast territory that extended through most of interior Alaska, bordered by the Arctic to the north and the temperate forests to the south. Included in this area were six subgroups: the Ingalik, the Koyukon, Tanana, Tanaina, Ahtna, and the Upper Tanana. While each group lacked a formal tribal system, they did occupy exclusive territory. Within each territory were smaller bands, which followed the seasonal migration of game, and families, who would, for part of the year, live separately in order to fish and hunt. Composed of people related by blood and marriage, bands were responsible for subsistence activities, territorial boundaries, and the settlement of disputes between families.

Men formed hunting partnerships; one killed the animal and the other distributed it. Resources were always shared. Because food was sometimes scarce, mobility and flexibility were imperative. There was little need to accumulate possessions. The Athapascan practiced what is termed "strategic hunting," in which fish were directed into weirs, caribou were corralled, and waterfowl were taken in their breeding grounds.

Neither primitive nor simple, traditional Native communities in Alaska were extremely well-adapted to the physical environment in which they lived, from the Arctic regions of northern Alaska to the rain forests of the southeast, to the cool and windy climates of the Aleutian chain. The Alaska Natives were also bounded by an intricate kinship system that usually specified who could marry and where the couple would live, as well as ownership of fishing and hunting places and leadership. Social and economic relations allowed for popular understanding and local initiative, equity, and community and kinship reciprocity of material goods and services. These relations also delineated the performance of social and religious obligations, such as potlatch exchanges, and other ritual reciprocities, such as performing funeral services for in-laws, as among the Tlingit. There was a precarious balance between the physical environment and the subsistence needs of each community. Natural disasters, population growth, or outside intrusion could easily upset the balance of human and natural environmental relations.

RUSSIAN COLONIALISM ♦ ♦ ♦ ♦ ♦ ♦ ♦ ♦ ♦ ♦ ♦ ♦ ♦ ♦ ♦

With the advent of European expansion in the eighteenth century, circumstances in Alaska began to change dramatically. The Russians were first. The voyages of Alexei Chirikof and

Vitus Bering in 1741 led to awareness of potential profit from sea otter and seal skins. Siberian fur hunters, the *promishleniki,* soon launched hunting expeditions in the area. An imperial decree was issued in 1766, claiming Russian dominion over the Aleutians, but there was little government regulation of Russian traders and hunters. In response to this anarchy and the competition with other Europeans, the Russian American Company was organized in 1799. The company's charter anticipated the conversion of Natives to Christianity and claimed that the "Islanders" (Aleut) would be treated amicably.

However, the relationship between Russians and Aleut was anything but amicable. Although the exact numbers are not known, it is estimated that 90 percent of the indigenous population was lost to disease or murder. The survivors were in a state of virtual servitude. The Russians used the men as pelagic (open sea) hunters and, as they moved into eastern Alaska, as warriors. Despite its brutality, Russian commercial expansion in Alaska was limited to the coast. There were occasional forays to the interior, but they were infrequent because of hostile tribes, impassable terrain, and severe temperatures. By 1867, when the United States acquired control of the territory, Russia ruled only a small portion of it.

◆ ◆ ◆ ◆ ◆ ◆ ◆ ◆ ◆ ◆ ◆ ◆ ◆ ◆ ◆ **AMERICAN COLONIALISM**

U.S. expansion into Alaska was propelled by an interest in fur and, more importantly, gold. In 1867, the Treaty of Cession was signed which transferred jurisdiction over Alaska to the United States. Article III was particularly important for Alaska Natives: "The Uncivilized tribes will be subject to such laws and regulations as the United States may, from time to time, adopt in regard to aboriginal tribes in that country." Congress recognized this obligation in 1884 when it passed the first Organic Act, which extended the civil and criminal laws of Oregon to Alaska: "Indians or other persons in said district shall not be disturbed in the possession of any lands actually in their use or occupation or now claimed by them but the terms under which such persons may acquire title to such lands is reserved for future legislation by Congress."

Despite this disclaimer in the Organic Act, land was usually available for the U.S. economic interests who needed it. The first fish canneries were built in 1878, and within six years they were spread along the entire southern coast of Alaska. In 1878, the first gold mining camp was constructed. Gold prospecting and disputes between miners resulted in the territory's first civil government. Legislation in 1891, 1898, and 1900 permitted trade and manufacturing sites, townsites, homesteading, rights of way for a railroad, and the harvesting of timber.

During World War II, national leaders became more aware of the strategic importance of Alaska. This realization, coupled with the influx of money and people, produced a viable effort to achieve admittance into the Union. In his State of the Union message in 1946, President Harry Truman recommended statehood. Owing to partisan opposition and doubts about the financial capability of the territory, recognition was delayed. Finally, a compromise was reached, and Alaska and Hawaii were admitted simultaneously. On January 3, 1959, President Dwight Eisenhower proclaimed Alaska the forty-ninth state.

THE LAND CLAIMS MOVEMENT ♦ ♦ ♦ ♦ ♦ ♦ ♦ ♦ ♦ ♦ ♦ ♦ ♦

The Alaska Statehood Act granted the state 104 million acres of land. As public officials began selecting land, imposing rules, and applying laws, Native opposition arose. For example, the Bureau of Land Management, the agency in the Department of the Interior responsible for federal lands, issued a license to the Atomic Energy Commission (AEC), which regulates the use of nuclear materials in the United States, to use sixteen hundred square miles around Point Hope, an Inuit village on the northwestern coast of Alaska, for an experimental nuclear explosion to create a deep water port. However, no one consulted the residents of nearby villages. Another issue was the enforcement of the Migratory Bird Treaty Act between Canada and the United States. The treaty prohibits the hunting of migratory birds between March 10 and September 1. In 1961, the Inuit staged a "duck-in" to protest the restrictions. Many were arrested.

In March 1961, the president of the Point Hope Village Council wrote to the Association of American Indian Affairs (AAIA), which was founded in 1923 to provide legal and technical assistance to Indian tribes, and asked for help. The AAIA and the Indian Rights Association, established in 1882 to protect the rights of American Indians, provided funds for intervillage meetings, at which experiences were shared, rights explained, and common solutions proposed. Within six years, twelve regional associations were formed to pursue their respective land claims. Early in 1967 regional leaders formed the Alaska Federation of Natives (AFN) to secure their rights, enlighten the public about their position, preserve their cultural values, and gain an equitable settlement (see the biography of Howard Rock).

Inuit children, Barrow, Alaska.

The first major bill to settle the claims of Alaska Natives was introduced in June 1967. The key to a congressional decision was oil. In the late 1960s, large quantities of oil were discovered in Prudhoe Bay on the north coast of Alaska. Several large oil companies worked to extract and transport the crude oil to refineries and markets in the lower forty-eight states. Indian land claims, however, prevented construction of the pipeline from Prudhoe Bay to the port at Valdez in southern Alaska. Native villages, in particular Stevens Village, an Athapascan village in the interior, claimed land over the pipeline route, and gained a court injunction against construction until Indian title to the land was clarified. Thereafter the oil companies actively lobbied Congress and President Richard Nixon in order to gain a quick settlement to Native land claims issues in Alaska. By late 1971, an unusual coalition of oil companies, the Alaska Native lobbying organization (AFN), the state of Alaska, and the federal government moved to settle Alaska Native claims through congressional legislation. President Nixon and the U.S. Senate wanted a domestic source of oil that would counter the increase in prices in 1970 and the shortage of fuel and heating oil. The state of Alaska needed the revenue that private development would generate. The oil industry and the House of Representatives wanted a permit to build the Alaska pipeline. Conservationists wanted more park and wilderness area, and Alaska Natives wanted their land. The Alaska Native Claims Settlement Act (ANCSA) was signed into law on December 18, 1971.

Under terms of the settlement Alaska Natives received $962 million and 44 million acres of land. In exchange, claims over the remaining 335 million acres were extinguished. ANCSA cleared the path for the construction of the Alaska pipeline. It also led to the withdrawal of millions of acres of public lands for national parks and forests, scenic rivers, and wilderness areas. State officials were also permitted to select the remainder of their land under provisions of the Statehood Act. In the end, 12 percent of Alaska will be privately owned by Alaska Natives, 28 percent by the state, and 59 percent by the federal government.

There are two important assumptions of the Settlement Act. First is the expectation that Natives will be assimilated into the American mainstream and away from a communal life-style to an economy based on private ownership, individualism, and free enterprise. Twelve regional profit-making corporations were established and given significant responsibilities, including the distribution of money to village corporations and individuals, the control of subsurface resources, the economic development of each region, the promotion of village interests, and the facilitation of intervillage cooperation. Village corporations were also created to use and manage the land and control local development. A second assumption of ANCSA was that the profit corporations and the market system would lead to more employment and educational opportunities, healthier communities, and increasing economic independence for Alaska Natives.

♦ ♦ ♦ SOCIAL AND ECONOMIC PROFILE OF ALASKA NATIVES

There are more than 100,000 Alaska Natives in the United States. Of the 85,603 who live in Alaska, 44,000 are Yupik or Inuit, 31,000 are Athapascan, Tlingit, Haida, or Tsimshian, and 10,000 are Aleut. The majority (56 percent) live in small villages ranging in size from 50 to 900 people. The total number of Alaska Natives is growing rapidly. During the decade of the 1980s, the Inuit and Yupik population grew by 30 percent, Indian peoples by 43 percent, and Aleut by 24 percent. However, the Native proportion of the total population of the state is dropping steadily from 26 percent in 1950, to 17 percent in 1980, to 15.6 percent in 1990. Natives, though, are the majority in five ANCSA defined regions: the Arctic Slope, Bering Straits, Bristol Bay, Calista, and the Northwest Arctic.

Alaska Natives are younger than the general population: 61 percent are under 29 years of age. Their median age is 23. The dependency of Native children on family employment is almost twice that of non-Natives. The average Native family has four children. Increasingly, Alaska Natives are moving to urban areas; 12 percent lived in cities in 1960, 31 percent in 1980, and 44 percent in 1990. Anchorage now has more Alaska Natives than any other area in the state. The populations of regional service centers such as Dillingham, Bethel, Nome, Barrow, and Fort Yukon, as well as small villages, have grown as well.

In the last twenty years, there have been improvements in the lives of Alaska Natives. Through contracts with the Alaska Area Native Health Service and other state and federal agencies, Native associations now administer most health programs. The results have been largely positive. Alaska Natives now live longer and with less fear of epidemic diseases like tuberculosis. Similar changes have occurred in Native education, housing, and employment. Secondary schools now dot the rural landscape, where none existed in the 1960s. The number of high school graduates and those enrolled in college or vocational training has increased. Through the creation of district and regional school boards, Native communities have gained some control over school curriculum and class scheduling. The majority of houses now have indoor plumbing, phones, and sewer and water outlets. Each region has a non-profit housing agency which, through funds from the Department of Housing and Urban Development (HUD), provides low-income housing assistance, builds new houses, and collects rents and mortgage payments. Unemployment has also been reduced in some areas because of the growth of local governments, private construction and organization, and expanding industries in fishing, oil, and gas. The major employer in rural Alaska is government. More than 60 percent of the labor force is employed by either federal, state, or local governments. Most jobs are related to public service and administration.

While the ANCSA and subsequent efforts have resulted in a few improvements, fundamental problems remain. The incidence of poverty among Alaska Natives is much higher than for non-Natives. From 2,500 to 3,500 Native families receive food stamps, Aid to Families With Dependent Children payments, and Adult Public Assistance. More than 18,000 rural households rely on low-income energy subsidies. More than 25 percent of the Native population live below the official poverty level. Unemployment among Natives is twice that of non-Native Alaskans. In the western region of the state, half the Native workforce is without a job. Native family incomes are less than half of the average family income in Alaska. Further, the costs of living in rural areas are much higher than in the cities. An average family in Nome or

Kotzebue will spend 62 percent more per week on food and 165 percent more for electricity than a family in Anchorage, the largest city in Alaska.

The lack of access to quality health services and preventive care, combined with poor living conditions, has led to higher death rates among Alaska Natives from preventable causes, such as infectious and respiratory diseases, congenital problems, and infant mortality. There are other statistics that indicate many Natives have difficult lives, since Alaska Natives die from violent causes, accidents, homicides, suicides, and alcoholism at a much higher rate than the general population. The Native suicide and homicide rates are four times the U.S. average. (Among young males 20 to 24 years of age, the suicide rate is twenty times the national average.) Death from accidents is five times higher; infant mortality and Sudden Infant Death Syndrome are two times higher; infant spinal disorders are thirty-six times the national rate; and so on.

Alaska Natives have addressed these and other problems in three major ways: through the protection of their subsistence life-style, the economic development of their villages and regions, and the strengthening of their tribal governments.

◆ **SUBSISTENCE**

Traditional subsistence economies in Alaska were small, self-sufficient, and practical household economies. People used what they produced. Alliances for trade did exist. Coastal communities would exchange seal oil for caribou skins, for example; but trading relationships were limited. Food and clothing were locally produced and shared among kin and within local camps. The sharing of resources was common. People were united through blood and marriage. Kinship was a way of organizing labor, establishing rights, forming groups, and distributing wealth. Aboriginal life was cyclic and inseparable from the patterns and turns of nature. Inuit whalers, for example, hunted caribou in the summer for clothing and bedding and snared small animals for food.

In the fall they returned to the coast for trade and the gathering of food on the beaches. Later, men hunted seals on the open sea, until the ice returned. In midwinter, seals, fish, and bears were hunted on the ice. By April, when the ice melted enough, boat crews were in pursuit of bowhead whales. Near the end of June, when the whales had migrated south, birds and seals were the primary sources of food.

The subsistence economy is central to the lives of most Alaska Natives. It is estimated that each person in rural Alaska consumes 354 pounds of traditional food per year. More than 50 percent of rural food comes from subsistence activities. These resources are also used for clothing, transportation (fish are given to dog teams), heating, housing, and arts and crafts. Traditional values of sharing, cooperation, and reciprocity also continue. Large extended families still live together. Customary rules guide distribution and consumption of subsistence resources. Many Natives consider themselves first and foremost hunters and fishermen. There is evidence, too, that subsistence economies are not only resilient but growing in certain villages.

Efforts to protect and nourish subsistence have borne some fruit and much rancor. In 1978, the state of Alaska passed legislation recognizing a priority to subsistence use in the event of a shortage of fish or game. Native rights to hunt and fish were extinguished by ANCSA but were partially restored in 1980 when Congress included a rural subsistence preference in the Alaska National Lands Conservation Act (ANILCA), which classified all federal lands in Alaska. The national government permitted the state to regulate fish and game as long as federal and state law were in agreement, i.e., contained a rural subsistence priority.

The Alaska law was then challenged in court because it excluded city residents who depend on subsistence and included people in rural areas who do not. In 1989, the Alaska Supreme Court agreed. It ruled that residency as a criterion for subsistence violates constitutional prohibitions against exclusive or special privileges to hunt and fish and was a denial of equal rights. Since state law was no longer consistent with the subsistence preference in ANILCA, the federal government assumed the responsibility for the management of fish and game. Alaska's governor then initiated a suit against the Federal Subsistence Board for overstepping its regulatory authority.

In response to the conflict over subsistence, Native leaders have made three recommendations: the adoption of a constitutional amendment that would enable the state to comply with federal law; the passage of state legislation that would protect the subsistence rights of individuals in cities; and the provision that tribal members be accorded a subsistence priority on traditional lands. At a summit meeting on subsistence in March 1992, Alaska Natives reaffirmed their opposition to any changes in the legal protection of subsistence and existing state policies with regard to the management of fish and game resources.

◆ ◆ ◆ ◆ ◆ ◆ ◆ ◆ ◆ ◆ ◆ ◆ ◆ ◆ **ECONOMIC DEVELOPMENT**

An important assumption of the Alaska Native Claims Settlement Act was that money and the profit orientation of village and regional corporations would lead to more employment and educational opportunities, healthier communities, and increasing economic independence for Alaska Natives. Regional corporations were given significant responsibilities, including the distribution of money to villages and individual Natives, the control of subsurface resources, and the economic development of their region. The corporations received over $440 million between 1972 and 1981.

The performance of these corporations in the last twenty years has been mixed. Few have achieved financial stability. Four of the corporations reported cumulative losses between 1973 and 1990, and eight increased their assets. But six of these achieved a positive balance only through the sale of their net operating losses to large outside companies for tax write-offs. Profitable corporations have relied on the development of their natural resources or investments in securities or the oil and gas industry. Of the nearly

$1.4 billion worth of assets held by the twelve corporations, half consists of buildings, equipment, and real estate; 18 percent is invested in securities; 20 percent is held in escrow by the Internal Revenue Service; and the rest consists of parcels of land, insurance policies, and miscellaneous payments.

The impact of these business ventures on the day-to-day lives of Alaska Natives has been, with a few exceptions, minimal. At-large stockholders (those not affiliated with a village corporation) have received about $6,500 from the settlement of land claims; village stockholders were paid $1,500. Only two corporations, the Arctic Slope Regional Corporation and the Northwest Arctic Native Association, employ a significant number of their shareholders. Of the 7,500 employees of the twelve corporations, only 33 percent are Native. Cook Inlet Region, Inc., is the only company to pay substantial dividends. There are over 25,000 younger Alaska Natives who are not members of a regional corporation, because they were born after December 18, 1971, and hence are not eligible to enroll as shareholders.

There are also 172 village corporations organized under the Alaska Native Claims Settlement Act. They own the surface estate to 22 million acres of land, and they received almost half of the compensation payments from Congress. The amount of money and land held by each corporation varies with the number of stockholders. These corporations are expected to manage their lands and guide the economic development of their communities. With the exception of a few of the larger villages or those with valuable resources, their impact on local economies has been limited. Most have been hampered by insufficient funds, bad advice, and litigation. For many village corporations, the minimum state requirements of incorporation have imposed intolerable costs.

TRIBAL SOVEREIGNTY ✦ ✦ ✦ ✦ ✦ ✦ ✦ ✦ ✦ ✦ ✦ ✦ ✦ ✦ ✦

Many Alaska Natives are convinced that the solutions to many of their problems lies in the development of strong and effective

Native Regional Corporations and Their Shareholders

Regional corporation	Total shareholders	Cumulative dividends	Equity per share	Native employees
Ahtna	1,100	$2,402	$23,336	55
Aleut	3,249	501	3,243	5
ASRC	3,738	1,857	12,850	827
Bering Straits	6,200	102	4,001	9
Bristol Bay	5,200	1,606	8,708	7
Calistal	3,306	59	482	n/a
Chugach	2,109	761	21,284	39
Cook Inlet	6,553	10,456	54,493	120
Doyon	9,061	1,062	14,591	69
Koniag	3,731	0	4,958	4
NANA	5,000	2,489	10,579	978
Sealaska	15,700	1,348	9,731	33

Source: Adapted from Steve Colt, "Financial Performance of Native Regional Corporations," Alaska Review of Social and Economic Conditions, volume 28, no. 2 (December 1991).

tribal governments. Villages have claimed to have an inherent right to self-rule and may therefore form their own governments, regulate their own affairs, manage their own assets, impose taxes, and so on (see the discussion of tribal sovereignty in the law sections).

Federal recognition of tribal governments has been uneven. Congress has passed legislation recognizing tribes in Alaska. After years of delay, the Department of the Interior approved a tribal constitution for an interior village in 1990. In 1991, the secretary of the interior, in a speech before the annual meeting of the Alaska Federation of Natives, expressed his support for strong tribal governments and self-determination.

Judicial decisions, though, have been more confusing. Two recent cases are particularly important. In 1987, two Native villages sued the state of Alaska for the money they were supposed
to have received under a revenue-sharing program. State officials
had withheld the funds, because they felt such payments would
favor a racial class. The Federal District Court dismissed the suit,
arguing that states are immune from suits. The Ninth Circuit Court
of Appeals reversed this decision on three grounds: each village
had a governing council organized under the Indian Reorganization Act, a 1934 act granting greater self-government to tribal
governments; the village's legal suit was constitutional because
federal power is supreme, something the state agreed to when it
was admitted to the Union; and, finally, the state was guilty of
racial discrimination by not distributing the money. Revenue-sharing was for political entities, such as village councils, a local form
of government, but not for ethnic organizations. However, in 1991,
the U.S. Supreme Court partially reversed this decision when it
ruled that a tribe or a village may not sue a state, since neither
tribes nor state have mutually surrendered their immunity.

A second case involving the village of Tyonek, a small Athapascan
village near Anchorage, recognized lands received under ANCSA
as "Indian Country" and upheld the power of the council to exclude non-Natives from their community. The state of Alaska has
vigorously blocked most Alaska Native efforts to gain greater tribal
self-government. In 1987, the Alaska Supreme Court ruled in a
dispute over a declaration of tribal sovereignty by a village government against an aggrieved contractor, that the village "does
not have sovereign immunity because it, like most Native groups
in Alaska, is not self-governing in any meaningful sense." Confident of their reasoning, the justices applied their interpretation
to all villages in Alaska. In 1991, the governor reversed an earlier
administrative order and proclaimed his opposition to "the expansion of tribal government powers and the creation of Indian
country in Alaska."

Despite these obstacles, Alaska Natives realize that powers not
exercised are powers not recognized. Therefore village councils
have established tribal courts, dissolved city governments, passed

restrictive ordinances, formed regional associations, claimed jurisdiction over their land and resources, and controlled entry into their communities. In the end, most are confident that their efforts will lead to better solutions for their problems and more control over their future.

David Maas
University of Alaska, Anchorage

BIOGRAPHIES

◆ ◆

William L. Hensley is an Alaska state senator whose district covers more than 150,000 square miles and has a population of nearly twenty thousand people, 90 percent of whom are Eskimos like himself. The term *Eskimo* is actually an Algonquian derogation meaning "raw meat eaters," which historically has been used to identify Inuit- and Yupik-speaking peoples living along the Arctic Rim in North America and Asia. Many modern descendants feel that the word Inuit would be more correct, but this term excludes the Yupik-speakers of Alaska.

William L. Hensley
1941–

Inuit state senator and lawyer

Born in Kotzebue, Alaska, in 1941, Hensley attended the University of Alaska in 1960 and 1961, then studied at George Washington University in Washington, D.C., and received his bachelor's degree from that school in 1966. He later studied law at the University of Alaska (1966), the University of New Mexico (1967), and the University of California, Los Angeles (1968).

Hensley has been active in land claims implementation and rural economic development since the late 1960s, when he served as chair of the Alaska State Rural Affairs Commission (1968–72) and also directed the Land Claims Task Force (1968). He was one of the founding members (1966) and president (1972) of the Alaska Federation of Natives (AFN), a state-wide organization that lobbied in Washington for resolution of Native land claims in Alaska during the 1960s. He played an active part in the passage of the Alaska Native Claims Settlement Act of 1971, which granted Alaska Natives $962 million and 44 million acres of land.

Hensley served in the Alaska House of Representatives from 1966 to 1970 and has been a member of the state senate since 1970. He has been active in many Native organizations over the years and served as executive director of the Northwest Alaska Native Association in 1968.

Howard Rock
1911–76

Inupiat activist and editor

Howard Rock was born at the Inupiat (Eskimo) village of Point Hope in northeastern Alaska. As a boy, he attended Bureau of Indian Affairs boarding schools, often traveling long distances from home. In the mid-1930s, he attended the University of Washington, Seattle. During the 1940s and 1950s, he worked as an artist, producing work with Inuit cultural themes, and much of his work was bought by tourists. Rock was not happy with his life or work as an artist. In the early 1960s, he returned to Point Hope, in search of some direction to his life within traditional Inuit culture.

In the late 1950s and early 1960s, the U.S. government was planning to use an atomic bomb to create a harbor near Point Hope. This project was billed as a peacetime use of atomic energy. The Inuit people in the area, however, hunted sea mammals like whales and seals, which would be exposed to serious radiation from an exploding atomic device. Since Rock had some writing skills, the village elders of Point Hope commandeered him to join in the protest movement called Inupiat Paitot, or The People's Heritage. In order to publicize the issue and to gather Native Alaskan and other supporters, the Inupiat Paitot created a newsletter and Rock became the editor. This newsletter became the means of publicizing Inuit and other Native issues, and, in 1962, it became the Native newspaper *The Tundra Times*. At first ,the *The Tundra Times* was published at Fairbanks, Alaska, but it soon moved to Anchorage, the largest urban center in Alaska. Rock was the first editor and served from 1962 until his death in 1976.

The early 1960s were a period of great activist ferment among Alaska Natives. After successfully preventing the use of atomic explosives at Point Hope, the Alaska Natives were confronted with a series of other issues, such as protection of their right to hunt game and the prevention of the Rampart Dam, which threatened to flood large areas of Athapascan hunting land in central Alaska. Perhaps the most important issue was the state of Alaska's claim to about ninety million acres of Native land. During the 1961–65 period, Alaska Natives tried to mobilize and protect their land. Through *The Tundra Times*, Howard Rock wrote editorials, printed articles, actively brought Native issues to the press, and helped Native villages and regional organizations form protests. In 1965, he helped organize the first Alaska Federated Natives (AFN) meeting in Anchorage. The AFN was a state-wide Native organization that represented the land, political, and social welfare issues of Alaska Natives. From 1965 to 1971, the AFN lobbied Congress for a solution to Native land issues in Alaska, and in 1971 helped gain passage of the Alaska Native Claims Settlement Act (ANCSA), which provided 44 million acres of land and $962 million to the Alaska Natives in return for surrendering claims to about 250 million acres.

Rock, as editor of *The Tundra Times*, published articles on Native culture, history, Native land claims, and social and welfare issues, and wrote many commentaries about the events leading up to passage of the ANCSA. *The Tundra Times* became revered as a representative of the Alaska Native communities, and Rock was honored throughout Alaska for his tireless and selfless contributions toward solving Native issues.

Native Peoples of Oklahoma

The land that is now encompassed within the state of Oklahoma appears on nineteenth-century maps as "Indian Territory." Even today, Oklahoma is the home of the largest number of Indian tribes and peoples within the United States. In the late twentieth century thirty-eight federally recognized Indian nations continue to exercise their sovereign tribal status within Oklahoma, on the lands once known as "Indian Territory." Ironically, only a few of these tribes occupied any part of the state prior to European contact.

The vast majority of Oklahoma Indian tribes were "resettled" in Oklahoma, most involuntarily, under the nineteenth-century federal Indian removal policy. In the formative years of American Indian policy, settlers and local communities pressured tribal communities to give up their large tribal land holdings. In response, the federal government adopted a policy to compel tribes to exchange their historic homelands for new "permanent" lands on unorganized federal domain in the West, where, theoretically, no conflicts would arise with non-Indians. Under treaty guarantees this new land was to remain forever in the hands of Indian tribes, who were promised that non-Indians would not be allowed to settle in their midst. At the beginning of the twentieth century, in violation of these agreements, Oklahoma was admitted to the Union as the forty-sixth state (1907).

In the late 1820s and throughout the 1830s, the earliest and most dramatic of the Eastern Indian removals to what is now Oklahoma were those of the Five Civilized Tribes (the Choctaw, Chickasaw, Creek, Cherokee, and Seminole). These tribes were called civilized because they adopted constitutional governments, some of their people adopted Christianity, and they formed tribal school systems. Driven out of the South on what historians know as "The Trail of Tears," tens of thousands of these Indians perished on forced marches that were often conducted in the dead of winter. As many as one-third of their tribal members, especially the very young and the very old, died before they reached the new Indian Territory. Prior to the American Civil War, other tribes, including the Quapaw, Seneca, and Shawnee, were also removed to what is now Oklahoma. Ultimately, at least sixty-five Indian nations came to be listed historically as having been, at one time or another, Oklahoma tribes. These included:

> Alabama, Anadarko, Apache, Apalachicola, Arapaho, Caddo, Cahakia, Catawba, Cayuga, Cherokee, Cheyenne, Chickasaw, Chippewa, Choctaw, Comanche, Conestoga, Creek, Delaware, Eel River, Erie, Hainai, Hitchiti, Illinois, Iowa, Kaskashia, Kansa, Kichai, Kickapoo, Kiowa, Kiowa-Apache, Koasati, Lipan, Miami, Michigomea, Modoc, Mohawk, Moingwena, Munsee, Natchez, Nez Percé, Osage, Oto and Missouri, Ottawa, Pawnee, Peoria, Piankashaw, Ponca, Potawatomi, Quapaw, Sauk and Fox, Seminole, Seneca, Shawnee, Skidi, Stockbridge, Tamaroa, Tawakoni, Tonkawa, Tuscarora, Tuskegee, Waco, Wea, Wichita, Wyandot, and Yuchi.

During the Andrew Jackson Administration (1830–38), a companion policy to removal was the proposed establishment of an Indian commonwealth or territory in the removal area (now Oklahoma), to be governed by a confederation of tribes. The Western Territory Bill of 1834 proposed an "Indian Territory" that was to be composed of Kansas, Oklahoma, parts of Nebraska, Colorado, and Wyoming. None of these proposals of the 1830s was enacted, and the territory set aside for Indians gradually shrank to what is now the state of Oklahoma. Unorganized Indian Territory west of

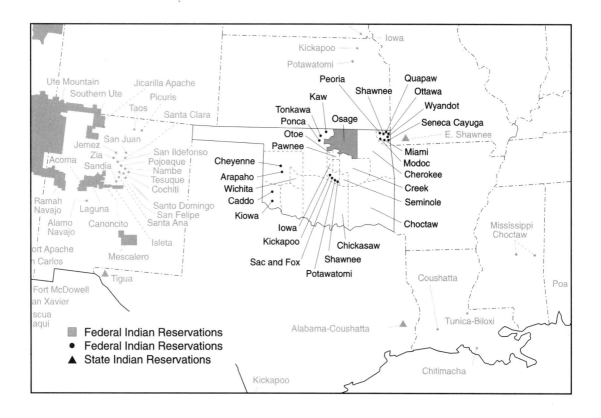

Ute Mountain
Southern Ute
Jicarilla Apache
Picuris
Taos
Santa Clara
Jemez
San Juan
Acoma
Zia
Sandia
San Ildefonso
Pojoaque
Nambe
Tesuque
Cochiti
Ramah Navajo
Laguna
Santo Domingo
San Felipe
Santa Ana
Alamo Navajo
Canoncito
Isleta
ort Apache
Carlos
Mescalero
Tigua
Fort McDowell
an Xavier
scua
aqui

Iowa
Kickapoo
Potawatomi
Peoria
Kaw
Shawnee
Quapaw
Ottawa
Tonkawa
Ponca
Osage
Wyandot
Otoe
Seneca Cayuga
Pawnee
E. Shawnee
Cheyenne
Miami
Modoc
Arapaho
Cherokee
Wichita
Creek
Caddo
Seminole
Kiowa
Iowa
Choctaw
Kickapoo
Mississippi Choctaw
Sac and Fox
Chickasaw
Shawnee
Potawatomi
Coushatta
Poa
Alabama-Coushatta
Tunica-Biloxi
Kickapoo
Chitimacha

■ Federal Indian Reservations
● Federal Indian Reservations
▲ State Indian Reservations

Contemporary Oklahoma Indian tribes.

the Mississippi disappeared, as one after another of the new territorial governments were established and states were admitted to the Union. When Kansas Territory was organized in 1854, the remaining unorganized area reserved for Indian tribes had boundaries almost identical to present-day Oklahoma. By 1868, the land that would later become Oklahoma was the only unorganized territory left in the lower forty-eight states. It was to this land that the federal government forced many remaining Indian nations. Although no territorial Indian government was ever established, the name *Indian Territory* gradually came into common use as the collective term for the lands of the Five Tribes and other Indian tribes settled amongst them. From 1865 until Oklahoma's admission to the Union in 1907, Congress frequently used the term in statutes and defined the boundaries of Indian Territory in laws passed in 1889 and 1890.

Indian tribes in Oklahoma have continuously operated their own sovereign governments, from pre-contact times through forced removal and statehood up to the present. After the end of the bloody Trail of Tears, the Five Tribes established comprehensive governments in Indian Territory and exercised self-rule relatively free of federal interference. The Five Tribes achieved a level of literacy and economic prosperity that exceeded many of the neighboring states. Before the American Civil War, these Indian tribes enjoyed a "golden age" in which tribal Indian traditions and the economic richness of this new land merged to produce a culturally diverse and prosperous Native civilization.

The Civil War had a dramatic impact on the Five Tribes. A number of tribal members owned slaves and supported the Confederacy. The Choctaw and Chickasaw Nations, whose lands adjoined Confederate Arkansas and Texas, sided with the Confederacy. The three most northerly tribes (Creek, Cherokee, and Seminole) were politically divided but nonetheless made treaties with the South. Loyalist factions continued to favor the North, and many tribal citizens fought on both sides. The Cherokee, Creek, and Seminole each lost as much as 20 to 25 percent of their population. In 1866 and 1867, the Five Tribes were compelled to accept new treaties and agreements that ceded western portions of their tribal territories, abolished slavery, granted railroad rights-of-way, and provided for the settlement of other tribes on their former lands and for the eventual allotment of tribal lands.

After the Civil War, other Indians—including many of the powerful Plains tribes, such as the Comanche, Kiowa, and Cheyenne—were removed to the western Indian Territory lands yielded by the Five Tribes and other strong tribal groups, such as the Apache. Thousands of U.S. settlers illegally moved into Indian Territory, and many lawless and violent drifters made Indian Territory a notorious haven for bandits and killers. In an effort to maintain law and order for non-Indians in Indian Territory, Congress established a special federal court for Indian Territory, over which Isaac C. Parker, known as "the Hanging Judge," presided. In 1889, the famous Oklahoma land run opened the so-called "unassigned lands" in central Indian Territory to U.S. settlers, and in 1890 the Oklahoma Organic Act reduced Indian Territory to its eastern portion, the lands of the Five Tribes and the Quapaw Agency Tribes. During this time an Organic Act created Oklahoma Territory in the western part of Indian Territory and established a U.S. territorial government. The Act expressly preserved tribal authority and federal jurisdiction in both Oklahoma and Indian territories. The status of Indian tribes in Oklahoma Territory was thus similar to that of tribes in other organized territories.

During the 1890s, the lands of many Oklahoma tribes were allotted or divided pursuant to the General Allotment Act of 1887. In 1893, the Dawes Commission was established to seek allotment of the lands of the Five Tribes, which were exempted from the General Allotment Act. In 1898, Congress passed the Curtis Act to speed up the allotment process. This act provided for allot-

Indian Territory, removal to 1855. Reprinted from Atlas of American Indian Affairs, *by Francis Paul Prucha, by permission of the University of Nebraska Press. Copyright 1990 by the University of Nebraska Press.*

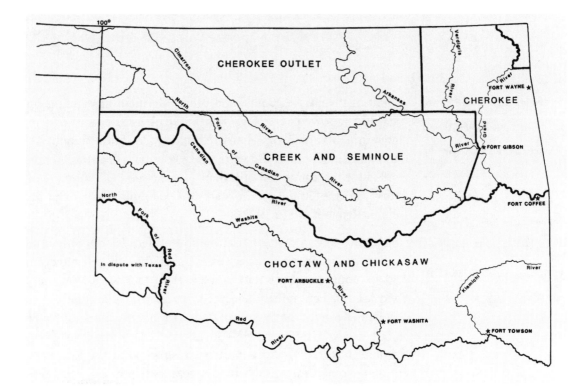

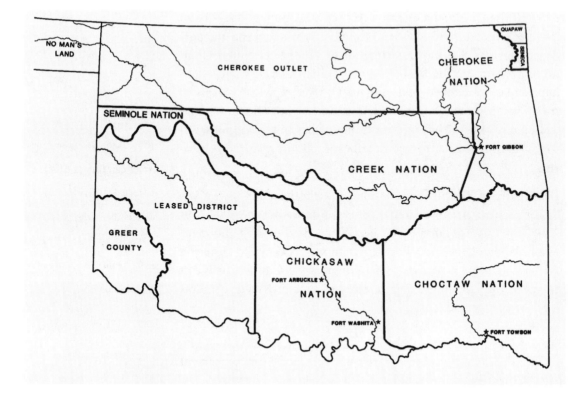

Indian Territory 1855–66.

Reprinted from Atlas of

American Indian Affairs, *by*

Francis Paul Prucha, by

permission of the University

of Nebraska Press. Copyright

1990 by the University of

Nebraska Press.

ment of Five Tribes lands, and other allotment agreements and statutes followed. The Five Tribes Act of 1906 preserved tribal governments and comprehensively addressed allotment and other Indian issues. Shortly thereafter, the Oklahoma Enabling Act provided for the admission of Indian Territory and Oklahoma Territory into the Union as the state of Oklahoma. Oklahoma proclaimed statehood in 1907.

Statehood was the bitter culmination of decades of conflict and self-righteous programs designed to transform Indian Territory into a U.S. commonwealth and to make the American Indian into a red farmer. Few non-Indians ever understood the depth of the Indians' agony at the passing of their nationhood. In the *Chronicles of Oklahoma* 26 (Winter 1948–49), Edward E. Dale, the dean of Oklahoma's historians, wrote with some surprise of the sadness an Indian woman still felt when she remembered the 1907 festivities to celebrate Oklahoma statehood. This Cherokee woman, married to a non-Indian, refused to attend the statehood ceremonies with her husband. He returned and said to her, "Well, Mary, we no longer live in the Cherokee Nation. All of us are now citizens of the state of Oklahoma." Tears came to her eyes thirty years later as she recalled that day. "It broke my heart. I went to bed and cried all night long. It seemed more than I could bear that the Cherokee Nation, my country and my people's country, was no more" (p. 382).

Since Oklahoma's statehood, the status of Indian tribes in Oklahoma has been similar to that of tribes in other states. The popularly held view that Oklahoma Indians are subject to special regulations generally applies only to narrowly defined property interests of individual members of the Five Tribes and the Osage Tribe. When Congress passed the Indian Reorganization Act of 1934, Oklahoma tribes were excepted from many of its important provisions. Two years later, Congress passed the Oklahoma Indian Welfare Act that authorized tribal organization in a manner similar to the Indian Reorganization Act and extended "any other rights or privileges served to an organized Indian tribe . . . ." Like all other Indian tribes, tribes in Oklahoma retain powers of self-government and sovereignty, except to the extent that their powers have been limited by treaties, agreements, or federal legislation. Although the land base of Oklahoma tribes has been substantially reduced by the allotment process, their inherent powers of self-government are undiminished.

The time before the American Civil War is remembered as the "golden age" of the Oklahoma Indian. For many Indians, this age followed the brutal, nearly genocidal expulsion from their original homelands. Such irony pervades much of Oklahoma's Indian life. The present Indian nature of the state results not from aboriginal Indian choice but from U.S. policy. Most Oklahoma Indians opposed coming to the state. Oklahoma's Indian people are largely descendants of nineteenth-century emigrants who had been driven by the U.S. government from almost every other section of the country. More bitterly ironic, Indians found in Oklahoma a quiet haven. Eventually, they came to love this land, and in the end it, too, was taken from them.

Generalizing about the coming of the Indian to Oklahoma is not easy. Tribes came at different times and for different purposes. Divisions of the same tribe were often split by migration. Oklahoma was historically a great and open hunting ground through which many Native peoples passed. State boundaries and formal tribal borders were unknown prior to U.S. occupation. Even the rigid recognition of formal tribal units was a political concept borrowed from the European legal tradition. Certainly fee-simple land ownership, with its feudal property implications, was foreign to the mind of the aboriginal American. Furthermore, in a society where splinter factions were free to move away from the main body of a tribe, portions of groups as large as the Seneca or the Osage or the Cherokee might be settled in several states as well as in Indian Territory. Still other tribes never settled anywhere, in the traditional European sense, but rather ranged from the plains of Texas into the Rocky Mountains and beyond.

Fewer than half a dozen of Oklahoma's tribes are indigenous. Only a few of the currently identifiable Oklahoma tribes were within the state when the Europeans arrived. Very early ancestors of the Oklahoma Indians, such as Plainview, Clovis, and Folsom man, as well as more immediate paleolithic ancestors, had disappeared. The great prehistoric Indian civilizations, with their mounds and their monumental art—such as those unearthed at Spiro in the 1930s—were gone when the first European explorers came to Oklahoma. By that time, Quapaw and Caddoan ancestors of the Wichita and Caddo had settled on this land with their village farming culture. Tribes like the Osage hunted in these domains, and nomadic bands, such as the Plains Apache and the Comanche, followed the migratory herds across the state. To appreciate the nature of Indian settlement in the state, we must distinguish among hunting, migration, and permanent residence. Further, we must appreciate the concept of a home base to which roving tribes might return with some regularity.

The major thrust of Indian settlement in Oklahoma resulted from U.S. policy, which consisted of formal negotiations; informal counsel, bribery, and threats; and military force. As early as 1803, Thomas Jefferson had spoken of a permanent Indian area or territory

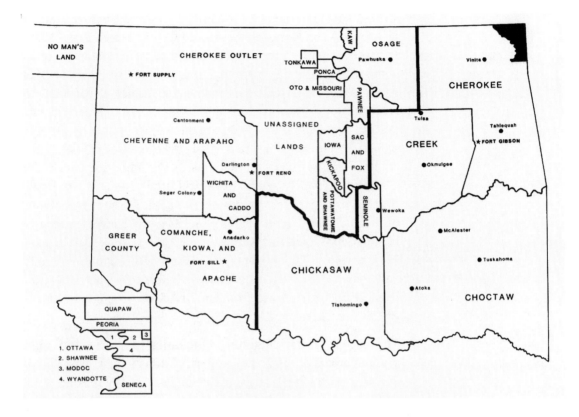

beyond the boundaries of U.S. society. Since before the founding of the nation, Indian tribes had been driven westward by both warfare and treaty negotiations. Through various inducements and the application of brute force more than sixty Indian tribes originally from other states were ultimately removed to and resettled in Oklahoma. One contemporary observer noted that this process "conformed in no phase or degree to any pattern," for "there was an infinite variety of methods, experiences, and details." Tribes were removed—particularly at the turn of the century for the northern Indians of Ohio, Indiana, Illinois, and New York—without plan or experience. Many once powerful tribes—such as the Shawnee, Sac and Fox, and Potawatomi—were fragmented, lost, or reduced in station before they arrived in the Indian Territory.

Voluntary migrations and inducements by treaty-settled portions of such tribes as the Seneca, Quapaw, Osage, Shawnee, Choctaw,

Indian Territory, 1866–69. Reprinted from Atlas of American Indian Affairs, *by Francis Paul Prucha, by permission of the University of Nebraska Press. Copyright 1990 by the University of Nebraska Press.*

Creek, and Cherokee in Oklahoma occurred before Andrew Jackson's Indian Removal Act was fully implemented in the 1830s. In these earlier removals there seemed to be no system or order. Some tribes were moved several times before they reached Oklahoma. Many tribal groups, sensing the futility of resistance to removal, sought a negotiated compromise that avoided the brutality of a forced military march to their new country. By the early 1830s, there were established tribal governments in Oklahoma of "old settler" or "western" factions of the Choctaw, Creek, and Cherokee, as well as separate political subdivisions of groups like the Osage, whose greatest numbers would not come to Oklahoma until much later. For example, in 1831, the Seneca exchanged land in Ohio's Sandusky Valley for 67,000 acres north of the western Cherokee, while a short time later another group of Seneca and Shawnee received a similar Indian Territory tract. In 1833, a band of Quapaw moved from the Red River to lands north and east of the Cherokee.

The tragedy of the brutal forced migration of almost sixty thousand members of the great southern nations—the Creek, Cherokee, Choctaw, Chickasaw, and Seminole—is known as the "Trail of Tears." As many as one-fourth of the Indians died from exposure and exhaustion during this migration. The agony of this experience is etched in the consciousness of the Five Civilized Tribes and of non-Indian Oklahomans as well. In turn, other tribes joined these southern tribes in Oklahoma, particularly northern woodland peoples, whose experiences were often as disastrous.

Between the end of the Civil War and the opening of Oklahoma's unassigned lands in 1889, the number of Indian tribes permanently living in Oklahoma changed. The many Plains and woodland tribes who joined the earlier inhabitants brought a diversity of Indian culture not present in any other state. In the northeast corner of the state, the Peoria, Modoc, Ottawa, Shawnee, and Wyandot joined the Seneca and the Quapaw. In the northeastern and central portions of the state were the Osage, the Kaw, the Pawnee, the Tonkawa, the Ponca, the Oto and Missouri, the Sac and Fox, the Iowa, the Kickapoo, the Potawatomi, and the Shawnee. Dominating the eastern half of the state and spilling into the west were Cherokee, Creek, Choctaw, Chickasaw, and Seminole. In the western part of the state, around the military outposts of Fort Reno and Fort Sill, the great tribes of the Plains were ultimately located. The Comanche, Kiowa, and Apache lands bordered on Texas. The Wichita and Caddo tribes nestled between this reservation and the reservation lands of the Cheyenne and Arapaho.

Ironically, more has been written and less is known about the history and culture of these Oklahoma tribes than about any other group of Native Americans. As many as 600,000 present-day Oklahomans identify themselves as Indians. Yet within the state of Oklahoma, there remains a widespread perception that the Indian and the Indian's culture is vanishing. "Non-Indians . . . are more ignorant of the Indian than the Indian is of them," according to a recent study of the population of Oklahoma City. "This is so because the majority of whites and blacks have had little personal contact with individual Indians and [even] that has been extremely superficial."

The contemporary facts are unmistakable. Oklahoma has more Indians from more varied tribes than any other state in the Union. It has more separate tribal groups historically associated with the state and more currently recognized tribes than any other state. A higher percentage of its population is Indian, and that population is more widely distributed among the state's counties than in Arizona, New Mexico, or the Dakotas. Indians once owned all the land in the state but now have a greatly reduced land base, the lowest income level, and the highest unemployment rate of any group in the state. Today more Oklahoma Indians are participating in more Indian-sponsored activities than in any period since statehood. The number of Oklahoma Indians is increasing. Indian tribes are again functioning as political and economic units, electing officials, administering programs, and dispensing justice.

The state is truly what Chief Allen Wright's Choctaw name for it, Okla Homma, conveys in a free translation: "Home of the Red People." More than sixty-seven tribes and bands have been located within the state and twenty-nine of them continue to be recognized. A population breakdown suggests that there are 100,000 sociocultural Indians, 220,000 persons recognized by the Bureau of Indian Affairs as legal Indians, and 600,000 Oklahomans of Indian descent. Tulsa and Oklahoma City rank second and third behind Los Angeles in Indian population within city boundaries. The sixty-five-mile trade radius of Tulsa constitutes the highest non-reservation concentration of Indians anywhere in the world.

The great diversity of Oklahoma's Indian population is lost in these statistics. Not only the Plains tribes and the Five Civilized Tribes reside in Oklahoma. Among the state's larger tribal groups are peoples as varied as the Ponca, the Apache, the Comanche, and the Choctaw. With urban migration, Indians from at least fifty other non-Oklahoma tribes have recently moved to the state. More and more of Oklahoma's Indians have ancestors from two to four, or more, tribes. An Osage-Cherokee, a Kiowa-Miami, and a Creek-Omaha are not unusual. The current generation is producing children who are such combinations as Choctaw-Ponca-Cheyenne-Delaware or Cherokee-Osage-Omaha-Creek-Apache.

Even among members of the same tribe there are great cultural and personal differences. Today as many as 10,000 Cherokee speak their native tongue in a tribe that began adopting European cultural variants in the eighteenth century. While Oklahoma U.S. Senator Robert L. Owen, an enrolled Cherokee, co-authored the Federal Reserve Act of 1913, the Cherokee Kee-Too-Wah, an ancient religious society, was reading ancient wampum belts and feeding the sacred fire with the blood of a white rooster.

Oklahoma has historically been a land of great contrasts between and among Indian people. Contemporary distinctions within the same or among different tribal groups are reflective of similar differences among Indians even before widespread settlement of non-Indians within the state. Nineteenth-century accounts of travelers, Indian tribal documents, missionary diaries, government negotiations, military reports, and trader journals clearly establish that there has never been a single, unified Oklahoma Indian culture. It is as rich and diverse as all of Indian America.

For convenience, Oklahoma's Indian tribes are often grouped into broad categories, such as the Five Civilized Tribes and the Plains Indians, or into semi-geographic, quasi-cultural divisions, such as Hunters of the Plains, Plains Farmers, Woodland Peoples, or Northern and Southern Woodland, Prairie, Plains, and High Plains Indians. Such artificial subdivisions are meaningful only when we remember the broad cross-cultural similarities and the genuinely unique aspects of each tribe. The Choctaw and Seminole, two "civilized" tribes, are in major respects culturally distinct, as are the Plains groups, such as the Kiowa and the Arapaho. To appreciate these varied cultures and what the Oklahoma Indian lost after the coming of white immigrants, one must understand the nature of Indian life on the prairie and in the woodland before the Civil War and the Treaty of Medicine Lodge. It is the culture of this "golden age" to which Oklahoma's modern Indians look with nostalgia.

The traditional Indian culture of Plains tribes such as the Cheyenne, Arapaho, Kiowa, and Comanche is familiar to most Americans. Their seemingly free and independent life has come to symbolize Oklahoma's Native peoples. These were hunter cultures, uniquely varied in many respects. Each depended on the existence of open lands that could be freely roamed and an abundant supply of wild game. Plains Indian thought, culture, and organization were complex. A civil, military, and religious structure preserved law and order, provided security, and assured economic and social well-being. It was a life intimately tied to the earth and to the natural cycles of life.

In absolute numbers, the Five Civilized Tribes and the Plains Indians historically constituted the largest blocs of Oklahoma Indians, but there were, and still are, other important and colorful Oklahoma tribes, such as the Sac and Fox, the Osage, the Potawatomi, the Quapaw, the Delaware, the Kickapoo, the Seneca, and the Shawnee. In addition, surviving portions of such tribes as the Catawba, the Natchez, and the Biloxi, and groups such as the Yuchi and the Hitchiti, were integrated into Oklahoma Indian governments, particularly those of the Choctaw, the Creek, and the Cherokee. During his tour of Indian Territory in the 1840s, Major Ethan Allen Hitchcock concluded that "fragments of Indian tribes are scattered in every direction."

The Oklahoma Indian tribes' viewpoints and problems are often lost in their cultural diversity and amidst their internal dissension. Yet even before the opening of Indian lands to non-Indian settlement, these tribes reacted to similar challenges and faced many of the same dangers from their common non-Indian and Indian enemies. As early as 1824, the tribes faced an invasion of commercial hunters and an assault on Native game. General Matthew Arbuckle reported two thousand hunters systematically killing fur-bearing animals in order to sell their peltries.

The U.S. challenge to the Indian way of thinking and living was a challenge to all Indian people. The unity among the Plains, woodland, and prairie tribes is not so readily apparent in material life and culture but emerges clearly at a philosophical and spiritual level. The great oneness of Oklahoma Indian tribes is spiritual. Peoples as seemingly diverse as the Cheyenne and the Cherokee reflect Indian attitudes in their perception of the earth, the supernatural, and the association of man's spirit and the spirits of animals.

For example, the Cheyenne Wolf Soldiers, the last of the seven great Cheyenne soldier societies to be organized, served as a defensive and protective association. The Cheyenne soldier-society warrior, draped in the skin of a wolf, sought protective power and acquired strength from the animal. Richard West, the Cheyenne artist, has captured this animal warrior as law man in his paintings and sculptures of the Wolf Soldier. The Cherokee, too, had many customs and legends about the wolf, which included wolf songs and medicine formulas. Even after the Cherokee had adopted their highly acclaimed constitutional government (1828–1907) and established peace officers or light-horsemen modeled after frontier sheriffs, they turned to the animal powers of the spirit world.

The close of the American Civil War and the 1867 Indian Treaty gathering at Medicine Lodge in Kansas signaled the beginning of the end of the old, free Indian nationhood. New treaties forced upon the Five Civilized Tribes at Fort Smith in 1866 contained provisions that ultimately opened the way for railroads to cross their domains and for the U.S. settler onslaught that followed. The signing of the Treaty of Medicine Lodge with leaders of Plains tribes—including the Kiowa, the Cheyenne, the Arapaho, and the Comanche—foreshadowed the federal government's effort to confine the tribes to reservations and to compel them to follow the "white man's road."

The Oklahoma Indian was caught on the crest of one of those great cycles that recur throughout American history. Westward expansion was itself an old story. Many of the Indians removed to Oklahoma, including the Shawnee, the Cherokee, the Seneca, and the Creek, had been caught in earlier stages of the cycle. But this expansion was somehow different. It was more determined, better organized, much faster, more efficient, and more difficult to resist. Powered by technological marvels such as railroads, the steam engine, and the mechanical harvester, the new expansion was also propelled by the "go-getter" spirit that infused the nation after the war. The military energy of the Union victory survived on the frontier. Congress, boardrooms, taverns, and churches shared a determination to thrust the nation westward. Landless Americans from older sections and newer emigrants who had temporarily settled elsewhere demanded Indian lands. There was no place left to remove the Indian to, and there was little sympathy for the preservation of a way of life that left farmlands unturned, coal unmined, and timber uncut.

By 1889, the life of the Oklahoma Indian was changing. The military balance of power rested with the white man. The great romantic, free, nomadic-hunter civilization of the Plains was past, or at least passing. The Plains Indian wars were coming to an end, with many Oklahoma tribal leaders held captive in distant jails. The brutal massacre known as the Battle of the

Washita (1868), in which George Armstrong Custer attacked Black Kettle's peaceful Cheyenne village, demonstrated the growing rift between the Indian "Spartans of the Plains" and U.S. soldiers. The "blue coats" appeared more frequently and grew larger and larger in the Indians' ledger-book drawings. Even the golden days of intense tribal creativity were ending for the Five Civilized Tribes, who were now left fiercely struggling to preserve whatever steps toward acculturation they had earlier made.

The year 1889 might appear on an Oklahoma Indian calendar as "the time when white farmers came with wives." Oklahoma Indian tribes were, in a real sense, still sovereign; they were "domestic dependent nations," in the words of former U.S. Supreme Court Chief Justice John Marshall. Until that fateful year, although they were subject to many federal regulations, Indians owned all the lands that were to become Oklahoma. Non-Indians within their domain were either government or military officials, who relied on Indian sufferance. Illegal intruders were subject to expulsion under existing treaties. These sovereign Indian nations were the only groups in Oklahoma whose political power and landed estate would diminish with the establishment of territorial government, which had begun in 1889 and culminated in the admission of Oklahoma to statehood in 1907.

A great drama opened Oklahoma's Indian lands and ended the exclusive Indian possession of these domains. Fifty thousand potential homesteaders vied to stake out claims to the ten thousand farms of 160 acres each. It was an epic, if condensed, enactment of the entire frontier-settlement process. The Oklahoma land rush of April 22, 1889, has been recreated in song and story, in novel and in film, but how the Oklahoma Indian came to that year of 1889 and what happened subsequently has been largely ignored.

Before 1889, when the United States acquired the disputed unassigned lands from the Creek and Seminole, Oklahoma was exclusively Indian country in a legal, political, and social sense. Not so after that eventful year of 1889, when the first of a series of runs opened these tribal lands to U.S. settlers. By 1975, the Bureau of Indian Affairs reported that Oklahoma Indian tribal lands encompassed only 65,000 acres and that Indians as private citizens owned only a million acres. The size of tribal acreage grows slowly from year to year but is still a fraction of the once great Indian Territories.

The long-range result of federal policy was that by the time of statehood in 1907, many Oklahoma Indians were handed land with a negotiable title. In many cases, this title was a fee simple, absolute title and in other cases was subject only to a limitation or restriction by supervision for a term of years. Most Oklahoma Indians were destined to become landless, because Indian tribes no longer held the land, and title soon passed to non-Indians. Indian land was thus lost, allotted to individuals despite the protests of the vast majority of Indians, who wished to retain tribal ownership.

Among the Five Civilized Tribes, tribal lands were shifted to individual members with remarkable speed. The Dawes Commission's preparation of the rolls began with the Curtis Act in June 1898 and continued through March 1907, with a few additional names being added in 1914. In all, the commission placed 101,526 persons on the final rolls of the Five Civilized Tribes. Of this number, full-bloods constituted 26,794; another 3,534 were enrolled as having three-fourths or more Indian blood; 6,859 were listed as one-half to three-fourths Indian; and 40,934 were listed as having less than one-half Indian blood. The commission also prepared a separate roll of 23,405 blacks, known as freedmen. Enrollments and land figures from the Dawes Commission's enrollment and allotment follow:

The total Five Tribe's tribal land base was 19,525,966 acres, 15,794,400 of which were allotted. The balance of 4 million acres included 309 townsites, which were sold, and segregated coal and timber, as well as other unallotted lands, sold at public auction.

Tribe	Enrolled	Acres	Allotted
Cherokee	40,193	4,420,068	4,420,068
Creek	18,712	3,079,095	2,993,920
Seminole	3,119	365,852	359,697
Choctaw	26,730	6,953,048	8,091,386
Chickasaw	10,955	4,707,904	(jointly with Choctaw and Chickasaw)

Today, Oklahoma Indians, especially full-blood descendants, suffer from these earlier federal programs to enroll Indians in tribes and to allot to individual Indians their tribally owned domains. When the Dawes Commission rolls were drawn at the turn of the century, many traditionalist Indians like the Crazy Snake Creek refused to enroll because they believed that the United States was violating its treaty promises. Many were enrolled against their will, but others escaped the roving enrollment parties. Thus Oklahoma's mixed-blood Indians are often federally recognized, while many full-bloods and their descendants are treated as non-Indian. Other full-bloods enrolled themselves as quarter-bloods or eighth-bloods so that they would not have restrictions on their lands and the need for guardians. As a result, in tribes such as the Choctaw, Seminole, Cherokee, Creek, and Chickasaw, whose rolls have been closed by act of Congress, enrollees' descendants are denied educational and other Indian benefits to which, by their correct blood quantum, they are entitled.

But the Indian and Indian attitudes were not so easily lost even in the statehood movement. Oklahoma may be the only state in which the Indian had a significant and long-lasting impact on the form of state government and on the nature of the constitutional legal system. Many important Oklahoma constitutional provisions, such as prohibition of alien ownership of land and limitation on corporate buying or dealing in real estate, were products of the unique Oklahoma Indian experience. The Five Civilized Tribes and the non-Indians who allied with them to control the Oklahoma Constitutional Convention dominated the attitudes and the development of the new Oklahoma government. Among the reasons for this influence was the experience gained in 1905 at the Sequoyah Constitutional Convention, a meeting called to prepare for the single statehood of the Indian Territory. William H. Murray held correctly that "some of the most important provisions of the [Oklahoma] Constitution derived their inspiration from the Sequoyah Constitution."

Oklahoma Indians have scattered throughout the world. Thousands of Oklahoma Indians living outside the state plan their vacations to come home for their tribal celebrations. Whether Comanche, Cheyenne, Kiowa, Shawnee, Ponca, Delaware, Quapaw, Creek, or Seminole, there is a time and a place for renewal, a need to call for strength from the arrows or the wampum. And there is also a time that brings together Indians from many tribes for pow-wows and gourd dances, rodeos and competitions, visits and quarrels, rekindled romances and revitalized disputes. Oklahoma's Red Earth celebration in June is now the largest Indian celebration in the world.

The summer and the summer dances bring scholars and tourists to see the Indians. But Oklahoma Indianness is hidden and confusing. Much of the Oklahoma Indian way is lost to the outsider because the Indian world has both a public and a private aspect and may, on occasion, involve both. An Indian legend shared by many Oklahoma tribes says that certain Indians can become transparent, turn into leaves on trees, or become small enough to ride on a bird's wing. Oklahoma Indians have been remarkably successful in doing just that. Indians have succeeded in hiding many aspects of their culture or camouflaging things Indian so that the Indianness is kept from the eye of the tourist or even the scholar. The outsider looking for a buffalo misses the deer, the raven, or the bright summer sun itself, which are all very Indian.

Much of the Indianness of Oklahoma is hidden because the Oklahoma Indian does not conform to non-Indian understandings of what is and is not Indian. A Boy Scout hobbyist in feathers and headdress is, by definition, Indian to students of the frontier myths, while a full-blood worshiper who wears blue jeans, a white shirt, and a Stetson hat and holds up the corporate seal of the Kee-Too-Wah is not Indian in the eyes of most U.S. moviegoers.

Furthermore, Oklahoma has few of the great geographic mountain and desert movie-set vistas that proclaim Indianness. There is no Oklahoma Monument Valley. No Oklahoma tribes have, like the Pueblo, drawn a whole school of painters and poets to record and romanticize their cultural ceremonies, crafts, and majestic landscapes. There are no Indian entrepreneurs who merchandise Oklahoma's Indian arts and crafts around a natural attraction such as the Grand Canyon. For this, most Oklahoma Indians are grateful.

Ponca Indian "Afternoon Dance" near Ponca City, Oklahoma.

Non-Indians imagine warbonnets and buffalo when they think of the Indian, but many of Oklahoma's Indian people have wood-

land or prairie heritages. They are the descendants of the front-line Indian soldiers of the seventeenth, eighteenth, and early nineteenth centuries. Their brave leaders were the Tecumsehs, the Osceolas, and the Little Turtles (see their biographies), the great warriors of the Seneca, the Shawnee, the Miami, the Creek, the Delaware, and the Seminole. These tribes fought the bloody pitched colonial and national battles of the eastern forests and the upland rivers. They learned early on the lessons of adaptation and acculturation that allowed them to adopt some U.S. cultural forms while retaining Indian substance. That these tribes survived is a testimony to their ingenuity. They saw that change was, paradoxically, their only hope of survival as an Indian people. Their lifeways, the summer rituals, and the reunions are no less Indian because they celebrate the fire or the green corn and not the buffalo.

Oklahoma Indians have historically loved to perform, to play and dance for themselves or crowds, to "play Indian," or just play. Colonial Indians traveling to Europe, Geronimo at the St. Louis World's Fair, the professional Indian dance troupe, the Osage ballerinas, Indians in Pawnee Bill's and the 101 Ranch shows all share the same tradition. Modern Indian teams and professional athletes reflect and continue the legacy of the great Indian professional football teams, Oklahoma's long list of Indian athletes, the successful Plains Indian baseball teams, and the most famous of all twentieth-century sports figures, Jim Thorpe (see his biography). No competitive sport in the world can be as exciting as a Sunday afternoon stickball game back in the Oklahoma hills. Nor can any group of actors be as proud or arrogant as a group of Oklahoma Indians dressed by a Hollywood director in make-believe Indian costumes. If one sees only the outward performance of the dances and the dancers and the Indians at play, one misses the spirit of the real world of Oklahoma's Indian people.

To Oklahoma Indians, the seasons still matter. To a people who are a part of the cycles of life of this planet, who live outside the artificial atmosphere of central heating and cooling and beyond the control of packaged goods and pre-planned public entertainment, the seasons are a measure of life. To the Oklahoma Indian, the summer celebrations bring more than oppressive heat and fresh tomatoes; they bring to life a world of family, tribe, politics, tradition, and ceremony. In its way, this world is as Indian and as real for this modern Oklahoma Indian as the world of his ancestors ever could be. As one young Indian explained, "Being an Indian doesn't depend upon how you dress or whether you have an old Ford or a young pony. Indians in bright cars and neat suits are still of the eagle race and as the people of the eagle race we are still a proud people who have kept alive a great spirit" (Jack Gregory and Rennard Strickland, *Adventures of an Indian Boy,* 1974, page 29).

The crucible of Oklahoma—the sharing of similar historical experiences and government policies—has helped produce this spirit and has contributed to the uniqueness of Oklahoma Indian culture. A great many factors have contributed to the evolution of this modern Oklahoma Indianness. For example, since most Oklahoma Indian tribes, as immigrant Indians, were separated from their historic homelands, the strong and ancient geographic-cultural ties that non-literate as well as literate peoples associate with landmarks do not exist within the state. For a relatively long period of time prior to the Civil War, many Oklahoma Indian tribes adapted themselves and their culture to their new location with neither the pressure of geographic-cultural ties nor the presence of many external non-Indian pressures. Dating from the first half of the nineteenth century, there is a history of tribal cooperation and intertribal meetings among the Indian groups in Oklahoma. Stimulated in part by the federal government's decisions to treat removed and reservation peoples alike and in part by a sense of common problems, these conferences reduced tribal hostility and stimulated united action.

The opening of Indian Territory to U.S. settlers and the general policy to end common ownership of Indian lands by allotting tribally held lands to individual Indians came at approximately the same time in Oklahoma history. They created a varied series of clashes and conflicts. The present-day absence of a large body of tribally owned land and the earlier federal failure to retain traditional reservations no doubt created a vastly different Oklahoma

Indian community, as did the aggressive manner in which the Dawes Commission distributed Indian farmlands and township lots, which were subsequently sold with government approval. Towns with sizable non-Indian population pockets therefore existed amidst Indian lands almost from the moment of settlement. The percentage of land in Indian hands was quickly reduced.

Yet another crucial factor was the fact that a number of Indian tribes, as well as the state of Oklahoma, shared the assumption that statehood in 1907 changed forever the nature and purpose of tribal government. Following statehood, the nation tended to legislate for the Indians of Oklahoma, particularly the Five Civilized Tribes, as separate legislative units not to be treated as the Indian tribes of other states. Added to this was the presence of a great body of mixed-blood Indian leaders who moved easily into the process of creating state governmental structures and who represented the interests of the entire state from positions of national or state leadership. Further, full-blood tribal leaders chose not to move into Oklahoma state government, retreating and withdrawing from the state political arena.

Much of Oklahoma Indian life has been culturally bifurcated. Since statehood, tribes have treated their recognized civil and traditional religious groups as separate tribal bodies, creating uniquely Indian religious and cultural pockets that are hidden within seemingly acculturated Native populations. Other issues divisive in many non-Oklahoma tribes, such as the role of women, have had little disruptive effect in Oklahoma, perhaps because those issues have few historic roots in this population. Oklahoma Indian women, many of whom are from matrilineal groups, exert a major and even dominant influence in many tribes and in most Indian families. Furthermore, Oklahoma Indian tribes have never developed a rigidly defined concept of "Indianness" and have encouraged the development of divergent cultural strains. There is a little historical evidence of tribal division based on degree of Indian blood, which indicates a strong degree of cultural confidence, a kind of Native sureness that Oklahoma tribes define as Indian pride and some non-Oklahoma Indians regard as arrogance. Voluntary separation and cultural segregation that is geographically intensified by traditional Indian settlement patterns combine to eliminate factional conflict. Finally, the size of the Indian population that is not physically identifiable as Indian, but is of Indian descent in proportion to the size of the non-Indian population of the state, creates a kind of "Indian culturality" that exists in no other state and, at least in the abstract, defines "being Indian" as socially desirable.

This particular set of cultural and historical circumstances occurred nowhere else in the Indian country of the West. None of these factors, alone, produced Oklahoma's unique Indian culture. Other factors, no doubt, contributed significantly to the development of Oklahoma Indian culture and values. Taken together, these attitudes and events helped shape the diverse tribal cultures of the immigrant Native American groups who are Oklahoma's Indians.

Today Oklahoma tribes seem to be undergoing a revived interest in the old ways and an increased pride in Indianness. As Wayne Wallace, of the Indian Job Corps, explains: "Indians have pride in who they are and where they come from. . . . The values of Indian people are just as good and important as the values of non-Indians." Yet numbers of modern Indians from all tribes choose to deny, ignore, or forget all that appears to be Native. Others retreat completely into the distant Indian hills, into an Indian world of the mind, to hide from the threat of the non-Indian world. The late Pam Chibitty, a Comanche-Shawnee-Delaware who worked with Indian people at the Native American Coalition of Tulsa, noted that for many Indians adjustment is not easy. "Some withdraw into an all-Indian world shunning non-Indians and modern society, others 'sell out' and go on to the modern white man's world and forget their backgrounds."

Within the individual Indian's life there are many distinctly personal values and attitudes that are influenced by an Indian heritage. Among Indians of the same generation and of the same tribe, there is no static view of Indianness. The world of the Oklahoma Indian is dynamic, varied, and diverse. And yet in some ways, Indian culture is becoming increasingly pan-Indian in the sense that many tribes share such events as powwows, gourd dances, and urban planning seminars. Oklahoma Indian life remains family-oriented, and the tribe is still important. The life of the Indian is more than dances at Anadarko, more than church-sponsored wild-onion dinners or public ceremonials. Events such as the birthday of Grandmother Anquoe or Mrs. Adair are at the heart of the real Indian world. Much of this personal Indian world remains hidden from non-Indian Oklahomans.

The notion that the contemporary Indian lives in two worlds has generated the misperception of a kind of Native American cultural schizophrenia. Oklahoma Indians, like Oklahoma non-Indians, live in a world that balances elements of diverse cultural traditions. The Indian brings a unique perspective to problem resolution. Two or more cultural currents may coexist so that the Indian must play many roles. Some of these roles are entirely consistent; others are hopelessly discordant. "Indian life does not fall into rigid categories," as one Oklahoma anthropologist, Carol Rachlin, notes. "It is, rather, a complex of interlocking circles, each exerting pressures and controls upon the others. An individual functions in different capacities in these circles or groups" (*The American Indian Today*, 1968, page 107).

The varied life of the real Oklahoma Indian exposes the bankruptcy of the stereotypic image of the Indian. The Indian lawyer in a three-piece suit can easily transform himself into a feathered championship fancy dancer. An elected county law-enforcement official returns to his office the morning after attending a peyote meeting. A nurse leaves the hospital and goes to have tobacco "treated." The computer worker has her house smoked with cedar. A man of 1/256 Indian blood sits in a French restaurant in Tulsa expounding on tribal genealogy, while the almost full-blood descendant of a great chieftain of the same tribe tells her high school history teacher not to tell her classmates that she is Indian. A gentle, hard-working full-blood is pulled from his job and charged with harboring an Indian felon because, as a religious leader, he has followed the traditional Indian legal ways of his people. A nationally honored scholar-author consults his medicine doctor when a witch is haunting him. An internationally famous Indian artist tours China and Russia to renew her art. Such is the world of the Oklahoma Indian.

The spirit of a civilization conveys more about the meaning of people's lives than do artifacts or documents. To understand cultural spirit is difficult, especially if one was not born into that culture. Attempting to capture the spirit of Christianity, an old Kiowa man went to a missionary service, contributed when the collection plate was passed, and settled down for the sermon. This Kiowa, Old Mokeen, who had already given what he thought to be generous, rose when the request for more funds came, squared his shoulders, and spoke to the missionary in broken English: "Whatza matter this Jesus—why he all time broke?"

The corn road, the buffalo road, and the peyote road are different from one another, but the spirit with which one follows the road, not the road itself, is the essence of Indianness. This Indian spirit, an Indian way of seeing and of being, makes a quarter-blood Chickasaw or an eighth-blood Comanche perceive as an Indian. "I believe that there is such a thing as Indian sensibility," T.C. Cannon, a Caddo-Kiowa, once explained. "This has to do with the idea of a collective history. It's reflected in your upbringing and the remarks that you hear every day from birth and the kind of behavior and emotion you see around you."

Rennard Strickland
University of Oklahoma

BIOGRAPHIES ♦ ♦ ♦ ♦ ♦ ♦ ♦ ♦ ♦ ♦ ♦ ♦ ♦ ♦ ♦ ♦ ♦ ♦

Black Kettle
1803–68

Southern Cheyenne
tribal leader

Black Kettle was a Cheyenne tribal peace leader whose band was attacked in the infamous Sand Creek Massacre during the Cheyenne and Arapaho War of 1864–65. During his youth, Black Kettle was actively engaged as a warrior against the Ute and Delaware, who were enemies of his tribe. He, however, advocated good relations with the Americans and ratified a treaty maintaining peace in Colorado and along the Santa Fe Trail. After traveling to Washington, D.C., in 1863, he met with President Abraham Lincoln.

Events such as the rapid settlement of Kansas and Nebraska territories after 1854 and the Colorado gold rush of 1859 promoted uneasiness between Indians and Americans, and reprisals on each side were not uncommon. Black Kettle and other Cheyenne and Arapaho chiefs met with the governor of Colorado near Denver and were assured that if each band would camp near army installations and regularly report to military officers, they would be safe from attack. Black Kettle moved his people to Sand Creek, near Fort Lyon in present-day Colorado, and informed the garrison of their peaceful presence.

On the morning of November 29, 1864, the Third Colorado Volunteers, under the command of Colonel John Chivington, took up position around Black Kettle's encampment. Over his tipi, he raised the American flag and a white truce flag. Nevertheless, Chivington's troops, many of whom were drunk, swept into camp, slaughtering and sexually mutilating the fleeing Indians. Black Kettle managed to escape, but about 150 others, mostly women and children, were killed.

The news of the slaughter caused a wave of condemnation. Chivington was brought before the Committee on the Conduct of the War, and was condemned, denounced, and forced to resign from the military. Meanwhile, the Cheyenne sought swift and destructive retribution; travel across the Great Plains to Denver was completely halted.

Despite this, Black Kettle still encouraged his people to remain at peace. He signed a treaty at the Medicine Lodge council in 1867 that granted reservations to the Southern Cheyenne, the Southern Arapaho, the Comanche, and the Kiowa within Indian Territory (Oklahoma). Black Kettle led his followers to the Washita River and traveled to Fort Cobb to assure the garrison there that he wanted nothing but peace. Nevertheless, U.S. officials refused to issue guns and ammunition to Southern Cheyenne men, for fear that they would raid settlers or other Indian tribes. Consequently, about two hundred Cheyenne raided several settlements in Kansas and caused U.S. troops to enter the field. Major General Philip Sheridan organized three columns of troops in an offensive aimed against the recently relocated Plains Indians.

Lieutenant Colonel George Armstrong Custer learned about the presence of Black Kettle's encampment on the Washita from Osage scouts. Disregarding the fact that the camp was on the reservation and had been guaranteed safety, he and the Seventh Cavalry attacked at dawn on November 27, 1868. Black Kettle rode out with his wife in a blinding snowstorm hoping to prevent the attack by parleying with the soldiers. Both were shot dead on sight and their bodies trampled by the advancing columns. The regimental band played "Garry Owen" as Custer and his men killed another one hundred Cheyenne, mostly women and children.

William W. Keeler
1908–87

Cherokee businessperson and tribal leader

In 1949, William Keeler was appointed principal chief of the Cherokee Nation in Oklahoma. He served as appointed principal chief until 1971 and, between 1971 and 1975, was the first elected principal chief since 1907. Keeler's initial appointment was made under laws that abolished the Cherokee government in 1907. Between 1907 and 1971, the Cherokee principal chief was appointed by the U.S. president and was responsible for administering the Cherokee land estate and attending to associated legal and political issues. It was thought that the Cherokee Nation would ultimately dissolve. In 1971, however, the Cherokee regained the right to elect their own leadership, and the nation continues.

Starting at age sixteen, as a part-time worker, Keeler pursued a corporate business career with Phillips Petroleum Company. In 1951, he was elected to the board of directors. In 1968, he was elected chairman of the board and vice-president of the executive department. Because of his reputation as a strong administrator, government agencies often tapped Keeler for advice on solving problems in the oil and refining industry. Keeler actively contributed his services to many public interest groups, including fraternal, veterans, civic, and business organizations.

During Keeler's administration as principal chief, he gained a reputation as an able administrator and leader. He served on two major government task forces, which investigated and reported on major issues in Indian affairs. One task force reported in 1961 with a critical review of government policies toward Indians during the 1950s, which included termination, or the dissolving of tribal reservations and governments. In 1962, Keeler also served on a task force that investigated conditions of Alaska Natives and their land claims. He also helped establish the Cherokee Foundation, which endeavors to promote the welfare and culture of the Cherokee Nation and its members.

As one of the principal chiefs of the Southern Cheyenne, Left Hand tread the delicate line between advocating peace and defending against U.S. encroachment. He also represented his people in negotiations with the federal government in the early 1890s.

Left Hand (Nawat)
1840–1890s

Southern Arapaho tribal leader

In 1864, Colonel John Chivington, a U.S. officer commanding some seven hundred soldiers, attacked the Southern Cheyenne and Southern Arapaho in order to open their hunting grounds for U.S. settlers. Left Hand tried to keep his people out of the conflict. He and his warriors were present with the Southern Cheyenne leader Black Kettle at the Battle of Sand Creek in November 1864, when about two hundred Cheyenne men, women, and children were indiscriminately killed by Chivington's troops. The incident was considered one of the most grievous of the Civil War. Left Hand was wounded during the shooting, but he refused to take up arms and return fire against Chivington's forces. His pacifist stance met with skepticism from some of his warriors, and a number of them adopted a more militant posture.

Left Hand became the principal chief of the Southern Arapaho in 1889, upon the death of Little Raven. In 1890, he agreed to allotment of Southern Cheyenne land in present-day Oklahoma, despite opposition from most Southern Cheyenne, who preferred traditional sharing and collective ownership of land. Allotment settlements allowed the U.S. government to divide Indian land and distribute it to individual Indians for farms, usually about 160 acres for a head of household. Any surplus land available after allotment usually was sold to U.S. settlers.

The allotment of land left most Indians in Oklahoma with a greatly reduced land base.

Lone Wolf (Guipago)
1820–79

Kiowa tribal leader

During the 1860s and 1870s, Lone Wolf became one of his tribe's most respected band chiefs and warriors. He was one of the signers of the Medicine Lodge Treaty of 1867 and later fought a series of military campaigns against U.S. forces.

During the first part of his life, Lone Wolf came to negotiate with U.S. agents in a spirit of peace and hope for close, friendly ties. In 1863, he visited President Abraham Lincoln as part of a delegation of southern Plains Indian leaders. In 1866, He became principal chief of the Kiowa. Lone Wolf was a compromised choice—between the militant Satanta and the pacifist Kicking Bird. As chief, Lone Wolf signed the Medicine Lodge Treaty of 1867, which established the boundaries of the combined Kiowa and Comanche Reservation in present-day Oklahoma. When members of his tribe refused to comply with the treaty, Lone Wolf was taken hostage by U.S. authorities.

Although Lone Wolf traveled to Washington, D.C., in 1872 to negotiate a peace settlement, the death of his son at the hands of federal soldiers in 1873 pushed him into war. For the next two years, he and other tribal leaders of the southern Plains met federal and state troops in a number of consequential engagements. Lone Wolf participated in the Red River War (1874–75), fighting alongside Quanah Parker, the Comanche leader. During the middle 1870s, the Kiowa and Comanche feared that the wholesale slaughter of buffalo by U.S. hunters would destroy their economic base and way of life. The Kiowa and Comanche started the Red River War to discourage buffalo hunters from killing the buffalo herds. After the battle at Palo Duro Canyon in September 1874, however, Lone Wolf's supply of horses and tipis was devastated. He was forced to surrender at Fort Sill in the Indian Territory in 1875. Lone Wolf, along with Mamanti, a Kiowa spiritual leader, were sent to Fort Marion in Florida. (The exiles had been handpicked by Kicking Bird, whom U.S. officials had appointed Kiowa chief.) Lone Wolf returned to his homeland in 1878 and died one year later of malaria.

Best known as chief of the Cherokee Nation, Wilma Mankiller was born at the Indian hospital in Tahlequah, Oklahoma. She gained an understanding of rural poverty early in life because she witnessed and experienced it. She spent her childhood in the wooded hills of the rural community of Rocky Mountain in Adair County, Oklahoma, where she now lives with her husband, Charley Soap, who is involved in community development. When she was eleven, her family moved to California as part of the Bureau of Indian Affairs relocation program. From a large family of eleven children, and with marginal employment for her father, Mankiller also gained insight into the meaning of urban poverty.

Mankiller became active in Indian causes in San Francisco in the late 1960s and early 1970s, and gained skills in community organization and program development. She earned a B.S. degree in social work and in 1979 completed graduate work in Community Planning at the University of Arkansas.

In 1983, she was the first woman elected deputy chief of the Cherokee Nation. When the Cherokee principal chief resigned in December 1985, Mankiller succeeded him. In the historic 1987 election, with 56 percent of the vote, Mankiller became the first woman elected Cherokee principal chief. Mankiller's service as the elected leader of the Cherokee Nation resulted in international media focus and public attention that enabled her to share the story of the Cherokee Nation with the rest of the world. But Mankiller insists that the achievements during her terms of office could not have been achieved without the work and support of others. She frequently praises the tribal employees, the tribal council, and Deputy Chief John Ketcher, who work together for the success of the Cherokee Nation.

Roman Nose was a leader of Indian warriors and a member of the Crooked Lance Society of the Cheyenne Indian tribe. During the wars of the 1860s, he became a prominent warrior and, because of his bravery in battle, earned the respect of a war chief.

Roman Nose fought in the Battle of the Platte Bridge in July 1865 during the Bozeman Trail dispute in present-day Wyoming and

Wilma P. Mankiller
1945–

Cherokee tribal leader

Roman Nose
1830–68

Southern Cheyenne
tribal leader

Montana. In 1866, Roman Nose fought alongside the Southern Cheyenne Dog Soldiers military society. In 1867, he was present at the Fort Larned Council with General Winfield Scott Hancock. Roman Nose declared to members of the Dog Soldiers that he intended to kill Hancock, but was prevented from doing so by Tall Bull and Bull Bear.

Roman Nose attended the preliminary meetings preparing for the Medicine Lodge Council of October 1867 but did not participate in the council itself or the signing of the Medicine Lodge Treaty. During 1867, he and the Dog Soldiers carried out numerous raids along the Kansas frontier, focusing on wagon trains and railroad work parties. In August 1867, he and his warriors defeated the U.S. Cavalry at the battle of Prairie Dog Creek in Kansas.

Roman Nose was killed in September 1868 in an engagement known to non-Indians as the Battle of Beecher's Island in present-day Kansas, and to Indian people as the Fight When Roman Nose Was Killed. Major George Forsyth and his troops had prepared for battle by digging themselves in on Beecher's Island, and during an afternoon charge, Roman Nose was shot. He died later that day. According to Cheyenne tradition, Roman Nose's "medicine" had been broken either when his feathered warbonnet was touched by a woman or when he ate food prepared with metal utensils.

John Ross

1790–1866

Cherokee tribal leader

John Ross was probably only one-eighth Cherokee and spoke halting Cherokee, yet he led the Cherokee Nation as principal chief from 1828 to 1866. His father was a Scottish trader, who married a part-Cherokee woman. For his early education, Ross's parents hired private teachers, and he later attended school in Kingston, Tennessee. While a young man, Ross became a successful merchant and plantation-slave owner. He strongly advocated agricultural and political change for the Cherokee as a means to preserve the nation from U.S. demands for cessions of land and Cherokee migration west of the Mississippi River. In 1811, he was appointed to the standing committee, which met to transact Cherokee government business while the national council, composed of about fifty village headmen, was not in session.

During the 1820s, the Cherokee incrementally adopted a constitutional government and became an agricultural nation. During much of the 1820s, Ross served as secretary to the Cherokee principal chief, Path Killer, who was greatly influential among the nation's conservative majority. Most conservatives preferred to remain in their eastern homeland and declined U.S. pressures to migrate west. After Path Killer's death in 1827, Ross inherited his great influence among the conservatives. In 1828, he served as chairman of the Cherokee Constitutional Convention and was elected principal chief by the Cherokee National Council. Between 1828 and 1866, Ross led the Cherokee conservatives, who formed the National party. The conservative majority consistently re-elected Ross as principal chief, and in return he worked to preserve Cherokee national and territorial independence from U.S. encroachments.

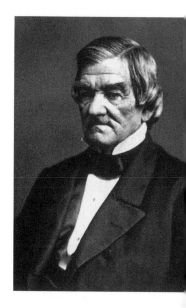

Sequoyah

1770–1843

Cherokee linguist

Sequoyah is justly celebrated for his development of the Cherokee syllabary, which is a set of symbols for each syllable sound in the language, rather than an alphabet in which symbols represent fewer but shorter sounds. Sequoyah's syllabary served the Cherokee people admirably for many decades and was the genesis of several Cherokee publications.

Sequoyah was born in Taskigi, near present-day Vonore, Tennessee. His mother was Cherokee and his father a U.S. trader. Sequoyah's early life was varied. He was a skilled farmer, hunter, and trader. He also served under General Andrew Jackson in the Creek War of 1813 to 1814.

The Cherokee language is still spoken by approximately ten thousand Cherokee whose families were deported to Oklahoma in the 1830s and the one thousand or so who remain in North Carolina. In 1809, while living in present-day Arkansas, Sequoyah began working on a written version of the Cherokee language. He recognized the importance of a written constitution and official records, and this was originally his main purpose in developing a written Cherokee language. At first, he developed a pictographic version of the Cherokee language, but soon abandoned this approach in favor of a syllabary of eighty-six characters representing the different syllable sounds. It took twelve years for Sequoyah to finish the project. It was a historic achievement in many ways. Despite limited proficiency in English and little in the way of formal education in writing, Sequoyah produced a workable syllabary of Cherokee characters. He was one of the few people in world history to single-handedly create an entire syllabary.

Sequoyah's achievement was initially met with some skepticism by his fellow Cherokee, but after a demonstration of how the system could be used to carry messages from an Indian family in Arkansas to relatives living in the east, it was adopted with enthusiasm. The Cherokee Council sanctioned the syllabary, and in a few short months, thousands of Cherokee were reading and writing. Christian missionaries, inspired by the translation of the Bible into Cherokee, helped obtain a printing press with a Cherokee syllabary font. In 1828, the *Cherokee Phoenix*, the first Cherokee newspaper, was published in both English and Cherokee. Also in 1828, the Cherokee constitution was ratified and written down. Sequoyah was invited to Washington, D.C., by the U.S. government, and his achievement was celebrated.

In subsequent years, Sequoyah continued to play an active role in politics and linguistics. In the late 1830s, as president of the Western Cherokee, he sponsored the Cherokee Act of Union, which united eastern and western parts of the Cherokee Nation. Before 1838, some Cherokee had migrated west as part of U.S. removal policies that encouraged eastern Indian tribes to exchange their land for territory in present-day Kansas or Oklahoma. The plan was designed to free more eastern Indian land for U.S. settlement. Most Cherokee refused to migrate west, but in 1838–39, most were forced on the "Trail of Tears" to migrate west. For several years the late Cherokee arrivals, who were the majority, and the earlier migrants, the "Old Settlers," could not agree on a shared government. The Act of Union in July 1839 helped provide a basis for a united government.

In 1842, Sequoyah set out on an expedition to locate a lost band of Cherokee who had migrated westward during the American Revolution. He hoped to locate them by cross-referencing languages. When he failed to return from the expedition, a fellow Cherokee named Oonoleh went searching for him. Sadly, Sequoyah had died during his quest for the lost band. In perhaps the most eloquent testimony to his lifetime achievement, the news of Sequoyah's death reached his people in the form of a letter written in the syllabary he had created. Sequoyah has been honored in many ways, including the naming of a distinct genus of giant redwood trees, sequoia, found along the northern California coast.

Standing Bear was a Ponca principal chief who won a U.S. federal case to bury his son in the Ponca homelands of Nebraska. Traditional enemies of the Sioux, the Ponca negotiated a treaty in 1858 that established boundaries between the two tribal groups. The treaty was abrogated when the government included Ponca lands within the Great Sioux Reservation in the Fort Laramie Treaty of 1868. In 1876, Congress passed a law to remove the Ponca from their homeland in present-day northern Kansas and forcibly relocate them to Indian Territory (Oklahoma).

Standing Bear (Mochunozhi) 1829–1908

Ponca tribal leader

One-third of the tribe perished from disease and hunger once they arrived. Two of Standing Bear's children died, and he set out to return his son's body to the old Ponca homeland. Accompanied by thirty warriors, the party set off on the journey. They were spotted by settlers, and, fearing an uprising, General George Crook ordered cavalry officers to arrest them. They were taken to Omaha, where they were interviewed by journalist Thomas H. Tibbles.

After the nature of the Ponca trip was understood, General Crook and others were sympathetic to Standing Bear's mission. However, federal attorneys argued that the Indians were not legally persons under the U.S. Constitution and therefore had no rights. Federal judge Elmer Dundy ruled against the attorneys, and Standing Bear's party was allowed to continue. He buried his son in northeastern Nebraska. Sympathy grew for the Ponca, and Standing Bear went on a lecture tour of the East. Congress formed a commission to study the Ponca case and granted Standing Bear and his party land in Nebraska in 1880. He lived until he was about 80 years old and was buried within the original Ponca homeland (see also the biography of Sarah Winnemucca).

Native Peoples of the Plateau, Great Basin, and Rocky Mountains

Numerous American Indian communities continue to live today in their ancestral homes on the Columbia Plateau of eastern Oregon and Washington State; in the Great Basin, largely Nevada, western Colorado, southeastern Idaho, and parts of eastern California; and in the Rocky Mountains, largely northeastern Colorado, Wyoming, and western Montana. The plateau Indians once enjoyed a rich environment oriented toward the region's rivers, where they traditionally fished for salmon. The lands on which they lived were lush with many varieties of roots, berries, and game. The plateau and mountain tribes lived on the edge of evergreen forests and high prairies, where they learned a deep respect for the earth. The Great Basin peoples, largely Paiute, Bannock, and Shoshoni, lived in the high deserts and intermountain regions. East of the Plateau tribes, the Bitterroot and Rocky Mountains rise majestically, separating them from the mountain Indians. Large portions of Washington, Oregon, Montana, and Idaho contain high deserts and plateaus, where a host of Native Ameri-

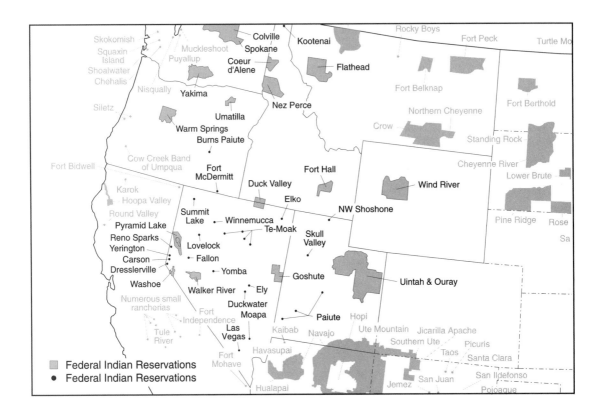

Contemporary Rocky Mountain Indian tribes.

cans lived by gathering an abundance of roots and berries, as well as by fishing and hunting. Similarly, the Paiute and Shoshoni of the Great Basin lived in small bands that hunted for food and gathered roots and berries.

In the plateau and mountain regions, the Indian nations shared many similar cultural traditions. Indian elders among the Flathead, Spokane, Wishram, Yakima, Nez Percé, Cayuse, Okanogan, and others say that the Creator placed them on the plateau and in the mountains at the beginning of time. Moreover, they argue that their history began when the earth was young, when plant and animal people interacted closely with the first humans. All of the tribes enjoy a rich oral tradition about their origins, and tribal elders consider the stories to be both literature and history. Many stories emerged from that time so long ago, and these stories form the basis of Native American cultural history.

One story recalls a time when five North Wind Brothers moved into the region and locked the plateau and mountain region in freezing cold. Coyote—the ever-present culture hero of many western Native peoples— whose actions often were the cause of both positive and negative events, became a follower of the North Wind. Many of the plants and animals chose sides, as either followers of the North Wind Brothers or antagonists against them. In particular, the North Wind Brothers encountered the Salmon people, who were large, edible fish that laid their eggs upstream of rivers that run to the ocean. In the stories of the Native peoples, animals often can communicate with humans, animals, and other beings. The Salmon Chief and his tribe lived in the Pacific Ocean, but in the spring of the year, they traveled up the rivers flowing into the Pacific. When the Salmon Chief led his people up one of the rivers, they were met by thick sheets of ice that prevented their traveling to their spawning grounds. The North Wind Brothers stood fast against the Salmon Chief, so the leader challenged the five brothers to a wrestling match on the ice. The Salmon Chief beat three of the brothers, but he lost to the fourth. The North Wind Brothers and their followers fell upon the Salmon Chief and all of his people, killing them in an attempt to destroy the entire tribe. They even cut open the wife of Salmon Chief, who carried numerous eggs. The North Wind Brothers smashed every egg, except one that fell between two deep and tightly wedged rocks. Believing that the egg would dry up, the North Wind Brothers left the area.

The Creator had watched the struggle between the Wind and the Salmon, and he took pity on the Salmon people. He sent a strong rain to wash the blood from the earth, and from the bosom of the rocks he washed the tiny salmon egg into the river. The Creator fertilized and nurtured the egg until a small salmon was born. The salmon returned to the ocean, where his grandmother cared for him and trained him to meet the future challenge of the North Wind Brothers. When Young Chinook Salmon was of age, he traveled upriver to meet the forces that had killed his mother and father. He met the five North Wind Brothers on the ice, and one by one he defeated them. However, Young Chinook Salmon did not kill the younger sister of the North Wind Brothers, and every winter she returns to bring a mild version of the cold once known when her five brothers ruled the region.

Like the battle between the salmon and the wind, the Indians of the plateau and mountains have long been engaged in a struggle for survival against European traders and settlers, who moved into the region and nearly destroyed the original inhabitants. In the nineteenth century, many Indian communities suffered a near-death experience, but like the small egg that survived, so did these Native people.

In the first decade of the 1800s, Indians living in present-day Oregon, Washington, Idaho, and Montana met Meriwether Lewis and William Clark, who led a U.S. expedition (1806–1809) to explore the Louisiana Purchase: land west of the Mississippi River bought from France in 1803. Indians from the plateau and mountains probably met European traders visiting the Chinook and Clatsop Indians living along the Columbia River and the coasts of Oregon and Washington. However, the interior tribes shared a common experience through their relations with Lewis and Clark.

When the explorers reached the Great Falls (near present-day Great Falls, Montana) of the Missouri River, they needed horses and information in order to cross the Rocky Mountains. With a small party, Lewis set out on foot to find the Shoshoni Indians. After some time, the men met several Shoshoni women, to whom they gave gifts. The women belonged to the Lemhi band of Shoshoni people, and their leader was Chief Kameawaite. After much effort, Lewis convinced Kameawaite to supply horses and guides to lead the U.S. exploring party over the Rocky Mountains. When the Shoshoni and explorers returned to Great Falls, Kameawaite willingly helped Lewis and Clark, because they had returned his long-lost sister, Sacajewea. Sacajewea and her husband, Touissant Charbonneau, served as guides for the Lewis and Clark expedition to Great Falls from a Hidatsa village in present-day central North Dakota. Some years earlier, enemies of the Shoshoni had stolen Sacajewea, who was sold into slavery and eventually bought by Charbonneau. Kameawaite contributed significantly to the safe journey of the famous explorers. The Shoshoni chief led the expedition through most of present-day Montana and showed them the way into the country of the Flathead Indians, in present-day western Montana. In like fashion, the Flathead guided Lewis and Clark westward across the panhandle of present-day Idaho.

In October 1805, the Lewis and Clark expedition entered the lands of the Nez Percé, who provided the explorers with kindness, food, and canoes to take them to the Pacific Ocean. With the aid of Nez Percé scouts, the explorers traveled quickly by canoe to the homelands of the Palouse Indians, safely reaching the Palouse village of Quosispah. Several Indians greeted Lewis and Clark at this village, and they celebrated the arrival of the *Suyapo*, "Crowned Heads" or "Crowned Hats," by singing long into the night. Palouse, Yakima, Wanapum, Wishram, Walla Walla, Cayuse, and a host of other tribes sent representatives to meet the U.S. explorers. The Indians and explorers traded goods, and Lewis and Clark honored some of the chiefs with special medals bearing the words *Peace and Friendship*. Relations between the two peoples were friendly, and the explorers soon continued their trip down the Columbia River, in present-day Oregon State, past the villages of the Skin, Wishram, Tenino, Wasco, Clackamus, Cathlapotle, Wahkiakum, and Cathlamet.

The explorers spent a rainy winter among the Clatsop Indians living south of the Columbia River before returning to the United States. The United States claimed the entire Northwest—including the plateau and mountains—for their country, and they encouraged others to relocate to the region. Lewis and Clark reported the many wondrous things they had seen, including the vast numbers of fur-bearing animals. By 1810, less than a year after Lewis and Clark's journey, British traders traveled through the Northwest in quest of a river route from the interior of Canada to the Pacific Ocean. Soon three major fur trading companies, the Northwest Company, the American Fur Company, and the Hudson's Bay Company, set up trading posts or factories in the Northwest.

Fort Astoria, in Oregon along the Columbia River, served as a key trading center for the Americans, but the British purchased the post in 1813 and renamed it Fort George. In 1824, the Hudson's Bay Company opened Fort Vancouver in present-day Washington, and they operated factories or posts on the plateau. While the company worked with Shoshoni, Paiute, and Bannock to procure furs, they depended on the plateau tribes for horses. Fort Nez Percé, Fort Okanogan, Fort Colville, and Fort Spokane, all named after plateau tribes, traded with Indians and supplied the Hudson's Bay Company with some furs and many horses. The British company enjoyed a prosperous Indian trade on the plateau and intermountain areas until the 1850s, when they had depleted the number of fur-bearing animals and when the United States took firm control of the region.

The traders and trappers became the first to occupy Indian lands in the region. A few of them tried to convert the Indians to Christianity, but the major thrust of the mission system on the plateau began in the 1830s. The Presbyterian missionary couples Marcus and Narcissa Whitman and Henry and Eliza Spalding established the first missions in the Northwest among the Cayuse and the Nez Percé. Catholic missionaries followed these early Presbyterian ministers, establishing missions among the Flathead, Sanpoil, Nespelem, Colville, Yakima, Umatilla, and others. Some Indians gravitated to Christianity, while others retreated into their own traditional religions. Controversy over whether to adopt Christianity split many plateau and mountain Indian communities into pro- and anti-Christians.

Between 1836 and 1843, the Presbyterian Whitmans and Spaldings worked diligently among the Indians with mixed results. In 1843, a significant event altered the course of events: Joe Meek, William Craig, and other former fur trappers opened a wagon road, later called the Oregon Trail, from Idaho across the Blue Mountains of Oregon, along the Columbia River, and into the Grande Ronde River Valley of Oregon. Soon many settlers and travelers used the Oregon Trail to travel to the Pacific Northwest Coast. The newcomers established territorial governments in the present-day states of Oregon and Washington, asserting political power over the indigenous peoples. Tensions mounted as disease, introduced by the newcomers, spread among the Indians, threatening their physical survival. In the interior, measles ravaged the Cayuse, and they blamed Dr. Whitman for the epidemic. A few Cayuse murdered the doctor, his wife, and eleven others. Oregon Volunteers marched to engage the Cayuse but eventually fought the Palouse, after the Volunteers tried stealing about 400 Indian horses. The conflict was settled after a few Cayuse surrendered and were later hanged.

Of equal importance, after Maidu Indians discovered gold in 1848 along the American River in northern California, miners invaded California, killing Indians with guns and viruses. The California mining frontier moved northward into the lands of the Modoc, Klamath, and Chetco. Gold was soon discovered on the plateau and in the mountains, where Indians resisted the invasion of their homelands by miners who had little or no regard for Indians or their rights. The miners extended their diggings north into Oregon and Washington and east into Idaho and Montana. The United States soon gave more attention to the area, and in 1853, it created two separate territories there. Oregon Territory included lands in present-day Oregon, Idaho, and Wyoming. Washington Territory included lands in present-day Washington, Idaho, and Montana. With the new government came American Indian policy bent on liquidating Indian title to the land, concentrating Indians onto smaller parcels of land called reservations, and establishing military and civil power over the tribes.

In 1854, Governor Isaac I. Stevens made a whirlwind tour of the coastal tribes of Washington Territory, coercing some of them into ceding their lands to the government. He made treaties at Medicine Creek, Point Elliott, and Point No Point. The Indians of Puget Sound secured for themselves only a small portion of their lands and fell victim to the power of the Bureau of Indian Affairs. Stevens had a more difficult time with the plateau Indians. In May 1855, Stevens made three treaties with the inland tribes, creating the Yakima, Nez Percé, and Umatilla reservations. Although he did not negotiate treaties with the Salish-speaking Indians of the plateau, he concluded a treaty with some Flathead, which forced the

Kutenai, Kalispel, and Flathead to move onto a reservation. Oregon Superintendent of Indian Affairs Joel Palmer helped Stevens with the Walla Walla Council before concluding treaties with the Tenino, Wasco, Wishram, and other people living along the Columbia River. He created the Warm Springs Reservation of Oregon south of the Columbia River, where he expected the tribes to live in peace with the Paiute of Oregon. Palmer negotiated treaties with several different tribes in Oregon, but over time, the U.S. government took nearly all Indian land in the territory, leaving Native Americans with virtually no land base. As a result of territorial government, the United States and its citizens took control of the plateau and mountain Indians but not without a fight.

Shortly after the Walla Walla Council of 1855, white miners discovered gold north of the Spokane River in Oregon Territory. Miners invaded the inland Northwest, and some stole and murdered a few Indians, which led to retaliation by Yakima warriors, who executed several miners. War resulted after two Yakima murdered Indian agent Andrew Jackson Bolon. Between 1855 and 1858, the Indians of the Columbia Plateau fought a series of fights with volunteer and U. S Army troops. After some initial successes, the Yakima retreated north. Volunteer troops from Oregon and Washington invaded the lands of Walla Walla, Umatilla, Cayuse, and Palouse Indians living near the Snake River in present-day Oregon. Few of these people had been involved in the conflict in the Yakima country, but the volunteer soldiers sought to punish all Indians. The Plateau Indian War concluded at the Battle of Four Lake and Spokane Plain when the combined forces of Yakima, Palouse, Spokane, Flathead, Okanogan, and others suffered a loss at the hands of the U.S. military, led by Colonel George Wright. Several tribes chose not to enter a war with the United States, but all of them felt the power of the federal government and the settlers who had taken their land.

Contact with settlers came relatively late for the Great Basin peoples, such as the numerous local bands of Paiute. But in the 1850s, many Great Basin Indians, who primarily lived by hunting animals and gathering roots and plants, went to work for U.S.

ranchers and farmers relatively quickly. Many worked for wages as cowboys driving cattle, and others performed a variety of wage-labor jobs, such as planting, cultivating, harvesting grains, and taking care of livestock. The ranchers and farmers were willing to hire the Indian workers, since farm and ranch hands were quite scarce in the Great Basin region.

The rapidly changing political and economic situation of the Great Basin region helped spark two social movements, which are often called the 1870 Ghost Dance and the 1890 Ghost Dance. The 1870 movement was started by the Paiute mystic Wodziwob, whose teachings spread primarily among the northern and western California Indians. The California Indians, at this time, were under great distress from disease, poverty, political subordination (see the California entry), and aggressive miners, who wanted the Indians out of the mining fields. Many California Indians adopted the Ghost Dance-associated hand game, a gambling game with ritual singing and betting while one team tries to hide bones and the other tries to guess who has the bones. The second, or 1890, Ghost Dance is more well known and was initiated by Wovoka, the son of a Paiute shaman. This Ghost Dance drew upon the early teachings of Wodziwob and emphasized the return of game and relatives who had died over the past several decades. Many Indians had died of diseases, and game, especially buffalo on the Plains, was noticeably declining. Many In-

The prophet Wovoka (seated) in his later years.

dian nations in the West were gravely concerned that changing conditions threatened their entire way of life. The Ghost Dance incorporated many Paiute traditions, such as a Round Dance. Performed to gain communication with or honor dead ancestors, the Round Dance became a central feature of the Ghost Dance, which, from 1888 to 1890, spread rapidly among many western Indian tribes, especially among the Plains nations. The dance was performed to achieve successful transition to the next world after death, and in some versions the dance was to help facilitate a great worldly change in which many dead ancestors would return to live on earth and the game would be replenished. These events would restore the Indian nations to their former, more prosperous condition, before the intrusion of U.S. settlers and government. The Ghost Dance movement declined rapidly after the 1890 massacre of Sioux at Wounded Knee in South Dakota. Units of the Seventh Cavalry killed at least two hundred Sioux, many of whom were women and children. After the Wounded Knee incident, the U.S. government officially discouraged the Ghost Dance, and because the Ghost Dance predictions of a cataclysmic worldly reorganization did not come to pass, within a few years the movement declined to only a few tribes, and occasional Ghost Dance spiritual leaders sprinkled among some of the Plains nations. Wovoka encouraged the Great Basin and other Indian people to keep the moral teachings he received in a vision from the Great Spirit by loving one another and living in peace with every one, teachings that he most likely adapted from Christian thought, with which he was familiar. As late as the 1920s, Wovoka told other Indians—usually avoiding discussions with non-Indians—that he had visited with God and a new world was coming for the Indians.

The Nez Percé of present-day Idaho lived peacefully with the United States until 1860, when "traders" found gold on their lands. Gold miners quickly moved into the Nez Percé country, and the Bureau of Indian Affairs responded by shrinking the Nez Percé Reservation to one-tenth its original size. All the Nez Percé chiefs refused to sign the treaty of 1863, except Chief Lawyer, who had no authority to sell Nez Percé lands. Still, he signed the "Thief Treaty," and the ultimate result was war. In 1876, General Oliver O.

Howard demanded that the non-treaty Nez Percé move onto the reservation in present-day eastern Idaho. When the people had no other choice but to accept peace or go to war, they chose to move to the reservation. Nevertheless, war erupted when three young men killed several settlers. In fear of U.S. retaliation, Chief Looking Glass led the Nez Percé out of Idaho, into Montana, and south toward the Crow Indians. When the Crow refused to help, the Nez Percé turned north toward Canada. U.S. forces, led by Colonel Nelson A. Miles, intercepted the Nez Percé near the Bear Paw Mountains of Montana and accepted the surrender of Chief Joseph, a central Nez Percé leader. Rather than return the Nez Percé to Idaho in accordance with the surrender agreement, U.S. General William Tecumseh Sherman transported the men, women, and children to Fort Leavenworth, Kansas, and to Indian Territory, present-day Oklahoma. The Nez Percé remained in Indian Territory until 1885, when the government permitted them to return to the Northwest. Some Nez Percé returned to Idaho, but others, like Joseph, were forced to live on the Colville Reservation in central Washington.

The Shoshoni, Bannock, and Paiute people also made a stand against the United States. Originally, the United States established the Fort Hall Reservation in present-day eastern Idaho for the Boise-Bruneau band of Shoshoni, but soon the government forced the Bannock to accept reservation life at Fort Hall. Many Bannock decided to go to the reservation and receive rations. The government, however, did not make good on its promises of food, and many Shoshoni and Bannock faced starvation. When the Bannock, Paiute, and Shoshoni living on the Fort Hall Reservation tried to continue their seasonal economic migrations for buffalo hunting and the gathering of roots and berries, it was only a short time before they began to feel pressure from the Bureau of Indian Affairs (BIA) and Christian missionaries to stop. Discontent spread at Fort Hall, and on May 30, 1878, a few Indians stole some cattle and killed two cowboys, which started a series of battles. By June 1878, it had escalated into a significant military conflict. Numbering only 700 people, the Bannock and Paiute joined forces in southeastern Oregon, where they fought the Battle of Camp

Curry. After the battle, the Bannock and Paiute moved north toward the Umatilla Reservation in present-day Oregon. U.S. forces subdued the Shoshoni and Bannock and returned them to the Fort Hall Reservation.

During the 1880s, reformers of American Indian policies determined that the trouble with Indians was that they held reservations communally and not individually. In an attempt to help Indians, liberal reformers decided to break up reservations into individual lots so that Indians would have private plots and want to productively work their ranch or farm. U.S. policymakers reasoned that this land policy would enable Indians to become "civilized," because they would have a direct stake in their own economic livelihood. Most reformers, however, knew little about Indian cultures or economic practices, such as their methods of hunting, fishing, and gathering. Few, if any, Indians in the plateau, mountain, or Great Basin regions farmed, and it would take years for them to alter their cultures to accommodate U.S. reformers. Many Indians refused to give up their traditional economic practices in order to adopt farming. Life on the reservations was hard: The people became dependent on U.S. government rations, and most reservations could not adequately support the small Indian populations that lived on the reservation.

In 1887, Congress passed the General Allotment Act, which called for the division of reservations into individual parcels of 160, 80, or 40 acres. Each Indian received an allotment, and the excess land was sold to non-Indian settlers. After twenty-five years, Indian allotees could sell their individual allotments.

The government began allotting the Yakima Reservation in Washington State in the 1890s and continued the process until 1914. Conservative Indians, particularly elders and worshipers of the Washani religion—a newly emergent religion that taught preservation of Indian land and many traditions—opposed allotment. Some Yakima agreed to take allotments, although many felt it contrary to tribal tradition. Between 1890 and 1914, the United States made 4,506 allotments on the Yakima Reservation, totaling 440,000 acres. Because many conservative Yakima resisted taking allotments, 798,000 acres of reservation land was not allotted and remained in tribal hands. The government also allotted land on the Spokane Reservation in Washington. On June 19, 1902, Congress passed a resolution directing the secretary of the interior to allot Spokane tribal lands. The Indians had little choice in the matter, because the United States forced 651 members of the tribe to accept allotments totaling 64,750 acres. The government sold the remainder of the Spokane Reservation to non-Indian timber, agricultural, and ranching interests.

Like many Indians, the Coeur d'Alene people of Idaho lost a huge portion of their original domain. On November 8, 1873, the president created the Coeur d'Alene Reservation with 598,500 acres. However, in agreeing to the executive order creating the reservation, the Coeur d'Alene lost 184,960 acres of their homeland in eastern Washington and western Idaho. When the government allotted reservation lands from 1905 to 1909, over the objections of Coeur d'Alene chief Peter Moctelme, the Coeur d'Alene and Spokane were left with only 51,040 acres of lands they traditionally had lived on.

A situation similar to that of the Coeur d'Alene occurred on the Flathead Reservation of Montana, where the Pend d'Oreille (also known as Upper Kalispel), Kutenai, and Flathead lived. Originally, these Indians controlled 1,242,969 acres of land. Between 1904 and 1908, the government allotted 80 acres to individuals interested in farmlands and 160 acres to Indians wishing to ranch. A total of 2,378 Indians received allotments on the Flathead Reservation. At the same time, the U.S. government sold 404,047 acres of former Indian lands to U.S. settlers, and the state of Montana took another 60,843 acres for school purposes. The United States kept 1,757 acres of the Indian lands for itself, thus assuming control over most of the original lands of the Flathead people. On May 2, 1910, the government opened the remainder of the reservation land for settlement and development by non-Indians.

During the late nineteenth and early twentieth centuries, Native Americans lost more than their estates. They also lost elements of their culture, language, and families through the efforts of the Bureau of Indian Affairs to "civilize" them. Indian reformers often wanted Indians to leave their Native cultures, which the reformers considered backward. U.S. policymakers believed that the best road for Indians to travel was to adopt U.S. culture and that education was the most effective way to civilize Native Americans. Indian schools emerged on several reservations, where U.S. teachers tried to discourage Indian students from practicing Indian languages, cultures, traditions, and religions. Churches established mission schools on some reservations, but, by the late nineteenth century, the Bureau of Indian Affairs controlled most reservation educational institutions.

Through the Indian agents and the superintendents of the Indian schools, the Bureau of Indian Affairs operated most of the reservation schools. Although both boys and girls attended these schools, the administrators and teachers focused their attention primarily on boys, mirroring the gender bias prevalent in U.S. society. Teachers taught Indian children to speak, read, and write English, and they punished the children when they spoke Indian languages. Indian students learned the subjects that were taught in most U.S. elementary schools of the time, but the major emphasis was on vocational education. Teachers trained girls to be waitresses, maids, and housekeepers, and Indian boys studied printing, masonry, and carpentry. Many Indian boys and girls were sent to work in nearby towns and homes, where they learned from on-the-job training but earned little or no money. Most reservations had elementary schools, but the Bureau of Indian Affairs sent older children—Shoshoni, Bannock, Nez Percé, Nespelem, Paiute, Okanogan, and others—to Carlisle in Pennsylvania, Haskell in Oklahoma, Sherman in California, or one of the other boarding schools. Some Indian boarding schools continue to function today, although their attitudes and curricula no longer directly discourage the expression of Indian cultures as they did in the early twentieth century.

While forced education dramatically altered Indian cultures of the Columbia Plateau, the Great Basin, and Rocky Mountains, other factors, such as disease, also influenced the lives of these Indians. While smallpox, measles, and venereal diseases ravaged the tribes in the nineteenth century, tuberculosis, pneumonia, and influenza killed thousands of Indians in the twentieth century. Between 1888 and 1930, among the Indians of the Confederated Yakima Nation, more deaths occurred between the time of birth and age one than in any other age category. Infant mortality most often resulted from the above-mentioned diseases. Each tribe had its traditional Native doctors, men and women who knew the healing herbs, medical techniques, prayers, and songs, but they were too often unable to fight the newly introduced diseases. Some Indians were treated by government doctors, but too many were not. The Native American population in the region suffered severely from disease until the 1930s, when the Indian Health Service received more funds for combating infectious diseases.

During the 1930s, Congress passed the Indian Reorganization Act, which allowed tribes to reassert themselves legally in a new way. Indians who accepted the Indian Reorganization Act could place their allotments in a trust so the lands could not be sold. The tribes could also reorganize into new political entities with tribal laws and constitutions. Some of the tribes of the plateau and mountains accepted the Indian Reorganization Act, while others did not. The Confederated Salish and Kutenai Tribes of the Flathead Reservation, the Confederated Tribes of the Umatilla Indian Reservation, the Confederated Tribes of the Warm Springs Reservation, and others voted to accept the Indian Reorganization Act. Regardless, all of the plateau and mountain tribes, and many of the Great Basin tribes, created tribal governments that helped guide them during the twentieth century. Certainly all of the tribes took advantage of the Indian Claims Commission established in 1946.

Prior to establishment of the Indian Claims Commission, the United States forced Indian tribes to take their cases directly to Congress, a branch of government not known for moving quickly to settle Indian land claims. For years the tribes had taken their problems involving land, water, and resources to Congress, without result. The Indian Claims Commission offered tribes a mechanism through which they could sue the federal government for treaty violations involving a host of issues. In every case settled by the Indian Claims Commission, the tribes received a monetary compensation rather than any land returned. Some Native Americans objected to this arrangement, but it was the only one used by the commission. For example, in settling claims of the numerous bands of Shoshoni and Bannock people, the Claims Commission separated the 1957 Shoshoni-Bannock claim into several parts, one of which dealt with the northern, northwestern, and western bands of Shoshoni. The case took so long that the U.S. Court of Claims made the determination of the case after the Claims Commission expired in 1978. On October 8, 1982, one section of the Shoshoni claim, which dealt with federal mismanagement of timber and grazing resources, was settled in favor of the Shoshoni bands, who were awarded $1.6 million.

In July 1951, the Nez Percé tribe of Idaho and the Nez Percé living on the Colville Reservation filed petitions with the Indian Claims Commission regarding compensation for the theft of their original homelands, particularly those in northeastern Oregon and western Idaho. The Claims Commission combined the petitions of the two groups into one claim on February 27, 1953. Finally, in 1971, the commission awarded the Nez Percé $3.5 million.

During the 1950s, the federal government sought to dissolve, or terminate, the reservation system and end its treaty and legal relationship with various tribes in the United States. Most notable was the government's attempt to terminate the Confederated Tribes of the Colville Reservation in Washington State. Colville tribal members living off the reservation generally favored termination because it would bring them a cash settlement. However, tribal members living on the reservation generally opposed termination, because it abrogated treaty rights and threatened to disperse Indian cultures and communities. The leaders of the Confederated Tribes struggled over the issue of termination during the 1950s and 1960s. The most vocal opponent of termination was Lucy Covington, a member of a prominent political family on the reservation. Covington stood nearly single-handedly against proponents of termination, and she never surrendered her position. As a result of her efforts, the tribe never agreed to termination, and it has been solidly opposed to the concept ever since.

Since the threat of termination receded in the 1960s, many tribes have made significant strides in health, education, and economic development. Each year the Colville Tribe sponsors workshops on cultural revitalization, and they encourage their young people to participate in their annual powwow and Circle Celebration held in Nespelem, Washington. The tribe owns a sawmill, a package log cabin sales business, and a trading post. Several young people attend colleges and universities in the region, and several students have returned to their reservation to contribute their expertise to developing the reservation economy and community. A similar situation has occurred on the Flathead Reservation, where the Kutenai, Kalispel, and Flathead have initiated a cultural heritage project to preserve their languages, oral histories, and songs. The Flathead tribe maintains a business relationship with Montana Power Company, which operates Kerr Dam on the reservation, and also operates a resort at Blue Bay along the shores of Flathead Lake.

The Shoshoni and Bannock tribal members from the Fort Hall Reservation are often employed in ranching, farming, and small businesses. The tribe owns its own agricultural enterprise as well as a construction business. Most important is the 20,000-acre irrigation project that the tribe operates, bringing water to Indians and non-Indians alike. The tribe enjoys its own health center, adult education program, and youth recreation program. The same is true at the Wind River Reservation in Wyoming, where suicide has plagued young people at a rate much higher than the national average. The Cayuse, Umatilla, and Walla Walla Indians living on the Umatilla Reservation in Oregon face similar problems, and they are responding by emphasizing both traditional culture and modern education. The tribe established a scholarship fund for college-age students, a day care center, and health education programs for young people. The emphasis on education and the encouragement of young people to seek post-secondary education is a common element of reservation life among the Indians of the plateau and mountains.

Nii'eihii No'eiihi', or the Eagle Drum, is the official ceremonial and social drum group of the Arapaho tribe. Their presence is required at any large gathering. Seated front left is Helen Cedartree, a noted elder of the tribe. Taken at the annual Ethete (Wyoming) Celebration Powwow.

Two of the most active tribes in the region in terms of educational and economic self-determination are the Warm Springs of Oregon and Yakima people in Washington. Indians of the Warm Springs Reservation have carefully logged the western edge of their reservation, and they have their own Warm Springs Forest Products Industries which include a sawmill and plywood plant. They also built their own resort and convention center called *Kah-Nee-Ta*, which has generated considerable money for programs in health and education. The elders encourage their young people to complete degrees in higher education, and some have returned to their homes to contribute to the well-being of their people. The Indians at Warm Springs have herds of wild horses, which they sell, and they manage a salmon hatchery through their own laws of fish and game. In 1982 the tribe became the first in the United States to open its own hydroelectric plant, the Pelton

Reregulating Dam, providing energy that is sold to the Pacific Power and Light Company. While the people of the Warm Springs Reservation have been successful in terms of education, health, and economic development, they have maintained a good deal of their traditional religion through the Washani religion—a spiritual faith they share with many Indians living on the Yakima Reservation.

Of all the tribes of the plateau and mountain region, the Yakima have been the most successful in maintaining their spiritual beliefs and promoting their own economic self-determination. The tribe manages its own forest products industry, annually cutting about 150 million board feet of lumber. They have their own furniture manufacturing plant, and manage 2.7 million acres of rangeland and 150,000 acres of farmland. The Yakima control their own water through the Wapato Project and have been highly successful in overseeing small businesses, banking, and fishing enterprises. With the funds the tribe has generated, it has initiated a major housing project, the Yakima Tribal Housing Authority. In addition, in 1980 the Yakima opened an extensive tribal cultural center, the largest of its kind in the country. Beautifully designed, shaped largely like a longhouse, the cultural center contains a library, museum, gift shop, theater, restaurant, and office space. The Yakima emphasize education, offering tribal scholarships to young people and a summer educational program that prepares students for college study. Each year, the Yakima people support numerous powwows and festivals to celebrate their heritage.

Programs for teaching Indian languages on the Colville, Umatilla, Nez Percé, Coeur d'Alene, Spokane, and Yakima reservations began in the 1970s and continue in the 1990s with even greater awareness of the need for language preservation. While the tribes themselves are responsible for the maintenance of language, university scholars have joined hands with some of the tribes to write and teach the language. Native Americans of the region consider language retention one of their most important projects.

Perhaps the most significant issue facing the Indians of the plateau and eastern mountain region is fishing rights. Native Ameri-

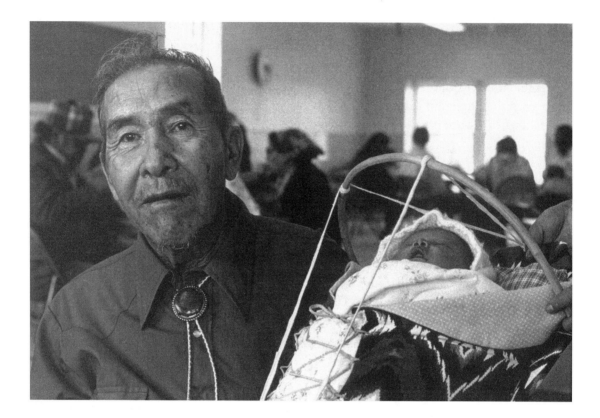

Ben Goggles was in his 70s when he died in 1978. He was the father of ten daughters and the head of the Arapaho Sun Dance for many years. His Arapaho name was Hoonino', or Quill.

cans in Washington, Oregon, and Idaho protested the destruction of the salmon, and they stood firm in their resolve to assert their treaty rights, which guaranteed them the right to fish, hunt, graze, and gather in all usual and accustomed areas on and off the reservations. The fight for fishing rights continued throughout the twentieth century. In 1974, the Boldt Decision acknowledged the right of Indians to fish in common with non-Indians, with Indians having the right to half of the harvestable fish catch. The Supreme Court has upheld the Boldt Decision, but opposition from state officials and recreational fishing organizations has not ended. The Nez Percé, Yakima, Palouse, Wanapum, and other tribes have continued to fight for their fishing rights and have stood against the discrimination they have suffered from state law enforcement agents, who refuse to recognize the federal treaty rights of the tribes.

The Boldt Decision has not ended the fishing rights struggle throughout the inland Northwest. During the 1980s, a case involving David Sohappy, an Indian elder of mixed Yakima and Wenatchi blood, illuminated the continual struggle of Native Americans to protect and defend their fishing rights. Sohappy represented the feelings of many northwestern Indians when he argued that his right to fish did not hinge merely on the articles of the Yakima Treaty of 1855. He insisted that the right to use the salmon had first come to the people as a result of Coyote—the trickster, changer—who, according to tradition, broke a dam guarded by monsters at the mouth of the Columbia River and led the salmon into the inland rivers.

As a result of exerting his traditional fishing rights, Sohappy was arrested by state and federal game and fish authorities. He was tried in a federal court and sentenced to prison in Spokane. He was later transferred to a federal jail in California. Ultimately, he was released from prison, but he continued to fight for fishing rights until his death. The fishing rights issue in the Northwest is an ongoing battle for Native Americans and those who support their rights. The fishing rights issue is such a major concern that it became a campaign issue during the race for Washington State governor in 1992. Times had changed, and many Washington State citizens supported Native people in their traditional and treaty rights to fish in their accustomed places. In November 1992, the state of Washington elected a governor who supported Indian treaty and fishing rights.

The Indians of the plateau, Great Basin, and mountains are a diverse people. All of them enjoyed a long history of

Cleone Thunder was born in 1903 and has lived most of her life in Wyoming. Her Arapaho name, Hiisei Nouuceh, or Woman Running out of the Lodge, was given to her by her father. It commemorates a brave Crow woman who ran from her tipi holding a baby and faced attacking Arapaho warriors.

growth and development before the arrival of Lewis and Clark. Yet all of them have been forced to contend with the United States as well as the state governments near their homes. They have lost most of their native estates and elements of their rich cultural heritages. They have all fought for their lives, sovereignty, and rights. They have all weathered many storms, and they all continue to exist today. Since the 1960s, the tribes have asserted themselves with greater vigor, offering tribally managed educational, health, and economic development programs. The tribes have attempted to preserve their languages and culture through diverse programs, projects, and institutions. The people of this region have a spirit about them tying their past traditions to life today. This spirit has sustained them since the time of creation, and this spirit will propel them into the twenty-first century.

Clifford E. Trafzer
University of California, Riverside

BIOGRAPHIES ✦ ✦ ✦ ✦ ✦ ✦ ✦ ✦ ✦ ✦ ✦ ✦ ✦ ✦ ✦ ✦ ✦ ✦

Ben Nighthorse
Campbell
1933-

Northern Cheyenne
U.S. senator

A successful politician, businessman, soldier, and athlete, Ben Nighthorse Campbell has served in the United States Congress since 1987. He was born in Auburn, California, and gave distinguished service in the air force during the Korean War. He also attended San Jose State College during the 1950s, becoming a judo champion there and graduating in 1957. Campbell's athletic career in judo was particularly outstanding, because he took the gold medal at the Pan-American Games in 1963 and won the United States championship in his weight division three times. He was also a member of the United States Olympic team in 1964 and wrote a judo manual, *Judo Drill Training* (1975).

Campbell became the second Native American elected to the Colorado legislature, where he served from 1983 to 1986. His committee assignments included agriculture and natural affairs, and business and labor. During this period he was also appointed as an advisor to the Colorado Commission on International Trade and the Arts and Humanities. He was named Outstanding Legislator of 1984 by the Colorado Bankers Association and was voted one of the Ten Best Legislators of 1986 in a survey of state legislators conducted by the *Denver Post* and News Center 4.

Campbell has always been a man of many talents. He founded a business called Nighthorse Jewelry Design and owns a horse ranch in Ignacio, Colorado. He was also inducted into the Council of 44 Chiefs by his native Northern Cheyenne tribe in Lame Deer, Montana.

A member of the Democratic party, Campbell was elected to the United States House of Representatives in 1987. Since then, he has served as a member of the House Committee on Agriculture and on the Committee on Interior and Insular Affairs, the latter of which includes a subcommittee on Indian affairs.

In November 1992, Coloradans elected Campbell to the U.S. Senate, the first Native American to serve there. Campbell is married and has two children.

Joseph (1840–1904)

Nez Percé tribal leader

Joseph was a Nez Percé born in the Wallowa Valley, in present-day Oregon. The Nez Percé lived in the area where the present-day states of Washington, Oregon, and Idaho adjoin. The various Indian tribes in this region signed the Isaac Steven's Treaty in 1855, ceding Indian lands in the Washington Territory in exchange for reservation lands, homes, tools, and money. As more settlers and miners arrived into the region, however, the treaty was ignored. Like his father before him, Joseph originally carried out a plan of passive resistance to U.S. land encroachment and efforts by the U.S. government to relocate his people to the Nez Percé Reservation, in present-day western Idaho.

A fragile peace was shattered in 1877, when U.S. settlers were moving into the Wallowa Valley. The government had recently overturned an earlier decision granting this land to the Nez Percé as a reservation, and they were given thirty days to relocate. On June 12, the inevitable fighting erupted when three young Nez Percé killed four settlers who had moved into the Wallowa Valley.

Joseph, Nez Percé Indian Chief, captured by Gen. Miles, Bear Paw Mountains, Montana, 1877.

After some initial battles, in which Joseph showed remarkable military skill by defeating superior U.S. forces, Joseph and the Nez Percé from the Wallowa Valley decided to attempt an escape into Canada. For roughly the next three months they eluded both U.S. troops and enemy Indian bands. In late September the Nez Percé group was only miles from the Canadian border when they found themselves surrounded and outnumbered by forces augmented with howitzer cannons and Gatlin guns, which were early machine guns. On October 5, 1877, Chief Joseph finally surrendered, but not before hundreds of Nez Percé escaped to Canada.

When the long odyssey was finally over, many of the Nez Percé leaders were dead or had escaped to Canada. The final surrender agreement was signed by Joseph. Subsequently, the exhausted leader is credited with giving a dramatic, often quoted, speech at the surrender. The actual text of the speech is unknown, and popular interpretations glowed in the hands of embellishing journalists. In the minds of the American public, Joseph became permanently identified with the courageous journey taken by the Nez Percé. According to historical accounts, the campaign of the Nez Percé in 1877 was characterized by restraint and relative nonviolence on the part of Joseph and the tribe. Sent to Indian Territory in Oklahoma, the Nez Percé were allowed to return to Idaho in 1883–84. Joseph spent the rest of his life on a number of different Indian reservations, but was allowed only a brief return to his homeland in the Wallowa Valley. He died on the Colville Indian Reservation in the state of Washington.

Ouray

c. 1820–80

Ute tribal leader

Ouray was born in what became Taos, New Mexico, and became a leader of the Ute, a nomadic tribe living in present-day Colorado. As a young man, Ouray was revered as a cunning and dangerous warrior, but his career shifted as he came to realize that white settlement in his tribe's territory was inevitable. With the growth of the mining frontier in western Colorado, the Ute had been forced by whites to cede more and more of their territory.

In 1863, Ouray helped negotiate a treaty with the federal government at Conejos, Colorado, in which the Ute ceded all lands east of the Continental Divide. In 1867, Ouray assisted Kit Carson, a U.S. Army officer, in suppressing a Ute uprising. In 1868, he accompanied Carson to Washington, D.C., and acted as spokesman for seven bands of Ute. In the subsequent negotiations, the Ute retained sixteen million acres of land.

The growth of the Colorado mining frontier continued, and more miners trespassed on Ute lands. In 1872, Ouray and eight other Ute again visited Washington, D.C., in an attempt to stress conciliation over warfare. As a result, the Ute were pressured into ceding four million acres for an annual payment of $25,000. For his services, Ouray received an additional annuity of $1,000.

Ouray encouraged his fellow tribesmen to increase their efforts at farming in an attempt to protect their claims to land. The Ute did not have a farming tradition, however, and many among them resisted, preferring their ancient hunting and gathering subsistence ways. Nathan Meeker, a new Indian agent who attempted to force farming upon the Ute, was evicted from the reservation. This resulted in a military confrontation that left twenty-three Ute dead, fourteen U.S. soldiers dead, and forty-three wounded. Ouray secured the release of Meeker's wife and daughter, who were captured during the battle.

Ouray traveled to Washington, D.C., again in 1880 and signed the treaty by which the White River Ute were to be relocated to the Unitah Reservation in Utah. Soon after his return from Washington, Ouray died while on a trip to Ignacio, Colorado, where the Southern Ute Agency had been relocated. He was buried at the Southern Ute Agency; however, his remains were later returned to Montrose, Colorado, for reburial.

Pocatello

1815–84

Shoshoni tribal leader

Born in the early 1800s, Pocatello became headman of the northwestern band of the Shoshoni Indians in 1847. This band was blamed for much of the violence along the California Trail, Salt Lake Road, and Oregon Trail as westward expansion and the California gold rush brought more and more settlers onto traditional Shoshoni lands in the northwestern corner of present-day Utah.

Pocatello was captured and imprisoned in 1859, but worked to maintain a delicate neutrality among the different Indian bands, Mormons, miners, ranchers, and missionaries who came into the Idaho region. In 1863, he signed the Treaty of Box Elder. From 1867 to 1869, he traveled and hunted with the Washakie's Wild River Shoshoni. By 1872, Pocatello's band was forced to relocate to the Fort Hall Indian Reservation in Idaho when the Union Pacific and Central Pacific railroads connected and brought further U.S. settlement into the region.

In order to be allowed to live on an off-reservation farm, Pocatello converted to Mormonism, a religion whose followers had settled at Salt Lake City, Utah. Ultimately, the local inhabitants requested federal troops to force Pocatello and other Shoshoni Indians to return to Fort Hall. Pocatello then rejected Mormonism and lived the remainder of his life at Fort Hall. He became known as General Pocatello to distinguish him from other members of his family. The town of Pocatello, Idaho, is named after this Indian leader.

Walkara (Walker)
1801–55

Ute tribal leader

Between 1830 and 1855, Walkara was probably the most powerful and renowned Native American leader in the Great Basin area, largely western Nevada. His daring bravery and cunning sagacity earned him nicknames such as Hawk of the Mountains, Iron-Twister, and Napoleon of the Desert. Walkara's sheer prowess, physical strength, and agility allowed him to gain enough influence to eventually surmount tribal feuds between the Ute, Paiute, and Shoshoni, and organize a corps of raiders who terrorized an area from the Mexican border almost to Canada, and from California to New Mexico.

A fierce opportunist, Walkara at various times collaborated with Indians, mountainmen, and Mormons, a religious sect that settled around Salt Lake in present-day Utah. In the winter of 1839, he and several companions stole more than three thousand horses in a daring night raid on the wealthiest Los Angeles rancheros. This escapade earned him the title Greatest Horse Thief in History. For over a decade, he and his followers raided villages for slaves and demanded goods and supplies from travelers on the

Old Spanish Trail, which passed through much of present-day Nevada. He became wealthy, kept a number of wives, and wore both Indian and American finery.

Accepting of the Mormons at first, Walkara even converted to their religion under the persistence of Brigham Young, an early founding leader of Mormonism. However, he soon became frustrated by their ubiquitous population of Ute tribal territories. Overgrazing of land, coupled with a measles epidemic, and an Indian-Mormon confrontation at Springville, Utah, led him to fight and lose the bitter "Walker War" in 1853. His power all but gone and his land now in the possession of the Mormons, Walkara died two years later. Fifteen horses were killed in his honor at his funeral.

Few Indians were as helpful to the westward passage of immigrants as Washakie. He was probably born in Montana's Bitterroot Mountains. When his father died, Washakie went to live with his mother's eastern Shoshoni family in the Wind River mountain chain of Wyoming. He was evidently a brave fighter as a young man against the Blackfeet and Crow. The Shoshoni in this area maintained friendship with mountain men and trappers. During the 1820s through the 1830s, Washakie met and became friends with Jim Bridger, the famous mountain man, and Christopher "Kit" Carson, the U.S commander who rounded up the Navajo in the 1860s.

Washakie became the principal head of his band in the 1840s. The Shoshoni became known for their hospitable relations with the United States. Washakie went as far as providing regular patrols of his men to guard and assist immigrants along that region of the Oregon Trail. During this time, he became friends with Brigham Young and spent part of one winter at the Mormon leader's home.

Washakie's band settled on the Wind River Reservation in present-day Wyoming. The Treaty of Fort Bridger in 1863 guaranteed safe passage for U.S. travelers in exchange for a twenty-year annuity paid to Washakie. The same year, he signed a second treaty giv-

Washakie (Gambler's Gourd) 1804–1900

Flathead-Shoshoni tribal leader

ing the Union Pacific Railroad Company right-of-way to lay track in the region. The Shoshoni served as scouts for the military against the Arapaho, Cheyenne, Sioux, and Ute in 1869, when Camp Brown was constructed in present-day Wyoming. In 1876, Washakie and two hundred warriors joined forces too late to help General Crook against the Sioux at the Battle of the Rosebud in southern Montana, but harrassed and pursued Crazy Horse's warriors to the Powder River region in present-day eastern Montana.

In honor of Washakie's assistance to the U.S. military, Camp Brown was renamed Fort Washakie in 1878. President Ulysses S. Grant gave Washakie a silver saddle that same year, and five years later President Chester A. Arthur visited Washakie during a trip to Yellowstone Park. In 1897, Washakie became a Christian and was baptized as an Episcopalian. He died three years later and was buried with full military honors at the fort bearing his name.

*N*ative Peoples of California

Without exception, the Native peoples of California believe they originated in North America. Despite unproven theories of a Siberian origin and migration favored by the non-Indian academics, traditional origin stories tell of a creator or creators whose wondrous powers brought forth the physical universe and all plant and animal life. The members of each group saw themselves as the center of that creation and viewed their neighbors as less favored. This cultural centrism created the precedent that tribal territories were sacred and intimately connected the divine intentions of the Creator. Consequently, land, place, and sacred sites all had a tie to the Creator and to traditional events that were the major events and symbols in Indian histories.

At the time of first contact with Europeans (1540), the population of the California Indians was approximately 310,000 to 340,000 people. These astounding numbers made it the most densely populated area in what is now the United States. The mild climate and abundance of wild foods proved more than adequate sustenance for such a population (see map below). Social organization among this population varied. The San Joaquin Valley Yokut and the Yuman along the Colorado River are examples of large tribes sharing a common language and possessing a well-defined territory and a degree of political unity. More common was the organization of populations that were essentially village centered, sometimes called tribelets. These groups, too, possessed well-defined territories. Villages ranged in size from 100 to 500 persons, with several villages displaying allegiance to a large central village where the headman or chief resided. Although neither type of social organization permitted chiefs more than limited ceremonial authority, they were most often wise and influential individuals who could galvanize community action, if supported by various types of councils made up of lineage elders. While female chiefs were not unknown, the majority were men whose succession to office was hereditary. Other authority figures included a shaman—a combination physician, psychologist, herbalist, and spiritual leader—and family lineage heads. Social and economic stratification existed to a varying degree throughout aboriginal California, but it was most pronounced in northwestern California, which in many ways resembled the hierarchical and ordered societies of the Pacific Northwest area.

Because of the varied ecological zones found throughout the state, several regional economic adaptive strategies shaped the economy and food quest. Northern coastal tribes fished, hunted sea mammals, and collected tidelands resources. Riverine and lakeshore dwelling groups hunted, trapped, and fished. Central valley, Plains, and foothill tribes hunted and gathered wild foodstuffs. The greatest variety of regional lifeways and economic activities were found in southern California. The Channel Islands, near present-day Los Angeles, and adjacent coast were

Contemporary California Indian tribes.

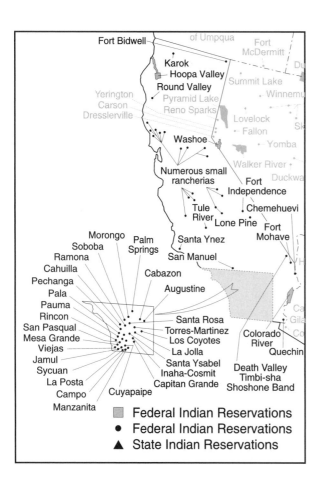

rich in sea-associated resources. Inland groups hunted and collected, while tribes living along the Colorado River, and a few neighboring groups, practiced the only agriculture found in aboriginal California.

Native Californian world view centered typically around seeking a balance between physical and spiritual well-being of the extended family and tribe. Such balance in both spheres is best understood in terms of reciprocity. For instance, individuals and villages made offerings to the Creator and earth spirits and, in return, expected a favorable relationship between themselves and the natural elements, such as access to game animals, wild foods, favorable winds, sufficient rain, fertility, and the like. Similarly, reciprocity formed the basis for economic relationships between individuals, extended families, and neighboring villages. Each group's territory and its resources were jealously guarded. Trespassing and poaching were serious offenses and were the principal causes of intergroup conflicts that periodically erupted.

♦ ♦ ♦ ♦ ♦ ♦ ♦ ♦ ♦ ♦ ♦ ♦ ♦ ♦ ♦ ♦ **EUROPEAN CONTACT**

The arrival of Europeans in California illustrates the profoundly different world views that clashed as various European empires scrambled to exploit the resources and peoples of the Americas. The story of one of the earliest European encounters illustrates this point well. In 1579, the English explorer Francis Drake anchored somewhere off the Sonoma County coast, in present-day northern California. The astounded Coast Miwok peoples exhibited behavior that seemed both incredible and incomprehensible to the English sailors.

English understandings of that encounter included a number of erroneous assumptions. Records of the Drake expedition refer to the headman of the local Indians as a "king," implying a European-like, highly centralized office of authority that could control both subjects' land and lives. In fact, no such offices of authority existed anywhere in Native California societies. The

The traditional tribal areas of the Indians of California.

English also claim this "king" gladly surrendered all of "his" territory and sovereignty to an unknown ruler half a world away. Finally, the English concluded the Coast Miwok regarded them as "gods."

The Coast Miwok, on the other hand, viewed all material objects of the pale strangers who arrived on their shores with fear and refused to accept the newcomers' gifts. At the same time, they offered gifts of baskets, food, and other ritual objects. While the men showed considerable awe and reverence towards the strangers, the Native women's behavior bewildered the sailors. Females tore at their cheeks and upper chests, crying and shrieking and throwing themselves on the rocky landscape while walking among the young Englishmen. Following a five-week stay, the newcomers departed, still baffled by the odd reception offered them by the otherwise hospitable Natives.

The mystery of the Indians' peculiar behavior was solved when anthropological data provided by Native traditionalists revealed elements of Coast Miwok culture that provided a reasonable explanation. The Coast Miwok Indians believed the land of the dead lay to the west; in fact, the path to that place passed directly beyond Drake's encampment. The women were exhibiting mourning behavior. The young English sailors had sparse beards (like Native men) and were furthermore deeply tanned from years of open-ocean sailing. The English gifts were refused because of strict sanctions about bringing back anything from the land of the dead. Clearly, the Coast Miwok believed they had been visited by their departed ancestors.

♦ ♦ ♦ ♦ ♦ ♦ ♦ ♦ ♦ ♦ ♦ ♦ ♦ ♦ ♦ **SPANISH COLONIZATION**

Permanent colonization created a catastrophe of indescribable proportions for the Indians of California. Spanish colonization began in earnest in 1769 with the establishment of a mission in the Native village of Cosoy, later called San Diego by the newcomers. The Spanish institutions of colonization were the military presidios (or forts) to protect the Franciscan missionaries, and later the Hispanic colonists who established pueblos (civilian towns). It was the missions, however, that had the greatest impact on the Native population. The Spanish empire's plan was to reduce the numerous free and independent Native hunting and collecting villages and societies into a mass of peon laborers. To accomplish this goal, the padres created a chain of twenty-three missions, with two missions on the Colorado River in the extreme southeastern tip of the state and a string along the coast from San Diego to Sonoma in the north. These institutions were much more than churches. When fully functional, they resembled Caribbean plantations. Under Spanish law, once baptized, the neophytes, as the Indians were called, would be compelled to move from their Native villages into designated areas adjacent to the mission. Between 1769 and 1836, about 80,000 California Indians were baptized and subjected to the mission labor and evangelization programs of the Spanish Empire.

At the missions, the Indians could be more closely controlled. At the age of five or six, the neophyte children were removed from their families and locked in dorm-like barracks under the vigilance of colonists. This served the dual purpose of indoctrinating the children and ensuring that their parents would not attempt to oppose colonial authority. Indian girls were locked up when not laboring or attending religious services, were freed only after marriage, and, if widowed, were again confined in the female barracks until remarriage or death. Adults were compelled to labor without pay. The soldiers and padres instituted floggings, incarceration, and various labor punishments to compel Native acquiescence to Spanish authority. Neither women nor children were exempt from beatings and other forms of compulsion. One Costanoan Indian neophyte named Lorenzo Asisara reported, "We were always trembling with fear of the lash."

The missions were only supposed to exist for ten years, a time limit the Spanish Crown deemed sufficient to convert the Indians into a disciplined and subservient labor force for a small elite of Spanish males. The sincerity of "religious conversions" under such circumstances is doubtful. Despite these harsh measures, considerable resistance erupted among the "converts." As Spanish borderlands historian David Weber observed, "Oppressed in body and spirit, many mission Indians sought ways to extricate themselves from the loving embrace of the sons of St. Francis."

Three types of resistance developed to the nightmare that Native groups found themselves caught up in. The first and most prevalent form of resistance was passive. Many mission Indians either refused to learn Spanish or feigned ignorance of commands given in that language. Slow and poorly performed labor was widely reported and can be seen today in the construction and work of the old missions. Native laborers covertly drew traditional Indian symbols on fired floor tiles and other surfaces throughout the mission's buildings. Both infanticide and abortions were practiced by Native women unwilling to give birth to children conceived through sexual assaults by the soldiers or to supply a new generation of laborers for the colonists. A fascinating aspect of passive resistance was the periodic outbreak of covert Native religious activities to reverse baptisms or offer solace to the terrified masses of neophytes.

Fugitivism or simply running away from the Franciscan labor mills seemed to be the simplest solution, once the unsavory and oppressive nature of mission life was revealed. But Spanish law and Franciscan practice permitted the soldiers to pursue runaway Indians. The padres kept detailed records of baptized Indians for each village, and squads of soldiers stationed at each mission routinely patrolled the surrounding territories. Furthermore, Native traditions forbade anyone not belonging to a village from demanding refuge there. Non-Christian villages soon learned that if they did offer refuge to runaways, they risked military assaults and hostage-taking. Worse still, the fugitives infected non-Christian village populations with the new diseases contracted at the missions. Murderous waves of epidemic diseases and the general poor health of the neophyte population kept many from even attempting the physical rigors of flight. Nevertheless, widespread fugitivism was reported. Thousands of Indian neophytes fled. However, only about 10 percent, or about 8,000, escaped the missions.

Overt resistance to Spanish domination took several forms. A type of guerrilla warfare became prevalent before 1820. Charismatic and talented ex-neophytes like the Coast Miwok Pomponio and the Northern Valley Yokut Estanislao organized stock-raiding attacks against mission, presidio, and civilian herds of cattle, horses, and sheep.

Individuals and groups of mission Indians sometimes poisoned the padres. Four padres were poisoned at Mission San Miguel, and one of them died in 1801. In 1811, a San Diego neophyte killed a padre with poison. The next year, Indians at Mission Santa Cruz smothered and castrated a padre there for making an especially terrifying new torture instrument and being unwise enough to announce he would employ it the next Sunday. In 1836, southern California Cahuilla Indians kidnapped the padre at Mission San Gabriel and horsewhipped him, as so many of their tribesmen had been whipped.

Mission Indian insurrections were spectacular, and several occurred. The earliest revolt occurred at Mission San Diego in October 1775, when 1,000 Kumeyaay warriors sacked and burned the mission and killed the padre. In 1781, the Quechan Indians living along the banks of the Colorado River utterly destroyed two missions established in their territory just the previous year. In that rebellion, they killed fifty-five colonists, including four padres, thirty-one soldiers, and twenty civilians. That military action denied access to the only known overland route to California from Mexico for the remainder of the Spanish era.

In 1785, San Gabriel Mission neophytes, organized by a female shaman called Toypurina, were thwarted in their attempt to destroy the mission and kill the padres. At her trial, the defiant holy woman declared, "I hate the padres and all of you for living here on my native soil . . . for trespassing upon the lands of my forefathers and despoiling our tribal domains."

That sentiment provoked the last large-scale revolt by mission Indians. The Chumash Indians of the Santa Barbara coast had endured nearly three decades of colonization when, in 1824, neophytes from missions Santa Barbara, San Ynez, and La Purisima rose en masse to protect their lives and regain their lost freedom and sovereignty. A pitched battle ensued at Mission Santa Barbara, and then the Indians fled. Santa Ynez neophytes also abandoned their mission and joined the others from Santa Barbara at Mission La Purisima, which they took over for longer than a month.

Although most of the rebellious Indians were eventually persuaded to surrender after a siege and full-scale assault by presidio troops using cannons, a significant number of them absolutely refused to return to the missions and instead sought refuge in the interior, where they issued this defiant message to colonial authorities who pleaded with them to return: "We shall maintain ourselves with what God will provide for us in the open country. Moreover, we are soldiers, stone-masons, carpenters, etc., and we will provide for ourselves by our work."

Despite their defiant sentiments, it was the introduced diseases that ultimately destroyed the majority of Native peoples in contact with the colonists. Native Americans had no immunities to even the most common European childhood diseases. A series of murderous epidemics swept through the mission Indian populations from 1777 to 1833. Thousands of Indian men, women, and children succumbed to the previously unknown diseases. When the missions finally collapsed in 1836, about 100,000 Indians had died.

The independence movement that created the Mexican Republic (1820) forbade the Franciscan padres from compelling labor from the Indians. The Mexican government allowed Indians to leave the missions, but corrupt officials conspired to prevent a distribution of developed lands to surviving ex-mission Indians. Those tribesmen whose native territories now included missions, presidios, and pueblos were nearly universally deprived of their lands and forced deeply into debt peonage, which resulted in further powerlessness. Many ex-neophytes fled into the interior or to their former tribal domains. But the landscape had changed profoundly. The horses, mules, sheep, pigs, and goats introduced into the California biosphere ravaged the delicate Native grasses and continued to multiply in alarming numbers. Mission agricultural practices began to systematically squeeze out Native vegetation. The California Indians were less able to live off the land than before Spanish colonization.

Some tribes and village populations had virtually disappeared from the face of the earth. So many lineages had been destroyed that the previous forms of aboriginal leadership no longer existed. Out of this political vacuum evolved new leaders, who assumed much more authority than had been previously allowed any single individual in aboriginal society. Some assumed the Spanish title of alcalde, or captain, and adapted aboriginal life to include the hunting and capturing of half-wild horses and mules, which provided food and valued trade items. Patterning their tactics on the mission Indian stock raiders of the recent past, a widespread and lucrative stock-raiding complex emerged in post-mission California. Among these new leaders was an ex-neophyte Plains Miwok called Yozcolo, who terrorized the Hispanic military and civilian populations around southern San Francisco Bay, until he was killed in battle near Los Gatos in 1839.

In southern California, Cahuilla, Mohave, and Gabrielino tribesmen joined forces with New Mexico mountain men in a decade-long series of raids that devastated the Californios' livestock. One spectacular raid in 1840 involved the theft of more than three thousand horses from ranches as far north as San Luis Obispo, to San Juan Capistrano in the south. The Californios pursuing the stolen horses suffered the indignity of having their mounts stolen while resting. Having no choice, they walked across the desert until they were picked up by another group of Californios.

The Swiss immigrant Johann August Sutter established a fortress deep in the interior of the Sacramento Valley, after promising Mexican authorities to stem the tide of stock-raiding that seriously threatened Mexican authority. Like other colonists of the period, he established a private army of Indians to protect his fort and enslave free Indians.

Despite a steady decline in the Native population throughout this period, the constant onslaught of stock raids began to push back interior Mexican outposts. After 1840, numerous interior ranches were abandoned under threat from the now well-mounted and armed groups of "horse thief Indians." Even Sutter began futile efforts to sell his fortress to the Mexican government after costly campaigns with interior Miwok warriors. But the Mexican government had, by 1845, lost control of the actions of its own citizens. The authority of the Mexican Republic was about to collapse. Meanwhile, both disease and violence had taken a grim toll on Native lives. By 1845, little over 100,000 California Indians survived the Mexican Republic's occupation of their territories.

The Bear Flag Revolt and the Mexican War (1846–48) brought momentous changes for the Native peoples of California. The majority of Indians who were involved in that conflict allied themselves with the Americans. Company H of the California Battalion was made up of Central Valley Miwok and Yokut warriors. In southern California, loyalties were split. Some, like the mountain Cahuilla chief Juan Antonio, fought for the Mexican Republic, while others participated on the U.S. side in the Battle for Los Angeles in 1847. However, the new U.S. occupation brought yet more death and labor exploitation to Native groups, whatever their loyalties.

Shortly after the Treaty of Guadalupe Hidalgo ended the Mexican-American War in 1848, a flood of gold miners descended upon California. Most of the Sierra Nevada and foothill tribesmen had been only indirectly affected by Hispanic colonization efforts, which were concentrated along the coast, but now they would bear the brunt of an incredibly violent horde of immigrants. Early in the gold rush, a few Indians were employed by miners or mined gold on their own. Soon Indians found themselves hunted like wild game.

Worse still was a series of state laws passed in the mid-1850s. These laws virtually enslaved Indians and institutionalized the legal kidnapping of Indian children for labor and sexual exploitation, despite the fact that California entered the Union as a "free state" in 1851. At the same time, the federal government was negotiating treaties with California Indians (1851–52). These treaties promised the Indians 7.5 million acres of land in exchange for surrendering the remainder of the state. A deluge of protests from non-Indian Californians fearing that the treaty lands might contain gold was sufficient to assure the treaties' defeat in the U.S. Senate, which must ratify all treaties. Afterwards, the bewildered and now hunted Indians were subjected to the earliest form of reservation life. The federal government began establishing reservations in the state in 1851. They were located on military reserves, where the Native population supposedly would be protected from U.S. citizens by the army.

The government reserves in reality served fewer than 2,000 Indians at any given time. The vast majority of California Indians survived the best they could, withdrawing into remote and marginal areas and attempting to avoid contact with U.S. settlers. But violence against them continued, ranging from casual homicide of individuals to vigilante raids and the occasional army massacre.

Protesting the taxation of their small cattle herd, the Kupa Indians of southern California fought a war against the citizens of San Diego in 1851. The Hupa Indians of northern California successfully fought vigilante and militia campaigns until 1864, when they were granted a reservation of their own, now the largest in the state. The last and largest war against California Indians was fought against the Modoc Indians of northeastern California. Under the leadership of Captain Jack (see his biography), fifty Modoc warriors and their families held off an army of over 3,000 for nearly a year. In the end, Jack and three others surrendered and were hanged by orders of a paramilitary court. Captain Jack and Schochin John were decapitated following their deaths; their heads were sent to Washington, D.C. and eventually wound up in the Smithsonian Institution.

By 1870, a new religious movement called the Ghost Dance swept west from Nevada, predicting the end of the world and promising the return of dead relatives and the game animals. Desperate Natives who had experienced first-hand the appalling widespread death, violence, and now real starvation, found the doctrines especially appealing. The movement lasted about two years and revitalized the Kuksu and Hesi ceremonies among the Pomo, Patwin, and neighboring groups. It also developed a new class of spiritual leaders called dreamer doctors. Finally, the Ghost Dance prophesy of the end of the world proved true, for the Indian world was gone.

It is no coincidence that the Ghost Dance swept through California when it did. Just prior to that event, the federal government had inaugurated a new policy to reform the widespread corruption in the Office of Indian Affairs (renamed the Bureau of Indian Affairs, or BIA, in the late 1940s). Part of that plan, called President Ulysses S. Grant's Peace Policy of 1869, called for the introduction of educational programs for Indian children. However, that policy once more unleashed hordes of missionaries upon the Indians to "save" them. Native ceremonies were outlawed on many reservations in a misguided effort to make Indians adopt U.S. culture and lifeways.

The federal campaign to educate Indian children was launched aggressively in 1879. Off-reservation boarding schools took Indian children thousands of miles from their homes and subjected them to military-type discipline. Native languages were forbidden, corporal punishment was used freely, and starchy foods

Spring Rancheria (Cahuilla), c. 1886.

dominated their diets. The dormitories echoed with children's homesick and lonely cries. The legacy of these social engineering policies was the creation of several generations of Indians who, abducted from their tribes, returned home virtual strangers, unable to communicate with their elders and ignorant of the skills and knowledge to continue practicing their culture. Even more sinister was the lack of parenting skills in the generations of Indian mothers and fathers. Preventing such practical skills from developing is an effective element in any plan to destroy a people.

The next approach was to divide the corporate tribally owned lands on reservations into tiny private parcels. This federal program, called the Dawes Allotment Act of 1887, was intended to introduce the Indians to private ownership of property. If an Indian moved onto his allotment, cut his hair, surrendered his children to the boarding schools, severed his tribal ties, and did exactly as told by the Indian agent for twenty years, he could receive title to his allotment, pay taxes on his land, and become a citizen of the United States. However, like other tribal peoples, California Indians considered this act yet another attack on their religious beliefs about the earth and the tribe's relationship to it. In practice, it proved to be a tool to deprive Indians of their remaining lands, and, almost everywhere, Indians opposed the Dawes Act. Nevertheless, the Office of Indian Affairs' missionaries and so-called reformers were unrelenting in these efforts, and countless others, to make the Indians into what they considered acceptable people.

By 1900, fewer than 18,000 California Indians survived after 130 years of colonization and foreign domination. This staggering population decline left the Indians dazed, reeling, and deeply demoralized. Hunger, destitution, homelessness, unemployment, and discrimination were widespread, yet a number of Native leaders worked diligently for their communities.

Following in the path of the activist Indian Rights Association of Philadelphia, a group of southern California citizens organized the Sequoya League. They assisted the Kupa Indians, who had

lost a bid in the Supreme Court to keep their ancestral home, now called Warner's Hot Springs in the mountainous interior of San Diego County. Through their efforts, Kupa leaders reluctantly selected a new home nearby at a place called Pala. Similar groups in northern California helped secure small homesite reservations, called rancherias, for homeless Pomo Indians at Manchester (near Point Arena in Mendocino County) and for Wintun Indians at Chico.

Sensioni Cibimoat, basket maker from Warner's Ranch, 1903.

One of the choice ironies of the boarding school experience was the unexpected development of a pan-tribal consciousness that emerged among Indian youth, which gave birth to pan-Indian reform groups. The first reform group to actually include California Indians was the Mission Indian Federation (MIF), founded in 1919. The MIF relentlessly attacked incompetent Indian administration officials and policies. Even urban Indians in Los

Angeles had an active chapter. The group worked for more autonomy for tribal governments, full civil rights for Indians, protection of Indian water rights, opposition to the Dawes Act, and the elimination of the Bureau of Indian Affairs. In 1921, fifty-seven MIF leaders were arrested for conspiracy against the government for their opposition to allotment. Eventually all charges were dropped.

The first all-Indian reform group, formed in northern California by Stephen Knight and other Pomo Indians, was the California Indian Brotherhood. That group sought rancherias for homeless Indians and integration of Indian children into public schools with free lunches and clothing assistance. This far-sighted group even sought opportunities for college education for Indian youth.

Gabrielino traditional homes, Mission San Gabriel.

The problems confronting twentieth-century California Indian survivors had many similarities, with some variation from com-

munity to community. One issue united them, however, like no other—the enduring sense of injustice regarding the broken federal treaties of 1851–52. There was little incentive for the treaties to be honored, since Indians had no voting rights and no way to pressure elected officials. But Native peoples never forgot those solemn promises and were determined to seek redress. Virtually all reform groups, as well as individual tribes, sought some kind of solution for more than half a century. Eventually, two settlements were reached. The first, in 1944, eventually paid $150 to every California Indian who could prove biological legacy to an Indian alive in 1850. A second effort, through the Indian Claims Commission (a federal entity established on the basis of the pioneering claims of the California Indians), resulted in payment of only $.47 an acre in compensation for lands outside treaty areas. Despite protests, the government per capita payments to individuals resulted in less than $800 per person paid in 1968. Few desperately poor Indians could turn down even that meager amount. However, a small number of Indians refused to cash those checks in hopes of yet a new settlement.

Another important contemporary issue remains education. Federal off-reservation boarding schools were supplemented by reservation boarding schools and day schools before 1900. These schools allowed families to remain in contact, but chronic illness and lack of clothing, food, and even shoes caused considerable absenteeism, which eventually closed many of them. By 1917, the public schools began to experience increased enrollment of Indian children. When Congress gave U.S. citizenship to all Indians in 1924, a gradual transfer of Indian students to public schools followed. But academic success did not. Racial and cultural prejudices in textbooks and among teachers led to isolation, shame, and feelings of low self-esteem for Indian children and set them up for failure. The classrooms became battlegrounds where Indian children had to endure the negative experience or fight back. The latter course ensured a perpetual cycle of academic failure, condemning generations of Indian children to economic failure and unemployment.

Ramona Lugu, Cahuilla, at her home.

One important focus of reform efforts was health access. While seven Indian hospitals had been established at boarding schools and other sites by 1930, local hospitals often refused to treat the Native population, claiming that was the federal government's responsibility. A growing chorus of criticism prompted the establishment of a separate division of health within the Bureau of Indian Affairs in 1924. Public health nurses were then allowed to provide services to Indians. However, services were still denied to unrecognized and homeless Indians, leaving as many as one-third of the Indian population without medical care. A new wave of indignation was forcefully expressed in a federal hearing conducted in 1929, but ironically these hearings only confirmed a 1912 survey that showed the health of the Indian population was dismal. Ultimately, the loss of their land base and food resources crippled their ability to rebound.

Approximately thirty reservations had been established by 1900. The northern California Indians' critical need for land was addressed in a series of congressional acts to provide homesites for landless Indians. By 1930, an additional thirty-six parcels of federal trust properties called rancherias were established. They had the same status as reservations but were substantially smaller, and they lacked developed water sources. Indians have been critical of the Bureau of Indian Affairs for failing to protect water rights, a problem that has plagued reservation leaders to this day. Allotment, or forced division of Indian trust lands into individual parcels, was pursued by the BIA despite the fact that these parcels were often of very small size. Considerable evidence points to the common practice of manipulating tribal leaders through assignment of choice reservation lands to Indians willing to cooperate with government interests. Numerous abuses and a national scandal concerning the loss of millions of acres of allotted lands finally prompted Congress to act. The new Franklin Roosevelt administration's Indian Reorganization Act of 1934 ended allotment and permitted formation of tribal governments. Despite this however, tribal governments effectively remained under economic control of the Bureau of Indian Affairs.

♦ **TERMINATION**

The end of World War II (1945) heralded an era of anti-communist xenophobia that ultimately stalled the slow but steady reform in the Bureau of Indian Affairs. The Hoover Commission study of 1948 recommended severing all federal relations with Indian tribes and peoples, including federal assistance to Indian peoples, whose poverty the government had engineered in the first place. That policy would be called "termination." The program called for an end to all health, education, and welfare assistance provided by the federal government and envisioned a division of tribal lands to individuals. In reality, it was a resurrection of the discredited Dawes Allotment Act of 1887.

California Indians were an early target; after allotment, Indian land would eventually be subject to state property taxation. Until then, immunity from state taxation allowed poverty-stricken Indians to retain their lands. Taxing them would bring about the final dispossession of the land through tax defaults. Furthermore, dispossession would bring disintegration to Native California's tribes, communities, and cultures—and the so-called Indian problem would finally be solved, at least as far as the government was concerned. By 1952, Congress had enthusiastically embraced termination. The BIA sold over 1,200 allotments. In the following year, California came under Public Law 280, an act that would further termination goals by turning over civil and criminal jurisdiction from federal authorities to state and local authorities. At first, state and local governments were enthusiastic, envisioning an expanded tax base. However, after several years of study, it became apparent that the burden of services it would have to assume would far outweigh any tax revenues. Consequently, their enthusiasm began to cool rapidly, though not before Congress passed the Rancheria Act of 1958. This act provided for reservation and rancheria members to decide whether to accept or reject termination. Federal authorities descended upon the isolated and powerless rancheria residents with exaggerated promises of new housing, road and domestic water system improvements, and even college scholarships for Native children. Oblivious to the looming threat of tax defaults, the BIA eventually convinced thirty-six of the most isolated and least sophisticated California Indian groups into committing tribal and cultural suicide by accepting termination. Sure enough, by 1970, 5,000 acres of tribal lands were lost to tax defaults and forced sales. The stunned and reeling tribesmen lost their recognition as Indians, and cultural and social decay of Indian community institutions accelerated.

CULTURAL REVITALIZATION ✦ ✦ ✦ ✦ ✦ ✦ ✦ ✦ ✦ ✦ ✦ ✦ ✦

The modern era of California Indian affairs can be divided into civil rights and cultural survival. The national sweep of the civil rights era from the mid-1960s to the present afforded new opportunities for national attention to the cause of the American Indians. On college campuses, racial minorities and their supporters demanded the hiring of minority faculty and staff, along with aggressive recruiting of minority students. The first college to establish a Native American studies program was San Francisco State University. The program's faculty, staff, and students were largely made up of non-California Indians relocated to the San Francisco Bay Area from other states, under part of a national termination program. Followed shortly by the University of California, Berkeley, and the University of California, Los Angeles (UCLA), these programs provided a multidisciplinary approach to the study of American Indians in the past and present.

Most importantly, the new Native studies programs addressed the future of American Indians and tribalism. The idea of actually controlling the future and shaping federal Indian policy made for an intoxicating euphoria that provided a kind of self-assurance not witnessed among Native leaders since the Indian wars of the last century. It furthermore produced a new generation of leaders, pressing legal and other avenues toward creating self-sufficient and responsible Native communities, new scholars contributing to the academic study of the American Indians, and numerous public school teachers in classrooms throughout the state. Both UCLA and UC Berkeley have developed important scholarly journals, the *American Indian Quarterly* and the *American Indian Culture and Research Journal*.

More access to health and legal services also emerged during this period. The California Rural Indian Health Board was established in 1968 to fund several demonstration projects in fifteen rural and reservation communities, restoring services that in many cases had been denied California Indians since 1956. Legal assistance on issues of land, water, and civil rights became available as part of the U.S. government's War on Poverty programs of the 1970s. California Indian Legal Services strengthened tribal ability to oppose still-archaic BIA policies. They continue to provide important leverage in fighting for civil rights of Indian individuals and tribes.

This era also gave rise to a succession of land occupations by Native peoples in California, setting a national trend. In fall 1969, fewer than one hundred Indian college students from UCLA, UC Berkeley, and San Francisco State landed on Alcatraz Island to reclaim that abandoned federal prison as Indian land, causing a media sensation around the world. The Native Americans cleverly pointed out that the island was just like reservations: no water, no electricity, no jobs! They also pointed out that it was isolated from the wealth that surrounds it. At last, Native peoples had discovered a vehicle that would focus attention on the current conditions of America's aboriginal people. Following the Alcatraz occupation, other land occupations occurred, such as the protest attempted by the Pit River Indians at a public utility campground in Shasta County in 1971. The Pomo Indian occupation of an abandoned national defense radio listening station in rural Sonoma County resulted in the establishment of Ya-Ka-Ama (our land), an educational and Native plant center. A similar occupation near the University of California at Davis resulted in the establishment of a fully accredited American Indian junior college called Deganaweda-Quetzelquatl University.

Unprecedented population growth in California during the 1970s and 1980s resulted in the construction of millions of new homes and businesses, unearthing thousands of California Indian burials and occupation sites. Traditionalists were dismayed that archaeologists intended to add the findings to existing inventories of skeletons and

Powwow singers,

Alcatraz Island, 1969.

other objects found in Indian burials, long neglected and seldom studied, gathering dust in warehouses, archaeology labs, and campus basements. Anthropologists claimed that they were the Indians' best friends and that much valuable information could be gained from the "data," as they euphemistically referred to the remains of Native ancestors. The Indians demanded to know why these human remains continue to be removed from the ground and why it only happens to Indians.

About this time, it was discovered that the skull of nationally known Modoc war leader (1872) Captain Jack was part of the physical anthropology collection of the Smithsonian Institution in Washington, D.C. Outrage over this case and thousands of other lesser-known Indian skeletons and burial goods led to a national program of repatriation of the thousands and thousands of Indian skeletons

Sign pointing to Pit River Nation, 1973.

to their tribes of origin. In 1978, Governor Edmund G. Brown, Jr. created the Native American Heritage Commission (NAHC), which took on the responsibility of mitigating human remains issues associated with construction. The NAHC attempted to compel universities and other state agencies holding human remains to submit plans for the ultimate disposition of the remains and associated burial goods. The NAHC has become an effective clearing house for these matters. Recent federal laws of 1990 mandate that federally funded museums inventory their American Indian human skeleton collections and develop a plan for repatriation to appropriate tribes. While a few archaeologists have argued against this policy, most agree that little new scientific information has been developed from collections that have already been in their possession for as long as a century. Native peoples often counter, that, if these human remains indeed possess such valuable data, why, then, are they not being systematically studied? For traditional peoples, it is a simple matter of dignity and the respect all citizens expect of their government and its laws.

TRIBAL RECOGNITION ✦ ✦ ✦ ✦ ✦ ✦ ✦ ✦ ✦ ✦ ✦ ✦ ✦ ✦ ✦ ✦

In retrospect, it seems miraculous that Native cultures in California survived at all, yet they have not only survived but have actually undergone a renaissance. Indian education centers throughout the state have developed Native language, culture, and dance classes. The first tribally controlled museum was established by Cahuilla traditionalists on the Morongo Indian Reservation in 1964. The Malki Museum also developed an impressive publication program, including the scholarly quarterly *The Journal of California Anthropology.* Several other reservation communities have followed suit.

In 1987, an entirely unique publication, called *News From Native California,* began publication. The widely read quarterly covers history, ethnography, current events, legislation, and the arts. Another event unique to California is the annual California Indian Conference, established in 1984. This event brings together scholars, Native traditionalists, and experts at state and federal levels to share their research and interests in the past, present, and future of California Indians. Usually, it is hosted by a major college; in 1992, it was held at Sonoma State University.

Recently, California Indian artists, both traditional and contemporary, have established a national reputation in the larger Indian art world. While late nineteenth- and early twentieth-century California Indian basketmakers have long been acknowledged as the finest in the world, a well-documented decline in the number of practitioners occurred over the last sixty years. With recent new interest in that important Native art form, a new generation of Native basketmakers now holds annual gatherings, notably at Ya-Ka-Ama, and promises to preserve and extend the artistic boundaries of their art. More contemporary California Indian artists, such as Jean LaMarr, Frank La Pena, Harry Fonseca, L. Frank Manriquez, James Luna, and Kathleen Smith, among others, are considered on the cutting edge of the modern Indian art world.

Despite the declaration by anthropologists, historians, and other writers that several California Indian tribes and cultures are extinct, it is well known among Native peoples that many of these groups are not in fact gone. Some have never been recognized by the government, like the Gabrielino and Juaneño of southern California. Others, like the Guidiville band of Pomo Indians, were terminated in 1966 and are seeking reinstatement or recognition. These disenfranchised groups have organized themselves and are currently aggressively pursuing their cause in the U.S. Congress.

In 1993, about 200,000 California Indians live in the state. Perhaps as many as 60,000 live on reservations and rancherias. The remainder live in nearby towns and cities. And while about two-thirds have some degree of non-Indian blood in their racial make-up, most today proudly claim their heritage.

Edward Castillo
Sonoma (California) State University

♦ **BIOGRAPHIES**

Captain Jack was a famous Indian leader in the Modoc War of 1872–73. The original territory of the Modocs was centered around lower Klamath Lake and Tule Lake in southeastern Oregon and northeastern California. Modern descendants of the tribe also live on reservations in Oklahoma.

Captain Jack
d. 1873

Modoc tribal leader

Born somewhere along the Lost River in present-day Modoc County, California, the man whom the U.S. settlers would call

Captain Jack was originally given the Modoc name Kintpuash. He became the leader of his band when his father died in 1846. Captain Jack was drawn into the Modoc Wars through a complex series of events that began in 1864, when the Modoc signed away much of their indigenous territory and were removed to the Klamath Reservation in Oregon. The living conditions on the reservation were miserable; there was much disease and not enough food to support both the Modoc and the Klamath tribe. The Modoc request for their own reservation in California was rejected.

Captain Jack and the Modoc returned to California anyway, but there were many complaints from white settlers and the federal government ordered troops to the area in 1872. A series of violent incidents ensued; then Captain Jack and his followers escaped and worked their way south to a volcanic area with lava formations that offered excellent natural fortifications. Another Modoc group joined them so that the rebel group consisted of about two hundred people, eighty of them warriors. They ambushed a wagon train on December 22, thus obtaining more ammunition, and in January 1873 they successfully repulsed a force of more than three hundred regular soldiers led by Lieutenant Colonel Frank Wheaton.

Shortly thereafter, General Edward Canby planned to lead another attack and gathered a force of about a thousand men. At the same time, a peace plan was set in motion. The first negotiation on February 28 produced no results, and at the second meeting Captain Jack produced a hidden revolver and fatally shot General Canby. Modoc warriors Boston Charlie and Schonchin John also fired on the peace commissioners that had been sent by President Grant, and the Modoc retreated to another lava formation to the south. Throughout these months there were scattered conflicts, such as the one that took place on April 26, 1873, when the warrior Scarfaced Charlie attacked a patrol of sixty-three soldiers and killed twenty-five, including all five officers.

Despite their successes, however, the Modoc were badly lacking for food and water, and their forces became less and less unified. General Jefferson C. Davis finally organized a relentless pursuit of the scattered bands that remained, and Captain Jack and other leaders were finally cornered in a cave and captured on June 1, 1873. Captain Jack was executed by hanging on October 3, 1873, and two other Modoc leaders were sentenced to life imprisonment on Alcatraz, a penal facility on an island in San Francisco Bay. On the night after the hanging, Captain Jack's head was stolen by grave robbers, embalmed, and put on display in a carnival that toured cities in the eastern United States.

The Modoc War was one of the few Indian wars that ever took place in California, since tribes of the California region were not highly organized militarily. Because of this and the relatively late date of the uprising, the Modoc War had a shocking effect on the public, gaining a great deal of national attention. A more detailed account of the events described here is given in Keith Murray's book *The Modocs and their War* (1969).

In 1911, this middle-aged Yahi from northern California became famous throughout the United States as "the last wild Indian." The Yahi (also called Southern Yana) originally lived along Mill Creek and Deer Creek, two eastern affluents of the Sacramento River in northern California.

Ishi

d. 1916

Yahi/Southern Yana survivor

In August 1911, Ishi wandered out of the mountains and found himself in the town of Oroville (Butte County). He was the last survivor of a tribe that had gone into seclusion more than forty years before. For much of this time, Ishi had been living in a band that never numbered more than a dozen for most of his adolescent and adult life. His last years before discovery were spent with just three other people: an old man and woman, probably his parents, and a middle-aged woman who was his sister. For the last several months, he had been completely alone, until finally—weaponless, pressed by hunger, and his hair still singed from mourning for his relatives—he gave up a lifetime of hiding and allowed himself to be captured.

Apparently, he expected to be killed but was instead placed in jail for a few days and soon afterwards was taken to the San Francisco Bay area. He was studied by Alfred Kroeber and other anthropologists at the University of California until his death in 1916. The researchers marveled at the genuineness of his aboriginal condition, which was also sensationalized in the press. Here, after all, was a completely unacculturated Indian who spoke no English and still practiced ancient skills such as flint shaping and bow making. A number of publications on Yahi language and culture came about because of Ishi's knowledge, but he is probably best known to most Americans because of Theodora Kroeber's book *Ishi in Two Worlds* (1960). For most Americans, Ishi is a romantic symbol of the last unspoiled Native, but to many Native Americans in California, he represents a terrible era of genocide and cultural devastation.

Ramona
1865–1924

Cahuilla (Kawia) basketmaker

Ramona was a Cahuilla Indian who lived in present-day San Diego County, California. She became something of a celebrity in the late 1880s, due to the fictional story *Ramona* by the famous historical novelist Helen Hunt Jackson.

The central character in the novel is a romantic figure who bears little resemblance to the real-life Ramona. Jackson came to California in 1881 as an investigative reporter for *Century* magazine. While gathering information, she became entranced with the picturesque life-style of the Roman Catholic past of southern California and wrote a sympathetic portrayal of the context and purposes of Spanish Catholicism and colonization in California. In contrast, *Ramona* was a work of social protest that underscored the plight of California Indians, often called Mission Indians, who were forced to live and work in the Catholic missions. In her investigative reporting, Jackson recorded the grave population decline of California Mission Indians and the role of the Spanish in this decline. Jackson became determined to write a work that would bring the plight of the Mission Indians to the American public's eye. *Ramona* was first serialized in 1884 by *Christian Union* magazine.

The real-life Ramona, a Cahuilla Indian living in present-day Temecula, California, had been married to Juan Diego, who was murdered in dramatic fashion by a local villain named Sam Temple.

The novel, which incorporated a fictionalized romance, became an instant success and spawned a movie in the early 1900s. The real-life Ramona became something of a celebrity, selling baskets and photographs of herself to eager tourists at a souvenir stand. Today, the myth of Ramona continues to live in numerous re-enactments and festivals celebrating her life and character.

*T*he Canadian Natives

Although the aboriginal peoples of Canada are a small segment of the total population, they have always played a significant role in Canadian history. Their historic and contemporary importance is now acknowledged in Section 35, Parts 1 and 2, of the Canadian *Constitution Act, 1982,* which states,

> 35(1) The existing aboriginal and treaty rights of the aboriginal peoples of Canada are hereby recognized and affirmed.

> 35(2) In this Act, 'aboriginal peoples of Canada' includes the Indian, Inuit and Métis peoples of Canada.

The constitutional recognition of aboriginal peoples and their rights, however, occurred only after a protracted struggle on the part of aboriginal leaders to convince federal and provincial government officials of the legitimacy of their claims. While constitutional recognition signifies a landmark achievement for Canadian Indians, Inuit, and Métis, it is only one step in their quest for an enlarged political and legal status within the Canadian confederation that will give them a greater degree of control over their future. Moreover, significant strides must be taken in the social and economic development of aboriginal peoples. The legacies of past government policies have left aboriginal peoples as the most disadvantaged group in Canadian society. The rates of social pathology among aboriginal peoples as evidenced by the degree of alcohol abuse, crime, incarceration, and suicide, as well as other indicators, are well over the levels of non-aboriginals. In addition, unemployment rates for aboriginal peoples far exceed those for the remainder of the Canadian population. Increasingly, aboriginal leaders see self-government for their peoples as the only way to escape these deplorable conditions. The mounting pressure by aboriginal leaders for the constitutional recognition of their right to self-government, coupled with an increased awareness among other Canadians of their plight, continues to give aboriginal issues a prominent place on the Canadian political agenda.

ABORIGINAL PEOPLES: A PROFILE ✦ ✦ ✦ ✦ ✦ ✦ ✦ ✦ ✦ ✦ ✦

Although Indians, Métis, and Inuit are now collectively recognized as aboriginal peoples, their cultural, legal, and political differences remain very important as the Canadian state attempts to accommodate their respective demands. Indians in Canada have traditionally been subdivided into three groups: status, treaty, and non-status Indians. A status Indian is a person registered or entitled to be registered as an Indian for purposes of the Indian Act, which was first passed in 1876, setting forth a policy of assimilating Natives into Canadian society. Status Indians are members of the 633 bands across Canada; "bands" are legal administrative bodies established under the Indian Act that correspond generally to traditional tribal and kinship group affinities.In the establishment of the Canadian reserve system, unlike that of the United States, different tribes were not placed together on the same reserve; nor were groups of Indians relocated to reservations far from their ancestral homelands. Most bands are located south of the sixtieth parallel on reserves, numbering 2,281, within the provinces. The Indian "register" (1990) estimates that there are 500,000 status Indians in Canada. (See map of Canadian Native areas in front pages.)

Treaty Indians are those persons who are registered members of, or can prove descent from, a band that signed a treaty. Most status Indians are treaty Indians, except those living in areas not covered by treaties, such as most of the province of British Columbia.

Non-status Indians are those persons of Indian ancestry and cultural affiliation who have lost their right to be registered under the Indian Act. The most common reason for loss of status was marriage of a registered Indian woman to a non-Indian. Loss of status has also occurred in other ways, such as voluntary renunciation, compulsory enfranchisement to non-Indian status, and failure of government officials to include some Indian families in the registry. Indians who served in the military during the world wars, for example, usually became enfranchised, losing their status as Indians. Non-status Indians do not have a distinct constitutional standing but are grouped with the Métis for jurisdictional and public policy purposes. The situation for many non-status Indians changed in 1985, when the federal government amended the Indian Act with Bill C-31 to restore registered Indian status to those women and their children who had lost it through marriage. Aboriginal women's groups welcomed this change. However, the response of Indian communities to Bill C-31 was not uniformly favorable; many Indian bands saw the bill as an unwarranted intrusion on their right to control band membership. The reinstatement process was largely completed by 1991, adding approximately 92,000 Indians to the registry.

The Inuit are those aboriginal people who inhabit Canada's northernmost regions, including the Mackenzie Delta, the Northwest Territories, the northern coasts of Hudson Bay, the Arctic Islands, Labrador, and parts of northern Quebec. The Inuit were classified with registered Indians for program and jurisdictional purposes in 1939, by a decision of the Supreme Court of Canada. They are the smallest group of Canadian aboriginal people, numbering around 35,000 (1990).

The Métis are people of mixed Indian and non-Indian ancestry. The term *Métis* originally referred to people of mixed ancestry living on the prairies. This is the definition now generally endorsed by the Métis National Council, which considers the contemporary Métis to be the descendants of the Métis community that developed on the prairies in the 1800s, and of individuals who received land grants and/or scrip under the Manitoba Act, 1870, or the Dominion Lands Act, 1879. Statistics Canada now includes in the category of Métis all people living in any part of Canada who claim mixed Indian and non-Indian ancestry. This classification corresponds to the definition of the Native Council of Canada, an umbrella group representing Métis and non-status Indians and now also identifying itself as the voice of urban Indians. The 1986 census set Canada's Métis and non-status Indian population at 400,000. Métis spokesmen themselves dispute the census figure and suggest the combined population of Métis and non-status Indians is close to one million. Approximately two-thirds of the Métis live in the provinces of Manitoba, Saskatchewan, and Alberta and in the Northwest Territories; the remainder are scattered throughout the rest of the country.

Finally, although aboriginal peoples remain widely distributed throughout rural Canada, recent decades have witnessed a growing migration of aboriginal peoples to urban areas. In western urban centers such as Vancouver, Edmonton, Calgary, Regina, Saskatoon, and Winnipeg, aboriginal peoples comprise a substantial portion of the population. The Department of Indian Affairs and Northern Development (DIAND) estimates that approximately one-third of status Indians now live off their reserves. (See map of Canadian Native languages in Chapter 12.)

THE INDIANS ◆

When Europeans first reached the Canadian east coast, every part of Canada was occupied by diverse Indian societies well established in their respective territories. Although European colonizers may have stereotyped all Indians as nomadic hunters, in Canada at the time of contact there were Indians living in villages in coastal British Columbia, southern Ontario, and western Quebec. Furthermore, Indians in central Canada were already engaged in agricultural activities. The Europeans "discovered" an inhabited land, and many historians believe that during the 1500s a catastrophic population decline resulting from the introduction of new diseases made possible European settlement of the continent.

The diverse Indian cultures encountered by the Europeans can be categorized according to the regions they occupied and the languages they spoke. On the Atlantic coast were the Beothuk, Micmac, and Malecite, whose economy centered on tidal and river fishing. Around the Great Lakes were Indian farmers—including the Huron and Iroquois—who lived in villages and grew crops such as corn and tobacco. The prairie Indians—the Assiniboine, Plains Cree, Blackfoot, Sarcee, Saulteaux, and Gros Ventre—followed the buffalo. In the coastal mountains, seashore and islands of British Columbia, salmon was the main source of food for the many different peoples who lived there. Stretching across the country throughout the northern forests were the Montagnais, Naskapi, Abenaki, Ottawa, Algonquin, Ojibwa, and Cree, nomadic peoples who hunted and fished. North of the treeline were the seafaring Inuit. Some of the regions were populated by linguistically homogeneous cultures; in others, such as British Columbia, a wide variety of languages were spoken within a small geographic area.

Today these diverse cultures are represented by a national Native organization, the Assembly of First Nations (AFN), formerly the National Indian Brotherhood. Twentieth-century Indian political activity in Canada began at the local and regional level, because national organizing of Indians was forbidden by the 1927 Indian Act. Even today, regional influences and differences are apparent in the operation of the AFN. Composed of the 633 (1992) band chiefs from across the country, the assembly regularly faces internal political splits. One of the most important issues dividing AFN constituents is the difference between "treaty" and "non-treaty" groups whose roads to self-government are not always parallel. Complicating the matter is the fact that Canadian Indian bands vary considerably in their degree of political militancy—from outright nationalist to much more accommodationist positions. Moreover, as demographic shifts have seen increasing numbers of Indian migrating into Canadian cities, the assembly's position

as the voice of reserve Indians has been challenged by more ur-
ban-based associations, such as the Native Council of Canada.
Still, a national event such as the 1990 confrontation over land
between the Mohawk and the Canadian Government at Oka,
Quebec, can galvanize widespread support and solidarity among
Canada's Indian peoples.

Indian-Government Relationships: Federal

Modern-day Canada was established by the British North America
Act of 1867. Prior to that point, relationships between Indians
and Europeans had involved the French and British Crowns, who
began negotiating Indian treaties as early as the 1600s. These early
agreements were usually "peace and friendship" treaties; the issues involved were military and political, and Indian nations often played a crucial role as ally or enemy of the European powers.
Later treaties, however, involved the surrender by Indians of large
tracts of land—a policy of the British Colonial Office. The policy
was articulated in the Royal Proclamation of 1763, which was
issued by King George III after the end of the war between England and France over their New World acquisitions. The main
purpose of the proclamation was to establish governments for
the territories that England acquired from France; however, the
last five paragraphs made reference to Indians, reserving certain
areas of the continent for them, and providing an elaborate mechanism by which other lands could be surrendered to the Crown.

The Robinson-Huron and Robinson-Superior treaties, concluded
in 1850 in Ontario, established the model for the later land surrender treaties numbered 1 to 11. The final treaty, Number 11,
was signed in 1921. Upon the surrender of land, Indian reserves
were established according to a formula which, since Treaty Three,
has been one "section" (640 acres) of land for every family of
five. The numbered treaties also typically contained a guarantee
of Indian hunting rights on surrendered, unoccupied Crown land;
made provisions for education and agricultural development on
the reserves; and included a system of annuities. What the various signatories of the treaties understood themselves to be agreeing to at the time has since become a matter for debate. Areas of
conflict cover a great deal of ground, including the contemporary

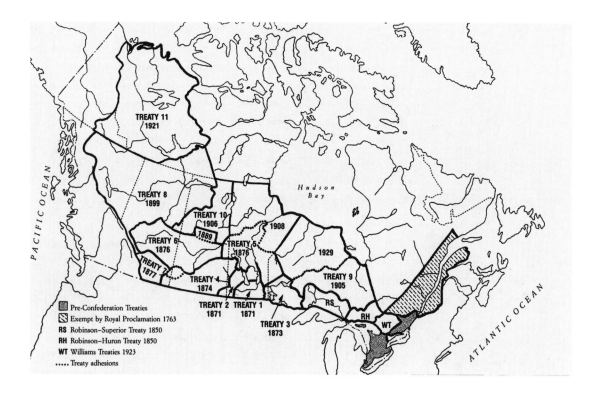

implications of certain treaty provisions. For example, a university education is now claimed by Indian groups as a treaty right; Indians also argue that the "medicine chest" provision in many treaties now obligates the government to provide universal health care for them. Some Indian leaders argue that Indian people were duped and cheated during the treaty-making process and that more lands, rights, and benefits are due; from this perspective the renegotiation or "renovation" of treaties is in order. (See the map of Canadian and Native treaties in the Canadian Chronology in Chapter 1.)

The treaty relationship between Indian peoples and the Canadian state has been paralleled by another legal relationship. Section 91(24) of the Constitution Act, 1867 established the federal government's responsibility for Indian peoples and lands. A major effect of this grant of authority was to continue a trust relationship between Indians and the federal government established

Indian treaty area in Canada. Maps by Brian McMillan from Native Peoples and Cultures of Canada *by Alan D. McMillan, 1988, published by Douglas & McIntyre. Reprinted by permission.*

by the Royal Proclamation. Put simply, the trust relationship involves an obligation on the part of the crown to ensure that the best interests of Indians are served where the management and protection of Indian proprietary interests are involved. The obligations created by this trust relationship have experienced an uneven history of compliance on the part of the federal government. This checkered attitude has also marked the judiciary's approach to interpreting the federal government's trust obligations to Indians.

A recent decision of the Supreme Court in *Guerin v. Regina* (1986), however, involving the Musqueam band near Vancouver, suggests that the courts may be more willing to provide judicial sanction for what Indian peoples have always considered a cornerstone of their relationship with the Canadian state. In this case, the court held that DIAND breached its fiduciary obligation to the Musqueam band by renting out part of the reserve for a golf course at a rate far below the commercial rental value of the land. The depth of feeling by Indians toward the trust relationship approaches the status of an article of faith and is consistently utilized by Indian leaders as a barrier against provincial encroachment against their lands.

To fulfill its responsibilities to Indians under Section 91(24), the federal government created a separate legal regime for them by passing the Indian Act, 1876. This act was revised in 1951 and 1985. Basically, the Indian Act had two major objectives: to establish a regime for administering the affairs of Indians and to create the conditions for their assimilation into the dominant Euro-Canadian society. For administering Indian affairs, the Indian Act established a reserve system, which included a system of Indian governments. Importantly, the Indian Act did not, and still does not, recognize Canadian Indians as retaining any right to self-government—inherent, constitutional, or otherwise. In setting up the reserve system, the Indian Act did several things: first, it defined legally who is entitled to be a status Indian; second, it established a system for the management of Indian lands and monies; third, it created legal units known as band governments to administer reserve communities and endowed band governments with a number of powers that would ordinarily be exercised by municipal governments; and fourth, it created a national administrative structure that has functioned as a microcosm of other Canadian governments for reserve Indians. Through the reserve system, the Department of Indian Affairs and Northern Development has traditionally provided services that other Canadians receive from provincial governments, such as health care, education, and law enforcement.

A significant effect of the Indian Act was the imposition on Indian bands of a council elective system that, in structure as well as underlying principles, resembles a non-Indian municipal government. The band council elective system represented a major attempt by the federal government to "civilize," that is, to assimilate Indian peoples. Within the broad objective of assimilation, the band council system was intended to accomplish two goals: first, to indoctrinate Indians into the Euro-Canadian system of political beliefs, ultimately preparing them ultimately to live within non-Indian municipal government systems; and second, to eliminate traditional Indian belief systems and governing processes. With the exception of a few Indian bands across Canada—most notably the Mohawk—who have fought vigorously to retain their traditional governing methods, the band council elective system is now widely established within Indian communities across Canada.

The colonial administrative nature of the Indian Act remains essentially unchanged today, even though the federal government appears to recognize a genuine need for changing it. The government is, moreover, attempting to accomplish this objective through several legislative and administrative initiatives for devolution of authority to band governments. However, ultimate authority over the management of Indian lands and finances still remains largely with the minister of Indian and northern affairs, should his or her office choose to exercise it. Moreover, the bylaw making authority of band governments is subject to ministerial disallowance, and money bylaws are subject to ministerial approval. The straitjacket of the Indian Act remains a thorn in the side of Indian bands that seek greater control over their own social, economic, and political development.

Indian-Government Relationships: The Provinces

The jurisdiction of the provinces over Indians is tied to Section 91(24) of the Canadian Constitution and the Indian Act's Section 88, which subjects Indians to all provincially enacted laws that generally apply to provincial citizens. Indians are therefore considered provincial citizens for purposes of these laws. Only in instances where such laws conflict with provisions of the Indian Act, or if they touch rights under treaty, or if they are discriminatory in respect to treatment of Indians, are such laws of general application considered not to apply. However, historically the interpretation of Section 88 by Canadian courts reveals an incremental pattern wherein the "declaratory" authority of the provinces over Indians has been expanded. Under this judicial doctrine, provincial laws apply by virtue of the provinces' general constitutional authority, without requiring the authority of Section 88 for validity. The courts have supported the view that unless there is clear evidence of a conflict with federal legislation, etc., that could interfere with federal activity or the application of federal laws, provincial laws of general application may apply to Indians even on reserves, unless they impair "Indianess," as defined by law, custom, or tradition. In cases where legislative vacuums have raised federal-provincial jurisdictional questions in regard to Indians, the courts have tended to expand provincial jurisdiction over Indians. In some instances, the courts have created overlapping federal and provincial jurisdictions. As a consequence, under some circumstances the exercise of authority by Indian bands is subject to both federal and provincial jurisdiction.

Since the 1950s, provincial jurisdiction over Indians and Indian lands has also been expanded by a number of tripartite administrative agreements. In several provinces, for example, the federal and provincial governments have negotiated tripartite agreements that extend provincial power over the administration of justice to Indian reserves, thus allowing the creation of reserve police forces under provisions of provincial police acts.

Federal responsibility for social and other services to Indians is also based in Section 91(24) of the Canadian Constitution. Even though this grant of authority is permissive and not mandatory with respect to providing services to Indians, the federal government has traditionally assumed responsibility for Indians living on reserves. On the other hand, it has taken the position that Indians living off the reserves fall under the general social responsibility mandate of the province. For the most part, provinces have accepted social responsibility for Indians living off-reserve. Provinces, however, have consistently refused to extend their social responsibility mandate to Indians living on reserves, despite the fact that no prohibitive constitutional barrier exists as long as the restrictions included in Section 88 of the Indian Act are observed.

A final aspect of Indian-government relationships involves jurisdiction over land. Outside of the Yukon and Northwest territories, the federal government owns very little land in Canada. Section 109 of the Constitution Act, 1867, as well as a number of federal-provincial agreements such as the Natural Resources Transfer Act, 1930 (pertaining to the prairie provinces of Alberta, Saskatchewan and Manitoba) gives the provinces control over nearly all Crown lands within their borders. While these federal and provincial agreements have established a patchwork of provincial obligations to surrender land for purposes established in treaties between the Crown and Indian nations where such treaties exist, provinces must concur in the way those obligations are defined and implemented. Consequently, all treaty claims by Indian bands located within provinces for lands outside of existing reserves or claims for land based on aboriginal title (that is, traditional occupancy) are laid against the provinces.

Jurisdiction over Land

The historical record of the provinces in accommodating Indian land claims has been a dismal one. In some instances, land transfer has taken place only after major confrontations. The Lubicon Lake Cree began to make progress on a forty-eight year old land claim in northern Alberta only after they blockaded access to nearly 10,000 square kilometers of oil- and timber-rich land, threatening the resource extraction industry in the area. However, negotiations between the Lubicon band and the federal government were stalemated from 1989 to 1993. The Lubicon and their American adviser blame government intransigence. Meanwhile, 125 Lubicon members joined with other Alberta Indians and formed the 450 member Woodland Cree Band, which received a settlement including a 143 square kilometer reserve and $19 million for economic development. In 1991, in a vote organized and monitored by DIAND, the Woodland Cree Band concluded an agreement amidst irregularities such as on-the-spot cash payments and a promise of $1,000 a head for a positive outcome.

Indians demonstrating in the early 1960s.

Another contentious land claim is that of the Kanesatake Mohawk, who in 1990 were able to force action on a land claim at Oka, in southern Quebec, by setting up blockades to prevent the development of a golf course on land that the Kanesatake have traditionally claimed as their own. After the failure of Quebec provincial police to remove the barricades, during which one provincial police officer was killed, the government of Quebec received authorization to use the Canadian armed forces to remove the barricades. In order to defuse the situation, the federal government purchased the disputed land at Oka and offered it to the Kanesatake as part of a negotiated settlement package that includes economic development and other benefits. However, the relationship between the Mohawk, the federal government, and the government of Quebec in particular remains tense and problematic.

Political confrontations such as these between the federal government and the Lubicon Cree or the Kanesatake Mohawk must be viewed against the background of the often desperate situations in which many Canadian Indians find themselves. The socioeconomic conditions on Indian reserves have been described as more typical of Third World countries than of a northern industrialized democracy. The statistical indicators (DIAND, 1990) are bleak. Indian life expectancy is ten years below the national average. The suicide rate is double that of the general population, and the rate of violent death is triple. Nearly a third of Indian families are headed by a single parent. Twenty percent of status Indians live in overcrowded dwellings, and 25 percent live in unheated houses. Government transfer payments are the major source of income for close to half of the Canadian Indian population. Over the last decade a number of these indicators have been improving; nevertheless, Indians remain one of the most disadvantaged segments of the population.

One area in which there have been some hopeful developments is education. As Indian populations have grown, there has been an influx of Indian students into all levels of the education system, which has caught the system off-guard. Indian children are staying in school longer and pursuing higher levels of education, in part due to the increased number of band-operated schools—of which in 1993 there were more than 300. In 1969, only 10 percent of Indian children remained in school until their last year of high school; in 1989, the number was over 40 percent. During these two decades, the number of federally sponsored students pursuing post-secondary education rose from 60 to 22,000. This has recently led to a "funding crunch" for Indian college and university students, most of whom rely on financial sponsorship from DIAND and/or their bands. Increasingly, Indian students are pursuing not only their individual aspirations but also community goals through post-secondary education. This creates challenges both for funders and for the institutions facing accusations about the irrelevance or ethnocentrism of their curricula. University education broadens the employment prospects available to Indian students and improves the human resource

Socio-Economic Development

Dene school children,

Northwest Territory.

base available to their communities. Yet the new generation of educated Indians are sometimes perceived as a threat to established power structures on their reserves, and, moreover, there are community concerns about the degree to which a "white" education may cause the students to become separated from their cultural roots.

The history of "Indian education" in Canada is a topic that has recently come in for much discussion, focusing on the system of residential boarding schools that engulfed multiple generations of Indian children. The schools, usually Catholic or Anglican, were a front-line tool in the project of assimilating Indians into the dominant Canadian society. Indian children were removed from their homes and families and placed in institutions, where they were indoctrinated with the tenets of Euro-Christianity, steeped in the practices of European culture, taught that their

Native ways were heretical and uncivilized, and punished for any attachment to indigenous language and culture. Contemporaneous photographs taken at the residential schools are evocative of the children's experience—rows of tidy Indian schoolchildren, dressed in white pinafores and buttoned up shirts, hair scraped back, faces unsmiling. But the process of "civilizing" Indian children was an abusive one, and the residential schools are retrospectively being viewed with horror by many. Boarding school continues to be a necessity today for some Indian students—especially those at the high school level—who live in communities too small and remote to sustain secondary schools; but the prospect of having to leave home for a high school education bars many from completing it.

This massive attempt at assimilation of Indian peoples was on the surface a failure—Indian languages and cultures, however fragile, survive in contemporary Canada. Yet the multigenerational experience of the residential school system has left scars that have been concealed for many years. Now former students are speaking out to their own peoples and to the Canadian public at large. The artistic community in Canada was one of the first mainstream participants to tackle the subject of abuse of Indian children at residential schools; a television drama about a young Blackfoot girl's experience received critical acclaim and the support of many aboriginal communities, despite a controversy over the fact that the script authors were not Natives. Another catalyst for discussion was the personal testimony of a prominent Indian leader from Manitoba who as a child had been the victim of both physical and sexual abuse at a Catholic boarding school. As the evidence from various quarters has mounted about the abuse of Indian schoolchildren, there have been calls from the Indian community for apologies and reparations. Few voices have been raised in defense of the missionary educators. In any event, the legacy of the residential school system, so recently brought to public consciousness, is likely to reverberate for some time in the relationship between Indian peoples and wider Canadian society.

THE INUIT ♦

The Inuit of Canada live in the far north of the country above the treeline, in small communities on the Mackenzie Delta, along the coasts of the Northwest Territories, on the shores of Hudson Bay, in Labrador, northern Quebec, and scattered across the Arctic Islands. They are thought to have been among the last of aboriginal peoples to migrate across the Bering land bridge from Siberia to Alaska, their ancestors arriving in Canada around 10,000 B.C. The Inuit were formerly known as "Eskimos," which comes from a Cree word meaning "raw meat eaters." Today they call themselves Inuit, which is the Inuktitut word for "the people."

The Inuit of Canada share one culture and one language, although there are different dialects of Inuktitut. Their settlement pattern along coastlines reflects a historical life-style tied to marine harvesting. They hunted seal, whale, and walrus in the waters of the north but would also travel inland for caribou, fish and waterfowl. Most Inuit lived in small groups of related families, sometimes coming together at fishing or sealing camps. Sharing the results of their hunt was a key aspect of Inuit culture; some communities had formal distribution systems for sharing out the catch. Life in the Arctic was difficult—starvation was always a possibility—but for centuries the ancestors of today's Inuit survived in this region.

Although Inuit in the eastern Arctic may have encountered the Norse explorers who reached Canada in the tenth century, sustained contact between Inuit and Europeans did not take place until the nineteenth century. American and Scottish whalers sailed north in pursuit of the bowhead whale, which they hunted to near extinction. The whalers hired Inuit to act as guides and crew, and some of them took Inuit wives. The trading posts established by the Hudson's Bay Company were another means of contact between Inuit and Europeans, and over the next century many Inuit forsook their traditional hunting pursuits in favor of fur trapping. They came to rely on European trade goods for survival, and when the fur trade collapsed in the 1940s, the effect on the Inuit was devastating. Hunger and disease afflicted many communities.

The Canadian government did not turn its attention to the plight of the Inuit until the 1950s. Relief supplies were sent to the starving communities, and the Inuit were encouraged to settle permanently around the Hudson Bay trading posts. The federal government undertook to provide the kinds of services for the Inuit that it did for Canadian Indians, and nearly all of the Inuit gave up their traditional way of life to settle in small northern villages. During this decade, the federal government also relocated a group of Inuit from northern Quebec to two different locations in the High Arctic as, among other motives, an assertion of territorial sovereignty in the north; four decades later the Inuit Tapirisat of Canada, the national political organization of the Inuit, called on the government for an apology and compensatory payments to the Inuit whose lives had been disrupted.

Because of the remoteness of Canada's Inuit from centers of government, their legal status was ambiguous for a number of years. The Inuit were brought into a direct relationship with the federal government in 1939. In that year, the Supreme Court of Canada decided in *Re Eskimos* that the Inuit come within the term *Indians* in Section 91(24) of the British North American Act. The Indian Act itself excludes Inuit from the operations of the Department of Indians Affairs, but as a result of *Re Eskimos,* the federal government's power to make laws affecting Indians and their lands also includes the Inuit. Today the Inuit are involved with several levels of government. In the Northwest Territories, Inuit and other Canadians are governed by the territorial government, which was moved from Ottawa to Yellowknife in 1967. In northern Quebec, the signing of the James Bay and Northern Quebec Agreement in 1975 established a regional government for Inuit in that area. And the province of Newfoundland and the federal government have negotiated a cost-sharing arrangement for provision of government services to the Inuit of Labrador, in which the provincial government retains primary administrative responsibility.

Inuit hunting seals on the ice. The Inuit and their way of life, as observed by Frobisher's men on Baffin Island in 1576–78. Engravings, after drawings by Captain G. F. Lyon on Melville Peninsula in 1822, published in W. E. Parry, Journal of a second voyage for the discovery of a North-west Passage, London, 1824.

Like Canadian Indians and Métis, contemporary Inuit are seeking a greater degree of self-determination for their people. The Inuit live in the only part of Canada where aboriginal inhabitants are in the majority, and they have sought a public, regional government in the north rather than an ethnically based one. A variety of organizations represent Inuit interests. The Inuit Tapirisat (Brotherhood) of Canada (ITC) was formed in 1971 as the "voice of the north." The impetus that gave birth to the ITC was the Inuit desire to negotiate a land claim with the federal government, a responsibility which has since been assumed by the Tungavik Federation of Nunavut (TFN). In 1979, the Tapirisat created the Inuit Committee on National Issues (ICNI), whose main role is to coordinate and present Inuit views on constitutional reform.

Inuit political aspirations are intimately tied to their pursuit of land claims. Unlike Indian groups who entered into treaties, the Inuit's claims to aboriginal rights were not dealt with (and were not made) before the modern era. In 1973, the federal government agreed to enter land claims negotiations with the Inuit, and the ITC submitted its claim on behalf of the Inuit of Nunavut (the eastern Arctic) to the federal government in 1976. Since 1982, the TFN has been responsible for land claims negotiations. The nine-member negotiating team has its head office in Ottawa, and there are regional offices in Coppermine, Rankin Inlet, Frobisher Bay, and Igloolik.

The Inuit were involved in the first modern land claims agreement to be reached in Canada, with the James Bay Cree and the Inuit of northern Quebec. The agreement, signed in 1975, guaranteed the aboriginal signatories exclusive hunting and fishing rights over parts of northern Quebec, "ownership" of other parcels similar to Indian "ownership" of reserve lands, the Kativik regional government for the Inuit of the area, education and language rights in Inuktitut, and a cash and royalties settlement, which for the Inuit amounted to $90 million. In return, the Inuit and Cree relinquished any further claim to lands covered by the agreement. A second land claim was settled in 1984 with the 2,500 Inuvialuit of the western Arctic, who obtained 242,000 square kilometers of land and a cash settlement of $45 million. The largest Inuit land claim involves the proposed division of the Northwest Territories into Denedah, Athapascan land in the west, and Nunavut, Inuit land, in the east. In 1976, the ITC submitted a land claim for the eastern Arctic and a proposal for the creation of a new territory called "Nunavut," to include all areas north of the treeline. The claim to Nunavut, which was settled late in 1991, involves a vast area of the Arctic. The settlement included a payment of $580 million and 350,000 square kilometers of land. Community ratification of the land claim settlement was expected to take place in 1992. In the process, the Inuit agreed to the "extinguishment" of their aboriginal rights claim to the rest of their traditional lands (1.6 million square kilometers).

Other groups besides the Inuit have an interest in the development of Nunavut, and their viewpoints have been far from uniform. In a 1992 territorial plebiscite, 54 percent of the Northwest Territories approved the western boundary for the new territory, an overwhelming endorsement on the part of the Inuit. However, there has been opposition to the creation of Nunavut from the Dene Indians, with whom the Inuit have had long-standing border disputes. The Assembly of First Nations criticized the deal for giving up too much in the way of aboriginal rights. Non-Native northerners, who have traditionally formed political coalitions with the Inuit and the Inuvialuit, are concerned about the makeup of future governments in the remainder of the Northwest Territory. While non-Natives are a slight majority in the west, the Dene are likely to be the dominant group after territorial division. A suggestion has already been made that non-Natives should be excluded from the cabinet of the new western territory. The development of Nunavut, however, is proceeding. It is expected that the new territory will be created by the end of this century. The federal government has given support to the Nunavut deal, which does not involve constitutionally entrenched self-government or the recognition of Inuit sovereignty. As a public government, rather than an ethnically based one, Nunavut would nevertheless give *de facto* self-government to the Inuit, who make up about 85 percent of the eastern Arctic population.

The Inuit economy has undergone an enormous change in the last forty years, from a hunting and trapping base to diversification involving tourism, arts and crafts, and development of both renewable and non-renewable resources. Government, however, is still the biggest employer in the North, accounting for 30 percent to 40 percent of the total. The outlook for mining and oil and gas exploration is not bright at present, and the tourism sector is poorly developed. The unemployment rate among the Inuit is very high, the population is young, and educational attainment is low. All the statistics point to an impending crisis. Many Inuit communities still rely on traditional hunting, fishing, and sealing activities both for a food supply and as a source of cash income. However, the recent outgrowth of environmental activism known as the "animal rights" movement has posed a serious threat to survival of northern aboriginal communities. In the late 1960s, a highly emotional campaign was organized against a non-Inuit commercial industrial kill of newly born harp seals in the waters of Atlantic Canada. The campaign developed into an attack on seal hunting in general, and it had a devastating effect on the Arctic Inuit and their traditional hunt for mature ringed seals. By 1982, the European Community had boycotted all seal product imports, a serious blow to the Inuit economy. Many Inuit were forced to leave the land for an uncertain future in communities with little wage employment; loss of economic self-sufficiency and social alienation have resulted in an escalation of health and social problems.

Canada's small Inuit population faces challenges on many fronts. Protection of Inuit culture is a priority for many, and there have been positive developments, notably in education. Inuktitut instruction has been introduced to elementary schools, and textbooks have been written in both Inuktitut and English, especially for the North. A Native press has developed, which prints newsletters and magazines in both languages, and the Inuit Broadcasting Corporation was established in 1981 to provide programming in Inuktitut. Canadian Inuit also participate in the Inuit Circumpolar Conference (ICC), which represents 115,000 Canadian, Alaska, Soviet, and Greenland Inuit on international issues affecting the Arctic. The ICC, a non-governmental member of the United Nations, meets every three years; the current president of the conference is Mary Simon, a Canadian Inuit from Kuujjuaq, Quebec.

◆ **THE MÉTIS**

Canada's Métis have been called "the forgotten people," and it was considered a major victory for them to have been included in the definition of "aboriginal people" in Canada's 1982 Constitution. The word *Métis,* "mixed," describes someone of mixed Indian and European ancestry. Originally, it referred to the children

Inuit meeting to discuss hamlet business, Cape Dorset, Northwest Territory.

of marriages between Indian women and the European men who participated in the Canadian fur trade. On the prairies, French fur traders often took Cree wives; in the north, English and Scottish traders married Dene women, and the offspring of both sets of relationships were the original Métis. In contemporary times, the term is used more broadly to refer to people of mixed Indian-European ancestry anywhere in Canada, regardless of where their ancestors lived. Two-thirds of the self-identified Métis are still concentrated in the prairie provinces of Alberta, Saskatchewan, and Manitoba. Another significant group of Métis live in the Northwest Territories and ally themselves with the Dene Nation for the purposes of pursuing land claims.

The Métis have also been called "the children of the fur trade." European fur traders derived many benefits from association with Indian women and their families—their familiarity with the forests and waterways, their Native technological skills, and their social and political "connections," which facilitated commercial trade. The children of these unions, in turn, were often involved with the business—acting as interpreters and middlemen in the trade. The Métis participated in the plains economy as hunters, trappers, traders, carters, and small farmers, developing a distinctive culture combining European and Indian traditions. Over time, the European influence over the Métis homeland continued to grow, and the traditional Métis way of life was threatened; a sense of Métis nationalism began to develop in response. In 1811, the Hudson's Bay Company made a large land grant in the Red River Valley of Manitoba for the purpose of establishing a new colony with an agricultural economy. Over the next half-century, homesteaders from eastern Canada settled along the Red and Assiniboine rivers, arousing Métis antipathy.

In 1869, the Hudson's Bay Company sold the Métis homeland to Canada, a union which was opposed by the Métis. A challenge to the new governor of the territory, "the Red River Resistance," was led by Louis Riel, Jr., the son of a prominent Métis. Riel and his followers established a provisional government, asserting their right to do so under the Law of Nations. They arrested several men for resisting Métis law and executed one of them—an easterner named Thomas Scott—causing an uproar. Negotiations with the government of Canada ensued, and in the Manitoba Act of 1870, many of the Métis demands were met, including allotments of land to individual Métis and their children. But in the following years, conflict continued between the Métis and the incoming settlers. The Plains economy was shifting further to the west along with the buffalo herds, and many Métis chose to follow. Canadian settlers were not far behind, continuing their disruption of the Métis way of life. In 1884, the Métis of Saskatchewan, finding the government of Canada unresponsive to their complaints, sent for Louis Riel, then living in the state of Montana. Riel returned to petition Ottawa for, among other things, land title for the Métis and provincial status for Saskatchewan, Assiniboine, and Alberta. The response was unsatisfactory, and Riel again set up a defiant provisional government. A series of armed conflicts followed, after which Riel was captured, put on trial, and hanged for treason in November 1885.

In the years following the "Riel Rebellion," referred to by the Métis as "The War of Resistance at Batoche," the Canadian government made some efforts to deal with the grievances that had led to conflict. Manitoba Métis were given 1.4 million acres of land to extinguish their "Indian title" in that province. Both land parcels and "scrip" (a certificate for the value of a parcel of land) were distributed to the Métis. Many chose to sell both land and scrip—rather than change their traditional life-style and engage in cash-cropping—and followed the dwindling plains economy west. However, by the twentieth century, large numbers of Métis had become impoverished and marginalized.

There is much contemporary debate about Canada's treatment of Louis Riel in particular and of the Métis in general. To some, Riel is a martyr; as the centenary of his death approached, a call was made for his posthumous pardon. To others, he is a more ambivalent figure, whose mental illness and religious mysticism are more interesting than his political activism. In any event, the life and person of Riel continue to fascinate Canadians—a favored subject for artists and writers as well as historians.

The demands that Riel made upon Canada have not been forgotten in the century since his death. Prior to 1982, the Métis had argued for many years that they were entitled to aboriginal rights, and today Métis spokesmen continue the battle for "equal recognition" with Inuit and Indians as one of Canada's three aboriginal peoples. Various political organizations—at the provincial, territorial and federal levels—carry on the struggle for Métis rights and jostle with other aboriginal groups for position and resources in Canadian society. The first Métis political organization was established in Saskatchewan in 1937, but it was not until the 1960s that provincial Métis organizations sprang up in Manitoba, Alberta, and British Columbia. In 1970 the Western Métis formed a new organization, the Native Council of Canada (NCC), to represent both Métis and non-status Indians and promote their social, economic, and political aspirations. The NCC has taken a "pan-Canadian" approach, defining a Métis as anyone of mixed European and Indian blood. However, in the 1980s, it faced a challenge from the prairie Métis, who define "the Métis" as a particular national group that arose in the historical Métis homeland during the development of the fur trade. The Métis National Council (MNC) was established in 1983 by those prairie Métis who felt the NCC was not adequately pressing for establishment of a Métis land base.

Métis politics are also carried on vigorously at the provincial level, and relations between the Métis and different levels of government vary considerably across the country. Alberta was the first province to recognize formally a distinct responsibility to its Métis population. The Métis Betterment Act was passed in 1938 after an investigation into the socioeconomic problems of the Métis. In 1938 and 1939, Alberta established twelve Métis colonies or "Settlements" in the northern part of the province; however, some of these communities were displaced when oil and gas were discovered, and real devolution of responsibility to the Métis has been a long, drawn-out process. By 1960, there were only eight communities left. In the following two decades, the Métis sought not only protection for these remaining lands but also compensation for oil and gas taken from their territory. An agreement was eventually reached in 1990 which saw 500,000 hectares and $310 million transferred to 5,000 of Alberta's Métis. Today the settlements, eight in number, are governed by elected councils with quasi-municipal powers over such areas as policing, housing, and land use; Métis who live outside the settlements are considered ordinary citizens by the government of Alberta.

Alberta's relationship with the Métis is an exception, however. In Saskatchewan, Métis "farms" have been established (with very small land bases), but special recognition of the Métis has been unusual elsewhere. In some cases, the Métis are pursuing their aspirations through the courts. The most important lawsuit is in Manitoba, where in 1992 the provincial Métis Association sought compensation for the 1.4 million acres granted to individual Métis by the 1870 Manitoba Act but largely lost to their descendants. The issues in this case involve detailed historical research into

Métis disposition of land and scrip from 1870 until the early twentieth century, with accusations of governmental deception and fraud being common (although unproven).

Apart from the prairies, the largest Métis population is located in the Northwest Territories. There many Métis adopted the lifestyle of their Indian neighbors; today the NWT Métis have both a higher educational level and a higher employment level than the Dene and Inuit of the area. The Métis Association of the NWT and the Dene Nation agreed in 1981 to negotiate a land claim jointly against the federal government. An agreement in principle was reached in 1988, but the deal fell apart in 1991 when some of the Dene chiefs balked at the principle that some of their aboriginal rights would be "extinguished" upon signing of the agreement. There is an internal split within the Dene Nation between the Dene of the northern Mackenzie Delta and the Dene of the south. The northern Dene are faced with the immediate prospect of oil and gas development; without a signed land claim in their possession they may have little influence over the course of development and few opportunities to ensure that it accrues to the benefit of local communities. For the southern Dene, resource development is a less pressing concern; their leaders have the luxury of time in which to argue for more philosophical points in land claims negotiations. When the overall Dene-Métis claim broke apart, Ottawa agreed to negotiate separate regional claims—one of which has already been signed with the Gwich'in Tribal Council. But the Métis, without the bargaining power afforded by a united front, seem once again likely to suffer in the now divided claims negotiations process.

The Métis elsewhere in Canada continue to experience the marginalization and impoverishment of many Native peoples. Despite their constitutional recognition as an aboriginal people in 1982, individual Métis continue to "fall through the cracks" of the Canadian social welfare structure. The relationship between national Métis organizations and other aboriginal groups has also been problematic. The Métis continue to point out that governments do not treat the Métis the same way they do the Indians and Inuit and insist that this is unjust: "equality for aboriginal peoples" is a Métis battle cry. The Métis national agenda is largely driven by a desire for a concrete land base, rather than for further constitutional amendment; this occasionally puts them at odds with Indian and Inuit organizations, whose assets and aspirations are different. Unlike the Inuit and Indians, the Métis have always been under provincial rather than federal jurisdiction; the "constitutionalization" of their status has not changed that fact. For program purposes, such as subsidized housing, the federal government deals with the Métis as "disadvantaged" people rather than as "aboriginal" ones. With one notable exception, Canadian Métis have been treated like other Canadian citizens; the exception is the Métis of Alberta. However, that province maintains that its special treatment of Métis was spurred by the social and economic needs of individual Métis, not by recognition of the Métis' aboriginal rights. Legally, and despite the Constitution Act of 1982, the Métis' claim for aboriginal status has not gone very far.

♦ ♦ ♦ ♦ ♦ ♦ ♦ ♦ ♦ ♦ ♦ ♦ ♦ **THE CHANGING STATUS OF CANADA'S ABORIGINAL PEOPLES**

The modern era of aboriginal politics can be dated from the release of the 1969 White Paper on Indian Policy by the federal government. The main thrust of the White Paper was a proposal to eliminate the special legal status of Canadian Indians and Inuit, who would then be provided government services through mainstream institutions, primarily provincial ones. Canadian Indians took immediate exception to this proposal and countered with their own Red Paper arguing in favor of special legal status on the grounds of aboriginal and treaty rights. However, the White Paper was more than a policy vehicle. It was also a statement of philosophy expressing the liberal individualistic vision of the state, in which the legal equality of individuals takes precedence over special benefits and status for groups. Specific questions of aboriginal rights in Canada have been entangled with a broader conflict: the vision of Canada as a liberal individualistic state versus the vision of Canada as a collection of historical communities.

The Trudeau government, which produced the White Paper, was strongly committed to the former, and the only grounds it acknowledged as justifying special treatment for Indians were social and economic disadvantage. The "liberal" ideology of the White Paper had very little appeal for aboriginal Canadians, however. The White Paper had also echoed the expectation dating from colonial times that aboriginal peoples would eventually be assimilated into larger Canadian society, but, since 1969 Canada's aboriginal peoples have consistently, publicly, and forcefully resisted assimilation.

The White Paper initiative of the federal government had some important consequences for Indian peoples. First, it accelerated a trend started earlier to bring Indians into a consultative role where Indian policy is involved. A significant outcome of this was the establishment of a program under the jurisdiction of the secre-

Chipewyan Indian houses, Smith Landing, Fort Smith.

tary of state to provide core funding to political associations representing aboriginal groups. This funding was originally intended to help aboriginal political organizations participate in the consultative process. During the 1970s and 1980s, however, the number of government departments involved in the funding of aboriginal political associations increased as well as the mandated purposes for which the funding could be used. Aboriginal peoples were given federal money to research land and treaty claims, to prepare constitutional proposals, and to provide limited delivery of social services.

In addition, the White Paper heightened Indian, and subsequently other aboriginal people's, awareness and appreciation of their cultural and political heritage. It provided a focal point around which Indian peoples across Canada could unite and rally in opposition to what they believed to be detrimental government policies. Consequently, the 1970s and the decades that followed have become periods of Indian political activism in Canada, and the National Indian Brotherhood (NIB; after 1981 renamed the Assembly of First Nations) for a time assumed a position of leadership among aboriginal peoples. Aboriginal organizations demonstrated in the streets, lobbied in the Cabinet, and sued in the law courts—seeking to shake off the bureaucratic yoke of Indian Affairs and acquire greater control over their own communities.

♦ ♦ ♦ ABORIGINAL PEOPLES IN THE CONSTITUTIONAL FORUM

Near the end of the decade, aboriginal aspirations became entangled with Canadian constitutional politics. In the face of a growing separatist movement in Quebec, the Liberal government of Prime Minister Pierre Trudeau took control of the national agenda with a project for renovating federalism, adopting the Constitution and entrenching a Charter of Rights much like the U.S. Bill of Rights. During the national debate, the leaders of the NIB came to realize that Canadian constitutional renewal was both a potential threat to their exclusive relationship with the federal government and an opportunity for wider assertion of their claims. The NIB leadership sought to participate with the prime minister and the provincial premiers in the "First Ministers' Conferences" on constitutional reform; when they were offered only observer status, they boycotted the meetings and carried out a successful lobbying effort in Great Britain to force their demands to be taken more seriously. In the end, when the Constitution was adopted in 1982, the "existing aboriginal and treaty rights of the aboriginal peoples of Canada" were recognized and affirmed, and a series of First Ministers' Conferences were scheduled to work towards definition of those rights.

The conferences were held in 1983, 1984, 1985, and 1987, attended by the eleven "First Ministers," representatives of the four main aboriginal organizations and government leaders from the Yukon and Northwest Territories. The agenda for discussion was extensive: aboriginal title over land; hunting, fishing, and trapping rights; preservation of aboriginal languages and cultures; delivery of government services; aboriginal sovereignty; equality of aboriginal women and men; and constitutional entrenchment of a Charter of Aboriginal Rights. Over the five-year period, however, discussion came to focus on one main issue: aboriginal self-government.

By the third conference in 1985, the item at the top of the aboriginal agenda was constitutional entrenchment of a right to self-government. Such an amendment was met with considerable resistance by Canadian governments, especially by provincial premiers in provinces with large numbers of aboriginal communities. British Columbia, for example, accounts for 1,629 of Canada's 2,281 Indian reserves. Would the province be forced to negotiate a self-government agreement with every one of them? The legal issue for debate was whether aboriginal self-government had to be clearly defined before it was entrenched in the Constitution (as most premiers insisted), or whether the principle should first be entrenched and then defined later through a process of negotiation (as aboriginal peoples demanded). Another way of looking at the question is whether the right to self-government is something to be delegated to aboriginal peoples by "higher" levels of government or whether (as aboriginal peoples insist) their right to self-government is "inherent," a right which they have never surrendered and which continues sovereign today. At the constitutional conferences, the former position prevailed and the conference process ended—in considerable bitterness—without any agreement on a self-government amendment of the Canadian Constitution.

The reluctance of the federal and provincial governments in Canada to legitimize claims of Native Indian peoples to self-government and to recognize their status as distinct societies was additionally illustrated by the 1987 Constitutional Accord, more commonly known as the Meech Lake Accord (signed at Meech Lake, Quebec). The accord, which excluded participation by aboriginal peoples, was drawn up in June 1987, just four months after the last constitutional conference on aboriginal rights ended in failure. The date of June 23, 1990, was set as the deadline for ratification of the accord by all provincial legislatures and the federal parliament, a condition necessary to give the accord the status of a constitutional amendment. The fundamental objective of the accord was to bring the province of Quebec into the constitutional fold through a form of renewed federalism. While the accord formally recognized Quebec as "a distinct society" with unique linguistic and cultural rights, aboriginal peoples were given only token recognition in a clause stating that their "rights" would not be affected. Aboriginal leaders reacted quickly to the accord, arguing that the sole recognition of Quebec as a "distinct society" denied that aboriginal peoples also comprise "distinct societies" within Canada.

Despite vociferous opposition to the accord by aboriginal leaders, only three provinces—Manitoba, New Brunswick, and Newfoundland—responded to their concerns that they be given greater recognition in the accord. None of the provincial proposals, however, came close to what aboriginal peoples were demanding as their proper place in the Canadian federal system. Moreover, the three provinces allowed their proposals to be watered down during a June 1990 First Ministers' meeting, called by Prime Minister Mulroney to break the impasse that had arisen among the provinces over the accord. Rather than include a new provision in the accord to deal directly with aboriginal rights and the unique nature of aboriginal societies, the First Ministers only agreed to resurrect the former mechanism for dealing with aboriginal self-government by adding another amendment to the Constitution Act, 1982 that would provide for future constitutional conferences devoted to matters of concern to aboriginal peoples. First Ministers also agreed to establish a parliamentary committee to study a so-called "Canada clause" as a basis for a future constitutional amendment, in which aboriginal peoples would be recognized as part of the distinctive fabric of Canadian society.

In effect, the constitutional agreement that arose from the 1990 First Ministers' meeting did two things to aboriginal peoples. First, it returned them to the constitutional position they occupied in 1982, prior to the original conferences on aboriginal rights. Second, it required aboriginal peoples to defend their arguments that they constitute a fundamental characteristic of Canadian society, even though their ancestors were the original inhabitants of Canada. Not surprisingly, aboriginal leaders reacted negatively to this new agreement, arguing that it perpetuated the myth that there are only two founding nations in Canada—English and French. Moreover, they felt that the second agreement continued the hierarchy of recognition established by the original agreement, which denied them the same status within Canada as provinces, a situation which many Indian leaders, for example, have been seeking.

Arguing that "we must put an end to the lie that there are two founding nations in Canada," Indian leaders in Manitoba supported Elijah Harper, the lone Indian member of the Manitoba Legislative Assembly, in his efforts to prevent the Manitoba legislature from ratifying the Meech Lake Accord and the 1990 agreement before the June 23 deadline. Manitoba, along with Newfoundland and New Brunswick, had not yet ratified the Meech Lake Accord. By utilizing the special procedural rules of the Manitoba legislature for considering constitutional amendments,

Harper was able to prevent the agreements from being approved before the deadline. The success of aboriginal leaders in blocking the constitutional entrenchment of the Meech Lake Accord forced the federal and provincial governments to finally recognize the growing political acumen and strength of aboriginal peoples. Moreover, during this process aboriginal leaders were able to create allies among those other groups in Canada that are reluctant to support a privileged status for Quebec in Canadian society or that wish to see their own interests protected in the constitution, such as women and other visible minorities.

During fall 1991, the federal government once again initiated a process for resolving Canada's constitutional difficulties. Entitled "Shaping Canada's Future Together," the process began with the establishment of a parliamentary Special Joint Committee on a Renewed Canada. The mandate of the committee was to receive recommendations from all levels of governments, interested groups, and individuals across Canada, after which the committee would enter recommendations about a renewed federalism into the grist of the constitutional mill. Perhaps as a result of the effective political maneuvering of aboriginal leaders and the growing public support for the demands of aboriginal peoples as evidenced in public opinion polls, the federal government decided to approach the participation of aboriginal peoples in a much different way than that used in the Meech Lake negotiations. Each national aboriginal organization was given a large federal grant to conduct a "parallel process" among their own constituents. The objective of this strategy was to allow the leadership of each national aboriginal organization to come up with a constitutional proposal dealing with the place of their peoples in a renewed federal system that would be rooted in the expressed needs of members. These proposals were then to be submitted to the Special Joint Parliamentary Committee for incorporation into its recommendations to Parliament as well as in future constitutional negotiations.

On September 25, 1991, the federal government tabled a number of constitutional proposals dealing with aboriginal peoples, particularly aboriginal self-government, before the joint committee.

Despite the caveat by the federal government that these proposals were not the final word on the subject, it was apparent that whatever ideas aboriginal leaders generate, the federal proposals were the baseline for future constitutional discussions.

In brief, the federal constitutional proposals affecting aboriginal peoples were divided into several groups. First, aboriginal peoples would be included in a "Canada clause" defining what it means to be Canadian. Essentially, the Canada clause would refer to the fact that aboriginal peoples have been historically self-governing and that aboriginal rights are recognized in Canada. Second, the right to self-government would be constitutionally entrenched. Negotiations could begin immediately on the forms and jurisdictions of aboriginal governments. Any agreement concluded would be constitutionally entrenched. After ten years, the right to self-government would be legally enforceable in the courts, meaning in effect that aboriginal peoples could ask the courts to define their right to self-government if negotiations did not succeed. Third, and unlike the Meech Lake process, aboriginal political organizations were to be allowed to participate in future constitutional discussions. Fourth, a continuing process to involve aboriginal peoples in constitutional matters that affect them was to be established. Fifth, aboriginal peoples would be given guaranteed representation in a reformed Canadian Senate. And last, the Charter of Rights and Freedoms would apply to aboriginal governments.

The Special Joint Committee on a Renewed Canada, however, turned out to be only a preliminary stage in the constitutional saga that occurred during 1992. Between January and March, a series of nationally televised "Renewal of Canada" conferences, consisting of constitutional experts, advocacy groups, and concerned citizens, took place in Canada's major cities. Following these conferences, a series of multilateral meetings were scheduled between the federal minister of constitutional affairs, governmental representatives from the provinces and territories, and the heads of Canada's major aboriginal political associations. On July 7, this group issued a status report of negotiations, which formed the basis of discussions for several First Ministers' meetings in late August. The result of these meetings was a consensus report on the Constitution, commonly known as the Charlottetown Accord, because of the location of the First Minister's meetings in Charlottetown, Prince Edward Island.

The Charlottetown Accord, after some legal fine-tuning, became the position on renewed federalism that Canadians were asked to either support or reject during an August 26 national referendum. The Charlottetown Accord incorporated, in modified form, a number of the constitutional positions on aboriginal peoples put forth previously by the federal government. It also included a number of the arguments advanced by aboriginal leaders during the 1992 constitutional discussions.

First, the Charlottetown Accord proposed that a new Canada clause be included as Section 2 of the Constitution Act of 1867. As it applies to aboriginal peoples, the suggested Canada clause held that the Constitution, including the Charter of Rights and Freedoms, should be interpreted in light of the fact that aboriginal peoples "have the right to promote their languages, cultures and traditions and to ensure the integrity of their societies, and their governments constitute one of three orders of government in Canada."

Second, the accord held that the Constitution should be amended to recognize that aboriginal peoples have the inherent right of self-government within Canada. The exercise of the right of self-government included authority to "(a) safeguard and develop their language, culture, economies, identities, institutions and traditions; and (b) develop, maintain and strengthen their relationships with their lands, waters and environment so as to determine and control their development as peoples according to their own values and priorities and ensure the integrity of their societies."

In contrast to the earlier federal proposal, however, the validity of the inherent right to self-government in the courts was only to be delayed for a five-year period, rather then ten years, in order to give aboriginal peoples time to work out the forms and jurisdictions of aboriginal governments with federal and provincial officials. The addition of the word *inherent* to the right of self-government marked a significant departure from the previous federal position. The differences between "a right to self-government" and "an inherent right to self-government" is far more than a question of semantics. In their insistence on inherency, aboriginal leaders claim that aboriginal peoples have always had a right to self-government, a right that precedes European colonization and formation of the Canadian state. Furthermore, that right continues to exist today as the foundation for aboriginal self-government. In contrast, the federal government's historic position arguing for a non-inherent right to self-government implies that self-government for aboriginal peoples derives from the authority of the Canadian state. Underlying the federal proposal have been two important, interrelated positions. First, the federal government rejects any claim of sovereignty in the international sense on the part of aboriginal peoples. This has been a consistent position. The federal government's treatment of the Mohawk claim to independence, for example, has been based on this principle. Second, federal officials were fearful that the word *inherent* could imply that no federal or provincial laws would apply to aboriginal peoples, except with their consent. Such a situation would represent a radical departure from traditional Canadian constitutional, legislative, and judicial doctrines.

The acceptance of the inherent right to self-government by federal and provincial governments was in part due to the pressure asserted by aboriginal leaders in particular and also due to public pressure on leaders to "get a constitutional deal" and move on the economy. Federal and provincial acceptance of the inherent right to self-government within Canada, however, was not left unqualified. The accord also stated that a constitutional provision should be added to ensure that laws passed by aboriginal governments would not be inconsistent with the preservation of peace, order, and good government in Canada. In essence this means that on the surface, any aboriginal law that is inconsistent with a fundamental principle of Canadian constitutional democracy could be nullified by the courts.

Third, the accord held that the Charter of Rights and Freedoms should apply to aboriginal governments. In contrast to the earlier federal position, however, the accord held that aboriginal governments should have access to Section 33 of Constitution Act, 1982, which allows parliament and the provincial legislatures to opt out charter provisions for a five-year period, if they desire. This represented a major concession to aboriginal participants in the constitutional discussions. Aboriginal leaders have consistently argued that the charter, which is based upon the individualistic values of Western liberalism, runs counter to the communal-based non-Western values of aboriginal peoples. In applying the charter to aboriginal governments, the federal government has traditionally desired to accomplish two objectives. One is to protect individual aboriginal persons from possible arbitrary actions on the part of their own governments. Another is the desire to extend the protection of the charter to aboriginal persons as Canadian citizens. The application of Section 33 to aboriginal governments stands a as partial reconciliation with the aboriginal position.

Fourth, the Charlottetown Accord continued to argue that some form of guaranteed aboriginal representation in any reformed Senate be put in the constitution and also suggested that aboriginal representation be considered for the House of Commons, Parliament's lower house.

Fifth, the accord recommended that the Constitution be amended to provide for four First Ministers' Conferences on aboriginal matters beginning no later that 1996 and following every two years thereafter.

Finally, in a radical departure from the current constitutional division of powers between the federal government and the provinces in Canada, the accord proposed that all aboriginal peoples be brought under Section 91(24), which has given the federal government constitutional authority over status Indians and, by judicial incorporation, authority over the Inuit. This provision implied access for the Métis to programs and funding available to status Indians under the Indian Act, an astonishing reversal of the federal government's position for over a century. Equally astonishing was the fact that Indian and Inuit leaders participating in the constitutional discussions also agreed. The financial implications of Section 91(24) recognition of the Métis were addressed only obliquely and deferred into a future political accord. Also deferred into a political accord was a provision committing five provinces and the federal government to negotiate an arrangement with the "Métis Nation" covering self-government, land and resources, and the financing of Métis institutions, programs and services.

On October 26, 1992, the Charlottetown Accord was decisively rejected by the Canadian electorate, and because the accord was voted on as a total package, the aboriginal right to self-government once again failed to achieve constitutional status, even though both pre-referendum and post-referendum analyses suggested the presence of a strong pro-aboriginal sentiment among the Canadian population. Reaction to the defeat of the accord by Indian and Métis leadership was characterized by anger and frustration, while that of the Inuit reflected moderate disappointment, probably owing to the fact that significant progress toward a non-constitutional based form of self-government had already occurred for this group. But while the feelings of the leadership toward the failure of the accord seemed to reflect the attitude of the Métis population in general, the reaction of a large number of status Indians, particularly treaty Indians, departed from that of the leadership. Many Indians felt that the provisions in the accord dealing with self-government did not go far enough, and they were especially fearful of the "peace, order, and good government" restrictions on Indian government authority. Others felt strongly that the constitutional proposals would weaken traditional treaty relationships by destroying the nation-to-nation basis upon which treaties had been originally negotiated. In fact, treaty areas number six and seven publicly disassociated themselves from the elected leadership of the Assembly of First Nations position on the accord. And there appeared to be a generalized concern over the future effects on financial support for Indians if Métis were to be brought under Section 91(24) of the Constitution. Ironically,

Elijah Harper, a key figure in the death of the Meech Lake Accord, had publicly expressed disapproval of the Charlottetown Accord. In the end, it appeared that the Assembly of First Nations leadership was unable to convince rank and file Indians of the merits of the accord since it failed to achieve the support of a majority of voters on Indian reserves.

The failure of the Charlottetown Accord has effectively placed constitutional recognition of aboriginal self-government in limbo for some time, although it will undoubtedly return to the constitutional arena in the future. In the meantime, aboriginal peoples will continue to strive for incremental gains to eventually acquire greater control over their own communities.

♦ ♦ ♦ ♦ ♦ ♦ ♦ ABORIGINAL PEOPLES IN THE LEGISLATIVE, ADMINISTRATIVE, AND JUDICIAL ARENAS

During the 1980s, the federal government introduced a number of initiatives dealing with aboriginal self-government and land claims. Federal policy in the area of aboriginal self-government is designed to allow a greater degree of aboriginal self-administration of their own communities in order that they can begin their own process of political, social, and economic development. These policy initiatives involved a recognition on the part of the federal government that, given the stalled constitutional negotiations on aboriginal rights, something must be done to accommodate the increasing demands of aboriginal leaders for self-government. The government's actions also responded to a 1983 report of a Special Committee on Indian Self-Government of the Canadian Parliament that delivered a scathing indictment of the restrictive nature of the present Indian Act as well as other governmental policies toward Indians. In all cases the federal government has insisted its policies will not prejudice any constitutional negotiations regarding aboriginal self-government or other negotiations involving land-claims and treaty rights.

Community-Based Self-Government

In the case of status Indians, the most significant of the federal policies is the "community-based self-government negotiations approach," which allows for a limited degree of structural change to band or tribal political institutions and a greater degree of self-administration of programs in the areas of education, health, child welfare, social services, and environment, among others. Since some of the matters involved in this approach touch upon provincial jurisdiction, the provinces must be involved in negotiations between the federal government and bands or tribal groups where provincial interests are involved. Once negotiations have been finalized, Parliament passes a special act removing the band or tribal group from the Indian Act regarding the negotiated points of agreement.

The major precedent for community-based self-government involves the Sechelt Band in lower mainland British Columbia. The Sechelt Act (1986) is an individualized piece of legislation designed to meet the specific needs of the Sechelt Indians in the areas of taxation and control over lands and resources. An earlier precedent the Cree-Naskapi Agreement (the James Bay Agreement) is, as discussed before, a much broader piece of legislation tied to a land claim settlement with Quebec. The form of government established is regional in nature, providing for a number of regional governments and authorities to deal with political, economic, social, and cultural matters affecting the signatories.

Despite their disappointment over the failure of the constitutional process, a large number of bands and tribal groups are now involved at some stage in the community self-government negotiations process. Several Indian bands and groups, including the Gitksan and Wet'suwet'en in British Columbia, the Alexander and Sawridge Bands in Alberta, the Kahnawake Mohawk in Quebec, and the United Indian Councils of the Mississauga and Chippewa Indians in Ontario, have signed framework agreements, the final step in negotiations before the agreements go before Parliament.

The interest expressed by many Indian communities in community-based self-government appears to be, in part, a pragmatic recognition that this approach presents them not only with an

opportunity to acquire a degree of autonomy not possible under the Indian Act but also a limited chance to restore some of their traditional governing practices. Moreover, given the uncertainty about the future of constitutionally based Indian government, many Indian leaders believe that it is better to move ahead on a modest scale than wait for something that may never be realized. Indian leaders understand that this approach basically involves self-administration and not self-government in the political sense. While this approach does provide them with a broader scope for action when compared to authority given to Indian governments under the Indian Act, it still involves devolution of authority from other levels of Canadian government and therefore does not alter the basic positions of the federal government and the provinces in Canada with respect to jurisdiction and responsibility over Indians. This approach certainly fits the present mode of Canadian federalism. It remains a long way, however, from meeting

Cree woman sewing.

the aspirations of Indian peoples for recognition of their inherent right to self-government.

Non-constitutional initiatives to bring about a greater degree of self-determination for the Métis have been complicated by the fact that, with the exception of those living in the territories, they remain under provincial jurisdiction and, apart from some of the Métis living in Alberta, lack a coherent land base. In 1985, however, the federal government signaled its willingness to participate in a tripartite negotiations process that would allow the Métis greater decision-making in areas such as housing, health care, economic development, social services, language use, and cultural development. Despite the willingness of the federal government to assume some financial responsibility for Métis peoples, progress in this area has been relatively slow, since these discussions must be initiated by the provincial governments. It also remains to be seen whether the federal government follows up on its apparent commitment to become more involved with the Métis as manifested in the failed Charlottetown Accord.

The Inuit quest for self-government as discussed previously is linked to two principles: land claims settlements and public government. The Nunavut government that will emerge from the Inuit land claims settlement in the Northwest Territories will be a public government and have powers similar to those of the existing Northwest Territories government. Also, the Labrador Inuit have expressed their intention to negotiate a self-government arrangement within context of their comprehensive land claim. Unlike the bilateral nature of the process to develop a Nunavut government in the Northwest Territories, the province of Newfoundland will be involved in any self-government agreement reached with the Labrador Inuit.

Land Claims   In addition to self-government, land claims have held a dominant position on the political agenda of aboriginal peoples for the last several decades. Land, of course, not only holds a unique status within aboriginal culture; in the eyes of aboriginal people, it is also the key to their social and economic development. Land is the basis of their survival as distinct peoples. As pointed out earlier, land claims in Canada have been divided into two general types—comprehensive and specific—and governments have formulated policies for both types of claims.

Comprehensive claims policy acknowledges that aboriginal peoples have inherent interests in certain lands based upon traditional occupation and that claims can be made when it can be shown that aboriginal interests have not been extinguished. Modern comprehensive claims policy emerged from a decision of the Canadian Supreme Court in the Calder case (1973), which involved a land claim based upon aboriginal title by the Nisga'a Indians of British Columbia. Although the Nisga'a claim was dismissed on a technicality, the Court was divided as to whether aboriginal title based upon traditional occupancy still existed, and therefore did not reject the concept of aboriginal title. Fearing that future court decisions might provide judicial sanction to aboriginal title, the federal government established a Native Claims Office in the Department of Indian Affairs and instituted a claims process for both aboriginal and specific claims, the latter involving disputes over treaty land entitlement matters.

Despite the fact that both structures and processes have existed since 1974 for dealing with aboriginal land claims, and despite the millions of dollars given to aboriginal political associations for land claim research, the record to the present in satisfying land claims for Indians and Métis has been poor. This record is a product of a number of factors. First, non-Indian stakeholders, including the provinces, have been reluctant to recognize aboriginal claims where land and other proprietary interests are involved. For example, in the case of natural resources, revenue from royalties can comprise a substantial proportion of government income. It is not surprising that the most progress toward comprehensive land claim settlements are involved has occurred in the Territories. Second, the federal government itself, due to a lack of both financial and administrative resources, has limited the number of claims it can handle at any one point in time, creating a backlog in the claims process. Third, there have been a number of disagreements between aboriginal peoples themselves over particular claims. Examples include disagreement between the

Inuit and Dene over the appropriate boundaries for territorial divisions, disputes between Métis and Indians where land claims cover mixed communities, divisions between regional and national political associations about the acceptability of proposed claim settlement packages, and disputes over proposed settlements with specific tribal groups themselves, such as the Lubicon band mentioned earlier. And finally, judicial doctrine regarding the existence of aboriginal title has been inconsistent. A prominent example of this situation is the land claim of the Gitksan-Wet'suwet'en Indians of British Columbia. This case, initiated in 1984, involved a claim of aboriginal title over 57,000 square kilometers of land in northwestern British Columbia. In a decision handed down on March 8, 1991, in the British Columbia Supreme Court, Chief Justice Allan McEachern argued that "the aboriginal rights of Natives were lawfully extinguished by the Crown in the colonial period." In the face of this decision the Gitksan-Wet'suwet'en tribal leaders appealed to the Canadian Supreme Court, while the federal government vowed to pursue an equitable negotiated land settlement.

TOWARD THE FUTURE ♦ ♦ ♦ ♦ ♦ ♦ ♦ ♦ ♦ ♦ ♦ ♦ ♦ ♦ ♦ ♦

The decade of the 1990s may become a watershed in the history of Canada's aboriginal peoples. The 1990s could witness Canada's historical policy of assimilation transformed to one of respect for the cultural and political diversity of aboriginal peoples. This decade could also see the marginal social and economic status of aboriginal peoples improved to bring them more in line with the rest of Canadian society.

Despite the failure of the Charlottetown Accord, the positive attitudes of both governmental leaders and public at large towards aboriginal peoples favors a just resolution of the concerns of aboriginal peoples. Constitutional entrenchment of the right to self-government that also preserves the integrity of treaties, even though it may take some years to achieve, would appear to be the most desirable solution in the long run, since it could provide aboriginal peoples with an identifiable constitutional footing for dealing with the federal and provincial governments as well as the courts. However, even if constitutionalization of aboriginal self-government does not take place, both the federal and provincial governments seem to be willing to develop new legislative, financial, and administrative initiatives, as well as continue present policies to redress aboriginal grievances. Governments, however, may confront the reality of fiscal pressures. Aboriginal Canadians, whatever their rights are determined to be, must compete with other Canadians for financial and other resources.

Even so, progress toward self-governing status will remain uneven among the three aboriginal groups. The Inuit will probably make the most rapid progress, because their massive land claims negotiations have been settled and the type of government they seek is of the inclusive, public kind. Status Indians will continue to face a number of impediments. The continued presence of intransigent non-Indian stakeholders at both the federal and provincial levels, plus the lack of progress by Indian leaders themselves in developing operational concepts of self-government, will remain significant stumbling blocks. Progress by the Métis toward self-government will continue to be the slowest among the three aboriginal groups. The lack of identifiable land bases, except for the Alberta Settlements, means that most Métis must seek some off-reserve organizational structure for self-government. This situation, when coupled with the ambivalent jurisdictional status of the Métis, indicates that progress toward Métis self-government will probably proceed at a snail-like pace.

Hopeful signs are also emerging that the land claims process, in both the comprehensive and specific land claims areas, will be accelerated in the 1990s. Reversing more than one hundred years of land claims policy, the British Columbia government has recently recognized the concept of aboriginal land title and the implications for aboriginal self-government that go along with it. British Columbia is now participating in a tripartite land claims process involving federal officials, provincial officials, and Indian leaders in an attempt to settle some of the decades old land claims in the province. In the Yukon, the federal government has, after two decades, finally reached an agreement with both status and non-status Indians, which provides for ownership of more than 41,000 square kilometers of land, self-government arrangements, and involvement in wildlife management, among other things. Finally, the federal government has established a new Indian Claims Commission to hear appeals from Indians dissatisfied with federal offers to settle specific land claims arising from treaty violations or other misdeeds by the government.

In the administration of justice, there appears to be a growing recognition that something must be done to ensure that Canada's legal system provides fair and just treatment of aboriginal peoples. During the past several years, three provinces—Nova Scotia, Alberta, and Manitoba—created commissions of inquiry to examine how aboriginal peoples are treated within their respective justice systems. In a broad indictment of the courts, law enforcement agencies, and the correctional system, all three commissions reported that aboriginal peoples have been subject to systemic discrimination by the legal system. In fact, the Manitoba justice inquiry stated bluntly that "Canada's treatment of its first citizens has been an international disgrace." Arguing that poverty, social inequality, and a lack of understanding of Native culture and beliefs underpin the inability of the justice system to treat aboriginal peoples fairly, the commissioners in each province recommended

Sally Karatak at museum in traditional Inuit beaded dress. Yellowknife, Northwest Territory.

that serious attention be given to the establishment of aboriginal controlled police, correctional, and judicial systems. The recommendations of the justice inquiries have been echoed by the Law Reform Commission, an agency created to advise the federal Minister of Justice on matters requiring legal reform.

And last, after years of lobbying by aboriginal leaders, the federal government has established a Royal Commission on Aboriginal Peoples. Co-chaired by Georges Erasmus, former grand chief of the Assembly of First Nations, the commission is charged with conducting a broad inquiry into the economic, social, legal, and political issues that affect the lives of aboriginal peoples. After extensive background studies, hearings, and deliberations, sometime in the mid-1990s the commission is expected to report back to the federal government with its findings and recommendations.

In the final analysis, however, the future of Canada's aboriginal peoples is integrally tied to the fate of Canada as a nation. The rejection of the Charlottetown Accord seems to have given renewed vigor to the leaders of the separatist movements in Quebec. If the province of Quebec establishes a quasi-independent political relationship with the rest of Canada, then new arrangements must be developed for the Indian, Métis, and Inuit peoples living within her borders. Developing these new arrangements will not be an easy or necessarily peaceful process. Moreover, what happens to the aboriginal peoples in Quebec, should that province withdraw from confederation, has significant implications for the recognition of aboriginal self-government, land claims, and culture in the rest of Canada. Within this context, the future of aboriginal peoples in Canada is dependent not only on the willingness of Canadian governments and citizens to understand and meet their needs, but also on the strength of aboriginal peoples themselves to survive as distinct cultures and continue their struggle for justice.

J. Anthony Long and Katherine Beaty Chiste
University of Lethbridge (Alberta)
Canada

BIOGRAPHIES ✦ ✦ ✦ ✦ ✦ ✦ ✦ ✦ ✦ ✦ ✦ ✦ ✦ ✦ ✦ ✦ ✦ ✦

Edward Ahenakew
1885–1961

**Plains Cree minister
and author**

Edward Ahenakew was one of the first people to collect and transcribe Cree legends. Born at Sandy Lake in Saskatchewan, Canada, in June 1885, he was named after Edward Matheson, an Anglican missionary who had taught at Sandy Lake. Ahenakew attended the missionary school until he reached the age of eleven, when he was sent to boarding school at Prince Albert, Saskatchewan. Upon graduation, Ahenakew returned to Sandy Lake, where he taught at local mission schools until his acceptance as a ministry candidate at Wycliffe College in Toronto. Throughout his years studying, Ahenakew returned to Saskatchewan during the summers to work in the Diocese of Saskatchewan. He completed his religious studies at the University of Saskatoon in 1912.

Following his ordination, Ahenakew traveled to a mission at Onion Lake, Saskatchewan, to assist Matheson's brother, the Reverand John Matheson, who had fallen ill. Ahenakew proved a vital assistant and friend to John Matheson and remained close to his family after Matheson's death in 1916. In the winter of 1918, a flu epidemic swept the reserves, and Ahenakew resolved to study medicine to help his people. Soon after beginning his new studies, however, Ahenakew himself fell very ill, partly because he had so little money to spend for food.

Ahenakew eventually recovered, but was unable to return to medical school. Instead, he set out to collect and transcribe Cree legends and stories, which were published in 1925 as *Cree Trickster Tales*. Ahenakew also helped to publish a Cree-English dictionary and edited a monthly journal in Cree syllabics. Another collection of Ahenakew's writings, *Voices of the Plains Cree*, was published posthumously in 1974. At the age of seventy-six, Ahenakew died while traveling to Dauphin, Manitoba, to help establish a summer school.

Big Bear (Mistahimaskwa) was born near Fort Carlton, Saskatchewan, and became head man and chief of approximately sixty-five Cree lodges. Concerned about the disappearance of the buffalo and the effects of European settlement on traditional Indian life, Big Bear fought for better treaty terms for his people until he died in 1888. He refused to sign his consent to Treaty Six, one of several treaties that Canada entered into with First Nations, because in his view it did not provide his people with sufficient compensation and protection against further settlement and development. Big Bear constantly spoke out against the relocation of First Nations onto reserves and the turn toward agriculture by Indian people. He maintained this view until the buffalo were gone and starvation took hold in his community.

Big Bear also strove to unite the Northern Cree people, and he once succeeded in attracting more than two thousand Indians to join him in his thirst dance at the Poundmaker Reserve near Battleford, Saskatchewan. Late in life, Big Bear began to lose the support of many of his followers who became more militant. Led by Little Bad Man (Ayimisis) and Wandering Spirit (Kapapamahchakwew), the militants killed several white settlers when they became involved in what is known as the second Northwest Rebellion. The rebellion was led by Louis Riel, leader of the Métis people, who sought to establish a provisional government in Saskatchewan against the wishes of Canadian authorities. They were captured shortly thereafter, and Big Bear subsequently surrendered. Big Bear was tried for treason-felony, found guilty, and imprisoned for three years in Stony Mountain Penitentiary. Big Bear became ill in prison and was released after serving two years of his sentence. He died within a year of his release.

Ethel Blondin was born in the northern community of Fort Norman, in the Northwest Territories, Canada. Blondin is a member of the Dene Nation, which includes a number of different peoples who live in the Northwest Territories. In accordance with the custom of her people, Blondin was adopted by her aunt and uncle at the age of three months and spent her early childhood living in various hunting-and-trapping communities with her

Big Bear
1825?–88

Cree tribal leader

Ethel Blondin
1951–

Dene member of
Parliament

extended family. As a child, Blondin attended residential school in Inuvik, Northwest Territories. She later attended a school designed to promote leadership among Native and northern Canadian youth. Blondin also received a bachelor of education degree from the University of Alberta, in Edmonton, Alberta.

From 1974 to 1984, Blondin taught in the remote Northwest Territories communities of Tuktoyaktuk, Fort Franklin, Providence, and Yellowknife. During this time, she was the recipient of an award from a private foundation for her work in developing a Dene teaching program. In the mid-1980s, Blondin's focus shifted first to public service and then to elected office. From 1984 to 1986, Blondin was first manager and then acting director of the Public Service Commission of Canada, the commission representing federal public servants in Ottawa, the nation's capital. Returning to the Northwest Territories, Blondin was appointed assistant deputy minister of culture and communications in Yellowknife. Blondin was first elected to the Canadian Parliament in November 1988, as member for the western Arctic.

Blondin is an active member of the boards of several aboriginal organizations including aboriginal education issues. The single mother of three children, Blondin divides her time between Yellowknife and Ottawa.

Matthew Coon Come
1956–

Cree tribal leader

Matthew Coon Come, the grand chief of the Council of the Cree of Northern Quebec, is the principal architect of the effort by the Cree to stop a hydroelectric development in northern Quebec known as James Bay II or the Great Whale project. Coon Come was born in northern Canada, and at the age of six, he was forcibly removed by Canadian authorities to attend school. He then went on to study at Trent University and spent two years studying law at McGill University. During his university studies, Coon Come maintained close ties with his people.

From 1981 to 1986, Coon Come served as a board member and an executive committee member of the Grand Council of the Cree, a province-wide organization devoted to advancing the interests of Cree in Quebec. While at law school in 1987, he was approached by Cree elders and asked to become grand chief to lead the struggle against the James Bay project, which threatened to flood much of the Cree homeland in northern Quebec. Coon Come accepted and began to chart an extremely successful campaign against hydro-electric development in the area. He quickly marshalled environmental, human rights, and indigenous communities on the local, national, and international levels to create a strong coalition opposing the project. Primarily targeting New York State as a likely hydro-electric consumer, Coon Come organized a canoe trip of Cree elders from James Bay, through Lake Erie, and down the Hudson River. Under his leadership the Cree people were able to renegotiate with Quebec the terms under which hydro-electric development would occur in the north.

Matthew Coon Come is married and is the father of five children.

Nellie Cornoyea was elected government leader of the Northwest Territories in Canada in 1991. She was the second of eleven children born near Aklavik in the Canadian Arctic to Nels Hvatum, a Norwegian, and Maggie, a member of the Inuvialuit who live in the western Canadian Arctic. Cornoyea spent her childhood in the bush, hunting, trapping, and fishing with her family and educating herself through correspondence courses. When she turned eleven, she worked as a volunteer secretary for the local hunters' and trappers' association. At the age of eighteen, she married and had two children. The marriage broke up soon thereafter, and Cornoyea obtained work at a new Canadian Broadcasting Corporation (CBC) station in Inuvik, a town in the far northwestern corner of the Northwest Territories, in order to support her young children. Cornoyea worked for the CBC for more than nine years, as an announcer and station manager, persuading many young people to take up radio as a career.

Nellie Cornoyea

1940–

Inuvialuit politician

Before her election to the Northwest Territories Legislative Assembly in 1979, Cornoyea was a founding member of the Committee for Original People's Entitlement (COPE), an organization devoted to the rights of the Inuvialuit of the western Arctic. She was also a land claims officer for the Inuit Tapirisat of Canada, a national agency mandated to promote Inuit culture and identity and to develop Inuit political, economic, and environmental policy. In 1984, the Inuvialuit of the western Arctic signed an agreement with the federal government in which they received title to large areas of land. Cornoyea coordinated aspects of the implementation of the agreement and served on the board of directors of the Inuvialuit Petroleum Corporation, the Inuvialuit Development Corporation, and the Enrollment Authority and Arbitration Board. Cornoyea has served in a volunteer capacity to many organizations, and in 1982 she received the Woman of the Year Award (Politics) from the Northwest Territories Native Women's Association.

Crowfoot
c. 1830–90

Blackfoot Confederacy tribal leader

Crowfoot (Isapo-Muxika) was born a Blood Indian at Blackfoot Crossing near present-day Calgary, Alberta, but, upon his father's death, moved with his mother to the Blackfoot lodge of her new husband. Crowfoot was known as Bear Ghost (Kyi-i-staah) among his people during his youth and was only thirteen years old when he participated in the first of nineteen battles as a Blackfoot warrior. He became known to settlers when he rescued a Roman Catholic priest from Cree Indians in 1866. In 1877, Canadian authorities treated Crowfoot as head chief of the Blackfoot Confederacy, which included at the time the Blackfoot, Blood, Peigan, and Sarcee tribes, at the signing of Treaty Seven, one of the several treaties that Canada entered into with First Nations. In the same year, Crowfoot was commended by Queen Victoria of England for refusing to assist Sitting Bull of the Sioux Nation during the wars between the Plains Indians and the American calvary. Following the Battle of the Little Bighorn (known as Custer's Last Stand), many Sioux fled to Canada, at which time Crowfoot and Sitting Bull shared tobacco and achieved peace between the two nations.

By the summer of 1879, the Blackfoot faced starvation and were forced to follow the last buffalo herds into Montana. Two years later they crossed back into Canada and faced continued shortages of food. Eventually, the Blackfoot were forced to sell many of their possessions, including their horses, to survive. In 1885,

Crowfoot's adoptive son, Poundmaker, led a Cree attack on the town of Battleford on the North Saskatchewan River, as part of a larger rebellion, known as the second Northwest Rebellion of 1885, in which Louis Riel, leader of the Métis people, sought to form a provisional government in Saskatchewan against the wishes of Canadian authorities. Crowfoot kept the Blackfoot out of the rebellion, although he encouraged his people to assist any Cree passing through their territory. Crowfoot lost most of his children to smallpox and tuberculosis.

Gabriel Dumont
c.1837–1906

Métis tribal leader

Gabriel Dumont was active in the second Northwest Rebellion of 1885, in which Louis Riel, another Métis leader, sought to form a provisional government in Saskatchewan. Dumont could neither read nor write, but he had a great reputation as a guide, hunter, canoeist, and warrior. Dumont first engaged in plains warfare at the age of thirteen, when he took part in the defense of a Métis encampment against a Sioux war party. At the age of twenty-four, with his father, Dumont concluded a treaty between the Sioux and the Métis, which helped bring peace to the Canadian prairie. Dumont also participated in the creation of a treaty between the Blackfoot Nation and the Métis. When he was twenty-five, Dumont was elected permanent chief of his community.

In 1884, Dumont traveled to Montana where Louis Riel was living in exile, and he obtained Riel's agreement to return to Canada to lead resistance to the settlement of what is now known as Saskatchewan. Dumont became the militant leader of approximately three hundred Métis, in what became known as the second Northwest Rebellion. They were victorious in several battles against Canadian authorities, including a violent attack on Frog Lake in what is now Alberta, where nine people were killed. While Riel subsequently surrendered to authorities, Dumont fled to the United States. Dumont attempted to organize an escape route for Riel, which never came to pass, and Riel was executed for treason in 1885. Dumont spent several years living with the Métis of Montana before returning to Canada in 1890. In addition to dictating two memoirs of the rebellion, Dumont continued to hunt and trade up until his death in 1906.

Georges Erasmus
1948–

Dene tribal leader

Georges Erasmus has been a central figure in aboriginal politics in Canada since the 1970s. He was born at Fort Rae in the Northwest Territories just after World War II. His people, the Dene Nation, are Athapascan Indians in the Northwest Territories. *Athapascan* is a Cree term that covers all the indigenous people from the interior of Alaska to the Hudson Bay whose languages are related to one another. In their own languages, these people refer to themselves as Dene or Dinneh.

Erasmus became president of the Dene Nation in 1976, during which time he successfully led efforts to stop the construction of the Mackensie Valley Pipeline, a proposed natural gas pipeline running south from Alaska through the Northwest Territories and British Columbia. In 1985, he was successful in persuading Greenpeace, an international environmental organization, to halt a proposed anti-fur campaign, arguing that it threatened his people's traditional ways of life.

Erasmus served from 1985 to 1991 as the national chief of the Assembly of First Nations, a national organization of First Nations in Canada. In 1991, Erasmus was appointed co-chair of the Royal Commission on Aboriginal Peoples. The commission was established by the federal government to examine and report on a broad range of issues concerning aboriginal peoples in Canada, including government, treaties, economic, social and cultural issues, as well as matters relating to the administration of justice and aboriginal people. Erasmus also serves as board member for many organizations and foundations across Canada dedicated to the advancement of human rights and ecological concerns. He is the co-author of *Drumbeat: Anger and Renewal in Indian Country* (1989) and has received an honorary doctorate of law degree from Queen's University.

Cuthbert Grant
1793–1854

Métis tribal leader

Cuthbert Grant was, perhaps, the first leader of the Métis. Grant played a large role in shaping a sense of Métis nationalism. He worked most of his life as a fur trader first for the North West Company, a group of Montreal traders formed in 1779, and later in life for the company that first capitalized on the fur trade, the

Hudson's Bay Company. When he was nineteen years old, he was put in charge of a small outpost in Fort Esperance, on the Qu'Appelle River in what later became Saskatchewan.

Historians claim that Grant was chosen by his superiors to foster a sense of Métis identity partly to solidify the North West Company's trading rights in the region, as it was facing stiff competition from the Hudson's Bay Company. Grant was named "captain of the Métis" by his superior in 1814 and led efforts to persuade, through friendly and unfriendly means, recent settlers, who put a strain on the community's resources, to return to central Canada. In 1816, Grant also led an attack on the Hudson's Bay Company, resulting in a massacre of approximately twenty people. Although charges were brought against Grant for these and other actions, they were eventually dropped. After 1821, when the Hudson's Bay Company and the North West Company merged, Grant worked for the Hudson's Bay Company in a number of different positions. He briefly served as a special constable at Fort Garry (later known as Winnipeg) and later as warden, justice of the peace, and sheriff. He served as captain of the Métis annual buffalo hunts, and in the 1840s, Grant mediated a temporary truce between the Métis and the Sioux, who had been fighting over territory and buffalo hunting.

Elijah Harper
1949–

Cree provincial legislator

Elijah Harper is, perhaps, best known in Canada for his opposition to the Meech Lake Accord, a 1990 federal proposal to amend the Canadian Constitution to respond to demands by the province of Quebec for greater autonomy. Harper became the voice of aboriginal people, who objected to the exclusion of aboriginal concerns from the accord. In June 1990, Harper blocked the accord's passage in the Manitoba legislature. The accord's demise heightened the awareness of political demands by aboriginal people in Canada and led to new talks on constitutional reform that placed aboriginal issues at the top of the agenda.

Harper was born at Red Sucker Lake, Manitoba, and attended residential school. After completing high school, he studied anthropology at the University of Manitoba in Winnipeg from 1970 to 1972. He married Elizabeth Ann Ross in the fall of 1973, and they have four children. During these years, Harper worked in a number of different community development positions and was elected chief of his home community's Red Sucker Lake Band in 1977. He held that post until his election to the Manitoba legislature in 1981, with re-elections in 1986, 1988 and 1990. Harper served as legislative assistant to the minister of Northern affairs between 1981 and 1986 and co-chaired the Native affairs committee of the provincial cabinet. In 1986, Harper was appointed minister responsible for Native affairs and in 1987 became minister of Northern affairs.

The image of Harper standing in the Manitoba legislature holding a single eagle feather, and depriving the legislature of the necessary unanimous consent to pass the Meech Lake Accord, struck a deep chord in the Canadian national psyche. Harper was awarded the 1990 Canadian press newsmaker of the year award and, in 1991, the Stanley Knowles Humanitarian Award. Harper continues to make his home in Red Sucker Lake, Manitoba.

George Manuel
1921–89

Shuswap tribal leader

George Manuel was born in the Shuswap village of Neskainlith, on the South Thompson River, about thirty miles east of Kamloops, in south-central British Columbia. The Shuswap people are one of four groups that comprise the Interior Salish people, the others being the Lillooet, Thompson, and Okanagan peoples. Salmon fishing is one of the major activities of the Interior Salish, and the Shuswap would spend summers and falls in mobile bands intercepting the spawning runs in numerous canyons that slice through the interior of the province. During the winter, they would form relatively permanent villages, living on stored food and engaging in major social and ceremonial activities. There they would live in pithouses, subterranean structures that protected them from the cold.

During his early years, Manuel was raised more by his grandparents than by his parents. He spent some time in a Kamloops residential school. He fell ill with tuberculosis, however, and was transferred to a hospital for children in Coqualeetza in the Lower

Fraser Valley. There he was able to improve his reading and writing skills. His formal education was never resumed.

Manuel became chief of his people in the late 1940s. He began to organize the Interior Salish people and in 1958 launched an organization called the Aboriginal Native Rights Committee of the Interior Tribes of British Columbia, which reconstituted itself as the North American Indian Brotherhood in 1960. Manuel was elected president of the brotherhood that year, and shortly thereafter he presented a lengthy brief to a parliamentary committee in Ottawa detailing his people's claims to land.

In 1966, Manuel was hired by the federal government to be a community development worker with the Cowichan Band on southern Vancouver island. His stint there was highly successful, although a subsequent assignment with the Nuu-chah-nulth on the western coast of the island was not, as the Nuu-chah-nulth were resistant to outside advisors. During this time, Manuel remained active in pressing the claims of aboriginal people in British Columbia with federal authorities. He was active in the formation of the Union of British Columbia Indian Chiefs in 1969, a province-wide organization devoted to the advancement of aboriginal claims and, in 1970, was elected president of the National Indian Brotherhood, a national organization of Indian groups. Manuel was also a major figure in the World Council of Indigenous Peoples, an international organization of indigenous peoples.

Leonard Stephen Marchand

1933–

Okanagan Canadian senator

Len Marchand has been a pioneer in the field of government. He was born in Vernon, British Columbia, on November 16, 1933. He attended residential school and then became the first Native person to graduate from his hometown's high school. Marchand went on to earn a bachelor of science degree in agriculture in 1959 from the University of British Columbia and a master's degree in forestry from the University of Idaho in 1964. During this time, Marchand became active in the North American Indian Brotherhood, a national organization devoted to advancing the rights of aboriginal people in Canada, working to obtain the federal vote, self-government, and improved education for aboriginal people.

In 1965, Marchand was the first Indian appointed as special assistant to a cabinet minister, and, in 1968, he was the first Indian to be elected to the Canadian House of Commons. Marchand was re-elected in 1972 and again in 1974. In 1977, Marchand was named minister of state for small business and became minister of state for the environment in 1977. Upon the defeat of the Liberal government in 1979, Marchand returned to British Columbia to work for four years as an administrator for the Nicola Valley Indian Bands (BC), an organization representing Indian bands located in the Nicola Valley, in south-central British Columbia. At this time, Marchand also became a director of the Western Indian Agricultural Corporation, a company designed to encourage the use of advanced agricultural techniques and production among Native people. Marchand also acted as a consultant on a variety of projects, among which was the Round Lake Treatment Centre, the first Native drug and alcohol treatment center, located near Vernon, his place of birth. Marchand was appointed to the Canadian Senate in June 1984 and has remained active on agricultural and aboriginal committees. He was named honorary chief of the Okanagans, a people who live in south-central British Columbia.

Matonabbee

1736–82

Chipewyan guide and translator

Matonabbee lived in the Hudson Bay region of northern Canada in the mid-1700s and was brought up in both European and Indian cultures. His ability to move easily between the two worlds made him a valuable liaison for European traders and explorers in the region.

Matonabbee was born near Fort Prince of Wales, located at the mouth of the Churchill River. When his father died, Richard Norton, a Hudson Bay Company manager, adopted Matonabbee and educated him. When Norton returned to England, Matonabbee returned to live among the Chipewyan people, who are Athapascan speakers who lived mainly by hunting large game animals and gathering wild plants. For the next few years Matonabbee learned Chipewyan ways and traveled about much of present-day northern Manitoba, northern Saskatchewan, and the eastern Northwest Territories.

When he was sixteen years old, Matonabbee returned to Fort Prince of Wales and took employment with the British as a hunter. Matonabbee's valuable background was soon noticed by the British, who asked Matonabbee to perform other duties as well, such as negotiating with Indian tribes and translating. While accompanying the British on southern trading trips, Matonabbee learned the Algonkian language of the Cree Indians. Matonabbee's prestige rose among his own people as a result of his growing stature among the British, and he soon became a respected leader.

In the 1760s, Englishman Samuel Hearne made two failed expeditions for the Hudson Bay Company to find the Northwest Passage and copper deposits. Many explorers sought a way across northern Canada because such a route promised efficient shipping and trade routes from Europe to China and Japan. Many sea captains and explorers tried to find a Northwest Passage, but there never was an easy route to find, since the Arctic Ocean freezes over much of the year and blocks any easy shipping lanes. During his second expedition, Hearne and his company were in danger of perishing from hunger, when Matonabbee, whom Hearne had met at Fort Prince of Wales, walked into his camp and helped him return safely to the English settlements. The two became friends, and, in 1771, they planned a third expedition to search for the Northwest Passage. Matonabbee provided Hearne with guides for the trip. Chipewyan bands followed the expedition and provided protection from enemies and provided food by hunting. In 1772, the expedition reached the Arctic Ocean, but Hearne was dismayed to find no passage. The return trip was brutal for the expedition and several Chipewyan died from starvation.

Ovide William Mercredi 1945–

Cree tribal leader

Ovide Mercredi is currently the national chief of the Assembly of First Nations, a national organization of first nations in Canada. Mercredi began his role as a political advocate in the late 1960s, when he observed first-hand the social upheaval resulting from a massive hydro-electric development project in his home community of Grand Rapids, Manitoba. He obtained a law degree from the University of Manitoba in 1977 and practiced criminal law in The Pas, Manitoba, for several years. In the 1980s, Mercredi turned his mind to constitutional reform, and ever since he has been actively involved in efforts by first nations to amend the constitution of Canada to recognize aboriginal rights to land and government. Mercredi was one of several aboriginal leaders to speak out against a constitutional reform package known as the Meech Lake Accord. Negotiated with a view to placating nationalistic concerns of the province of Quebec, the accord did not address first nations' concerns. Mercredi provided key advice to Elijah Harper, an elected member of the Manitoba legislature, who succeeded in blocking the accord's passage. In 1992, as national chief, Mercredi entered into successful negotiations with the federal government on constitutional reform.

Before his election as national chief, Mercredi represented and served his people in a number of different ways. He represented the Assembly of First Nations in Geneva in 1989 in seeking improvements to the International Convention on the Rights of the Child and acted as the assembly spokesperson for the United Nations Indigenous Peoples Working Group. He served as a commissioner for the Manitoba Human Rights Commission. He has advised various agencies on aboriginal family and child services issues, in addition to numerous other community-oriented activities. Mercredi lives with his wife Shelley and their daughter Danielle in Orleans, Ontario. He was recently given the name Gebezhkong by Ojibway elders, which means "the One Who Walks the Land."

John Norquay
1841–89

Métis politician

John Norquay was a Métis politician who served as the premier of Manitoba from 1878 to 1887. He was born in 1841 to Métis parents, persons of mixed Indian-European heritage. Norquay's mother died when he was only two years old, and he was left in the care of his grandmother. He excelled at school, attending a parish school during his childhood. With the help of a scholarship, he attended St. John's Academy. He then turned to teaching, first at the parish school that he attended as a child and later at a school known as Park's Creek, where he met, courted, and, in 1862, married Elizabeth Setter. After the wedding, Norquay took up farming in High Bluff, and for four years he worked the land.

His interests quickly turned to political matters, however, and he was elected by acclamation to Manitoba's first legislature in 1870. He quickly moved up through the political ranks, becoming the minister of public works and then minister of agriculture. When the premier of Manitoba resigned in 1878, the lieutenant-governor of the province called upon Norquay to form a new government and serve as premier. During his nine-year tenure, he was faced with difficult and divisive political issues dealing with French representation in the government, among other matters. His government eventually collapsed on the issue of extending the railway through the province. In an effort to force the hand of the federal government, Norquay proposed the construction of a railway to the United States. His plan backfired, however, and he was forced to resign shortly thereafter. Norquay died soon after leaving office, in 1889.

Also known as Payepot (One Who Knows the Secrets of the Sioux), Piapot was a respected leader and warrior during a time of many conflicts for the Cree. He was raised by his grandmother after his parents were killed by a smallpox epidemic introduced by settlers. Piapot and his grandmother were captured by the Sioux and lived among the Sioux people for fourteen years until a Cree raiding party freed them. After his rescue, Piapot became an important source of information to the Cree, due to his knowledge of the ways of the Sioux. Following his selection as chief of his community in Manitoba, Piapot led a number of successful raids against the Sioux and the Blackfoot. In 1870, he took approximately seven hundred warriors into Blackfoot territory and destroyed several lodges. The Blackfoot, with the assistance of their kindred allies, the Peigan, counterattacked, killing at least half of Piapot's warriors. According to historians, the counterattack led to a significant adjustment of power between the Cree and the Blackfoot on the Canadian Plains.

Piapot was also known for his resistance to white settlement of the western Plains and, in 1874, he refused to sign a treaty with Canadian authorities that would have resulted in his people moving to a reserve. He reluctantly signed a year later but continued

Piapot

c. 1816–1908

Cree tribal leader

to resist the containment that its terms imposed. Piapot moved his people westward into Saskatchewan and disrupted the building of the Canadian Pacific Railroad by pulling up surveyor stakes and erecting tipis in the path of crews laying track. The Mounties responded by dismantling the tipis, and Piapot again moved his people to a nearby stretch of barren reserve land. Approximately one quarter of Piapot's people died before they relocated to the more fertile valley near Regina, Saskatchewan. Piapot was eventually "deposed" as chief by white authorities after his people held a forbidden "Sun Dance," an annual tribal renewal ceremony. The Cree remained loyal to Piapot until his death in 1908.

Poundmaker

c. 1842–86

Cree tribal leader

A trader who met Poundmaker in the 1860s described him as "just an ordinary Indian, [an] ordinary man as other Indians." Poundmaker's life changed several years later, however, when, during a truce between the Cree and the Blackfoot, he was noticed by a wife of the Blackfoot chief Crowfoot. The two were struck by Poundmaker's resemblance to a son who had been killed by Cree warriors before the truce. Crowfoot immediately adopted Poundmaker as his son and gave him a Blackfoot name, Makoyi-koh-kin (Wolf Thin Legs). Poundmaker's stature increased when he returned to his people in central Saskatchewan and was chosen to be one of several spokespersons for the Plains Cree in negotiations over a treaty with Canadian authorities in 1876. During negotiations, Poundmaker pressed for better terms, including education and assistance, stating that once the buffalo were gone, he and his people would have to learn how to farm and survive in a new world. His pleas fell on deaf ears, however, and he eventually signed the treaty and agreed to a reserve for his people in central Saskatchewan.

Poundmaker and his followers participated in the second Northwest Rebellion of 1885, in which Louis Riel, leader of the Métis people, sought to form a provisional government in Saskatchewan against the wishes of Canadian authorities. Poundmaker's followers ransacked the abandoned village of Battleford in what is now central Saskatchewan. A military force of some three hundred men were sent in retaliation. When they attacked Poundmaker's camp, however, they suffered heavy casualties. When he learned of Louis Riel's surrender in 1885, Poundmaker also surrendered to Canadian authorities. He was convicted of treason and after serving a year of his three year sentence, Poundmaker fell ill and was released. He died four months later.

Also known as Mekaisto, Red Crow was born and raised in what is currently Alberta in the Canadian Plains. Descended from a long line of Blood chiefs, including his father, Black Bear, Red Crow continued the family tradition. The Blood people, together with the Blackfoot and Peigan nations, were part of the powerful Blackfoot Confederacy that lived on the Canadian Plains. Red Crow became a warrior in his teens, and, during his lifetime, participated in at least thirty-three raids against the Crow, Plains Cree, Nez Percé, Assiniboine, and Shoshoni peoples. He was known for his remarkable ability to remain unscathed and late in life boasted, "I was never struck by an enemy in my life, with bullet, arrow, axe, spear or knife."

Red Crow

c. 1830–1900

Blood tribal leader

Red Crow became leader of his people, the Fish Eaters band, when smallpox claimed the life of his father in 1869. He forged alliances with the North-West Mounted Police and Plains Indian leaders and became the leading chief of the Blood people. During the 1870s, the buffalo were virtually destroyed by American hunters in Montana Territory, and Red Crow realized that his people would have to change their ways in order to survive. In 1880, he selected a reserve for his people and organized the construction of log shanties. He and his people turned to agriculture and cattle raising. Unlike many other Plains Indian communities, Red Crow's people did not participate in the 1885 Northwest Rebellions, in which Louis Riel, leader of the Métis people, sought to form a provisional government in Saskatchewan against the wishes of Canadian authorities. In fact, Red Crow joined a delegation of Blackfoot chiefs on a tour of eastern Canada provided as a gesture of thanks from Canadian authorities for not participating in the rebellions. After visiting the Mohawk Institute in Brantford, Ontario, a school for Mohawk students, Red Crow became a strong supporter of education and encouraged the schooling provided by various missionaries on the reserve. Red Crow died quietly in 1900 on the banks of the river that ran through his reserve.

Louis David Riel, Jr.
1844–85

Métis leader

Louis Riel was a leader of the Métis people. He led what have become known as the Northwest Rebellions of 1870 and 1885. Riel was born to a French-Ojibway father, Louis Riel, Sr., a political leader in his own right, and a French mother, Julie Lagimodiere, in the Red River Settlement in what is now Manitoba. He began his education in St. Boniface, Manitoba, and went on to study languages, philosophy, mathematics, and the sciences in a Montreal seminary, and then went on to study law.

After traveling throughout the United States, he returned to the Red River in 1868 and became involved in the first Northwest Rebellion, in which he and his followers drove away federal surveyors planning to section off the territory into townships contrary to Métis patterns of landholding that divided the land into strips extending out from the river. A group of Canadians responded with an attempt to organize a militia, but Riel formed his own "Comité National des Métis," peacefully seized Fort Garry in Winnipeg, took numerous prisoners, and declared a provisional government in 1869. After declaring an amnesty of all prisoners, his government re-arrested one William Scott, who had plotted an attack on Fort Garry. Scott was found guilty and sentenced to death. When Riel supported the verdict, sentiment in the rest of Canada hardened against him. Riel fled to the United States shortly after his government reached an agreement with Canada to create the province of Manitoba. Riel was elected twice in absentia to the Canadian Parliament, returning once to claim his seat only to be evicted by a motion of the House of Commons. Shortly thereafter he suffered a nervous breakdown and was admitted for a short time to a mental institution. Released in 1878, Riel moved to Montana where he became an American citizen, married, and worked as a schoolteacher. He returned to Canada to help lead Métis resistance to the settlement of Saskatchewan in 1884, seizing a local church and again establishing a provisional government. He surrendered two months later, and was convicted of treason and executed in Regina, Saskatchewan, in 1885.

Ralph Steinhauer, the first Native person to serve as lieutenant-governor of a Canadian province, was born in 1905 in Morley, a small town in east-central Alberta. His great-grandfather, Henry Bird Steinhauer, was a distinguished Ojibway missionary. Ralph attended the Brandon Indian Residential School. Until the age of twenty-three, he also worked on his father's farm in Saddle Lake during the summer and at a local store during the winter. In 1927, Steinhauer met Isabel Davidson, who had recently moved from the eastern United States to Alberta with her widowed mother. They were married the following year and moved to the Saddle Lake Indian Reserve in east-central Alberta to farm in earnest. The Steinhauer farm grew steadily, and he became an enormously successful farmer, teaching others to use the reserve system to maximize agricultural opportunities.

Steinhauer began to develop an interest in politics, serving as chief of the Saddle Lake Reserve for three years. In 1963, he was nominated by the Liberal party to run for election to the federal House of Commons, although he did not get elected. However, his successes were many. He was a founder of the Indian Association of Alberta, a province-wide organization devoted to the advancement of aboriginal rights. In 1974, Steinhauer was sworn in as the lieutenant-governor of Alberta, a position he held until 1979. In light of his contribution to his community, Steinhauer was named a Companion of the Order of Canada, an award conferred by the governor general of Canada to select Canadians in recognition of exemplary merit and achievement. He also received honorary doctoral degrees from the Universities of Alberta and Calgary.

Bill Wilson is well-known in Canada for advancing the rights of aboriginal people. Born in 1944 to Charles William Wilson and Ethel Johnson, Wilson is a Kwawkgewlth Indian. The Kwawkgewlth live on the northern coast of Vancouver Island and the nearby coast of British Columbia. Wilson began to work for his father when he was twelve at a fish purchasing plant in Comox, BC, on Vancouver Island while attending grade school and high school. Although he wanted to quit school when he turned fifteen, his parents persuaded him to continue, and Wilson went on

Ralph Garvin Steinhauer
1905–87

Métis politician

Bill Wilson
1944–

Kwawkgewlth tribal leader

to obtain a bachelor of arts degree from the University of Victoria on Vancouver Island in 1970 and a bachelor of laws from the University of British Columbia in 1973. During his summer vacations and weekends, he worked at numerous jobs, including stints as a taxi driver, fisherman, logger, laborer, pulpmill worker, bartender, and car salesman.

Wilson became involved at an early age in Indian political activities. At fourteen, he joined the Native Brotherhood of British Columbia, a province-wide organization devoted to advancing the cause of Indian rights. His early involvement with the Native Brotherhood of British Columbia developed into a full-time commitment to aboriginal politics that has spanned more than three decades, during which time he has actively participated in countless aboriginal organizations.

While in law school, Wilson was instrumental in the creation, and became an executive director, of the Union of British Columbia Indian Chiefs, an organization representing Indian bands across the province. In 1976, Wilson was the founding president of the United Native Nations, an association designed to represent aboriginal people by tribe instead of according to bands defined by Canadian authorities. In 1990–91, Wilson was a vice-chief of the Assembly of First Nations, a national organization representing Indian bands across the country, and in 1991, he became the political secretary of the Assembly of First Nations. As the chairman of the First Nations Congress, Wilson succeeded in commencing negotiations on land claims in the province for the first time with the government of British Columbia. Wilson has two daughters and a son and currently lives in Comox, BC.

Native North American Languages

The term *North American Indian languages* is used here to refer to the Native languages of the continental United States and Canada, including Aleut and Eskimo. However, the Inuit (eastern) branch of Eskimo is also the principal language of Greenland (under Danish administration); and several languages of the southwestern United States, such as Pima-Papago (O'Odham), are also spoken in northern Mexico. In addition, certain important language groups of the United States, such as the Uto-Aztecan family (to which O'Odham belongs), are also represented in Mexico and southward into Central America as far as El Salvador.

The Native North American languages may have originally numbered as many as three hundred. However, many have become extinct as a result of contact with European society and have been replaced by English, French, or Spanish. The study of such languages depends on materials written down by missionaries, travelers, educators, anthropologists, and linguists. Nevertheless, more than one hundred languages may still be spoken, although some of these may survive mainly in the memories of a few elderly speakers. Still others are spoken by thousands of people and are still learned by children as their first language; Navajo, with around 100,000 speakers, probably leads the list.

Nevertheless, because of the trend toward extinction among American Indian languages, their study is increasingly aimed at three goals: (a) interpreting written data on extinct languages, (b) obtaining data from the last speakers of obsolescent languages, and (c) encouraging the maintenance of languages still spoken by substantial communities. In the history of the linguistics of North America, the study of Native American languages has played a vital role. Indeed, these languages have provided a living laboratory for the analysis of a great variety of languages. (In the following discussion, the present tense refers to extinct and obsolescent languages as well as those which are still viable.)

North American Indian languages are as diverse as they are numerous; no single set of characteristics is shared by all of them. They can be grouped into some fifty-seven families, comparable to language families in Europe such as Romance (Italian, Spanish, French) and Germanic (German, Dutch, English). This diversity tends to be concentrated in the western part of the continent: thirty-seven families lie west of the Rockies, with twenty in California alone, so that California shows more linguistic variety than all of Europe. This linguistic diversity of Native North America suggests that the area may well have been populated by several waves of migration from Asia, across the Bering Straits, by peoples of distinct linguistic stocks; many of those stocks perhaps have no modern survivors in Asia.

CLASSIFICATION ✦ ✦ ✦ ✦ ✦ ✦ ✦ ✦ ✦ ✦ ✦ ✦ ✦ ✦ ✦ ✦ ✦ ✦ ✦

When a group of languages shows similar vocabulary items, with regular correspondences of sounds, the group is said to have a genetic relationship; that is, the languages are "sister" languages descended historically from a single origin. Examples in the Romance languages are sets of words like Italian *vacca*, Spanish *vaca*, French *vache* 'cow,' and Italian *bocca*, Spanish *boca*, French *bouche* 'mouth'; these distinguish the Romance family from the Germanic family, which has contrasting sets: German *Kuh*, Dutch *koe*, English *cow*, and German *Mund*, Dutch *mond*, English *mouth*. Such sets of words also occur among American Indian languages, as with Fox *okimaaw*, Menominee *okeemaaw*, and Ojibway *okimaa* 'chief,' which help identify the Algonkian family and assist in reconstructing a proto-language, or prehistoric parent, under such a name as Proto-Algonkian.

Beyond this level of relationship, however, some families show more distant degrees of similarity, indicating some shared history at a more remote chronological period. For instance, European language families like Romance and Germanic can be grouped together into Indo-European, which also includes families like Slavic and Indic. In North America, similarities between the Siouan family and the Iroquoian family suggest such a higher-order grouping, which can be called Macro-Siouan. This type of grouping is often called a phylum (plural phyla), referring to a family at a high level of classification. Within a phylum, however, it may also be necessary to recognize some languages that have no close relatives and do not fall into families; these are language isolates (or simply isolates). Thus the Yuchi language, in the southeastern United States, may be such an isolate within Macro-Siouan. The classification of languages in these terms helps correlate the history of languages with what archaeology and Native tradition reveal about the history of cultures (see Language and Culture section, below). Taken together, these types of evidence aid in the reconstruction of prehistoric homelands, migrations, and culture contacts.

Some other language families, and even language isolates, are not generally recognized as falling into any of the familiar phyla; such "unclassified" units are the Salishan and Wakashan families of the Pacific Northwest and the Kutenai language isolate of northern Idaho. The possibility remains, of course, that further research will uncover historical links for these languages.

However, at the more remote historical levels, it is not always clear that similarities among languages are to be explained in terms of common origins. An alternative explanation is that prehistoric contact among languages may have resulted in the borrowing of vocabulary items, of sounds, and of grammatical features. Such phenomena of language contact are discussed in Language Contact section, below.

At present, the classification of Native American language families in terms of phyla is a matter of intense controversy. Almost the only agreement is that the organization into some fifty-seven families, as presented by J. W. Powell (1891), is approximately correct. One of the most influential scholars of American Indian linguistics, Edward Sapir (1929), published a classification of these languages into six phyla, and at one time this was widely accepted. In more recent years, however, re-evaluation of Sapir's work has suggested the revised scheme of C. F. Voegelin and F. R. Voegelin (1977), which recognizes six phyla—not identical with Sapir's—but also several unclassified families and language isolates. Still more recently, opinions have become increasingly divided. Scholars known as "splitters," such as Campbell and Mithun (1979), have cast doubt on all groupings of the phylum level; by contrast, a "lumper" such as J. H. Greenberg (1987) has proposed that all linguistic families of both North and South America—except for Na-Dené and Eskimo-Aleut, in the far north—can be assigned to a single macro-phylum that he calls Amerindian.

Various proposals have been made to relate North American Indian languages to language families of Asia; none of these have gained wide acceptance, except for a possible connection of Eskimo-Aleut to some languages of adjacent Siberia. To be sure, Greenberg has suggested connections of his Amerindian with several major language families in Eurasia; however, he has provided little evidence to date.

✦ ✦ ✦ ✦ ✦ ✦ ✦ ✦ ✦ ✦ ✦ ✦ ✦ ✦ ✦ ✦ ✦ ✦ **PHYLA AND FAMILIES**

The following list of phyla, families, and languages follows the "middle-of-the-road" system of Voegelin and Voegelin (1977), which provides a useful point of reference in terms of its familiarity, and use in many reference works. For an overall map, see the next page.

In some cases, either a phylum or a family must be divided into two or more branches. Sometimes it is not clear whether local speech variants should be called languages of a single family, or dialects of a single language; in such cases, the neutral term varieties is used. Where languages have changed location in historic times, both older and newer locations are listed. The names of languages believed to be extinct are followed by an asterisk (*). Some extinct languages on which virtually no information is available are omitted.

Phylum: Eskimo-Aleut
    Family: Aleut, a single language (Aleutian and Pribilof Islands, in Alaska; and Komandorskiye Islands, in Siberia)
    Family: Eskimo
        Branch: Yupik, with the following languages:
        Central Siberian Yupik (Chukotski Peninsula; St. Lawrence Island, Alaska)
        Central Alaskan Yupik (southwest Alaska)
        Alutiiq (southwest Alaska)
        Branch: Inuit, a language with many local dialects, including Inupiaq (Alaska), Inuktitut (eastern Canada), and Kalaallisut (Greenland)

Note: It has been suggested that Eskimo-Aleut is related to certain native languages of the Chukotski area in Siberia, across the Bering Straits from Alaska. In Canada the label Eskimo is disfavored; the term Inuit is generally used to refer to the people, and Inuktitut to their language. In Greenland, Kalaallisut is an official language along with Danish.

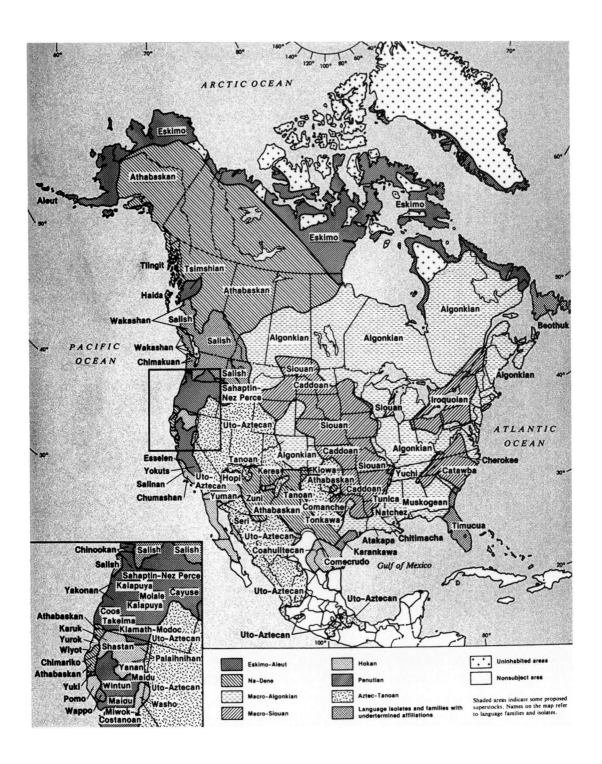

ARCTIC OCEAN

Eskimo

Athabaskan

Aleut

Eskimo

Eskimo

Tlingit
Tsimshian
Athabaskan

Haida
Algonkian

Wakashan Salish
Algonkian
Beothuk

Salish

PACIFIC
OCEAN Wakashan
Salish Algonkian Algonkian

Chimakuan

Salish
Siouan

Sahaptin-
Nez Perce Caddoan
Iroquoian

Siouan

Uto-Aztecan

ATLANTIC
OCEAN

Siouan

Esselen Tanoan Algonkian Caddoan
Algonkian
Cherokee

Yokuts Keres Kiowa Siouan Yuchi Catawba

Salinan Uto- Hopi Athabaskan

Aztecan Tanoan Caddoan

Chumashan Zuni Tunica Muskogean

Yuman Comanche Natchez

Athabaskan

Seri Tonkawa Timucua

Uto-Aztecan Atakapa Chitimacha

Coahuiltecan Karankawa

Comecrudo *Gulf of Mexico*

Uto-Aztecan

Uto-Aztecan

Uto-Aztecan

Chinookan Salish Salish

Salish

Sahaptin-Nez Perce
Yakonan Kalapuya
Molale Cayuse
Kalapuya

Coos

Athabaskan Takelma
Karuk Klamath-Modoc
Yurok Uto-Aztecan
Wiyot Shastan

Chimariko Yanan Palaihnihan

Athabaskan Maidu

Yuki Wintun Uto-Aztecan

Pomo Maidu Washo

Wappo Miwok-
Costanoan

	Eskimo-Aleut		Hokan		Uninhabited areas
	Na-Dene		Penutian		Nonsubject area
	Macro-Algonkian		Aztec-Tanoan		
	Macro-Siouan		Language isolates and families with undetermined affiliations		

Shaded areas indicate some proposed superstocks. Names on the map refer to language families and isolates.

Phylum: Na-Dené
    Family: Tlingit, an isolate (southeast Alaska)
    Family: Haida, an isolate (northwest British Columbia)
    Family: Athabaskan
        Branch: Eyak,* an isolate (southeast Alaska)
        Branch: Northern Athabaskan, including the following languages (grouped geographically):
            Interior Alaska: Tanana, Koyukon, Han, Tutchone, Tanaina, Ingalik, Nabesna, Ahtena
            Alaska and Yukon: Kutchin
            Northwest Territories: Dogrib, Bear Lake, Hare, Chipewyan, Slave, Yellowknife, Tahltan, Kaska
            Alberta: Beaver, Sarsi
            British Columbia: Sekani, Carrier, Chilcotin
        Branch: Pacific Coast Athabaskan, including the following languages (grouped geographically):
            Southwest Oregon: Chasta Costa,* Galice,* Tututni* Northwest California: Tolowa, Hupa, Kato,* Wailaki,* Mattole*
        Branch: Southwestern Athabaskan or Apachean (Arizona, New Mexico), including the following varieties:
            Navajo, Western Apache, Chiricahua, Mescalero, Jicarilla, Lipan, Kiowa-Apache
Note: Athabaskan peoples carried out migrations from the sub-Arctic in two southward directions, as shown in a map on facing page.
Phylum: Macro-Algonkian
      Branch: Algic, with three families:
        Yurok, an isolate (northwest California)
        Wiyot, an isolate (northwest California)
        Algonkian or Algonquian (grouped geographically):
            Central and eastern Canada: Cree, Naskapi, Montagnais
            Northern Great Lakes region: Ojibway (Chippewa), Ottawa, Algonkin, Saulteaux
            Maritime Provinces and New England: Micmac, Malecite, Abnaki, Penobscot, Passamaquoddy (and several extinct languages, such as Massachusett*)
            Central Atlantic coast: Delaware (later moved to Oklahoma and elsewhere)

Opposite: Map of Native North American Language, Families, and Phyla. From International Encyclopedia of Linguistics, *volume 3, edited by William Bright. Copyright 1992 by Oxford University Press, Inc. Reprinted by permission.*

Southern Great Lakes region: Menominee, Fox, Sauk, Kickapoo, Potawatomi (partially moved to Oklahoma)

South central United States: Shawnee

Western Great Plains: Blackfoot, Cheyenne, Arapaho, Atsina

Branch: Gulf, including the following families (all isolates):

Natchez* (Louisiana)

Atakapa* (Louisiana, Texas)

Chitimacha* (Louisiana)

Tunica* (Louisiana)

Tonkawa* (east Texas)

Muskogean, including the following languages:

Choctaw (Mississippi, Oklahoma)

Chickasaw (Oklahoma)

Alabama (Alabama, Texas)

Koasati (Alabama, Texas)

Mikasuki (Florida)

Hitchiti (Florida)

Muskogee or Creek (Georgia, Oklahoma)

Seminole (Georgia, Florida, Oklahoma)

Phylum: Macro-Siouan

Family: Siouan, including the following languages (grouped geographically)

Northern Plains: Crow, Hidatsa, Dakota (Sioux)

Central Plains: Omaha, Osage, Ponca, Kansa, Quapaw

Wisconsin: Winnebago

Gulf Coast: Tutelo,* Ofo,* Biloxi*

Southeastern United States: Catawba*

Family: Iroquoian, including the following languages (grouped geographically)

Northeastern: Seneca, Cayuga, Onondaga, Mohawk, Oneida, Wyandot or Huron (in New York State and adjacent Canada)

Southeastern: Tuscarora (North Carolina, later New York), Cherokee (southern Appalachians, later also Oklahoma)

Family: Caddoan, including the following languages: Caddo, Wichita, Pawnee, Arikara (central Plains)

Family: Yuchi, an isolate (southern Appalachians)

Phylum: Hokan or Hokan-Coahuiltecan, including the following families:

Karuk, an isolate (northwest California)

Chimariko,* an isolate (northwest California)

Shastan, a family with two branches:

Shasta* (north-central California)

Palaihnihan, including Achomawi and Atsugewi (northeastern California)

Yanan, a family including North Yana,* Central Yana,* Southern Yana,* and Yahi* (all in north-central California)

Washo, an isolate (east-central California)

Pomoan, a family including Northeast Pomo,* Northern Pomo, Central Pomo, Southwest Pomo or Kashaya, Southeast Pomo, and Southern Pomo (all in north-central California)

Esselen,* an isolate (central California coast)

Salinan, including Migueleño* and Antoniano* (central California coast)

Chumashan, a family including Obispeño,* Ynezeño,* Barbareño,* Ventureño,* and Island Chumash* (all on the southern California coast)

Yuman, a family (languages grouped geographically): Northwest Arizona: Walapai, Havasupai, Yavapai

Lower Colorado River: Mojave, Yuma, Cocopa

Southern California: Diegueño

Baja California: Paipai, Kiliwa*

Seri, an isolate (northwestern Sonora, Mexico)

Comecrudan, an extinct family (southern Texas, northwestern Mexico)

Coahuiltecan, an extinct family (southern Texas, northwestern Mexico)

Note: Also hypothesized as belonging to the above phylum are Tequistlatecan, in southern Mexico, and Jicaque, in Honduras.

Phylum: Penutian, including the following families:

Yokutsan, a group of dialects including Chuckchansi, Wikchamni, Yawdanchi, Yawelmani, and Tachi (south-central California)

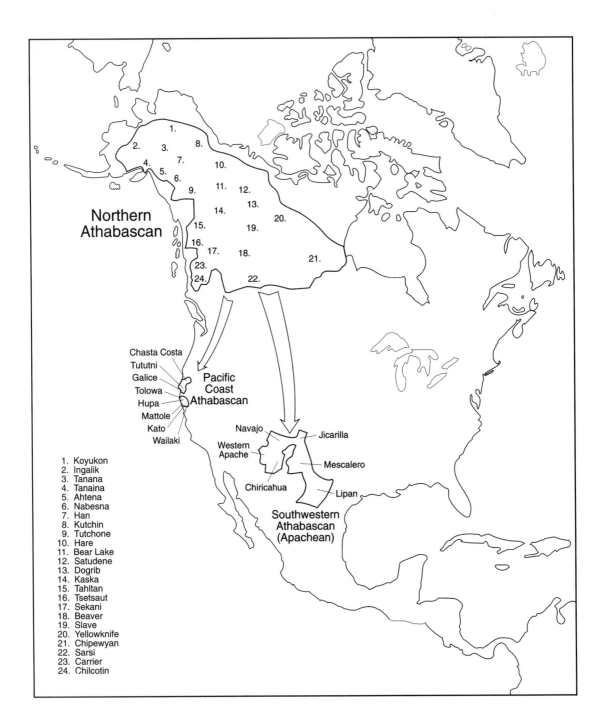

Northern
Athabascan

1. Koyukon
2. Ingalik
3. Tanana
4. Tanaina
5. Ahtena
6. Nabesna
7. Han
8. Kutchin
9. Tutchone
10. Hare
11. Bear Lake
12. Satudene
13. Dogrib
14. Kaska
15. Tahltan
16. Tsetsaut
17. Sekani
18. Beaver
19. Slave
20. Yellowknife
21. Chipewyan
22. Sarsi
23. Carrier
24. Chilcotin

Chasta Costa
Tututni
Galice
Tolowa
Hupa
Mattole
Kato
Wailaki

Pacific
Coast
Athabascan

Navajo
Western
Apache
Chiricahua

Jicarilla
Mescalero
Lipan

Southwestern
Athabascan
(Apachean)

Miwokan, a family including Sierra Miwok, Plains Miwok, Lake Miwok,* and Coast Miwok* (central California)

Costanoan, a family including Mutsun,* Rumsen,* and Ohlone* (central California coast)

Maiduan, a family including Northeast Maidu, Concow, and Nisenan (north-central California)

Wintun, a family including Wintu, Nomlaki, and Patwin (north-central California)

Klamath-Modoc, an isolate (south-central Oregon)

Takelma,* an isolate (southwest Oregon)

Coos,* an isolate (southwest Oregon)

Yakonan, a family including Alsea,* Siuslaw,* and Lower Umpqua* (west-central Oregon)

Kalapuyan,* an extinct family (west-central Oregon)

Molale,* an isolate (north-central Oregon)

Cayuse,* an isolate (northeast Oregon)

Sahaptian, a family including Sahaptin (north-central Oregon) and Nez Perce (west-central Idaho)

Chinookan, a family including several varieties, such as Lower Chinook,* Wishram, and Wasco (northern Oregon, southern Washington)

Tsimshian, an isolate (west-central British Columbia)

Zuni, an isolate (west-central New Mexico)

Phylum: Aztec-Tanoan

 Family: Kiowa-Tanoan, including two branches:

  Kiowa (Oklahoma)

  Tanoan, including three languages: Tiwa, Tewa, Towa (pueblos of New Mexico and Arizona)

 Family: Uto-Aztecan, including the following branches:

  Numic branch, including the following languages:

   Mono (east-central California)

   Northern Paiute (northeast Great Basin)

   Panamint (east-central California)

   Shoshoni (central Great Basin)

   Comanche (southern Plains)

   Kawaiisu (southeast California)

   Ute, including Southern Paiute and Chemehuevi (southern and eastern Great Basin)

Opposite: Map of Athabaskan migrations from the sub-Arctic to the Southwest.

Tubatulabal, an isolate (south-central California)

Takic, including the following languages: Serrano, Kitanemuk,* Gabrielino,* Cupeño, Cahuilla, and Luiseño (all in southern California)

Hopi, an isolate (Arizona)

Sonoran, located in Arizona and northwestern Mexico, including O'Odham or Pima-Papago, Yaqui, and several other languages of northern Mexico, such as Tarahumara

Note: The Uto-Aztecan family includes the Huichol and Cora languages of western Mexico, and the Nahuatl (Aztec) language, spoken not only in central Mexico, but also as far south as El Salvador.

Unclassified family: Salishan or Salish (languages are grouped geographically):

Interior British Columbia: Lillooet, Shuswap, Thompson, Okanagon

Eastern Washington and northern Idaho: Middle Columbia, Wenatchee, Coeur d'Alene, Flathead

Coastal British Columbia: Bella Coola, Comox, Sishistl, Squamish, Halkomelem, Straits Salish

Western Washington: Twana,* Chehalis, Cowlitz, Quinault, Puget Sound Salish

Western Washington: Tillamook*

Unclassified family: Wakashan (languages are grouped geographically):

West Central British Columbia: Kwakiutl, Bella Bella, Heiltsuk, Kitamat, Haisla

Vancouver Island: Nootka, Nitinat

Northwestern Washington: Makah

Unclassified family: Chemakuan, including two languages:

Chimakum* (northwestern Washington)

Quileute (northwestern Washington)

Unclassified family: Yukian, including two languages:

Yuki* (north-central California)

Wappo* (north-central California)

Unclassified language isolates:

Beothuk* (Newfoundland)

Kutenai (northern Idaho)

Keresan (pueblos of New Mexico)
Karankawa* (southeast Texas)
Timucua* (Florida)

♦ ♦ ♦ ♦ ♦ ♦ ♦ ♦ ♦ ♦ ♦ ♦ ♦ ♦ ♦ ♦ **LANGUAGE CONTACT**

Like all languages of the world, North American Indian languages have always existed in contact with each other, with many degrees of bilingualism or multilingualism, determined by sociocultural factors. The effects of this are shown in various amounts of borrowing between languages, involving not only loan words but also features of pronunciation, grammar, and semantic organization. Such long-term borrowing can result in a language area, a geographical region in which families of different families or phyla have come to share numerous features on all levels of language structure. The importance of such areas will be discussed further in the Geographical Areas and Language Areas section, below.

In some areas, tribes who lacked a common language but needed to communicate with each other (e. g., for purposes of trade) developed a type of mixed language called a lingua franca or trade language. When Europeans arrived on the scene, they often learned to use such trade languages and contributed new vocabulary from European sources. The best known such language is Chinook Jargon, used in the Pacific Northwest; its bases were in the Chinook language and other native languages such as Nootka, but it acquired many loan words from French and English before its eventual obsolescence. Some examples of French loan words in Chinook Jargon are *kosho* 'pig,' from French *cochon*; *lapush* 'mouth,' from *la bouche*; and *saiwash* 'Indian,' from *sauvage*. (For typographical reasons, Indian language examples are given here in a practical spelling—e. g., using 'sh' as in English *ship*—rather than in the technical phonetic alphabet. Another such trade language is Mobilian Jargon, used in the southeastern United States and based primarily on Muskogean sources.

A special kind of lingua franca is the Plains Sign Language, a language of gestures used among tribes of the Great Plains (and later learned by many whites as well; see Mallery, 1881). The tribes of this area spoke many unrelated languages, such as Dakota, a Siouan language, and Cheyenne, of the Algonkian family. But their highly mobile life-style made it difficult to cultivate extensive bilingualism in any single spoken language; the need for communication was therefore met by an organized system of gestures.

An unusual result of language contact has occurred in a few areas, where an intimate mixture of vocabulary and grammar has given rise to a new language spoken natively by a local community but not clearly classifiable as belonging to the family of either of its parents. The best-known example is Michif or Métchif, currently spoken by part of the Indian population of North Dakota: in this language, noun forms are predominantly French, but verb forms are predominantly Algonkian. A sample sentence is *Kee-ouyashkinastow li feezee avik lee kartoush* 'He loaded the rifle with cartridges,' which begins with an Algonkian verb form, but continues with French *le fusil* 'the rifle,' *avec les cartouches* 'with the cartridges.'

Another unusual example comes from a mixture of Aleut and Russian, which was formerly spoken on Medny Island in the Komandorsky Islands off the coast of Siberia. In this dialect, Aleut verb stems were combined with Russian endings, as shown in the comparisons given below. (Capital *X* is a 'back velar' fricative; see Sounds in Types of Language Structure, below.)

	Unmixed Aleut	Medny Aleut	Russian
'I sit'	*unguchi-ku-q*	*unguchi-ju*	*ja sizh-u*
'you sit'	*unguchi-ku-Xt*	*unguchi-ish*	*ty sid-ish*
'he sits'	*unguchi-ku-X*	*unguchi-it*	*on sid-it*

In addition to the European words that have entered trade languages such as Chinook Jargon, words from English, French, Spanish, and (in Alaska) Russian have frequently been borrowed into native languages. Among the Native peoples, the type and degree of such linguistic borrowing has varied greatly, depending on socio-cultural factors. For example, in the southwest, after several centuries of contact with Spanish, Navajo has borrowed almost no Spanish loan words, but the Pueblo tribes have borrowed a few more, and O'Odham (Pima-Papago) has borrowed a very large number. Sample loan words from Spanish in O'Odham are *káwal* 'sheep' (from Spanish *cabra* 'goat'), *lúulsi* 'candy' (from *dulce*), and *wákial* 'cowboy' (from *vaquero*).

Among the Karuk of northwestern California, a tribe that suffered very harsh treatment at the hands of Anglo-Americans, there are only a few loan words from English; for example, *ápus* 'apple(s)', and a few adaptations based on English; thus 'pears' are called *vírusur,* the native word for 'bear', because English *pear* and *bear* become merged in Karuk pronunciation. In such languages, which disfavor borrowing, new vocabulary items are frequently formed by new combinations of native materials; thus the Karuk word for 'hotel' is *am-naam,* literally 'eating-place'.

One other result of language contact, of course, has been borrowing of words in the opposite direction—from Native American languages into European languages. The oldest known loan into English from a North American Indian language is *raccoon,* borrowed from an Algonkian language; the word occurs in a letter written by Captain John Smith from Virginia in 1608. This was quickly followed by many other borrowings from Algonkian, as Europeans made contact with tribes along the Atlantic seacoast. The following examples indicate the major semantic categories of such borrowings, and their earliest dates from which they are known.

Animal names:

Caribou, 1610	Terrapin, 1672
Opossum, 1610	Menhaden (fish), 1643
Moose, 1613	Woodchuck, 1674
Skunk, 1634	Muskellunge (fish), 1799
Quahog (clam), 1799	Chipmunk, 1841

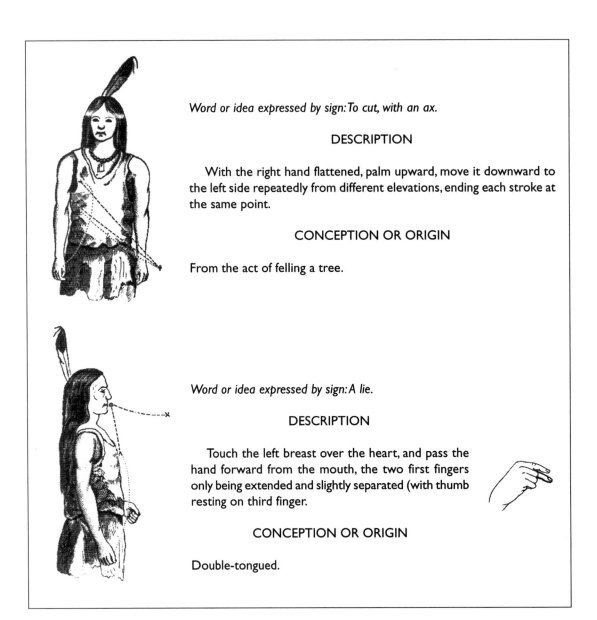

Word or idea expressed by sign: To cut, with an ax.

DESCRIPTION

With the right hand flattened, palm upward, move it downward to the left side repeatedly from different elevations, ending each stroke at the same point.

CONCEPTION OR ORIGIN

From the act of felling a tree.

Word or idea expressed by sign: A lie.

DESCRIPTION

Touch the left breast over the heart, and pass the hand forward from the mouth, the two first fingers only being extended and slightly separated (with thumb resting on third finger.

CONCEPTION OR ORIGIN

Double-tongued.

Examples of Plains sign language.

Plant names:

Persimmon, 1612	Pecan, 1778
Hickory, 1629	Tamarack, 1805
Squash, 1643	Scuppernong (grape), 1825
Chinquapin (nut), 1676	

Prepared foods:

(Corn)pone, 1612	Succotash, 1751
Hominy, 1629	Pemmican, 1804

Cultural features:

Totem, 1609	Wigwam, 1628
Moccasin, 1612	Manitou (a deity), 1671
Tomahawk, 1612	Toboggan, 1829
Powwow, 1624	

As Europeans moved westward across the continent, words were added from other language families, such as *teepee* from Siouan. In a more recent period, words such as the following have been borrowed from Native languages of the far west:

Potlatch (a type of Native celebration), from Chinook jargon

Hooch (illegal liquor), from a Tlingit place name in Alaska

Abalone (a shellfish), from Costanoan of central California

Chuckwalla (a kind of lizard), from Cahuilla of southern California

Hogan (a Native house), from Navajo

Kiva (a Pueblo ceremonial chamber), from Hopi

Kachina (a Pueblo deity), probably from Hopi or Keresan

In addition to such borrowings, English took many words from Spanish that had originated in Indian languages of Latin America. Examples are *maize, potato,* and *barbecue* from languages of the West Indies; and *tomato, chile,* and *coyote* from the language of the Aztecs in Mexico.

Still more numerous are borrowed place names; one of the earliest is *Massachusetts,* originating as the plural of the name of an Algonkian tribe. Many other place names of the northeastern and central parts of the continent are also from Algonkian: *Connecticut, Ottawa, Manhattan, Potomac, Allegheny, Illinois, Michigan, Wisconsin, Chicago, Mississippi* (literally 'big-water'), *Manitoba,* and *Saskatchewan.* In the Great Lakes area and in the South, names of Iroquoian origin are common, such as *Ticonderoga, Conestoga, Niagara, Chautauqua, Ohio, Kentucky,* and *Tennessee.* The Midwest has many Siouan place names, including *Iowa, Missouri, Arkansas, Kansas, Nebraska, Minnesota,* and *Dakota.* In the South, many names are from Muskogean sources, such as *Alabama, Appalachia,* and *Oklahoma.* The diverse languages of the far west have also contributed many place names to English, such as *Arizona* and *Tucson,* both from Pima-Papago; *Utah,* from the Ute language (Uto-Aztecan family); *Seattle,* taken from the name of a Salishan chief in the Puget Sound area; and *Alaska,* from the Aleut language. The name of the western state of *Wyoming,* however, is not from a western American Indian language: it was transferred from a place name in Pennsylvania, which in turn was borrowed from an eastern Algonkian language.

The Native place names of North America have had a certain attraction for the white population, and it has been argued that even more such names should be used. The poet Walt Whitman was so much in favor of Indian names that he proposed substituting them for all others: "California," he wrote, "is sown thick with the names of all the little and big saints. Chase them away and substitute aboriginal names . . . The name of *Niagara* should be substituted for the *St. Lawrence* . . ." Whitman had a point about the place names of California, but many Native place names are in use there, such as *Shasta* and *Yosemite.* The name *Sequoia,* given to one of California's most famous trees and national parks, is not local: it was borrowed from the name of *Sequoyah,* the Indian inventor of the Cherokee writing system. On the other hand, the name *Pasadena* is not Spanish, as one might guess; invented during a period when it was popular to apply Indian place names, regardless of their authenticity, it is in fact a garbled version of a phrase taken from Chippewa (Ojibway), an eastern Algonkian language. And the Pasadena that is a suburb of Houston, Texas, is named after the city in California!

TYPES OF LANGUAGE STRUCTURE ✦ ✦ ✦ ✦ ✦ ✦ ✦ ✦ ✦ ✦ ✦

Some false stereotypes about Native American languages have long been in circulation: that they spoke only in guttural grunts; or that they spoke languages with rudimentary vocabulary, or with "no grammar"; or that they only communicated by gestures. (As previously explained, the Plains Sign Language was only a supplement to spoken languages such as Dakota or Cheyenne.) In fact, members of each tribe spoke a language with thousands of vocabulary items and with elaborate grammatical structures. These are not primitive languages; they draw upon the same linguistic resources as the languages of Europe and display both the regularities and the typical complexities of languages all over the world. For sketches of several Native American structures, see Hoijer and others, 1946.

To be sure, no writing systems were used in North America until the nineteenth century (though writing was developed by the Maya in Mexico and Central America). So the Native North Americans lacked the notion of "standard language" that often accompanies a written tradition; and of course they had no grammars in the sense of books that codified their languages. But they did not lack literary traditions: huge bodies of myth, legend, and song were composed orally and transmitted by memory from one generation to the next—just as the *Iliad* and the *Odyssey* were transmitted in ancient Greece before the invention of the Greek alphabet (see the Traditional Literature section, below).

Sounds

In their systems of pronunciation, American Indian languages show as much diversity as in other parts of language structure. A linguist will generally begin the study of a Native American language by transcribing it in terms of phonetic symbols. As work progresses, it is possible to simplify the phonetic transcription by reducing it to the phonemes of the language, the basic sounds that contrast with one another. Some languages have very few such contrasting sounds; for example, Wichita, a Caddoan language of the southern Great Plains, has only ten consonant phonemes; in contrast, English has twenty-one. Languages of the Pacific Northwest are famous for having large numbers of consonants; Nootka has thirty-seven (see figure below). Certain languages of the Northwest, such as Bella Coola

(Salishan, British Columbia), are also famous for words containing long sequences of consonants—*qnqnklxitXw* 'lower it!'—and even some with no vowels at all—*sk'lxlxc* 'I'm getting cold.'

Many Indian languages display contrasts of sound that are unfamiliar in European languages. In English, consonants may be voiced—pronounced with vibration of the vocal cords, or voiceless—without such vibration; they may be stops—produced by shutting off the air momentarily, or fricatives—letting the air pass through with audible noise; and they may be produced in several parts of the mouth. Indian languages use these mechanisms and several others also.

Phonetic table for Nootka.

PHONETIC KEY

Consonants

	Labials	Dentals	Palatal Sibilants	Alveolar Sibilants	Laterals	Gutturals	Labialized Gutturals	Velars	Labialized Velars	Glottals	Laryngealized Glottals
Voiceless Stops and Affricates											
Simple	*p*	*t*	*č*	*c*	*ƛ*	*k*	*kʷ*	*q*	*qʷ*	*ʔ*	*!*
Glottalized	*ṗ*	*ṭ*	*č̓*	*c̓*	*ƛ̓*	*k̓*	*k̓ʷ*	*q̓*	*q̓ʷ*		
Spirants			*š*	*s*	*ł*	*x*	*xʷ*	*x̣*	*x̣ʷ*	*h*	*ḥ*
Voiced Continuants Nasals											
Simple	*m*	*n*									
Glottalized	*ṁ*	*ṅ*									
Semivowels											
Simple	*w*	*y*									
Glottalized	*ẇ*	*ẏ*									

Vowels

	Front		Back	Back Rounded	
High	*i*	*iˑ*		*o*	*oˑ*
Mid-wide	*e*	*eˑ*		*ɔ*	*ɔˑ*
Low			*a aˑ*		

A common sound is the glottal stop—an interruption of the breath caused by closing the vocal cords momentarily, as in the middle of English exclamations like *Oh-oh!* Transcribed with an apostrophe, the glottal stop is frequent in many Native American languages, such as in Yurok (northwestern California), which has many words like *'o'rowi'* 'dove.' This phenomenon is partly responsible for the stereotypes of American Indian languages as guttural.

Especially in western North America, a common phenomenon is the use of consonants with glottalization—as a consonant is produced in the mouth, there is also closure and reopening of the vocal cords, producing a popping or cracking sound. This feature is also usually transcribed with an apostrophe; for instance, in Hupa, an Athabaskan language of northwestern California, it distinguishes words like *t'eew* 'raw' from *teew* 'underwater.'

Another common characteristic in languages of western North America is the expansion in number of consonants by using a larger variety of tongue positions than in most European languages. Many languages distinguish velar consonants, made with the rear part of the tongue (like English *k*) from uvular consonants, produced even farther back in the mouth (written with *q*, as in Arabic *Iraq*). Some languages, especially in the Pacific Northwest, even differentiate a front-velar *ky*, a plain-velar *k*, and a backed *q*. In addition, labiovelars, i.e. velars with simultaneous lip-rounding, are common. Thus, whereas English has only the velar stops *g* and *k* (and the combinations *kw, gw*), Tlingit has twenty-one velar phonemes: *g, k*, uvular *G, q*, glottalized *k', q'*, labiovelar *gw, kw, k'w, Gw, qw, q'w*, with the corresponding fricatives *gh, x*, uvular *X*, glottalized *x', X'*, and labiovelar *xw, Xw, x'w, X'w*.

In some Indian languages, as in English, stressed syllables are significant in distinguishing the meaning of words. In others, musical pitch plays a role, as it does in Chinese. For example, in Navajo, high pitch can be written with an acute accent, as in *tsé* 'stone,' and low pitch with a grave accent, as in *hài* 'winter.' Then there are contrasting words like *biní* 'his nostril,' *bìnì* 'his face,' and *biní* 'his waist.'

Native American languages, like most languages of the world, have changes of sound associated with distinctions of grammar; compare English *f* versus *v* in *half, halves, to halve*. In some languages, such changes of sound give a diminutive meaning, referring to "smallness." So Luiseño, in southern California, changes *r* to *d* when it adds a suffix referring to small things: *ngarúngru-sh* 'a pot' becomes *ngadúngdu-mal* 'a little pot.' Other languages show vowel harmony, a process in which vowels change to resemble vowels in nearby grammatical elements. The Yurok language, for example, has an unusual vowel that can be written *r*, similar to the vowel in English *bird*; when this occurs in a suffix, vowels of the preceding stem change to agree with it, so that *lo'oge* 'black' plus the suffix *-'r'y* gives *lr'rgr-'r'y* 'black animal.'

In several Native American languages, linguists have reported systematic differences of pronunciation depending on whether the people speaking and spoken to are men or women. A famous example is in the Yana language of northern California, in which "men's speech" was used only among men; in contrast, "women's speech" was used both among women and between the sexes. The linguistic differences had to do with how words were pronounced in isolation or at the ends of sentences; thus, in men's speech, 'deer' was pronounced *pana,* but in women's speech it had a shorter pronunciation, as *pah.* Similarly, in men's speech, 'Dance!' was *puri'i',* but in women's speech it was *puri'.*

The concept of grammatical structure refers both to the traditional category of morphology—the ways that words are made up of stems, prefixes, and suffixes; and syntax—the way that words are combined into sentences. Many Native American languages are termed polysynthetic: they put great emphasis on morphology, combining large numbers of elements to express within a single word what European languages may express by an entire sentence. Here is an example from Wichita:

kiyaakiriwaac'arasarikita'ahiiriks
'He carried the big pile of meat up into the top of the tree.'

This is composed of the following elements:

kiya- 'information is from hearsay'
a- '3d person singular subject'
ki- 'past tense'
riwaac- 'big'
'aras- 'meat'
a- 'object is plural, i. e., in pieces'
ri- 'action is performed on an object'
kita- 'goal of action is up above' (e. g., in a tree)
-'a- 'come' (verb root)
-hiiriks 'action is repeated' (here, 'piece by piece.')

Some languages especially favor incorporation, the compounding of a noun with a verb. This happens only rarely in English, as in *to baby-sit*; but it occurs in the Wichita example above ('to meat-carry'); and it is common in Iroquoian, as in Mohawk *ke-weNna-weieNhoN*, literally 'I-language-understand.' (The capital N is used in this article to represent nasalization of a preceding vowel.)

Some other widespread grammatical characteristics are the following:

(a) In verbs, the person and number of the suffix are often marked by prefixes; for example, Karuk has *ni-áhoo* 'I walk,' but *nu-áhoo* 'we walk.' Sometimes the prefix indicates the object of the verb as well as the subject, as in Karuk *ní-mah* 'I see him', *ná-mah* 'he sees me.'

(b) Tense of verbs and related features are usually marked by suffixes, as in many languages of the world; but in some areas, as in the Athabaskan languages, prefixes are used. So, in Chipewyan (Northwest Territories), *hE-tsagh* means 'he is crying' (*E* is the vowel of English *met*), *ghiN-tsagh* is 'he cried,' and *ghwa-tsagh* is 'he will cry.'

(c) In noun forms, the concept of possession is often expressed by prefixes indicating the person and number of the possessor. Thus Karuk has *ávaha* 'food,' *nani-ávaha* 'my food,' *mu-ávaha* 'his food,' etc. When the possessor is a noun, as in 'man's food,' the language uses a construction like *ávansa mu-ávaha* 'man his-food.' Many languages have inalienable nouns, which cannot occur except in such possessed forms. These generally refer to such things as kin or body parts; to illustrate,. Luiseño has *no-yó'* 'my mother,' *o-yó'* 'your mother,' etc., but no word for 'mother' by itself. The closest one could come would be *a-yó'* 'someone's mother.'

(d) Nouns in many languages take case suffixes (like those of Latin or Slavic languages) to indicate that they are the subject or object of a sentence, or in some other relationship such as location or direction. Thus a Luiseño noun stem like *kii-* 'house' has the subject form *kíi-cha,* the object form *kíi-sh,* and other forms like *kíi-k* 'to the house,' *kíi-ngay* 'from the house,' *kíi-nga* 'in the house,' and *kíi-tal* 'by means of the house.'

(e) In many languages, first person plural pronouns show a distinction between an inclusive form ('we' meaning 'you and I') and an exclusive form ('we' meaning 'I and someone else other than you'). For example, in Cree, inclusive *ni-nikamo-naw* means 'we sing (including you),' but exclusive *ni-nikamo-naan* means 'we sing (I and my friends, but not you').'

(f) The process of reduplication, the repetition of all or part of a stem, is used in many Uto-Aztecan languages to indicate the plural of nouns, such as Pima *gogs* 'dog,' *go-gogs* 'dogs.' Such reduplication is used in many other languages to indicate repeated or habitual action of verbs, as with Karuk *imyah* 'to breathe,' *imyáh-yah* 'to pant.'

(g) In many languages, verb stems are distinguished on the basis of the number, shape, or other physical characteristics of the associated noun. Thus Karuk has *ikpuh* 'one swims,' *ithpuh* 'two swim,' and *ihtak* 'several swim.' In Navajo, in order to refer to the motion of an object, one uses the verb stem *'áN* for round objects, *táN* for long objects, *tíN* for living things, *lá* for ropelike objects, etc.

(h) Verb forms often specify the location or direction of an action by using prefixes or suffixes. Thus, in Karuk, from the verb stem *path-* 'throw,' we have *páath-roov* 'throw upriver,' *páath-raa* 'throw uphill,' *paath-rípaa* 'throw across-river,' and as many as thirty-eight similar forms. Some languages also specify the instrument of an action, generally by prefixation, as with Pomo *phi-de-* 'to move by batting with a stick,' *phu-de-* 'to move by blowing,' *pha-de-* 'to move by pushing with the end of a stick.'

(i) Some languages have constructions called evidentials, indicating the source or validity of the information reported. Thus Hopi distinguishes *wari* 'he ran, runs, is running,' as a reported event, from *wari-kngwe* 'he runs (e. g., on the track team),' a statement of general truth, and from *wari-kni* 'he will run,' an anticipated event. In other languages, verb forms consistently distinguish hearsay from eye-witness reports. In fact, the Wintu language of north central California has four contrasting evidential suffixes: 'non-visual sensory' -*nthere,* meaning 'it sounds or feels so to me'; 'hearsay' -*kele,* meaning 'I heard it said' (used in stories, gossip, or any other second-hand report); 'inferential' -*re,* meaning 'it must logically be true'; and 'experiential' -*'el,* meaning 'I judge from experience that it is true.'

(j) Some American Indian languages, notably in the Pacific Northwest, have numeral classifiers, a type of grammatical element that is required in counting objects and that differentiates the form or shape of the objects counted. (Such elements also occur in Chinese, Japanese, and other languages of the Far East, and in many American Indian languages of Mexico.) Thus, in Yurok, the number 'two' is *ni'iyelh* when counting human beings, but *nr'r'r'y* for animals, *no'oh* for round objects (like stones), *nr'rpi'* for tools, *na'a'r* for trees, *na'ak'wo'n* for smaller plants, *na'a'n* for body parts, *na'ak'* for long flexible objects (like ropes), *no'ok's* for flat objects, *na'a'li* for houses, and *na'ey* for boats; such differences apply to all the numbers through ten.

(k) A striking feature of syntax, found in some Native American languages, is the ergative construction, a pattern in which the direct objects of certain verb forms are treated grammatically as if they were the subjects of those verbs. Thus, in Yupik Eskimo, an intransitive verb (one that takes a subject but no direct object) occurs with its subject in the absolute case:

Arna-q yurartuq 'The woman is dancing.'
woman-abs. is-dancing

But with a transitive verb (one that may take both a subject and a direct object), the absolute case is used not for the subject, but for the object. With such verbs, the subject is in the relative case:

Arna-m neraa neqa 'The woman is eating the fish.'
woman-rel. is-eating fish-abs.

Vocabulary

Words in Native American languages, like those of other languages, are composed both of simple stems and of derived constructions. The derivational processes commonly include prefixation, suffixation, and compounding. A few languages use internal sound change, as when English derives the noun *song* from the verb *sing*; thus Yurok has *pontet* 'ashes,' *prncrc* 'dust,' *prncrh* 'to be gray.' Some languages also acquire new vocabulary items by borrowing, as mentioned above.

In Native American languages, like other languages of the world, the meaning of a word cannot always be guessed from a knowledge of its historical origin or from knowing the meaning of its parts. For instance, in the early nineteenth century, Karuk borrowed the name of a Canadian trapper, Jean-Baptiste McKay, in the form *mákay*, to refer to white people in general. It was then combined with *váas* 'deerskin blanket' to give the new word *makáy-vaas*, used to mean 'cloth' (literally, 'white-man's blanket'). This in turn was compounded with *yukúku* 'moccasin' to give still another new word, *makayvas-yukúku* 'tennis shoes' (literally, 'cloth shoes').

In the area of vocabulary, American Indian languages are especially likely to present surprises to the outsider. Where European languages label things by different terms, an Indian language may use a single term—or vice versa. Thus, where English distinguishes 'airplane,' 'aviator,' and 'flying insect,' Hopi calls them all *masa'ytaka*, literally 'flyer'; but conversely, where English has only the single term 'water,' Hopi differentiates *paahe* 'water in nature' from *keeyi* 'water in a container.'

Again, natural phenomena may be classified by different languages on the basis of totally different criteria. In talking about directions in space, European languages use words like 'north, south, east, west,' which are basically defined in terms of the rising and setting of the sun; and many Native American languages have terms corresponding to these. But Karuk and Yurok, along with other languages of northwestern California, use terms defined not in relation to the sun, but rather in relation to the Klamath River, which follows a winding course through their territory. So the principal directional terms of Karuk are *káruk* 'upriver' (borrowed by whites as the name for the tribe), *yúruk* 'downriver,' *máruk* 'away from the river, up-hill,' and *sáruk* 'toward the river, downhill' —supplemented by *ithyáruk* 'across-river.'

Another semantic area in which languages may differ greatly is that of terms for kin. For example, where English has the single term 'uncle,' the Seneca language (Iroquoian) makes a distinction: my father's brother is simply called *ha'nih* 'my father,' while my mother's brother is called by a separate term, *hakhno'seNh*. But this latter term also refers to my mother's nephew or niece, whom in English I would call 'my cousin.'

Another area that shows many differences among languages is that of counting. Of course English and many European languages have a counting system based on the number ten and its variant forms, so that *thir-teen* was originally 'three [plus] ten,' while *thir-ty* was 'three [times] ten,' this clearly reflects that a person's ten fingers represented a historically important aid to counting. In Native American Indian languages, 'five' (the fingers of one hand) and 'twenty' (the fingers plus the toes) are also sometimes used as basic units. For example, in the old counting system of Luiseño in southern California, six was called, literally, 'five adding one,' ten was 'both my hands finished'; fifteen was 'both my hands finished and one of my feet'; and twenty was 'my other foot finished also.' In a few languages, 'four' rather than 'five' is used as a basis for counting: Thus Ventureño, a Chumashan language of Southern California, had *pakéet* 'one,' *eshkóm* 'two,' *maség* 'three,' *skumú* 'four—followed by *iti-pakés* 'five, literally one more (than four)'; *yeti-shkom* 'six, literally two more'; *iti-maség* 'seven, literally three more.' The numbers for eight, nine, and ten are unitary words; but twelve is *maség skumú*, literally 'three fours,' while thirteen is *maség skúmu kam-pakeet* 'three fours plus-one.' The next unitary number is sixteen, the square of four, and after that one starts adding again: seventeen is literally 'sixteen plus one.' Continuing with this strategy of multiplying fours, one logically arrives at numbers like thirty-two, which is literally 'two sixteens.' The use of four as a base may go back to counting one's fingers without the thumbs or to a system of counting the slots *between* one's fingers (and thumbs).

It should be noted that many Native American societies have no name for their own tribe or their own language: they simply call themselves 'the people,' and their language is called 'the language of the people' or 'our language.' This is in general true among the Athabaskan peoples: thus, in Navajo, *diné* means 'person, people, human being(s),' but also 'Navajo'; and *diné bi-zaad,* literally, 'person his-tongue,' means 'the Navajo language.' Other tribes, however, do have names for their own groups; for example, the Hopi in fact call themselves *hopi.*

In any part of the world, the number of words that people use in a particular semantic area depends on the importance of that area to them. For example, one might expect the Inuit (Eskimo) to distinguish several types of snow, and in fact they do. But the 'exotic' qualities of Native American semantic systems need not be exaggerated. Many writers have repeated the claim that the Inuit language has "a hundred distinct words for snow." This has been shown to be false. In fact, Boas (1911) reported that Inuit has four words in this semantic area—referring to 'falling snow,' 'snow on the ground,' and two types of 'drifting snow'—and this was exaggerated by various writers and journalists. Of course one might equally well say that English has at least four words in the same area: besides the word *snow,* we have terms like *slush, sleet,* and *blizzard.* After all, snow is also important in many parts of the English-speaking world!

GEOGRAPHICAL AREAS AND LANGUAGE AREAS ♦ ♦ ♦ ♦ ♦ ♦

As an alternative to the classification of languages given in the Phyla and Families section above, it is useful to consider Native American languages in terms of the geographical areas in which they are found, understanding these areas in terms both of physical habitat and shared cultural patterns and in terms of the distribution of features of language structure, such as those described in the Types of Language Structure section, above. Eleven such areas may be distinguished, which are listed and described below. Some of these prove to be quite close-knit linguistically, reflecting a long history of language contact and structural borrowing; others show much greater diversity of linguistic structure, reflecting situations in which language contact was less important, or had a shorter history.

The Arctic Area

Constituting the northern edge of the continent, the Arctic area is occupied by two language families, Aleut and Eskimo, comprising the Eskimo-Aleut phylum. The two families are clearly related but there was relatively little language contact between communities in former times, so that similarities between language can be explained mainly in terms of their common origin.

The Western Sub-Arctic

In the Yukon and the western part of the Northwest Territories, the western sub-Artic is monopolized by languages of the Athabaskan family; thus the genetic similarities among languages far outweigh those possibly due to contact.

The Eastern Sub-Arctic

Extending from the Northwest Territories through northern Ontario and Quebec, the eastern sub-Arctic is occupied entirely by Algonkian languages; once again, the genetic relationship is predominant.

The Northwest Coast

Extending from southeastern Alaska to southwestern Oregon, the Northwest Coast presents a very different picture. There is a high degree of genetic diversity: the genetic groups represented include Tlingit, Haida, and Athabaskan (the hypothesized Na-Dené phylum); Tsimshian, Chinookan, and several Oregon languages which have been assigned to the Penutian phylum (which is also represented in the Plateau and California areas); and three families found only in the Pacific Northwest—Salishan, Wakashan, and Chimakuan. Nevertheless, this area is the most striking example in North America of structural similarities that cut across genetic boundaries. Some features that especially characterize the Northwest Coast (as discussed in the Types of Language Structure section, above) are complex consonant systems, including glottalized consonants; the use of numeral classifiers; and reduplication in verbs. The spread of such areal features was probably associated with high population density, along with widespread trade and intermarriage among tribes.

The Plateau Area
Occupying eastern British Columbia, Washington, Oregon, as well as Idaho, the Plateau area contains languages of the Penutian phylum, the Salishan family, and the Kutenai isolate. It resembles the Northwest Coast area in combining genetic diversity with borrowed structural features. Characteristic traits of the area include elaborate consonant systems (though not quite as complex as those on the Northwest Coast) and the use of sound changes to mark diminutive meaning. Communicative factors seem similar to those in the neighboring Northwest Coast area, though with less intensity.

The California Area
With boundaries roughly identical to the state, the California area is genetically one of the most diverse on the continent: languages of this area belong to the Hokan and Penutian phyla, each containing several distinct families; and also to the Athabaskan, Algic, Yukian, and Uto-Aztecan families. In terms of structural features, the area is also highly diverse; no single features are found throughout the entire area. Nevertheless, there is evidence for a complex history of structural borrowing among adjacent families and for relatively recent intrusions by the Athabaskan family from the north and Uto-Aztecan from the east. Rather than being regarded as a single language area, California may be   considered as a set of sub-areas, partly interlocking and partly discontinuous.

The Southwest Area
Roughly including Arizona and New Mexico, the Southwest area is also highly diverse, containing languages of the Kiowa-Tanoan and Uto-Aztecan families (grouped into the Aztec-Tanoan phylum) as well as the Athabaskan and Keresan families and the isolated Zuni language. As has been noted above, the Athabaskan languages are relatively recent arrivals and as such have quite different structural features from their neighbors. However, even among the non-Athabaskan languages there is little structural uniformity. As for California, a description in terms of sub-areas may be preferable. The limited amount of structural borrowing is ap-

parently related to an attitude reported in the Pueblo communities, where languages of "outsiders" are traditionally viewed with mistrust.

The Great Basin

Nevada, Utah, and parts of adjacent states make up the Great Basin, which is occupied entirely by Uto-Aztecan languages except for the presence of Washo, a Hokan language, on the western edge. Like the sub-Arctic, this is an area with low population density, limited language contact, and little evidence for borrowed linguistic structure.

The Plains Area

Occupying the Great Plains region of both Canada and the United States, the Plains is an area of genetic diversity. It contains languages of the Algonkian, Athabaskan, Caddoan, Kiowa-Tanoan, Siouan, and Uto-Aztecan families—most of which are also found outside the Plains. Structural features of Plains languages tend to be with their genetic relatives in other areas, rather than with their geographical neighbors. Thus Blackfoot, Arapaho, and Cheyenne, the Algonkian languages of the Plains, are much more like their Algonkian sister languages in the eastern United States than they are like the nearby Siouan languages. This may be because many Plains languages moved into their historic locations only in relatively recent centuries, especially after horses had been introduced to America by the Spanish. Also, as noted above, the use of Plains Sign Language made communication possible even in the absence of much bilingualism.

The Northeast Area

Reaching from the Great Lakes region eastward to New England and the Maritime Provinces of Canada, the Northeast is occupied predominantly by the Algonkian and Iroquoian families, with a small representation of Siouan. There is little areal influence cutting across genetic boundaries; it is definable as a unit on geographical and cultural grounds, but not linguistically. Low population density may have discouraged language contact and bilingualism in this area.

The Southeast Area

Occupying the southeastern region of the United States, the Southeast contains languages of the Gulf, Iroquoian, and Siouan families, plus the isolated Yuchi language. Areal traits are not strongly marked.

Classes of Geographic Areas

It seems possible to distinguish four classes among geographical areas:

(a) Genetically uniform areas, with sparse population—the Arctic, the western and eastern sub-Arctic, and the Great Basin—where structural borrowing across genetic lines has been largely irrelevant.

(b) One genetically diverse area, the Plains, in which structural borrowing has conspicuously not occurred, primarily because the historical distribution of tribes is relatively recent.

(c) Genetically diverse areas—California, the Southwest, the Northeast, and the Southeast—where structural borrowing has been local rather than sweeping.

(d) Finally, two genetically diverse areas—the Northwest and the Plateau—where structural borrowing has been at its maximum. Causal factors seem to include high population density and cultural attitudes that encourage intimate contacts between tribes.

As noted above, cases of mutual assimilation such as those found among the northwest languages create serious problems for attempts at genetic classification. It may not be meaningful to ask whether the similarities between the Salishan and Wakashan families, for instance, are the result of common origin or result from prolonged contact and borrowing within the Northwest Coast language area. It may be best to say simply that the two families must have a great deal of shared history; once that is granted, particular similarities may be examined to determine whether they are more likely to result from common origin or from borrowing.

LANGUAGE AND CULTURE ♦ ♦ ♦ ♦ ♦ ♦ ♦ ♦ ♦ ♦ ♦ ♦ ♦ ♦

The striking differences that the semantic organization of American Indian languages show from those of European languages, both in grammar and vocabulary, have led many people to think about the degree to which differences in language are correlated with differences in culture, with differences in patterns of habitual thought, and with differences in world view, that is, the unconscious philosophical outlook held by the members of a society. It is clear that differences in language may be correlated with nonlinguistic differences: that the Karuk use directional terms like 'upriver, downriver' results from the fact that the Klamath River is the basis of their habitat. A much more difficult question is whether the language structures people learn as children may, in some ways, provide them with 'ready-made' habits of thought, and so in part determine the way they view the world.

The most famous discussion of this problem is that by B. L. Whorf (1939), based on material from Hopi. Whorf points out that Hopi words referring to units of time (e.g., 'day') are different from other nouns in that they have no plural form; in addition, they cannot be counted with the cardinal numerals (one, two, etc.) but only with the ordinals (first, second, etc.). Comparing English and Hopi, Whorf remarks that English speakers say "ten days," as if the days were a collection of separate units (like ten apples), whereas the Hopi speaker means "ten days" to be a cycle, or ten recurrences of the same unit of time. Whorf advances the idea that Hopi speakers think about time differently from English speakers, a contention he supports by pointing to a nonlinguistic aspect of Hopi life: their ceremonial cycle, which involves repeated preparation for future events (such as planting, or harvest). Whorf reasons that the Hopi really view each day as a recurrence, rather than something new, so that it is reasonable for them to believe that the daily repetition of ceremonial acts will have a cumulative effect on the future. As Whorf points out, the Hopi attitude seems just the opposite of English-speakers' idea that "Tomorrow is another day."

Such ideas remain controversial; however, the study of the interaction of Native American languages and cultures continues to provide a rich laboratory for study. An interesting problem is found in northwestern California, where several small tribes share most features of culture but use languages of very diverse types. The languages concerned are Karuk, classified as Hokan; Yurok and Wiyot, of the Macro-Algonkian phylum; and Hupa and Tolowa, of the Athabaskan family. Whorf might suggest that the difference among these languages would have led to greater diversity in their cultures—or, failing that, the languages might have grown more similar to each other. In fact, it seems that something of a compromise has taken place: linguistic diversity and cultural uniformity have made modest accommodations to each other. An example may be found in the systems that the Yurok and the Tolowa use for semantic groupings of animals. The Yurok language has more generic terms, like *hoore'mos* 'animal' and *nunepuy* 'fish,' as well as specific words like *puuk* 'deer' and *regork* 'trout.' This seems consistent with relatively high degree of complexity in Yurok culture generally, especially with its emphasis on ranks and hierarchies. By contrast, Tolowa has only the specific terms for species of animals, and this may be correlated with the relatively lower emphasis on hierarchy that characterizes Tolowa culture.

A different kind of relationship between language and culture is of more interest from the viewpoint of North American prehistory: the fact that language retains traces of changes in culture. Thus the historical study of Native American languages, along with archaeological findings and knowledge of Native historical traditions, helps reconstruct remote past cultures and migrations. Edward Sapir holds that the original homeland of a group of languages is likely to be found in the area of greatest linguistic diversity, noting that there are many more different European languages and dialects now spoken in Europe than in continents more recently colonized by Europeans, such as North America, South America, or Australia. To take an American Indian example, Sapir points out that the Athabaskan languages spoken in Alaska and Canada are much more diverse than the Pacific Coast or Southwestern families of Athabaskan, suggesting that the original center of Athabaskan migration was in the sub-Arctic. To confirm this, Sapir (1963) reconstructed parts of prehistoric Athabaskan vocabulary, showing, for instance, how a word meaning 'horn' or 'spoon' came to mean 'spoon' or 'gourd,' as the ancestors of the Navajo migrated from the far north (where spoons are made of deerhorn) to the Southwest (where they are made of gourds).

♦ ♦ ♦ ♦ ♦ ♦ ♦ ♦ ♦ ♦ ♦ ♦ ♦ ♦ **TRADITIONAL LITERATURE**

Verbal art has always been highly cultivated among Native Americans—though until recent times it was limited to the oral medium. The repeated recitation of myths, legends, and ceremonial formulas by elders and the performance of songs constituted the educational system of the tribe. These practices made it possible for younger people to learn the religion, the morals, the history, the aesthetic values, the humor, and the music of their ancestors. In modern terms, the traditional literature has provided rich resources for American Indian storytellers and poets expressing their own experience in English or, in some cases, in Native American languages.

Ethnopoetics refers to the study of traditional literature in which linguists and anthropologists try to understand how the Native languages—the words, the sounds, the grammatical constructions, the pauses, the tone of voice—are used to create artistic effect. It has been pointed out that many traditional Native American narratives are not simply prose texts, but that they are organized in terms of lines: sequences which are somehow parallel in structure.

In traditional European literature, poems are organized in lines that often show parallelisms of rhyme or meter, as well as other types. Though the oral literature of the American Indian does not generally use rhyme or meter, it uses many other types of parallelism. The following short myth, from the Karuk of northwestern California, illustrates both the grammatical structure and the literary structure of such texts. The protagonist is Coyote, the divine trickster who stars in hundreds of traditional narratives told by the tribes of western North America. The story consists of two parallel acts, each with two parallel scenes. In scene 1, act 1, an aspect of the primeval world is presented; in scene 1, act 2, Coyote tampers with it, so that male humans will have to work harder. In scene 2, act 1, another aspect of the world is presented; and in scene 2, act 2, Coyote again interferes, this time to put a heavier burden on female humans.

Coyote Lays Down the Law

Scene 1, act 1:
Kun-piip,
they-say

'It was said,

Xâatik ápap yúruk u-vuu-núp-ahi-ti,
let one-side downriver it-flow-down-condition-durative

**"Let the river flow DOWN-stream
on one side,**

káru ápap káruk u-vuu-nôovu-ti.
and one-side upriver it-flow-up-durative

and UP-stream on the other side.

Xâatik vaa u-kupi-ti.
let thus it-do-durative

Let it be so."

Kári xás chémi.
and so all-right

And so it was agreed.

Vaa uum vúra pa-yúruk tá-kun-vîit-rup,
thus they just when-downstream already-they-paddle-down

Whenever they traveled downstream,

t-u-thívruuh-rup yúruk.
already-it-float-down downstream

the boat would drift DOWN-stream.

Ithyáruk kúna ú-p-viit-roov-eesh,
across-river but they-again-paddle-upriver-future

**But they would travel back upriver
on the OTHER side,**

u-thívruuh-roov-eesh káru,
they-float-upriver-future also

they'd drift UP-stream too,

káruk u-vuu-nôov-ahi-ti pa-íshaha.
upriver it-flow-up-condition-durative the-water

it was flowing upriver, that water was.

Scene 1, act 2:
Kári xás pihnêefich u-piip, pûuhara,
and then coyote he-say no

> And then Coyote said, "No,

xáyfaat vaa u-kupi-ti.
don't that it-do-durative

> let it not be that way,

koovúra yúruk kám-vuu-nup-ahi-ti.
all downriver let-flow-down-condition-durative

> let it all flow DOWN-river.

Vaa uum vúra káan ifmaará-piit kam-íktaat-roovu-ti,
thus they just there husband-new let-push-upriver-durative

> Let the young husbands
> PUSH their way up there,

pa-káruk u-vít-roovu-ti.
when-upstream they-paddle-up-durative

> when they travel UP-stream."

Scene 2, act 1:
Kári xás kúna kun-piip,
and then but they-say

> But then it was said,

*asiktávaan pa-mukun-átimnam máruk tá-kun-sá-
naa-n,*
woman when-their-packbasket uphill already-they-carry-
up-pl.

> "When women carry their packbaskets uphill,

púyava máruk xás áhup sú' tá-kun-máhyaan,
so uphill then wood inside already-they-put

> then uphill they put wood into them,

túr tá-kun-íkyav.
basketload already-they-make

> they make basketloads.

Kári xás tá-kun-pá-vyiih-ship pa-asiktavaan-sa.
and then already-they-back-go-start the-woman-plural

> And then the women start back home.

Kári xás vaa vúra káan tá-kun-íitshur pa-mukún-tur.
and then thus just there already-they-
leave the-their-basketload

> And they just leave them there,
>   those basketloads."

Xás kun-piip,
then they-say

>   And they said,

vaa vúra kun-írunaa-ti-heesh pa-tur.
thus just they-walk-durative-future the-basketload

>   "They'll just WALK home,
>   those basketloads will."

Scene 2, act 2:
Kári xás pihnêefich u-piip, xáyfaat, pûuhara.
and then coyote he-say don't no

>   And then Coyote said, "No, don't!

Vúra uum yarará-piit vúra kám-tuun-ti.
just they wife-new just let-carry-durative

>   Let the young wives just CARRY the loads."

Kári xás vaa u-kupí-ti payêem,
and so thus it-do-durative now

>   So that's the way it is nowadays,

tá-pu-áhoo-tih-ara pa-tur.
already-not-walk-durative-negative the-basketload

>   now they can't walk any more,
>   those basketloads.'

WRITING SYSTEMS ✦ ✦ ✦ ✦ ✦ ✦ ✦ ✦ ✦ ✦ ✦ ✦ ✦ ✦ ✦ ✦ ✦

Opposite: Cherokee Syllabary (mistakenly called "Alphabet"). From Beginning Cherokee, *by Ruth Bradley Holmes and Betty Sharp Smith, 2d ed. Norman: University of Oklahoma Press, 1977.*

Before the arrival of Europeans, some American Indian peoples kept records by means of pictographs, simplified pictures drawn on skin or on wood, as a way of recording their history. These records are not the same as written language, however, since people can not read them back in a uniform and unambiguous way. Of the writing systems that have been developed for Native American peoples, most have been invented and introduced by Europeans—sometimes by missionaries, sometimes by linguists and educators.

Several types of writing have been introduced at various times and places. Early in the settlement of New England the European

Cherokee Alphabet

D a	**R** e	**T** i	**Ꮹ** o	**Ᏹ** u	**i** v
Ꮪ ga **Ꮠ** ka	**Ᏺ** ge	**Ᏹ** gi	**A** go	**J** gu	**E** gv
Ꮤ ha	**Ꮲ** he	**Ꮑ** hi	**Ꮅ** ho	**Ꮎ** hu	**Ꮗ** hv
W la	**Ꮄ** le	**Ꮅ** li	**Ꮕ** lo	**M** lu	**Ꮅ** lv
Ꮉ ma	**Ꮉ** me	**H** mi	**Ꮽ** mo	**Ᏼ** mu	
Ꮻ na **Ꮏ** hna **Ꮐ** nah	**Ꮑ** ne	**Ꮒ** ni	**Z** no	**Ꮔ** nu	**Ꮕ** nv
Ꮖ qua	**Ꮗ** que	**Ꮜ** qui	**Ꮚ** quo	**Ꮙ** quu	**Ꮛ** quv
Ꮪ sa **Ꮝ** s	**4** se	**Ꮞ** si	**Ꮠ** so	**Ꮡ** su	**R** sv
Ꮣ da **W** ta	**Ꮪ** de **Ꮦ** te	**Ꮧ** di **Ꮨ** ti	**V** do	**S** du	**Ꮫ** dv
Ꮬ dla **Ꮯ** tla	**L** tle	**C** tli	**Ꮲ** tlo	**Ꮰ** tlu	**P** tlv
Ꮳ tsa	**Ꮴ** tse	**Ꮵ** tsi	**K** tso	**Ꮷ** tsu	**C** tsv
G wa	**Ꮺ** we	**Ꮻ** wi	**Ꮼ** wo	**Ꮽ** wu	**6** wv
Ꮿ ya	**ß** ye	**Ꭰ** yi	**Ꭱ** yo	**G** yu	**B** yv

Sounds Represented by Vowels

a, as <u>a</u> in <u>father</u>, or short as <u>a</u> in <u>rival</u>

e, as <u>a</u> in <u>hate</u>, or short as <u>e</u> in <u>met</u>

i, as <u>i</u> in <u>pique</u>, or short as <u>i</u> in <u>pit</u>

o, as <u>o</u> in <u>note</u>, approaching <u>aw</u> in <u>law</u>

u, as <u>oo</u> in <u>fool</u>, or short as <u>u</u> in <u>pull</u>

v, as <u>u</u> in <u>but</u>, nasalized

Consonant Sounds

<u>g</u> nearly as in English, but approaching to <u>k</u>. <u>d</u> nearly as in English but approaching to <u>t</u>. <u>h k l m n q s t w y</u> as in English. Syllables beginning with <u>g</u> except **Ꮪ** (ga) have sometimes the power of <u>k</u>. **A** (go), **S** (du), **Ꮫ** (dv) are sometimes sounded <u>to</u>, <u>tu</u>, <u>tv</u> and syllables written with **tl** except **Ꮯ** (tla) sometimes vary to **dl** .

alphabet was adapted to write the Massachusett language. In the nineteenth century, a hieroglyphic system was developed for the Micmac language in Nova Scotia by Jesuit priest Father Chrestien Le Clercq; but this proved difficult to learn, and in recent years the Micmac have used an alphabetic system. Among the Cree people of Canada a syllabary was introduced, in which each symbol stands for a combination of consonant plus vowel. In this system if a given symbol is rotated 45°, 180°, or 225°, the value of the consonant remains the same, but the vowel changes from *e* to *i*, to *o*, and to *a*, respectively. A modification of this symbol was adopted by the Inuit people of Baffin Island and continues to be widely used in the Canadian North.

The most famous of North American writing systems, however, is that invented for Cherokee in the nineteenth century by Sequoyah, who knew no English, but had seen materials written in English. Deciding that his language should have its own writing system, he succeeded in inventing one: not an alphabet, but a syllabary, in which each symbol indicates a combination of consonant plus vowel (see Cherokee Syllabary; an example of how the syllabary is used is given below). Note that Sequoyah borrowed the shapes of some letters in the English alphabet but without regard to their sounds; so Cherokee *D, R,* and *T* are pronounced *a, e,* and *i,* respectively.

In most other languages, alphabetic writing systems have been used, adapted from European alphabets when necessary by using additional letters and accent marks. In the nineteenth century the Russian alphabet was adapted to write Aleut; elsewhere, the Roman alphabet was generally used.

However, some Native Americans distrust the use of writing systems for their languages and prefer to emphasize the continuance of the oral medium. In 1991, the president of the 28,000-member Oglala Sioux tribe announced that Lakota was the language of tribal business on the Pine Ridge Reservation; nevertheless, he stated that he does not approve of writing the language down. "Writing it is bad," he said, "because you have a tendency to lose some of the spirituality when it's down in black and white." In spite of such feelings, the development of literacy in traditional languages may make it possible for tribal people to transmit and elaborate their literary tradition—not only in the oral medium, and not only in English translation—but also in writing systems adapted to their individual languages and developed with their active cooperation.

♦ ♦ ♦ ♦ ♦ ♦ ♦ ♦ ♦ ♦ ♦ ♦ ♦ ♦ **LANGUAGE MAINTENANCE**

Since their first contact with Europeans, Native Americans have been under pressure to learn European languages; this pressure has been applied by administrators and educators, as well as by the European-dominated society in general. However, in the early to middle nineteenth century bilingualism was common in many Native communities. Especially in the eastern and central parts of the continent, many people used English or French for dealing with whites; but some schools, churches, newspapers, and government services used Indian languages. This situation changed during the late nineteenth and early twentieth centuries, especially in the United States, when the government began to stamp out the use of Native languages; many individuals were forcibly removed from their homes and taken to boarding schools, where they were punished for speaking anything but English. After the Indian Reorganization Act of 1934 there was some reversal in official attitudes, and attempts began to be made to revive literacy in Native languages. But by this time, many Indian parents had come to believe

Example of Cherokee in Sequoyah's syllabary, in phonetic transcription, and in translation. From Beginning Cherokee, *by Ruth Bradley Holmes and Betty Sharp Smith, 2d ed. Norman: University of Oklahoma Press, 1977.*

Syllabary:	WΡᏟ ᏣᎳᎩ ᎠᏦᎸᏗ
Pronunciation:	Ta?-li:ʼ-ne Tsa-la-giʼ Go-hwe-lv:ʼ-i
Translation:	Second Cherokee Lesson

The Inuit people of the Arctic try to preserve their language by providing reading material in Inuit for their young people.

that assimilation to Anglo-American language and culture offered the only hope for their children. The result was the obsolescence and extinction of many languages. Today it is common to find languages that are remembered only by a few elders. Since the Native language is the principal medium for teaching traditional culture, the loss of languages has been accompanied by the loss of much cultural knowledge.

Since the 1970s, various efforts have been made in Native American communities to revive or preserve traditional languages, sometimes through the teaching of literacy in those languages. In some groups children are growing up as active bilinguals; examples can be found among the Inuit and Cree in Canada, Athabaskan groups in both Canada and Alaska, the Sioux reservations in South Dakota, the Cherokee in North Carolina and Oklahoma, some Pueblos in New Mexico, and the Navajo in New Mexico and Arizona. However, each succeeding generation tends to be less fluent in Native languages than the one before it. It has been estimated that by the mid twenty-first century not more than a dozen Native American languages will still be actively spoken. Nevertheless, studying extinct and living Native languages broadens understanding of the resources offered by human language and provides insight into the past history of the North American continent.

William Bright
University of Colorado

R*eligion*

NATIVE AMERICAN RELIGIONS:
CREATING THROUGH COSMIC GIVE-AND-TAKE ♦ ♦ ♦ ♦ ♦ ♦

From time immemorial, Native American religiousness has grown out of encounters with spirit, plant, animal, and human "others" who often seemed like dangerous strangers. Grounded in the actual world with its very real threats, neither contemporary nor traditional Native American religions are belief systems. Unlike the idea of belief, which stresses some other-worldly, mysterious, and unseen reality, the term *worldview* suggests that religion has to do with the ways in which people see the world practically in cooperative or competitive terms. Native American respect for nature, for example, has always been admired. What has not been appreciated is that Native Americans have always understood that the world is a dangerous place. If respectful trust exists, it has been earned. Disaster, whether personal, social, military, or ecological, may therefore be the result of the people's failings.

Traditional stories over the centuries have pointed out that the people are threatened, as well as helped, by other beings. American Indians learn hard lessons through the oral tradition and relearn them in ceaseless struggle for intercultural understanding. Navajo mythology recounts this key religious insight: Navajo exist because they struggled to learn from, rather than about, the many strange peoples they met along their path. Navajo have learned, are still learning, from Protestants, Catholics, Mormons, Peyotists, and from the Lakota of the northern Great Plains. All the while, they have continued to create in their traditional ceremonies that exquisite balance in the world they call *hoz'ho*, a term that expresses beauty, harmony, knowledge, and well-being. Such a condition has always been, in fact, a main objective of Native American ritual life. The people understand that the world itself has always been and, especially now, is threatened. Traditional Hopi call post-contact life *koyanisquatsi* (life out of balance), and so they all the more diligently perform their ritual responsibilities to keep their earthly lives in balance.

Native American religiousness comes from a profound and astute understanding of the relatedness of all beings. The Navajo concept of *hoz'ho*, for example, balances thought and speech, correct understanding and responsible action. In this way, Navajo religion exists in the actual, everyday life of the people. The Wabanaki of the Canadian-American Northeast say of their world-transforming culture hero, Gluskap: "He lives here in my story." In this way, the Wabanaki declare that religion comes into being in the speech of the people. The stories of Gluskap and other stories are upheld, brought to life, by their remembrance and retelling, and by the moral guidance and resulting moral conduct engaged in by the listeners. Unlike Christianity, traditional Native American religions do not emphasize personal salvation in the next life or in preordained, godly commandments. While the Lakota and many other Plains Indian people evoke the Great Spirit, they also address many other beings as "all my relatives." These beings, understood as kin and addressed as "grandfather" and "grandmother," express a morality of caring relationships with all beings and forces within the universe. Indeed, at the heart of Native American languages exists the religious insight that the entire universe is composed of powerful beings who either help or hinder human beings.

In all the American languages (more than 250 are still spoken), there is no word, no abstraction, for "religion." Yet American Indians have always had religious institutions, and these institutions are as complex and diverse as the people themselves. For example, shamans, people with special spiritual gifts, guided the hunting and gathering peoples, while song and dance groups, in the larger societies, performed ancient rituals celebrating solidarity with the great powers of mythology: Sun; Moon; Stars; the Winds; the Animals; the Three Sisters, Corn, Bean, and Squash; and with the ancestors. Both male and female medicine people still guide the people today, as do new kinds of religious practitioners, including Christian priests and ministers and roadmen in the pan-Indian Native American Church. American Indian people care little for institutional religions constructed on the written word and revelation fixed in dogma; they understand that their religiousness "seeks the path of life."

Ceremonies at the death of a chief or of priests. Drawing by Le Moyne; engraving from T. de Bry, America, *part II, 1591, plate XL. Courtesy of American Heritage Press.*

The religions of North America have always been poorly understood by Europeans. Writing about his first encounter with indigenous people in 1492, Christopher Columbus told Queen Isabella and King Ferdinand of Spain that the "New World" Natives were "very deficient in everything." It seemed to him that they had no religions, no governments, and no laws. At the same time, however, Columbus assured his monarchs "that in all the world there cannot be a people better or more gentle." Columbus, as did many Europeans after him, wondered how a people could be civilized without organized religion. Columbus thought, as do many still, that those humane qualities associated with religion—ethical behavior, moral leadership, a search for justice—could not be obtained outside the God-given institutions of European church and state. Columbus did not realize that Native Americans have always located morality in the personal and communal lives of the people.

Traditional Native American religions should not be thought of as "pure"; to the contrary, these traditions have always been muddied with life. They evolved over centuries, as Native peoples moved from place to place in North America, discovering new plants and animals and meeting new peoples with different ways of being religious. This process of religious discovery was not always peaceful. When Native Americans intruded on the lands of others, they met resistance. Thus war became part of life's struggle, and so conflict helped shape religious change.

The Peace Council, a spiritually guided conference, arose out of the need to end conflict between nations and people. The peace councils often opened with smoking the Sacred Pipe with friends or enemies to affirm the relatedness of all living things and to explore and seek understanding of political and cultural differences. Native Americans often celebrated their encounters with European strangers, or early explorers and colonists, with the lighting and sharing of a peace pipe or burning of tobacco. Tobacco was ceremonially burned when the Wampanoag Indians of present-day Massachusetts met with the Pilgrims, and thereafter in countless councils to seek peace. Today the rituals take the form of talking circles, in which urban Indians from many once hostile tribes seek mutual understanding and support. The act of seeking peace and harmony with nature and with fellow human beings lay at the heart of Indian religiosity. The long tradition of spiritually guided meetings suggests that Native religiousness has always expressed itself in cautious but mutual and respectful conversation with others.

Stories of the Beginning

The enduring and dynamic character of Native American mythologies has often been misunderstood. One popular misunderstanding is that because their cultures were based on the spoken word, Native Americans lost over the years their pure, original traditions. Nonetheless, Native American culture is generally transmitted from generation to generation by the retelling of stories and myths and reenactment of rituals and ceremonies. Some North American Indians kept records with sacred symbols written on wooden sticks or embroidered into wampum belts, but there was no written sacred book like the Christian Bible. Instead all Indian peoples had long traditions of transmitting religious ceremonies and ideas through storytelling and ritual reenactments. The stories and rituals carry the traditions and history of Native American people. A second and related misinterpretation is that mythology is fictional and therefore an inadequate way of thinking about the world.

Mythology is historical, because it reflects upon the traditional values of the past in order to make sense of the moral challenge of the present. Mythology makes an unspoken but underlying assumption: the future depends not on what people believe, but on their responsible actions in the here and now. Myth is not narrowly historical in concerning itself factually with what happened, where, and when. To the contrary, myth addresses urgent issues of personal and social existence and boldly offers Native American peoples basic answers to basic questions: "I am because—" and "We are because—" Myths, especially origin myths, answer for a people where they came from, describe the purposes people have on earth, and establish the relations of the individual and the nation to the universe

Native American

Mythology

and to the spiritual world. The answers to such questions are given in the details and symbols of the origin and other myths.

The myth of earth-divers is probably the most widespread way in which Native Americans have dealt with the question of origin. There are many earth-diver stories throughout North America, and often specific details of the stories vary. Nevertheless the central symbolic theme of the origin of solid earth (symbolic of order and a haven) emerging within a chaotic and formless universe is usually the same. Unlike the all-powerful God of Judeo-Christian religions, these creators needed the cooperation of various birds and animals to form the earth, or solid ground. Confronted with a pre-existing, boundless, and chaotic water world, the creator-transformer sought the assistance of animals or birds, who dove deep into an almost bottomless sea attempting to seize a tiny bit of mud to form the earth island. These were compassionate, sacrificial acts, because the animal persons often died in their attempts. In the end, one of them succeeded. The creator then expanded the bit of earth into the earth island, where people and animals live. The stories vary about which animal is successful in gaining the bit of earth from under the sea, but that animal is usually highly revered by the people. In an Iroquoian version of earth-diver, Turtle generously offered his back as a foundation to hold up the earth. Similarly, among many Indian cultures, the earth island is considered the turtle's back, who swims in the great sea of water, which is symbolic of chaos and disorder. In Delaware culture, the Turtle clan or social division was considered politically and religiously the most the prominent, because the Turtles symbolically hold up the society and, mythically, support the earth island. In all variants of the earth-diver stories, cooperation, service, and self-sacrifice bring order into a formerly chaotic universe.

In many other stories, great beings, who anthropologists often call culture heroes and who often resemble earth-diver transformers by their actions, wisdom, and sometimes direct law, show people how to act powerfully and responsibly. Like transformers all over the continent, the Wabanaki Gluskap changed the shape of the earth itself. He created the rivers and streams that flow throughout the Northeast by killing a selfish frog who hoarded all the world's water, just as Coyote, the transformer figure of the western Indians, did in California. In the Southeast among the Cherokee, a powerful bird formed the landscape by lifting and lowering mountains and valleys with his wings as he inspected the newly formed earth. Gluskap also reduced giant animals like beaver to their present size so that they would live cooperatively with human beings. He created the coming and going of the seasons, thus assuring that the great person Winter interacted reciprocally with Summer.

Besides Gluskap in the Northeast, similar culture hero stories are found throughout North America, although the culture hero's name usually changes from region to region. Similar culture hero roles are taken up by Raven in the Northwest Coast and Arctic, by Rabbit in the Southeast, and Old Man in the Plains. The actions and deeds of the culture heroes help explain the importance of human responsibility. About each culture hero there are many stories, but invariably they are stories about the culture hero's immoral or irresponsible actions that lead to negative consequences. For example, the cause of death and pain in the world is attributed to the irrational and selfish actions of the culture hero. The lessons taught by the story is that selfish, irresponsible, proud individuals will suffer negative consequences such as illness, death, or other misfortunes. The culture hero stories give an account for the origin of harshness of life—the existence of poverty, suffering, death, the need to labor, the dispersal of the tribes, and the nature of war. Culture heroes also establish safe limits to such negative facts of life. At the same time, the culture hero stories are usually very funny and are told for both moral edification and entertainment. The culture heroes take their misfortunes in stride and thereby provide examples for how individuals are to endure the sufferings of life. Furthermore, the culture heroes are great gift givers because, in many mythical histories, they form people and instruct them about edible plant and animal foods, and they create the tools—pots, baskets, nets, spears, digging sticks, canoes, and snowshoes—that make human work economically and morally productive. The ritual knowledge and technological gifts of the culture heroes help the Indian people to live either in the desert heat or the Arctic frost. Often, as among the Tlingit of the Northwest Coast, the culture hero—in this case Raven—gives the people their primary ceremonies and their primary social relations. The Tlingit are divided into two moieties, two social halves, called Raven and Eagle. It was Raven who organized Tlingit society into this two-fold division, which the Tlingit continue to honor.

The emergence tradition is another widespread form of creation history, developed with complexity by the Pueblo, Navajo, and Apache in the Southwest, and by the Creek in the Southeast. Emergence stories have the people climbing out from under the earth, their existence bound up with the character of the world itself. In these accounts, emergence becomes a rich metaphor for moral development or, in the Navajo case, *hoz'ho*—greater harmony, beauty, and order with the beings of the universe (e.g., the sun, the sky, the wind, men and women, the animals, and other peoples). Living within the earth, the peoples face serious troubles. Often their world lacks light and warmth. Sometimes the planet is too small, and spinning rapidly makes the people dizzy. Such inhospitable conditions drive the people to seek more suitable living conditions. Traveling upward, some animals flying, others carried by tall plants that reach the vault of the heavens, the people (often animal persons as well as humans) seek their proper, balanced place in the cosmic scheme of things. The people, sometimes animals or insects, are cast out of the lower worlds for their moral indiscretions, and they must find a way to the next world in order to survive and attempt to live more morally ordered lives, or that world will also be destroyed by the cosmic beings whom the people offend.

In the Navajo creation history, humans do not live in the first three worlds that exist beneath the present world. A people of flying insects, Air Spirit People, occupied the First World. Because the Air Spirit People were quarrelsome and committed adultery, they were forced by powerful spirit beings to flee to the next higher world, where they met a people of swallows. By committing adultery with the swallow leader's wife, the Air Spirit People were forced to fly up to the Third World. There they soon committed the same sins with the beings of the Third World and were forced to fly up to the Fourth World, where they met the Holy Beings, who are immortal spirits who made the First Man and First Woman. Much of the story of life in the Fourth World revolves around difficulties encountered by the first people over reconciling gender differences and developing harmonious sexual and husband-wife relations. Because Coyote, also created in the Fourth World by the Holy People, kidnapped two children of the water spirit, a great flood forced the people, with the aid of actions by two spiritual leaders, to ride a reed up to the fifth, or present, world. For the Navajo, the fifth world is not the last possible world. If the people do not maintain moral and harmonious lives in the fifth world—the present world—then this world will also be destroyed, and perhaps only a few lucky survivors will be able to climb to the sixth world, the next higher world. Navajo emergence mythology emphasizes a search for moral responsibility, seeking a state of being in which humans, plants, animals, sun, and moon exist in a stabilized, moral, and harmonious relationship.

As one result, Navajo understanding of world discovery contrasts dramatically with that of Western Europeans. For European discoverers, the strange, new peoples of the Americas failed to pose new questions about the nature of reality. Judging by their own cultural standards, European discoverers declared that Native Americans were culturally and religiously incomplete. Assured of the godly superiority of their own culture, Europeans, from contact to the present, have attempted to impose their way of life on Native Americans. To the contrary, Navajo emergence mythology describes a cooperative, open-minded approach to other cultures.

The earth-diver, culture hero, and emergence stories are similar in that they teach that all persons, human and otherwise, must share power and responsibility. Otherwise they risk upsetting the ordered relations of the universe and thereby will cause disorder, suffering, disease, misfortune, and death among the people. The Winnebago of Wisconsin have another case in point of this cosmic give-and-take. Although most of their story's variations on how the world came to exist discuss the origin of the Winnebago clans, a few do focus on the vague figure of Earthmaker. In these stories (here there is the possibility of missionary influence), the Winnebago declare that Earthmaker established a universe largely independent of himself, and one in which human beings were an afterthought. As he created the Sun, Moon, Earth, the four Winds, plants, and animals, he endowed each with particular and exclusive powers, such as the ability to fly for birds and great strength for the bear. Human beings alone were powerless. To correct his mistake, Earthmaker gave human beings a special gift of power. He created tobacco and promised that as long as human beings tended the plant with care and offered it to the powerful persons of the cosmos, their needs would be met. It is also telling that Earthmaker gave human beings something that he and all spirits greatly desired. In this way, Earthmaker endowed the Winnebago with tremendous power and an opportunity to express respect

Native leaders often consulted shamans on important issues. Drawing by Le Moyne; engraving from T. de Bry, America, part II, *plate XI. Courtesy of American Heritage Press.*

towards the great others. As with many other Native American peoples, tobacco and the pipe thus became the way in which the Winnebago obtained spiritual harmony and order with the beings of the universe.

Similarly, New Mexican Zuni mythology describes a time when human beings and the Kachinas, ancestral spirit beings, competed with each other over ownership of the deer and other game animals. After a prolonged battle in which humans and Kachinas found themselves equally powerful, humans decided to use trickery to win the contest. Rather than seek a mutually beneficial sharing of the deer, which the balance of power suggested as the only positive outcome, humans imprisoned all the game in a place that the Kachinas could not find. When the battle continued, humans prevailed. The result was a reciprocal balance that declared the uselessness of conflict: the Kachinas acknowledged human ownership of the deer and, in return, humans recognized that the Kachinas had control of corn and other seeds. Since each group desired the resources of the other, interdependence and reciprocity became a cosmic necessity.

Although Native American mythologies view the cosmos and its formation in very different ways, depending on their ecological setting, they share some common religious insights such as the need to establish constructive relations among themselves and with the great beings of the cosmos, including the plants and animals who sustain life.

Celebrations of the Life Cycle

Throughout North America, Indian peoples express gratitude towards plants who feed, herbs who cure, and deer and bear, who make human life possible. They understand that animal bones must be treated with respect and that animal reincarnation, the understanding that the spirits of respectfully treated animals are reborn and replenish the earth, depends on human action. In the Pacific Northwest, for example, the first-catch ceremony celebrates the gift of salmon. Here, the first fish of the year was placed on evergreen bows, themselves symbols of enduring life, and the people thanked the salmon for willfully sacrificing its life so that humans can live. The salmon was then carefully cooked, and each person in the village ate part of this special fish. Finally, the salmon's bones were returned to the water so that they will live again. In the same way, first-fruit ceremonies across the continent acknowledged the cosmic cycle of life. On the eastern seaboard, the widespread Green Corn ceremony, an annual new year and purification ritual, honors and gives thanks to the corn for its life-giving qualities. In a variety of Iroquois rituals, like "Thanks to the Maple" and the Strawberry festival, the people sing and dance to express gratitude to maple trees and strawberries for doing their part to support the lives of humans.

After the 1750s and the development of the high Plains horse cultures, human ritual responsibility differed on the Great Plains. There the well-being of buffalo and horses and the need to achieve success in war were the focus of ceremonial activity. The Plains Pawnee, southwestern Pueblo, and California peoples, among others, keyed ritual performance and human responsibility to seasonal and celestial cycles. All of these ritual performances represent variants of a single insight, as stated by the Northwest Kwakiutl: Life is about eating and being eaten. Human life plays an essential role in the cosmic cycle of birth, growth, death, and rebirth.

In effect, various North American mythologies teach very similar lessons. The stories explore the meaning of human life in relation to a threatening universe. Despite their emphasis on the dangerous nature of existence, the stories also hold out hope. The great others of the beginning teach responsible cooperation. Cosmic councils, in which animals, birds, plants, insects, and other beings come together, identify what would become the heart of Native American religious action: each being has a unique power or ability and the responsibility to contribute and cooperate. Native American mythologies also explore the terrible things that happen when people—human and otherwise—fail to play their part in this cosmic drama.

The unprivileged role that human action takes in Native American religions is startling to a Judeo-Christian. For Christians, reality is divided into three spheres that derive from a great chain of being: above all stands an all-powerful God, who is creator of an impersonal, machine-like universe; directly below this God and closely associated with him are angels, who are devoted to his worship. (Some angels, associated with rebellious Lucifer, refused such submission. In punishment, God excluded them from his presence, although they remain powerful and destructive.) Below this exalted heavenly order stands the realm of God-created nature in which humans are the highest beings, served in their turn by a subordinate, exploitable nature. Judeo-Christian religions are ones in which "higher" beings are superior to lower ones, and therefore one in which grace, or empowerment, comes from on high.

Native American religions, in contrast, strike a balance. Native piety differs from Christian prayer and worship, and leading a devout life means performing rituals and moral behaviors that create human and world order in the present life, with less emphasis on salvation in the next life. One essential characteristic of Native American piety has to do with acknowledgment. For example, traditional Hopi begin the day by greeting the Sun, the great person whose light and warmth makes life possible. Similarly, in the traditional Southeast, people bathed daily, for bathing was an act that admitted the possibility of both transgression and personal and collective purification. In a related way, Mountain Wolf Woman, a twentieth-century Winnebago, recounts that, after a successful deer hunt, her father directed her and her sister to express thanks by offering tobacco to the thunders, trees, stars, and moon, thus nurturing these beings in return for their gift of meat. Concluding the ritual by fasting, the Winnebago girls experienced humility and gratitude for gifts generously given and gratefully returned.

Differing views on origin and order also influenced how European colonists labeled Native Americans. Judging by their own standards, European discoverers declared that Native Americans were culturally and religiously incomplete and, thus assured of the godly

Native American Perspectives Different from Those of Judeo-Christian

superiority of their own culture, Europeans still attempt to impose their way of life on Native Americans. To the contrary, Navajo emergence mythology is one example of the cooperative, open-minded approach to other cultures that Native Americans carry.

Religious Power and Social Life

Just as councils have always been central to the give-and-take of Native American social, economic, and political life, religions express the collective processes through which the peoples share in creating, maintaining, and transforming relations with others. The relationships of importance include those with one another, with the great persons of the four directions, with the great persons of the above and the below, and with the great persons co-existing with human beings on the earthly plane. Native Americans choose to symbolize these persons and their cosmic domains in various ways. For many, the four directions are fundamental; for others, up-river and down-river describe the central relationships. Whatever the symbolic orientation to the world's persons, Native American ritual action aims for balance, cooperation, and mutual interdependence.

Importance of Collectivism

The collective goal of religious action cannot be over-stressed for any of the Native American peoples. Although some interpretations view hunting peoples as religiously individualistic and peoples with permanent settlements and ampler resources as more devoted to communal religious activity, these interpretations miss the mark in several ways. Particularly, they reveal a misunderstanding of the diversity of religious outlooks within the various tribal traditions.

In traditional Native American contexts, religion meant very different things to different people, depending on age, gender, knowledge, and power. Hunting peoples lived in very small kinship groups, and usually only a few persons (male and/or female) were religious specialists. Only some had the special power to evoke the spirits, foretell the future, find game, and cure. But, far from encouraging individualism, power spread from the few throughout the group: everyone encountered the spirits in dreams, and in everyday work life they contributed their share to make a communal whole. Moreover, religious specialists in hunting societies were no more motivated by self-interest than were their counterparts in larger-scale agricultural or marine-fishing societies.

Indeed, at first glance, important differences do seem obvious between hunting and agricultural societies. In addition to hunting-gathering societies, North America witnessed many large-scale tribal developments apparently associated with technological evolution. In all probability, agriculture—in the milder regions of the Northeast, along the Eastern seaboard, in the Southeast, along rivers on the Great Plains, and even in the desert Southwest—made town life possible. Also striking is the fact that the seagoing, big-canoe cultures of the Pacific Northwest, which won an ample livelihood from fishing and hunting marine mammals, created a complex tribal life, even one divided into upper and lower classes. Similarly, on the Great Plains, a dynamic combination of French guns from the Northeast and horses from the Spanish Southwest apparently helped to create the classic, stereotypical Plains tribes.

Despite these developmental differences and the varying degrees of tribal-wide religious rituals, the scale of these societies did not force them to depart religiously from the rituals of the hunter-gatherers, nor did they separate religion from other parts of culture. Tribal rituals—like the Green Corn ceremony, an annual world renewal ritual, of the Huron and Iroquois in the Northeast and the Cherokee, Chickasaw, Choctaw, and Creek in the Southeast; the medicine societies, or ritually exclusive groups of shamans with specialized curing knowledge, of the Ojibwa, Odawa, Menominee, and Winnebago of the Eastern Woodlands; the Sun Dance, an annual purification ceremony, among the Hidatsa, Cheyenne, Lakota, Crow, and Blackfeet on the Plains; the Kachina rituals, for bringing rain and community well-being, of the Southwest Pueblo; the world-renewal rites, ceremonial reenactments of origin histories that ensure the life of the world for another annual or ritual cycle, among the Luiseño, Kumeyaay, and Chumash of California; and the winter ceremonials of the Salish,

Kwakiutl, Tsimshian, Haida, and Tlingit of the Pacific Northwest—all share an ancient American religious logic. Just as the hunter-gatherers acknowledged life freely given, thus empowering its reincarnation, most major tribal rituals, such as those mentioned above, celebrate human interdependence and reciprocity with the great persons of the cosmos.

Far more important, to say that hunting peoples were religiously individualistic denies their collective orientation. In fact, even small social groups had an intensely religious communalism. Hunting peoples like the Inuit of the Arctic, the Algonquin in the sub-Arctic Northeast, and the hunting and gathering peoples—Ute, Shoshoni, and Paiute of the Southwest and desert areas of the Great Basin and California—all depended on kinship cooperation for their very lives. Hunting and gathering were collective activities conducted by men and women in their respective work groups. These societies were relatively unspecialized in their economic activities, although individuals certainly had special skills in crafting canoes, snowshoes, bows and arrows, spears, nets, pots, and baskets. The telling point is that everyone—religious specialists included—did more or less the same kind of work, usually as part of a group effort.

In both small- and large-scale Native American societies, all contributed to the collective good. Young boys proudly gave their first-kill to elders who thanked them for their skill and gift. Similarly, young girls learned from their mothers, aunts, and grandmothers the importance of service. Unmarried men presented their game to headmen, who served as redistributive agents making sure that no one—whether young or old, married or unmarried, healthy or sickly—went without food, clothing, or shelter. Selflessness and unvarying attention to others' needs (including the need for courage in defending the people from their enemies) were the hallmarks of "chiefly" status. Individualism did, of course, exist. But self-interest expressed itself in relation to the well-being of the group, since people used laughter, gossip, and social contempt as powerful ways of controlling deviant individualist behavior that threatened the well-being of the group. When people turned their backs on a wayfaring person, he felt the pain of isolation and soon mended his ways to comply with the general will of the tribal community. Otherwise, Native Americans both respected and valued responsible individuality.

Hunting and gathering peoples thus reveal the religious and cultural challenges all Native American peoples have always faced. They lived in hostile environments peopled by beings who could injure, maim, and kill as easily as they could sustain life. Loners could not survive, and this may be one reason why orphans figure so prominently in Native American stories. Cast adrift from sustaining social contact, orphans were pitied, often treated with contempt, and sometimes cautiously admired. The frequent outcome of orphan stories drives home a collective moral: noticed by benevolent spirits, orphans were given powers—extraordinary knowledge and special skills—withheld from ordinary people. Thus, having been given abilities that people need, orphans become an important part of society, using their power to serve the very persons who had scorned their social isolation.

Social Challenges

Like the life challenges posed by the environment, the social world within the tribes also posed great moral challenges to both individual and collective well-being. Selfishness, envy, jealousy, lust, anger, hatred, and revenge have always been destructive facts of life. Additionally, in patrilineal societies (in which ancestry is descended through fathers), women often came to live with their husbands and their husbands' relatives. As a result, wives were not only separated from their closest kin, but they sometimes lived out their lives among a group of strangers. The opposite was often the case in matrilineal groups (among whom identity flowed from maternal kin). Here (as among some Apache tribes) a husband found himself put to the moral test by his mother-in-law. Tradition dictated that a husband could not even speak to his mother-in-law, yet she could demand unflinching service from him. Many Apache stories explore the mutual resentment resulting from these traditions. Serious tensions also played themselves out in sibling rivalries. Such contests were particularly true among brothers whose competitive hunting and aggressive warfare created dangerous personalities. Not surprisingly, then, in many tribes purification rituals reoriented warriors to the peaceful values of community life.

The same tension between individualism and collectivism undercut the mythic and religious ideal among American Indian religious specialists. Defined by their unique possession of great power given by the spirits who wished to assist human beings, these specialists could dream the future, call the spirits, destroy enemies, cure disease, find game, and even control the weather. Ideally, they carefully held the people's welfare in their hands. They were guardians of traditional knowledge and values, and in their own lives they were to be exemplars of the moral meaning of tradition. Yet they too were men and women, and so subject to every human failing. This truth the people knew all too well, as their emotional reactions declared. The people sought assistance and leadership from their religious specialists, and for those contributions they were grateful. But they also combined respect and admiration with fear. If power could be used to help, it could also serve the religious specialist's own purposes: religious rivalries, duels, love medicine, poisonings, and witchings were destructive facts of life.

Social struggles within even the smallest Native American group must be understood in a religious context. The struggles represent not the kind of impersonal meaninglessness that has come to characterize so much of contemporary American life (with which present Native Americans struggle). Rather, Native American religious life reaches for collective order in the face of individualistic chaos. Such a moral challenge derives, in actuality, from the relational laws of the universe as declared by mythology. The unvarying need to grapple with such troubles is one major reason why Native American religions have seemed so perplexing, at least when their differences with mainline Judeo-Christianity have been honestly encountered. As anthropologist Paul Radin noted: "Native Americans do not have fixed, dogmatic religions with which to read the challenge of life. Rather, they read life in order to understand the religious challenge demanding their active response. They ask not what they must believe. To the contrary, they study troubled situations to discover what they are called upon to do."

With European contact, an era of rapid religious change began. Between 1492 and 1820, significant impact was limited to the French, English, and Spanish/Mexican colonial spheres in Canada, the Southwest, and California. As part of a larger economic, political, and military colonialism, missionaries single-mindedly stressed the superiority of Christian religion. Destructive as the colonial years were to the American Indian, they were also a time of tremendous creativity, as the tribes applied the lessons of mythology to assess their troubled situations, examine the claims of the missionaries, and work on revitalizing their communities.

Native American Religious History: The Colonial Period

The Northeast

Missionization in Canada had various outcomes—some people were destroyed, while others adapted. Given the devastating impact of European diseases, intertribal wars, and the loss of lands, it is remarkable that Algonkian-speaking peoples (the Micmac, Wabanaki, Montagnais, and Algonquin) continued to practice important parts of traditional religion.

The French priests who introduced Catholicism to the Algonkian condemned many traditional Indian religious practices. While many Indians came to trust Catholicism, it would be incorrect to say that they converted to what they perceived as a superior religion. Rather, in their conversations with French missionaries, the Algonkian rediscovered traditional values. Catholic sacraments were used to preserve several religious functions and to recreate tribal communities at the same time that the sacraments established an important alliance with the French. The fact that the English threatened the Eastern Algonkian (the Wabanaki and Micmac) almost continually between 1675 and 1760, and that the French offered a powerful military alliance, also strengthened the religious alliance.

The Algonkian adapted some Christian rituals to fill their traditional needs. In many instances, for example, baptism was used to cure people afflicted with diseases against which traditional medicine was ineffective. The ritual also was used to maintain contact between the living and the dead. Jesus Christ began to appear in Algonkian dreams as the one who empowered medicine people to predict the future, cure disease, communicate with the dead, and hunt and make war successfully. In all these ways, the French God struck Algonkian as similar to their culture hero. Algonkian believed that when their culture hero withdrew from this world, he promised to return in some future time of need. And up to the present, Algonkian have continued to balance tradition and Christianity in a way that maintains their traditional relationships with the land and the plant and animal persons who still populate it.

For New England Algonkian, change proved much more damaging. Here the impact of disease and territorial displacement was much greater, and intertribal and colonial war also played an important role. After 1640, survivors of once powerful tribes regrouped in Indian praying towns, which were settlements of remnant Indian communities, adopted Christianity and New England town government, and reconciled themselves to live under colonial law. In the Indian praying towns, English ministers were more critical of traditional life than were the French Catholic priests. Caught between the demanding English and an inability to return to a traditional ecological life-style, the praying Indians endured English and Indian attacks during Metacom's (King Philip) War, only to survive thereafter on the margins of English life.

The Southwest and California

A fundamental religious conflict emerged in the Spanish Southwest in the early 1600s, when the Spanish violently asserted control over the Pueblo peoples of New Mexico and Arizona. Because intolerant Franciscan priests, with military backup, attacked the practice of Pueblo religions and used gang labor to create mission centers, the Pueblo remained unimpressed with Catholicism. In addition, the new religion simply did not address their urgent religious need to preserve reciprocal relations with the ancestral powers who ensured rain and successful crops.

The traditional political independence of each pueblo made the Spanish conquest easier, but ceaseless oppression eventually united the Pueblo. Under the leadership of San Juan Pueblo's medicine man, Pope, and with the active support of many religious leaders, the Pueblo tribes drove the Spanish out of the Rio Grande Indian pueblos in 1680. The Pueblo returned to independent political action but were reconquered by 1696. But times had changed. After 1700 the Spanish became more tolerant, and the Pueblo had learned an important lesson. They practiced Catholicism in public, especially in celebration of their pueblo's feast day, usually named by the Spanish after a Catholic patron saint, but all the while, traditional religious practice went underground where it remains, largely invisible, to the present day.

The humpback flute player Kokopelli, with horned serpent (Utah).

Other peoples under Spanish control fared differently. As they had in the Southwest, the Spanish, beginning in 1769, created an immense mission system in California from San Diego to San Francisco. There was some acceptance of Catholicism in these missions, but traditional religions survived as well. Among the Gabrielino and Chumash a new religion emerged, called Chingichngish, which asserted the truth of tradition and warned the people that they would die if they accepted baptism. The collapse of the mission system after the Mexican War of Independence in the 1820s created conditions of economic, political, and social marginality, but even in the twentieth century traditional religious practices survive among the former mission Indians of southern California.

The collapse of the mission system in Arizona and northwest Mexico created conditions that encouraged the emergence of Sonoran Catholicism. The missions had less impact on the desert-dwelling Papago (Tohono O'Odham) and Pima. Once free to follow their own interests, these Sonoran peoples continued to maintain positive relations with the patron saints the missionaries had introduced. Some Catholic holidays, like All Souls Day, have developed into community celebrations of solidarity with dead relatives. Likewise, Easter has come to mark the seasonal shift from winter to summer. To this day, Native chapels (independent of the Catholic church) are dispersed throughout the immense Tohono O'Odham reservation in southern Arizona. At the same time, traditional singers and curers survive, and the culture hero I'itoi is still important to the people.

Native American Religious History: The American Era

Algonkian, Pueblo, and the peoples of southern California and Sonora all largely maintained ties with their ancestral lands—this was an important factor in the preservation of traditions. Beginning with the American Revolution, however, many Native American peoples found themselves ecologically displaced. They became either surrounded by American settlers or forcibly removed to reservations far from original homelands. Native peoples responded to these changes with various degrees of success. Among the peoples of the Eastern seaboard, the Iroquois-speaking Six Nations Confederacy have been the most successful in religious adaptation. The peoples of the Midwest (the Shawnee, Miami, Fox, Potawatomi, and Illinois, to name a few) and those of the Southeast (the Cherokee, Creek, Chickasaw, Choctaw, and Seminole) struggled through periods of resistance, adaptation, missionization, and removal to Oklahoma reservations in the 1830s. In the process, they lost much, but not all, of their traditional culture.

The Iroquois and Handsome Lake

Between the end of the French empire in 1763 and the War of 1812, the Six Nations, or Iroquois Confederacy (before European contact the prophet Deganiwidah abolished the law of revenge between nations and so created the confederacy consisting of the Cayuga, Mohawk, Oneida, Onondaga, and Seneca, and, after 1716, the Tuscarora) experienced severe disruption of their traditional way of life. Iroquois warriors and diplomats once held formidable power, playing an important role during the French and Indian Wars between 1689 and 1763. Acting also as middlemen in the fur trade, the Iroquois were prosperous, especially since Iroquois women were highly successful agriculturalists. As the American colonies began to seek independence, the Iroquois attempted to maintain diplomatic neutrality, but found it impossible. By 1800, the confederacy had disintegrated—the individual nations were confined to separate reservations surrounded by American farms and settlements, traditional male roles no longer existed, and alcohol began to take a harsh toll on the people.

The Iroquois situation can be understood as a breakdown of the give-and-take of life. Although the confederacy had once been a respectful relationship between younger and elder brothers, these relations collapsed. Reciprocity no longer shaped clan, village, national, or confederate life. Women's political influence had been undercut by male warriors and diplomats, then male status disappeared as drinking, vicious politics, and loss of territory replaced hunting, warfare, and diplomacy. The Iroquois disagreed among themselves about whether to accept U.S. economic and political institutions and whether to accept Christianity. As a means to survive under vastly changed political conditions, some, led by the Seneca leader Cornplanter, favored adoption of Christianity and U.S.-style government and agriculture. Others, led by the Seneca conservative Red Jacket, favored retention of Iroquois culture and institutions and rejection of Christianity and agriculture. Red Jacket argued that if the Iroquois adopted U.S. institutions and Christianity, they would lose their character as a distinct people, and there would, in effect, be no Iroquois people or culture. In 1794, a smallpox epidemic, compounding an already difficult situation, cut the U.S. Iroquois population by more than half to some 4,000 people.

In 1799, the prophet Handsome Lake, a former warrior and a chief within the Iroquois Confederacy, arose to reflect upon the people's physical, social, economic, political, and moral condition. In 1799, Handsome Lake woke from a vision-in-death and, speaking an ancient form of the Iroquois language, called his people to renewal and adaptation. His vision was diagnostic: the people suffered because of their sins and, he said, if they did not repent the world itself would end. Handsome Lake particularly condemned the drinking, interpersonal violence, and sexual promiscuity that undercut his people's family life. He stressed traditional values, particularly the close relationship between individual and collective well-being. In this way the prophet affirmed the primary value of kinship. Even while he taught the Iroquois to tolerate American culture, he also urged caution, warning that a capitalist economy would only further divide the people. He identified sharing as a prime moral directive. To some extent Christianity influenced Handsome Lake (he stressed the ideas of God, sin, repentance, confession, and salvation), but he still emphasized the importance of public rituals, especially those ceremonies that thanked all the powers of the universe with whom the people were interdependent. One result of Handsome Lake's religious movement was establishment in the 1830s, some fifteen years after his death, of the Longhouse religion, which professes Handsome Lake's teachings and which survives to this day.

Tenskwatawa

Handsome Lake was neither the first nor the last prophet to urge Native peoples to reform. In the early nineteenth century (1806–11), Tenskwatawa, the Shawnee prophet and brother to Tecumseh, the great pan-Indian war leader, influenced religious, social, and political change along the entire Eastern seaboard. Moved by Tenskwatawa's call to reject American culture, several tribes in the Northeast and a conservative faction among the southeastern Creek went to war against the United States. In these years, religious leaders led resistance to—though sometimes urging compromise with—the growing American presence in their territories. At the same time, the new religious leaders urged their peoples to ritually renew their relations with plant, animal, and cosmic persons on whom their lives depended. The Shawnee prophet taught the tribes to return to the old traditions of economic self-sufficiency, avoid trade with U.S. traders, adopt old style dress, and throw off political leaders who were willing to sell land to the

United States. Tenskwatawa's influence ended after the Battle of Tippecanoe in November 1811, when his power failed against U.S. Army bullets. Thereafter, he had few followers, and his movement was over.

Religious Change on the Great Plains

Europeans had a less direct but still tremendous impact on the Great Plains. Responding to economic, political, military, and technological forces, great migrations of eastern and western peoples converged on the Plains in the eighteenth century, prompting a period of explosive cultural and religious change. The Plains people entered a prolonged period of intertribal warfare as they attempted to establish territories for themselves, yet cultural rebirth also occurred, as the tribes created new or modified religious and political societies, such as soldier societies, tribal councils, sacred bundle keepers, and the Sun Dance, to help ensure victory in war, cure horses, and ensure the well-being of the buffalo.

The Cheyenne exemplify the sorts of religious changes that came to affect all of the Plains tribes. Originally living in present south-central Canada, the Cheyenne were forced by colonial expansion to migrate west, eventually entering the Plains area. Soon after entering the Plains, the prophet Sweet Medicine gave the Cheyenne the great person-bundle, Mahuts—the four Sacred Arrows—considered a living being by the Cheyenne. Mahuts gave the Cheyenne men power in hunting and war and was a symbol of the Creator's covenant to preserve the Cheyenne people and culture. By accepting the Mahuts, the sacred bundle, the Cheyenne agreed to obey the sacred laws and perform the annual renewal ceremonies required by the Creator, and given by his prophet Sweet Medicine, and in return the Creator promised to preserve the Cheyenne in war and to provide for their material welfare through abundant access to game. On behalf of the Creator, Sweet Medicine also gave instructions for organizing soldier societies and for creating a council of forty-four chiefs for management of the annual buffalo hunt, the annual summer tribal ceremonies, and national Cheyenne affairs. The leading chief, who was selected by vote each ten years with each new council, represents the prophet Sweet Medicine, and his place in the Council was called the Center of the Universe, where he is in communication with the Creator. On the Plains, the Cheyenne met another Algonkian-speaking people, the Suhtai who, in making an alliance with the Cheyenne, brought their great person-bundle, Is'siwum, the Sacred Buffalo Hat. Is'siwum was responsible for world fertility, especially for the reproduction of the buffalo, and she obligated the Cheyenne to perform special rituals, such as the purification rites of the sweat lodge, a cleansing steam bath and ceremony in a small lodge, and the world-renewing powers of the Sun Dance.

Ghost Dance

As was true on the Great Plains, religious change was also accelerating in the far west. From California to British Columbia, the tribes experienced sudden and devastating contact with fur traders, missionaries, fishermen, and miners. Also as elsewhere, territorial loss and epidemic sickness caused the tribes to look to religion for answers to their crises. Some peoples sought help in Catholic and Pentecostal forms of Christianity, while many more turned to tradition, discovering that old stories, foretelling continental devastation, called the people to renewal. Taking various forms, the so-called 1870s Ghost Dances, special songs and dances, sought to reestablish solidarity between the people and their long-dead relatives and, as a result, to recreate the world as it was before white contact. As had happened earlier in the East, prophets reminded the peoples that they had to take moral responsibility for their condition. While these Ghost Dance movements were not always successful, they did lead to several enduring religious adaptations. In California, the Ghost Dance eventually gave way to the Bole Maru religion, sometimes called the Dreamers, whose practitioners revealed new ceremonial rituals, cured disease, and warded off witches. Significantly, the Dreamers democratized access to religious power and so stressed individual responsibility for communal good. As a result, Dreamers condemned drinking, arguing, stealing, and any failure to cooperate religiously.

By the 1890s, Ghost Dance teachings of world renewal and return of dead relatives, given by the Nevada Paiute prophet Wovoka, reached the Great Plains. The Indians there had suffered greatly because the buffalo had been all but eliminated and their people placed on reservations. They hoped that religious resistance would achieve world renewal. The infamous 1890 massacre of Lakota at Wounded Knee, South Dakota, where some of the people were practicing the Ghost Dance, marks the general decline of the Ghost Dance movement. Nevertheless the Ghost Dance persisted in small groups in the Plains area and farther west. Among the Pawnee, the Ghost Dance enabled individuals to communicate with dead medicine men and so to recreate many religious rituals that had been lost. Most important, the Ghost Dance encouraged the people to practice their traditional values in their daily lives by emphasizing traditional cultural understandings about ritual world renewal and the value of ritual to affect world change, even though the United States outlawed many of their religious ceremonies.

Arapaho Ghost Dance.

Salish Rituals in the Pacific Northwest

The Salish of Washington faced cultural annihilation in the 1870s and 1880s, and as was true for the Plains Indians, the Salish intensified religious activity in order to save themselves. While local settlers understood that Indians would act to preserve their way of life, they did not understand Salish rituals. Salish ceremonies were occasions when people danced and sang about their spirit power in order to avoid and to cure sickness. Settlers tended to interpret Salish religious rituals as war dances, because they understood little about Salish culture, and the fact that the rituals were practiced frequently amplified settler anxieties. As a result, in 1871, Salish rituals were outlawed and religious leaders were jailed. These measures were doubly problematic for the Salish: because their principal ceremonies drew together large numbers of people, they were difficult to perform secretly. And, since the rituals were held less frequently after 1871, the need for them increased.

Thus U.S. government policy struck at the center of Salish life. As with many other Native American groups, guardian spirits not only empowered Salish shamans to cure, they also gave most people the craft, hunting, gathering, and fishing skills upon which life depended. Unlike many groups in which guardian spirits were personal and secret (although still used to serve the group), spirits among the Salish required public acknowledgment of their freely given gifts. The spirits also threatened people when they failed to give public ceremony of the gifts received from friendly helper spirits. Failure to acknowledge the gifts, the Salish understood, led to retribution in the form of some material misfortune at the hands of the formerly allied spirit being.

Shaker Church

In 1882, John Slocum, a Coast Salish Indian man, fell dead, only to revive and reveal a religious vision. He reported that God required the Salish to abandon spirit dancing and shamanism for a new source of power. When Slocum again fell dead, he was revived by his wife Mary, who was possessed by a shaking that many interpreted as the promised gift of power. By 1892, Slocum and his followers, who became known as the Shakers, formed a church that by 1910 was incorporated in the state of Washington.

Although Slocum repudiated much of the past, especially shamanism, and adopted Christian symbols, the Shaker church only gradually shifted allegiance from traditional spirit helpers to the Christian God. In time, an understanding developed that allowed continuity between old and new. Although Shakers refer to Jesus and God, they vitally depend on the "Spirit of God," the spirit who gives the Salish powers to cure, foretell the future, and counter malicious shamans. Similar to the ancient winter ceremonies, the Shakers publicly witness the abilities they have received and thus address the well-being of the individual. At the same time, the Shaker church celebrates communal solidarity in Sunday gatherings, charismatic meetings often held to cure sickness, weddings, and funerals. Above all, Shakers express in Christian terms the ancient truth of interdependence between humans and the spirits: mutual charity among people makes it possible for the Spirit of God to work effectively among them.

Peyotism

The cultural changes of the late nineteenth and early twentieth centuries paved the way for new forms of pan-Indian, as opposed to tribal, religions. Increased contact among different tribes, especially in Oklahoma, led to the development of powwows, or festivals of dancing and socializing, which still continue as celebrations of Indian identity. Although the American era weakened relations between the tribes and animal persons, a great plant person, Peyote, whose visionary effects and teaching abilities derive from the cactus *Lophophora williamsi,* emerged on the southern Plains as a new guide to a distinctive religious life. The Peyote religion has a long history among American Indians. Early in the eighteenth century, peyote entered the Southwest from Mexico, with the Mescalero Apache integrating it into their curing rituals. Peyote did not begin to spread northward until the 1880s, when the Plains tribes experienced their greatest despair at reservation life.

Under reservation conditions, and facing religious persecution from the U.S. government, Indian people experienced social alienation, psychological confusion, and a loss of religious faith. Peyote addressed these problems and helped people to reorient their lives. The new religion affirmed cultural identity by preserving old world views of worldly interdependence and traditional ritual style, and gave heightened value to being Native American. At the same time, it eased the conflicting demands of traditional religion and Christianity. Finally, peyote helped the embattled peoples to resist cultural assimilation.

The Peyote religion gave the people ways to reassume religious responsibility: in the church they confessed their sins, achieved purification, cured sickness, recovered from alcoholism, and created powerful bonds of brotherhood—even among tribes which, in the nineteenth century, had been enemies. In many ways, the spread of peyote in the late nineteenth century was the most significant experiment in Native American religious change.

The early peyote prophets were innovators in drawing together various religious strands to create a new tradition. When mixed blood John Wilson (Delaware, Caddo, and French) first took peyote at an Oklahoma Ghost Dance in 1890, he received a great vision. Taking pity on him, plant person Peyote showed him the road Jesus took and assured him that if he traveled the same road, he would reach heaven. Hence Wilson added elements of Christianity, such as belief in Jesus as a major spirit helper and individual moral responsibility, to traditional peyote religious practice.

The Christ of Wilson's vision related to Indian peoples differently than he did to Christians. Wilson taught that Christians were given the Bible because they were guilty of killing Christ; Native Americans had no responsibility for this terrible act and so had a closer relationship to God. He thus taught that while Christians needed the Bible to communicate with God, Indians could learn God's truth directly from the Peyote spirit. Although other prophets insisted that peyotism and Christianity were the same religion, over time a consensus emerged that Christ and Peyote had special concern for Indian people. As did many other peyotists, Wilson declared that Native Americans, unlike Christians, could communicate personally with divinity.

Another prophet, John Rave, had experiences that illustrate the religious quest for meaning that Peyote addresses. Rave had been a restless child and a troubled adolescent. He participated in traditional Winnebago rituals, but they made little impression on him. Rave eventually left his home and became an alcoholic.

Rave's first experience using peyote, in Oklahoma, had been frightening. He confronted a huge, threatening snake, a symbol of powerful and destructive force in Winnebago mythology. As Rave's vision continued, he saw God, and he prayed for mercy and guidance. In time he received assurance and understanding that in all his life he had never known anything that was truly holy.

Rave's experience with peyote was typical. Confused, rootless, unhappy people came to Peyote, and the spirit gave them knowledge and healed them by giving them access to spiritual life, and by developing an ethic of personal responsibility and morality. According to Rave, peyote could heal because all sickness was merely a symptom of deeper troubles rooted in the soul. As in traditional Indian religious views, peyote, by healing and providing knowledge to the individual spirit, would clear the way for curing illness and other troubles. He taught that public confession of sin and trust would achieve redemption and salvation.

Just as Americans suppressed traditional religious practices, they also attacked the use of peyote. Believing that Indian rituals were un-Christian and uncivilized, reservation officials and missionaries spread false rumors that peyote led to wild sexual orgies. Traditionalists in some tribes opposed the new religion, and Indian progressives in the pan-Indian Society of American Indians joined forces with non-Indian critics and organized nationally against peyotism, claiming that the religion was an excuse to take drugs. They also said that peyote deprived people of real medical care, even though peyotists testified that peyote cured disease. Moreover, peyotists all opposed alcohol and attempted to lead morally upright lives. As a constructive response to this angry opposition, Oklahoma peyotists incorporated as the Native American Church and began a battle for religious freedom that still continues.

By providing a new moral ethic and spiritual guidance, peyotists stress that their medicine and ritual often cures the physical, psychological, and spiritual ills of reservation and urban life. Peyote leaders emphasize the moral unity of all Indian people and have integrated many tribal religious symbols into their religion. The Native American Church is a religion created by Indians to meet modern Indian needs.

Reemergence of Traditional Rituals

As powerful as peyotism has been in addressing the religious needs of Native American peoples, it has not displaced, or replaced, traditional religions. The traditional religious rituals that went underground in the early twentieth century began to reemerge in increasingly vigorous forms since the 1930s. The earliest public reintroduction of apparently lost rituals occurred as Native Americans responded to the needs of their men during and after World War II. War ceremonials became vehicles through which Lakota and Navajo, among others, prepared men for service in the armed forces; prayer sustained them during the conflict; and healing ceremonies reintroduced them to community life after their return home. The Native American Church also addressed these needs, but it was far from unique in adding the force of prayer to what many saw as a necessary national war effort. World War II, the Korean War, and the conflict in Vietnam not only provided the focus for a resurgence of traditional and pan-Indian religious practice; these wars also led many Native Americans to a growing realization that their participation required a prayerful hope for peace for all peoples.

Since the 1960s, then, such forms of participation in national wars brought Native American life into an intensified relationship with U.S. national life. Increasingly, Euro-Americans came to realize that Native Americans possess living rather than dead religions. As the civil rights movement gained momentum, Native Americans themselves became more outspoken against an oppressive system that continued to attack a traditional life that Indians saw as fundamentally religious. They felt they were oppressed by the trust relationship between the tribes and the United States; that the U.S. government had reneged on its promises to protect tribal territories and Indian access to sacred sites and had failed to devise forms of government sensitive to tribalism and traditional religious leadership; they criticized programs that undermined religion, including culturally insensitive educational programs, forced relocation to cities, and a variety of other programs designed to detribalize and assimilate the peoples.

The leaders of the American Indian Movment (AIM) have been protesting the woefully inadequate educational, economic, and political situation of all Indians. AIM thus speaks to the full complexity of Native American needs, although not always with the support of traditional leaders. Its agenda expresses the need to strengthen a tribal base that young and old recognize: communal life is inseparable from constructive association with the spirits; the need to sustain pan-Indian religious forms that speak to urban Indians' situations; and the need for common political action.

AIM is only one voice addressing these concerns. Vine Deloria, Jr., wrote about the unique character of Native American religions in *God Is Red.* In other works—*Custer Died for Your Sins* and *We Talk, You Listen*—Deloria expressed urgent Indian concerns and called for Euro-Americans to recognize a failed pluralism, especially the nation's economic system that has marginalized the tribes and devastated their remaining lands.

Religiousness and Contemporary Native American Peoples

Unlike Christianity, which concentrates all power in the hands of God who bestows it on human beings as an act of grace, Native American religions emphasize the interdependence of all beings. Even the Great Spirit needs humans, just as they need him, because if people live beyond the pale of spiritual order by not honoring the other beings and forces of the universe, they will create disturbances that will cause destruction and chaos. Mother Earth reminds her people that her well-being depends on responsible human action. The Yaqui people of Arizona, for another example, do Jesus's work, and they think of him as being like their little brother, the Deer. Both Deer and Jesus are perfect innocents who give their lives so that others may live. The Yaqui perform ceremonies in honor of Jesus: At the end of the Easter Ceremony, in which they em-

A Sun Dance at Pine Ridge, a Sioux reservation in southern South Dakota.

power Jesus to resurrect Himself, they ring the bell of their church to call St. Michael to carry to heaven the flowers that bloom from their ritual labor. Every year, in a ceremony that attracts thousands of people, the Zuni of New Mexico perform Shalako, a ceremony in which the great powers of the universe enter the pueblo and dance with the people. In the Pacific Northwest, the Salish sing and dance the powers given them by their spirit helpers, thereby acknowledging the religious obligations that make life possible.

These, then, are key insights expressed in past and present Native American religious activity: the world is composed of persons, not things; some persons, including some human beings, are powerful; some are not; some persons act in caring, respectful, and nurturing ways; many do not. In brief, all people have responsibilities toward others, whether or not they act accordingly. These insights were formed in the mythic period in which Native American cultures came into being, play themselves out in various religious community structures, and are embodied in religious, kinship, political relations, and economic activity. The insights are renewed in ritual performances, great and small. In all these ways, the American Indians create themselves in powerful acts that renew solidarity with all the world's people.

Kenneth M. Morrison
Arizona State University

◆ ◆ ◆ ◆ ◆ ◆ ◆ ◆ ◆ ◆ ◆ ◆ ◆ ◆ **PLURALISTIC RELIGIOUS BELIEFS**

Native Americans are very spiritual people. Before European conquest, in fact, spiritual life was the foundation of indigenous society. For the most part, Native American religion had not become institutionalized as it had among the so-called great or world religions, such as Christianity, Judaism, Islam, Buddhism, etc. Indeed, Indian government and religion were integrated: the political leaders were usually also the spiritual leaders. Until the late 1800s, for example, the Cheyenne Nation was governed by a council of forty-four Peace Chiefs composed of four clan chiefs from each of the ten bands and four sacred leaders. These last four leaders presided over the great tribal religious ceremonies—the Arrow Renewal, Medicine Hat, Sun Dance, and Massaum or Animal Dance—which integrated the tribe and gave it its collective consciousness or social solidarity.

Traditionalists in the Native American context are those who follow the traditions—the beliefs and rituals—of the old culture. Traditional Indians find it difficult to define or explain religion, because to them spirituality is metaphysical and not material. Navajo Community College, which integrates medicine people and traditional elders into its school curriculum, therefore prefers the term "sacred" instead of religion. Sacred ways and practices are at the heart of living and the essence of cultural survival. The sacred ways of tribal, non-western peoples the world over do not try to explain or control all of the phenomena of the universe. They do not, as organizations, seek to dominate other people's thought, ways of worship, or their societies in the name of religious orthodoxy. This is what makes the sacred different from schools of philosophical thought or the denominations of organized religion.

French sociologist Émile Durkheim contended that religion embraced more than the ethnocentric "state religion" prevalent in Europe, a property-owning institution with a hierarchical structure of religious specialists who intervene on behalf of the devotees with a supreme being and who officiate over church dogma. According to Durkheim, the elementary forms of the religious life are found among all peoples, the essence of which is not theoretical directive but, instead, its sacred community of believers. The true heart of religion may be defined, therefore, as a unified system of belief and practices relative to sacred things that unite its devotees into a single moral community called a church.

All peoples, Durkheim noted, divide the world into two separate domains—the sacred and the profane, or secular—but how human beings conceptualize this division, where they make the cutting points, differs from society to society. The sacred can include an object, such as an eagle feather or stone pipe of traditional Indian ceremonies or a crucifix in the Catholic church. It can include a place, such as a Sun Dance enclosure, a Navajo hogan during curing ceremonies, a sacred mountain, like the Papago Indians' Baboquivari Mountain, or a Jewish synagogue. It can include a rite—for instance a Lakota "sweat" (purification), an Apache woman's "coming out" (puberty) ceremony, or a Protestant baptism. Among all cultures, the dead are consecrated, and burial places are considered sacred ground no matter what the form of burial or belief in the hereafter. Durkheim rejected the definition of religion as a belief in gods or transcendent spirits or as synonymous with magic. Religious beliefs are determined by the group—the society—and how the sacred and profane are demarcated in practice is called a church. In contrast to non-Native culture, traditional Native Americans live spiritually. Their religion permeates every facet of their daily lives and is not merely relegated to attending service once a week.

Although all peoples, including non-Western indigenous peoples, practice religion, important differences exist between the religions of Native North America and the Judeo-Christian tradition. Nature has been called the Indians' church, because worship in traditional religions was out-of-doors and also because of the widespread belief that all creatures great and small, all things, both animate and inanimate, possess a spiritual life force, sacred power, or "mana." Vine Deloria, Jr. pointed out that the concept of space—relating land, community, and religion into an integrated whole—is the dimension of traditional Native American religions. Indian spirituality is circular, not linear; it is feeling, not thinking; it is being, not becoming. The Judeo-Christian concept of religion, on the other hand, emphasizes the dimension of time, from creation to apocalypse, a founding or founder, and doctrine.

What, then, has been the ideological impact of the European conquest of North America on the religious life of Native Americans? What has been the result of 500 years of Christianization? In fact, every conceivable religious process has occurred, so that, today, we find significant numbers of Native Americans in each possible category. These include (1) acceptance of Christianity through acculturation; (2) rejection of Christianity through the retention of traditional religious beliefs and practices; (3) reaction to Christianity and Anglo or Canadian domination through the rise of revitalization movements and new religions; (4) the blending or mixture of Christian and traditional Indian religious practices and beliefs, or syncretism; (5) and pluralism, where forms of both Christianity and traditional or new religions are embraced. Few

Apache Crown Dance, White Mountain Apache Reservation, Whiteriver, Arizona, 1971. This traditional puberty rite is performed to this day, blessing the participant with a prosperous future.

Native Americans today adopt a purely secular world view, one of agnosticism or atheism. The contemporary beliefs of Native Americans in terms of their acculturative, syncretic, and pluralistic practices and associated social movements are examined below.

Christian Influences
A 1950 survey of Christian missions identified thirty-six Protestant denominations with 39,200 Indian communicants, having increased their Native believers only a little over 8 percent since a previous 1921 survey. In addition, Protestant missions claimed influence among 140,000 additional Indians, but this may be an exaggeration. Whereas the majority of Native Americans have been introduced to Christianity, many also participate in one or another of traditional ceremonies and practices. Although staff members were predominately non-Indian, these missions claimed 213 Native Americans as having entered the mission field. Today there are probably several hundred ordained Christian ministers of Native American descent. By 1974 the United Presbyterian, Protestant Episcopal, United Methodist, American Baptist, United Church of Christ, and Reformed and Christian Reformed listed 452 Indian parishes with a total staff of 177 missionaries.

Contemporary statistics are difficult to obtain primarily because much religious work falls within standard diocesan categories that contain non-Indians as well. Nevertheless, Catholics have been active in the Indian mission field since early colonial times, such as among the Iroquois in the east and among the Pueblo and the Indians of the Southwest and California. Thus they claim a number of Native American communicants today.

Most Christian churches and missions adopt an admittedly assimilationist philosophy, that is, make Indian people into "brown-skinned white men," but there are exceptions, especially in recent years. A 1958 National Council of Churches study found that although 35 percent of Protestants favored outright assimilation for Indians, 51 percent took a middle ground and said they found "some Native values worth preserving." Thirty-one percent of Catholics favored a blend of the cultures. On the other hand, only a small percentage in both groups actually expressed strong sympathy for traditional customs and beliefs. Only 22 percent of the Protestant mission churches utilize Native leadership in any capacity, compared to half of the Catholic missions. The use of Native languages for both Protestant and Catholic missionaries, except for the Navajo Nation and the Lakota-Dakota (Sioux) reservations where most Indians still speak or understand the indigenous tongue, was very small. Most denominations, especially the Protestant fundamentalists, believed that traditional Indian beliefs and practices were "almost entirely unreconcilable" with Christianity. Exceptions were the Episcopalians (81 percent), Congregationalists (75 percent), Catholics (74 percent), and Methodists (53 percent), who said that elements of traditional Indian religions were complementary with Christian teachings.

The Catholic position is guided by the 1977 Letter of the U.S. Catholic Bishops on American Indians: "The Gospel must take root and grow within each culture and community. Faith finds expression in and through the particular values, customs, and institutions of the people who hear it. It seeks to take flesh within each culture, within each nation, within each race, while remaining prisoner of none."

Thus St. Stephen's Indian School in Wyoming, a Catholic mission, has celebrated an Indian mass at Christmas, where the priest is dressed in traditional Indian robes and wears a feathered headdress. St. Stephen's was founded in 1884 for Arapaho and Shoshoni Indians. Today it consults with tribal elders, and the pulpit is shaped like a Thunderbird.

Catholic priests on the Lakota-Dakota reservations sometimes incorporate use of the sacred pipe at mass, and in Oklahoma Catholic Indians have worn traditional regalia for the offertory procession and chant Indian songs. Indian fry bread is consecrated, instead of wafers. Wisconsin Chippewa sing their own hymns at seasonal services. Sage and cedar (traditional Indian purifying herbs) have been used at other services. At San Juan Capistrano Mission in California there are eagle feather blessings. St. Joseph's Church in Los Angeles held a Native American Mass in April 1991. There is also the City of Angels (Los Angeles) "Kateri Circle." Kateri Tekakwitha was a Mohawk Indian who converted to Catholicism in the seventeenth century. In 1980, at St. Peter's Basilica in the Vatican, the Beatification of the Blessed Kateri Tekakwitha took place. This is an important step to sainthood, and, if realized, this Catholic Mohawk woman will become the first American Indian saint for North America.

The *Peace Pipe Line* is the publication of the Native American United Methodist Church of southern California. The church has sponsored an American Indian festival, a caring center for emergency shelter for Indians, a job board, and a Seventh Generation Walk to promote Indian pride. (Seventh generation refers to the traditional Indian concept of planning today in terms of the future generations.)

A Native American Awareness Sunday emphasizes what Native American people have added to the life of the church. In 1978, it was the United Methodists who opened their national headquarters in Washington, D.C., to the coordinators of The Longest Walk—the walk from San Francisco across the country to the nation's capital to press congressional legislators to protect traditional Indian religious freedom.

The Religious Society of Friends (Quakers) has been active among Native Americans, especially in the last century among the Iroquois and today among the Alabama Choctaw, the Mesquakie of Iowa, and the Oklahoma tribes through the Associated Committee of Friends on Indian Affairs. The American Friends Service Committee, a Quaker service organization, has for a number of years maintained an Indian program with fieldworkers on Indian reservations and in urban areas. Yet, although influenced by Friends' religious ideology, few Indians consider themselves Quakers.

The Charles Cook Theological School in Tempe, Arizona, founded by the Presbyterian church, is an ecumenically supported institution to educate Native Americans and other indigenous people "to serve God and their people in the context of their own culture." In 1991, for example, a Rosebud Sioux woman trained at Cook Theological School was appointed Episcopal lay pastor for the Gila River Indian Reservation.

In addition to ministering "Christian charity" to the Indians, proselytization remains the central mission of most Christian faiths. The American Ministries International, for example, publishes and distributes scriptures and other Christian literature to both Indians and Inuit, and among Native people in hospitals, schools, correctional institutions, nursing homes, and missions. It also distributes blankets, quilts, baby layettes, and children's clothing.

One of the most active missionary churches among American Indians is the Church of Latter-Day Saints, or Mormons. It is part of Mormon belief that American Indians are descendants of Lamanites—the degenerate progeny of Laman derived from a lost tribe of Israel. The Lamanites produced the prophetic Book of Mormon discovered by Joseph Smith, the founder of the Mormon religion. The church, therefore, conceives as part of its task the reconversion of the Indians, that they might once again become a "white and delightsome people." The expansion by early Mormon settlers into the lands of the Shoshoni and Ute in the middle of the last century earned them the enmity of these Indian people whom they displaced. Although few Ute have ever converted, Mormonism has made inroads among the Hopi and Dine (Navajo). Again, as with a number of the other Christian faiths, many of the converts claimed by the Mormon church appear to be nominal Christians.

Most Native Americans have contradictory feelings about Christianity. Although a significant number of Native Americans today claim membership, it is even more remarkable, after several hundred years of active missionary and Christianizing work, that so many remain only nominal adherents, and still others actively participate in traditional (pre-Christian) ceremonies or are members of syncretic religions like the Native American Church. Christianity, because it was closely identified with the original land dispossession, genocide, and exploitation of the Native peoples, was considered to be the state religion of an oppressive Anglo-American nation. By identifying through the Christian ethic with Anglo-America, Native Americans felt they were weakened ideologically and therefore more easily divided. For example,

"Christian" and "pagan" were the oppositional epithets used by the missionaries and the federal government to differentiate the "good" from the "bad' Indians up until the Indian New Deal of the 1930s; that is, those Indians who cooperated with the federal government versus those who opposed it. Sharp religious differences very early divided the Tohono O'Odham (Papago), Apache, Lakota-Dakota, Chippewa, and many others.

This divide-and-conquer strategy, whether always consciously intended by the Christian churches or not, is still seen operating today. For example, in one small Apache community of only several hundred inhabitants studied in the 1960s, there were at least eight competing religious ideologies. The most prominent church in the community was the Lutheran church. It was the official Christian religion in the early reservation days on the Apache reservations in Arizona, so that it became "politically correct" for Apache leaders to be associated with Lutheranism. There was also a small Catholic mission where a priest said Sunday Mass. Traditional curing "sings" by the medicine men were common, although the Mormon church and its "elders" (young men doing two years of church service) were also quite active. The Assembly of God church was usually well attended, sometimes by those also attending other Christian churches. The fact that hymns could be sung in the Apache language was especially attractive. The new Miracle Church, which emphasized Pentecostal principles and faith-healing, was Apache led, and it also held services and camp meetings in the native language. It had split in a factional dispute so that there were actually two functioning Miracle Churches in the community at the time. Finally, there was also the Holy Grounds religion. This movement to revitalize Apache culture, combining Catholic, Protestant, and Apache values, had been started by Silas John in the 1920s. Although suppressed by the authorities because of Christian missionary influence, it nevertheless survived into the 1960s.

Another kind of factionalism occurred between the established Christian churches, on the one hand, and emergent, Native churches, on the other. In the Southwest, for example, Indians already converted to Presbyterian, Baptist, and Lutheran religions rebelled against being part of a national religious organization and set up their own independent churches. Indian churches grew up from the Baptist congregations on the San Carlos Apache Reservation and from Presbyterian congregations on the Mohave Reservation. They then adopted new names such as Hopi Mission Church, Mohave Mission Church, San Carlos Apache Independent Church, and Pima Independent Church, and the Miracle Church was also active on the San Carlos Apache Reservation in the 1960s under an independent Apache lay ministry.

A political struggle that manifested itself as a Christian denominational dispute arose in the Navajo Nation in the 1920s and 1930s between two strong Indian leaders. J. C. Morgan, a layworker for the Reformed Church, used anti-Catholicism in his bitter rivalry with Chee Dodge, a Navajo Catholic. Morgan later founded an independent Navajo church and was elected tribal chairman in 1938. Morgan's independent church then affiliated with the Methodists.

There were other changes in evolving Indian Christianity. Often these involved the relationship of form to meaning. The form—for example, hymn singing—might be the same, but the meaning to the Indian converts could be somewhat different. One researcher recently examined Iroquois texts of Anglican and Presbyterian Christian hymns used on the Seneca reservations in western New York State. (The hymns are actually paraphrases, not literal translations, because Seneca words are much longer than their English equivalents and thus do not fit the meter and length of Christian songs.) He found that the source of language in Christian tunes is pre-Christian ritual expression, augmented by special ways to express new Christian ideas. For example, the Seneca expressions for God (there are several, including a female equivalent) are retained. One such term is "Sky Guardian," an archaic Seneca belief. In some cases, Christian expressions are translated literally into the Seneca language, although they do not make complete sense to the native speaker unfamiliar with Christian traditions. A few words, such as Jesus, Christ, and place names are taken directly from the Bible.

Baptism of Paiute Indians.

As with language, a considerable part of hymn theological motifs also reflect pre-Christian cosmology and ceremony, such as the various medicine societies in traditional Seneca culture. At times sophisticated Christian ideas find their equivalency in like sophisticated Seneca expressions and at other times in archaic Seneca language. Finally, many Christian ideas have been accepted wholesale with no particular influence by Seneca traditional religious values. In sum, this suggests that there is an Iroquois Christianity apart from non-Indian (mainstream) Christianity, or at least different from the established Protestant denominations, such as the Anglican and Presbyterian, which undertook the task of translating and promoting the hymns.

Historically, Christian influences have played an important role in the Indian community—especially on the reservations—until the termination and relocation period of the 1950s and the rise of the "new" Indian movement of the 1960s. The oldest Presbyterian churches in Idaho and South Dakota are Indian. The First Presbyterian Church of Kamiah on the Nez Percé Reservation was founded in 1891 and had Indian pastors after 1898. The First Presbyterian Church at Flandreau in South Dakota was established in 1869. Both churches functioned as Indian community centers for the next century. Henry Roe Cloud, the pioneer Indian educator, noted that the Christian church was effective in developing some of the first college or seminary-trained Indian leaders.

For example, on the Nez Percé Reservation, Catholic laymen organized a council of chiefs in the late nineteenth century. More recently, in the 1950s, the Presbyterian church at Barrow, Alaska, provided Native community leaders with opportunities for leadership that was unavailable elsewhere, and Episcopal lay leaders exerted similar informal power for the 'country" Lakota Sioux on the Pine Ridge Reservation in the 1960s. Such as they were, in the Protestant and Catholic churches, opportunities for leadership in men's, women's, and youth groups represented some areas for Native advancement after traditional forms of worship and religious organization were outlawed (from the late nineteenth century until 1934, Indians who practiced Native religious ceremonies and customs could be fined and jailed).

Conversion to Christianity among the Native peoples often occurred only after other forms of struggle had failed. The Santee Sioux, for example, resisted conversion until after their defeat in the Sioux uprising of 1862. As a "benefit," conversion offered access to non-Indians who could help secure Indian land tenure in some instances. For example, a group of Presbyterian laymen on the Nez Percé Reservation responded to the problem of white encroachment on reservation land by organizing the Nez Perce Indian Home and Farm Association in 1923. Presbyterian laymen founded the Alaska Native Brotherhood in 1912, a pan-Indian, secular organization which pressed for integrated schools, Indian citizenship, and the settlement of Alaska Native land claims.

Alaska was first Christianized by the Russian Orthodox religion, which worked with the Aleut as well as the Tlingit and Haida Indians of the Aleutian Island chain and southeastern Alaska. The Moravians, who had long maintained missions in eastern Canada and Greenland, were persuaded by the missionary Sheldon Jackson in the 1880s to take up mission work among Alaska's Inuit population. They have been especially active among the villages along the Kuskokwim River in the vicinity of Bethel, among the Yupiak. The Catholics, too, have had a firm presence, particularly in education. In the 1970s, for example, young people from St. Mary's Boarding School seemed to be making a better adjustment to college life at the University of Alaska in Fairbanks than Native students from the public schools, and some became leaders in the Alaska Native nationalism emerging around the Native land claims issue, strongly supporting traditional Native language and culture.

Urbanism increased dramatically in the United States in the 1950s due in large part to the federal policy of reservation termination and urban relocation for the "surplus" reservation populations. The reservation-based Christian missions and churches failed to keep pace with this development, but pan-Indian ceremonials such as powwows and the secular social service centers became the new focus of Indian identity and social solidarity in the cities. Kiowa migrants to San Francisco, for example, felt unwelcome at non-Indian Protestant churches, which lacked extensive social interaction with the Kiowa churches of Oklahoma. Some Kiowa

Native American

revitalization movements.

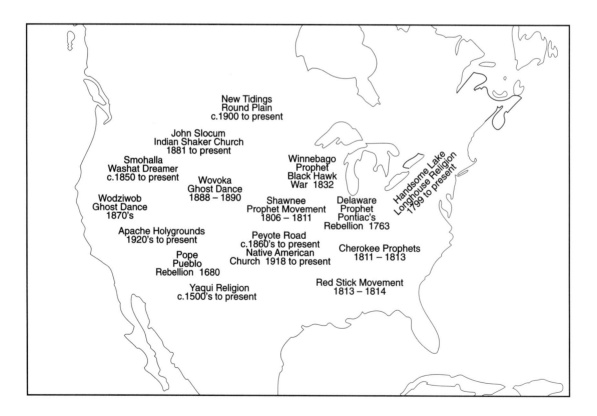

attended one of the three inter-tribal Indian Protestant churches in the San Francisco Bay area, but most became increasingly involved in traditional Kiowa religion and culture. Understandably, Indian Christian church attendance is lower in urban areas than it is on many reservations. Non-Indian domination and control of Indian churches, especially in urban areas, undoubtedly explains the decline of the Indian Christian church after the 1960s. During the late 1960s and early 1970s, urban Indian leadership developed outside of the Christian churches in organizations such as the Survival of American Indians, American Indian Youth Council, United Native Americans, and the American Indian Movement. A resurgence in traditional Indian religion has since been noted in the cities, in Indian country, on the reservations and in the historic Indian areas of Oklahoma and Alaskan villages.

New Religions

A frequent response to European conquest and aggression in past centuries was the formation of new religious movements among Native American peoples in both Canada and the United States. In some cases, such as with some of the early prophet movements, both the form and meaning of the new religions were entirely indigenous, but in other instances there was a recombination of Christian and Native spiritual traditions and practices. The latter have been termed syncretic religions. In fact, Sam Gill, a Navajo specialist and a prolific writer on American Indian religions, identifies three broad religious responses made by indigenous peoples of North America: (1) traditionalism, either retained secretly in the early Indian-non-Indian relations, or else revived at some later point in the contact history when political climate improved; (2) pan-Indianism through intertribal ceremonials; and (3) becoming Christianized or acculturated. The peyote religion combined all three paths in a spiritual form that did not directly threaten non-Indians. At the same time, it remained distinctly Indian and crosscut different tribal religious traditions.

Native American Church

Peyote (*Lophophora williamsii*) is a small, turnip-shaped cactus grown in the arid Rio Grande Valley of northern Mexico and Texas. Its substance is not addictive and should not be classified as a narcotic. People eat the bitter, dried top, or "button," to induce heightened perceptions of sound and color. It enhances concentration and highlights religious truths with vivid imagery during ceremonies.

Spanish chroniclers observed peyote use in the religious ceremonies of northern Mexico in the sixteenth century. Its use in these indigenous community festivals, however, was different from the organized peyote church which later developed. Peyote use was first recorded in the United States among the Lipan Apache in the 1870s, who then taught its use to the Kiowa, Comanche, and others. As a religion, it spread through Oklahoma (formerly Indian Territory), the Great Plains, the Great Lakes area, and in various parts of the Northwest during the same 50 years that Christianity was being spread by paid, federally backed missionaries. In 1918, several peyote groups incorporated under the state laws of Oklahoma as the Native American Church.

Peyotism took hold in the United States when the Native population had reached its lowest point: Indian peoples, hungry and defeated, were confined to reservations as captured nations; indigenous political economy was all but destroyed; individualism and the capitalist ethic conflicted with Indian values and traditions; and Native religions were outlawed. Under these extreme conditions new Indian religions arose, and the peyote church offered its adherents a means of religious expression by which they could maintain a positive identity as Indian people but also obtain personal security (both health and general well-being) in a hostile, non-Indian environment.

An important figure in the diffusion of the peyote church was John Wilson, of mixed Delaware, Caddo, and French parentage. After taking up the peyote religion in 1880, he claimed he had received a number of revelations instructing him in certain ceremonial procedures and preparation of religious paraphernalia, such as the construction of the moon-shaped altar since used in most peyote ceremonies. Wilson's version incorporated a number of Christian elements. Wilson reported being transported, during a peyote-induced out-of-body experience, to the "sky realm," where he learned of events in Christ's life as well as relative positions of spirit-forces, such as the sun, moon, and fire. The Peyote Road, which led from Christ's grave (which he found empty) to the moon, is the road Christ traveled in his ascent into Heaven. To follow the Peyote Road, then, means to follow the way of Christ's teachings and to obtain knowledge by use of peyote.

Wilson also taught specific revealed rituals still in practice today, and he gave a set of moral instructions: abstinence from liquor; restraint in sexual matters; matrimonial fidelity; and prohibitions against angry retorts, falsehoods, vindictiveness, vengeance, and fighting. Witchcraft and malevolent conjuring were also prohibited in the ethics of the Peyote Road. To purge oneself of sins is the function of peyote.

The Christian elements of the peyote religion, or the Native American Church, are obvious. Traditional non-Christian beliefs and practices, however, render it uniquely Indian, for they underlay the religion and make the whole greater than the sum of its parts. The peyote religion incorporates many traditional Native features. Such traditional aspects include communicating with the Creator through spirit forces by means of visions, which lead to power. Curing ceremonies, a central feature of peyotism using the water drum and eagle fan, were traditional among many Indians, especially on the Plains. Medicine men had many powers, including prophecy, control of weather, locating lost objects, and giving

John Wilson introduced many elements of Christianity into the peyote religion. His version is the generally recognized version of the religion today.

advice on where the enemy could be found. Many Native peoples practiced the vision quest, which involved self-torture for power to protect oneself from evil powers of others. Traditional ceremonies also used special plants— including tobacco, mescal bean, jimson weed, and peyote—as a means of obtaining visions and hence power. Most of these spiritual practices are still used in traditional Indian religions today.

The Native American Church demonstrates its integration of both Christian and traditional Indian religious beliefs and practices in its articles of incorporation:

> The purpose for which this corporation is formed is to foster and promote religious believers in Almighty God and the customs of the several tribes of Indians throughout the United States in the worship of a Heavenly Father and to promote morality, sobriety, industry, charity, and right living and cultivate a spirit of self-respect and brotherly love and union among the members of several tribes of Indians throughout the United States . . . with and through the sacramental use of peyote.

Quanah Parker, Comanche leader who greatly facilitated the spread of the peyote religion among the Plains Indians during the 1880s and 1890s.

In 1954, the peyote religion became international, with the incorporation of the Native American Church of Canada, and by the 1970s there were as many as 250,000 Indian members. It is, without doubt, the largest and fastest-growing Indian religion in North America. Its legal status today, however, is in doubt. The Comprehensive Drug Abuse Prevention and Control Act, passed in 1970, prohibits peyote use except in an Indian religious ceremony, but permits must be obtained from the U.S. attorney general's office. Twenty-four states consider its use a misdemeanor, with imprisonment up to a year in jail and fines of from $2,000 to $5,000. Until recently, a number of states, such as Arizona and California, allowed peyote use in ceremonies. In 1990, however, the U.S. Supreme Court struck down federal religious protection for the peyote church in the case of *Employment Division of Oregon v. Smith* and left it up to the various states to decide whether to criminalize peyote use as a religious sacrament by Native Americans. This is one of the main reasons why many Native Americans today say that religious freedom is being denied them and, as a legal precedent, First Amendment rights for all Americans are threatened.

Early Prophet Movements

Prophets and prophecy are an integral part of Native American religions, as with Deganawida and Hiawatha's founding of the League of the Iroquois (Hau-De-No-Sau-Nee, or People of the Longhouse) and its great Binding Law in the fourteenth century at a time of conflict among the Iroquoian nations. A prophet or messiah traditionally arises to give the people hope and direction in times of adversity or crisis. In recent decades, Hopi, Iroquois, and other Native religious leaders have been reinterpreting their age-old prophecies to better guide them in their dealings with western culture, especially in terms of racism and destruction of the environment.

Since Native Americans are deeply spiritual, it was natural for them to draw upon their traditions of prophecy in order to cope with the new problems brought by European conquest, including genocide and the dispossession of their lands. Prophets received their messages from the spirit world and often implored their people to return to the old way of life. Frequently, however, new religious practices and beliefs through songs, dances, ceremonies, and paraphernalia were needed to combat the evils of non-Indian society, such as alcohol, lying, and cheating. The prophecies often included the promise of divine intervention and the restoration of the old order, when Indian peoples would again be sovereign and free of colonial domination. Often they recommended military resistance to U.S. authority, while other prophecies counseled accommodation or non-violence and that ethnic survival would come through new religious practices that promised spiritual intervention.

Revivalistic Movements

In his study of the Seneca Indians and the Handsome Lake religion, Anthony F.C. Wallace coined the term revitalization to indicate the attempt on the part of a group of people to reinstitute values and social solidarity when faced with cataclysmic changes. Other terms characterizing this phenomenon are resistance, nativistic, or millenarian movements. In the Native American case, many of these movements have been or are prophet-based or prophecy oriented. The seventeenth-century Pueblo Indian patriot Popé was one of the first messiahs to emerge in response to European Christianization and subjugation. In 1680, Popé led the autonomous Pueblo villages in a war of independence which succeeded in freeing the Indians from Spanish tyranny for fifteen years. After experiencing a heavenly visitation, he prophesied that an Indian millennium was near and that it was the sacred duty of Native people to rise up and fulfill the prophecy.

In eastern mid-eighteenth-century United States, the Delaware Prophet sought to unite the Delaware people who lost their land and were greatly disrupted by British colonial expansion. Directed by the Great Spirit, he preached that Indians should shed European ways so the British would mysteriously disappear and the former Indian life be restored. It is believed that Pontiac, the Indian leader who organized the tribes of the Old Northwest against the British at the close of the French and Indian War, drew upon the widespread influence of the Delaware Prophet.

A second Delaware Prophet, the Munsee Prophetess, emerged from the regeneration of the tribes of the Old Northwest (northeast United States) in the late eighteenth century, influencing the Shawnee leader, Tecumseh, to found an all-Indian republic to block the westward advance of the United States. Tecumseh was assisted by his brother, Tenskwatawa (the Open Door), a prophet, who preached pan-Indian living and what he called "the Way." Creek prophet Josiah Francis rallied a traditionalist segment of Creeks, called the Red Sticks, against American influence in the same conflict and during the War of 1812. Somewhat earlier than the Red Stick movement, between 1810 and 1813, several prophets emerged among the Cherokee, and several visions were reported that called on the Cherokee to protect their sacred sites and villages and slow down the pace of economic and political change. The Cherokee movement soon died away with the outbreak of the War of 1812 and after several prophetic predictions failed to materialize.

However, some of the prophetic movements sought accommodation with U.S. society. Kickapoo prophet Kenekuk for example, urged his followers in Illinois to engage in passive resistance. He and his followers ignored government demands to vacate their eastern lands and migrate to Indian Territory in Kansas. Directed by the great Holy Force Above, Kenekuk instructed the Kickapoo people to return to their ancient traditional culture, to live abstemiously, and to worship through meditation and the use of prayer sticks.

Handsome Lake and the Longhouse Religion

A religious renaissance occurred on a number of the Iroquois reservations between 1799 and 1815 called Gaiwiio, the Old Way of Handsome Lake, and it survives today among many, if not most, contemporary Iroquois. The U.S. revolution had divided the Iroquois Confederacy and seriously weakened its old unity. Jesuit missionaries had helped to instigate pro-British and other migrations to Canada; the Seneca population had been decimated by half through warfare, disease, and alcoholism; and they had lost most of their lands. Depression and suicide were widespread, and charges of witchcraft were on the rise. Many Iroquois men became alcoholics. The Iroquois villages were slums in the wilderness. Although defeated, starving, and impoverished, they believed the new U.S. government honored their treaties. But land loss was rapid: the treaty of Fort Stanwix in 1784 had recognized Iroquois land rights to most of central and western New York, but by 1800 only a few small reservation areas remained.

Only two paths seemed open to the dispirited Iroquois: to convert to the ways of the Christians or to preserve Indian ways. Into this cultural abyss came the Philadelphia Quakers, who sent missionaries to the Allegany Seneca to teach literacy, crafts, and technical skills. Cornplanter, the chief warrior of the Seneca, had long advocated that the Indians adopt the economic practices of non-Indians, such as men working in agriculture. The Quakers promoted plow agriculture by men, a gender role reversal for the matrilineal Iroquois where women owned the fields or gardens. In 1799, Cornplanter, his family, and a growing number of others supported the Quaker reforms. Into this situation stepped Handsome Lake, the degenerate brother of Cornplanter, with his drunken fellow warriors. However, through a terrible sickness and near-death state, Handsome Lake had several visions which were recorded by the Quakers and remembered in Iroquois oral tradition.

In the first vision, Handsome Lake received four evil words: whiskey, witchcraft, love magic, and abortion-and-sterility-medicine. Persons guilty of any of these wrong-doings should repent and never sin again. Subsequently he had two more visions, and these constitute the *Gaiwiio*, or Good Word. His teachings from 1799 to 1801 constituted an apocalyptic first gospel, dealing with the immanence of.world destruction, a definition of sin, and a prescription for individual salvation. The second is the social gospel and includes the following themes: temperance, peace and unity, land retention, limited acculturation (Western technology and the English language), and a revised domestic morality. Following the social gospel of the code would lead to personal salvation, social betterment, and the postponement of the apocalypse. Although not Christian, the code of Handsome Lake was inspired by Christian teachings, especially those of the Quakers. Christian rituals and symbols were combined with those of traditional Iroquois religion. Impressed by the positive changes among the Iroquois, non-Indians held the prophet in high esteem; and Thomas Jefferson described the religion of Handsome Lake as "positive and effective." Handsome Lake also preached against theft, alcoholism, malicious gossip, witchcraft, adultery, wife-beating, and jealousy. Husbands and wives were to love each other and remain faithful, and they were to treat their children with kindness. Compassion should be shown to all those who are suffering. Certain ceremonies were to be conducted in the long-house (a place of worship), and all were to revere the Great Spirit and all of Creation.

Unlike the Native American Church, which is pan-Indian in scope, the longhouse religion is uniquely Iroquois in faith and practice so that its practice today is confined to the Iroquois nations, where perhaps half are followers of the Old Way, or Code of Handsome Lake.

Reservation-Era Religious Movements

Once confined to reservations by the U.S. military at the close of the nineteenth century, Indian peoples in the western United States came to hold the unenviable status of captured nations. All the old tribal institutions—the aboriginal economy, sovereignty and the system of government, the kinship group and the extended family—were destroyed or else drastically changed. In their place non-Indian authority instituted the 1887 Indian Allotment Act "to break up the tribal mass," the federal boarding school system "to save the man but kill the Indian," and the office of Indian Affairs superintendency. The superintendent or Indian agent was a virtual dictator, and his authority was backed by the Indian police and a code of "Indian crimes." Native Americans, now unfree and powerless, were rendered paupers, and the daily roll call and ration system effectively checked organized resistance. Then arose new prophets—Smohalla, Squasachtum, Wodziwob, and Wovoka—and new revitalization movements. The best known of these was the Ghost Dance in the late nineteenth century.

Ghost Dance Religious Movement

The first phase of the Ghost Dance movement actually appeared around 1870 among the Northern Paiute soon after the transcontinental Union Pacific Railroad was built. An Indian prophet, Wodziwob ("White Hair"), had a vision that a big train would bring back the dead ancestors, at which time a cataclysm would engulf U.S. society but miraculously leave its material goods behind for the Indians; then, the Great Spirit would return. This event could be hastened by new songs and religious dancing. After a time, this early Ghost Dance petered out, although many elements were incorporated into the beliefs and practices of California Indians that continue to this day.

In 1889, a new prophet arose among the Paiute—Wovoka. Known also as Jack Wilson, Wovoka was born at Pyramid Lake, Nevada. His father, Tavibo, was a leader of the Paiute community and a "weather doctor"; that is, he could control the weather. Wovoka, too, became a weather doctor and led the traditional circle dances. Between dances he preached universal love. Wovoka, "the Cutter," had worked for a non-Indian rancher named Wilson and became familiar with the Christian Bible, learned about Jesus Christ, and watched non-Indian people in their round dances.

On January 1, 1889, a total eclipse of the sun occurred, and Wovoka, while very ill, experienced a powerful vision. When the sun "died" that winter day, he was taken up to Heaven, where God gave him a message of peace and right living. Now a prophet, his preaching influenced even Mormon settlers, who thought for awhile that he might be the messiah prophesied by their founder, Joseph Smith. Had the son of God appeared in Nevada and as an Indian? Using religious paraphernalia from traditional Indian culture (such as red ochre paint and magpie feathers), Wovoka taught a new circle dance "to embrace Our Father, God." The celebrants were to move in harmony sunward, singing Ghost songs, and thus live and work in harmony in actual life.

Although Wovoka himself never left his native land, Paiute believers and visiting delegations of other Indians soon spread the new prophecy. Disappointed in Wodziwob and the first Ghost Dance, the Indians of California and Oregon rejected the new message, as did also the Pueblo Indian theocracies and the deeply traditional Navajo. But many other tribes took up the new religion.

Wovoka explained that non-Indians had been sent to punish Indians for their sins but that they could soon expect deliverance. He also promised that their ancestors would return as would the game and the old Indian world, and U.S. settlers would mysteriously be eradicated. And until the Indian world regenerated it could be visited through a new religious dance, by wearing spirit regalia, by singing Ghost songs, and through self-hypnotic trances.

My father will descend
the earth will tremble
everybody will rise,
stretch out your hands.
—Kiowa Ghost Song

A dancer would fall down in a trance, "dying," and then speak of traveling to the moon or the morning star and come back with "star flesh" in his fist that had turned into strange rocks. By these means, one could "visit" the long-dead relatives and see the promised world. Thus the religious celebrants joyously awaited the coming cataclysm that was supposed to occur sometime in 1890.

Among the Lakota Sioux, however, Wovoka's non-violent message took a militant turn. The Great Sioux Nation had been broken up, and the sacred Black Hills were seized for their rich gold deposits in 1877. By 1889, many Sioux were dying of starvation due to a severe drought. They were forced to eat their seed corn and to butcher even their stud bulls. Food rations promised by Congress were slow in coming, and disease epidemics ravaged the population. Local holymen like Kicking Bear took up the Ghost Dance, which became a form of spiritual resistance to U.S. authority; it was said that warriors wearing ghost shirts could even turn back soldier bullets.

Sitting Bull was one of the principal Indian leaders who sympathized with the new religious movement. The Indian agents and local settlers, however, feared an Indian uprising like the one at Little Bighorn in 1876 that resulted in George Custer's defeat, and they set out to suppress the new religion. When Sitting Bull was assassinated by the Indian police, the terrorized followers of the Ghost Dance movement fled south to Pine Ridge Reservation to seek protection from Chief Red Cloud. Just a few miles from Pine Ridge, at Wounded Knee Creek, on December 24, 1890, Custer's old regiment, the Seventh Cavalry, opened fire on the Indians with Hotchkiss (machine) guns. These guns poured two-pound explosive shells at the rate of nearly fifty a minute, mowing down everything alive—warriors, old people, women, children, ponies, and dogs. Chief Big Foot and the elders in the council circle were killed, and the warriors were no match for the army's guns. Of the 370 Indians massacred that day, 250 were women and children. Thus ended the Ghost Dance among the Sioux and with it also the twenty-five-year-long Plains Indian war of resistance.

The Ghost Dance nevertheless survived for a number of years among other tribes in both the United States and Canada. The Dakota-speaking Sioux of Saskatchewan Province, Canada, for example, incorporated much of the original Ghost Dance into their New Tidings religion. These Wahpeton Sioux, descendants of refugees from the 1862 Minnesota uprising, created a

Revival of the Ghost Dance, May 1974.

new form of Ghost Dance that included their traditional Medicine Feast.

Fred Robinson, an Assiniboine, introduced the Ghost Dance to the Dakota at the Round Plain Indian Reserve in Canada about 1900. He had learned it from Wovoka by way of Kicking Bird, a Teton Sioux (Lakota) leader. Believers pray daily and gather as a congregation to pray together and to sing holy songs that remind them of the prophet's journey to God and His promise of eternal life. A communion of meat, corn, berries, and rice with raisins is held. Some people wear Ghost shirts, to protect the wearer from evil temptation. They are to follow the "good Red path" of ochre paint on the earthen altar and the incense rising to Heaven from the sacred pipe and sweetgrass. Medicine bundles, symbolizing the good message of the New Tidings religion, are brought to these prayer meetings and purified in the incense smoke.

The New Tidings, the Holy Dance prayer communions, were part of the Round Plain Reserve community for much of the twentieth century.

Washat or Seven Drums Religion

Another major religious movement was the Washat religion originating along the Columbia River in the present-day states of Washington and Oregon. Although influenced by Roman Catholicism, the movement urged Indian people to return to their ancient ways and values. Followers of Washat, called Seven Drums, peacefully resisted government attempts in the late nineteenth century to herd Indians of the region onto the reservations and to give up their lands and traditional way of life. They chose, instead, to remain on their ancestral lands near the river, to continue to live according to their traditions, to fish, dig roots, pick berries, and maintain their "first foods" and other religious ceremonies. To this day, Washat is practiced along the river and on the Yakima, Nez Percé, and Warm Springs reservations.

Around 1860, Smohalla, called Preacher, a Wanapum Indian, revitalized the old Washani religion of the Pacific Northwest. He taught that the Indian world invaded by Anglo-American settlers was on a course of self-destruction. It could only be averted by human efforts to restore the original balance of nature and creation. Called the Dreamer religion because of Smohalla's frequent trances and the meditation practiced by his followers, Smohalla prophesied the coming of the millennium and the resurrection of the old Indian world. After this world cleansing, only the followers of the Seven Drums religion would regain their lands and live as they did before the coming of non-Indians.

Smohalla was adamantly opposed to U.S. government policy to make farmers out of Indian fishermen and hunters. As a result, he was frequently jailed. He preached, "My young men shall never work. Men who work cannot dream, and wisdom comes to us in dreams [visions]." He said also, "You ask me to cut grass and make hay . . . . But how dare I cut my mother's hair?"

In 1877, inspired by the teachings of Smohalla, Chief Joseph of the Nez Percé refused a government order to abandon the rich Wallowa homeland and remove to a reservation in Washington under the terms of a bogus treaty. Before being forced to surrender just thirty miles from the Canadian border and freedom in "Mother Canada," he led his people on a 1,300-mile trek in which he continually out-fought and out-foxed the army and its best generals.

A basic belief of the Washat religion is that Mother Earth provides all sustenance, the salmon being the foremost. This tradition came in conflict with the dominant society in the post-World War II decades when the Columbia River was dammed, which inundated Indian villages and fishing sites and depleted salmon runs. Things came to a head in the 1970s and 1980s in the clash over Indian fishing rights in opposition to the interests of commercial and non-Indian sports fishermen on the Columbia River. A number of Indian families still live along the Che Wana (Columbia River), such as Celilo Village and Little White Salmon Indian Settlement, refusing to relocate to nearby reservations. In 1983, David Sohappy, Sr., and thirteen other traditional fishing Indians were convicted of illegally selling fish under the 1981 Lacey Act. Sohappy and the others, all adherents of the old Seven

Drums religion and its healing cult, the Feather religion, were sent to federal prison.

Sohappy and the others readily admitted to ignoring federal and reservation fishing regulations and welcomed the chance to bring their treaty and religious rights to fish "in their accustomed places" into court. Sohappy, a lineal descendent of the Indian prophet Smohalla, had been instrumental from 1959 to 1974 in getting the courts to issue the Boldt decision, awarding the Indians 50 percent of the salmon catch. Traditionally the fish are shared by a wide extended family network of poor Indian families. Today there are more than 2,000 of Smohalla's followers living along the river and carrying on the religion.

David Sohappy, Sr. spent two-and-one-half years of a five-year sentence in federal prison. Through the intervention of the Yakima Tribal Court and his attorneys, he was released from prison in 1988. He had suffered three strokes, a series of prison transfers, and separation from his traditional life and spiritual sustenance on the Che Wana (Columbia River). A year later he died.

Other New Religions

In the 1880s, the Indian Shaker church began among the Coast Salish in the southern Puget Sound area of Washington State, although there is no connection with the Shaker Church of Anglo-America. Both the Indian Shaker church and the Prophet Dance enjoyed increasing influence in the Pacific Northwest in these years and eventually spread to California.

John Slocum, a Nisqually Indian of Mud Bay, and his wife, Mary Johnson Slocum, received their basic inspirations for the Indian Shaker religion in 1882. The church itself was organized as an association in 1892, at Mud Bay, Washington, and incorporated in 1910 in Olympia, the state capital. It is a syncretic religion, incorporating elements of both traditional practices and beliefs and Christian theology. Liturgical aids, such as bells and candles to conduct services, are featured, along with prayers, songs, and dances.

Like other Indian prophets, Slocum "died" and went to Heaven following a serious illness. There he spoke to the angels and received a message from God. The creed is simple, requiring no familiarity with the Bible or Christianity (in fact, Bibles are not to be used or directly quoted in the Shaker church). Healing is the single most important element of the religion. This is accomplished through the Holy Spirit, to restore health and balance. Trembling with power (hence, the word *shaker*) cures diseases and gives a purpose to living. Alcoholics, for example, can recover through the "shake."

Among the Tolowa of California, Christianity made little headway because it was perceived as a state religion of an oppressor nation. The Shaker church, on the other hand, provided a midway point in the accommodation process. Christian beliefs have infused old spiritual practices that sometimes appear similar to pentecostal services, but the Indian Shakers maintain their religious independence. On the Warm Springs Reservation in Oregon among the Simnasho, and at Umatilla, Shakers have an obvious presence. The religion is very much alive today.

Syncretic, Pluralistic, and Other Religious Processes in the Southwest

E. H. Spicer, social anthropologist, cultural historian, and past president of the American Anthropological Association, has written extensively on the Indian peoples of the American Southwest and northern Mexico, especially the Yaqui. In *Cycles of Conquest*, he detailed the religious changes that took place among the various indigenous peoples in the southwestern United States and Sonora, Mexico, as a result of the Spanish conquest and then the Mexican and Anglo-American contact periods. Similar changes have occurred among other Native American groups.

In the Southwest, where one-quarter of all Indian people reside, a majority consider themselves Catholic, employing the Spanish word *catolico*. These include the Tarahumara, Yaqui, Mayo, and Opate of Sonora, Mexico, and the lower Pima, many Papago and Gila River Pima, and the Yaqui barrios in the United States. In addition, most Yuma, some Navajo, some Apache, and some Zuni also speak of themselves as Catholic. These Catholic Indians, in particular the Mayo, the Tarahumara, the Yaqui, and the Eastern

Pueblo of New Mexico, have developed beliefs and practices so different from mainstream Catholic doctrine and organization that they are held to be syncretic religions, distinctly Indian when observed and practiced by Native Americans.

Spicer described three different types of Catholic syncretism. The Eastern Pueblo added some Catholic elements to their otherwise little changed traditional religion, which Spicer called compartmentalization. The Yaqui, on the other hand, were influenced by the Jesuits in the 1500s and reworked their entire traditional religion until a wholly new religion resulted, which Spicer called fusion. And the Papago accepted certain elements of Catholicism without integrating them into their traditional systems of religion, identified as addition. Many of these Indian "Catholics" do not accept the European ideas of heaven and hell; many hold little interest in the Virgin Mary or in Jesus; and almost all reject the organized Catholic church. The Papago, for example, do not allow priests into their village chapels. From a Native American perspective the Pueblo Indian response could be considered pluralism: the practice of more than one religious tradition. In the Pueblo case, the early Franciscan missionaries physically discouraged Native religious practices, which forced Pueblo religion underground. After the Spanish put down a Pueblo revolt under Popé in 1680, they considered the Indians nominally Catholic but allowed them to practice their religious kiva ceremonies. But from the late 1800s until 1934, the Pueblo religion underwent suppression from Anglo-American authorities. Again the Pueblo peoples retrenched through their religious organizations and actions, developing protective and isolationist mechanisms. Thus today they are both Catholic and traditional Indian in their religious observances.

The Yaqui Easter Festival appears to be a complex integration of indigenous ceremonial dance practices with an overlay of Christian liturgy and beliefs. For example, one dancer group, the Pascolas, or "old men of the fiesta," predate Christian influence. To the accompaniment of drum, flute, harp, and violin, they dance wearing sleighbells around their hips and cocoon rattles on their ankles, and carrying a rattle. The Yaqui Deer Dancer, who performs during Easter and at other ceremonial times of the year, also predates Christian influence.

The next largest Christian faith in the Southwest are the Presbyterians. They include more than half of the Gila Pima, a fourth or more of the Papago, many Navajo, some Apache, Mohave, Maricopa, and Hopi.

Beginning in 1869, under the Grant administration, it became federal policy to assign the running of Indian reservations to the various Christian missionary groups. The Presbyterians and the Christian Reformed (Lutheran) were the first prominent Protestant churches in the Southwest. The Lutherans took over the education and Christianization of all Apache groups, the Navajo, the Gila Pima and, later, the Zuni. The Presbyterians later took over responsibility for the Gila Pima and shared religious responsibility for the Papago with the Catholics, and then Mohave, and the Laguna Pueblo. Next were the Mennonites among the Hopi, the Episcopalians among the Havasupais, and, later, among the Navajo. The American Baptists worked among the Hopi, the Methodists among the Yuma and Navajo, and the Plymouth Brethren among the Walapai, Eastern Pueblo, and Navajo. At the same time, the Franciscan Catholics entered the field among the Navajo, Apache, Gila Pima, and Papago. By 1915, there were eight Christian denominations conducting schools and religious services.

In 1920, Apache leaders on the San Carlos Reservation petitioned their Bureau of Indian Affairs superintendent to be free of religious persecution at the hands of the two established churches, the Lutherans and the Catholics. They asked for religious freedom and pointed out that their movement was devoted to the best beliefs and values of both Christian and traditional Apache religions. They also complained that the established Christian sects were not making adequate progress. The Holy Grounds movement grew until 1938 when its founder, Silas John, was sentenced to jail for fifteen years. He had been arrested on the charge of murdering his wife, although many Apache still say he was framed by the government under pressure from the Christian missionaries. In 1954 he was released and then resumed his position as head of this religious movement. The new religion continued to grow until the early 1960s, when it began to be displaced by the independent evangelical Apache church, the Miracle Church.

Finally, on all reservations and in the various Indian communities, whether rural or urban, there are Indian people who have constantly rejected Christian ways and who continue to practice their traditional religions, which in some ways are only slightly modified since European entry into the region several hundred years ago. This has been the case for the majority of Navajo, the Eastern Pueblo generally, and some of the Papago and Seri. Since the 1960s, due to the "new" Indian movement and religious revitalization, there has been a resurgence of traditional religious practices. For example, the International Indian Treaty Council, which supports traditional culture and religion, organized a gathering of Indian nations on the Papago Reservation in 1982, and a Lakota medicine man led a Plains sun dance on the Navajo Nation in the early 1980s.

Starting with the decade of the 1980s, a second phase of the "new Indian" movement occurred: whereas the earlier political organization and militancy of the 1960s and 1970s began with the urban Indians of the cities, the new wave of religious revitalization and cultural renaissance is reservation-based. Today younger Indian people, both urban and reservation, are orienting themselves to their grandparents' generation; that is to the elders and traditional people.

Religious Revitalization Today

Native American religion, including modified traditionalism, peyotism, and other syncretic forms, is again the centerpiece of what it means to be Indian for many Native Americans. Medicine men like the late Lakota holy man Henry Crow Dog and other reservation traditionalists have taken American Indian Movement (AIM) militants under their tutelage. Sweat lodges have been set up in the prisons; the use of sacred pipes and purification ceremonies of the Sun Dance is spreading throughout the United States. The Tipi Religion (or peyote cult of the Native American Church) has become an increasingly important form of therapy and recovery for that part of the Indian population suffering from alcohol and drug addiction. Not only traditional religion, but also native Indian languages, singing and drumming, long suppressed ritual practices like "piercing" (as a form of a sacrifice in the Sun Dance), storytelling and the oral traditions, have all seen a revival.

During most of this century, social scientists as well as the federal government promoted the idea that Native American culture was dead or on its way out, that Indians were "the vanishing Redman." Anthropologists held the belief, which was the basis for their acculturation studies, that the Indians were giving up aboriginal culture and language and would assimilate into the mainstream society. But more recently, Indian scholars like Vine Deloria, Jr. have taken exception to this view. In *God Is Red* and other works, Deloria compares Native American traditional religious principles to Christianity and underscores the persistence of traditionalism in contemporary Indian culture. More recently, Ake Hulkrantz, a specialist on Indian religion, points out in *Religion in Native North America* that the nineteenth-century emergence of Indian revitalization movements should have made it obvious that Indian culture and religion were not dying but, instead, were only changing. In the same work, Amanda Porterfield compares the present-day Indian spirituality movement to the earlier revitalization movements. Religion, language, and culture have seen a new stage of development, if not rebirth, in Native North America today; the evidence is everywhere.

Along the Northwest Coast, the Salish traditional religious dances are being revived, where for many years they were eclipsed by Christian Methodism and the Indian Shaker Church. Among the Eastern Cherokee in North Carolina, there has emerged a Cherokee Christianity, a blend of both traditional and Christian religion. And the Abenaki of Newfoundland today practice a syncretic blend of Catholicism and traditional religion. Traditionalism has gained in prominence. A growing number of Indian people are becoming "sweataholics," participating in the ancient practice of cleansing both body and spirit in a sweat lodge. Native Americans from the Aztecs to the Delaware to the Inuit observed this rite of purification. Today it is practiced widely on a number of reservations, and it is not uncommon for Indians who live in metropolitan areas to have personal sweat lodges in their own backyards. They invite Indian and even non-Indian friends and relatives to "sweats" which often end with the participants sharing a meal and socializing.

Vision quests, the ancient puberty rite for young men, have returned to Indian country after being almost stamped out by federal authorities in past decades. Women, too, are "going on the hill," or "crying for a dream," as the Lakota call this practice. Not unlike the early Christian prophets, contemporary Indian people can be healed or help heal others through prayer to the Great Spirit, and even obtain spiritual helpers for life's trials and tribulations. By cleansing oneself in an Indian "sweat," making tobacco tie offerings, fasting, and "locking" oneself in an altar on a sacred hill, mountain, or in a vision pit, Indians can receive spiritual instruction for walking the "good Red Road" or "Way" of Native American culture and values.

Reconstructed Iroquois longhouse in Brantford, Ontario. A False Face Society mask grimaces in the foreground.

Summertime, especially, is a season of going home to the reservation, visiting Indian country, seeing one's friends and relatives at the Crow Fair, the Navajo Fair, the powwows, the Sun Dances, and other tribal ceremonies. For the Yaqui of Arizona, in their syncretic Indian-Christian religion, Easter is one of the special times in the ceremonial calendar. For the various Pueblo villages along the Rio Grande in New Mexico, and for the western

Pueblo, frequent ceremonial occasions include important religious dances and rituals that they have been practicing for thousands of years, even though most Pueblo Indians are nominally Catholic.

One of the lessons that contemporary Native Americans are endeavoring to teach non-Indian America is that the urban versus reservation Indian dichotomy is a false one; that one cannot separate urban Indians in terms of values and beliefs from their reservation or rural brothers and sisters. The new revitalization movement makes this clear. For example, on the door of the Intertribal Friendship House, an Indian community center in Oakland, California, one may see the notice "Ceremony Tonight!" Typically, a Lakota medicine man from one of the South Dakota reservations will have flown in to administer to Indians and others in the Oakland-East Bay area. The center's community hall will be darkened with black plastic placed over the windows, tobacco prayer ties will be made, a floor altar constructed, and, drumming and singing, the medicine man will begin to heal and prophesy. The ritual will end with a giveaway of gifts to the attendees by those healed. It is almost the exact ceremony performed back home on the reservation.

Or, to take another example, twenty-five miles south of Washington, D.C., on the Potomac River lies Moyoane, ancestral home of the Piscataway Indians. At present, however, it lies within the Piscataway National Park under control of the Alice P. Furgeson Foundation, with its colonial farm, the Smithsonian Institution, and the National Park Service. Since 1974, the hundred or so traditional Piscataway living in the area today, survivors of an original population of 12,000, have been waging a ceaseless struggle to regain possession of their sacred burial ground—only twenty-five acres of the 4,200-acre park. Yet they are continually harassed in their attempt to carry on traditional ceremonies at Moyoane and in the exercise of their religious freedom. Living a "stone's throw" from the nation's capital, they are "urban Indians," yet they persist and endure as a traditional people.

The new revitalization movement, too, has sparked political protest for Indian land rights and sovereignty, as in the late 1960s when the Indian, Inuit, and Aleut peoples of Alaska organized the Alaska Federation of Natives to press for their land rights, and again in 1973 in the occupation protest at Wounded Knee on the Pine Ridge Reservation. In Nevada, led by the Dann sisters, Chief Yowell, and traditional elders, the Western Shoshoni Nation has been waging a long struggle against the U.S. government and its Bureau of Land Management over the issue of Indian land rights and nuclear testing. Under traditional beliefs, Mother Earth cannot be sold. It is therefore maintained that the 1863 Treaty of Ruby Valley did not cede Shoshoni lands to the United States but was, instead, a treaty of peace and friendship. Traditional religious beliefs support the struggle for land and sovereignty, and liberal Catholic and Protestant clergy, ministers and lay leaders, have joined Indian religious leaders in supporting this religious freedom issue on a number of occasions.

Due to the resurgence of Indian traditional culture, over 18,000 Indian human remains held by the national Smithsonian Institution in Washington, D.C., are scheduled for return to their respective tribes for sanctified reburial. Indian remains in the states of Georgia, Alabama, Kentucky, and Kansas have already been removed from public display. Indian leaders and their supporters have long criticized the "specimen collecting complex" of the dominant culture as sacrilegious, racist, and demeaning. One of the most infamous sites, the Dickson Mounds Museum in Illinois, displayed 200 skeletons from a 900-year-old burial mound. It was closed in April 1992 with an Indian sacred pipe ceremony.

Religion, whether pluralistic or syncretic, has now been given a decidedly traditionalist emphasis and has become the foundation of the Native American cultural renaissance, a modern revitalization movement.

Steve Talbot
San Joacquin Delta College

BIOGRAPHIES ✦ ✦ ✦ ✦ ✦ ✦ ✦ ✦ ✦ ✦ ✦ ✦ ✦ ✦ ✦ ✦ ✦ ✦ ✦

Thomas Banyacya, Sr.
1910–

Hopi tribal and spiritual leader

Thomas Banyacya, Sr., is a Hopi elder and traditionalist who has spoken out against the relocation of the Navajo and other possible effects of U.S. Public Law 93-531, which mandated that the Navajo should be relocated, ostensibly so that the land could be returned to the Hopi. The Hopi are a Pueblo tribe whose Native territory is located in northeastern Arizona.

Born in the village of New Oraibi around 1910, Banyacya was one of four young men chosen by Hopi elders in 1948 to be their "ears and tongue"; that is, they were selected as interpreters to tell the outside world of certain direful warnings contained in the ancient Hopi prophecies. Among other things these prophecies mentioned a "gourdful of ashes" (the atomic bomb) and predicted that the world would end in a global explosion or "purification" unless human beings changed their destructive ways and prayed to the Great Spirit. Banyacya is the last surviving member of the group, and in recent years he has also become recognized as a major spokesman for the traditionalist viewpoint on controversial issues, such as the future of a huge expanse of land surrounding the area of Black Mesa in northeast Arizona.

The so-called Hopi-Navajo Land Dispute involves an area of 1.8 million acres of high desert plateau where Navajo herders have lived on little-used Hopi land for generations. In 1972, the Congress passed Public Law 93-531, which involved the forced removal of more than ten thousand Navajo and the erection of a barbed wire fence 285 miles long.

When the Navajo protested during the 1970s, many others joined them, including Hopi traditionalists such as Thomas Banyacya and his son, Thomas, Jr. The Banyacyas and others believe that the government is mainly interested in clearing the land so that puppet tribal councils can be established and mining companies can gain access to the area's immense deposits of coal, uranium, and oil shale. According to the elder Banyacya, the depredations of the Americans and their ultimate self-destruction were all revealed ages ago in certain traditional Hopi prophecies.

Deganawida is the founder of the Iroquois Confederacy. Its origin is unknown, but it is generally dated before the landing of Columbus in 1492. In Iroquois history, Deganawida lived in a time when there was little peace among the Iroquois-speaking nations, of which the Huron, Deganawida's tribe then residing in present-day Ontario in southern Canada, is one. These nations were often at war with one another because there was no agreed-upon means of resolving conflict between the various nations. A murder of one man by a man of another nation led to revenge raids and war between the nations.

Deganawida had a vision from the Great Spirit that instructed him to give the Great Law, a set of rules and procedures for working out differences and settling hostilities between nations. Deganawida traveled among the Iroquois Nations in present-day New York and Ohio spreading the message of peace. Most rejected the message, but on his travels he met Hiawatha, a member of the Iroquoian-speaking Mohawk Nation living near present-day Albany, New York. Since Deganawida had a speech impediment, Hiawatha, a powerful orator, became the spokesperson for the message of Deganawida and the Great Spirit. Both Deganawida and Hiawatha traveled among the Iroquois Nations, and after some resistance among the Onondaga, convinced the Seneca, Cayuga, Onondaga, Oneida, and Mohawk to form a confederacy of forty-nine chiefs. Through ceremonies and agreements they settled their disputes peacefully at the annual gatherings of the Confederate Council, which met at Onondaga, near present-day Syracuse, New York. Decisions of the Confederate Council required unanimous consensus among all nations, thereafter called the Five Nations. The elderly clan matrons nominated and deposed the chiefs of their own lineages from office if they did not conform to the will of the lineage. The purpose of the league was to create peace and to spread the Great Law of peace to all nations in the world.

Deganawida

fl. 1300?

Huron spiritual leader

Delaware Prophet
fl. 1760s

Delaware (Lenape)
spiritual leader

During the early 1760s—a time of threatened trade, military, and diplomatic domination by the English— several religious leaders emerged among the Delaware Nation living in the eastern Ohio region. In North America, the French and Indian War had just been concluded in December of 1759 when Montreal in New France fell to Indian and English troops. The defeat of the French left many Indians who had fought with the French cause without allies and military support. The British threatened to gain monopoly control over the fur trade, the distribution of guns and manufactured goods, and threatened to establish military control over the Ohio and Great Lakes region by occupying the old French forts at places such as Detroit.

With their economy potentially in crisis, the Delaware responded to the rise of new leaders who attempted to reorganize their society. Although we do not have their names, the strategies of two of them are sufficiently different to distinguish them as a militant prophet and a church-building prophet.

The militant prophet had a vision that he died and visited heaven, where he was given a message for gaining the spiritual and political salvation of the Indian people. He preached that because the Indians gave up the traditions and life-style of their forbears and traded and accepted the goods of the Europeans, the path to heaven for the Indians was blocked. Concepts of heaven and the strong emphasis on personal salvation were ideas borrowed, probably indirectly, from the Christian religion. Pontiac, an Ottawa leader, supported the teachings of the militant prophet as a means to forming a multi-tribal military alliance that would push the English out of Indian territory in the Great Lakes region. In 1763, Pontiac initiated a coordinated military attack on the British-occupied forts, but he was not able to sustain the fight or evict the English.

The church-building Delaware prophet, unlike the militant prophet, had a religious message only for the Delaware, not for a multi-tribal coalition. This Delaware prophet brought together elements of Delaware religion and formed a centralized

Delaware national ceremonial and religious order, often called the Bighouse Religion. Previously, the Delaware were formed into about forty small bands, which were severely disrupted during the 1600–1760 colonial period. The prophet reorganized the kinship and political organization of Delaware society and instituted a system of three phratries, often called Turtle, Turkey, and Wolf, and each of which was subdivided into twelve smaller clans or subdivisions. This prophet created a system of chiefs for the Delaware with ceremonies of installation, and one chief, who led the Turtle phratry, was designated principal chief, although he had little authority over the other two major chiefs. The three major divisions were recognized with the Bighouse Religious ceremonies and each had complementary religious and political duties.

After 1765, the Delaware prophets appear to disappear from the record.

The name Handsome Lake is the sachem title of the Turtle clan from among the Seneca, the westernmost nation of the Iroquois Confederacy. The Iroquois Confederacy consisted of six nations and forty-nine sachems, or chiefs, chosen from historically privileged families. Handsome Lake obtained his title sometime before 1799 and held it until his death in 1815. A relative within the Turtle clan, reckoned only through the female line, assumed the name and leadership role after his death.

Handsome Lake

d. 1815

Seneca spiritual leader

As a young man, Handsome Lake participated in the forest wars of the period: the French and Indian War (1755–59), Pontiac's War (1763), and the American Revolutionary War (1775–83). By the late 1790s, the once-powerful Iroquois lost most of their territory and were relegated to small reserves in upstate New York. While the Iroquois were experiencing social and cultural depression resulting from their recent losses, starting in 1799 Handsome Lake reported a series of visions and preached the *Gaiwiio*, or Good Word, to the Iroquois. He quickly obtained many followers and taught that the Iroquois must reorganize central aspects of their economic, social, and religious life. Under Handsome Lake's guidance, many Iroquois communities adopted new moral codes, men took up agriculture and constructed family farms, and many individuals adopted new religious ceremonies and beliefs. Handsome Lake's message combined elements of Quakerism, Catholicism, and traditional Iroquois beliefs. The new religion helped the Iroquois make the transition from a hunter society to a reservation agricultural community. In the 1830s, after his death, Handsome Lake's followers formalized his teachings into a church, known as the Handsome Lake Church; his teachings are still practiced today by many Iroquois.

Kenekuk (Kickapoo Prophet) 1785–1852

Kickapoo tribal and spiritual leader

Kenekuk was the religious and political leader of a community of Kickapoo, which was later joined by some Potawatomi. The Kickapoo lived in Illinois, while the Potawatomi occupied parts of present-day Michigan, but a small group of them joined Kenekuk and his Kickapoo community when they were removed to Kansas after 1933. Kenekuk was influenced by the Shawnee prophet, who before the War of 1812 advocated strong and overt military resistance to U.S. settlers and territorial expansion. The War of 1812 left the Kickapoo and other northern Great Lakes Indian nations in a state of disarray and destitution. In 1819, the Kickapoo ceded half of the present-day state of Illinois to the U.S. government. Thereafter during the 1820s, some Kickapoo bands migrated to Texas, while others sought refuge in Mexico.

Kenekuk, like the Shawnee prophet before him, claimed he had a vision, containing a message from the Great Spirit for the Indian people, but for the Kickapoo in particular. Kenekuk's vision differed from the Shawnee prophet's message in that it preached accommodation to U.S. culture and land demands. The Kickapoo prophet worked to create a new moral and religious community for his followers, one that drew on elements of Catholic, Protestant, and traditional Kickapoo religious beliefs. He advocated the taking up of agriculture, the formation of self-sufficient Indian farming communities. He banned alcohol, instructed his followers to maintain friendly relations with U.S. settlers, and developed a self-contained religious moral community, which tried to preserve its land and identity from the onslaught of U.S. settlers and the demands of the U.S. government.

In 1832, Kenekuk's community did not join with Black Hawk in his war to regain parts of Illinois. Nevertheless, he tried hard to avoid the removal of his people from Illinois to present-day Kansas. In 1833, however, he and 350 followers were required to move. In Kansas, Kenekuk continued his preaching, and he attracted some converts from among the Potawatomi. He died in 1852, but his community continues to survive until this day, and the people retain the distinct religious teachings of the Kickapoo prophet.

In the decades following the American Civil War, the American military turned its attention to pacifying and destroying American Indian groups, including those in the southern Plains. At the Medicine Lodge Council of 1867, several Comanche leaders agreed to move onto reservations. Indian groups who refused to relocate became outlaws. One of the most fearless and powerful of these "renegade" groups was led by Quanah Parker.

Quanah Parker
1845–1911

Comanche tribal and spiritual leader

Parker was the son of Peta Nocona, chief of the Kwahadi band in Texas, a subgroup within the Comanche nation, and Cynthia Parker, a non-Comanche captive. Throughout the 1860s, Parker led numerous attacks against U.S. soldiers. He and his band escaped capture longer than most of the Comanche bands in their final days living freely on the Plains. In the 1870s, however, new high-powered rifles and increasing numbers of U.S. hunters were systematically killing buffalo and destroying the way of life for the Plains Indians. Hunters were now killing buffalo year long. In 1875, after years of battle and their buffalo nearly gone, Parker and his warriors turned themselves in, defeated by hunters with repeating rifles. The Comanche were among the last American Indians to roam freely over the southern Plains.

Parker quickly adapted to reservation life in present-day Oklahoma. In a few short years he became a successful cattle rancher. He counseled his people to adapt to the reservation without surrendering their Comanche customs and heritage. Parker adopted the peyote religion, which offered a modified world view, different in many ways from traditional religions, but offering many Indians a new form of religious belief that provided moral and spiritual support in the reservation setting. Parker helped spread the peyote religion to the Indian peoples of the Plains when they were desperately depressed and disoriented from the early reservation captivity of the 1880s and 1890s.

Parker became an appointed judge and served in the court of Indian affairs from 1886 to 1898. By 1890, he was the chief representative for the Comanche people in the allotment of tribal lands, which divided up tribal domains into small individual plots of 160 acres or less, while government officials made the surplus available to U.S. settlers. Parker also negotiated for the release of Geronimo by offering refuge to Apache warriors on the Comanche Reservation.

Juan de Jesus Romero (Deer Bird) 1874–1978

Taos tribal and spiritual leader

If there was one cause in life for which Juan de Jesus Romero fought, it was the return of the sacred Blue Lake (Maxolo) to the Taos Pueblo. He was hereditary *cacique* or headman of Taos Pueblo as well as its spiritual leader.

As early as 1906, Romero began a personal campaign for the return of the ancestral lands surrounding Blue Lake that the U.S. government had expropriated from the Taos Indians. Romero met with little success in this endeavor, but vowed to keep up pressure on the government. The Taos believe that Blue Lake, in present-day eastern New Mexico, is a sacred site where the world was created and, therefore, has great religious and symbolic significance in Taos Pueblo culture. Ceremonies acknowledging the creation of the world and of man were annually celebrated by the Taos community at Blue Lake. Forty-five years passed before the tribe filed a lawsuit against the government for the area including the lake and the land. In 1965, the Taos were awarded cash compensation in lieu of their claims, but this was rejected by them in favor of their original claim.

Romero was adamant that the lake be returned, and he traveled to Washington, D.C., in 1970 to plead his case before President Richard M. Nixon. A motion was put before the U.S. Senate and passed, with seventy senators for and twelve against, for the return of Blue Lake to the Taos along with 48,000 acres of surrounding land. Nixon signed the bill in 1971, and Blue Lake was again within the Taos domain. For his lifelong efforts in the fight for Blue Lake, Romero won the prestigious Indian Council Fire Award in 1974. He passed away at the age of 104.

John Slocum was a member of the Squaxin band of Southern Coast Salish Indians and achieved importance as the founder of the Indian Shaker Church. Slocum was born near Puget Sound, Washington, during the early 1830s, but there was nothing particularly remarkable about his life until the fall of 1881, when he became sick and apparently died. Friends had been summoned and preparations were being made for the funeral when he suddenly revived. He then announced that he had been to visit the judgment place of God and received instructions about certain ways in which Indian people needed to change their lives if they wanted to achieve salvation. This visionary experience became the basis of Tschaddam or the Indian Shaker Church as it is known in English.

**John Slocum
d. 1896–98**

Coast Salish spiritual leader

This religion is exclusive to Indians and has no connection to millenarian Shakerism as practiced by ascetic Protestant communities in New England. Indian Shakerism incorporates Christian beliefs concerning God, heaven, hell, and the relationship between sinfulness and damnation, but in this religion these ideas are combined with Native concepts, particularly beliefs relating to sickness as a penalty for spiritual offenses.

The element of "the shake" developed out of a later incident. About a year after his "resurrection," Slocum became ill again and was expected to die. Faced with the impending catastrophe of his death, his wife Mary became hysterical; she approached his prostrate body praying, sobbing, and trembling uncontrollably. When her convulsion had passed, it was observed that Slocum had recovered slightly. This was attributed to her seizure, which was understood as a manifestation of divine power. Thus, curing through "the shake" and laying on of hands became a basic element in Shaker services which continues to this day.

The Indian Shaker religion is still flourishing among coastal Indians of British Columbia (Canada), Washington, Oregon, and northwestern California. John Slocum died between 1896 and 1898, and the religion has undergone many changes since its inception in 1881.

Smohalla
1815–1907

Wanapam spiritual leader

Smohalla was a member of the Wanapam Indian tribe, which lived along the upper Columbia River in present-day eastern Washington State. He left this area around 1850 after a dispute with a local chief. Smohalla traveled for several years. Despite being influenced by Catholic missionaries, Smohalla became a warrior. He was wounded and left for dead during an encounter with a Salish war party. When he returned to his homeland he claimed to have visited the Spirit World during this near-death ordeal. He brought back a message which, to the Wanapam, had the ring of authenticity due to his death-and-resurrection experience.

Smohalla's preaching was a combination of nativist sentiment, cultural purity, and resistance to the U.S. government and Christianity. His popularity came at a time when the Indian population of the region was declining due to diseases and land losses to U.S. settlers. According to Smohalla, religious truths came to him in dreams, thus the name of his religion: "Dreamer Religion." Among Smohalla's teachings was the repudiation of U.S. culture, including alcohol and agricultural practices. Smohalla has been credited with the oft-mentioned quotation, "You ask me to plow the ground. Shall I take a knife and tear my mother's bosom? You ask me to cut grass and make hay and sell it and be rich like white men. But dare I cut off my mother's hair?" Smohalla also prophesied that Indians would be resurrected and banish whites from their lands. He taught that Indians would be saved though divine intervention, but did not advocate violence. His teachings and sermons were often accompanied by ceremonial music and dance.

Smohalla spread his message throughout the region and had many converts, including Old Joseph, a former Christian. His teachings got him into trouble with U.S. authorities, and Smohalla was often jailed. Smohalla's teachings influenced a number of later prophets who also preached a message of resistance and cultural identity.

Kateri Tekakwitha, whom many Catholics call "Lily of the Mohawks," converted to Christianity in the 1670s and became a nun. She was a person of uncommon religious conviction and is currently a candidate for canonization by the Roman Catholic Church.

Kateri Tekakwitha 1656–80

Mohawk Catholic nun

Tekakwitha was born near present-day Auriesville, New York. Her father was a Mohawk chief and her mother an Algonquin who had been captured by the Mohawk. Tekakwitha's mother was a Christian convert. Her parents died when she was four years old, and she grew up with her uncle in the village of Caughnawaga, near present-day Fonda, New York.

Jesuits visited Tekakwitha's village in the 1670s, and she was baptized at the age of twenty by Jacques de Lamberville, a Jesuit missionary. Her uncle, also a Mohawk chief, opposed her conversion, and her religion caused her ridicule and made her an outcast among her people. In 1677, Tekakwitha fled her village with some visiting Christianized Oneida Indians. She settled near a Christian Mohawk community outside of present-day Montreal. Tekakwitha hoped to establish a convent on Heron Island. Church authorities rejected her plan, but did accept her into an order of nuns. Tekakwitha's religious fervor never wavered, and her almost fanatical devotion and commitment to helping others were well known among her people. Many stories have grown around Tekakwitha, including the account that when she died in 1680, scars from a childhood case of smallpox disappeared.

Tekakwitha became a candidate for sainthood in the Roman Catholic Church in 1884. In 1943, the Church declared her "venerable," and in 1980, she was declared "blessed." These are the first two steps toward sainthood.

**Tenskwatawa
(Open Door)
1778–1837**

Shawnee spiritual
leader

Tenskwatawa, better known as the Shawnee Prophet, was the brother of Tecumseh, the famous Indian leader who tried to rally Indian forces against U.S. expansion before and during the War of 1812. Tenskwatawa was born at Piqua near present-day Springfield, Ohio, of a Shawnee war chief and his Cherokee-Creek wife. As a result of their defeat at the Battle of Fallen Timbers in 1794 and the Treaty of Greenville the next year, the Shawnee were left leaderless and demoralized throughout Tenskwatawa's childhood. He became an alcoholic and lost the sight in his left eye in a hunting accident. In 1806, while living in the Delaware villages in present-day Indiana stretching from Indianapolis to Munsee, Tenskwatawa was influenced by the cultural and ceremonial revival created by the Munsee prophetess, who in 1804–1805 reformed the Delaware Big House religion. Since 1675, many Shawnee had lived with the Algonkian-speaking Delaware, or Lenape, and some groups within both nations became very closely tied. In February 1806, Tenskwatawa had an out-of-body experience and a vision that he died and went to heaven to see the Great Spirit, and brought back a message to the Indian people.

Tenskwatawa began to preach a return to traditional Shawnee customs, condemned intermarriage with Europeans, and rejected contact with them. He promoted claims that he could cure sickness and prevent death. The brothers Tenskwatawa and Tecumseh envisioned a vast Indian confederacy strong enough to keep the colonists from expanding any further west. Tenskwatawa's influence began to grow with other Indians, and he and Tecumseh traveled extensively among tribes from Wisconsin to Florida spreading the message. Indiana governor William Henry Harrison challenged him to "cause the sun to stand still" and "the moon to change its course." Tenskwatawa promptly did as much in accurately predicting the total eclipse of the sun on June 16, 1806. Thousands of Indians quickly became believers and hastened to join the new religion.

Tecumseh and Tenskwatawa founded Prophetstown along the confluence of the Wabash River and Tippecanoe Creek in Indiana, and many Indians came to live there. Tecumseh began to exert a larger presence than his brother in the organization of the town and its operations. When he left on a trip in 1811, leaving Tenskwatawa in charge, Tecumseh cautioned his brother to avoid any confrontation with Harrison's troops. Perhaps seeking to regain preeminence, Tenskwatawa was drawn into attacking Harrison at the Battle of Tippecanoe in November 1811. During the battle, he stayed at the rear using magic to drive the U.S. soldiers into retreat. Tenskwatawa had no power that day, and the Indians were soundly defeated at Tippecanoe. After the battle, the prophet was left without influence and could no longer command believers.

As a result, upon his return, the enraged Tecumseh broke with his brother. Tenskwatawa fled to Canada, returning fifteen years later in 1826 and eventually settling in Wyandotte County, Kansas. George Catlin painted Tenskwatawa in 1830. The oil-on-canvas portrays a pensive old man wearing a nose ring. Holding his once-powerful firestick wand in his right hand, and in the left, a sacred string of beads given to him during the long-ago vision, his portrait seems to contemplate what once was to be.

Wabokieshek (White Cloud) was an important supporter of Black Hawk, the Sac and Fox leader, during the final conflicts for the old Northwest Territory in the 1830s. Due to his prophetic visions, he has also been called the Winnebago Prophet. The Winnebago are a Siouan-speaking people who currently live in Nebraska and Wisconsin.

Wabokieshek was born in the heart of what was to become the final battle ground for control of the old Northwest Territory, now known as the Great Lakes region. His homeland was situated near the present-day site of Prophetstown, Indiana, at the junction of the Tippecanoe and Wabash rivers. Although Wabokieshek had long preached for resistance to U.S. encroachment and culture, he had advocated peace with the United States during the Winnebago uprising of 1827. Five years later, however, he agreed to take up arms in support of Black Hawk in the so-called Black Hawk's War of 1832.

Winnebago Prophet (Wabokieshek) 1794–1841

Winnebago spiritual leader

Wabokieshek came to Black Hawk in 1832, when the Sac and Fox leader was gathering forces for his return to Saukenuk, a major Sac village in present-day Illinois. Wabokieshek told Black Hawk of his visions, in which the Great Spirit would help defeat their enemies. He promised that with the aid of certain ceremonies, he could create an army of spirit warriors who would aid Black Hawk in defeating the U.S. Army. Thereafter, the Indians could reclaim their homelands that were occupied by the United States. Prophecies of this sort were not uncommon. Both the Delaware Prophet (1760–63) and Tenskwatawa, the Shawnee Prophet (1806–11), had made similar prophecies in their people's conflicts with European colonists and U.S. settlers. Wabokieshek's alliance with Black Hawk resulted in the enlistment of a number of Sac and Winnebago warriors to Black Hawk's cause. Wabokieshek remained with Black Hawk throughout the conflict and was at his side when the Indian leader surrendered at Prairie du Chien in present-day Wisconsin. Wabokieshek was imprisoned with Black Hawk and traveled with him as a kind of war trophy in the eastern United States. After his release, Wabokieshek lived for a number of years in relative obscurity, first with the Sac and later with the Winnebago.

Wovoka
(Jack Wilson)
c. 1856–1932

Paiute spiritual leader

The Ghost Dance religion of 1890 originated with this Paiute visionary and prophet, who grew up in the area of Mason Valley, Nevada, near the present Walker Lake Reservation. His proper name, Wovoka, means "The Cutter" in Paiute. On the death of his father he was taken into the family of a white farmer named David Wilson and was given the name Jack Wilson, by which he was known among local American settlers.

During the late 1880s, Wovoka became ill with a severe fever at a time that happened to coincide with a solar eclipse. In his feverish state, Wovoka received a vision, and an account of this experience as told in Wovoka's own words was documented by James Mooney in his book *The Ghost Dance Religion and the Sioux Outbreak of 1890* (1896): "When the sun died," Wovoka said, "I went up to heaven and saw God and all the people who had died a long time ago. God told me to come back and tell my people they must be good and love one another, and not fight, or steal, or lie. He gave me this dance to give to my people."

This vision became the basis of the Ghost Dance religion, which was based upon the belief that there would be a time when all Indian people—the living and those who had died— would be reunited on an earth that was spiritually regenerated and forever free from death, disease, and all the other miseries that had recently been experienced by Indians. Word of the new religion spread quickly among Indian peoples of the Great Basin and Plains regions, but it is said that Wovoka himself never traveled far from his birthplace. A complex figure, he was revered by Indians while being denounced as an impostor and a lunatic by the local settlers throughout his entire life.

Health

TRADITIONAL INDIAN HEALTH
PRACTICES AND CULTURAL VIEWS ♦ ♦ ♦ ♦ ♦ ♦ ♦ ♦ ♦ ♦ ♦

**Health Systems and
the Role of Culture**

The health care system of a society reflects the ways in which that society organizes to care for its sick, based on commonly held ideas about wellness and unwellness. These sociocultural theories encompass the causes of unwellness and death, and the appropriate interventions to prevent or heal unwellness. For example, most modern societies have a disease theory model that attributes many illnesses to bacteria or viruses. This model also has fairly rigid ideas about the types of interventions that are necessary, as well as the appropriate agency or person to treat those illnesses. In this model, treatment of illness, especially major illness, is carried out by a physician who is expected to utilize scientific means in the diagnosis and treatment of the malady.

The health care system of most modern societies is easily identifiable by its social institutions—hospitals, clinics, and doctors' offices. During times of illness, patients and sometimes their families interact with health care providers within these institutions where diagnosis, treatment, and recuperation take place. The health care-seeking behavior of patients using these institutions often indicates that they have faith in the providers and share with them ideas concerning the causes and characteristics of the illness process as well as its treatment.

If an illness cannot be cured or successfully treated by providers or institutions of the modern health system, patients and their families may seek alternative resources. Thus faith healing, biofeedback, meditation, and other forms of unconventional treatments may be sought, and it is usually provided by practitioners who are not part of the formalized medical institutions. In this context, healing and religion and/or faith often come together.

Health and religion overlap also for members of the society who do not subscribe to the same beliefs about illness etiology and the appropriate course of action for treatment of various illnesses. For example, members of the Church of Christian Scientists largely hold to the belief that faith and prayer, not medication or surgery, are the critical elements in healing. This group therefore has developed its own health care resources, which use prayer as the central therapeutic intervention.

Because illness is a sociocultural construct, illnesses are viewed differently by different cultural groups. In most cultures, illness is defined as the inability of a person to perform his or her normal role in society (i.e., the absence of health), and therefore the person is expected to seek a relief or cure. Society generally accepts and excuses its members during times of illness but only if the patient actively seeks treatment. A sick person is not only expected to seek appropriate relief but also to comply with the recommended treatment process. Any abuse of the sick role (such as feigning illness) is neither condoned nor supported.

An important aspect of the sociocultural understanding about wellness and unwellness is that society not only provides culturally relevant diagnoses or causes but also a framework for appropriate intervention. Within this framework there may be ways to explain "why" an illness occurred. These ideas are important in the treatment process of any illness and also in the prevention of illnesses.

A culture's health care resources and beliefs about health may not readily be visible to others. Health beliefs may be so integrated into the religion of the culture that healing is one of the

primary responsibilities of the religion. Thus religious practices may represent an important part of that culture's health care system. This is often the case, for example, with many American Indian tribal groups and Alaska Natives.

As a minority population colonized by Europeans and forced to assimilate into majority culture, American Indians and Alaska Natives today are subjected to health policies and practices based on Western cultural values and models. However, access to quality health care for this population is far from adequate because of poverty, isolation, misunderstanding of jurisdictional responsibilities, and a variety of other governmental policies. The situation is further aggravated by the fact that access to health care is greatly influenced by the race, language, and socioeconomic circumstances of an individual.

Mode of treating the sick.

Drawing by Le Moyne,

engraving from T. de Bry,

America, *part 2. Courtesy of*

American Heritage Press.

Although a segment of the U.S. population wants health care to be a right and therefore accessible to all, the U.S. government continues to view health care as a commodity to be purchased. Because of this governmental stance, there is also a growing expectation within the general public that the federal government should finance a greater portion of the health care cost. This inconsistency between the social expectation and the country's socioeconomic reality continues to foster a health care system that is not only substandard but is also largely unavailable to the poor or the near poor in America. A majority of the American Indians and Alaska Natives are in the lower socioeconomic strata of U.S. society and therefore experience greater rates of poor health and are more likely to have inadequate health resources.

Although it is not clear how much inaccessibility to modern health care influences the use of indigenous traditional health care providers, many American Indians and Alaska Natives do use this resource. Those who live in the cities or away from the rural reservations frequently travel back to the reservation to participate in healing ceremonies. Sometimes the indigenous healers also come to urban areas to assist patients and/or health facilities.

Native American Cultural Views

In 1854, the great American Indian orator and leader Chief Seathl summarized a basic belief held by many Indians about the concept of harmony and the place of humans in the universe:

The deer, the horse, the great eagle, these are our brothers. The Earth is our mother. All things are connected like the blood which unites one family. Whatever befalls the earth, befalls the sons of the earth. Man does not weave the web of life. He is merely a strand in it. Whatever he does to the web, he does to himself.

The notion of such interrelatedness between people and their environment and the inclusion of various deities or a great spirit (called "grandfather" in some tribes) is a common thread in the concept of wellness and well-being for many American Indians and Alaska Natives, despite the heterogeneity of culture, language, and values. Although there are variations on the theme and its symbolic meaning, notions of interrelatedness and harmony are illustrated in dances and healing ceremonies that seek to reaffirm the oneness with the universe and restore harmony as a part of treating illnesses and misfortunes.

The concepts of harmony and balance within the health context are often expressed by the use of various symbols, often presented within a theoretical framework that emphasizes wholeness, for example, a circle as opposed to a linear progression. It is often emphasized that the circle has no beginning or end and that the spiritual being continues even after a person's physical body has become dust. Sometimes this is illustrated by the idea of a person born into a lineage continuing that lineage even after death because, as he or she dies, others are born to take his or her place. Likewise, persons leaving the physical world continue their journey or purpose in the afterworld or the spirit world. Thus, in many tribes, funeral ceremonies help prepare those persons for this next phase of life in the spirit world.

Harmony and Health

Like the concept of the yin and the yang in various Asian cultures, Indian tribes may include within the symbolic circle other elements of life that represent harmony or the equilibrium that is needed to maintain health and well-being. These elements may take the form of the four cardinal directions, the four winds, the four worlds, or the four elements in the medicine wheel. Within these four elements are various sources of energy, power, and knowledge. Sometimes these elements are symbolized by sacred colors that in turn may represent such elements as fire, wind, water, and earth. At another level, these four elements may be viewed as sources of strength that symbolize the innate qualities of a person's being—physical, mental, emotional, and spiritual. In order to maintain health, these elements must be in balance within as well as without. For example, a pregnant woman is often told to avoid unpleasant experiences in order to keep her unborn child healthy in mind and spirit.

Most traditional Indian concepts of health and daily living center on wellness, not illness. In fact, most tribal taboos and other practices are observed and stressed to prevent illness or misfortune.

MEDICINE LODGE.

Plains Medicine Lodge. The central figure, apparently the medicine man, holds a pipe in his right hand and the patient's wrist in the other, as if taking the pulse. From "Life of an Indian," Harper's Illustrated Weekly, *June 20, 1868. From* American Indian Medicine, *by Virgil J. Vogel. Copyright © 1970, University of Oklahoma Press.*

In many communities, healers are sought in time of illness, but, more importantly, they are also called upon to provide protection; to bless happy occasions such as weddings, a birth of a child, and a new home; to offer thanks for a successful hunt or a bountiful harvest; or to ensure success on an expedition, on a hunt, or in a new occupation. Healers in most American Indian and Alaska Native communities therefore are an important resource in helping prevent illness or misfortune for individuals, families, or the entire community.

Some of the annual ceremonies that help ensure the safety and health of the communities are conducted seasonally and include the participation of all the members of the tribe. These ceremonies may bless the planting, hunting, or fishing season, and may involve praying for rain for crops. In other instances, special ceremonies may be conducted to mark the initiation of new clan members or puberty rites for young men or women who are ready to assume the role of adults. Other ceremonies, such as a "give-away" or potlatch where the host honors his guests by giving them gifts, may be done to fulfill a vow or to celebrate achievements. Large public ceremonies may also be given to introduce a new healer into the community.

As in many cultures, American Indians and Alaska Natives are also very pragmatic about dealing with some of life's problems, including minor illnesses. For example, before calling on physicians or their own traditional healers, they will most likely have tried various home remedies. Sometimes this may entail a prayer to call on the help of the appropriate guardian spirit or an ancestral totem. A totem serves as a helping spirit that may be represented in the spirit of a special animal or a bird. If these interventions do not bring relief, then the patient is most likely to go to the physician or an indigenous healer.

Although most tribes have different names for their traditional healers, words such as *medicine man, medicine woman, shaman, Native practitioners, and traditional healer* are some of the terms borrowed and used by non-Indians to describe healers. For example, the word *shaman* was borrowed from the Siberian Tungusic word *saman*, which translates as "spiritual medicine men." Today, the term *shaman* is usually used for healers whose primary practice is treating illnesses associated with or attributed to malevolent spirits. Medicine men or medicine women, on the other hand, tend to treat illnesses caused by both natural and supernatural causes. Native practitioners are sub-specialists who limit their practice or speciality to a specific form of intervention, for example, herbalists or diagnosticians.

Healers and Healing

When treating an ill patient, most healers work with their patients in the patient's home where the healing ceremonies may be less public and involve primarily the patient and his or her family. Depending on the tribe, the type of illness, and the type of intervention, some healing ceremonies may require a few minutes, while others require days or a series of different ceremonies over a period of one or two years. In some instances, the preparation for the ceremony such as a Sun Dance may take months. And depending on the nature of the rituals or healing ceremonies, there may be more than one healer or one patient involved. The ceremony also may require singers, dancers, drummers, persons to prepare ceremonial objects, persons who serve as mentors, and elders who may help prepare the dancers.

Except in very rare instances, most healers are also generally acknowledged as spiritual or religious leaders, not only because of their skills but also because of their knowledge of religion. It is not uncommon, for example, to find in some of the traditional Indian leadership models a religious leader and a war chief serving as key advisors to the tribal chief. Among many of the Pueblo in the Southwest, for example, the religious leader selects or nominates the governor for the pueblo each year. While the latter are elected or nominated, the position of religious leader is a lifetime position.

Today, in addition to their responsibilities as healers and religious leaders, healers are often sought to provide consultation on a variety of cultural issues and public health matters of the tribe. Some healers, in fact, have concentrated their efforts in working with mental health programs or working with schools to ensure appropriate cultural content in the school curriculum.

The career of a healer in most tribes does not bring wealth. In most cases, healers charge small or no fees for their services. Because in some tribes healers are an important resource to the community, members of the tribe may provide food and other necessities for the healer so that he or she might devote full time to the welfare of the community. Within this role, however, the healer also spends considerable time training and teaching others various ceremonial dances, songs, and supervising restoration or creation of ceremonial objects to be used by tribal members.

While ministering to the sick is often considered a curative role, most healers in Indian communities view their roles as more of a catalyst in the healing process. For example, with the various rituals and ceremonies, they help set the stage for the initiation of a healing process. Through prayers, songs, and other related activities, they evoke the appropriate spiritual forces to help heal patients and/or empower patient so that they can heal themselves with the aid of the spiritual forces. Among the Navajo, this preparation may include replication of some of these deities in a sand painting; whereupon the appropriate spiritual forces are asked to assist the patient who will be sitting on the painting during part of the ceremony. The ritual or ceremony must therefore be conducted in a specific manner and matched with the appropriate deities.

During healing ceremonies, the traditional healers may wear special garments with a special mask that symbolizes the specific healing spirit. Certain sound instruments, such as drums or flutes, may be used to invite, accompany, or thank the helping spirits. Similarly, sage, feathers, and steam may be used to purify and prepare for the arrival of the deities as well as mentally prepare the patient for the healing process. This preparation is comparable to what may take place before a patient is examined by a physician, that is, the nurse takes the patient's temperature, blood pressure, and obtains some key information in preparation for the examination by the physician.

In some healing ceremonies, the healer may be assisted by a cadre of dancers who impersonate in their clothing, dances, and songs the various important deities central to the ceremony. Many of the healing ceremonies also require specific settings or require that the ceremony be conducted only during certain seasons of the year or only during the night.

In addition to healers, other sub-specialists or practitioners are often an important part of most healing systems. Some help the healers while others practice independently and may be utilized because of their expertise in such procedures as bone setting, treating wounds, making diagnoses, assisting with births, or in making herbal medicine. Although the introduction of modern medicine has all but replaced some of the functions of these various specialists, diagnosticians, herbalists, and birth attendants are still active in some tribes.

Even though most Native American babies are now delivered in hospitals and persons requiring surgery or other acute medical interventions are generally served by physicians in hospitals, traditional healers are

Medicine man ministering to a patient. Notice the bowl and pestle for mixing medicines. The medicine man is shaking a gourd rattle and may be singing a medicine song. From History, Condition and Prospect of the Indian Tribes, *by Henry R. Schoolcraft. Courtesy of Chicago Historical Society.*

nevertheless still utilized. They are sought out by patients who have mental health problems or other forms of chronic health problems that may not be amenable to the standard interventions by modern medicine. Other illness such as recurrent bad dreams may readily call for the intervention of a traditional healer. The use of traditional healers in these contexts is also largely determined by the degree of acculturation or assimilation of the patient or the patient's family.

In the past and today, the traditional healing system of a tribe may consist of a highly organized social structure with full-time healers who preside over and coordinate a variety of ceremonial and other religious activities for the tribe. In other instances, a healer in a tribe may be a part-time solo practitioner who is engaged to assist patients or families. During the rest of the time, the healers may be employed in other occupations.

Depending on the tribe or culture, the healers may also treat a number of patients at one time. For example, during a Sun Dance, there may be as many as a dozen participants in the piercing ceremony. Among the Pueblo in the Southwest, all but a few participate in most of the major ceremonies, and children as young as three years of age are encouraged to practice and participate in these dances.

Natural Causes of Unwellness

In many American Indian and Alaska Native groups illness and misfortune are attributed to numerous causes, ranging from taboo violation or wrongdoing to other forms of supernatural interventions that may occur as a result of witchcraft or sorcery. For example, in one tribe a condition such as epilepsy may be viewed as the consequences of unsanctioned behavior such as incest. In another, the same condition may be attributed to supernatural causes such as soul possession or witchcraft. The explanations for illness and misfortune in many tribes, therefore, generally fall in the realms of either natural or supernatural causes.

Natural causes of disease are those conditions caused by known or easily explainable factors. For example, the injuries suffered by a person who falls off a horse would be attributed to natural causes. Those who develop diarrhea as a result of eating something that disagrees with them would also have their illness attributed to "natural causes." Many of the illnesses that fall under natural causes are generally mild and easily treated at home or by modern medicine. Other more traumatic or devastating forms of illness or disability may not be as easy to explain or treat. For example, certain traumas or disabilities resulting from an accident may also be viewed as caused by natural causes, but "why" the accident occurred may require the assistance of traditional healers. Finding the answer to "why" is important in order to prevent future mishaps and to ensure that the health problem does not worsen.

Illnesses or conditions attributed to breech of cultural taboos may be attributed to natural causes in some instances. For example, a child's cleft lip may be punishment for the parents' breach of tribal marriage rules forbidding members to marry a clan member. Ceremonies that include confession and reparation are often called for to prevent future episodes.

Supernatural Causes of Unwellness

Within the supernatural explanations, illnesses or misfortunes are thought to be caused by agents or evil forces that intend to do the individual harm. These agents or forces may be conceived by willful beings. It may be believed that a person becomes ill or dies as a result of some supernatural force or agent engaged by another who desires harm or misfortune to its victim. Sometimes the willful agent or agents are the deities themselves. For example, a series of unexplainable misfortunes such as severe drought or devastation from a new disease epidemic may be attributed to the wrath of angry gods or ancestors as a form of punishment for failing to observe certain rites or customs. Confession of wrongdoing as well as re-institution of cultural taboos and ceremonies to restore "harmony" are often means of dealing with these sources of illness and the resulting problems.

At the level of the individual patient, various agents may also be identified as methods of creating illness. For example, the method used may consist of object intrusion, whereby unsuspecting victims of witchcraft may become ill due to foreign objects placed in or on their bodies. A diagnostician or healer therefore has to remove such objects by a ritual ceremony that may involve sucking or cupping.

Soul loss may be the diagnosis, as in the case of a patient who suddenly becomes unconscious or exhibits other forms of incoherent behavior such as autism, where one is unable to relate to the environment or external stimulus. Ceremonies and treatments utilized in these cases often require procedures to coax the return of the soul to the body. Sometimes persons with soul loss are seen as victims of witchcraft. At other times, soul loss may be attributed to the influence of other spirits, usually those of departed ancestors who wish the patient to join them.

The role of supernatural forces is also central in cases of soul possession, in which the soul of the individual is replaced by an unnatural force. In some tribes seizure disorders or other forms of violent outbursts may fall under this diagnosis. The treatment for these conditions requires various rituals of exorcism.

Illnesses and misfortunes can also be attributed to other forms of witchcraft such as placing spells on objects intended to do harm or to bring death to an individual. Sometimes these items contain pieces of a victim's clothing, hair, nail paring, and other personal items. The intervention in this instance is focused on retrieving or removing these objects, thereby breaking the intention or spell.

Most Indian tribes view humans, nature, and the supernatural as being on equal footing. Thus, any disturbance of this balance or harmony places the individual or group in a vulnerable position, easy prey to those wishing to inflict misfortune or illness. The consequences of the imbalance are also seen as affecting the offender's family or close kin. For example, the visible congenital anomalies of a child may be linked to the child's parent who failed to obey tribal taboos concerning marriage laws or to observe tribal prenatal rules. Individuals in this particular society, therefore, are responsible not only for their own healthy behaviors, but also for the others in their family as well as future family members.

Within the context of one's network, nature, plants, animals, birds, and sacred places have great importance. Many tribes view certain animals, such as eagles, bears, deer, buffaloes, and ravens, as powerful allies, whose spirits or totems may serve as an important source of protection. Other forms of plant and animal life may also be central to many of the sacred ceremonies, and some of these may consist of important food sources such as buffalo, salmon, rice, corn, and acorn. Many tribal ceremonies or rituals are performed to honor these elements for their contribution to the welfare of humans. For example, tribes who honor the buffalo often imitate this power source in their dances and dance regalias. These animal spirits or their power sources are often called upon during times of illness and misfortune.

Spirits of certain plants are also important in diagnosis or healing. For example, some tribes may use Indian tobacco in diagnostic procedures. Tobacco is still used today in many of the healing ceremonies as well as in offerings to the helping spirits. Prior to the European conquest, tobacco was rarely smoked except in healing ceremonies to seek wisdom or as a gesture of good will in the company of visitors when important topics were to be discussed. In some tribes, Indian tobacco may be given to a healer as a token of a request for help or as thanks for the healer's help.

In addition to tobacco, other plants such as sage, cedar, and sweet grass may be utilized in healing or purification rituals. Roots, leaves, blooms, or the fruit of many plants are still used in many herbal teas and medicines.

Plant and Animal Spirits

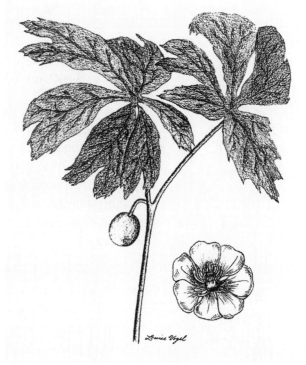

May apple (Podophyllum peltatum L.). *American Indian purgative. From American Indian Medicine, by Virgil J. Vogel. Copyright © 1970, University of Oklahoma Press.*

Modern and Traditional Ways

The initial introduction of European-style medicines to most Indian tribes came from traders, missionaries, and periodically from army physicians in the 1700s. An integral part of the work of missionaries was not only handing out government relief rations but also dispensing drugs and sometimes caring for the sick. Physicians, nurses, and hospitals, however, gradually became a familiar sight in Indian communities and modern health care became available to increasing numbers of American Indians. Some tribes, in fact, negotiated for medical supplies or services of a physician as part of their treaty agreements with the U.S. government. Thus, a number of tribes prepaid for their health care by ceding all or a portion of their land to the government.

During the nineteenth century, a number of physicians were contracted by the federal government to visit Indian children in boarding schools and/or in times of epidemics to see Indian patients on nearby reservations. Until the use of antibiotics in the treatment of infectious diseases became commonplace, the only preventive health service provided by these physicians was vaccination, especially against communicable diseases such as smallpox.

The ravages of communicable diseases were well known by the time physicians and other health care providers became visible in most Indian communities. Communicable diseases had decimated many tribes and depopulated the Americas after European contact. Not until the mid-twentieth century were certain communicable diseases such as tuberculosis, trachoma, and diphtheria brought under control on a number of Indian reservations.

Many tribal members were reluctant to accept Western health care because it was difficult for some to accept the idea that germs or microorganisms (invisible to the naked eye) could cause an illness such as tuberculosis—a condition which they also could not see. Even more baffling was the treatment for tuberculosis that required isolation and bed rest. Indian families did not welcome this treatment regime because patients were separated from their families for months and sometimes years as they recuperated in faraway sanitariums. Although practitioners of modern medicine and traditional healing shared a common concern to help patients, the choice between traditional and modern medicine often presented a major conflict for some of the patients with tuberculosis.

The following comparison between traditional Indian medicine and modern medicine builds on the work of Dr. J. T. Garrett, a Cherokee health professional:

Indian Medicine	Modern Medicine
Is wellness-oriented	Is illness-oriented
Patient treated in family or community setting	Patient is treated alone and isolated from family
Focuses on "why" illness occurred	Focuses on "how" illness occurred
Includes natural and supernatural causes	Emphasizes natural causes
Expects multiple causalities	Usually links illness to a single cause
Treatment approach is primarily holistic	Treatment approach is primarily physiological
Treatment is personal and reciprocally oriented	Treatment is often impersonal and complaint-oriented

As previously mentioned, most traditional Indian health systems historically have been wellness oriented in that cultural rules and values emphasize a healthy life-style, and healers spend a good portion of their time ensuring the wellness of their patients. The conquest by the Europeans drastically changed the traditional life-style of those tribes that survived. By means of warfare, removal, and displacement, the European conquest also decimated many tribes' health care resource people. Thus a number of Indian tribes today do not have indigenous healers or religious leaders and must rely on healers from other tribes.

Where it still exists, traditional Indian medicine is often concerned with *why* an illness or misfortune occurred, whereas modern medicine searches for *how* an illness came about. In both instances, however, appropriate interventions are determined by the diagnoses. In traditional Indian medicine, the etiology may be linked to supernatural causes. In some Indian tribes, one symptom or illness may be linked to multiple causes. For example, in some Indian communities, problems of alcoholism may be attributed to failure to adhere to traditional customs as a result of colonization and culture change. In other tribes, recurrent unpleasant or violent dreams may be important indications of unwellness. Among the Cherokee, for example, a healer may inquire about dreams when called upon to diagnose an illness. The healing approach of most Indian healers is holistic in that their interventions treat the whole person—physical, spiritual, emotional, and mental well-being—and almost always in the context of the patient's family or community.

The indigenous healer-patient relationship within most Indian communities is also based on some form of reciprocity or kinship obligation. Generally the patient and the healer come from the same culture and also share a common socioeconomic background or experience. Within the modern medical model, physicians and patients often do not share similar socio-economic or life experiences. In addition, in most physician-patient encounters, professional detachment or impersonal relationships are expected and are taught to the physicians and other health care providers.

Treatment Modalities

Until about the 1950s, when modern medicine became more accessible and more widely accepted, traditional healers and other practitioners used many other forms of therapy. For example, phlebotomy or blood letting was a common procedure used to relieve headaches, fever, swelling, or edema. Boils, tumors, or abscesses were also frequently treated with herbal poultices after the infected area was incised, drained, and cleaned.

The use of an herbal antiseptic was probably administered more frequently by Native Americans than by European healers until this procedure was accepted as standard medical practice. Most

Native Americans learned early how to treat wounds and lacerations, often by bathing them in various hot herbal solutions and then dressing them with poultices of the same or different types of herbs. To relieve pain or to speed up tissue healing, some indigenous practitioners also performed cautery and moxa by localized burning, usually using certain reeds or woods. Herbal enemas were also utilized as part of home remedies to treat various ailments such as constipation and diarrhea. Bladders of small animals and hollowed bones or reeds were used as enema instruments.

Various heat treatments were commonly used by many tribes. Sweats using herbs were common as was the use of a variety of herbal fumigants that were burned or poured over heated stones or coals. Smoke treatments were used for various complaints such as insomnia, headaches, head colds, and respiratory disorders. Fever treatment often called for rest, use of a sweat lodge, a special liquid diet, and anti-fever herbal medicine. In some tribes, ritual herbal baths would be prescribed for treatment of fever, skin conditions, and/or to heal skin rashes or abrasions. Hot mud mixed with various herbs were used in conjunction with some of these procedures. Mineral springs or natural hot springs were utilized by many tribes for arthritis, muscle aches, and other therapeutic purposes.

Massages with herbs and ointments were also common. Sometimes the massage followed ritual sweat treatments and involved applying pressure to affected areas. Bone setting, for example, often included massages using oil or herbs as well as other materials for splints. Wet raw hide was often applied to splints, so that when dried, the splint became immobilized. Crutches, stretchers, and arm slings were also commonly used by various tribes.

Diet therapy is frequently used by various practitioners as a form of treatment. Soft or special liquid diets may be used to treat abdominal pain, diarrhea, or other internal disorders. Diet therapy was also used to cleanse the body of substances that were considered toxic or illness causing. It is not uncommon, for example, for a woman to be on a special diet (to restore her strength) for a few days after delivering a baby. Certain foods are considered therapeutic and useful for restoring a sick person's physical strength. Special diets may also be prescribed or used by healers for purification.

Most tribes, until they were placed on reservations, practiced various forms of isolation techniques with certain illnesses. Sometimes clothing, bedding, and properties of the sick or the deceased were burned and the camp area abandoned. Similarly, climatic changes were prescribed for some illnesses. Most tribes based the location of winter and summer camps not only on food sources, but also on particular sacredness of a locale that was critical in some of the healing ceremonies or prescriptions. Treatment of certain mental disorders such as depression often called for moving back to a familiar homeland.

The use of herbs, in particular, continues to be an important part of the healing practices of most American Indians and Alaska Natives today. However, it is not the biological properties as much as the healing spirit or essence of the plants that is considered important. Most of the plants used for healing are considered to have these qualities, and therefore the healing spirit of the plant must be approached and harvested in a special way. For example, various songs and prayers are said before the plants are harvested and often some of these plants may only be

Flowering dogwood (Cornus florida L.). *American Indian febrifuge (fever reducing agent). From* American Indian Medicine, *by Virgil J. Vogel. Copyright © 1970, University of Oklahoma Press.*

harvested or prepared by herbalists. In addition, most Indian families also keep their own supplies of "home remedies" for minor illnesses. Depending on the region, sassafras, fern, goldenrod, or prickly pear teas may be prepared in various strengths and used as diuretics.

From observation of nature and from experimentation, most Native peoples learned to utilize plants from their region. They saw the effects of certain plants on the body and could predict certain outcomes with some of these plants. Because plants are viewed as living beings, many of these plants were not only recognized for their healing abilities but also warranted special songs and prayers to enhance their healing abilities.

For example, peyote, an alkaloid plant containing mescaline, is an important plant used as a sacrament and healing plant in the Native American Church (NAC). The plant is valued for its healing properties as well as for its teaching abilities. In other words, the plant heals, but it can also be used to teach (via vision) the patient about the cause of his or her illness or misfortune.

Because the Peyote Way stresses moral codes that emphasize the care of the family, the Protestant work ethic, and abstinence from alcohol, many Indian families faced with problems of alcoholism have begun to follow the NAC. NAC ceremonies contain elements of both Christianity and traditional Indian beliefs. The peyote songs and prayers contain gospel messages as well as reflect some of the cultural values of most American Indian tribes. During the ceremony, in addition to the peyote plant, the prayers and songs are accompanied by familiar sacred elements such as sage, cedar, tobacco, water, and special foods that are used in various other tribal religious ceremonies and activities.

The peyote ceremony, which usually lasts one night, is used for a broad range of illnesses in addition to being used for blessing and the ritual of thanksgiving. Peyote meetings are often requested by family members of the patient and may be utilized to ensure a successful outcome for a major surgical procedure such as open heart surgery.

Contribution to Modern Medicine

Because of the value of traditional herbal remedies among Indians of the Americas, many of these herbal medicines have become integrated into modern medicine. In the 1970s, historian Virgil Vogel identified at least 170 botanical drugs in the *Pharmacopoeia of the United States* and in the *National Formulary* previously discovered and used by Indian tribes in pre-European times. Some of the more well known drugs include digitalis, quinine, belladonna, cocaine from coca leaves, curare, and ipecac. In the search for cures for cancer, AIDS, and other diseases, a number of researchers have returned to the jungles of South America or other non-Western communities to question indigenous healers about plants and herbs and conduct research on indigenous plants and herbs used for medicinal purposes.

Euro-American Views of Indian Healing Practices

Because they are often at the center of most religious and healing ceremonies, indigenous healers became targets of oppression by missionaries and government officials. The healers were labeled as heathen witch doctors who only served as barriers to progress and therefore had to be discredited wherever and whenever possible. Sometimes this meant subjecting the sacred healing ceremonies to ridicule and condemnation. The preservation and use of ceremonial healing objects were likewise discouraged. As recently as 1976, families in one Navajo community were asked by their minister to bring their traditional medicine bundles to be burned. Such actions were applauded by the church as an act of true conversion to the Christian faith. The Navajo tribal government, however, not only expelled this particular minister but passed a tribal law that prohibited any burning of sacred ceremonial objects.

Any effort to incorporate some of the traditional healing practices of Indian tribes into the modern health care delivery system was especially criticized by many missionaries. Such proposals were viewed as a glorification of paganism. Until recently in many Indian communities, some non-Indian health care providers who tolerated or attended healing ceremonies were shunned or considered atheist by the missionaries. The influence of the missionary was especially felt by the government doctors who often joined the missionaries in verbal attacks against the healers. On the

Navajo reservation, the traditional healers were accused of per-petuating superstition and failing to recognize the limits of their healing skills. Some physicians and missionaries also blamed tra-ditional healers for preying on the poor and furthering the poverty of their patients. While these allegations were often unfounded, such rumors and criticism did nothing to improve the perception of Indian medicine or the relationship between traditional healers and Western health care providers.

Traditional medicine and the healers, however, continue to re-main important to tribes and to Native communities, despite the fact that various institutional and governmental policies have worked against these traditional resources. Mandatory education has eliminated the chance for many young people to learn the skills of traditional healing. Thus, in many Indian communities, there are very few opportunities for training a new cadre of traditional healers.

The need for traditional healers has greatly increased in recent years as more Indian communities are assuming greater responsi-bility for directing and managing their own health programs. Moreover, there is now a greater appreciation and understanding of traditional Indian healing by physicians and other health care providers who work with American Indians and Alaska Natives. The importance of traditional Indian healing has been particu-larly noted for a variety of "new" health problems faced by Native peoples. Diabetes, cancer, hypertension, alcoholism, and other forms of chronic health problems are relatively new to most In-dian communities but represent health problems for increasing numbers of Native Americans. While most of these health prob-lems are also new to the practice of most indigenous healers, the healers are able to utilize their skills to help patients cope with these conditions or to accept modern medical treatment.

For most Indian communities the rediscovery and renaissance of traditional medicine has been welcomed. Needless to say, the right to practice traditional ways has only occurred after years of court battles or as a result of lobbying for these rights in the halls of Congress. For example, the passage of the American Indian

Renaissance in the Use of Traditional Healers

Religious Freedom Act (Public Law 95-341) in 1978 formally allowed Indian tribes the freedom to practice their religion. The actual words of the legislation resolves "that henceforth it shall be the policy of the United States to protect and preserve for American Indians their inherent right of freedom to believe, express, and exercise [their] traditional religions."

This new law also allowed tribes to regain access to sacred sites on federal lands and the right to possess sacred objects such as eagle feathers. The congressional hearings on this subject contain extensive testimony and statements identifying sacred sites that have been destroyed by governmental action, such as the deliberate or accidental flooding of burial sites or the building of recreational facilities on sacred grounds that have served as worship sites for many tribes. Despite the passage of this act and recent efforts to reauthorize the legislation, access to sacred sites and difficulties in obtaining and using bald eagle feathers and peyote remain a problem.

Over the last few decades, the right of Native Americans to use peyote in the Native American Church has continued to be questioned in various state and federal courts. While peyote is one of the substances subject to control under the Federal Comprehensive Drug Abuse Prevention and Control Act, approximately nine states do exempt the status for "the non-drug use of peyote in religious ceremonies of the Native American Church." Although some courts have supported the right of Native Americans who are members of the Native American Church to possess and use peyote, other courts do not grant the same recognition. The legal battles continue.

Likewise, legal debates continue concerning the right of Native Americans to use bald eagle feathers and to hunt animals that are protected by the Endangered Species Act. Court decisions regarding these issues also continue to surface as a result of litigation.

Traditional and Modern Medicine

In most Indian communities, patients generally utilize a variety of health resources—government hospitals, private physicians, or traditional healers who may or may not be members of the patient's tribe. The patients often do not see any conflict between these alternatives and, depending on the symptoms and perceived cause of the illness, will select what they deem to be the most appropriate intervention.

The health picture of the Native Americans for the last two decades has begun to slowly mirror that of the majority society. A greater share of the health problems today are the consequence of unhealthy life-styles rather than substandard health care. Accordingly, many Indian tribes are now searching for ways to teach and instill in the young the need to improve their nutrition, participate in physical exercise, and, more importantly, to view themselves more positively. These are challenges many tribes face today, and some of the answers lie in the return to some of the traditional values and teachings of the traditional healers. At the forefront of this movement are the increasing numbers of Native Americans who are completing their medical education and returning to work with tribal groups. The inclusion of more Native American health professionals in the modern health care delivery system in Indian communities has meant more culturally sensitive health care providers and greater appreciation for the "culture" variable in health care.

Jennie R. Joe
University of Arizona

A*rts*

NATIVE ART IN NORTH AMERICA ♦ ♦ ♦ ♦ ♦ ♦ ♦ ♦ ♦ ♦ ♦ ♦

The visual arts of Native North Americans have a history of some 25,000 years. The diverse arts produced today by artists of Native ancestry throughout Canada and the United States are part of a living cultural tradition with deep roots in the past and much promise for the future. This is because artists of Native heritage not only express traditional values and draw upon past images and styles in their works, but they also address social, political, spiritual, and environmental issues of relevance to the entire human family.

Until recently, Native North American arts were viewed in the past tense, but now a static perception of Native art is no longer acceptable. Thanks to the investigations of archaeologists, art historians, and ethnohistorians and to the revitalization of Native art and culture especially since the 1960s, the vitality and continuity of Native North American art is readily apparent.

Its history is in many ways far more complex and interesting than that of the European newcomers to Canada and the United States, who for a long time merely imported European art styles and traditions to the New World. Native art history, on the other hand, is unique and indigenous to North American soil for most of its long history, with European aesthetic influences coming into play mainly in the nineteenth and twentieth centuries.

Native art history may be divided into prehistoric, colonial or historic, and contemporary periods, the precise dates of which vary enormously from one region of the continent to another. Transitions between these periods, moreover, are gradual, with many continuities as well as sharp distinctions between them. In addition, contemporary Native art falls into at least three or four major subdivisions, each fulfilling different functions and each catering to a different audience: (1) traditional art forms such as sacred drums and ceremonial costumes produced for use within the Native communities themselves mainly for spiritual occasions and powwows; (2) "tourist" or "popular" art forms for sale to non-Native travelers and collectors at such places as airports and "Indian Art and Craft" shops; (3) "contemporary" Native art for sale in art galleries specializing in Indian and Inuit carvings, prints, and various crafts; and (4) what could be described as "main-stream" or "high" art, created by artists of Native ancestry trained in major Euroamerican art schools and universities, who perceive themselves primarily as self-expressive individualists but work with Native values, beliefs, and concerns always uppermost in their practice. The latter also exhibit in the major galleries of urban North America, and their works are now acquired by provincial, state, and national art institutions.

Prehistoric Native Art

Depending on when first contact with Europeans occurred in each culture area, North American art may date anywhere from between 25,000 B.C. to A.D. 1500–1800. Most prehistoric art work has been recovered from the earth by archaeologists using scientific techniques of recovery and analysis, but also by farmers plowing their fields, by bulldozers at construction sites, or illegally by looters from as early as the eighteenth century. Not surprisingly, few actual artworks so far recovered can be dated much before 3000 B.C. This is because most Native art forms were made of perishable wood, hide, or vegetable and animal fibers, all of which rarely survive in moist North American soils. Nevertheless, the kind of work produced by the earliest Native Americans may be inferred in the most general way upon analogy with prehistoric and surviving archaic traditions in both the Old and New Worlds. Best known in earliest archaeological records are works in stone, bone, antler, and, with the introduction of ceramics in the New World after 3000 B.C., objects in clay such as figurines and decorated pottery.

What is known as "rock art" belongs to the oldest of Native North American artistic traditions. This includes paintings (pictographs) and engravings (petroglyphs) both of which are found throughout the continent on vertical cliffs, rock shelters, boulders, and flat bedrock surfaces. Pictographs, shapes like mounds, petroglyphs, and drawings on the wall are almost always impossible to date precisely, but they are part of an ancient and worldwide genre produced mainly by nomadic hunters and gatherers of wild foods, one that goes back at least 30,000 years to the cave art found in Spain and France. The

Petroglyph, Galisteo, New Mexico, 1991.

New Mexico petroglyph.

tradition of painting and carving on rock surfaces was no doubt brought to North America by the earliest Native peoples, perhaps some 25,000 years or so ago, although no examples that old have ever been found and dated. Rock art continues in importance, even today, as many contemporary Native artists, such as Norval Morrisseau, Jane Ash Poitras, and Jaune Quick-to-See-Smith, have been inspired by the images and meanings of this ancient pictorial genre.

Hundreds, if not thousands, of rock art sites are known. These have been grouped by specialists—archaeologists, art historians, and amateur enthusiasts—into various style areas that correspond roughly to the archaeological and ethnographic culture areas of

North America. In Canada, a major rock art region is the Canadian Shield, which extends from central Quebec to northern Saskatchewan. In this vast sub-Arctic region, hundreds of pictograph sites as well as a small number of petroglyph sites have been discovered, clustered mainly between Lake Superior and Lake Winnipeg. Petroglyph sites are more common in the Eastern Woodlands of the United States and are likely older than pictographs found in the Canadian Shield. Among the most outstanding petroglyphs in North America are those found at Nanaimo on Vancouver Island, British Columbia, at Writing-on-Stone Provincial Park in southern Alberta, at the Jeffers Site in Minnesota, and at Petroglyphs Provincial Park Near Peterborough, Ontario. At Writing-on-Stone, for example, hundreds of petroglyphs as well as some pictographs occur on sandstone bluffs along twenty miles or so of the Milk River. Most distinctive are narrative scenes describing battles and other activities in graphic detail. Images of horses, carts, and rifles at this site give evidence of the continuity of rock art well into the post-contact period.

The most vivid pictographs in all of Native North America are located in the territory of the Chumash people of southern California. Painted on rocks and in caves in the mountainous landscape, the brilliantly colored images of humans, animals, and abstract circular motifs in pulsating hues served a religious function and were most likely inspired by trance-induced visions.

Throughout North America, prehistoric art varies in genre, style, function, imagery, and meaning from one culture area to another, and these diverse traditions have also undergone changes over time, even in prehistory. Change accelerated almost everywhere after about 1000 B.C. as a result of a number of influential factors, mainly the introduction of agriculture and settled village life in the American Southwest, the Southeast, the Midwest, and the southern Great Lakes area of Canada and the United States.

There are a number of particularly noteworthy traditions of prehistoric art in North America. In the Arctic, major developments occurred in western Alaska and in the Northwest Territories of Canada and in Greenland. Between 500 B.C. and

A.D.1000, for example, an "Old Bering Sea" style of ivory carving prevailed in westernmost Alaska and the islands of the Bering Strait, a tradition that may be subdivided into the Okvik, lpiutak, and Punuk phases. These archaeological cultures are noteworthy for their small-scale and exquisitely carved bone, ivory, and antler objects depicting humans, animals, sea mammals, and birds. In subject matter and style, they have often been compared with the Ancient Stone Age art of Siberia and occasionally with the so-called Scytho-Siberian "animal style" of the Eurasian Steppes, the grassy plains areas of nomadic peoples in north central Asia.

In the Canadian high Arctic in the meantime, the prehistoric Dorset culture (800 B.C. to A.D. 1000), an early Eskimo culture is noted for its abundance of miniature carvings in bone, antler, and ivory, which differ from those in Alaska by their greater emphasis upon plastic, sculptural forms and an iconography (art objects with religious themes), wherein multiple images coexist in a single work. Around A.D. 1000, however, the more graphic, linear, and pictorial style of the Thule culture, another early Eskimo culture, overtakes the earlier archaeological styles in both Alaska and Canada. Everyday "genre" scenes of hunting activities and ceremonial dancing are introduced in Thule narrative art, a tradition that leads directly into the post-contact period, indeed well into the present-day expressions of contemporary Inuit art.

On the Northwest Coast, the prehistoric Marpole culture (500 B.C. to A.D. 500) centered on the Fraser River delta and the Gulf Islands, is known for its remarkable stone and bone carvings, mainly of ceremonial bowls, human and animal effigies, and various utensils. In style, the Marpole material as well as archaeological finds in the Prince Rupert area of northern British Columbia dated similarly to 500 B.C., anticipate historic Northwest Coast art styles of the nineteenth century, and indicate the great time-depth and persistence of Northwest Coast aesthetic expression. Contrary to the older view, Northwest Coast art is not a product of European contact but evolved *in situ* out of an ancient North Pacific maritime tradition dating back to about 2000 B.C. In fact, the art and architecture of the Northwest Coast peoples has more in common with that of ancient China and Siberia than with Europe.

In New York State and southern Ontario, the prehistoric Iroquoian between A.D. 900 and 1600 produced pottery decorated with representational and geometric motifs, as well as antler and bone combs and figurines, and stone and clay effigy pipes. The latter, produced in abundance, depicted the spiritual guardians of their owners and wereused in the ritual smoking of tobacco. The pipes were carved out of stone or modeled in clay and depicted humans as well as zoomorphic images of birds, lizards, turtles, snakes, and bear. This prehistoric Iroquoian art most likely represents the northernmost area of influence from the more complex Southeastern and Mississippian archaeological cultures (A.D. 800 to 1600), which were themselves affected by contacts with high culture influences coming from Mexico.

Carving of Hopi kachina.

The entire Eastern Woodlands area in prehistoric times is noted for its complex, large-scale ceremonial centers, in which large burial mounds and flat-topped temple mounds, open plazas, and elaborate artworks in such exotic materials as copper and mica, as well as stone, shell, and clay, evidence a more stratified society. Art fulfilled not only utilitarian, spiritual, and social functions, but also political and diplomatic ones connected with the emergence of chieftaincies and status groups and with patterns of economic exchange and long-distance trade.

Of all the prehistoric art traditions in Native North America, however, those of the American Southwest— the Mogollon, Hohokam, Anasazi, and Mimbres archaeological cultures—are most notable. Mimbres painted pottery, in particular, appeals to the present day, with its charming and humorous black and white images executed in a rather abstract, geometric style. The Anasazi tradition, however, is the most significant, because it leads directly into the living culture of contemporary Pueblo peoples, who occupy ancient villages in northern New Mexico and Arizona, alongside their Navajo neighbors.

The Anasazi tradition begins with the Basketmaker archaeological culture dating between A.D. 1 and 700, noted for its underground houses which survive into contemporary Pueblo cultures in the form of ceremonial underground kivas. The Basketmaker people also produced basketry objects with geometric patterns, characteristic of the "decorative" arts of numerous Native North Americans well into the 1700s. Artistic production among the Pueblo people centered, then as now, upon spiritual beliefs that were focused upon activities in the sacred, highly symbolic kivas, their walls decorated with many colored painted murals. Supernatural "kachina" spirits were believed to visit from time to time and were depicted in the form of painted leather masks and some 400 different Kachina (special series) dolls, the latter created for the instruction of young children. The Pueblo peoples also produced ceramic vessels in abundance, which were painted in a variety of geometric and figurative motifs in red, black, and white. Pottery making has also survived into the historic and contemporary periods, produced today mainly for sale to Euroamerican tourists and collectors.

Native Art in the Colonial Period

The colonial period of post-contact, historic Native art, during which time written accounts of Native art and cultures become available, may date in each region anytime between A.D. 1500 and 1900. In this Western perspective, history is seen to begin, for example, in the sixteenth century for the American Southwest, and the seventeenth century in the Great Lakes area. From the Native perspective, however, historical records do not have to be in the form of writing. In Native societies, "oral tradition" and pictorial records painted, embroidered or incised on hides, bark, wood, and other materials, such as the Iroquoian "wampum" belts, served as memory aids in the narration of oral history and are considered equally valid as records kept by means of alphabetical writing. Such oral and pictorial records are only now being investigated as vitally important documents for the reconstruction of Native art and cultural history.

Very few colonial period artworks remain within their Native communities. Most were "collected" (purchased, stolen, received as gifts, or appropriated) by early explorers, traders, missionaries, travelers, settlers, and various governmental agencies. Thousands upon thousands of North American Native artworks are stored in art galleries and museums throughout the world, from New York City to St. Petersburg, Russia, and mainly in Europe, Great Britain, the United States, and Canada. Some of the earliest sixteenth-, seventeenth-, and eighteenth-century works are in Spain, England, France, and Russia, which colonized North America between the sixteenth and nineteenth centuries. In some cases, however, Native art works have been returned to their original communities.

Decorative elements of Hopi architecture. Detail from photo by Owen Seumptewa.

Native art of the colonial period—also referred to as "post-contact," "historic," or "ethnographic" Native art—is better known and understood than prehistoric art. Examples have been collected, sketched, or described by explorers, traders, missionaries, artists, and scholars for over 300 years and are now available for study in museums throughout the Western world. In Canada, colonial period art is best known in the eastern sub-Arctic, occupied mainly by speakers of Algonkian languages, such as the Naskapi, Montagnais, Cree, Algonquin, and Ojibwa, and along the St. Lawrence River and lower Great Lakes area, where first French and then British settlers established themselves between the seventeenth and early nineteenth centuries. In the United States, Spanish colonists settled the Southwest as early as the sixteenth century, and between A.D. 1600 and 1800 the British and other Western Europeans in New England and elsewhere along the Atlantic seaboard arrived in such large numbers that Native cultures were severely overwhelmed by colonial influences. Along the Pacific coast from southeastern Alaska, the British Columbia coast, to northern California, colonization occurred later, mainly in the early nineteenth century. Art works collected in the late eighteenth and early nineteenth centuries on the Northwest Coast were still relatively uninfluenced upon comparison with many other areas in North America, as was also true for the Inuit of Alaska and the Canadian Arctic.

What has come to be labeled "tourist," "souvenir," or "airport" art is a category of Native art and craft production that arose to satisfy the Euro-American market for Indian souvenirs. The sale of traditional Native artworks to colonists and travelers gradually gave way, especially at the beginning of the nineteenth century, to new kinds of objects produced specifically for sale in the marketplace. These included the black argillite, a stone carving of the Haida of British Columbia, as well as miniature wooden "totem" poles and canoes. Bead-worked and embroidered moccasins, pouches, and decorative pincushions and other Victoriana were popular sale items for tourists visiting Niagara Falls throughout the nineteenth century. In the American Southwest, Pueblo women produced both traditional and new styles of pottery for sale, and the Kachina dolls, traditionally made for the education of Hopi and Zuni children, were produced en masse for sale to outsiders. Navajo blankets, too, became an important commodity in the Southwest, with dealers at trading posts acting as middlemen between the weavers and tourist trade. Today the tourist art business is booming so much so, that "Native" art for sale in curio shops is sometimes produced not by Native North Americans, but by workers in Taiwan, Japan, and Korea. Production of Native arts and crafts has also been stimulated and promoted by both American and Canadian governmental agencies as make-work projects for the economic improvement of Native communities. This has been the case especially in the Canadian Arctic, where contemporary Inuit sculpture and print-making have been sponsored by the federal government since the 1950s. While much contemporary Inuit art has achieved high standards of creativity and individual artists have become well known, the market has also been flooded with mass-produced imitations and second-rate works, which many Westerners interpret as representing Native creativity.

Contemporary art by Native North Americans varies widely in form, function, and meaning. These diverse expressions may be located between two poles, depending upon the degree to which they are rooted in either indigenous Native or Euro-American aesthetic and cultural traditions. On the one hand, for example, there is the continuing production of traditional art objects made for use within still vital or newly revitalized Native communities. The clearest illustration is that of the Canadian Northwest Coast, where the carving of totem poles and masks and the production of dancing blankets and other ceremonial regalia are once again flourishing, now that the Canadian government has repealed Bill 87. This was the law of 1884 that banned the potlatch—an important ritual feast that provided the social, mythic, and spiritual context for the dramatic ceremonial arts of many Northwest Coast peoples. Carvers and painters, such as the Haida Bill Reid (b. 1920) and the Kwakiutl artist Tony Hunt (b. 1942), produce artworks today that are grounded firmly in Northwest Coast tradition for use in ceremonial dances associated with the potlatch as well as for sale on the open market to non-Native collectors. This continuity with tradition among most contemporary Northwest Coast artists had been maintained in the late nineteenth and early twentieth centuries by a handful of such great artists as Charles

**Contemporary
Native Art**

Edensaw (1839–1920; see his biography) of the Haida Nation and Willie Seweed (1873–1967) and Mungo Martin (1881–1962) of the Kwakiutl. Once again, totem poles are being carved, painted, and raised in Native villages along the coast, the first in 1969 by Bob Davidson in the Haida village of Masset on the Queen Charlotte Islands of British Columbia. In the Hazelton area of northern British Columbia, too, the 'Ksan community project initiated a program for the revival of traditional arts and ceremonialism among the Tsimshian, once considered the finest artists on the Northwest Coast in the years before the 1884 ban of potlatches. Tsimshian artists, for example, are known to have been commissioned to decorate the houses of even Alaskan Tlingit chiefs living hundreds of miles to the north.

Artwork produced by Northwest Coast artists for sale to non-Natives, however, may often include such traditional ceremonial items as masks, rattles, boxes, and bowls, but more popular are works that cater to Euroamerican aesthetic preferences and which are adapted to Western techniques, materials, and functions. Bill Reid, for example, was at first best known for his silver and gold jewelry, bracelets, rings, and brooches, which were engraved with Haida mythological images such as Bear, Killer Whale, Raven, and Frog. He later became more widely known for his argillite and wood carving and for his prints, the former often adapting traditional Haida imagery to contemporary needs, as in the case of carved Western-style doors and dividing screens in architectural settings. Most recently he has become internationally recognized for his monumental public sculpture, including "Raven Discovering Mankind in a Clamshell" (1983) carved in wood for the University of British Columbia's Museum of Anthropology; a large bronze "Killer Whale" (1984) for the Vancouver Aquarium in Stanley Park; and his most important commission, "The Spirit of Haida-Gwaii" (1991), a blackened bronze, mythic canoe, for the new Canadian Embassy in Washington, D.C. This monumental sculpture measures some 6 meters long by 4.3 meters high and depicts Reid's myth-animals on a canoe voyage. Its black patina suggests argillite, the traditional Haida stone found and mined on the Queen Charlotte Islands. Haida carvers favored argillite throughout the nineteenth century to illustrate the myths and family traditions so important to Haida social and cultural life.

Contemporary artwork produced by Northwest Coast artists is tied more strongly to traditional coastal style and iconography than many other contemporary Native expressions. While Northwest Coast printmakers and easel painters may deviate radically from traditional imagery, forms, and compositions, their works are nevertheless composed with an established range of pictorial elements and motifs traceable to the so-called "classic style" of Northwest Coast art, that is, to that of the Tlingit, Haida, and Tsimshian printers of the nineteenth century.

Almost equally tied to tradition is the contemporary art of the Inuit of the Canadian Arctic and Alaska, who produce today sculpture, prints, drawings, and wall-hangings, all of which have had great success in the marketplace. Carving in contemporary style began first between 1949 and 1953, when, under the inspiration of the Canadian artist James A. Houston and with the encouragement and promotion of the Canadian Handicrafts Guild, the Hudson's Bay Company, and the Canadian government, the Inuit produced soapstone, ivory, and bone carvings for sale in Canada and abroad. Often under the influence of specific guidelines as to subject matter, scale, and style from Houston and other interested parties and agencies, the Inuit produced carvings that departed in certain important respects from prehistoric and early historic sculpture. In particular, contemporary sculptures were provided with flat bases, giving them a Western single-gaze, more static perspective than was traditional.

In the late 1950s, too, Houston introduced the Inuit to the Western and Japanese techniques of drawing on paper and of various methods of printmaking. In the 1960s and 1970s, Inuit prints—stonecuts, silkscreens, engravings, and etchings—became enormously popular among collectors, eventually outstripping sculpture by the 1980s. Subject matter for both sculpture and prints in contemporary Inuit art is derived for the most part from the traditional hunting, ceremonial, and nomadic life-style of the Inuit and from myths, legends, and shamanic beliefs and practices of traditional Inuit culture. More recently, however, the Inuit have begun to depict elements of living in the twentieth century, and their prints may include airplanes, snowmobiles, Christian iconography, and various Westernized social activities.

In the 1970s and 1980s, interest in the creativity of individual artists overtook interest in the group work of cooperatives. This led to new interest in the original drawings previously stored away and to a demand for information on the art and life of such noted artists as Ashoona Pitseolak (1907–83), Ashevak Kenojuak (b. 1927), Karoo Ashevak (1940–74), Jessie Oonark (1906–85), and Ruth Annaqtuusi Tulurialik (b. 1934).

In spite of all these changes in subject matter, techniques, materials, and the fact that art is made now for sale to foreigners, contemporary Inuit art maintains fundamental continuities with the past in theme and principles of compositional order. These are continuities that extend as far back in time as that of the Old Bering Sea, Dorset, and Thule prehistoric arts and have to do with how the Inuit perceive and interpret the world around them in terms of space and time, being and becoming. Such socio-cultural values have survived so long because the Inuit themselves have survived and adapted to the realities of the modern world. This remains true for many other Native North American traditions as well.

The aesthetic cultures of the American Southwest have been equally persistent, in spite of massive Western cultural influences. Especially noteworthy are the Navajo, Hopi, San Ildefonso, and Zuni Pueblo peoples, who continue to produce handwoven textiles, painted pottery, basketry, and silver jewelry for sale to collectors which maintain both historic and prehistoric traditions dating back some 2,000 years. The fame of potters, innovating new techniques and styles with a traditionalist base, such as Maria Martinez (d. 1980) of San Ildefonso, inspires younger Pueblo potters. These include both men and women potters, such as Juan Tafoya of San Ildefonso and Elizabeth Naranjo of Santa Clara.

The most magnificent expressions of cultural and aesthetic continuity in the Southwest today, however, are the handwoven blankets still being produced on the Navajo Reservation. More recent "pictorial" patterns have appeared, but the older geometric patterns persist and outshine them in beauty, with their innumerable variety of patterns worked painstakingly, still mainly by women, on the traditional vertical loom.

In the Southwest, one of the earliest "schools" of Euro-American-influenced painting emerged and persisted between 1910 and 1960. The so-called Southwest Style was associated with the influence of Dorothy Dunn of Santa Fe, another non-Native patron who played a role in the Southwest akin to that of James Houston in Canada. In these works, historic Southwestern ceremonial dances, hunting scenes, and various domestic activities are depicted in a flat, two-dimensional decorative style that favored a pale color scheme.

On the Plains, a similar stylistic mode of expression is evident in painting encouraged and promoted in the 1940s by the Philbrook Art Center in Tulsa, Oklahoma. Here, too, a non-Indian artist and patron was involved, Oscar Jacobson. Paintings embodied a romanticized nostalgia for past cultural ways, and favorite subjects were buffalo hunts and brilliantly colored and costumed warriors engaged in ceremonial dancing. Noted Southwest and Plains artists still working in this manner include Cheyenne artist Archie Blackowl (b. 1911), Comanche Rance Hood (b. 1941), Choctaw Jerry Ingram (b. 1941), and Navajo Harrison Begay (b. 1917), Gilbert Atencio of San Ildefonso (b. 1930), and Millard Dawa Lomakema (b. 1941). This flat and decorative style of painting extended as far north as the Canadian Prairies, where Gerald Tailfeathers (b. 1925), also occasionally printed in the Oklahoma style.

Tradition informs the work also of Ojibway painter Norval Morrisseau (b. 1932), who began painting in the 1960s and was the inspiration in the 1970s for an entire "school" of younger artists, now known as the Woodland School or the Legend Painters. Working in a style and with related systems of images, these include, for example, Carl Ray (1943–78), Roy Thomas (b. 1949), Josh Kakegamic (b. 1952), Saul Williams (b. 1954), and Blake Debassige (b. 1956). Linked with this

Indian artist Norval Morrisseau at work.

group is Odawa (Ottawa) painter Daphnie Odjig (b. 1925), whose style developed independently but along lines similar to that of Morrisseau.

Morrisseau's work can be positioned midway along the continuum between Native and Euro-American aesthetic traditions in both form and subject matter. His brilliantly colored and often large canvases are executed in synthetic acrylic paints, a characteristically Euro-American technique of the 1960s. Both subject matter and style are inspired to a large extent by traditional Algonkian pictography as found in the birch bark pictorial manuscripts used in the Chippewa Grand Medicine Society, a group of religious leaders and healers, and in the prehistoric rock art of Northwestern Ontario. But Morrisseau's sources also include the stained glass windows of his childhood Catholic church, with their glowing colored images outlined by dark lead. Native Ojibway legends learned at the knee of his maternal grandfather, a shaman, combine with Christian symbols and themes, and in the 1970s, with ideas taken from the Eckankar religion, one which appealed to his mystic vision of the world (see Morrisseau's biography).

Most akin to Euro-American tradition and artistic practices are the works of a wide network of contemporary artists of Native background who are no longer trained in traditional techniques nor are self-taught, as was Morrisseau, but studied in the leading art schools of Western society. The best-known Native artists in the United States are as follows:

T. C. Cannon (1946–78), Caddo/Kiowa
Harry Fonseca (b. 1946), Maidu
Richard Glazer Danay (b. 1942), Mohawk
R. C. Gorman (b. 1932), Navajo
Oscar Howe (1915–84), Sioux
Peter Jemison (b. 1945), Seneca
Frank LaPena (b. 1937), Wintu-Nomtipom
George Longfish (b. 1940), Seneca-Tuscarora
George Morrison (b. 1919), Ojibwa
Jaune Quick-to-See-Smith (b. 1940), Cree-Shoshoni
Fritz Scholder (b. 1937)

Best-known Native artists in Canada are the following:

Carl Beam (b. 1942)
Bob Boyer (b. 1948)
Robert Houle (b. 1947)
Alex Janvier (b. 1935)
Laurence Paul (b. 1957)
Edward Poitras (b. 1953)
Jane Ash Poitras (b. 1951)
Métis Joane Cardinal-Schubert (b. 1942)
Pierce Sioui (b. 1950)

These are all individualists who perceive themselves as artists first and foremost, for whom their Native ancestry is a constituent and vital aspect of their identity as persons. At the same time,

Watercolor of Southwestern Indian children by Earl Sisto for 1992 UCLA Indian Child Welfare Conference.

they do not negate, but take pride in that identity and see their role as artists in a traditional way. That is, their focus is upon making a personal statement through their art about any or all of the social, political, racial, and environmental issues concerning both Native and world society at large. They are informed at all times in this mission, by the spiritual and cultural values of their respective Native traditions.

The work of Ojibway artist Carl Beam, for example, reveals that his concerns are the loss of spiritual values in society at large; the destruction of the natural environment and animal life through pollution, industrialization and wanton disregard; the inhumanity of humans to other humans through assassination, betrayal, and genocide; the threat of over-reliance upon technology and science and their effects upon the dehumanization of mankind; nostalgia for the loss of a more humane and spiritual past; the place of the self in history and the passage of time. His works juxtapose images derived from photographs and newspapers with painted representations that include writing and numbers, as well as three-dimensional objects such as feathers and even stuffed birds. His most notable recent work consists of a three-year cycle of paintings, prints, sculpture, and installations entitled "The Columbus Project," completed in 1992.

Joan Vastokas
Trent University

♦ ♦ ♦ ♦ ♦ ♦ ♦ ♦ ♦ ♦ ♦ ♦ TRADITIONAL AND CONTEMPORARY CEREMONIES, RITUALS, FESTIVALS, MUSIC, AND DANCE

Through music, dance, ceremony, rituals, and festivals, Indian peoples of North America distinguish themselves not only from other North Americans, but also from each other. Despite these differences, scholars have tried to find cultural or musical groupings of these events for purposes of study. Because music and religion are abstract and invisible forms, they are not as easy to classify and study as other, visible components of culture such as art work, textiles, ceremonial dress, and dance. Even ceremonies that have been described for centuries by European and Euro-American observers may have secret and invisible meanings and may not fit into neat categories when interpreted by the Native performers. The reader will find, when visiting specific events, that the differences are what enliven the activities, not the similarities. For example, Iroquois and Cherokee music and dance share many resemblances, such as counterclockwise motion, small steps, and call-and-response singing, but they do not sound or look alike when heard indoors (in the longhouse of the Iroquois) as opposed to outdoors (at the open-air ceremonial grounds of the Cherokee). Even in using the same tunes, the two groups of singers produce different sound qualities and create different song forms. The same kinds of conclusions can be drawn from dozens of other examples in North America.

Indian music and dance occur everywhere in North America— on large U.S. reservations, like the Navajo; on Canadian reserves; on small California rancherias, like Morongo; in big cities, like Los Angeles; and in rural settings, like the mountains of North Carolina; at specific sacred places, like Canyon de Chelly, Arizona; and at public gatherings, such as fairs and graduation ceremonies. While some Indian music exists without dance, no Indian dance exists without music. The music enables the dance to occur, and the dance makes the music visible. Even the earliest accounts of Indian music and dance from explorers and settlers mention the parallel and interdependent natures of these two art forms. Ordinarily, in ceremonies, music, and dance, women perform lesser roles. In social occasions for music and dance, women are increasingly taking larger roles.

Before the European colonization of America, there is archaeological evidence of music, dance, and ceremony through surviving musical instruments, ceremonial regalia, ritual paraphernalia, and depictions of music and dance in pottery, pictographs, and petroglyphs. After European contact, explorers and settlers give detailed and sometimes sensationalized descriptions of many events, including their ideas of the sounds, colors, and movements.

In Marc Lescarbot's *The History of New France* (1617), a compilation of various explorers' accounts of the Northeast, there is a first attempt to notate Native music. Using a seventeenth-century method, Lescarbot shows tunes that use three- or four-tone scales, have the range of a fourth, and feature a soloist with chorus response. The text includes both translatable words and non-translatable vocables. From earliest times some Indians, such as the Ojibway or Chippewa, have used their own mnemonic writing systems (picture symbols) to record their songs on birch bark or other materials.

Even though some music and dance has always been performed solely for entertainment, religion, life-ways, and world view affects most of the performances. Many Indian ceremonies are practiced to renew the world or keep it in balance. Others, such as those of the Tewa Pueblo Indians, maintain relationships with deities, supernaturals, each other, and strangers through music, dance, and ceremony. These activities range from extremely private and sacred gatherings, restricted to initiated or birth clans, to some that are extremely public and joking in nature and that may be accompanied by carnivals and concession stands. Strangers, and sometimes even other Indian people, are barred from private events, while they are welcomed at the public ones.

After Europeans and later American, Mexican, and Canadian colonists converted many Indians to Christianity (often by coercion), they removed them from their homelands by waging warfare, making treaties, and using other economic and political forces.

After some groups of Indians disappeared altogether, other smaller groups, often from necessity, intermarried with neighboring peoples, both Indian and non-Indian, or were adopted by larger tribes. Then the governmental agencies grouped these peoples together arbitrarily, or because of language, cultural similarities, or geographical proximity. Often territorial enemies found themselves living side by side.

Frequently, missionaries were hired to perform what should have been the governmental jobs of supervising the education (including extermination of Native practices, religions, and languages), health, welfare, and Christian life of these Native Americans. After that, many singers, dancers, and traditional religious practitioners could not perform their arts and life-ways in the appropriate places and at the accustomed times, and some of this heritage was lost forever.

Repeatedly, Indian religious practices and ceremonies were forbidden by the churches and colonial governments. After the 1680–96 Pueblo Indian Revolt in New Mexico and Arizona, which forced the Spanish conquerors and missionaries south to El Paso, the Indians achieved some compromises concerning taxation, governance, and some alleviation of religious persecution. Later these Native Americans practiced their religions and dances, to some extent, alongside Catholic rituals. While the U.S. government's ban on Indian religions in the late nineteenth century targeted especially the Sun Dance and Ghost Dance, it also affected all other religions. After prohibiting Northwest Coast Indian potlatches (huge Native giveaway celebrations, such as those held by the Kwakiutl), the Canadian government seized many beautiful sacred and ceremonial objects and much dance regalia, making performances difficult, if not impossible, without these artifacts.

In the 1990s, many Indians living on U.S. reservations, on Canadian reserves, and in rural areas carry on the indigenous religions and music that are necessary to Indian life. As long-established activities, they are regionally or tribally specific, and the leaders conduct the events in Native languages following age-old calendars and belief systems. These activities include dances such as the Lakota Sun Dance (a yearly spiritual renewal for the community that sponsors it) and "sings" (gatherings for performing and sharing songs) like those held by the Iroquois singing societies; fiestas (Malki Museum Fiesta, Cahuilla); healing ceremonies (Navajo Enemy Way or "Squaw Dance"); seasonal celebrations (Yuchi Green Corn ceremony); hunting dances (Pueblo game dances); agricultural celebrations (Hopi Bean Dance); Native games (Creek ballgame and dance); courting (Indian flute playing); influencing nature or one's fellows (spiritual songs and prayers); lullabies; and giveaways (Native customs for redistributing wealth). A few other examples of areas of retention include, but are not limited to, the following: southern California (Cahuilla Bird Dance, recounting the creation); Great Basin (Ute Bear Dance, welcoming spring); northwest Alaskan Eskimo (Wolf Dance, honoring the hunter); Northwest Coast (Kwakiutl potlatch, strengthening community ties); Eastern Woodlands (Iroquois Thanksgiving, ending the harvest season); Southeast (Cherokee Stomp Dance, honoring the sacred fire); Plains (Blackfeet Medicine Lodge ceremony, similar to the Sun Dance); Pueblo (San Juan Turtle Dance, celebrating the winter solstice); southern Athapascan (Navajo Kinaalda', recognizing girls' puberty).

Some Indian people are specialists in language, religion, ceremony, and customs. They are necessary members of their tribes and nations and work hard at sharing their knowledge so that their groups can maintain these crucial practices. If young people are willing to learn the oral traditions from the elders and stay with their own people, some of this cultural richness, indigenous to America, will certainly be retained in the future.

Preservation and Revival

Knowledge of Indian life has always been passed from generation to generation through oral tradition. Starting in the nineteenth century, non-Indian scholars (and a few Indian scholars) of history, folklore, anthropology, linguistics, and music began trying to preserve Indian culture, especially knowledge of ceremonies, music, dance, stories, languages, and customs. They used written, drawn, photographic, and electronic means to achieve their aims. Later in the twentieth century, more Indian people embraced these same media to achieve their own cultural documentation.

Some younger Indian leaders have fervently begun recording traditional music and dance and their instructions for performance. They have also recorded stories, sacred narratives, oral histories, and ritual sayings. These efforts culminate in a new trend by Indian people themselves to gather recordings from archives, make recordings of elders, and combine the two to recreate or preserve some partially remembered dance or ceremony. The Federal Cylinder Project at the U.S. Library of Congress and the California Indian Project at the Lowie Museum, Berkeley, have returned many old recordings to these tribal groups.

Music and Musical Instruments

In Indian music, whether sacred or secular, the voice is the most important instrument. As a result, melody and vocal style become paramount, and texture (layering of parts to create a thick sound) takes the place of harmony in most instances. Performing as a rule in native languages or vocables (non-translatable syllables), the singers utilize solos, responsorial songs (leader and chorus taking turns), unison chorus songs, and multipart songs. Most are accompanied by some sort of rattle or drum, or both rattle and drum.

Excerpt from Creek Gar Dance with leader-chorus responses and alternation of words and vocables.

Members of some Great Lakes and Plains tribes historically played small, shallow drums in unison, keeping time together to accompany their own singing. At the end of the nineteenth century,

after many of these groups adopted the large drum, singers began sitting or standing around a single drum, playing together. In the pueblos of the Southwest, several men play large cylindrical or kettle-shaped drums together, each holding his own instrument.

The water drum is unique to North America and is played by only one person at a time. It is made from a small container of wood, pottery, or metal, partially filled with water for tuning, covered with a dampened, soft hide stretched tight, and beaten with a hard stick. It is found among the Eastern Indians (e.g., Iroquois, Cherokee, Creek, and others), the Apache and Navajo, and members of the Native American Church (a Native peyote religion, widespread in North America).

Adding to the texture of the music are various rattles and scrapers. Ordinarily, singers accompany themselves with vessel rattles (globes, cylinders, or irregularly shaped containers enclosing pebbles, fruit seeds, or other noisemakers, fixed with a handle). These may be played by lead or backup singers, dancers, or even by people who are simultaneously dancing and singing. The rattles can be made of carved wood, baskets, gourds, bark, rawhide, moose feet, clay, metal shakers, turtle shells, cow horns, copper, coconut shells, buffalo tails, or other materials.

Other rattles are strung and fastened to sticks, hoops, hides, or textiles and held or attached to the bodies or clothing of dancers. These are made from bird beaks, cocoons, deer hooves, tin cans, turtle shells, petrified wood, sea shells, or metal cones. A few are hollow and may contain pebbles or seeds and then be strung— for example, cocoons, turtle shells, or tin cans. Other instruments such as notched-stick rasps or scrapers, wooden box drums, bullroarers, flutes, whistles, musical bows, fiddles, split-stick clappers, and pairs of clapping sticks are less common.

Simple, short songs with many repetitions and song cycles (several different songs sung in sequence) are the most common musical forms among Native Americans. Vocal style, scales, rhythms, and meters vary according to geographic area, tribe, ceremony, and sometimes even by neighborhood or individual family. Even without knowing a particular song, a knowledgeable listener can usually tell the tribal or regional origin of a song from the vocal style, instrumentation, rhythm, and direction of the melody. Some musical characteristics are true for many but not all tribes: songs are in duple (2/4, 4/4, etc.) meter; scales (number of non-duplicated pitches in an octave) are pentatonic (various 5-tone scales); melodies start high and descend throughout the songs, ending on the lowest or next to lowest pitch (musical tone defined by its frequency, such as A440); songs are vocal with rattle, drum, or other percussive accompaniment.

The most common and easily recognizable form is the Plains Indian powwow, or intertribal song. It features a lead singer (also the lead drummer among several seated around the big drum) who usually starts the song with one phrase, as high as he can (using a letter for each phrase; for simplicity, the first phrase is

Plains rawhide drum, played by several men simultaneously.

A). His chorus members (who are both singing and drumming) then answer him, repeating that phrase (*A´* same as *A* but slightly modified), and all sing the melody together, with the pitch getting lower and lower throughout the middle (*B*, next phrase) and last (*C*, last phrase) sections, resting on the lowest or next to lowest pitch. This last or next to last note is often more than an octave (the distance between two notes whose frequency ratio is 2/1; e.g., A440 and A880) and a half lower than the starting pitch. All singers then repeat the middle (*B´*, slightly modified) and last (*C´*, slightly modified) sections before repeating the whole. This can be shown as *AA´BCB´C´ AA´BCB´C´*, etc. Often the *B´C´* section contains words in an Indian language and a change in the drum pattern. Sometimes there is a long pause at the end of the entire rendition, and the singers repeat the *B´C* section as a "tail," or *coda*, and finish off the dance. The male dancers wear loud ankle bells, and some blow whistles to show their delight with the singers and to ask for another repetition. The "pulsation," or intentional quivering of the voices, enhances the sound and helps to define the style.

Much of the music that is best known by the public belongs to nonprivate ceremonies and social occasions. However, private songs for medicine and curing, prayer, initiation, hunting, trying to control nature, putting children to sleep, telling stories, performing magic, playing games, and courtship are equally important. Many musical, dance-related, and cultural characteristics—such as the words,

Peter Garcia, drummer, at San Juan Pueblo Yellow Corn Dance.

the number of repetitions, the instrumentation, ceremonial dress, body and face paint, and the way the singers and dancers work together—arise from world view, growing out of long-lasting religious and social customs. Music, dance, religion, and ceremonial life are wholly integrated, and one can hardly exist without the other. For example, if the words to a song mention east, north, west, and south in that order, as they do in some Cherokee songs, the dancers probably start in the east and move counterclockwise throughout the dance. If colors also are mentioned by the Cherokee, they would probably be ordered as red (east), blue (north), black (west), and white (south). Other tribes have different schemes for ordering their worlds and ceremonies. There is no one "Indian Way."

Although the origins of many songs lie in the past, Indian composers and singers continue to play the major roles in creating and passing on the music through oral tradition. Changes do occur, even though many people still cherish the older songs and forms. Some modern instrument makers now use metal bells, tin cans, metal salt shakers, rubber, and plastic materials for musical instruments and dance outfits. Various song makers add English words to Rabbit Dance (a couples, social dance), Forty-nine (a group social dance), and Peyote songs (songs to accompany religious practices of the Native American Church). A few American popular melodies have inspired Indian composers, and these words or melodies have found their place in contemporary Indian songs. New songs are composed every year and spread across the nation during the powwow season (the period of time from Memorial Day to Labor Day in the United States, when most powwows are held).

Dance

Dance, along with music, is still a major pursuit for many Indian groups still practicing the old religions important to their ways of life. Due to their spiritual and supernatural origins, and because these dances are often tied to seasonal or life-cycle events, they are regionally or tribally specific, the singers usually perform in native languages, and the ceremonies themselves unfold according to local customs. Rather than expressing individual prowess, dancers usually adhere to established patterns and movements.

As with music, there are few solo dances but many group events. Some dances have a leader and chorus; some are unison groups acting together; others are groups with featured soloists; a few offer individual dancers the freedom to "show off." Occasionally, dancers can play a variety of roles in multipart dances. While many dances have vocal and drum accompaniment, often the dancers themselves, activating the rattles and bells that adorn their ceremonial dress, set their own beat.

Cloud Dance, San Juan Pueblo. Men are playing gourd rattles.

Indian dancers often use restrained movements, without large motions or leaps. Generally the dancers stay close to the earth, both for religious and practical reasons. Because they must conserve their strength to dance all day or all night to satisfy a particular custom, because of limited space, or because of a large

number of participants, they typically take small steps. The torso and head have the most freedom of movement, with little twisting. The feet and legs ordinarily act as a unit when extended, as do the hands and arms. Small movements of the forearms and wrists are limited to times when the dancer shakes an implement, such as a rattle, stick, or branch. Some dances require crouching or bent-over postures; the dancer usually stays in that position for a the length of a musical phrase or section. At times, specific dancers are called on to mimic animals (such as in the Creek Buffalo Dance), or birds (as in the Taos Eagle Dance), or the work of hunting, fishing, planting, harvesting, preparing food, other occupational duties, or warfare.

Dancers often conceive their space in terms of circles, moving either clockwise or counterclockwise, as defined by their cosmology. Other possibilities include lines of people dancing in place, moving forward or backward in unison, or moving into and out of larger dance areas in a procession. As an example, many Pueblo dances require the dancers to dance, moving forward into the plaza, dance in lines (mostly in place with some turns to right, left, or behind), and then move together to the next dance plaza in what becomes a circling of the village. Often four repetitions of the dances take place in order to cover all four directions in the proper order.

In northern Alaska and Canada, the lines and circles frequently become almost stationary or wind around to use all of the small interior spaces. For the most part, Plains and urban Indian dances, such as powwows,

Northern Plains Traditional dancer at Red Earth, Oklahoma City, Oklahoma.

follow clockwise directions. Many Eastern and formerly Eastern tribes dance counterclockwise. A few tribes dance in either or both directions at different seasons or for different ceremonies. Many Navajo social dances allow the dancers to go clockwise during one song and counterclockwise during the next one.

Although some individual expression is allowed in most North American Plains dances, most Pueblo dances require unison action and strict rules of motion, broken up from time to time by the relatively free movements of the ritual clowns (specially initiated members of the Pueblo). One of the most individualistic dances, the Hoop Dance, has been adopted as an exhibition dance by many tribes. It showcases an individual who manipulates at least a dozen large hoops over and around his torso, legs, and arms to create a variety of geometric shapes. Usually, Indian dances mirror each group's norms and types of community interaction: for example, leader and followers, unison action, cooperation of individuals assuming differing roles, and the ideal of several generations working together.

Games

Almost every game played by North American Indians has music and sometimes dance associated with it. The most popular games are handgames or stickgames. As social and sometimes religious activities, these guessing games are found almost everywhere in North America. Ordinarily, the players sing while hiding an object or the mark on a stick. Their opponents guess the location of the hidden object or mark, and then it is their turn to sing and hide. Each team scores points for fooling its competitors, and the first team to reach a specified point total wins the stakes. Each team has lucky songs and experienced guessers, and the game cannot exist without the music.

Ordinarily, the melodies are simple and easy to sing, with short, repeated phrases, so that the players can concentrate on winning the game. Among the Northwest Coast and northern California tribes (such as the Tolowa), stickgame songs have complicated rhythms and often contain multipart singing. In the Great Basin (Nevada, California east of the Sierras, Utah, Idaho, and parts of

Colorado and Wyoming) and Central California—for example, among the Washoe and Pomo—men and women play entirely separate games and have gender-specific songs. Instrumental accompaniment is supplied by drums, sticks, rattles, or clapping sticks.

Eskimos (referring here to the many Arctic peoples called Yupik, Inupiat, Inuit, etc.) have other musical games—the women's throat games (vocal contests between two women at a time) of Baffin Island; the string figure games of northwest Alaska (often accompanied by songs or stories); and the insult-singing contests (to settle differences of opinion) of the Netsilik. The Iroquois in the northeast United States and Canada have a snow snake game played in specially constructed tracks, something like bobsled runs. In the southeastern U.S., the Cherokee, Creek, Choctaw,

Cheyenne children playing hand games at Red Earth, Oklahoma City, Oklahoma.

and Seminole have ballgame songs and dances preceding and following the highly ceremonial stickball game (played with pairs of laced sticks and a small ball, remotely similar to lacrosse). Although some of these songs are similar in style to other southeastern Indian dance music, others resemble curing or hunting songs. Women vocalists are an integral part of the ceremony in these southeastern ballgame songs, singing encouraging words for their own teams and insults against the opposing teams. In the twentieth century these games are sometimes played only for "show" and frequently leave out many of the songs, dances, and ceremonial aspects.

Arctic and Sub-Arctic

Midwinter gatherings in their large community houses are the most important occasions for music and dance among the Eskimo in Alaska and Canada. At those celebrations, several men gather and sing together in unison while each singer also plays a large frame drum. These round, shallow drums are constructed from the bladders of large sea animals (or sometimes plastic), stretched over driftwood hoops with attached handles. They are played sometimes from above and other times from underneath with long slender sticks hitting either the rim or the drum head. Mostly the male and female dancers act out hunting, fishing, and other daily activities. They often wear gloves or hold decorated dance fans woven from grass and animal hair.

Northern Athapascan and northern Algonkian-speaking tribes have many songs and dances devoted to their traditional occupations of fishing and hunting. For social occasions many of these peoples of the sub-Arctic region play fiddle-guitar music based on European models.

Northwest Coast and Northern California

Indian music and dance are often part of compelling ritual dramas and ceremonies in the Northwest Coast area of the United States and Canada. These rituals (such as the Kwakiutl potlatch), with their elaborately painted screens, highly decorated ceremonial dress, and multipart singing (accompanied by rattles, drums, and whistles), rival European opera in conception and execution. Often they are held to install a totem pole, a new chief, or to validate other honors and titles of a family or clan. When many

Northwest Coast Indians became members of the Russian Ortho-dox church, they then translated appropriate hymns into their native languages. They also adopted some of the Russian harmo-nies and incorporated them into a few Native songs, like the Tlingit Death Chant.

In Washington State, an Indian Shaker movement began near the turn of the century. It was not similar to, nor was it affiliated with, the New England Shaker church. Its members concentrated on ritual healing, accompanying the ceremonies with singing and the ringing of bells. The new religion became popular locally and also spread to regions adjacent to Washington and to northwest California.

Until the Gold Rush in the late 1840s, Indians of northwest Cali-fornia saw few non-Indians. Much of their ceremonial life cen-ters around world renewal and healing ceremonies like the Hupa White Deerskin Dance and the Yurok Brush Dance. Their ensemble music and dance are characterized by a sobbing, pulsating vocal quality, layers of vocal *ostinatos* (short rhythmic parts repeated over and over) underlying the soloist, and relative lack of instru-ments. The female dancers move up and down, mostly in place, activating pieces of abalone shell sewn to their dresses to serve as a high, rattling instrumental accompaniment. Meanwhile the men execute varying postures and more vigorous steps. Personal songs exist—such as those for hunting and attracting a lover-—and are used primarily to affect nature and one's daily affairs. Organized, ceremonial, team gambling is a popular venue for music. This primarily male activity used to require religious fasting and pray-ing to ensure luck for the game. The singers use rectangular frame drums and deer-hoof rattles strung on a stick.

Central and Southern California

In central and southern California, the vocal style is somewhat relaxed, rattles of various types serve as primary instruments, and drums are practically nonexistent. Among the Kashaya Pomo of central California, the dreamer-shamans (frequently women) and their helpers (both men and women) sing, dance, and play double whistles and splitstick clappers to accompany healing rituals and ceremonial and social dances.

In southern California, the most common contexts for music and dance are fiestas and funerals. Bird songs commemorating the creation of the world comprise the main repertoire. Here one also finds little influence from outsiders except for the presence of a few Spanish loan words in Diegueño bird songs from the area near the Mexican border.

Southwest In the Southwest, Spanish accounts, starting in 1540, and kiva murals from the fourteenth to sixteenth centuries show that masks, decorative textiles, and body painting have always been important arts to Pueblo Indian culture. Prehistoric evidence shows the hump-backed flutist Kokopelli portrayed on many petroglyphs and pieces of ancient pottery throughout the area. Archaeologists have also found prehistoric pottery depicting dance and have unearthed copper bells worn by dancers.

The large Pueblo rawhide, wooden drums, hand-held gourd rattles, and the turtle shell, deer hoof, and marine-shell strung rattles, worn by the dancers, are the most important instruments. The singers rehearse together to create a full, unison, choral sound. Many of the dances involve men singing and dancing simultaneously in lines or moving in a procession. Women participate in the winter, as featured dancers in front of the men, and in the summer, in couples dances and large, group dances.

Most Pueblo ceremonies are seasonal, are organized, directed, and regulated by clans and moieties, and feature prescribed roles for ceremonial leaders, singers, dancers, and supporters. Many are called feast days because the members of the Pueblos expect their friends and relatives to visit and accept their hospitality. While some ceremonies are completely closed, others are open to outsiders if they respect the religious aspects of the events, behave with decorum, and do not take pictures or make recordings without permission. Some of the more famous ceremonies are the Zuni Shalako (a masked winter dance), Hopi Snake Dance (a biennial summer dance), San Ildefonso Corn Dance (a harvest dance), and the San Juan Deer Dance (a winter game-hunting dance).

Among the Apache and Navajo (southern Athapascan), curing rituals and girls' puberty ceremonies are the best-known contexts for music and dance. The White Mountain Apache Sunrise Dance (for a girl who is becoming a woman) and the Navajo Enemy Way (sometimes called the Squaw Dance) exemplify these ideals. Each reinforces group beliefs and brings a person into the community or back into the community from outside. Apache and Navajo song style are similar: tense, nasal voices; rhythmic pulsation; clear articulation of words in alternating sections with vocables. Both Apache Crown Dancers and Navajo Yeibichei (Night Chant) dancers wear masks and sing partially in falsetto or in voices imitating the supernaturals.

The hand-held rattle, the voice, and the water drum (an instrument unique to North America) are the most important elements for music-making. The bullroarer (a thin wooden plaque attached to a string and swung in a circle), which survives in popular American culture as a child's toy, is still used today for ritual and ceremonial events in the Southwest. The Navajo use it in the Yeibichei and the Apache in the Mountain Spirit or Crown Dance (a masked dance in which humans impersonate deities of the mountains).

In the desert area and urban sprawl of southern Arizona (Tucson and Phoenix) and in northern Mexico, the Pima and Papago (O'Odham) and the Yaqui continue to carry out traditional ceremonies alongside innovative and hybrid ceremonial forms. An older ceremony, the O'Odham Chelkona, serves as entertainment and is often performed as a contest dance for local powwows, rodeos, and other events. It includes gift-giving, a hopping or skipping dance, feasting, speeches, and games. The Yaqui Deer Dance (a traditional, sacred ceremony) and the Yaqui Pascola (an Easter, Catholic Indian ceremony) exist side by side, reinforcing both the tenacity and the adaptability of these people.

Plains

The Plains area, stretching from Canada to Texas, is home to many tribes who lived there originally and to some who were moved there in the nineteenth century by their respective governments. As a result of this forced commingling of peoples, some ceremonies and dances spread across tribal boundaries, and new contexts were created for music and dance, most notably the popular, intertribal powwow. Although predecessors of both the Ghost Dance and Sun Dance existed in the mid-nineteenth century, these ceremonies became more widespread and popular at the end of the century. Even in the 1990s, one can find singers and dancers performing these ancient songs and ceremonies.

Before the widespread use of the horse, and before the U.S. Civil War, the smaller, more isolated bands of Plains Indians did not have the large drums that are associated with twentieth-century Indians. For sacred ceremonies, such as opening sacred bundles, they used small, hand-held frame drums, each beaten by a singer. If several men were singing together, each held a drum and played it in unison. The pulsating vocal style (a variation both in pitch and loudness), often loud and somewhat individualistic, is a hallmark of the Plains singer. In addition to drums, rawhide rattles accompanied singing.

The flutes were reserved primarily for love songs. The courting flute deserves special mention as a male instrument. Its music echoes and embellishes well-known melodies, often drawn from love songs, and its influence draws a player's sweetheart to him.

Eastern   Music of the Eastern Woodlands, the Northeast and Southeast, share many common traits. Many of the dances and songs are responsorial, incorporate shouts and animal cries, are performed by both genders, and circumscribe a counterclockwise dance area. Most feature hand-held rattles and water drums along with strung rattles worn on the dancers' legs. Vocally, the singing tends to be nasal and somewhat high-pitched. Among the Iroquois of the Northeast, many of the ceremonies occur in the longhouses, particularly in midwinter. In the Southeast most occur outdoors with the summer first-fruits or green corn ceremony as the centerpiece.

Innovations   Although pre-Columbian evidence is difficult to find for stringed instruments, the Apache fiddle (made from a mescal stalk) and musical bows, found in various cultures, are examples of early string instruments. Taking into account the rapid adoption and adaptation of stringed instruments such as guitars, fiddles, and the like, especially in the Mexican and French borderlands, either a few stringed instruments existed in the past, or the novelty was too appealing to resist. In Eskimo, northern Athapascan, Plains, Pueblo, Yaqui, Papago, Métis, Ojibway, Pima, Choctaw, and Cherokee cultures of the twentieth century, fiddle-guitar music and the accompanying dancing is widespread and, in a few cases, overshadows traditional music and dance. For example, the Athapascan Fiddle Festival, held every November in Fairbanks, Alaska, is the premiere Native music and dance event of that area. The Alaskan Kutchin Indians also dance to European fiddle-guitar music imported by Scottish settlers from the Orkney Islands. In addition, Indian fiddlers and guitar players can be found almost everywhere. During the annual Cherokee National Holiday in Tahlequah, Oklahoma, a national Indian fiddler's contest is held.

Early in their careers, missionaries recognized that Indians loved music and began to capitalize on that tendency. Often Indians were lured or forced into the missions to learn and sing the new songs. Then they were proselytized, became Christians, and began translating and composing their own hymns. In California, they became the primary musicians for the Catholic Spanish mission system. In the East, they were both Catholic and Protestant converts. While most sang melodies without harmony, the Cherokees and Tlingits are famous for their improvised harmonies based on the European models. Indian people throughout North America still compose their own hymns and translate others for their own use.

In the 1990s, the Indian churches provide a place for worship, a meeting place for Christians, and a locus for Indian singing. In rural and reservation areas, worshipers attend services held in Native languages with songs in those languages; the ministers are local men with some theological training. In the cities, intertribal groups of Indians come together within specific denominations. Usually conducted in English, these urban services feature songs both in English and in Native languages, and the ministers are usually well-educated Indians.

The "Sings" or "Singings" held at these churches draw Indians from far and wide. Indian choirs, quartets, trios, duets, and soloists travel far to participate in them. Although some groups sing unaccompanied, many use piano, guitar, bass fiddle, organ, or other available Western instruments for accompaniment. In the 1990s, some singers use tape-recorded sound tracks or even synthesizers and electronic keyboards. Many groups harmonize, but in much of the Christian music, early Indian vocal techniques remain. We still hear leader-chorus responsorial patterns, upward-gliding attacks and downward-gliding releases to musical phrases, and generally nasal voice production. The themes of the songs represent basic human needs and communication with God and are not always direct translations of their English counterparts. Just as traditional ceremonies and urban powwows draw Indians together, so do Indian churches, especially through their music. Several choirs and quartets have published commercial recordings.

The renewed interest in Indian flute playing represents another revival and innovation. A first-year recipient of a National Heritage Fellowship from the National Endowment for the Arts, Doc Tate Nevaquaya, a Comanche from Oklahoma, taught several young Indian men through his recordings and personal efforts to play old songs, compose new songs, and adapt Indian vocal melodies and non-Native songs, such as hymns, for the flute. Dick Fools Bull, Sioux, had similar influence on the northern Plains. Among the other Indian flutists who have enjoyed success as concert artists are Kevin Locke (also a National Heritage Fellowship recipient), R. Carlos Nakai (popular also with symphonic and New Age audiences), Edward Wapp, Jr., John Rainer, Jr., Gordon Bird, Fernando Cellicion, Robert Tree Cody, Herman Edwards, Daniel C. Hill, Frank Montano, Cornel Pewewardy, D. M. Rico, Stan Snake, Douglas Spotted Eagle, Robert Two Hawks, Woodrow Haney, and Tom Ware. Nakai also composes and performs in ensembles with synthesizers and other electronic or amplified instruments, carrying the music forward into contemporary life. A few of the other flutists also cross over to contemporary or New Age.

In the 1990s, Indian traditional singers and dancers frequently perform out of context at all kinds of fairs, receptions, national Indian conferences, political rallies, museum and college programs, political demonstrations and the presidential inauguration of 1993, graduation ceremonies, tourist attractions, and in various Indian education programs. Indian traditional music can be studied in schools ranging from preschool to university.

Many Indian people also take their tape recorders to powwows, stomp dances, and other Indian gatherings to record music for pleasure. They may be recording the proceedings to learn the songs or merely for entertainment. This widening influence of Indian music has created an interest among the Indian and non-Indian record-buying public, with at least six commercial record companies now catering to this new market.

Although Indian tribes perform music unique to their own traditions, some tribes have adopted music and accompanying religious ceremonies from others. The most important ceremonies that spread pan-tribally across the West and into the Great Lakes area were the Sun Dance, the Ghost Dance, and the Native American Church, or Peyote religion. In each ceremony there is some borrowing along with incorporation of local styles.

Of these three, only the Ghost Dance has almost disappeared, and even it survives in the song repertoire of Shoshoni women on the Wind River Reservation in Wyoming. The Sun Dance, after spreading from its origins in the central Plains north into Canada with the Plains Cree and Plains Ojibwa, south into Indian Territory with the Kiowa, west into Idaho and Utah with the Kutenai, Shoshoni, and Ute, and east into South Dakota and Minnesota with the Santee Dakota, finally began to vanish from the Great Plains by the end of the nineteenth century. Beginning in the 1970s, the Sun Dance has seen a revival on the Plains, in the mountains with the Ute and Shoshoni, and, newly transplanted, in California and other non-traditional sites.

Some modern Sun Dance performances retain the old ways, some revive ceremonies that were temporarily forsaken, and some borrow the ceremony from the Plains to benefit all Indian tribes. The Sun Dance religion requires that candidates for redemption do not withdraw from the world but live here and struggle for the good of all. Proper life requires a good heart, sacrifice for others, and selfless behavior toward family, kin and friends, and the entire Sun Dance community.

These universalist values draw Indians, young and old, from the cities and rural areas to the Sun Dance. Whether sponsored by an ancient tribal group or by a modern organization like the American Indian Movement, the music is so sacred that only the social songs have been released on commercial recordings. The style echoes that of other Plains social dance songs.

The Native American Church and its peyote religion and music are also widespread. Urban Indians participate in ceremonies near their cities, while reservation and rural Indians set up teepees in sacred places or in their own yards. Peyote music is so popular that dozens of albums have been released by the two major Indian record companies, Indian House and Canyon. Featured together on these albums are singers from tribes whose indigenous ways contrasted greatly.

Wherever one finds peyote music, the general musical style, as defined by ethnomusicologist David P. McAllester, applies to all areas: peyote music is fast, uses a ceremonial water drum and rattle to accompany the singers, and the melody descends. The speed and driving pulse of the drum characterize the music. The worshipers take turns passing the drum in a clockwise direction around a sacred area upon which fire, sage, a peyote button, water, and cedar have been placed. At special times during the ceremony an eagle-bone whistle is blown outside in the four directions.

The most common pan-tribal music is found at powwows (urban, reservation, and rural). The singers and dancers at powwows often represent many tribes. Sponsored by an organization or club, each powwow group raises money and plans months ahead for this major event. The planners take great care in choosing a good head singer, head man dancer, and head woman dancer. Although the powwow is a gathering that includes activities like feasting, giveaways, arts and crafts sales, raffles, and the crowning of a princess, the emphasis is on singing and dancing. The singers perform Plains Indian music—northern, southern, or often both—with some regionally specific music and dance performed before, after, or as interludes during the powwow.

To open many powwows on the southern Plains and sometimes in the cities, members of a Gourd Dance Society may dance. Representing southern Plains warrior societies, Gourd Dancers, who are members of this honor brotherhood, have prescribed clothing and use special rattles and fans. In contrast to the general powwow fare of War Dances (dances featuring older, traditional clothing and stylized movements), Fancy Dances (dances exhibiting brightly colored clothing and innovative footwork), or Grass Dances (dances based on older northern Plains dances, with modern dress including fringe), the Gourd Dance seems slow and the songs extremely long. The music resembles other southern Plains music but uses a narrower vocal range. The dance is also less vigorous as are most honoring dances.

Frequently, the dancers warm up with Round Dances (slow friendship dances using a side-together step, in a clockwise circle) before the formal opening of a powwow (after the Gourd Dance, if it is performed), and Round Dances may be interspersed among War Dances, Grass Dances, Trick Songs (special songs for contests), etc. These social dances, together with the couples dances, such as the Oklahoma Two-Step, Rabbit Dance, Snake Dance, and Owl Dance, offer a chance for audience members to participate freely. At these times, visitors often dance without observing all the formal etiquette and dress requirements for the more serious dances.

Extra or specialty dances include the Navajo Ribbon Dance (a mirror-image dance by one or two sets of partners), the Swan Dance (an imitation of the bird), the Hoop Dance, the Shield Dance (a mock duel by dancers using shield and spears), or one of the pueblo Buffalo Dances (an imitation of male and female buffalos). These dances in a powwow setting are strictly for show, and often the dancers receive payment for demonstrating them. In recent years most powwow clubs have added contests to attract the best dancers and singers to the events they sponsor. The Men's War Dance or Fancy Dance contests offer the top prize money, sometimes one thousand dollars or more.

In the complex social and sometimes religious setting of the pow-wow, the leaders choose the head singer and head dancers not only for their superior knowledge of song and dance repertoire, but also for their community status and network of family and friends. If these powwow leaders have prestige and command respect, other good singers and dancers will join to show their support. Becoming a head singer requires a strong voice, musical talent, a superior memory, and an ability to guide the group of singers constituting the "drum." A head dancer must know and observe proper etiquette and decorum, must have stamina, must know all genres of powwow dance, be skilled at executing them, and be an easy leader to follow.

The Forty-nine Dances, social dances performed mostly by young people after powwows, may last all night. The dress is casual, and the drum, central to most Plains music, may be replaced by any sonorous surface. Done mostly for fun, the dances and songs may contain words about love, sweethearts, and problems. Changing the words to fit the locale or tribe involved is common; for example, Oklahoma may become New Mexico, or Kiowa may become Pueblo.

These pan-tribal (or pan-Indian) songs contain many vocables (or nonlexical syllables). Because the styles spread across geographical and tribal boundaries, using vocables allows a group of singers from different tribes and language families to sing together with ease. When songs at powwows are language specific, many singers have to drop out unless the members of the group all speak the same Indian language.

Because of Indian migration to cities and towns, and, because of generations of intermarriage with Indians of other tribes and with non-Indians, many young people have never experienced traditional Indian life and have come to rely on powwows, Indian community organizations, and Indian studies programs at schools as sources for reinforcing their "Indianess." Music and dance have contributed greatly to the search for identity by these young Indians. Drums, or groups of Indian men singers, have sprung up in community centers and in schools all across the nation. Although the purpose of these drums is to perform at powwows and other gatherings, the result is a weekly or monthly intertribal gathering of men who practice songs from various tribes in northern or southern Plains style.

In the past, most young women participated only in dancing, doing beadwork, or practicing other Indian crafts, but recently women have taken a visible role in singing and composing, often joining male drums or creating their own.

Intertribal choirs and bands enjoy popularity at Indian schools throughout the country. Depending on local tastes, the choirs may perform Western art or popular music, Christian music, or indigenous Indian music in new choral arrangements. The bands range from marching bands to jazz swing bands with corresponding repertoires. The Navajo Nation Band even marched once in the Pasadena, California, Tournament of Roses parade, performing Navajo social songs on brass instruments.

Louis Ballard, a Quapaw-Cherokee composer, did much to promote Indian choral singing. By traveling throughout the country to present Indian music workshops, conduct Indian choirs, and produce records and films, Ballard spread his idea of using Indian motifs in traditional Western forms.

A few of the school choirs and bands gaining recognition and producing record albums are Brigham Young University (Provo, Utah), the Institute of American Indian Arts (Santa Fe, New Mexico), Fort Lewis College (Durango, Colorado), Haskell Indian Junior College (Lawrence, Kansas), and Bacone College (Muskogee, Oklahoma).

Professional Indian musicians perform in many styles, including classical, jazz, country, folk/protest, contemporary, rock, rap, and New Age. Some blend Indian tunes with mainstream rhythms, instruments, and styles. Most use some themes, instruments, or melodies from traditional Indian music. Among these are Tom

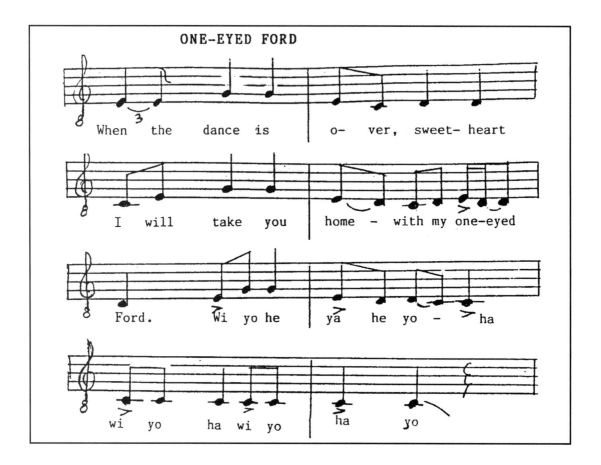

ONE-EYED FORD

When the dance is | o- ver, sweet- heart

I will take you | home – with my one-eyed

Ford. Wi yo he | yá he yo – ha

wi yo ha wi yo | ha yo

Excerpt from Forty-nine Dance song, "One Eyed Ford," with English words and vocables.

Bee, Robby Bee, Joe Manuel, Sand Creek, Winterhawk, Cody Bearpaw, Borderline, El Cochise, Eddie and Brian Johnson, Joe Montana and the Roadrunners, Jimi Poyer, Rockin' Rebels, Wingate Valley Boys, Jim Boyd, Arliene Nofchissey Williams, Vincent Craig, Chief Dan George, Burt Lambert and the Northern Express, Frank Montano, Tomas Obomsawin, A. Paul Ortega, Sharon Burch, Jim Pepper, Buddy Red Bow, Joanne Shenandoah, Gene T, Buffy Sainte-Marie, Bruce Hamana, Floyd Westerman, the Fenders, Undecided Takers, the Navajo Sundowners, the Zuni Midnighters, Apache Spirit, Louis Ballard, Brent Michael Davids, XIT, Redbone, Billy Thunderkloud, and John Trudell.

Chicken Scratch (*waila*), popular dance music of the Indians of southern Arizona, relies heavily on European dance forms such as polkas and schottisches. Similar to Mexican-American Norteño music, employing guitars, concertina, and saxophone, Chicken Scratch finds popularity among the Tohono O'Odham (Papago), Pima, Quechan (Yuma), and Yaqui.

Like other Americans, Indians and Eskimos will sing or dance to almost any variety of music that catches their fancy while reserving their own music for special occasions. Indian musicians have composed music to fit the times while keeping many of their old styles, forms, and contexts to reinforce traditional values. Music pervades Indian life starting from creation stories and ending with death and memorial. American Indian music is important not only because it influences modern American society, but also because it emphasizes the traditions and values of Indian people. This oral tradition has survived solely because the music and dance were too important to be allowed to die.

Indians of North America have been dancing, playing, and singing music, performing speeches and ceremonies, and carving and painting walls, ornaments, and everyday household items that have exhibited group and individual artistry for many centuries. The legacy remains.

Charlotte Heth
University of California, Los Angeles

♦ ♦ ♦ ♦ ♦ ♦ ♦ ♦ **NATIVE NORTH AMERICAN VISUAL ARTS**

In every American Indian society, the visual arts—textiles, architecture, sculpture, pottery, painting, and photography—are inextricably linked with the arts of music, dance, festival, and religious performance. Artistic objects were and still are used for their powerful qualities in ceremonies, both of the group, and of the individual who sought spiritual power. Masks, dance costumes, carved rattles, and other items of ceremonial regalia add to the power and impressiveness of any ceremony—in the eyes of the beholders as well as of the supernaturals. During the twentieth century, some Native artists created paintings and sculptures that are made principally for sale to an international community of art lovers. These arts may draw inspiration from traditional Indian arts as well as from arts of the European tradition.

Art and Environment

In each region of the North American continent, Native people made art that reflected the environment around them and that best expressed their own unique social structure and world view. In coastal British Columbia and southern Alaska, Tlingit, Haida, Kwakiutl, and other Northwest Coast people have used the wood of the cedar tree in their arts for over a thousand years. The thick trunk can be carved into imposing totem poles. The straight-grained wood of the trunk splits long and true, enabling the architect to fashion planks as long as forty feet to make the great carved and painted houses so characteristic of this region. Cedar is also easily carved to make the masks, dance rattles, great storage boxes and feasting bowls that were used in extraordinary numbers by all Northwest Coast peoples. The cedar's bark, thin branches, and roots can be pounded to make soft, flexible weaving material for capes, hats, bags, baskets, and mats. The rich coastal environment of the Northwest not only provided plenty of cedars but also an abundance of foodstuffs—fish, game, and fruit. This abundance allowed people more leisure time to devote themselves to art and other expressive aspects of culture.

Kwakiutl totem poles at Alert Bay (circa 1910).

In contrast to the large, settled communities of Pacific Northwest, the small-scale societies that stretched across the mid-section of the United States and the prairies of Canada during the eighteenth and nineteenth centuries were characterized by a high degree of mobility. Sioux, Cheyenne, Kiowa, and other tribes rode their horses over the Plains, following the seasonal migrations of the buffalo herds. All of their arts had to be small and easily portable. Unlike the great wood houses of the Northwest Coast, Plains peoples lived principally in tipis. Women assembled these structures quickly by setting up the long, strong lodge poles and wrapping and anchoring buffalo-hide tipi covers around them. If the band needed to break camp quickly, tipis could be disassembled even more rapidly.

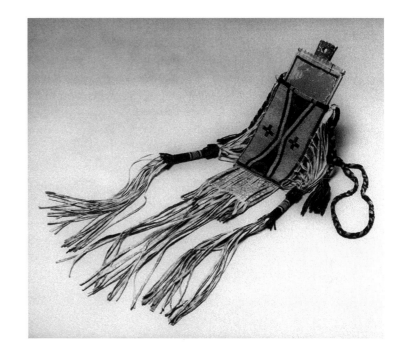

Crow beaded mirror with case, Montana, circa 1880. Philbrook Art Center, Tulsa, Oklahoma.

Small-scale portable arts included many items of personal adornment. Painted shields; hide garments decorated with paint, beads, quills, and hair; soft and sturdy beaded mo-ccasins; and ornate feather and fur headgear were important aspects of Plains arts. As the cedar tree was so fundamental to art and life on the Northwest Coast, the buffalo was the primary artistic material on the Plains. The animal's hide provided skins for tipi covers and clothing, the sinew provided thread to sew these items together, and the horn was used for jewelry and carved utensils.

In the harsh Arctic region of Canada and Alaska, where the only plant materials are tiny flowers and lichen blooming for a brief growing season in the summer, life as well as art traditionally depended on the bountiful animal world: caribou, polar bear, salmon, walrus, whale, and seal. Men carved walrus tusks, caribou antlers, and whale bones into fishing and hunting implements, such as harpoon heads, knives, buttons, and toggles that were both practical and beautiful. Women sewed animal skins into fine and warm garments to protect the wearer and to please the spirits of the animals who had sacrificed their lives so that humans could eat and stay warm. Especially fine garments were required for the shaman, the spiritual protector of the people, whose role it was to communicate with the spirits of the game animals and of the ancestors.

In the southwestern regions of Arizona and New Mexico, Hopi, Zuni, and other Pueblo people have been sedentary farmers for over fifteen hundred years. Their relationship with a fixed place on the land is reflected in many of their arts. The unique architectural form of the multi-story apartment compounds—some of which have been continuously in use for hundreds of years—allows for a community of people to live together with both privacy and communal space. These housing compounds are made of stone and adobe brick, the interior walls plastered with clay and painted. Clay pottery is made from the "flesh" of mother earth herself, in an unbroken tradition that extends back well over one thousand years. Clothing was traditionally made from harvested cotton fibers and other plant materials. Shell and turquoise jewelry reflected a trading network that, even a thousand years ago, extended for hundreds of miles in every direction.

Art and Power   While modern Western culture customarily characterizes aspects of life as either secular or sacred, there are no such arbitrary divisions in Native American thought. Neither can art be divided easily into religious arts as something distinct from arts of daily life. In some arts, the spiritual aspects may be the most obvious ones, but even arts made for daily life or for sale to outsiders can carry spiritual meaning if they are made in the proper way.

A Zuni altar is a highly sacred construction made up of individual artistic forms: carved and painted figures adorned with feathers, painted pottery bowls for cornmeal, and dry paintings made of sand and crushed minerals. Not only do the individual items have power, but they are activated as a constellation of sacred forms when the proper ceremonies are performed over them by initiated members of a society. Centuries of custom and ritual dictate how the component parts are to be made and used, and who may be allowed to see them.

A Comanche or Crow shield is a power object as well as an art object. A Plains warrior might have a dream or a vision in which a particular animal, insect or other natural phenomenon appeared to him in a significant fashion. He would then paint his war shield with elements from his vision, and it would bestow upon him power and protection in combat. Each such object is a highly personal and individual work of artistry.

In contrast to these two examples, it might seem that a Navajo rug made for sale would be a completely secular object (see photo on following page). Yet further knowledge of the conditions under which it is produced reveals that, for the Navajo, weaving is a sacred activity. In Navajo creation stories, the universe itself was woven on a giant loom by a sacred ancestor named Spider Woman, who used the materials of the natural world as she wove. Lightning, clouds, rainbows, and sunrays were woven together to create the world. Navajo women think about Spider Woman as they combine different products of the natural world (the wool from sheep, the dyes from plants, and their own human creativity) into their weavings.

The designs on many Navajo rugs are geometric patterns that are not symbolic but simply demonstrate the weaver's powers of creativity and graphic design. In the example illustrated here, however, the imagery on the rug relates to the sacred arts of medicine and astronomy. It is a design taken from the Navajo art of sand painting, used for physical and spiritual healing. In this design, Mother Earth is depicted by the large figure on the right. Corn, beans, squash, and tobacco (the four most important Native American plants) grow out of her belly. The black figure beside her is Father Sky. In his belly the sun and moon are depicted most prominently, while the background is dotted with constellations, including Orion, the Pleiades, and the Dippers.

An art object may give the viewer only hints of the complex technological, spiritual and social processes that stand behind it. While anyone may admire the beauty of a Navajo rug or the impressiveness of a Haida totem pole, it is only by learning more about the culture and ideas that stand behind their creation that we can appreciate the true eloquence of these works of art. In many areas

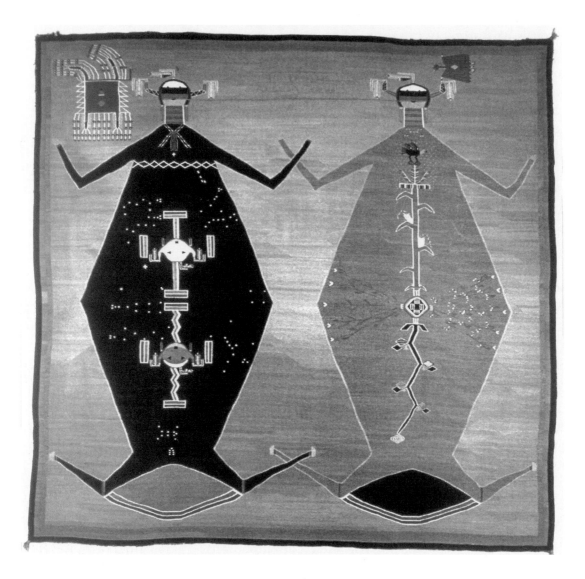

Navajo sandpainting rug woven by Altnabah. Early twentieth century. Museum of Northern Arizona, object no. E3716.

of life, art may be used for personal power and prestige or to reveal the power of the entire social group.

In the nineteenth century, a Sioux man would advertise his personal feats of bravery in warfare by painting his exploits on the buffalo robe he wore or on the tipi in which he lived. He owned the rights to these scenes, for they were his own personal history. So, too, he would own the rights to any images he discovered through his dreams and might paint these on his tipi as well. These power symbols could be bought or inherited by others, just like other kinds of property. In similar fashion, a Cheyenne woman who ornamented her own and her family's clothing with carefully sewn designs in dyed porcupine quills owned the rights to these designs. She gained power and prestige through her role as a fine artist, just as a Cheyenne man gained honor through his role as a warrior.

Among the Iroquois of upper New York State and southern Ontario, a man who needed to draw upon the power of the spirit world to aid in healing would dream of a spirit face, and would then carve a mask of this spirit from the trunk of a basswood tree while the tree was still growing. This "False Face" spirit mask would be used in conjunction with tobacco to purge the community of diseases, or to heal a particular individual. To the Iroquois, such masks are more than just inanimate art objects; they are

Masked dancers participating in a Kwakiutl winter ceremonial.

believed to have spiritual power and must be handled respectfully and are ritually offered cornmeal and tobacco.

While artists and artmaking can be powerful, myth and folklore sometimes give warnings about abuses of such power, especially if too much attention to making art means that an artist is not leading a balanced life. A Tlingit myth from southern Alaska cautions that cooperation within the human community is the proper model for an artist's life (rather than the Euro-American stereotype of the isolated artist who is totally devoted to art). According to this myth, in ancient times there was a young Tlingit woman whose most compelling desire was to perfect the art of weaving, an art form not yet commonly practiced on the Northwest Coast. But the demands of her many male admirers made it difficult for her to devote sufficient time to her art. For this reason, she decided to go live in seclusion in the wilderness. She was discovered there by Raven and Marten (two animal heroes in Northwest Coast mythology), who masqueraded as a high-ranking chief and his son in order to get to know her. The chief asked her to marry his son, but she agreed to do so only on the condition that they could remain in isolation in the woods, so that she could continue her weaving undisturbed. Only when the men agreed did she consent to show them her house, which was filled with the most beautiful weavings in the world. While she slept, Raven and Marten stole all of her weavings. They flew back to the human communities on the coast and distributed the weavings as gifts to all the women in the communities. From these items, women learned to weave the Chilkat Tlingit blankets that soon became the most valued textiles along the Northwest Coast.

This myth serves as a cautionary tale for those artists whose involvement in their own work leads them to seek isolation from the human community and to withhold knowledge that would be helpful to others. For that lack of moral generosity, the myth says, the artist may lose her art.

Learning to Be an Artist

Among some tribes, all people may reasonably be considered to be artistic, and all are responsible for making and ornamenting their own clothing, shelter, and other goods. Even within such societies, however, it is generally recognized that certain people excel at art. If an individual needed a finely made object for a ceremony or to give as a special gift, he or she might contract with a particularly talented carver or quill-worker, for example, in order to ensure a truly fine piece of work. In societies where artistic practice is widespread, children typically learn from their parents or other adult members of the extended family—uncles, aunts, or grandparents. A young Eskimo boy watched and then ultimately helped his father carve walrus tusks into small amulets. A young Navajo girl helps her mother herd sheep, spin the yarn made from their wool, and finally weave a fine blanket or rug.

In some societies, the making of art is considered to be a specialty. Like any other specialized profession, one must study hard and apprentice oneself to an expert in order to become an accomplished artist. A young Tlingit or Kwakiutl boy on the Northwest Coast who was interested in being a carver would typically become the apprentice of a master artist. His jobs at first would be menial: keep the fire going, sharpen the master's tools, grind up the mineral pigments to make the paints. As he got older and proved himself worthy of more responsibility, he would be allowed to use the sharp carving tools to remove the bark from a piece of log and rough out the facial features of a mask. The fine finishing work would then be done by the master artist, while the boy carefully observed. The more advanced apprentice might work as the "other side man": The master carver would plan out a totem pole design and carve the entire right side of it while the apprentice would, on the left side, follow the carver's example, striving to replicate his teacher's work with every stroke of the carving tool or every dab of the paint brush.

In societies like those of the Northwest Coast, where art was a specialist's pursuit, elaborate payment schemes and contracts would be worked out between artist and patron. Among the Kwakiutl, for example, a man might host a public feast to announce his intention to commission a new totem pole. The guests at this feast would serve as the witnesses to the oral contract between patron and artist; their participation would ensure that all aspects of the contract would be honored.

Among many Native American societies, people report that one of the principal ways that they get ideas for art is through dreams. A Pueblo potter may dream of the complex design she wants to paint on the water jar she has just made—a pattern that incorporates many elements of traditional design, yet is uniquely her own. An Iroquois carver may dream of a particular False Face Spirit, whose facial expression is slightly different from any mask he has carved before. A Sioux beadworker may dream of the ways that the colors of her new beads will fit together into an innovative pattern; or she may dream of the supernatural spirit of Double Woman, who is the patron of Sioux quillworkers and beadworkers. It is said that if a woman dreams of Double Woman, she will be an extraordinary artist.

Most of the Native American art that was put in museums before the mid-twentieth century was collected anonymously. The collectors and scholars who acquired it did not bother to find out the names of the artists who made these works. A visit to most museums gives the false impression that Native American art is anonymous art—few labels bear the names of the makers. Yet, in any tribe, people recognized each other's individual styles and distinctive markings: the particular way one carver might carve the eye socket of a mask, or paint the markings on its face, or the unusual and distinctive way one weaver would finish off the edge of her blanket. It was not necessary to put one's name on the carving or basket for others to recognize or appreciate the achievement, when all lived closely within a small society.

In some regions, early in the twentieth century, artists were encouraged by their non-Native patrons to sign their works, for this had been the custom in Euro-American art since the Renaissance. The famous potter from San Ildefonso Pueblo, Maria Martinez, was urged around 1920 to sign the bottoms of her famous blackware pots, for buyers would pay more money for her signed works (see photo below). Over the next two decades, Maria signed her name to pots made and painted by others, and she polished and signed pots that other women had formed. To the modern, Western way of thinking, this may seem to be a misrepresentation; within the Pueblo world view, where community balance and group harmony are valued over individual achievement, this was a mechanism by which other artists could share in the high prices brought by Maria Martinez's overriding fame. This insured that jealousies and unfairness were kept to a minimum.

Artists everywhere are curious about the work of other people. They typically draw upon the work of past centuries as they experiment with imagery and motifs. At the same time, new materials and new ways of doing things also stimulate artists to take their work in new directions. Native American artists are no exception.

In ancient times, around A.D. 1100, Anasazi potters of the present-day U.S. Southwest learned how to manufacture pottery that was beautifully painted and skillfully fired in open-air kilns. The Anasazi potter was not only a master of the elegant vessel form, she painted complex abstract designs using only simple decorative motifs like straight lines, zig-zags, cross-hatching, and spirals. In ancient Anasazi pottery there were many regional traditions. Potters learned technical information within their own families, but might draw inspiration for decorative patterns from other pots that were widely traded within the Southwest.

To the south of the Anasazi, the Mimbres people of southwestern New Mexico were also experts at pottery-making and painting. The Mimbres pottery tradition shares some features with Anasazi pottery—both usually used black and white designs. But Mimbres pottery painters were

Tradition and Innovation

Maria Martinez, potter of San Ildefonso Pueblo, New Mexico, and her blackware designs, 1940s.

Agents of Oppression. Diego Romero, contemporary artist/ potter. This bowl combines traditional Mimbres (A.D. 500-1100) pottery with a concern for contemporary Native American issues. Romero is a graduate of the Institute of American Indian Arts, Santa Fe, New Mexico, and received the Master of Fine Arts degree from the University of California, Los Angeles.

interested in depicting scenes from daily life, from religious stories, and from the animal world. The unique Mimbres pottery-painting tradition died out by A.D. 1200, as drought set in and Mimbres villages were abandoned. People migrated, new communities were formed, and new artistic traditions established. Mimbres pottery painting was not rediscovered until archaeological excavations brought it to light after 1910. Today, twentieth-century descendants of ancient Mimbres and Anasazi potters experiment not only with new ways of doing things but with very old ways as well. Early in the twentieth century, Maria and Julian Martinez incorporated Mimbres serpent and feather designs into their painted pots. Contemporary Pueblo potters at the village of Acoma, too, continue to draw creative inspiration from fine Mimbres designs.

On the Great Plains, in the centuries before the coming of Europeans in the early nineteenth century, artists from Crow, Cheyenne, Sioux, Kiowa, and other tribes experimented with materials and designs in quillwork, hide-painting, and other diverse arts of clothing and personal adornment. Through their trading networks, such goods were exchanged over long distances across the Great Plains. When horses became a fundamental part of Plains culture, these long-distance trading networks grew even more extensive.

While today we think of beadwork as a "traditional" American Indian art, especially on the Great Plains, there was a time when beads were an exciting new material for artists to experiment with. French fur traders brought beads to Western Great Lakes Indians by the early seventeenth century. When the trader François Laroque visited the Crow Indians on the northern Plains in 1805, they were already using blue glass beads obtained from Shoshoni intermediaries, who had, in turn, obtained them from Spanish traders in the Southwest. At that time, beads were such a highly prized commodity that the Crow would trade one horse for only 100 beads. Later, beads became widespread and inexpensive. Artists quickly recognized the artistic potential of these wonderful new materials. Strong and durable, with a vivid range of non-fading colors, beads were easy and comparatively quick to work with, compared to the laborious process of quillwork traditionally done by female artists on the Great Plains. At first, beads were used alongside quillwork as an extra form of ornamentation; but, by the mid-nineteenth century, in many areas, beads came to replace quillwork. At the start of the reservation era in 1869, the use of beadwork intensified, becoming a symbol of the ethnicity of the tribes, at a time when Indian cultures were under great pressure to change and assimilate to Euro-American ways. All-over beading of vests, dresses, moccasins, and cradles became common.

When beadwork replaced quillwork as the primary form of female artistry, some of the customs and beliefs associated with quillwork were transferred as well. Among many Plains tribes, quill and beadworkers were members of professional artistic guilds. It was through such work that women proved their artistry, diligence, and power. George Bird Grinnell, who lived among the Cheyenne in the 1890s, found that for women, good artistry was considered to be the equivalent of bravery and success in war for men. Grinnell observed that in meetings of the artists' guild, the women would recall and describe their previous fine works similar to the way in which men would "count coup," recalling their bravery in war. Counting coup, the ultimate act of courage in war, demands that a man touch his opponent with a coup stick, showing his boldness and finesse. That women's arts demand these traits as well is a persistent idea among some Plains people. Even today, expert Crow beadworker Winona Plenty Hoops of Lodge Grass, Montana says, "A good design is like counting coup."

Just as female artists on the Great Plains embraced new materials like beads and brightly dyed and printed fabrics to use in their art, male artists, too, found new materials of interest. In the eighteenth and nineteenth centuries, men painted on buffalo hides, depicting scenes of their own personal history and war exploits. When they observed visiting Euro-American artists like George Catlin and Karl Bodmer paint highly realistic scenes of Plains life, Native men began to transform their own painting styles, making them more detailed and realistic. They used inks and other materials obtained from these artists and subsequently from traders. As Euro-American hunters ruthlessly slaughtered the great buffalo herds during the second half of the nineteenth century, hides became scarce, and Plains painters turned once again to imported materials to record their autobiographical exploits. Ledger books and muslin cloth became their new canvases. As the end of the century brought even more dramatic changes in their way of life—settlement on reservations, conversion to Christianity, abandonment of some long-held traditions—Plains painters transformed their art of painting from one which recorded ongoing heroic deeds to one which recorded the past that was so rapidly slipping from their grasp.

Native American Art in the Twentieth Century and Beyond

As many other essays in this reference book demonstrate, Native American life of the past century is characterized by great diversity within and among cultures. Some individuals live in a manner that would not be unfamiliar to their ancestors—hunting animals or planting corn, and speaking little English—while others have doctorates in engineering and work in the aerospace industry. Native American artistic traditions of the last few decades are as diverse as this also. Some artists continue to work in traditions that have been handed down through countless generations; Pueblo women at Hopi, Acoma, Santa Clara, San Ildefonso, and elsewhere continue a pottery-making style and technology that has its roots in Anasazi and Mimbres traditions of a thousand years ago.

In some communities, artists today are reviving artistic traditions that had languished for decades. When Haida artist Bill Reid erected a totem pole in his ancestral community on the Queen Charlotte Islands in Canada in the 1970s, it was the first pole carved and raised in almost a hundred years. Since then, other Haida artists have turned to carving, printmaking, and the revival of ancestral ceremonial traditions with new commitment and vigor. They want their children to respect and practice the arts that had defined them as Haida since time immemorial.

Yet another way of being a Native American artist in this century is to merge one's own ethnic art tradition with styles and symbols learned through the study of world art history. Many Native artists have earned fine arts degrees in painting, sculpture, and photography in universities. Their work is a dialogue between Native American art history and European art history. T. C. Cannon (1946–78), whose ancestry included Caddo, Choctaw, Kiowa, and European, lived in Oklahoma and studied both at the Institute of American Indian Art in Santa Fe, New Mexico, and at the San Francisco Art Institute. His self-portraits depict him variously as an artist, a cowboy, an Indian dressed in "traditional" dress, and an art collector. His painting, *Collector #5* (1975), while not an exact self-portrait, stands for Cannon as a contemporary artist who draws strength and identity both from his Indian heritage and his love and knowledge of European art history. This painting turns upside-down the customary position of Indian artist and non-Indian patron. Here it is the Indian man, sitting in a wicker chair atop a Navajo rug, dressed in late nineteenth-century tribal finery, who is the collector and connoisseur of the Van Gogh painting on the wall. Cannon's work displays a motif common in much contemporary Native art—an impulse toward social critique, often done with humor and a sense of irony. Many artists play with this idea of cultural mixtures. This may reflect their own ethnically mixed ancestry or simply the mixture of cultures they feel as Native artists making their way through a culture dominated by European-American history and art.

Nora Naranjo-Morse, from Santa Clara Pueblo in New Mexico, merges her family tradition of pottery- making with her own ironic

Nora Naranjo-Morse, Pearlene Teaching Her Cousins Poker, 1987. *Mixed media.*

sense of humor and love of figural sculpture. In *Pearlene Teaching Her Cousins Poker* (1987), Naranjo-Morse takes the Pueblo image of ritual clowns (characterized by their striped bodies), makes them female instead of male, and depicts them playing a game of poker, which they are learning from a book. By making this work of art in clay, Naranjo-Morse identifies with her sisters, mother, and earlier female ancestors, all makers of fine Santa Clara pots. Yet her own wit and sense of play links her with the larger community of contemporary Native American artists working today, whose work speaks across ethnic boundaries to a shared cultural condition.

Jolene Rickard, a Tuscarora (Iroquois) artist from New York State, uses the contemporary mediums of photography, color xerox, and collage, to express her views on contemporary Native art. In *Self Portrait—Three Sisters* (1988), her use of photography links her to experimentation in this artistic medium throughout the world.

The subject matter—two ears of corn and her own image—relates to the deeply held belief of Iroquoian people (and some other Native Americans as well) that human beings are related to "the corn people." In Iroquois tradition, women in particular are identified with this precious food substance because of a mythical ancestress who caused corn to be planted on the earth and taught women how to farm. The title of the work also evokes the "three sisters" of Iroquois belief—the corn, beans, and squash that are the staples of all life to many Indian nations.

The last twenty-five years have witnessed a tremendous explosion of creativity among Native artists throughout North America—from the Canadian Inuit (Eskimo) printmakers of Cape Dorset and Baker Lake who sell their images of Arctic life worldwide, to the mask and totem pole carvers among the Haida and Kwakiutl who make works for local Native use as well as for an international art market, to the painters, photographers and sculptors discussed here. Native American artists, using diverse materials and with many strong and different statements to make about creativity, Native identity and personal artistry, will continue unabated into the next century as well.

Janet Catherine Berlo
University of Missouri–St. Louis

♦ **BIOGRAPHIES**

Paul Apodaca was born in Los Angeles, California, of Navajo, Mexican, and Spanish descent. Apodaca is actively involved in the Native American, Hispanic, and arts communities on the state and national levels.

Paul Apodaca
1951–

Navajo artist and community organizer

Since the early 1970s, Apodaca has been associated with the Bowers Museum, the largest museum in Orange County, California, as an exhibiting artist, artist-in-residence, and curator of Native American art. Apodaca is also in charge of the California History and Folk Art Collections that are part of

the museum's 72,000 object holdings. The Bowers Museum is a museum of the cultural arts of the Pacific Rim, the Americas, African art, and California history.

Apodaca has worked with many arts funding agencies, including the California Arts Council (CAC), the Arizona Commission on the Arts, the Los Angeles Cultural Affairs Department, and the Corporation for Public Broadcasting. He is a board member of the Native California Network and the prestigious California Council for the Humanities (CCH). The state of California has hired Apodaca to design CAC arts programs and develop a new administrative plan for the California State Indian Museum. In 1992, Apodaca worked as the principal consultant for Knott's Berry Farm, a Western style entertainment park in Buena Park, California, on the design and operation of the "Indian Trails" cultural arts area in the park, which sees 4–5 million visitors each year. The Los Angeles Festival, a major Los Angeles multi-cultural event, uses Apodaca as a committee member and consultant. In addition, he served as master of ceremonies for the 1990 Pacific Rim beauty pageant. Currently, Apodaca works as a consultant for the Smithsonian Institution National Museum of the American Indian.

Apodaca has held the position of professor at Chapman University in Orange, California, and has taught and lectured at California State University, Fullerton, as well as at the University of California, Irvine. He is book review editor for *News From Native California* and a writer for the *San Francisco Review of Books*. He was a contributing scholar for the *Macmillan Dictionary of Art*, a writer for the *American Encyclopedia of Ideas*, and worked as an educational consultant for the Scott-Foresman textbook, *California—Our State, Its History*. He has also illustrated many Bowers Museum publications.

Apodaca has been honored with numerous awards and grants, including the Orange County Human Rights Award, the Smithsonian Institution Museum Professional Award, and the Academy of Motion Pictures Arts and Sciences Award for the feature documentary *Broken Rainbow* (1986), a film which helped to stop planned government relocation of 12,000 Navajo from their reservation in Arizona. Apodaca wrote and performed the musical score for *Broken Rainbow* and provided historical research. In response to legislation sponsored by Apodaca, Henry Koerper, a faculty member of Cypress College, and Jon Erickson, a faculty member at the University of California, Irvine, the state of California passed a bill making the State Prehistoric Artifact, an 8,000-year-old carving of a bear found in San Diego County, the state symbol of California's indigenous population.

Michael Chiago is an illustrator whose art reflects his experiences as a powwow dancer.

Michael Chiago
1946–

Tohono O'Odham
illustrator and dancer

Born in Kohatk Village on the Tohono O'Odham (formally Papago) Reservation in Arizona on April 6, 1946, Chiago started dancing and drawing when he was just a boy. He attended St. John's Academy High School in Laveen, Arizona, then joined the marines and served in Vietnam and Okinawa.

On returning home, Chiago studied commercial art and magazine layout techniques at the Maricopa Technical School. He is best known for a style of painting that he developed by himself. He uses water color and adds a special coating or glaze to certain parts when the painting is finished, thus producing a surface of unusual depth and brilliance.

Chiago's paintings are surrealistic in character, rather than being strictly representational, and they often depict dramatically costumed Indian dancers, thus drawing on Chiago's own personal experiences as a powwow dancer who has toured throughout Arizona, California, Nevada, and has even performed in concerts on the East Coast. Chiago has been recognized as an outstanding dancer since he was a young man, and he often attends powwows to watch and learn from the techniques of other dancers. All these images find a place in his paintings, which are included in the permanent collection at the Heard Museum in Phoenix, Arizona, and are often exhibited throughout Arizona and New Mexico.

**Datsolalee
(Luisa Keyser)
d. 1925**

Washo basketmaker

Datsolalee was a Washo woman who became famous for her skills as a basketmaker. The Washo are a Hokan-speaking tribe occupying the eastern slopes of the Sierra Nevada Mountains in northern California and Nevada.

She was born near Carson City, Nevada, around 1835 and learned the refined art of traditional basketry as a girl. Basketry is particularly developed among the California tribes, and Washo styles are among the more intricate, involving designs with as many as thirty-six stitches per inch. In 1844, Datsolalee was one of the Washo who welcomed John C. Fremont, the famous early explorer of territories west of the Mississippi River, when he arrived in the Carson City area. She later married a Washo man named Assu and had two children by him. Upon Assu's death, she married another Washo man named Charlie Keyser, and thus she also became known by an English name, Louisa Keyser.

Datsolalee's historical importance is owed at least partly to the bravery she showed in a marketing conflict with the Paiute. During the 1850s, this neighboring tribe had defeated the Washo in battle, and they prohibited the Washo from selling baskets to U.S. settlers, in order to increase their own sales. Without this source of income, the Washo suffered extreme poverty. Finally, however, Datsolalee decided to defy the ban, and in 1895 she took several of her finest pieces and sold them to Abram Cohn, a merchant in Carson City. This was the beginning of a long-standing relationship, and over the years Cohn bought some 120 works from Datsolalee, who is said to have produced about 300 baskets in her lifetime.

Datsolalee worked on baskets until she died, even though she had become nearly blind long before then. Her baskets, the largest and most intricate of which took more than a year to produce, became very valuable after her death, and one of them is said to have sold for $10,000 only five years later.

Charlie Edenshaw was a prosperous and renowned Haida artist, member of the Eagle clan, and chief of Yatza village on Graham Island located in the Queen Charlotte Islands of British Columbia. Named Takayren (Noise in the House) at birth, Edenshaw was schooled in Haida tradition by his uncle, Eda'nsa, who himself was a chief of the Sta Stas Eagle clan of Graham Island. It is said that upon reaching adulthood, his mother gave him a small pistol. He promptly held it to his head and pulled the trigger three times. The gun went off on the third try, wounding him slightly in the face. In celebration of his brush with death, he held a potlatch, a Haida traditional ceremony and feast involving the giving of food and goods, in which he demonstrated the episode to others. Charlie Edenshaw also became known among his people as Nngkwigetklas (They Gave Ten Potlatches for Him), perhaps in recognition of his repeated participation in potlatches. Charlie Edenshaw married and had five children. The early death of his only son, Robert (Gyinawen), profoundly affected him, and it is said that he never fully recovered from the loss.

Charlie Edenshaw demonstrated artistic talent at an early age and became a skilled carver of wood and argillite, a type of black slate. His work, noted for its flowing sculptural design, grew in popularity, and he became one of the first professional Haida carvers. Edenshaw was equally talented as a silversmith, goldsmith, and woodcarver. He frequently met with anthropologists and art collectors, and so provided others with insight into Haida culture and art. Many of his carvings, including model totem poles, as well as drawings and sketches, were collected by museums and art patrons. His work dramatically illustrates the intricacy of Northwest Coast art.

Charles Edenshaw
1839–1924

Haida artist

Harry Fonseca grew up in the Sacramento, California, area and once said in an interview that he did not truly appreciate his Indian heritage until he reached his mid-twenties. It was while pursuing an art degree at Sacramento State College that he became interested in Indian and other Native cultures and the power of imagery invoked by ancient mythologies. At that point, he says, he became drawn to the old myths "like a magnet" and would sit

Harry Fonseca
1946–

Maidu artist

for hours listening to stories told by his uncles and cousins. He states that he did some library research then but found that the writings of anthropologists and scholars lacked the excitement and personal involvement in stories told by his own relatives.

Fonseca is probably best known for paintings and other graphics depicting Coyote, the cunning but also reckless and irresponsible trickster of Maidu mythology. In these works, Coyote is typically rendered in ultra-modern clothing or absurd situations that some-how produce satirical images of contemporary American society. One painting from the early 1980s depicts Coyote and his female counterpart, Rose, performing a ballet step in the Tchaikovsky opera *Swan Lake*.

Fonseca had already mastered formal painting techniques and established a reputation as an artist before becoming involved with Coyote and other subject matter based on Maidu mythol-ogy. His career took a major leap when the Coyote paintings first appeared at the Wheelwright Museum in Santa Fe, New Mexico, during the 1970s. Countless delightful manifestations have been produced in the years since then. The artist is currently living in Santa Fe, exploring new images and new techniques in painting and print-making.

Carl Nelson Gorman

1907–

Navajo artist

A distinguished artist, Carl Gorman was among the first to em-ploy traditional Navajo motifs in producing modern works of art. He was born on the Navajo Reservation at Chinle, Arizona, on October 5, 1907. A member of the Black Sheep clan, Gorman comes from a distinguished family. His parents founded the first Presbyterian mission at Chinle; his father was also a cattleman and Indian trader, while his mother focused on the arts. She was a traditional weaver and translated many religious hymns from English into Navajo. Others in the family were also tribal leaders and well-known silversmiths.

During World War II, Gorman served in the U.S. Marine Corps and became one of the famous Navajo Code Talkers, whose mes-sages in their native language confused the Japanese military in the Pacific campaigns. On leaving the service, Gorman used the

GI Bill to support formal art studies at Otis Art Institute in Los Angeles, California, and since then he has worked as a technical illustrator for Douglas Aircraft, established his own silkscreen design company, and taught Indian art at the University of California, Davis.

Gorman's works have appeared in numerous solo and group shows and is represented in many public and private collections. His works include a variety of styles and media. Always an innovator, yet also firmly grounded in tradition, this creative figure once even originated a Navajo Gourd Rattle Dance, a new dance based on a combination of traditional elements.

R.C. Gorman is one of the leading contemporary American Indian artists and is the son of artist Carl Nelson Gorman.

R.C. Gorman

1932–

Navajo artist

Born on the reservation at Chinle, Arizona, on July 26, 1932, Gorman is the descendant of distinguished artists and traditionalists on both sides of his family. He was encouraged while still quite young to follow in his father's footsteps, and he once said in an interview that he could remember making his first drawings when he was three years old by tracing designs with his fingers in the sand and mud of the wash at the base of the Canyon de Chelly, a beautiful and famous Navajo landmark.

As a youth he lived in a *hogan* or traditional Navajo-style dwelling and herded sheep with his grandmother, but he soon became exposed to wider influences and developed a cosmopolitan art style of considerable range and depth. After graduating from Ganado Presbyterian High School, he went on to study art at the Northern Arizona University at Flagstaff and at San Francisco State University. He later received a grant from the Navajo Tribal Council to study art at Mexico City College. This was the first time the tribe had awarded a grant for study outside the United States.

Gorman has received an extraordinary number of awards and honors and is probably the most heralded of all contemporary Indian artists. In 1973, he was the only living artist to be included in the show "Masterworks of the Museum of the American Indian," held at the Metropolitan Museum in New York, and two of his drawings were selected for the cover of the show's catalog. In 1975, he was honored by being the first artist chosen for a series of solo exhibitions of contemporary Indian art at the Museum of the American Indian in New York.

Over the years, Gorman has published several articles about some of his other interests, which include Mexican art and artists and cave paintings or petroglyphs.

Allan Houser

1914–

Chiricahua Apache artist and art instructor

Allan Houser is an internationally recognized sculptor and painter whose works have a serene but powerful quality that reflects Chiricahua Apache culture. Born in Apache, Oklahoma, on June 30, 1914, he attended Santa Fe Indian School in New Mexico and later studied art at Utah State University. A muralist and painter during the late 1930s, Houser had to give up his artwork during a long period when he lived in the Los Angeles area in the 1940s and supported his family by working as a pipefitter and at various construction jobs. During this period he turned to wood carving and got a commission to create a stone monument at Haskell Institute, a junior college for Indian students in Lawrence, Kansas. The resultant work, entitled *Comrade in Mourning*, was a memorial to the Indian casualties of World War II carved from a half-ton block of marble.

In the following year (1949), Houser was awarded a fellowship from the Guggenheim Foundation and from that point his career was established. He later had many solo shows at places such as the Museum of New Mexico in Santa Fe; the Heard Museum in Phoenix, Arizona; the Southern Plains Museum in Anadarko, Oklahoma; and the Philbrook Center in Tulsa, Oklahoma. He won many prizes during his mid-career, including the Palmes Academique, awarded to Houser by the French government in 1954.

In 1962, Houser became a teacher at the Institute of American Indian Arts in Santa Fe, New Mexico, and he remained on the faculty there until retiring as head of the sculpture department in 1975. Since then he has been living in Santa Fe, where he continues to work and show his paintings and sculptures in stone and bronze.

Born at Joe Creek, South Dakota, on the Crow Creek Reservation in 1915, Oscar Howe's Sioux name was Mazuha Koshina (Trader Boy). He graduated from Pierre Indian School in South Dakota (1933), then studied painting at the U.S. Indian School in Santa Fe, New Mexico (1934–38), and had special training in mural techniques at the Indian Art Center in Fort Sill, Oklahoma. He later received a bachelor's degree (1952) from Dakota Wesleyan University in Mitchell, South Dakota, and a master of fine arts degree from the University of Oklahoma at Norman (1954).

Oscar Howe
1915–83

Yankton Sioux graphic artist

Howe served as an assistant instructor during his years at Dakota Wesleyan and taught art at Pierre High School in South Dakota from 1954 to 1957. He then became a professor of fine arts and artist-in-residence at the University of South Dakota at Vermillion; he remained on the faculty there until well into the 1970s. Howe employed a modern style to depict poignant images of Indian culture in transition and once wrote, "One criterion for my painting is to present the cultural life of the Sioux Indians. It is my greatest hope that my paintings may serve to bring the best things of Indian culture into the modern way of life."

Kevin Locke is a performer and teacher interested in preserving Indian, especially Lakota, artistic traditions. Born in 1954 on the Standing Rock Reservation in South Dakota, Locke is a member of the Lakota tribe. Fluent in Lakota (a subgroup of the Sioux) languages and a preeminent traditional flute player and hoop dancer, he received master's degrees in educational administration and community education from the University of South Dakota.

Kevin Locke
1954–

Lakota musician and dancer

Locke is also a popular performer and storyteller, working to ensure that his cultural heritage survives and prospers. He traveled throughout the world, to Canada, Australia, Africa, and Europe, his goal being to show people, through the Lakota hoop dance, that humanity can be unified through an appreciation of diversity. Locke uses twenty-eight hoops to tell a story, depicting such things as flowers, butterflies, stars, the sun, and an eagle. The hoops represent unity, and their colors—black, red, yellow, and white—represent the four directions, the four winds, the four seasons, and the four complexions of people's skin.

In 1982, Locke performed in the play *In Deo* and in *The Night of the First Americans* at the Kennedy Center in Washington, D.C. In his performances, he uses a traditional flute, which for the Lakota/Dakota Nations is the essence of the wind. The flute gives voice to the beauty of the land, and its sound is the sound of the wind rustling grass and leaves. The instrument consists of seven notes; four represent the directions, one represents the heavens, another the earth, and the last one represents the place where the six come together—the heart of the people listening to it.

Locke also organizes children's interactive and participatory workshops involving games, music, dancing, and storytelling, as well as lectures on American Indian issues, value and belief systems, social structure, and education. In the early 1990s, he participated in various festivals and programs such as the Hunter Mountain Festival in Hunter Mountain, New York; the Frontier Folklife Festival in St. Louis, Missouri; and the First Annual Storytelling Festival in Reno, Nevada. In 1992, he was appointed a delegate for Earth Summit 1992, an international environmental conference held in Rio De Janeiro, Brazil.

In 1990, Locke was awarded a National Heritage Fellowship by the National Endowment for the Arts for his contributions to the preservation of his cultural heritage and for his efforts to make it known and appreciated around the world.

Charles Loloma

1921–91

Hopi artist

Charles Loloma's jewelry is among the most distinctive in the world. The originality of his designs stems from the combination of non-traditional materials, like gold and diamonds, with typical Indian materials like turquoise. He has received great recognition as a potter, silversmith, and designer.

Loloma was born in Hotevilla, Arizona, in 1921. He grew up and was educated on the Hopi Reservation in northern Arizona; he attended the Hopi High School in Oraibi and the Phoenix Indian High School in Phoenix. In 1939, Loloma painted the murals for the Federal Building on Treasure Island in San Francisco Bay, as part of the Golden Gate International Exposition. The following year, he was commissioned by the Indian Arts and Crafts Board to paint the murals for the Museum of Modern Art in New York. Also in 1940, Loloma was drafted into the army, where he spent four years working as a camouflage expert in the Aleutian Islands off the Alaskan coast. After his discharge, he attended the School for American Craftsman at Alfred University in New York, a well-known center for ceramic arts. This was an unprecedented move on Loloma's part, since ceramics was traditionally a woman's art among the Hopi, but it was also indicative of his future course.

In 1949, Loloma received a Whitney Foundation Fellowship to study the clays of the Hopi area. After that, he and his wife set up a shop in the newly opened Kiva Craft Center in Scottsdale, Arizona, which was intended to become a center for high-quality arts and crafts. From 1954 to 1958, he taught pottery during the summers at Arizona State University, and in 1962 he became head of the Plastic Arts and Sales Departments at the newly established Institute of American Indian Arts in Santa Fe, New Mexico.

In 1963, Loloma exhibited his work in a private showing in Paris and then returned to the institute in Santa Fe until 1965, when he moved back to the Hopi Reservation in northern Arizona. By this time, his reputation as a jeweler was well established, and his pieces were winning first prizes in Indian arts competitions. By the mid-1970s, his jewelry was exhibited throughout the country and in Europe. Loloma spent the rest of his years on the Hopi Reservation, where he continued working and teaching his art to several apprentices. He was one of the first prominent Indian craftsmen who worked outside the traditional Indian influence; a variety of influences resulted in his unique personal style, which has been widely imitated among Indian artisans.

Linda Lomahaftewa

1947–

Hopi-Choctaw painter and educator

Linda Lomahaftewa is a painter whose works highlight the culture of the Plains Indians. She was born on July 3, 1947 in Phoenix, Arizona. In 1962, she entered the Institute of American Indian Arts in Santa Fe, New Mexico, where, in 1965, she received her diploma in art. She also received a bachelor of fine arts degree and a master of fine arts degree (1971) at the San Francisco Art Institute.

Since 1970, Lomahaftewa has been an art educator, first as a teaching assistant at the San Francisco Art Institute and, from 1971 to 1973, as assistant professor of Native American Art at California State College in Sonoma. From 1974 to 1976, she was an instructor of painting and drawing in the Native American Studies Program at the University of California in Berkeley.

During the seventies, Lomahaftewa's paintings were shown in more than forty exhibitions, including "New Directions," an Institute of American Indian Arts alumni traveling exhibition, and "Contemporary Native American Artists" at the Alternative Center for International Arts in New York City in 1977. In 1977, her works were also presented in the exhibition "Eleven Women Artists" at the Elaine Horwitch Gallery in Santa Fe, New Mexico.

Lomahaftewa's paintings were featured in a solo show in 1978 at the C. N. Gorman Museum at the University of California at Davis. Her work was exhibited in the "Pintura Amerindia Contemporanea" tour, organized by the United States Communication Agency in 1979. In 1980, she exhibited her paintings at the special exhibition organized by the Indian Arts and Crafts Board's Southern Plains Indian Museum and Crafts Center in Anadarko, Oklahoma. Lomahaftewa was listed among other prominent figures of the contemporary Native American artistic scene in two editions of *Who's Who in American Indian Arts*, in 1976 and in 1978.

Solomon McCombs

1913–

Creek Nation of Oklahoma painter

Solomon McCombs is an artist and former vice-chief of the Creek Nation of Oklahoma. Born in Eufaula, Oklahoma, he attended Bacone College and Tulsa University, both in Oklahoma. As an artist, McCombs uses traditional Native American themes in his paintings. His work has been honored with many accolades, including the Five Civilized Tribes Museum Seal and the Waite

Phillips Special Indian Artists Award for contributions in Indian Art over a period of five years, and Grand and Grand Masters Awards in 1965, 1970, 1973, and 1977 from the Philbrook Art Center, Tulsa, Oklahoma. In 1976, McCombs was commissioned by the U.S. Army to paint one of the American Indian Congressional Medal of Honor recipients of World War II. McCombs is also interested in graphics, architectural design, and the history of traditional American Indian painting.

Considered an expert on American Indian art and painting, McCombs has conducted a number of exhibits and lectures on this subject in the Middle East, Africa, India, and Burma, sponsored by the U.S. Department of State.

McCombs has served on the board of directors of the American Indian National Bank from 1973 to 1975. He is a member of the National Congress of American Indians (NCAI) and the Five Civilized Tribes Council, composed of representatives from the Cherokee, Choctaw, Chickasaw, Creek, and Seminole. Between 1976 and 1992 he served as a member of the National Council of the Creek Nation.

Norval Morrisseau

1932–

Ojibway artist

Norval Morrisseau is a renowned, self-taught Ojibway artist, perhaps the first Indian to break through the barriers of the non-indigenous professional art world in Canada. His unique style of painting, which combines European easel painting with the pictography of indigenous rock paintings, has been described as "x-ray art" or "legend art." With his bold and brilliant use of color and lines, he shows simultaneously the interiors and exteriors of figures—animals and humans, often using figures within figures. Morrisseau's style has given rise to a genre called "Woodlands art," which younger artists have embraced with enthusiasm and which has received international acclaim.

Morrisseau, whose Ojibway name means "Copper Thunderbird," was born at the Sand Point Reserve near Lake Nipigon, Ontario, north of Lake Superior. His Ojibway heritage was instilled in him at an early age by his maternal grandfather, Moses Nanakonagos. The initial inspiration for his art came from the legends of his people and from Ojibway images on birch bark scrolls and rock paintings. Early on in his career, he came into conflict with his elders because some of his work broke a taboo against depicting legendary figures outside of Ojibway spiritual rituals. Morrisseau was first noticed by the broader Canadian art community in 1962, when he displayed his work at the Pollack Gallery in Toronto, Ontario. His work demonstrates a deep commitment to religious and spiritual values, and Morrisseau continues to study Ojibway shamanistic practices, which he believes assist him in his creative work.

R. Carlos Nakai
1946–

Navajo-Ute musician

R. Carlos Nakai is a composer and musician. His instrument of choice is the Native flute, and in many regards, he has kept its tradition alive by defining both its presence and its haunting sound throughout his recordings. Nakai was born in Flagstaff, Arizona, and raised on the Navajo Reservation. His father, Raymond Nakai, was a Navajo tribal chairman.

Nakai began playing trumpet in the 1960s but switched to Native flute in 1972 after failing to be accepted at the Juilliard School of Music in New York City. He blames this on evidently "being the wrong color." He was encouraged by elders of the central and northern Plains people during the time that he was beginning to learn how to play the Native flute. Around 1982, he met the founder of Canyon Records, Ray Boley, and made his first record, *Changes*. Since then, he has released a number of recordings on the Canyon label, including *Winter Dreams* and *Carry the Gift* with guitarist William Eaton; *Spirit Horses*, a concerto for Native American flute and chamber orchestra; and *Natives* and *Migrations* with pianist Peter Kater.

Nakai has been a folk and visual artist in the artist-in-education program for the Arizona Commission on the Arts. In 1985, he performed at the Magic Flute Festival in St. Paul, Minnesota, with flutists from around the world. Currently, he is devising a methodology and theory of the Native flute within its own cultural context, using the influences of Western European music theory and practice for descritive and technological terminology. In this endeavor, he has worked with musicologists, ethnomusicologists, composers, and instrumentalists, as well as the San Diego Flute Guild.

Nampeyo is a world-recognized potter who, besides developing her own style, was instrumental in bringing about a revival of traditional Native American ceramics.

Nampeyo
c. 1860–1942

Hopi-Tewa potter

Nampeyo was born at Hano Pueblo in Arizona. In the 1890s, Nampeyo took an interest in pottery and concluded that the ceramic work being done by the artisans of her time was inferior to that of ancient potters. Her husband, who was working with an archaeologist at the time, helped her to find shards of ancient pottery. Using these pieces as a model, Nampeyo developed her own style based on these traditional designs. Nampeyo and her husband often traveled to Chicago to display her work. Nampeyo's beautiful designs evoked images of an era long past, and were quickly embraced by the art world. The Smithsonian Institution purchased her pottery and soon it was sought after by collectors from around the world. For years, her work was sold at the Grand Canyon Lodge of the Fred Harvey Company.

Nampeyo has been credited with bringing about a renaissance of pottery-making among her people. Furthermore, it was her ideas and inspiration that elevated pottery among her people to an art form, as it had been centuries ago.

Daphne Odjig, a well-known and influential Native Canadian artist, was born on the Wikwemikong Indian Reserve on Manitoulin Island in Lake Huron, Ontario, in 1919. Her father was a Potawatomi Indian and her mother was English. Her father and grandfather were both artists in their own right, and they encouraged young Odjig to explore artistic activities as she was growing up.

Daphne Odjig
1919–

Potawatomi artist

Odjig lived, painted, and worked on the reserve until 1938, when she moved to British Columbia. Her move did not signal a change in career, however, as she was subsequently elected to the British Columbia Federation of Artists. Odjig has also lived in Manitoba, where, in 1970, she opened a museum in Winnipeg devoted to indigenous art and formed an association of Native artists, including the renowned Norval Morrisseau. This had a powerful effect on her work, which combines Western techniques and styles with an emphasis on Native modes of artistic statement. Many younger Native artists owe a debt to Odjig's style, which continues to be influential in the Native artistic community.

Odjig has exhibited in Europe, Israel, and Japan, as well as in numerous cities in Canada. The National Arts Centre in Ottawa, Ontario, is home to a magnificent mural by Odjig, entitled *The Indian in Transition*. Odjig has received a number of honorary degrees from universities in Canada, and in 1987, she was made a member of the Order of Canada, an award conferred by the governor general of Canada to select Canadians in recognition of exemplary merit and achievement.

Kevin Redstar
1942–

Crow-Northern
Plains artist

Kevin Redstar is a Crow Indian born on the Crow Reservation in Lodge Grass, Montana. His father had an abiding interest in music, and his mother is a skilled craftswoman. In this nurturing environment, Redstar developed an early artistic capability. He studied at the Institute of American Indian Art (IAIA) in Santa Fe, New Mexico, from 1962 to 1964, then at the San Francisco Art Institute, and, later, at Montana State University.

In 1965, Redstar won a scholarship to the San Francisco Art Institute. As a freshman there, he was awarded the governor's trophy and the Al and Helen Baker Award from the Scottsdale National Indian Arts Exhibition. Redstar's first one-person exhibition was in 1971 at the Museum of the Plains Indian in Browning, Montana, where he drew heavily upon his Plains Indian culture, using Crow art and design concepts to inspire his own interpretation of the life force that exists beyond the surface of decorated objects. In 1974, after having worked as an assistant art instructor at his alma mater, Lodge Grass High School, Redstar was invited to return to IAIA to participate in the artist-in-residence program and became the first graduate of IAIA to return as an artist-in-residence. While in Santa Fe, he expanded his art to include lithography, serigraphs, and etchings and was selected as Artist of the Year by *Sante Fean* magazine in 1976–77.

Redstar returned to his own community to teach art and served as Crow tribal art consultant, helping to form the Crow-Cheyenne Fine-Arts Alliance to organize art exhibitions. Redstar has emerged as one of the premier Northern Plains fine artists. His latest works include exciting use of color and refined graphic design. Redstar continues to work daily, primarily in oils. With galleries all over the country, he is free to live where he chooses. Redstar's goal is to move to his native Pryor area to create a studio for monotypes and ceramics and to focus on art and music. Redstar has been recognized as being among the masters of Indian artists.

Bill Reid is a renowned Haida sculptor, known around the world for his monumental sculptures of Haida life. He was born in Vancouver, British Columbia, in 1920 to a Haida mother and a Scottish-American father and was unaware of his indigenous background until he was a teenager. It was only in the 1950s, after studying jewelry and engraving in Toronto and working as a broadcaster for the Canadian Broadcasting Company, that Reid began to explore Haida art and sculpture in earnest. He continued with his artistic education, studying at the Central School of Art and Design in London, England. He eventually returned to British Columbia where he quickly became known as an accomplished expert on Haida art, while simultaneously transforming the tradition to include his work. Perhaps his best known piece is a four-and-a-half ton cedar sculpture on display in the University of British Columbia School of Anthropology entitled *Raven and the First Humans*. It depicts an enormous raven perched on top of a half-open seashell from which human beings are peering out at the world. Other noteworthy works include a bronze killer-whale sculpture entitled *The Chief of the Undersea World* on display at the Vancouver Aquarium. Reid is accomplished in a number of media and has illustrated and collaborated on a number of books. He was awarded an honorary doctorate from the University of British Columbia in 1976. Most recently, Reid has been active in efforts to preserve South Moresby Island, located in the Queen

William Ronald "Bill" Reid 1920–

Haida sculptor

Charlotte Islands off the coast of British Columbia, from economic development and the logging industry.

Buffy Sainte-Marie
1942–

Cree singer and composer

Buffy Sainte-Marie is a well-known folk singer and Academy Award-winning songwriter. Throughout her career as a recording artist, she has remained an advocate for Indian rights.

Sainte-Marie was orphaned as an infant and was raised in Massachusetts by a Micmac Indian couple. In college, she studied Oriental philosophy. Sainte-Marie has been playing guitar and writing songs since she was sixteen years old. In the 1960s, spurred on by the positive reaction to her singing, Sainte-Marie went to New York City, where she began singing in the numerous folk clubs in the Greenwich Village section of the city. In a short time, she was offered a recording contract with Vanguard Records. Over the years, she had numerous hit singles, including "Universal Soldier" and "Until It's Time for You to Go." Her most recent (1992) recording, entitled *Confidence and Likely Stories*, marked a departure for the artist. The new songs included lush strings and multi-rhythmic textures that set them apart from her earlier pop and folk recordings.

Sainte-Marie has infused both her recording career and her general life with a sense of purpose relating to Indian culture and concerns, both past and present. She has contributed writings to *The Native Voice*, *Thunderbird*, *American Indian Horizons*, and *Boston Broadside* in the field of North American Indian music and Indian affairs. Sainte-Marie is the author of *Nokosis and the Magic Hat* (1986), a children's adventure book set on an Indian reservation. She has traveled and lectured throughout western Europe, Canada, and Mexico.

Fritz Scholder
1937–

Luiseño artist

Fritz Scholder is recognized as a leading modern artist in the United States. His work often deals with themes relating to the Native American experience.

Scholder was born in Breckenridge, Minnesota. His grandmother was a member of the Luiseño tribe, although Scholder describes himself as "a non-Indian Indian." He earned his master of fine arts degree from the University of Arizona in 1964. For five years, Scholder was instructor of advanced painting and art history at the Institute of American Indian Arts.

Although Scholder's upbringing was not acutely focused on his Native American heritage, his art awakened in him a desire to explore this background. Scholder's work often combines surrealist pop imagery and Native American mysticism. The artist has frequently addressed issues facing American Indians, including alcoholism, assimilation into mainstream U.S. society, and the degradation of Native American culture. In some ways, Scholder has been controversial. His critics complain that he has not taken Native American problems seriously enough and that his pop art has reduced their culture to kitsch—popularized art with little aesthetic value. Some would like to see Scholder use his high profile as a popular artist to advance Native American causes. Scholder himself prefers to communicate through his work. He states, "I'm not at all militant. I have a way out: I can put something down on canvas or do a lithograph."

In 1980, Scholder made a promise to himself to no longer paint "Indians." The decision was based entirely on artistic grounds. In 1992, he broke that rule, for a lithograph titled *Indian Contemplating Columbus*. The forty-by-sixty-inch work is the largest ever made by Scholder. "I'm very divided about Columbus," Scholder states, "because I grew up thinking of him as a hero. When I was a boy, I didn't think about my being part-Indian. . . . But now, I can understand the other side, and now, after much more reading as an adult, I realize that Columbus's trip was the beginning of the end for many cultures." The lithograph portrays a silhouetted figure sitting in a chair, facing the corner. A brightly colored moccasin on his foot is the only clue that the figure is Indian. Concerning the celebration of the 1992 Columbus Quincentenary, Scholder believes all viewpoints have a right to be heard: "If someone puts up a statue to Columbus, they have that right, and people should be dignified about it and not protest. But the American Indian should also make his stand clear."

Diosa Summers-Fitzgerald
1945–89

Mississippi Choctaw artist

Diosa Summers-Fitzgerald was an educator and artist who worked with Native American art forms, and she developed and designed art programs to teach Native American art and traditions.

Born in New York, New York, she earned a bachelor of arts from State University College at Buffalo (1977), and a master in education (Ed. M.) from Harvard University (1983). The focus of her work and studies was Native American art. She was both an artist herself and a teacher of Native American art traditions. In the classroom, Summers-Fitzgerald worked to foster a clearer understanding of the roots of Native American tradition through art.

From 1975–77, Summers-Fitzgerald was the director of education of the History and Continuing Education Department at the State University College of New York College at Buffalo, and an instructor at Haffenreffer Museum of Anthropology, in Bristol, Rhode Island from 1979 to 1980, at which time she was also acting tribal coordinator of the Narragansett Tribal Education Project. From 1982 to 1985, she was artist-in-residence at the Folk Arts Program in Rhode Island State Council on the Arts in Providence, Rhode Island, and also an artist working with the Native American Art Forms Nishnabeykwa Production in Charlestown, Rhode Island. From1985 until her death in 1989, she was the education director of the Jamaica Arts Center, in Jamaica, New York.

Summers-Fitzgerald was the author of Indian museum brochures including "Native American Food," "Fingerweaving," "Narrative and Instruction," and "Ash Sapling Basketry."

Gerald Tailfeathers
1925–75

Blackfoot artist

Gerald Tailfeathers, one of the first Native Canadian artists to pursue a professional artistic career, was born in 1925 at Stand Off, Alberta. His talent was apparent to others early in his life; in his teens, he received a scholarship from the Anglican Church to study art and was not yet twenty when he had his first exhibition. He trained in art at the School of Fine Arts in Banff, a small resort town in the Rocky Mountains in Alberta, and at the Provincial School of Technology and Art in Calgary,

Alberta. Tailfeathers's career began to flourish while he was in his twenties; apart from a stint as a technical draftsman for a petroleum company, he worked as a fulltime artist.

Tailfeathers's painting style was pictorial and nostalgic. His paintings often depicted his people, the Blackfoot and Blood Indians, as they lived in the nineteenth century, hunting buffalo, setting up camp, and engaging in ceremonial practices. He was influenced by other Indian painters of his generation, as he traveled often to view the work of others. He spent a summer studying at the Summer Art School in Glacier National Park in Montana, for example, with several portrait painters, including Winold Reiss and Carl Linck from New York. Later in his career, after a visit to the Arizona studio of the sculptor George Phippin, Tailfeathers began to experiment with bronze sculpture depicting life on the plains. Tailfeathers died in 1975, without being able to fully realize his vision of indigenous sculpture, on the Blood Indian Reserve in Alberta.

Roger Tsabetsye
1941–

Zuni Pueblo artist

Roger Tsabetsye was born in Zuni, New Mexico. The Zuni Pueblo is one of nineteen pueblo villages in eastern New Mexico known for their strong ties to their traditional religion, ceremonies, and culture. Tsabetsye was educated at the Institute of American Indian Arts, the government-operated Indian art school in Santa Fe, New Mexico, and also studied at the School for American Craftsmen, where he majored in silver and metal processing, and the Rochester Institute of Technology.

He is one of the first people, along with Fritz Scholder, the famous California Indian artist, to actively express their combined traditional and modern artistic training gained from the arts program at the Institute of American Indian Arts. Tsabetsye taught art at the institute and helped develop the school's curriculum and philosophy.

Working principally in three different media, painting, ceramics, and silver, Tsabetsye has exhibited at the Heard Museum, Phoenix (Arizona), the Scottsdale (Arizona) Indian National Art Show, the Museum of Santa Fe, the New York American

Indian Art Center, and numerous other exhibitions. His work has received many awards and honors, and in 1968 he was asked by President Lyndon Johnson to create a squash blossom for the president of Costa Rica. During this time, Tsabetsye was an Indian representative at several conferences in Washington, D.C., to help initiate President Johnson's War on Poverty.

Tsabetsye is also the founder and owner of Tsabetsye Enterprises, a company specializing in the merchandising (retail and wholesale) of Zuni jewelry. The company illustrates Tsabetsye's personal philosophy that American Indians should be partners with the rest of U.S. society.

Pablita Velarde
1918–

Santa Clara Pueblo
painter

Pablita Velarde is an acclaimed Native American painter, whose works reflect the culture and heritage of her people.

Velarde was born in the Santa Clara Pueblo of New Mexico and educated at the Santa Fe Indian School. Her love for art and talent as an artist has been traced to a childhood eye disease that temporarily restricted her sight. According to one biographer, when Velarde's sight was regained, it gave her a new appreciation of visual perception. Velarde studied art under Dorothy Dunn, a pioneer among Indian artists. In 1938 Velarde built a studio for her work in Santa Clara and began her career in earnest.

One of Velarde's first works is still her most renowned—a series of painted murals containing composite pictures depicting the day-to-day life and culture of the Rio Grande Pueblos. In 1956, Velarde developed a unique painting technique that employs colored rocks that are ground and mixed to create a pliable, textured painting material. With this material, Velarde has produced works that recall the art of her ancestors and that make effective use of traditional designs and pictographs in her work. Another of Velarde's paintings that has received widespread acclaim is *Old Father, the Story Teller* (1960). With a unique and insightful composition, the painting links traditional Native American legends and universal human beliefs.

Velarde is also the author and illustrator of *Old Father, the Story Teller* (in which the painting of the same name appears).

Exhibitors of Contemporary Native Arts

The focus of this section is on tribal cooperatives—Native-operated not-for-profit enterprises. For more complete listings, including for-profit galleries, see *Indian, Eskimo, Aleut Owned and Operated Arts and Crafts Businesses: Source Directory,* published by Indian Arts and Crafts Board, Room 4004, U.S. Department of the Interior, Washington DC 20240; (202) 208-3773.

Alaska

MUSK OX PRODUCERS'
COOPERATIVE,
"OOMINGMAK"
604 H St.
Anchorage, AK 99501
or
Musk Ox Farm
Box 69
Unalakleet, AK 99684
(907) 272-9225

NANA MUSEUM
OF THE ARCTIC
CRAFT SHOP
Box 49
Kotzebue, AK 99752
(907) 442-3304 or
(907) 442-3747

ST. LAWRENCE ISLAND
ORIGINAL IVORY
COOPERATIVE, LTD.
Box 189
Gambell, AK 99642
(907) 985-5112 or
(907) 985-5649

TAHETA ARTS AND
CULTURAL GROUP
605 A St.
Anchorage, AK 99501
(907) 272-5829

YUGTARVIK REGIONAL
MUSEUM SHOP
Box 388
Bethel, AK 99559
(907) 543-2098

COLORADO RIVER INDIAN
TRIBES MUSEUM
Rte. 1, Box 23-B
Parker, AZ 85344
(602) 669-9211, ext. 213

GILA RIVER ARTS AND
CRAFTS CENTER
Box 457
Sacaton, AZ 85247
(602) 562-3411

HATATHLI GALLERY
Navajo Community College
Development Foundation
Tsaile, AZ 86556
(602) 724-3311, ext. 156

HONANI CRAFTS
Hopi Cultural Center, Shop #4
Box 317
Second Mesa, AZ 86043
(602) 734-2238

HOPI ARTS AND
CRAFTS–SILVERCRAFT
COOPERATIVE GUILD
Box 37
Second Mesa, AZ 86043
(602) 734-2463

NAVAJO ARTS
AND CRAFTS ENTERPRISE
Postal Drawer A
Window Rock, AZ 86515
(602) 871-4090

  BRANCH SHOP:
Box 464
Cameron, AZ 86020
(602) 679-2244

  BRANCH SHOP:
812 North Highway 666
Gallup, NM 87301
(505) 722-6709

SAN JUAN SOUTHERN
PAIUTE YINGUP WEAVERS
ASSOCIATION
Box 1336
Tuba City, AZ 86045
(602) 526-7143

Arizona

AMERICAN
INDIAN CONTEMPORARY
ARTS GALLERY
685 Market St.,
Suite 250
Monadnock Bldg.
San Francisco, CA
94105-4212
(415) 495-7600

INDIAN ARTS GIFT SHOP,
NCIDC, INC.
241 F St.
Eureka, CA 95501
(707) 445-8451

INTERTRIBAL TRADING POST
523 East Fourteenth St.
Oakland, CA 94606
(415) 452-1235

California

Florida   MICCOSUKEE GIFT SHOP
& CULTURAL CENTER
Box 440021, Tamiami Station
Miami, FL 33144
(305) 223-8380

SEMINOLE CULTURAL
CENTER
5221 Orient Rd.
Tampa, FL 33610
(813) 623-3549

Idaho   TRADING POST CLOTHES
HORSE
Box 368
Fort Hall, ID 83203
(208) 237-8433

Kansas   INDIAN MUSEUM GIFT
SHOP
Mid-America All-Indian
Center
650 North Seneca
Wichita, KS 67203
(316) 262-5221, ext. 41

Maine   BASKET BANK,
AROOSTOOK MICMAC
COUNCIL, INC.
8 Church St.
Presque Isle, ME 04769-2410
(207) 764-1972

Michigan   INDIAN EARTH ARTS &
CRAFTS STORE
124 West First St.
Flint, MI 48502
(313) 239-6621

INDIAN HILLS TRADING
COMPANY & INDIAN ART
GALLERY
1681 Harbor Rd.
Petoskey, MI 49770
(616) 347-3789

NATIVE AMERICAN ARTS
AND CRAFTS COUNCIL IN-
DIAN ARTS 7 CRAFTS STORE
Box 1049
Goose Creek Rd.
Grayling, MI 49738
(517) 348-3190

SWEETGRASS ARTS & CRAFTS
206 Greenough St.
Sault Ste. Marie, MI 49783
(906) 635-6050

IKWE MARKETING
Rte. 1
Osage, MN 56570
(218) 573-3411
or
(218) 573-3049

CHOCTAW MUSEUM OF
THE SOUTHERN INDIAN
GIFT SHOP
Rte. 7, Box 21
Philadelphia, MS 39350
(601) 656-5251

COUP MARKS
Box 532
Ronan, MT 59864
(406) 246-3216 or
(406) 644-2267

FLATHEAD INDIAN
MUSEUM, TRADING POST
& ART GALLERY
Box 464
St. Ignatius, MT 59865
(406) 745-2951

EARTH WINDOW
Nevada Urban Indians, Inc.
401 West Second St.
Reno, NV 89503
(702) 786-5999

CROWNPOINT
RUG WEAVERS'
ASSOCIATION
Box 1630
Crownpoint, NM 87313
(505) 786-5302

PIPESTONE INDIAN
SHRINE ASSOCIATION
c/o Pipestone National
Monument, Box 727
Pipestone, MN 56164
(507) 825-5463

NORTHERN
PLAINS INDIAN
CRAFTS
ASSOCIATION
Box E
Browning, MT 59417
(406) 338-5661

PLAINS GALLERY
Box 126
Lame Deer, MT 59043
No telephone

STEWART INDIAN
MUSEUM TRADING POST
5366 Snyder Ave.
Carson City, NV 89701
(702) 882-1808

INDIAN PUEBLO
CULTURAL CENTER, INC.
2401 Twelfth St. N.W.
Albuquerque, NM 87102
(505) 843-7270 or
(800) 288-0721

Minnesota

Mississippi

Montana

Nevada

New Mexico

INSTITUTE OF AMERICAN
INDIAN ARTS MUSEUM
108 Cathedral Pl.
Santa Fe, NM 87504
(505) 988-6212

JICARILLA ARTS AND
CRAFTS SHOP/MUSEUM
Box 507
Dulce, NM 87528
(505) 759-3515

NAVAJO GALLERY
Box 1756
Taos, NM 87571
(505) 758-3250

OKE OWEENGE ARTS
AND CRAFTS
Box 1095
San Juan Pueblo, NM 87566
(505) 852-2372

New York AMERICAN INDIAN
COMMUNITY HOUSE
GALLERY/MUSEUM
404 Lafayette St.
(708 Broadway, 2nd Floor)
New York, NY 10003
(212) 598-0100

MOHAWK IMPRESSIONS
Box 20
Mohawk Nation
Hogansburg, NY 13655
(518) 358-2467

NATIVE AMERICAN CENTER
FOR THE LIVING ARTS, INC.
25 Rainbow Mall
Niagara Falls, NY 14303
(716) 284-2427

PUEBLO OF ZUNI ARTS
AND CRAFTS
Box 425
Zuni, NM 87327
(505) 782-4481 or
(505) 782-5531

TA-MA-YA
CO-OP
ASSOCIATION
Santa Ana Pueblo
Star Rte., Box 37
Bernalillo, NM 87004
(505) 867-3301

ZUNI CRAFTSMEN
COOPERATIVE
ASSOCIATION
Box 426
Zuni, NM 87327
(505) 782-4425

NATIVE PEOPLES ARTS
AND CRAFTS SHOP
North American Indian Club
of Syracuse and Vicinity, Inc.
Box 85, 210 Fabius St.
Syracuse, NY 13201
(315) 475-7425

SENECA-IROQUOIS NATIONAL
MUSEUM GIFT SHOP
Box 442
Broad Street Extension
Salamanca, NY 14779
(716) 945-1738

SWEETGRASS GIFT SHOP
Akwesasne Museum
Rte. 37
Hogansburg, NY 13655
(518) 358-2240

HALIWA-SAPONI TRIBAL
POTTERY AND ARTS
Box 99
Hollister, NC 27844
(919) 586-4017

THREE AFFILIATED
TRIBES MUSEUM, ARTS &
CRAFTS DIVISION
New Town, ND 58763
(701) 627-4477

CHEROKEE ARTS &
CRAFTS CENTER
Box 948
Tahlequah, OK 74464
(918) 456-0511, ext. 307

CHEROKEE NATIONAL
MUSEUM GIFT SHOP
TSA-LA-GI, Box 515
Tahlequah, OK 74464
(918) 456-6007

FIVE CIVILIZED TRIBES
MUSEUM TRADING POST
Agency Hill, Honor Heights Dr.
Muskogee, OK 74401
(918) 683-1701

LENNI LENAPE
HISTORICAL SOCIETY
R.D. 2, Fish Hatchery Rd.
Allentown, PA 18103
(215) 797-2121 or
(215) 434-6819

OYATE KIN CULTURAL
COOPERATIVE
c/o Wesley Hare, Jr.
Marty, SD 57361
No telephone

QUALLA ARTS AND
CRAFTS MUTUAL, INC.
Box 277
Cherokee, NC 28719
(704) 497-3103

OKLAHOMA INDIAN
ARTS AND CRAFTS
COOPERATIVE
Southern Plains Indian
Museum, Box 966
Anadarko, OK 73005
(405) 247-3486

WEWOKA TRADING POST
C.R. Anthony Indian
Arts and Crafts Center
Seminole Indian Museum
Box 1532
524 South Wewoka Ave.
Wewoka, OK 74884
(405) 257-5580

ST. JOSEPH'S LAKOTA
DEVELOPMENT COUNCIL
St. Joseph's Indian School
Chamberlain, SD 57326
(605) 734-6021, ext. 307

North Carolina

North Dakota

Oklahoma

Pennsylvania

South Dakota

TIPI SHOP, INC.
Sioux Indian Museum
Box 1542
Rapid City, SD 57709
(605) 343-8128

Texas **TIGUA INDIAN RESERVATION CULTURAL CENTER & RESTAURANT**
Box 17579
El Paso, TX 79917
(915) 859-3916

TRIBAL ENTERPRISE
Alabama-Coushatta Indian
Reservation
Rte. 3, Box 640
Livingston, TX 77351
(409) 563-4391;
Texas only, 800-392-4794

Virginia **PAMUNKEY POTTERY AND CRAFTS TRADING POST**
Rte. 1
King William, VA 23086
(804) 843-2851

Washington **DAYBREAK STAR ARTS GALLERY**
Discovery Park
Box 99253
Seattle, WA 98199
(206) 285-4425

SACRED CIRCLE GALLERY OF AMERICAN INDIAN ART
607 First Ave.
Seattle, WA 98104
(206) 223-0072

MAKAH CULTURAL RESEARCH CENTER
Box 95
Neah Bay, WA 98357
(206) 645-2711/2

SUQUAMISH MUSEUM
Box 498
Suquamish, WA 98392
(206) 598-3311

POTLATCH GIFTS
Northwind Trading
Company
708 Commercial Ave.
Anacortes, WA 98221
(206) 293-6404

BUFFALO ART CENTER
Box 51
Bayfield, WI 54814
(715) 779-5858

ONEIDA NATION MUSEUM
Box 365
Oneida, WI 54155
(414) 869-2768

WA-SWA-GON ARTS AND CRAFTS
Box 477
Lac du Flambeau, WI 54538
(715) 588-7636

Wisconsin

American Indian Cultural Events

This is a partial list of cultural events and gatherings (primarily powwows, ceremonials, and feast days) throughout the United States and Canada. While many of these events include art markets and fairs, an additional listing of those events follows this one.

The anticipated months or dates for the events and entrance fees may change from year to year. Contact tribal offices, American Indian cultural centers or clubs, university American Indian studies programs, national parks, rodeo associations, museums, travel/visitor's bureaus, and BIA offices for more complete or current information. Inquiries into certified Indian artists' and artisans' arts and crafts and dress, photo taking, and conduct while attending cultural events should be directed to the sponsoring organization. Respect and cooperation are appreciated at all events.

The events are listed alphabetically by state according to title. Addresses listed indicate the location or mailing address. For additional listings you can contact the following organizations:

EIGHT NORTHERN INDIAN PUEBLOS COUNCIL
P.O. Box 969
San Juan Pueblo, NM 87566
(505) 766-3170

HOPI CULTURAL CENTER
P.O. Box 647
Second Mesa, AZ 86043
(602) 734-2441

INDIAN PUEBLO CULTURAL CENTER
2401 12th St. N.W.
Albuquerque, NM 87102
(505) 843-7270

LAKOTA TIMES
(A monthly periodical)
Karen and Garfield Magpie
P.O. Box 359
Brisbane, CA 94005-0359

**NATIONAL
NATIVE AMERICAN CO-OP**
Native American
Information and Trade Center
P.O. Box 1000
San Carlos, AZ 85550-0301
(602) 622-4900
Fred Snyder, Director

**NEWS FROM INDIAN
COUNTRY**
(A monthly periodical)
Oklahoma Indian Affairs
Commission
4010 North Lincoln, Suite 200
Oklahoma City, OK 73105
(405) 521-3828

TOURIDAHO
State Capitol Bldg., Rm. 108
Boise, ID 83720
(800) 635-7820

◆ **UNITED STATES**

**CREEK INDIAN
THANKSGIVING DAY
HOMECOMING AND
POW WOW** (November)
HCR 69A, Box 85-B
Atmore, AL 36502
(205) 368-9136

Alabama

**NORTHWEST
NATIVE TRADE FAIR**
(July)
Arctic Circle
Chamber of Commerce
P.O. Box 284
Kotzebue, AK 99752

**WORLD ESKIMO AND
INDIAN OLYMPIC GAMES**
(July/August)
Parry Gymnasium,
University of Alaska
Fairbanks Convention and
Visitors Bureau
P.O. Box 2433
Fairbanks, AK 99707
(907) 452-6646

Alaska

Arizona

COYOTE MOON GALA
(June)
HOLIDAY CELEBRATION
(November)
TRIBUTE POW WOW
(November)
P.O. Box 457
Sacaton, AZ 85247
(800) 472-6298

NAVAJO NATION FAIR
(September)
Pow Wow Grounds
Window Rock, AZ 85615
(602) 871-6702

O'ODHAM TASH-CASA
GRANDE INDIAN DAYS
(February)
Tohono O'odham Nation
(Papago Reservation)
P.O. Box 837
Sells, AZ 85634
(602) 383-2221

TEWANIMA FOOT RACE
(September)
Hopi Public Relations
P.O. Box 123
Kykotsmovi, AZ 86039
(602) 734-2441

WHITE MOUNTAIN
APACHE TRIBAL FAIR AND
RODEO (September)
Fort Apache Reservation
P.O. Box 700
White River, AZ 85941
(602) 338-4346

California

AMERICAN INDIAN
LEADERS OF TODAY AND
TOMORROW
CONFERENCE (Fall)
AMERICAN INDIAN
STUDENT COUNCIL
ANNUAL POW WOW
(Spring)
CSULB American Indian
Student Council
c/o American Indian Studies
Department
F03 Building, Room 310
1250 Bellflower Blvd.
Long Beach, CA 90840
(310) 985-5293

ANNUAL CHRISTMAS
POW WOW (December)
United Indians in Christ and
Mothers and Others for
American Indian Children
3947 Second Ave.
Los Angeles, CA 90008
(213) 294-4528

ANNUAL UCLA CONTEST
POW WOW (May)
University of California, Los
Angeles - 3220 Campbell Hall
405 Hilgard Ave.
Los Angeles, CA 90024-1548
(310) 206-7513 or
(310) 825-7315

CHRISTMAS POW WOW
(December)
DQU POW WOW
(February)
GRADUATION POW WOW
(June, second Saturday)
NATIVE AMERICAN
STUDENT UNION POW
WOW (April)
VETERAN'S POW WOW
(November)
D-Q University
P.O. Box 409
Davis, CA 95616
(916) 758-0470

CHUMASH INTERTRIBAL
POW WOW (July)
Santa Ynez Reservation
P.O. Box 517
Santa Ynez, CA 93460
(805) 688-7997

FOUR MOONS POW WOW
(June)
P.O. Box 1258
Fontana, CA 92334
(714) 822-8302

GATHERING OF THE
TRIBES POW WOW
(February)
GATHERING SOCIAL POW
WOW (November)
MEDICINE WAYS ANNUAL
POW WOW (May)
University of California,
Riverside
Native American Programs
224 Commons
Riverside, CA 92521
(909) 787-4143

HUTASH HARVEST
FESTIVAL AND
POW WOW (October)
Santa Barbara, CA
(805) 965-4688 or
(805) 684-1925

INDIAN INTERTRIBAL
AGENCY
COMMITTEE POW WOW
(June)
P.O. Box 1296
Bishop, CA 93515
(619) 873-6394
Rena Brown

MALKI MUSEUM
FIESTA AND POW WOW
(May)
11795 Fields Rd.
Banning, CA 92220
(714) 849-7289

SCIC, INC. ANNUAL
POW WOW
(August)
CHILDREN'S XMAS
PARTY/POW WOW/
TOY DRIVE/BOUTIQUE
(December)
Southern California Indian
Center, Inc.
12755 Brookhurst Ave.
Garden Grove, CA 92643
(714) 530-0221

STANFORD UNIVERSITY
POW WOW (May)
P.O. Box 2990
Stanford, CA 94309
(415) 725-6944

Colorado

DENVER POW WOW (March)
Denver Coliseum
P.O. Box 19178
Denver, CO 80219
(303) 936-4826

OYATE/AISES SPRING POW
WOW (Spring)
Box 184
University of Colorado
Boulder, CO 80302
(303) 492-8874

SOUTHERN UTE BEAR
DANCE (May)
SOUTHERN UTE
TRIBAL FAIR AND
POW WOW
(September)
Southern Ute Tribal
Council
P.O. Box 737
Ignacio, CO 81137
(303) 563-4525

Connecticut

ANNUAL CONNECTICUT
RIVER POW WOW
(August)
ANNUAL PAUCATUCK
AND PEQUOT HARVEST
MOON POW WOW
(October)
ANNUAL STRAWBERRY
MOON POW WOW
(June)
(203) 684-6984

EAGLE WING PRESS POW
WOW (August)
Black Rock State Park
Watertown, CT 06357
(203) 238-4009

MOHEGAN TRIBE POW
WOW (August)
Fort Shantok Park
Mohegan Nation
P.O. Box 387
Norwich, CT 06360
(203) 376-4525

Delaware

NANTICOKE
INDIAN POW WOW
(September)
Millsboro
Delaware State Travel
Service
99 Kings Hwy.
P.O. Box 1401
Dover, DE 19901
inside Delaware:
(800) 282-8667;
outside: (800) 441-8846

PANTHER BEND POW-WOW
(December, second weekend)
P.O. Box 226
Lacoochee, FL 33534
(904) 567-0314

**SEMINOLE INDIAN
TRIBAL FAIR (February)**
Seminole Okalee Indian Village
Seminole Tribal Council
6073 Sterling Rd.
Hollywood, FL 33024
(305) 583-2435

**SOUTH FLORIDA POW
WOW (January)**
c/o Native America, Inc.
P.O. Box 282
Fall Rock, KY 40932
(606) 598-6623

Florida

CHEROKEE GOLD
(September)
Highway 225
Calhoun, GA 30701
(706) 629-8151

**INDIAN AWARENESS DAYS
(July or September)**
Etowah Indian Mounds
813 Indian Mounds Rd. S.W.
Cartersville, GA 30120
(404) 387-3747

Georgia

**CHIEF JOSEPH AND
WARRIORS MEMORIAL
POWWOW (June)**
Nez Percé Tribal Office
P.O. Box 305
Lapwai, ID 83540
(208) 843-2253

**FOUR NATIONS POW
WOW (October)**
P.O. Box 222
Lapwai, ID 83540
(208) 843-2003
Jessica Redheart

**SHOSHONI-BANNOCK
INDIAN FESTIVAL AND
RODEO (August)**
Shoshone-Bannock Tribes
Pow Wow Grounds
P.O. Box 306
Fort Hall, ID 83203
(208) 785-2965

Idaho

**ANNUAL CHICAGO AND
REDCLOUD POW WOW
(February & November)**
1631 West Wilson
Chicago, IL 60640
(312) 275-5871

INDIAN POW WOW
(September)
619 Iowa St.
Gavenport, IL 52803
(319) 323-7955

Illinois

Indiana   AMERICAN INDIAN
COUNCIL, INC.,
TRADITIONAL POW WOW
(August)
1302 Victoria Dr.
Lebanon, IN 46052
(317) 482-3315

POTAWATOMI FESTIVAL
(September)
P.O. Box 408
Attica, IN 47918
(317) 762-3340

Iowa   MESQUAKIE INDIAN
POW WOW (August)
Pow Wow Association
Sac and Fox Reservation
Rte. 2, Box 56C
Tama, IA 52339
(515) 484-4678

Kansas   ANNUAL INDIAN
ARTS SHOW
(September)
University of Kansas
Museum of Anthropology
Spooner Hall
Lawrence, KS 66045
(913) 864-4245
Maria Martin, coordinator

Kentucky   TRAIL OF TEARS
INTERTRIBAL POW WOW
(September)
Recreation Complex
P.O. Box 4027
Hopkinsville, KY 42240
(502) 886-8033

SUMMER
POW WOW (June)
Wildwood Acres
Hartford City, IN 77348
(317) 348-1223

KICKAPOO POW WOW (July)
Kickapoo Reservation
P.O. Box 271
Horton, KS 66349
(913) 486-2131

**MID AMERICA INDIAN
POW WOW** (July)
Wichita Chamber of Commerce
Wichita, KS 67201
(316) 262-5221

LOUISIANA INDIAN
HERITAGE ASSOCIATION
POW WOW (May)
Tchfkunchte Campground
Folsom, LA
(504) 244-5866

Louisiana

CEREMONIAL DAY
(August)
Pleasant Point
Passamaquoddy
P.O. Box 343
Perry, ME 04667
(207) 853-2551

Maine

BALTIMORE AMERICAN
INDIAN CENTER
POW WOW
(August)
113 South Broadway
Baltimore, MD 21231
(410) 675-3535

MARYLAND INDIAN HERI-
TAGE FESTIVAL AND POW
WOW (June & August)
Maryland Indian Heritage
Society
P.O. Box 905
Waldorf, MD 20604
(301) 372-1932

Maryland

HASSANAMISCO
NIPMUC INDIAN
COUNCIL POW WOW
(July)
(508) 839-7394

HOMECOMING POW
WOW (October)
American Indianists Society, Inc.
15 Mattson Ave.
Worcester, MA 01606
(508) 852-6271

Massachusetts

FIRST PEOPLES POW
WOW (May/June)
P.O. Box 861
Warren, MI 48090
(313) 756-1350

SAULT TRIBES
POW WOW (July)
Sault Ste. Marie Tribe of
Chippewa
206 Greenough
Sault Ste. Marie, MI 49783
(906) 635-6050

Michigan

Minnesota

HEART OF THE EARTH POW WOW (February)
Minneapolis Convention Center
209 Fourth St. S.E.
Minneapolis, MN 55414
(612) 331-8862

MEMORIAL DAY POW WOW (May)
Minnesota Chippewa Tribal Office
Rte. 3, Box 100
Cass Lake, MN 56633
(218) 335-8200

Mississippi

CHOCTAW INDIAN FAIR (July)
Choctaw Reservation
P.O. Box 6010
Philadelphia, MS 39350
(601) 656-5251

Montana

CROW INDIAN FAIR (August)
Crow Tribal Council
P.O. Box 159
Crow Agency, MT 59022
(406) 638-2303

NORTH AMERICAN INDIAN DAYS CELEBRATION (July)
Blackfeet Tribal Council
P.O. Box 850
Browning, MT 59417
(406) 338-7521/2

NI-MI-WIN CELEBRATION (August)
Spirit Mountain
9500 Spirit Mountain Pl.
Duluth, MN 55810
(218) 628-2891 or
(218) 897-1251

TRADITIONAL INTERTRIBAL POW WOW (Spring)
1426 Fourth Ave. S.E.,
No. 207
Rochester, MN 55904
(507) 281-4772

NORTHERN CHEYENNE POW WOW (July)
Northern Cheyenne Tribal Council
P.O. Box 128
Lame Deer, MT 59043
(406) 477-8283

ROCKY BOY POW WOW (August)
Chippewa Cree Tribe
Rocky Boy Route, Box 544
Box Elder, MT 59521
(406) 395-4708

OMAHA TRIBAL
POW WOW
(August)
Omaha Reservation
P.O. Box 368
Macy, NE 68039
(402) 837-5391

SHOSHONI-PAIUTE
ANNUAL POW WOW (July)
VETERAN'S DAY POW
WOW (November)
Shoshoni-Paiute Tribal Council
P.O. Box 219
Owyhee, NV 89832-0219
(702) 757-3161

GALLUP INTERTRIBAL
CEREMONIAL (August)
Red Rock State Park, Gallup
Intertribal Ceremonial
P.O. Box 1
Churchrock, NM 87311
(505) 863-3896

GATHERING OF NATIONS
POW WOW (April)
P.O. Box 75102
Albuquerque, NM 87194
(505) 836-2810

INSTITUTE OF AMERICAN
INDIAN ARTS STUDENT
POW WOW (April)
GRADUATION CLASS (May)
HIGH SCHOOL
COMPETITION (October)
Institute of American Indian Arts
P.O. Box 2007
Santa Fe, NM 87504
(505) 988-6440
Clifford LaFromboise

WINNEBAGO POW WOW
(July)
Winnebago Reservation
Attn: Pow Wow
687 Winnebago Tribal Council
Winnebago, NE 68071
(402) 878-2272

Nebraska

SNOW MOUNTAIN
POW WOW
(May)
Pow Wow Committee
Las Vegas Paiute Tribe
1 Paiute Dr.
Las Vegas, NV 89106
(702) 386-3926

Nevada

LITTLE BEAVER ROUNDUP
(July)
Jicarilla Apache Tribe
P.O. Box 507
Dulce, NM 87528
(505) 759-3242

New Mexico

SANTO DOMINGO PUEBLO
FEAST DAY (August)
P.O. Box 79
Santo Domingo Pueblo, NM
87052
(505) 465-2214

New York

IROQUOIS INDIAN
FESTIVAL
(September)
Schoharie Museum of the
Iroquois
Box 7, Caverns Rd.
Housi Cave, NY 12092
(518) 296-8949

PAUMANAUKE POW WOW
(August)
Babylon Citizens
Council on the Arts
71 Sawyer Ave.
West Babylon, NY 11704-6622
(716) 532-4900

SENECA NATION INDIAN
FALL FESTIVAL (September)
Saylor Complex,
Cattaraugus Reservation
1490 Rte. 438
Irving, NY 14081
(716) 532-4900

SHINNECOCK
INDIAN POW WOW
(September)
Shinnecock Reservation
Rte. 27A, Montauk Hwy.
Southampton, NY 11968
(516) 283-6143

TURTLE POW WOW
(May)
Native American
Center for the Living Arts
25 Rainbow Blvd. S.
Niagara Falls, NY 14303
(716) 284-2427

North Carolina

CHEROKEE POW WOW
(June)
Eastern Band of Cherokee
Indians
P.O. Box 455
Cherokee, NC 28719
(704) 497-2771

HALIWA-SAPONI
POW WOW (April)
P.O. Box 99
Hollister, NC 27844
(919) 586-4017

North Dakota

MANDAREE CELEBRATION
AND POW WOW (July)
Three Affiliated Tribes
Fort Berthold Reservation
P.O. Box 220
Mandaree, ND 58757
(701) 627-4781

STANDING ROCK POW
WOW (August)
Standing Rock Reservation
Cave Fort Yates Committee
Fort Yates, ND 58538
(701) 854-3431

UNITED TRIBES
INTERNATIONAL
CHAMPIONSHIP
POW WOW (September)
Bismarck Civic Center
3315 University Dr.
Bismarck, ND 58504
(701) 255-3285, ext. 217

ANNUAL OGLEWANAGI
POW WOW (November)
1960 Byron Dr.
Brunswick, OH 44212
(216) 225-3416

INDIAN MOUND FESTIVAL
(October)
15 Shady Ln.
The Plains, OH 45780
(614) 797-4091

AMERICAN INDIAN
EXPOSITION (August)
P.O. Box 908
Anadarko, OK 73005
(405) 247-6651 or
(405) 247-2733

ANNUAL PONCA POW
WOW (August)
Ponca Tribe of Oklahoma
Box 2 White Eagle
Ponca City, OK 74601
(405) 762-8104

CHEROKEE NATIONAL
HOLIDAY (September)
Cherokee Nation of Oklahoma
P.O. Box 948
Tahlequah, OK 74465
(918) 456-0671

MIAMI VALLEY
COUNCIL FOR NATIVE
AMERICANS POW WOW
(June/March)
P.O. Box 637
Dayton, OH 95401-0637
(513) 275-8599

Ohio

CHOCTAW NATION
LABOR DAY FESTIVAL
(September)
Choctaw Nation of Oklahoma
P.O. Drawer 1210
Durant, OK 74702
(405) 924-8280

PAWNEE INDIAN
HOMECOMING
AND POW WOW
(July)
Pawnee Tribal Council
P.O. Box 470
Pawnee, OK 74058
(918) 762-3624

Oklahoma

RED EARTH NATIVE
AMERICAN CULTURAL
FESTIVAL (June)
Myriad Convention Center
2100 Northeast 52nd
Oklahoma City, OK 73111
(405) 427-5228

Oregon AMERICAN INDIAN ART
SHOW (April)
CHRISTMAS WINTER
HOLIDAY POW WOW
(December)
CULTURAL AWARENESS
WEEK (includes Salmonbake
and Pow Wow, May)
United Indian Students in
Higher Education
P.O. Box 751
Portland, OR 97207
(503) 725-5671

PENDLETON ROUND-UP
(September)
Pendleton, OR
(800) 524-2984

PI-UM-SHA POW WOW
AND TREATY DAYS
(June)
Warm Springs Tribal
Council
P.O. Box C
Warm Springs, OR 97761
(503) 553-1161

Pennsylvania COUNCIL OF THREE
RIVERS
POW WOW
(September)
Indian Center
200 Charles St.
Pittsburgh, PA 15328
(412) 782-4457

MOUNTAIN SPRINGS POW
WOW AND FESTIVAL
(July)
Mountain Springs Camping
Resort
P.O. Box 365
Shartlesville, PA 19554
(215) 488-6859

Rhode Island ALGONQUIN INDIAN
SCHOOL POW WOW
(July, tentative)
270 Vermont
Providence, RI
(401) 781-2636

NARRAGANSETT INDIAN
FALL FESTIVAL (October)
Indian Longhouse, Rte. 2,
Charlestown
Rhode Island Department of
Economic Development
7 Jackson Walkway
Providence, RI 02903
(401) 277-2601

BLACK HILLS
POW WOW AND
ARTS EXPO
(July)
Harold Salway
P.O. Box 8131
Rapid City, SD 57709
(605) 341-0925

CHEYENNE RIVER
SIOUX FAIR AND RODEO
(CHERRY CREEK POW
WOW; September)
H.V. Johnston Cultural
Center
P.O. Box 590
Eagle Butte, SD 57625
(605) 964-4685 or
(605) 964-7275

FALL FESTIVAL AND POW
WOW (October)
Native American Indian
Association of Tennessee
211 Union St., Suite 932
Nashville, TN 37271
(615) 726-0806

AMERICAN INDIAN
VETERANS OF NORTH
TEXAS SOCIETY
POW WOW (Monthly)
717 Vickie
Azle, TX 76020
(214) 333-3908,
Frank Tongkeamha
or (817) 444-2770,
Dick Green

FOURTH OF JULY POW
WOW (July)
Glacial Lakes Association
P.O. Box 1113
Watertown, SD 57201
(605) 886-5814

OGLALA NATION POW WOW
AND RODEO (August)
Pine Ridge Reservation
P.O. Box H
Pine Ridge, SD 57770
(605) 867-5821

ROSEBUD SIOUX FAIR
AND POW WOW
(August)
Rosebud Tribal Office
P.O. Box 430
Rosebud, SD 57570
(605) 747-2381

NAIA POW WOW
(June)
P.O. Box 11473
Memphis, TN 38111
(901) 276-4741

NATIONAL
CHAMPIONSHIP
POW WOW
(September)
Traders Village
2602 Mayfield Rd.
Grand Prairie, TX 75051
(214) 647-2331

South Dakota

Tennessee

Texas

TEXAS RED
NATIONS
POW WOW
(November)
P.O. Box 758
Cedar Hill, TX 75104
(214) 264-2283

TIGUA SAINT ANTHONY'S
DAY CEREMONY (June)
Ysleta Del Sur Pueblo
Tigua Indian Reservation
P.O. Box 17579
El Paso, TX 79917
(915) 859-7913

Utah NATIVE AMERICAN
WARRIOR VETERANS
MEMORIAL POW WOW
(August)
70 North Terrace Dr.
Clearfield, UT 84015
(801) 775-0808

OGDEN POW WOW
(September)
Circle Center
530 24th St.
Ogden, UT 84401
(801) 392-1638,
Judy Butler

NORTHERN UTE POW
WOW AND RODEO (July)
UTE TRIBAL BEAR DANCE
(April)
Uintah and Ouray Tribal
Council
P.O. Box 400
Fort Duchesne, UT 84026
(801) 722-5141

Virginia ANNUAL DAVIS LAKE
INTERTRIBAL POW WOW
(April)
200 Byrd St.
Suffolk, VA 23434
(804) 539-1191

Washington CHIEF SEATTLE DAYS
(August)
Suquamish Tribe
Port Madison Reservation
P.O. Box 498
Suquamish, WA 98392
(206) 598-3311

LUMMI STOMISH
WATER FESTIVAL (June)
Near Gooseberry Point
Lummi Indian Tribe
2616 Kwina Rd.
Bellingham, WA 98226-9298
(206) 734-8180

MAKAH INDIAN DAYS
(August)
Makah Tribal Council
P.O. Box 115
Neah Bay, WA 98357
(206) 645-2205, ext. 36

MASON SCHOOL POW WOW
(January, second weekend;
February, March, and
December, first weekend)
Tacoma Public Schools
Indian Education
P.O. Box 1357
Tacoma, WA 98401-1357

NORTHWEST INDIAN
YOUTH CONFERENCE
POW WOW
(April/Spring)
102 Prefontaine Place S.
Seattle, WA 98104
(206) 343-3111

ANNUAL UW-OSHKOSH
POW WOW (Month varies)
751 Algoma
Oshkosh, WI 54901
(414) 424-1246

HONOR THE EARTH
TRADITIONAL POW WOW
(July)
Lac Courte Oreilles Reservation
Attn.: Earth Traditional
Commission
Rte. 2, Box 2788
Hayward, WI 54843
(715) 634-2100 or
(715) 634-8934

SEAFAIR INDIAN DAY
POW WOW (July, third
weekend)
Daybreak Star Cultural Arts
P.O. Box 99100
Seattle, WA 98199
(206) 285-4425

SPOKANE FALLS
NORTHWEST INDIAN
ENCAMPMENT (August)
E905 East Third Ave.
Spokane, WA 99202
(509) 535-0886

TIINOWIT
INTERNATIONAL POW
WOW (June)
WEASELTAIL POW WOW
(May)
P.O. Box 151
Toppenish, WA 94948
(509) 865-5121

MENOMINEE NATION
CONTEST POW WOW
(August, first weekend)
Menominee Indian
tribe of Wisconsin
P.O. Box 910
Keshena, WI 54135
(715) 799-5166

ONEIDA POW WOW
(July)
Oneida Reservation
P.O. Box 365
Oneida, WI 54155-0365
(414) 869-2214

Wisconsin

Wyoming

CHEYENNE
FRONTIER DAYS
(July/August)
Frontier Park
P.O. Box 2477
Cheyenne, WY 82003
(800) 227-6336

ETHETE POW WOW AND
RODEO (July)
Northern Arapaho Business
Council
P.O. Box 396
Fort Washakie, WY 82514
(307) 332-6120

SHOSHONI INDIAN FAIR
(August)
Shoshoni Cultural Center
P.O. Box 1008
Fort Washakie, WY 82514
(307) 332-9106

CANADA ✦

Alberta

BRIDGING THE
GAP POW WOW
(May)
140 Second Ave. S.W.
Calgary, AB T2P 0B9
(403) 264-1155

ERMINESKIN INDIAN
DAYS (August)
P.O. Box 219
Hobbema, AB T0C 1N0
(403) 585-3741

LAC LA BICHE
POW WOW DAYS
(July/August)
Travel Alberta
P.O. Box 2500
Edmonton, AB T5J 2Z4

British Columbia

FIRST PEOPLES
CULTURAL FESTIVAL
(August)
Capilano Park
North Vancouver BC
(604) 873-3761

KAMLOOPS
POW WOW (August)
315 Yellowhead Hwy.
Kamloops, BC F1H 1H1
(604) 828-9716

MINI POWWOW
(July, 2nd wknd)
St. Mary's Campus
34110 Lougheed Hwy.
Mission, BC V2V 1G4
(604) 826-1281

SEABIRD ISLAND
FESTIVAL
(May)
P.O. Box 650
Agassiz, BC V0M I80
(604) 796-2177

OPASQUIA INDIAN DAYS
(August)
The Pas Indian Reserve
Travel Manitoba Tourism
Dept. 2001, Box 940
The Tas, MB R9A 1K9
(204) 623-6478

Manitoba

WIKWEMIKONG INDIAN
POW WOW (August)
Unceded Indian Reserve
Box 112
Wikwemikong, ON P0P 2J0
(705) 859-3122

Ontario

SAKIMAY ANNUAL POW
WOW (June/July)
Sakimay Band Office
P.O. Box 339
Grenfell, SK S0G 2B0
(306) 697-2831

Saskatchewan

American Indian Art Markets and Fairs

UNITED STATES ✦ ✦ ✦ ✦ ✦ ✦ ✦ ✦ ✦ ✦ ✦ ✦ ✦ ✦ ✦ ✦

Arizona

ARIZONA STATE FAIR
(October)
P.O. Box 6728
Phoenix, AZ 85005
(602)252-6771

FESTIVAL OF NATIVE
AMERICAN ARTS
(June–August)
Coconino Center for the Arts
P.O. Box 296
Flagstaff, AZ 86004
(602)779-6921

GILA RIVER ARTS AND
CRAFTS FAIR (January)
SPRING FESTIVAL (March)
P.O. Box 457
Sacaton, AZ 85247
(800)472-62948

HEARD MUSEUM INDIAN
MARKET (March)
Heard Museum
22 East Monte Vista Rd.
Phoenix, AZ 85004
(602)252-8848

HOPI AND NAVAJO SHOWS
(June–July)
ZUNI EXHIBITION
(May)
Museum of Northern
Arizona
Rte. 4, Box 720
Flagstaff, AZ 86001
(602)774-5211

NATIVE AMERICAN
ARTS AND CRAFTS
MARKET
(November–April, first
weekend)
Native American Tourism
Center
4130 North Goldwater Blvd.
Scottsdale, AZ 85251
(602)945-0771

O'ODHAM-TASH INDIAN
DAYS (February)
P.O. Box 11165
Casa Grande, AZ 85236-1165
(602)836-4723

PUEBLO GRANDE
MUSEUM ART AND
CRAFT SHOW
(December, second full
weekend)
4619 East Washington St.
Phoenix, AZ 85034
(602)495-0901

AGUA CALIENTE
CULTURAL MUSEUM
HERITAGE FIESTA
(Spring)
Agua Caliente Tribal Council
960 East Tahquitz Canyon
Way, No. 106
Palm Springs, CA 92262
(619)325-5673

AMERICAN INDIAN FILM
FESTIVAL (November)
225 Valencia St.
San Francisco, CA 94103
(415)554-0525

AMERICAN INDIAN EXPO
(various)
American Indian Traders'
Guild, Inc.
3876 East Fedora Ave.
Fresno, CA 93726
(209)221-4355
Fresno-February;
Marin County -February;
Monterey-March and November;
Pleasanton-February and July;
San Diego-June;
San Jose-April and December;
San Mateo-January and July;
Ventura-July and November

WHITE MOUNTAIN NATIVE
AMERICAN FESTIVAL AND
INDIAN MARKET
(July, last weekend)
Pinetop Chamber of Commerce
P.O. Box 266
Pinetop, AZ 85935
(602)367-4290

ANNUAL CALIFORNIA
INDIAN MARKET (May and
September, first weekend)
San Juan Indian Council
Mission San Juan Bautista
San Juan Bautista, CA 95045
(408)623-2379

CALIFORNIA INDIAN
DAYS (September)
California Indian Manpower
4153 North Gate Blvd.
Sacramento, CA 95834
(916)920-0285

SANTA MONICA INDIAN
SHOW AND SALE AND
POW WOW
(January and June)
c/o Bullock Productions
8291 Carburton St.
Long Beach, CA 90808-3302
(310)430-5112

California

Colorado	COLORADO INDIAN MARKET AND WESTERN ART ROUND-UP (January) P.O. Box 17187 Boulder, CO 80308 (303)447-9967	
Florida	MICCOSUKEE INDIAN FAIR (December–January) Miccosukee Cultural Center P.O. Box 440021 Miami, FL 33143 (305)223-8380	
Iowa	ANNUAL INDIAN CREEK TRADES EXPO (April) P.O. Box 841 Council Bluff, IA 51502 (712)325-1779	
Kentucky	CHIEF REDBIRD HOMECOMING AMERICAN INDIAN FESTIVAL (May) P.O. Box 282 Fall Rock, KY 40932 (606)598-6623	
Michigan	CHICAGO ANTIQUE AMERICAN INDIAN ART SHOW AND SALE (April and October, first weekend) 15746 Bradner Rd. Northville, MI 48167 (313)420-3237	
Montana	BIG SKY INDIAN ART MARKET (June) Eastern Montana University P.O. Box 531 Billings, MT 59101 (406)657-2200	GREAT FALLS AMERICAN ASSOCIATION ART SHOW AND SALE (March) P.O. Box 2429 Great Falls, MT 59403 (406)791-2212

STEWART MUSEUM ARTS
AND CRAFTS FAIR AND
POW-WOW
(June, third weekend)
5366 Snyder Ave.
Carson City, NV 89701
(702)882-1808

CREATIVITY IS OUR
TRADITION EXHIBITION
(Ongoing);
STUDENT SALES
(December–January)
Institute of American Indian Arts
P.O. Box 2007
Santa Fe, NM 89504
(505)988-6440
Clifford LaFromboise

CROWNPOINT RUG
WEAVERS ASSOCIATION
NAVAJO RUG AUCTIONS
(Monthly)
P.O. Box 1630
Crownpoint, NM 87313
(505)786-5302

EIGHT NORTHERN
PUEBLOS INDIAN ARTS
AND CRAFTS (April)
P.O. Box 969
San Juan Pueblo, NM 87566
(505)852-4265

GALLUP CEREMONIAL
(August)
Red Rock State Park at Gallup
Gallup, NM 87301
(505)863-3896

STEWART MUSEUM
CHRISTMAS INDIAN ARTS
AND CRAFTS BOUTIQUE
(November)
5366 Snyder Ave.
Carson City, NV 89701
(702)882-1808

INTERTRIBAL INDIAN
CEREMONIAL
(August)
Red Rock State Park at
Gallup
P.O. Box 1
Church Rock, NM 87311
(505)863-3896

NATIVE AMERICAN
MUSIC FESTIVAL
(August)
El Morro Theatre
P.O. Box 1265
Zuni, NM 87327
(505)782-2217

NEW MEXICO STATE FAIR
(September)
State Fairgrounds
P.O. Box 8546
Albuquerque, NM 87898
(505)265-1791

SANTA FE INDIAN
MARKET (August)
Southwest Association of
Indian Affairs
320 Galisteo, Suite 600
Santa Fe, NM 87501
(505)983-5220

Nevada

New Mexico

North Carolina

ANNUAL CHEROKEE
HERITAGE ART
SHOW
(October)
P.O. Box 1599
Cherokee, NC 28719

KITUWAH AMERICAN
INDIAN EXPOSITION
(September)
46 Hayward St.
Ashville, NC 28801
(704)252-3880

Oklahoma

AMERICAN INDIAN
EXPOSITION
(August)
P.O. Box 366
Anadarko, OK 73005
(405)247-2733

CHRISTMAS
EXHIBITION OF
CONTEMPORARY INDIAN
ARTS AND CRAFTS
(December)
Southern Plains Indian Museum
P.O. Box 749
Anadarko, OK 73005
(405)247-6221

Oregon

ANNUAL
CULTURAL EVENT
(October)
405 Northwest Despain
Pendleton, OR 97801
(503)278-0115 or
(503)276-8500

Pennsylvania

A TIME OF
THANKSGIVING
(November, second Sunday)
CORN PLANTING
CEREMONY
(May, first Sunday)
ROASTING EAR OF CORN
FOOD FEST
(August, second Sunday)
Museum of Indian Culture
R.D. 2, Fish Hatchery Rd.
Allentown, PA 18103
(215)797-2121

GREAT PLAINS ART SHOW
AND SALE (February)
Augustana College
Center for Western Studies
P.O. Box 727
Sioux Falls, SD 57197
(605)336-4007

AMERICAN INDIAN ART
FESTIVAL
(February or March)
2700 Albany, Suite 203
Houston, TX 77006
(713)521-0133

AMERICAN INDIAN ART
FESTIVAL AND MARKET
(November)
American Indian Arts
Council, Inc.
725 Preston Forest Shopping
Center, Suite B
Dallas, TX 75230
(214)891-9640

AMERICAN INDIAN
EXPOSITION AND
SALES
San Antonio, TX
(April and October)
Austin, TX
(May and November)
c/o American Indian Traders'
Guild, Inc.
3876 East Fedora Ave.
Fresno, CA 93726
(209)221-4355

ANNUAL VETERAN'S
HONOR DINNER/POW
WOW
P.O. Box 4948
Suquamish, WA 98392
(206)598-3311

INDIAN ART MARKET
(October–April, second
weekend)
Cultural Arts
P.O. Box 99100
Seattle, WA 98199
(206)285-4425

NATIVE AMERICAN ART
FAIR (April)
Suquamish Tribe
P.O. Box 498
Suquamish, WA 98392
(206)598-3311

SPEELYI MI INDIAN ART
AND CRAFT FAIR (March)
Yakima Nation Cultural
Center
P.O. Box 151
Toppenish, WA 98948
(509)865-2800

CANADA ✦ ✦ ✦ ✦ ✦ ✦ ✦ ✦ ✦ ✦ ✦ ✦ ✦ ✦ ✦ ✦ ✦ ✦ ✦

ONTARIO   NATIONAL INDIAN ARTS
AND CREE REGIONAL
CRAFTS CORPORATION
1106-1 Nicholas St.
Ottawa, ON K1N 7N5
(613)232-2436

Literature

Out of their long tenure on the North American continent, American Indians have developed rich and varied literatures that reflect the diversity of indigenous American cultural traditions and languages. With the arrival of Europeans came many new languages and cultures to which Native peoples have been forced to adapt. What we refer to as "American Indian literature" reflects that wide range of linguistic and cultural experiences.

Major themes in American Indian literature include a place-centered view of the physical world and of time, a reverence for the power of the word, kinship ties (to living and dead relatives, to supernatural beings, to animals and other spirits in nature), and a belief in the importance of renewal of the world through rituals associated with seasonal cycles. Contact with Europeans has led to changes in traditional themes related to warfare and cultural continuance, particularly since the nineteenth century. Indian resistance has been reflected not only in writings in English, French, and Spanish, but also in oral literatures. Such traditions form the basis for writings from tribal cultures, even when the written content is not explicitly about traditional life.

Today, American Indian writers produce works in the English language that can be counted among the most innovative and engaging in contemporary fiction, poetry, drama, and the non-fictional essay. Meanwhile, oral traditions continue to enrich the lives of the people as they have for countless generations, especially as traditional religious ceremonies are being revitalized.

Whether writing from specific tribal traditions or from a pan-Indian point of view (a view that sees indigenous Americans' experience as a shared experience), American Indian literary artists present unique and imaginative new perspectives on what it means to be an "Indian" today and often attempt to recover a history that has been ignored, distorted, or dismissed.

ORAL LITERATURE ♦ ♦ ♦ ♦ ♦ ♦ ♦ ♦ ♦ ♦ ♦ ♦ ♦ ♦ ♦ ♦ ♦ ♦ ♦

Oral literature exists always and everywhere in human communities. In contemporary American Indian settings and communities, storytelling plays an essential role in the revitalization and preservation of culture. To better understand the place of oral literatures within the body of works referred to as American Indian literature, we must recognize that oral literature is a continual aspect of all peoples' lives and that the weaving together of oral literary expressions with writing reveals the unique features and values of many particular cultures across time.

Oral literature can be defined as that body of literary works that a people have disseminated and preserved for many generations through oral performance with relatively standard features. Myths, legends, ritual dramas, prayers, chants, songs, speeches, anecdotes, and even jokes can all be considered forms of oral literature. While the oral literature studied in classrooms may appear on the page to be like other poems or stories, the reader should nonetheless keep in mind that specific audiences and settings figure significantly in the shape and content of oral literatures. For example, while a written American Indian myth may seem sparse in its language and focused primarily on plot development, that same story when told by a Native speaker to a Native audience comes to life through their shared history, that is the shared knowledge of the characters, tribal customs, and geographical region, as well as family and

personal histories. The pieces that find their way into print, however, are generally representative of crafted oral works that have enjoyed a long life among a people.

Creation myths form the cornerstone of American Indian cultures' world view—perhaps of every culture's world view. A simple definition of myth is "sacred story," and even though the content of myth is fantastic, that is, beyond the realm of fact as we know it—people who hold their myths to be sacred see a deep, holistic truth in them. Readers outside of the cultures being studied see through the windows of myths, as it were, into the culture—by no means seeing all, yet glimpsing the life of a people. On the

Early American Indians often recorded histories and stories on rocks and cliffs at sacred sites. The above petroglyphs were found in San Gabriel Canyon in Southern California. Courtesy of the Los Angeles Public Library.

North American continent, there are at least three common types of creation myths (with variations among different groups). The first is the Earth-Diver Myth, in which the world is covered by water, as after a great Flood, often referred to as a Deluge. In nearly every form of this myth, an animal dives down below the surface of the water and succeeds in retrieving mud or earth to begin the habitable world, after three companions before him had failed. The second type is the Emergence Myth, in which humans, animals, and plants who live in a cave below the world as we know it emerge by climbing a reed, tree, or root into the sun. The third type is the Two Creators myth, in which two godlike beings (sometimes brothers, sisters, or other relatives) create the world in their efforts to compete with one another. Because creation myths occur as an integral part of a set of stories, which folklorists call "cycles," they are best understood in relation to other stories of that culture. Myths are always geographically situated; they help explain a people's history on a particular landscape, and they illustrate the intricately balanced relationship between the natural environment and its human inhabitants.

Other forms of oral literature related to storytelling include legends, trickster tales, and specialized types of stories (such as coup stories). Most tribes have their own literary terms for their various types of literature. Legends, as opposed to myths, arise from events within historical memory. Over time the story of the event takes on symbolic significance and may be exaggerated in dimensions related to time, place, or factual detail. A legendary American folk hero, for example, Daniel Boone supposedly could kill a bear with his bare hands. By contrast, a common Native American mythic figure, Trickster, often referred to as the Trickster/transformer, takes the shape of Coyote in the Southwest, Ikhtomi Spider in the High Plains, Hare in the Great Lakes and the Southeast, Raven in the Northwest, and Jay or Wolverine in Canada. Depending on the tribal tradition, stories about such characters may be used to teach proper behavior to children, to instruct and inspire adults, to entertain through humor, to present a culture hero who saves the people or otherwise makes the world better by his brave acts, or to tell of how the universe came to be as we know it. When Plains warriors would tell of their brave deeds in battle through their "coup" stories, they too played the part of culture heroes, but on a smaller scale than legendary figures. The other warriors who witnessed the event also had to be there to swear to the truth of the teller's version of what happened. Other types of specialized stories might include stories related to how one acquired one's name.

Another category of recorded oral literature arises from the practice of Native religions, the verbal parts of rituals performed for specific purposes, such as preparing for spring planting or fall harvesting. Early anthologies of American Indian lore, like George Cronyn's *The Path on the Rainbow* (1918), were intended both to enlighten the public regarding the rich literary materials of Native cultures and to further the preservation of Native

Stories and legends were often re-enacted through dances. Here the American Indian Dance Theatre performs an Eagle Dance.

cultural materials. Toward the end of the nineteenth century and into the early twentieth century, there was much concern among ethnologists and others that American Indian cultures were dying out and that there would be no record of Native cultural practices if great efforts weren't made to record them. Before the 1960s, anthologies designed for a popular audience were frequently compiled from those ethnographic materials. Taken out of context, however, the pieces often raise more questions than they answer. In other words, the meanings a non-Native person may derive from reading them may be entirely different from what a Native would find in them.

Northwest Coast dancers embodied spiritual beings and re-enacted creation histories and traditional stories.

Another consideration in reading oral literatures relates to whether or not the particular American Indian tribe would prefer that such specific knowledge of their ceremonies remain only within their tribe. Back when much of the ethnographic material was first collected, individuals may have revealed sacred tribal information without realizing that it would be published, or had it stolen from them by people who claimed they would not publish it. Some tribal groups, however, believe it is proper to share some of their ceremonies and rituals with non-Native and other tribal audiences. The Iroquois, for instance, have published their Ritual of Condolence, a rite conducted after the death of a high chief to install a new chief to take his place in the council of forty-nine chiefs. The new chief embodies the spirit of the chief who has died, who in his time was believed to embody the spirit of the chief before him, all the way back to the original council chief.

Songs and chants accompany virtually all Native ceremonies. Some are generations old, but others are composed for the occasion, often continuing to be part of the ceremony in the future or simply remaining with the individual involved in the particular ceremony, as in the instance of naming or perhaps healing. Songs created for social occasions, often called "forty-nines," may be in English, a native language, or both. Among Lakota people, young men composed flute songs, usually with the help of a medicine man, for courting a young woman whom they desired to marry. The young man would sit on a hill behind her tipi and play the song, which might contain words she had spoken. If she wanted nothing to do with him, she would ignore him and his song. If she was interested in him, she might go out with an older female relative to listen to the song. While composing songs and chants continues to be an important aspect of American tribal peoples, flute courting songs are part of a custom that has fallen into disuse.

Perhaps the most widely known form of American Indian oral literature is oratory, and a prominent orator is Chief Seattle, after whom the city in Washington State is named; he was known by his own people, the Suquamish, as Chief Sealth, and he lived between about 1786 and 1866. Chief Seattle's speech, frequently quoted for its environmental message that on earth all people, plants, and animals were interrelated, has been the subject of much controversy. Questions persist about the reliability of the earliest existing draft of his speech (1887), written down twenty years after his death, and about details added later as the speech became popular through film and printed media. Other famous American Indian speeches raise similar questions; however, there can be no doubt that before earliest contact with Europeans, Native Americans prided themselves on their public speaking abilities. In 1772, Samson Occom (Mohegan, 1723–92) published his *Sermon Preached at the Execution of Moses Paul*, the first example of a literate American Indian (i.e., someone who could read and write English) who controlled the publication as well as the public presentation of his speech. The sermon, an indictment of non-Natives for supplying alcohol to American Indians, was popular in its day, going through multiple printings. Peter Nabokov's *Native American Testimony: A Chronicle of Indian-White Relations from Prophecy to the Present, 1492-1992* contains many other fine examples of American Indian oratory, as well as excerpts from autobiographies.

LIFE HISTORIES AND AUTOBIOGRAPHIES ✦ ✦ ✦ ✦ ✦ ✦ ✦ ✦

Taken up with the political causes of their peoples and with the need to record their histories and religious beliefs, early writers such as Samson Occom, William Apes (Pequot, b. 1798), David Cusick (Tuscarora, d. c. 1840), George Copway (Ojibway, 1818-69), Peter Jones (Ojibway, 1802-1856), and others provided a body of works that contain both literature (oral and autobiographical) and literary and historical scholarship. While many early writings were not intended to tell a life history, the personal histories contained in those works legitimate and enliven the whole. Since the writings of other Americans who are important to the founding of the United States (John Smith, Cotton Mather, Henry David Thoreau, and Ralph Waldo Emerson) are studied as literature—that is, their sermons, speeches, other types of oral literature, histories, and memoirs—so too should early American Indian writers be regarded as contributing essential voices to the canon of American literature.

Native American autobiography is a unique literary form in that over 80 percent of what is usually referred to as American Indian and Alaska Native autobiography has been collected and edited by non-Native people. Lack of literacy figures in the reasons why American Indians are less inclined than their non-Indian counterparts to write autobiographies, but there are other reasons as well. The way tribal people define themselves tends to be in relationship to their communities as a whole, rather than as individuals within nuclear family structures or as individuals opposing themselves to society in general. That does not mean that American Indians have no stories about themselves to share with one another. Rather, they do not usually tell personal stories for broad dissemination to outsiders, particularly in the form in which autobiography has evolved in Western civilization. Tribal people, among whom each person—even in his or her private life—is quite well known by the group, would find it odd to hear the tale of a person's psychological struggles in the shaping of his or her personality. Hence, until quite recently, American Indian autobiography has been written mostly for non-Native audiences or for generations of tribal people to come.

A Son of the Forest (1829), by William Apes (also spelled Apess), is the earliest known autobiography in English by a Native person. Apes had converted to Methodism after many sad years as a foster child and writes about the abuses he and other American Indian peoples have suffered at the hands of Europeans as well as about his own faith in Christianity. Thus, his narrative compares to conversion narratives of the time, but differs in important ways. Another autobiographer, George Copway had already become well-known as a lecturer before he published *Life, History, and Travels of Kah-ge-ga-gah-bowh* (1847), a popular book republished six times in its first year. Like Apes before him and Charles Eastman (Dakota, 1858-1939) after him, Copway explained that he believed that Christianity offered hope to American Indians.

The first autobiography by an American Indian woman, *Life Among the Piutes,* also arose from its author's popularity as a lecturer. Sarah Winnemucca Hopkins (Paiute, c. 1844-91) was an advocate for her people, the Paiute, who were badly mistreated by their Indian agents and by neighboring U. S. settlers. She speaks out strongly and forthrightly both about the virtues of her people's ways and about the need for government reform to protect Paiute and other tribes from exploitation and abuse. Her stories of her early years are engaging and endearing, and her dramatic stories of Native women's courage are inspiring. Throughout most of her life, Sarah Winnemucca acted as a liaison between her people and non-Native officials.

Charles Eastman wrote two autobiographies, *Indian Boyhood* (1902) and *From Deep Woods to Civilization* (1916), as well as many books on Dakota culture. In his autobiographies, he chronicles his years before contact with non-Indians at age fifteen up through his eastern education and his many professional jobs— as a medical doctor on two reservations, as a Young Men's Christian Association (YMCA) and Boy Scout leader and organizer, as a public lecturer and writer, and as a government records clerk. His presence as the Pine Ridge reservation physician at the time of the Wounded Knee Massacre (1890) makes his narrative particularly valuable as a historical record. Throughout his life he worked to further the causes of American Indians, including over twenty years spent lobbying to reinstate his people's (the Santee Sioux's) treaty rights, which were taken from them after the Sioux Uprising of 1862.

Luther Standing Bear (Lakota, c. 1868-1939) began writing, with the editorial help of E.A. Brininstool, after Standing Bear had spent time traveling with Buffalo Bill's Wild West Show, acting in movies, lecturing, and engaging in activities associated with American Indian political causes. He wrote three books with autobiographical content, the most famous of which is probably *Land of the Spotted Eagle* (1933). Standing Bear's children's book, *My Indian Boyhood* (1931) and Eastman's book with a similar name were both preceded by Francis LaFlesche's (Omaha, 1857-1932) account of his years in a Presbyterian boarding school, *The Middle Five* (1900). Although the boarding school experience often traumatized American Indian youth, in the most extreme cases to the point of suicide, the story told in *The Middle Five* is heartwarming as well as tragic. The experience of the young people there differs from that of other Native children elsewhere in two important ways: Because the school was close to the Omaha camps, the children were able to see their loved ones more frequently; and the philosophy of the teachers seems less oppressive and punishing than that of educators of other Christian denominations.

Within the special subcategory of American Indian autobiography, "as told to" narratives seem to attract the largest mainstream reading audience. Whether these can rightly be called autobiography or should instead be referred to as life histories depends on the extent of the editorial assistance or intrusion. Whichever they are, they differ from biographies in that the person whose life is being presented participates substantially in their production. *Black Hawk, an Autobiography* (1833), the great war chief's popular story recorded and translated by Antoine Le Claire and edited by John B. Patterson, was the first "as told to" autobiography to appear. Black Hawk wanted his side of the story of the Black Hawk War (1832) to be known, since all the newspaper accounts ignored the injustices done to his Sauk people.

Since then, a number of "as told to" autobiographies, too numerous to name, have been published. Some of the most best-known, with the recorder/editor identified in brackets, include: Blowsnake [Paul Radin], *Crashing Thunder* (Winnebago); Mountain Wolf Woman [Nancy O. Lurie], *Mountain Wolf Woman* (Winnebago); Don Talayesva [Leo Simmons], *Sun Chief* (Hopi); Maria Chona [Ruth Underhill], *Papago Woman*; John Stands In Timber [Margot Liberty], *Cheyenne Memories* (1967); and Nickolas Black Elk [John Neihardt], *Black Elk Speaks*. Collaborators frequently add their own sense of narrative structure, particularly regarding the ordering of events, to conform to Western notions that an autobiography should begin with childhood events. Some editors/collaborators, however, regard the way the Native person orders his or her own narrative to be essential to the whole of the story. In Julie Cruikshank's introduction to her recent collaboration with three Alaska Native women, *Life Lived Like a Story* (1990), she claims that landscape and kinship do more than add background to the women's narratives, they actually determine how those narratives are shaped.

In the tradition of nature writing, John Joseph Matthews (Osage, c. 1894–1979) wrote *Talking to the Moon* (1945), a contemplation of nature, Osage history, and the struggles of humankind in general. Two decades later, N. Scott Momaday's *Way to Rainy Mountain* (1969) appeared; it also relies on nature as teacher and as guide. His text contains drawings by his father, depicting aspects of Momaday's three-sided view of his journey to Rainy Mountain—

the mythical, the historical, and the personal. Leslie Silko's *Story-teller* (1981) also combines several kinds of writing, and contained within her work are photographs showing the southwestern landscape of her stories and of her family.

Two recent autobiographies represent a marked departure from previous forms: Gerald Vizenor's *Interior Landscapes* (1990) and Ray A. Young Bear's *Black Eagle Child: The Facepaint Narratives* (1992). Both are highly metaphorized versions of the authors' lives. Despite the appearance of innovative and imaginative autobiographies by literary American Indians (Vizenor's and Young Bear's other creative writing will be discussed below), "as told to" narratives continue to be produced. *Lakota Woman,* by Mary Crow Dog with Richard Erdoes, is the story of a young woman who chronicles her participation in the AIM (American Indian Movement) activism of the 1970s, her life as the wife of a medicine man, and her growing awareness of her place as a mixed-blood in the Indian world.

FICTION AND POETRY ✦ ✦ ✦ ✦ ✦ ✦ ✦ ✦ ✦ ✦ ✦ ✦ ✦ ✦ ✦ ✦ ✦

During the nineteenth century and early twentieth century, Indian writers of fiction and poetry were more rare than Indian collectors of their peoples' histories and oral literatures and autobiographers of all types. Bernd C. Peyer's recent collection of early short stories by North American Indians, *The Singing Spirit* (1989), however, attests to the fact that Native American intellectuals, most of them born in the 1870s, were writing and publishing fiction; these authors include Gertrude Bonnin, Francis and Suzette LaFlesche, William Jones, Alexander Posey, Charles Eastman, Pauline Johnson, John Joseph Mathews, D'Arcy McNickle, and others.

The first American Indian novel, *Life and Adventures of Joaquin Murieta,* was written in 1854 by John Rollin Ridge (1827–67), a Cherokee who had relocated to California after the removal of his tribe to Oklahoma in the 1830s and the murder of his father and brother, because the two men favored removal. He became a newspaperman and eventually owned his own paper. The novel's hero, an outlaw with a heart, avenges the downtrodden and the wronged as he goes from one wild adventure to another.

Although not much in the way of long fiction appears until after the turn of the century, Alexander Posey (Creek, 1873–1907) wrote satirical pieces called the Fus Fixico Letters. In the "letters," which appeared in local as well as regional newspapers, he creates conversations wherein local dialect characters make fun of politics, politicians, and the government. After his death, his widow published a collection of his poetry, one of the earliest by an American Indian poet.

With the rise of the novel form among American Indian writers comes the theme of mixed-blood ancestry and the dilemma of being "caught between two worlds," by virtue of having parents who are from different cultures. In the 1920s, Mourning Dove (Christine Quintasket, Colville, 1888–1936) takes up that theme in her novel, *Cogewea, the Halfblood* (1927), the first published by an American Indian woman. It is about a young woman trying to decide between two suitors, one half-Indian and one non-Indian. In finally choosing the man with Indian heritage, she affirms her cultural values and sheds some of her girlish ways. Three other American Indian authors of the early decades of the twentieth century produced novels with mixed-blood or mixed-influence themes: John Milton Oskison (1874–1947), John Joseph Mathews, and D'Arcy McNickle (Cree/Salish, 1904–77). Variations on that theme would continue well into the 1970s, but as a greater number of writers enter the scene, both subject matter and aesthetics expand.

In 1959, a new phase in American Indian writing was ushered in by the republication of *Black Elk Speaks*. Although an "as told to" autobiography, the text merits discussion under the fiction category both because it is an unusual collaboration and because it spurred a renaissance in Native writing. As John G. Neihardt's study of the life of Nick Black Elk, it is an expression of Neihardt's poetic and visionary aesthetic and, most importantly, a partial, though powerful, record of the Oglala (Sioux) medicine man's vision. As such, many have said that *Black Elk Speaks* ranks among the holy books of the world. Carl Jung, a famous psychologist, intrigued by what he saw as its thematic similarity to other religious autobiographies, figured in the revived interest in the book and its subsequent republication in 1959. It became what Vine Deloria, Jr., terms a "veritable Indian Bible" to youth of the 1960s and 1970s. Despite its somewhat fatalistic tone, *Black Elk Speaks* has moved Indians and non-Indians alike beyond fixed or static ideas of American Indians as defeated and has shown the beauty and value in traditional Native religious ways.

In the early 1970s, American Indian writers began producing fiction and poetry as never before and in a manner that suggests the emergence of a writing community. The literary renaissance, spurred by works like *Black Elk Speaks* and *Bury My Heart at Wounded Knee* by Dee Brown (1972), found its first voice in N. Scott Momaday. His book *House Made of Dawn* (1968), winner of the 1969 Pulitzer Prize for literature, along with Vine Deloria's *Custer Died for Your Sins* (1969), coincided with the Indian occupation of Alcatraz Island in California, which caused a tremendous stir in the public imagination. The continued presence of Indians in America was beginning to be felt, and American Indian college students particularly began writing and publishing as never before.

James Welch (Blackfeet, b. 1940) took his place among the writers of that generation, when his first novel *Winter in the Blood* (1974) was reviewed on the front page of the *New York Times Book Review,* prompting the republication of his first book of poetry, *Riding the Earthboy 40* (1971; 1976). Themes of alienation and loss dominate both works, as well as his second novel, *The Death of Jim Loney* (1979).

Many writers took up those themes as well as others and chose poetry as the medium of expression. Duane Niatum (Clallam, b. 1938), with two books of poems already to his credit at the time, edited the much-celebrated *Carriers of the Dream Wheel,* a collection of poetry by American Indians, in 1975. It was followed four years later by Geary Hobson's *The Remembered Earth* (1979), a collection that takes its title from Momaday's *The Way to Rainy Mountain.* Niatum's and Hobson's collections became popular classroom texts.

Leslie Silko's *Laguna Woman* (1974) and *Ceremony* (1977) affirm both cultural continuities and change, as do Simon Ortiz's early works: *Going for the Rain* (1976), *A Good Journey* (1977), and *Howbah Indians* (1978). Both authors come from the Southwest, and in their works they evoke the long history American Indians have had with both Spanish and English colonizers in that part of the country. Along with the themes of alienation and loss comes the theme of healing, and Silko's *Ceremony* depicts the struggles of its mixed-blood protagonist, Tayo, in his attempts to find healing after World War II. Like Momaday's Abel in *House Made of Dawn* and Welch's nameless narrator in *Winter in the Blood,* Tayo must also come to terms with conflicts arising from the colonization of his people, the Laguna. Silko's novel *Almanac of the Dead* (1991) was published to great acclaim. Momaday and Welch have also continued their writings with *Ancient Child* (1989) and *The Indian Lawyer* (1990), respectively.

Louise Erdrich, an Ojibway (b. 1954) from North Dakota, achieved what many writers hope for: her first novel, *Love Medicine* (1984), became a best-seller. Set mostly on the Turtle Mountain Chippewa Reservation, the novel is a weaving together of a number of first-person voices and perspectives as well as that of an omniscient narrator. Erdrich's other novels, *Beet Queen* (1986) and *Tracks* (1988), are also set in North Dakota, where she grew up. She claims that her fictional works are produced in collaboration with her husband, Michael Dorris (Modoc, b. 1945), author of the novel *A Yellow Raft in Blue Water* (1987) and *The Broken Cord* (1989), his personal story as an adoptive parent struggling to raise a fetal alcohol syndrome child. Erdrich also has two books of poetry to her credit.

Paula Gunn Allen (Laguna/Lakota/Lebanese, b. 1939) and Wendy Rose (Hopi/Miwok, b. 1948) both began writing poetry in the 1970s. Allen has gone on to write in many forms—as a literary critic (*The Sacred Hoop*, 1986), editor (*Studies in American Indian Literature*, 1983, and *Spider Woman's Granddaughters*, 1989), and novelist (*Woman Who Owned the Shadows*, 1983). Allen's voice in contemporary American Indian literature and literary studies is a unique and essential one; as suggested by the subtitle of *The Sacred Hoop*—"Recovering the Feminine in American Indian Traditions"—her work often focuses on the concerns of women. Autobiographical pieces by both Allen and Rose appear in *I Tell You Now* (1987), edited by Brian Swann and Arnold Krupat.

Among that generation of writers, Joy Harjo (Creek, b. 1951) and Ray A. Young Bear (Mesquakie, b. 1950) have distinguished themselves as important voices in mainstream American poetry, as well as American Indian poetry. It is important to make that distinction clear, because all too often the talent of Native writers is not recognized by audiences outside ethnic studies circles. Although Harjo's first book of poetry (*What Moon Drove Me to This*) was not published until 1979, her presence on the writing scene was felt long before that. Women's themes, particularly related to suffering, are central to her work, thus the moon figures as a symbol throughout this collection. Horses become a metaphor for human energy and struggle in *She Had Some Horses* (1983). Harjo's latest work, *In Mad Love and War* (1990), contains mostly prose poems (poems in paragraph form), and is perhaps her strongest work to date. Ray A. Young Bear's poetry reflects his bilingual language use and his belief in the importance of cultural sovereignty, Native control of cultural development, transformation, and preservation. *Winter of the Salamander* (1980) and *The Invisible Musician* reflect his Mesquakie heritage both in theme and symbolism and in the syntax of his aesthetic.

The phases of writing since the Native renaissance began have become an interweaving of past re-envisioning and recovering by remembering the past. This is the past left out of history books and American literature written by James Fenimore Cooper, who wrote the Leather Stocking Tales series that featured several Indian personalities, and Henry Wadsworth Longfellow, who wrote a long poem about the mythical Indian figure Hiawatha. James Welch's third novel, *Fools Crow* (1986) and Simon Ortiz's *From Sand Creek* (1981) engage a re-memory to recapture some of the more traumatic events in Indian history, such as in Ortiz's case the 1864 Sand Creek Massacre of Cheyenne Indians in Colorado. Linda Hogan (Choctaw, b. 1947), who began as a poet of the stature of Young Bear and Harjo, has also written short fiction and a novel of historical recovery, *Mean Spirit* (1990). Set among the Osage in Oklahoma in the 1920s, the novel depicts the traumatic and unjust circumstances of Osage people when oil was discovered on their land. In many details, the work is historically accurate.

Hogan, like Beth Brant (author of *Mohawk Trail,* 1985, *Food and Spirits,* 1991, and editor of *A Gathering of Spirit,* 1984), also treats the role of women in Native communities. Both present female characters and relationships between women in realistic and unique ways. With these works come a reassertion of the woman's place in Native communities, as well as an assertion of feminist ideals and issues, conjoined but not necessarily in harmony with mainstream feminist thought and goals.

Of all contemporary writers, none is more prolific or diversified than Gerald Vizenor (Ojibway, b. 1934), who has written at least twenty books. Formerly a journalist, Vizenor writes about a range of topics from tribal history to contemporary legal struggles and other issues, such as tribal gambling. His poetry reflects the time he has spent in Japan, since he often utilizes the Japanese haiku form. Vizenor is perhaps best known for his novels. In his more recent work, he continues themes begun in his first novel, *Darkness in Saint Louis Bearheart* (1978). The work develops a world in which contemporary tricksters attempt to find a tribal way to live in the post-modern, post-industrial world. Vizenor has also edited a collection of essays on American Indian literature, with contemporary, post-modern theoretical approaches.

New Native American writers emerge and new literary works surface every day. With each new wave of Native American literary creativity, a measure of cultural sovereignty is achieved. New writers like Luci Tapahonso, Nia Francisco, and Rex Lee Jim, all Navajo, write bilingual works and incorporate Native song into their works. Playwrights like Hanay Geiogamah (Kiowa/Delaware, b. 1945) and William S. Yellow Robe, Jr. (Assiniboine, b. 1957) produce plays that are gaining international recognition. As a newly recognized field within American literature, Native American literature is destined to grow and to change the ways America sees itself.

Kate Shanley
Cornell University

BIOGRAPHIES ◆ ◆ ◆ ◆ ◆ ◆ ◆ ◆ ◆ ◆ ◆ ◆ ◆ ◆ ◆ ◆ ◆ ◆

Sherman Alexie
1966–

Spokane-Coeur d'Alene
poet and novelist

Sherman Alexie grew up in Wellpinit, Washington, on the Spokane Indian Reservation. Winner of a 1991 Washington State Arts Commission poetry fellowship and a 1992 National Endowment for the Arts poetry fellowship, Alexie has published more than two hundred poems, stories, and translations in publications such as *Another Chicago Magazine, Beloit Poetry Journal, Black Bear Review, Caliban, Journal of Ethnic Studies, Hanging Loose Press, New York Quarterly, Red Dirt, Slipstream, ZYZZYVA,* and others. His first book of poetry and short stories, *The Business of Fancydancing* was published by Hanging Loose Press in January 1992 and quickly earned a favorable front-page review from *The New York Times Book Review.* This first poetry book was the result of poems and stories written in Alexie's first creative writing workshop at Washington State University in Pullman. Alexie soon published a second collection, *I Would Steal Horses,* which was the winner of Slipstream's fifth annual Chapbook Contest in March 1992. In January 1993, he published a third poetry book, *Old Shirts & New Skins* (UCLA American Indian Studies Center). By early 1993, Alexie had written three books. Atlantic Monthly Press contracted to publish a collection of Alexie's short stories, *The Lone Ranger and Tonto Fistfight in Heaven* (published in September 1993), and a novel, *Coyote Springs,* in 1994. Another book of poetry, *First Indian on the Moon,* was published in late 1993 by Hanging Loose Press. Alexie lives in Spokane, Washington.

Paula Gunn Allen is a distinguished literary figure of mixed ancestry. She was born in Cubero, New Mexico, in 1939. Her father is a Lebanese-American and a former lieutenant-governor of New Mexico, and her mother is Laguna Pueblo and Scots on one side and Sioux-Métis on the other. Thus, she grew up in a multi-cultural household where Spanish, German, Laguna, English, and Arabic were all spoken and understood. This mixture of ancestry—with all its blessings and difficulties—has been a primary fact of life for Allen and a theme that figures in various writings such as her novel *The Woman Who Owned the Shadows* (1983).

As a scholar and literary critic, Allen has worked to encourage the publication of Native American literature and to educate others about its themes, contexts, and structures. Her book *The Sacred Hoop: Recovering the Feminine in American Indian Traditions* (1986) analyzes the fiction of several Indian writers and has done much to improve understanding of this new literature. She has also introduced the reading public to emergent Native American writers in anthologies such as the award-winning collection *Spider Woman's Granddaughters: Traditional Tales and Contemporary Writing by Native American Women* (1989). These are only a few titles to her credit, as Allen has been an extremely prolific critic and also has published several volumes of poetry.

Allen has won several awards, including fellowships from the National Endowment for the Arts (1978) and the American Indian Studies Program at UCLA (1981), and the Native American Prize for Literature, 1990. She has served on the faculties at San Francisco State University, the University of New Mexico, the University of California at Berkeley, and UCLA, where she now teaches in the English Department.

The mother of three children, Allen is also a dedicated feminist who has stated that her convictions can be traced back to the woman-centered structures of traditional Pueblo society. She has been active consistently in American feminist movements and in antiwar and antinuclear organizations. She is the sister of the Laguna Pueblo writer Carol Lee Sanchez and cousin of the novelist Leslie Marmon Silko.

Paula Gunn Allen
1939–

Laguna Pueblo and Sioux novelist, poet, and professor

Beth Brant
1941–

Mohawk writer and
poet

Beth Brant is a widely published writer and poet. Many of her works appear in *Kitchen Talk, An Anthology of Canadian Women's Prose and Poetry* (1992); *Getting Wet* (1992); *An Anthology of Native Canadian Literature in English* (1992); *Talking Leaves* (1991); and *Piece of My Heart* (1991). A variety of magazines and journals have published her stories, and "Turtle Gal" was adapted and aired by the CBC in Toronto, Ontario, in 1990. Among her recent publications are *Mohawk Trail* (Firebrand Books, 1985) A *Gathering of Spirit* (Firebrand Books, 1989); and *Food & Spirits* (Firebrand Books, 1991).

Brant was a lecturer at the University of British Columbia in 1989 and 1990 and has contributed to numerous writing workshops, such as the Women of Color Writing Workshop in Vancouver, British Columbia, and the Michigan Festival of Writers in East Lansing, Michigan, both in 1991.

In 1992, she participated in the Festival of North American Native Writers in Norman, Oklahoma, at the International Feminist Book Fair in Amsterdam, Holland, and at the Flight of the Mind, Writing Workshop for Women in Eugene, Oregon.

In 1993, Brant was the writer-in-residence at the Kanhiote Library on the Tyendinaga Mohawk Reserve in Canada, and guest lecturer in women's studies and Native studies, at New College, University of Toronto, Ontario. She has received many grants and awards including grants from the Michigan Council for the Arts (1984 and 1986) and the Ontario Arts Council (1989), and in 1991, she received the National Endowment for the Arts Literature Fellowship. In 1992, Brant was awarded the Canada Council Award in Creative Writing.

Joseph Bruchac
1942–

Abenaki author and
poet

Joseph Bruchac is an author and poet whose work draws on his Native American heritage and especially on stories that he heard from his Abenaki grandfather. He lives with his wife Carol in the Adirondack foothills where he was raised by his grandparents. Much of Joseph's writing draws on that land and the Abenaki heritage from the maternal side of his family. Although his Indian heritage is only part of an ethnic background that includes Slovak and English, his Native roots are deepest and he has cultivated them the most.

Born on October 16, 1942, Bruchac received his bachelor's degree in English from Cornell University (1965), then went on to complete a master's in English from Syracuse University in 1966. From 1966 to 1969 he lived and taught in Ghana, West Africa and on his return to the United States founded the Greenfield Review Press. From 1972 to 1974, Bruchac completed the doctoral program at Union Institute Graduate School in Yellow Springs, Ohio. His stories and poems have appeared in more than four hundred anthologies and have also been translated into several different languages. Most of his work emphasizes spiritual balance and his deep and continuing concern for the health of the world environment.

He has recently published collections of short stories entitled *Keepers of the Earth* (with Michael J. Caduto, 1991) and *Thirteen Moons of a Turtle's Back* (1992). Perhaps the best-known anthology of his poetry is *Entering Onondaga* (1978). Bruchac has won several awards for his writing over the years, including fellowships from the National Endowment for the Arts (NEA) and the Rockefeller Foundation, and a PEN Syndicated Fiction Award.

Barney Bush is a poet of Shawnee and Cayuga descent. Born in August 1945, Bush left home at sixteen and traveled throughout the United States, Canada, and northern Mexico. He studied graphic arts at the Institute of American Indian Arts in Santa Fe, New Mexico, then completed a bachelor's degree in humanities at Fort Lewis College in Durango, Colorado (1972). He later completed a master's degree in English and fine arts at the University of Idaho (1978).

Barney Furman Bush
1945–

Shawnee and Cayuga poet and teacher

Bush's poetry appears in dozens of anthologies and magazines, as well as in his own published collections *Longhouse of the Blackberry Moon* (1975), *My Horse and a Jukebox* (1979), *Petroglyphs* (1982), and *Inherit the Blood* (1985). He has taught Native American literature and related subjects at Milwaukee Technical

College, New Mexico Highlands University, and the Institute of the Southern Plains (Cheyenne Indian School) and has also been a writer-in-residence at several universities and arts councils.

Elizabeth Cook-Lynn
1930–

Sioux poet, author, and professor

Elizabeth Cook-Lynn comes from a family of political leaders and scholars. Her father and grandfather served on the Crow Creek Tribal Council for years, and her grandfather (Gabriel Renville) was a Native linguist who helped develop early Dakota dictionaries. Cook-Lynn herself was raised on a reservation and speaks Dakota, one of the dialects of the Sioux Nation.

Born on the Crow Creek Reservation in South Dakota, on November 17, 1930, Cook-Lynn received a bachelor's degree in journalism and English from South Dakota State College (1952) and later completed the master's degree in education, psychology, and counseling at the University of South Dakota (1970). She completed additional graduate work in literary criticism at the University of Nebraska, Lincoln, and at Stanford University.

Early in her career, she worked as a journalist and teacher at the secondary level, but since 1970 Cook-Lynn has been on the faculty at Eastern Washington State University and, in 1993, was professor emeritus (retired) of English and American Indian studies. She is a founding editor of *The Wicazo Sa Review*, a journal of Native American studies and continues to teach part-time.

Cook-Lynn's poetry and short stories focus on the geography of the northern Plains and on her own Dakota heritage, and she has been described as one of the most authentic of Native American "tribal" voices. After the age of forty, her stature as a poet grew with publication of *Then Badger Said This* and *Seek the House of Relatives*. Her short stories have appeared in journals such as *Prairie Schooner*, *Pembroke Magazine*, *South Dakota Review*, *Sun Tracks*, and *The Greenfield Review*; and she has presented numerous papers on Native American literature at various scholarly meetings.

Michael Dorris is a novelist and anthropologist who has taught Native American Studies at Dartmouth College in New Hampshire.

Born in Dayton, Washington, on January 30, 1945, Dorris was raised in Washington, Idaho, Kentucky, and Montana. He studied English and classics at Georgetown University, graduating with honors in 1967. He then received a master's degree in anthropology from Yale University in 1970.

Since leaving Yale, Dorris held various teaching positions and became a professor of anthropology and Native American studies at Dartmouth in 1972. He has many scholarly publications in this area, most importantly the books *Native Americans: Five Hundred Years After* (1975) and *A Guide to Research on North American Indians* (1983), co-authored with Arlene Hirschfelder and Mary Lou Byler.

In recent years, Dorris has become better known as a novelist. His first novel *A Yellow Raft in Blue Water* was published in 1989, and he has since written a best-selling novel entitled *The Crown of Columbus* (1991) with his wife Louise Erdrich, a well-known fiction writer. Dorris also is the author of *The Broken Cord: A Family's On-Going Struggle with Fetal Alcohol Syndrome* (1989); this non-fiction book describes the effects of the syndrome on Dorris and his adopted son Adam.

Michael Dorris
1945–

Modoc novelist and scholar

The daughter of a German-American father and a Chippewa mother, Louise Erdrich was born at Little Falls, Minnesota, in 1954 and raised in Wahpeton, North Dakota. She was among the first group of Native American women to be recruited and accepted to Dartmouth College shortly after it began accepting women, and graduated with a major in English and creative writing in 1976. After graduation, Erdrich returned to North Dakota and conducted poetry workshops throughout the state under the auspices of the Poetry in the Schools Program of the North Dakota Arts Council. She later returned to graduate school and completed a master's degree in creative writing from Johns Hopkins University, after which she moved to Boston and became editor of the Boston Indian Council newspaper.

Louise Erdrich
1954–

Turtle Mountain Chippewa novelist and poet

As a novelist Erdrich has often collaborated with her husband, Michael Dorris, and together they have been writing a four-volume family saga, published under Erdrich's name: *Love Medicine* (1984), *The Beet Queen* (1986), *Tracks* (1988), and *The Bingo Palace* (1993). Erdrich and Dorris have also co-authored a recent best-seller entitled *The Crown of Columbus* (1991).

Joy Harjo
1951–

Creek poet and
educator

Joy Harjo was born in Tulsa, Oklahoma, in 1951 and is an enrolled member of the Creek Nation. She graduated in 1968 from the Institute of American Indian Arts in Santa Fe, New Mexico, and from the University of New Mexico in 1976. In 1978, she received a master of fine arts degree in creative writing from the Iowa Writer's Workshop at the University of Iowa. She also completed the filmmaking program at the Anthropology Film Center. She has published four books of poetry, including *She Had Some Horses* (Thunder's Mouth Press, 1983) and the award-winning *In Mad Love and War* (Wesleyan University Press, 1990). *Secrets from the Center of the World* (University of Arizona Press, 1989) is a collaboration with photographer/astronomer Stephen Strom. In 1993, she was professor of English in the creative writing program at the University of New Mexico. Harjo has received the Josephine Miles Award for Excellence in Literature from PEN Oakland, the William Carlos Williams Award from the Poetry Society of America, the Delmore Schwartz Award from from New York University, the American Book Award, the Poetry Award from the Mountains and Plains Booksellers Association, and two National Endowment for the Arts Creative Writing Fellowships. She is also a screenwriter and is working on an original dramatic screenplay, "When We Used to Be Humans," for the American Film Foundation. A children's book, *The Goodluck Cat,* is forthcoming from Harcourt Brace & Jovanovitch, as well as two book projects for W.W. Norton & Co. and an anthology of Native American women's writing, *Reinventing the Enemy's Language,* from the University of Arizona Press. Harjo gives poetry readings nationally and internationally, and she plays saxophone with her band, Poetic Justice.

Linda Hogan is a writer and poet whose work reflects ideas and images of Chickasaw life. She was born in Denver, Colorado, in 1947, but raised mainly in Oklahoma. She received a master's degree in English and creative writing from the University of Colorado at Boulder and is currently an associate professor of Native American Studies at the same school. Hogan's poetry has appeared in several important anthologies devoted to Native American writers, including *Carriers of the Dream Wheel* (1975) and *Harper's Anthology of Twentieth Century Native American Poetry* (1988). Her own poems are featured in the collections *Eclipse* (1983) and *Seeing through the Sun* (1985).

Besides her poetry, Hogan has published a collection of short stories entitled *That Horse* (1985) and the novel *Mean Spirit* (1990). She received a fellowship for fiction from the National Endowment for the Arts in 1986 and has been poet-in-residence for the Oklahoma and Colorado state art councils.

Linda Hogan
1947–

Chickasaw author and poet

Pauline Johnson was an internationally acclaimed Mohawk poet and performer who lived and worked in the second half of the nineteenth century. A distant relative of Joseph Brant, a Mohawk chief who fought alongside the British during the American Revolution, Pauline Johnson was born to a Mohawk father, George Johnson, and a non-Native mother, Emily Howells. The Johnsons lived in Chiefswood, across the Grand River from the Six Nations Indian Reserve located near Brantford, in southwestern Ontario. Pauline wrote poetry as soon as she learned to write, and as a young child she was a voracious reader. She was educated mostly at home until she went to college in Brantford, where she performed in plays and pageants and decided to become a poet and performer. During her teens, she wrote many poems and had several minor publishing successes with local and regional magazines.

When her father died in 1885, Pauline moved with her mother to Brantford, where she often attended recitals and theater productions. Johnson's career blossomed when she started to re-

E. Pauline Johnson
1861–1913

Mohawk poet

cite her poetry in front of audiences. As a result of her successes, she saved enough money to travel to London, England, where she gave numerous recitals and arranged publication of a book of her poems, entitled *The White Wampum,* released in 1895. Upon her return to Canada, Johnson traveled from Newfoundland to Vancouver, performing and reciting her poetry. She also toured throughout the United States.

Besides being a poet, Johnson was also one of the first Indian women to publish short fiction. Especially interesting is *The Moccasin Maker* (1913), a collection of short stories on diverse subjects but mainly focusing on the lives of Indian and non-Indian women in Canada. Some are love stories, some focus on pioneer women who established homes for their families despite great hardships, and several deal with what would become a dominant theme in American Indian literature of the twentieth century: the mixed-blood's search for his or her proper place in the modern world. One story called "A Red Girl's Reasoning" tells of a mixed-blood woman who remains true to her Indian values even when the decision forces her to leave her husband, who is critical of such ideas. Johnson also was a prolific author of essays and magazine articles. She died in 1913 after a lengthy illness.

N. Scott Momaday
1934–

Kiowa novelist and poet

N. Scott Momaday is recognized as one of the premier writers in the United States. In 1969, his novel *House Made of Dawn* was awarded the Pulitzer prize for fiction.

Born of Indian parents who themselves were teachers, artists, and authors, he grew up in the Southwest, living on a number of reservations and attending government Indian schools. He later attended the Virginia Military Academy and the University of New Mexico. Momaday began writing poetry while teaching on the Jicarilla Apache Reservation. His writings have always reflected his attachment to land and the mystical beliefs of his Kiowa people. The poems he wrote during this period led to a Creative Fellowship from Stanford University where he earned master's and doctorate degrees. He taught first at the University of California, Santa Barbara, and later at the University of California, Berkeley.

At Berkeley, Momaday created an Indian literature program. For Momaday the need for Indian writers has a special urgency. He believes Indians must become writers to collect and preserve traditions and legends handed down from one generation to another. Momaday further believes only Indians can interpret Indian culture and history.

The Pulitzer prize-winning *House Made of Dawn,* which was written over a three-year period, reflects the author's background growing up in the Southwest. The plot focuses on the role confusion experienced by a young Indian, recently returned from World War II, who no longer feels "at home" on the reservation, but also experiences displacement in U.S. urban society.

Many readers believe that Momaday's second novel, *The Way to Rainy Mountain,* is his best one. Really two stories in one, the book is a description of the three-hundred-year-old migration of the Kiowa from the headwaters of the Yellowstone to the Black Hills as well as Momaday's own remembrances of his family and culture. *The Ancient Child,* published in 1985, is the story of an Indian artist who searches for his identity. Though mainstream audiences know Momaday best for his novels, the author himself prefers to write poetry. According to Momaday, Indians express themselves naturally in poetic, artistic terms.

Momaday believes that there is not enough awareness of what Indians can do and their artistic capabilities, but he hopes his own acclaim indicates a growing public awareness and appreciation for Native American contributions.

Carlos Montezuma was a successful physician who advocated the abolition of the Bureau of Indian Affairs. In 1915, he wrote the pamphlet "Let My People Go," and in 1916, he founded the Indian magazine *Wassaja: Freedom's Signal for the Indian,* which remained in press from 1916 to 1922.

Montezuma was born among the Yavapai Indians in Arizona, but as a boy was captured by the Pima Indians who sold him to Carlos Gentile, a white photographer, who named him Carlos

Carlos Montezuma
1867–1923

Yavapai physician and journalist

Montezuma. After Gentile's death, Montezuma was shuttled between a number of non-Indian benefactors. In 1884 he graduated from the University of Illinois with a bachelor of science degree, and in 1889 graduated from the Chicago Medical College. After an attempt at private medical practice, Montezuma was appointed physician-surgeon by the Indian Service at the Fort Stevenson Indian School in North Dakota. Montezuma practiced medicine at a number of reservations until his frustration with conditions led him to take a position at Carlisle Indian School in Pennsylvania. In 1896, Montezuma opened a private practice in Chicago, specializing in stomach and intestinal diseases. The practice was successful, and Montezuma turned his attention to activist work on Indian rights.

Montezuma's experiences working in the reservation health system made him an advocate for the abolition of the Bureau of Indian Affairs and the reservation system. His criticisms were acknowledged by government officials. Presidents Theodore Roosevelt and Woodrow Wilson asked him to become the Commissioner of Indian Affairs. Montezuma refused and continued his calls for the abolition of the BIA. He wrote essays against the institutions and people he believed exploited and suppressed Indian people.

For the rest of his life, Montezuma urged citizenship and equal rights for Native Americans, though not at the cost of sublimating cultural identity. Montezuma continually stressed the importance of maintaining "Indianness" in Native American society. He died in 1923 of tuberculosis at the Fort Dowell Reservation in Arizona, where he was born.

Duane Niatum

1938–

Klallam poet

Duane Niatum is the author of four volumes of poetry and a number of short stories and essays. Much of his work focuses on the realities of being a Native American in contemporary U.S. society.

Niatum was born in Seattle, Washington, and is a member of the Klallam tribe. As a young man, he changed his name from McGinnes to Niatum—a family name given to him by an older relative. He received his undergraduate degree in English at the University of Washington and his master's degree from Johns Hopkins University.

Niatum's first volume, *After the Death of an Elder Klallam,* was published in 1970 under the name Duane McGinnes. Later works include *Digging out the Roots* (1977), and *Ascending Red Cedar Moon* (1974) (Harper & Row). A 1981 collection from the University of Washington Press, *Songs for the Harvester of Dreams,* received the National Book Award from the Before Columbus Foundation in 1982. From 1973 to 1974, Niatum was the editor of the Native American authors series at Harper and Row. In 1975, he was the editor of *Carriers of the Dream Wheel,* one of the most widely read books on contemporary Native American poetry. In 1988, he edited a second anthology entitled *Harper's Anthology of Twentieth Century Native American Poetry* (Harper & Row).

Much of Niatum's work deals with what it means to be Native American in contemporary U.S. society. Some of his most poignant writing juxtaposes modern urban landscapes with traditional Native American imagery. Niatum lives in the Seattle area and has taught at Washington State University.

Simon Ortiz
1941–

Acoma Pueblo poet

Simon Ortiz is one the most respected and widely read Native American poets. His work is characterized by a strong storytelling voice that recalls traditional Native American storytelling.

Ortiz was born in Albuquerque, New Mexico, and raised at Acoma Pueblo, located in eastern New Mexico. He attended Bureau of Indian Affairs (BIA) schools on the Acoma Reservation. He originally attended college with the goal of becoming a chemical engineer but eventually quit and joined the army, where he hoped to expand his knowledge of people and places. In 1966, he enrolled at the University of New Mexico. It was during this time that his first poems were published in a number of small magazines. Eventually, Ortiz received a master of fine arts degree from the University of Iowa. Ortiz has taught creative writing and Native American literature at San Diego State University, the University of New Mexico, and Sinte Gleska College in Rosebud, South Dakota. Ortiz's career has included stints as a journalist, public relations director, and newspaper editor. In 1969, he received a Discovery Award from the National Endowment for the Arts. In 1981, his collection of poetry, *From Sand Creek,* received the Pushcart Prize for poetry.

Ortiz has stated that his work reflects his Native American heritage and oral tradition. He also points to the social and political movements of the 1960s as major influences on his work. It was during this era that expressing a tribal literary voice took on a special poignancy for Ortiz, who has remarked pointedly that writing about his heritage and culture was considered revolutionary, because there was none in the previous literature.

Ortiz's published works include *Going for the Rain* (1976), *A Good Journey* (1977), and a collection of short stories entitled *Fightin'* (1983). Ortiz was also editor of *Earth Power Coming* (1983), an anthology of Native American short fiction.

Alexander Posey

1873–1908

Creek journalist and poet

Alexander Posey was a well-known Creek poet and journalist. His skillful satirization of U.S. culture provided his people with an important source of identity during a time when their lands and culture were being stripped from them.

Alexander Posey's father was Scotch-Irish and his mother was Creek. He was raised in Creek culture by his mother near Eufaula, Oklahoma. He mastered English as a teenager while going to Bacone Indian University in Tahlequah, Oklahoma. At the university, Posey learned to set type and began writing.

Some of Posey's most direct work was done in the *Indian Journal*, a Native Oklahoma newspaper, in which he regularly satirized U.S. society. He especially liked to point out American fondness for material possessions, including Indian land. Posey cleverly mixed pidgin English, puns, and inside jokes with a recurring cast of characters who dealt with attempts to change Indian ways through new names, haircuts, and slogans. One of Posey's most beloved characters was Hotgun, a droll, seasoned veteran of the conflict between Indian cultures and U.S. culture. Hotgun's humorous comments helped Indians maintain a sense of belonging and identity. Posey's humor was a much-needed witty tonic for Indians whose way of life and lands were under siege in the late 1900s.

Posey was also directly active in tribal affairs and was superintendent of public instruction of the Creek Nation. In 1905, he helped draft a revised Creek constitution. Sadly, Posey died at the early age of thirty-four during a swimming accident.

Carter Revard
1931–

Osage writer

Carter Revard is a nationally acclaimed writer whose works combine traditional images of Native American culture with contemporary issues. He is considered to be part of the new generation of promising Native American writers.

Born in Pawhuska, Oklahoma, he grew up in Buck Creek on the Osage Reservation. The Osage are a people who lived near the Mississippi River in present-day Oklahoma, and were most likely one of the Mississippian Culture mound-building societies that flourished from A.D. 800 to 1500. Revard was raised by his stepfather, Addison Jump, in a large family that included his Ponca aunt and cousins. In 1952, he went to Oxford University as a Rhodes Scholar, showing exceptional promise both as an athlete and as a scholar. When he returned to the United States from Oxford University, one of the oldest and most prestigious universities in England, Revard went to Yale University and earned a Ph.D. in English.

Presently Revard teaches English at Washington University in St. Louis, Missouri, and serves on the board of the American Indian Center in St. Louis. He is also a Gourd Dancer, a sacred traditional dance among the southern Plains Indians (with origins among the Kiowa) and considered by many Indians to be a sacred part of contemporary powwows.

Revard's writings have been published in several anthologies of Native American writing, including *Earth Power Coming, The Remembered Earth, Voices of the Rainbow, Voices of Wahkontah, American Indian Literature*, and *The Clouds Threw This Light* (1983).

John Rollin Ridge
1827–67

Cherokee journalist and author

John Rollin Ridge was the son of John Ridge (1803–39) and the grandson of Major Ridge (1771–1839), both Cherokee leaders who favored Cherokee removal from Georgia in the 1830s. Both Ridges were assassinated in 1839, in part because they led the Treaty party, a group of economically well-off Cherokee slaveholders, merchants, and plantation owners who agreed to migrate west to present-day Oklahoma by signing the Treaty of New Echota in 1835. Most Cherokee were not in favor of removal

to the West, and many conservative Cherokee blamed the elder Ridges and other Treaty party leaders for the deaths of their relatives during the Trail of Tears (1838–39), when the U.S. Army forced most Cherokee to migrate from the East to present-day Oklahoma.

John Rollin Ridge grew up in the ensuing internal political disturbances among the Cherokee. In 1849, he killed a member of the conservative anti-Treaty party and was forced to flee for his life. He traveled to California and worked as a newspaper editor and author. Ridge often wrote in defense of the political rights of the Cherokee, Creek, and Choctaw. Although California Indians of his day were suffering greatly from political oppression and even genocide, Ridge did not take up a consistent defense of the California tribes. In 1854, he published *The Life and Times of Joaquin Murieta, the Celebrated Californian Bandit,* which was a romantic and probably fictitious story about a Spanish-American bandit who raided the American gold fields. The book on Murieta became his most famous work and is well known in Mexican and Chilean literature. Ridge lived a lively, but short life, and left a legacy of writings in politics, fiction, and poetry.

Wendy Rose
1948–

Hopi and Me-wuk poet

Wendy Rose is a poet whose work explores the conditions of Native Americans in modern urban society. Several collections of her poetry are published, and she teaches at the Fresno City College where she is also affiliated with the American Indian Studies Program.

Rose was born in Oakland, California, and descends from Hopi and Me-wuk parentage. She studied at Contra Costa College and the University of California at Berkeley. Growing up in a large city influenced her later writings, which focus on the experiences of urban Indians in America. Rose also confronts in her writing the "hybrid" nature of her heritage and culture. She states, "The poetry, too, is hybrid—like me, there are elements of Indian-ness, of English-ness, of mythology, and of horse-ness." Besides writing and teaching, Rose has been active in a number of Indian organizations, including serving as editor for the *American Indian Quarterly,* a scholarly journal in the Indian studies field.

Published works by Rose include *Hopi Roadrunner Dancing* (1973); *Long Division: A Tribal History* (1976); *Academic Squaw: Reports to the World from the Ivory Tower* (1978); *Builder Kachina: A Home-Going Cycle* (1979); *Lost Copper* (1980); *What Happened When the Hopi Hit New York* (1982); *The Man Who Dreamed He Was Turquoise; Dancing for the Whiteman; Halfbreed Chronicles & Other Poems* (1985); *Letters Home: Neon Scars* (in progress).

Leslie Marmon Silko is an acclaimed novelist. She is the author of the highly praised novels *Ceremony* (1977) and *Almanac of the Dead* (1991).

Leslie Marmon Silko 1948–

Laguna Pueblo novelist and poet

Silko was born in Albuquerque, New Mexico, although she spent her childhood at the Laguna Pueblo in eastern New Mexico, where she was surrounded with the culture and lore of the Laguna and Keres people. It was during these years that she learned about the traditions of Native American storytelling, principally through her grandmother and aunt. Silko received a bachelor's degree in English from the University of New Mexico, at which time she wrote her first short story, "The Man to Send Rain Clouds." Published in 1969, the story, based on an incident that had occurred at Laguna, gained Silko a National Endowment for the Humanities Discovery Grant.

Silko temporarily considered a law degree but, after three semesters, left law school to pursue a career in writing. In 1974, *Laguna Woman,* a book of poetry, was published. In 1977, *Storyteller,* a collection of short stories, and *Ceremony,* a novel, were published. *Ceremony,* the story of an inner journey that takes a young Indian back to his roots, established Silko's reputation as a leading U.S. author. This novel had crossover appeal for the larger audience of serious readers. Largely on the basis of *Ceremony,* Silko received one of twenty-one "genius" fellowships awarded by the MacArthur Foundation, which granted her a five-year annual stipend of $33,600 to pursue her writing.

In 1991, *Almanac of the Dead* was published. The seven-hundred-page novel was called by one reviewer, "the most ambitious literary undertaking of the past quarter century." The novel interweaves an apocalyptic depiction of declining Western society with sacred traditions of the Native American people. Underlying the entire work is the tragedy and anger Silko feels for the violation and humiliation Native Americans have suffered since the 1500s.

Silko believes that "our identity is formed by the stories we hear when we're growing up. Literature helps us locate ourselves in the family, the community and the whole universe." Consequently, Silko's work has the "feel" of traditional Native American storytelling, interweaving tales that she has remembered and imagined.

Mary TallMountain
1918–

Athapascan poet

Mary TallMountain is a widely respected Athapascan author and poet. Her writing focuses on the years she spent as a child in Alaska, in the Yukon River region.

TallMountain was born Mary Demoski on the Yukon River in the Alaska Territory, of Athapascan-Russian and Scots-Irish parents. At age six, because her mother was sick with tuberculosis, she was adopted by a non-Indian couple. Although her adoptive parents could teach her little about her culture, she retained vivid memories of her early childhood, and much of her poetry captures a delighted child's view of village life among the Athapascan of central Alaska.

As an adult, TallMountain moved to San Francisco, where she worked as a legal secretary and began to write poetry, which was featured in a number of anthologies, such as *Earth Power Coming, The Remembered Earth,* and *That's What She Said.* In 1960, she came under the tutelage of Pueblo poet and author Paula Gunn Allen. TallMountain has published two collections of poems, *The Light on the Tent Wall* in 1990 and, in 1991, *A Quick Brush of Wings.*

Currently, TallMountain lives in Petaluma, California, and is compiling an oral history of her life and working on a novel. TallMountain's works and papers are deposited in the archives at the University of Alaska, Fairbanks.

Gerald Vizenor is a teacher, novelist, and poet. He was born in Minneapolis, Minnesota, and spent a difficult childhood as a consequence of his family's poverty and his father's death. Both of these elements have been incorporated as metaphors in a number of his works.

Vizenor was educated at New York University, received a bachelor of arts from the University of Minnesota, and later studied at Harvard University. He has been a social worker, civil rights organizer, journalist, and community advocate for tribal people living in urban centers. He organized an Indian studies program at Bemidji State University in Minnesota and taught tribal history and literature at Lake Forest College, Macalester College, and the University of California at Berkeley.

Vizenor has been recognized as a multifaceted writer, and his published works include novels such as *Darkness in Saint Louis Bearheart* (1978), *Griever: An American Monkey King in China* (1987), and *The Trickster of Liberty* (1988). His volumes of haiku, a Japanese form of writing poetry, including *Raising the Moon Vines and Seventeen Chirps* (1964), and *Empty Swings* (1967). Narratives and traditional tales and songs are *The Everlasting Sky: New Voices from the People Named Chippewa* (1972), *Wordarrows: Indians and Whites in the New Fur Trade* (1978), *Anishinabe Adisokan* and *Anishinabe Nagamon* under the title *Summer in the Spring* (1981).

Gerald Robert Vizenor
1934–

Chippewa author and teacher

M*edia*

AMERICAN INDIAN TRIBES IN THE MEDIA AGE ✦ ✦ ✦ ✦ ✦ ✦ ✦

Since the relatively short time span between the mid-1960s and the present, American Indian tribes have entered what Marshal McLuhan and other American cultural sages have called the Media Age. No single event or happening, as an expression of the period would have labeled it, occurred to mark this cultural process; Indian Americans have always moved slowly and cautiously toward change. The national culture itself was in the midst of a radical make-over, and ethnicity as a human and economic reality for millions of citizens was claiming a large share of the nation's attention via television, the printed press, radio, and films.

American Indians quickly became aware that the tumult and creative excitement generated by the civil rights movements were opening up opportunities in ways that could not have even been imagined in the late 1950s and early 1960s. Here was a challenge to advance an agenda of grievances, demands, and moralistic concerns that had solidified over centuries, when American Indians were at the bottom of the ethnic ladder in the American melting pot. But to effect true, meaningful change, new skills needed to be learned and adapted, old concepts and attitudes discarded, and organized, unified campaigns involving many tribes and tribal groups needed fielding. The images of the Indians—both in their own views and in the minds of non-Indians—would need revision, make-over, and retooling. The non-Indian public would no longer easily envision a party of braves sending smoke signals to convey a coded message from a perch on a far mesa to another on a distant horizon. The much-misrepresented system of sign language, which for centuries served as a *lingua franca* for the millions of Native peoples in North America, would become a quaint relic of the past. Native peoples now communicated and expressed art through many contemporary media, such as satellite communication, weekly and monthly newspapers, journals and magazines, radio programming, and videotape. In addition, Indian actors read scripts written by Indian writers, and Indian writers write poems, plays, and novels about Indian life.

For tribal peoples the primary means of communication from time immemorial was always oral and intensely focused in a personal mode. Nevertheless, American Indians are engaging in a complex transformative process, which is developing everything from professional associations for journalists and writers to an American Indian theater movement, as well as a filmmaking community and plans for a satellite television network to link tribal groups from the top of Alaska to kindred people and communities in all parts of the lower forty-eight states and Canada. Whether this fundamental change in communication modes and systems will prove a positive, beneficial advancement for Indian people and their traditional cultures and belief systems is a question that won't be answered completely any time in the near future. But already this revolution is redefining the identity and role of American Indian communicators and artists, and a productive track record from it has been established and is growing. Some major milestones are presented here.

In the 1970s, a group of American Indian journalists in Washington, D.C., established the American Indian Press Association, which sought to establish a pan-tribally representative news bureau to gather and disseminate political, economic, and cultural information to dozens of reservation and community newspapers and publications across Indian Country. The creative and entrepreneurial energy generated by the press association encouraged many tribal communities and groups to sponsor news publications

for their constituents, many for the first time ever, and helped to firmly implant the concept and practice of freedom of information across Indian America. The press association's successor organization, the Native American Journalists' Association, in 1993 boasted a professional staff of eight American Indians at its Boulder, Colorado, offices and represents over 150 newspapers, magazines, and other publications, which serve an estimated readership of nearly one million.

Also in the 1970s, the American Indian Theatre Ensemble, later the Native American Theatre Ensemble, was founded in New York City. The ensemble was the first professional acting company of American Indian performing artists. This group provided impetus and encouragement for the subsequent development of more than a dozen Indian theaters across the United States: the Red Earth Performing Arts Company in Seattle, Washington; the A-Tu-Mai

Fancy Shawl Dance. A highlight of the American Indian Dance Theatre performance is the Women's Fancy Shawl Dance in which female members of the company exhibit their grace and virtuosity as they spin around the stage, displaying intricate dance steps while twirling colorful shawls to the beat of the drum.

Southern Men's Traditional Dance. Morgan Tosee, a member of the Comanche tribe of Oklahoma, is a champion Southern Men's Traditional dancer with the American Indian Dance Theatre.

Community Theater on the Southern Ute Indian Reservation in Colorado; the Navajoland Outdoor Theater in Window Rock, AZ; Spiderwoman Theatre in New York; and the American Indian Theatre Company of Oklahoma, in Tulsa, among others. More than one hundred original plays, musicals, revues, and assorted theater works have been produced by these groups, and a new generation of trained, experienced actors, writers, directors, producers, and technicians has emerged from this movement.

In the early 1980s, in Lincoln, Nebraska, Indian filmmakers created the Native American Public Broadcasting Consortium (NAPBC) to support and encourage Native work in television, video, and motion pictures. The 1993 catalog of NAPBC lists over 250 entries of original works that its members and contributors have produced for tribal educational, cultural, and arts

development programs around the country. NAPBC has also strongly supported American Indian television programming on numerous public television stations across the country and has addressed tribal economic and cultural concerns in all aspects of its agenda.

In 1983, the American Indian Registry for the Performing Arts was established in Los Angeles. The registry serves as an advocate for, and promoter of, American Indian actors, directors, producers, and technical personnel who are entering mainstream professions in film and television. In the registry's nearly ten years of struggle and survival in Hollywood, it has played a major part in changing the long-stereotyped and abused image of the American Indian in numerous feature films and television series. In late 1992, American Indian creative talent was poised to write, produce, and direct the first movies and television productions about American Indians.

As an outgrowth of the work related to the Native American Public Broadcasting Consortium, in 1990, about seventy-five Native video artists, filmmakers, directors, writers, and producers founded the American Indian Producers Group, which actively pursues an agenda of self-sufficiency and self-determination within the media industry. The group proclaims its goal as

> commitment to quality and culturally appropriate productions involving Native Americans. Our Native American vision, as film and television producers, is to empower ourselves to produce our stories. We will enable our future generations to continue this work from the culture of our people. We say our people deserve their inherent right to dignified and respectful presentation.

Indian communicators/artists in the past, e.g., storytellers, musical composers, poets, oral historians, and performing artists, lived a life significantly different from their counterparts in contemporary times. There was, in times past, very little "art for art's sake" in tribal societies. Just about everything had a specific purpose, and the communicators were not apart from the rest of the tribe in any special sense, nor did they want to be. Their place, and they never questioned it, was with their people. It was from the people and from their practical needs that the communicators drew their inspiration.

Richard La Course, a Yakima tribal journalist-historian and founder of the American Indian Press Association in Washington, D.C., in the early 1970s, has been a defining presence in introducing the Media Age into Indian Country. He has chronicled the changes and challenges he has experienced. In 1972, La Course said:

> In more secure times than these, everything the Indian individual needed to know for self-definition and for tribal definition was made available with the luxury and times of years. For children, winters were for stories. For all, summer was for dances, and feasts were held in the early fall. In the different tribal orders of time, the pace of growth and the pace of understanding was assured.
>
> But in many tribal sectors today, these classic lines of Indian communications have suffered from intermittent and contradictory federal policies of suppression of the ceremonies, the enforced separation of parents and children, the continuing loss of the ability on the part of many to converse in their original tribal languages, and the overweening presence of the majority American culture and its alternate system of knowledge.
>
> Much of the knowledge, the definition of Indian life borne in the life of one's own grandfather and grandmother, is vanishing with time and death. It is timely and mandatory to seek avenues not to replace those traditional modes of communication but rather to restore and enhance them toward a truly Indian future.

La Course's basic identification of artist and tribe still holds true today in some cases, but it is no longer so simple or easy for the communicators to fulfill their role in the vanguard of much that keeps the tribal spirits vibrant, strong, and constantly renewed. Ironically, as the 1990s head for a countdown to close the twentieth century, and with all the uncertainties this decade holds for America and for the world, it appears that now, more than ever, Indian people need the age-old elements of life that bind them together, unify their style into a living force, and give them strength and pride as a people.

In 1993, the nearly two million Americans who identified themselves as Native Americans and who were registered members of one of the 427 tribes were seeking ways to strengthen their tribal identities and sovereignty. They were searching for strategies to protect their land base and to develop tribal economies and business plans that will provide housing, education, and health programs. They were keenly aware of the fragilities of their natural resources and traditional and spiritual heritages.

As emerging nations with their variously complex agendas for development, the tribes find themselves long on ambition, creative energy, and determination, and short on resources, especially investment capital. Tribal members must be informed, educated, and culturally stimulated, and the world outside the tribal communities must be dealt with similarly. Many tribal leaders share a strong belief in the potential power of the media as an effective tool that, if used cautiously, can contribute significantly to finding answers and achieving goals. The avenues that La Course spoke of in 1972 are now clearly visible in the myriad new technologies abundantly and even cheaply available, but incorporating them into a balanced, creative process that respects old traditions while making new ones is the far more difficult half of the challenge.

It is in the areas of film, video, and television that much of the creative ferment of the 1990s is centered, and a number of Native American and Alaska Native creative artists have entered these fields of work. A critical review of Indian-produced works in film and video suggests that immediate tribal and family concerns have been the primary focus of much of their output as they sought to explore means of preserving cultural traditions and values as well as problems arising from struggles to retain cultural integrity in the face of strong demands for acceptance of Western culture and general rejection of Native culture by non-Indians.

Artists such as Victor Masayesva (Hopi), Bob Hicks (Creek-Seminole), Phil Lucas (Choctaw), Chris Spotted Eagle (Houma), and Sandra Osawa (Makah) have produced films and documentaries that present positive, culturally sensitive images of American Indians and Alaska Natives. They have shown impressive skills in writing, producing, and distributing a wide variety of video works, documentaries, and short films produced primarily for Native Americans.

Phil Lucas, whose body of creative work has been primarily for television, sees the present explosion in technological advances as a crucial time of opportunity when Native people must take control of their image in the media through applying their creative gifts and energies. "We must be working to replace the outdated, stereotyped images of ourselves with truth, knowledge, understanding and appreciation for the differences in our respective cultures. And as we work for these goals, we must ply our trade in whatever manner and with whatever means we are able to draw unto ourselves."

Bob Hicks, whose award-winning short film *Return of the Country* (1982), a satirical comedy about identity reversal, offers a pragmatic view of what strategies contemporary Indian communicators should follow.

> We need to develop a strong, durable support base to provide funding, housing for production activities and advocacy to sustain us in our work. We need to get the tribes more involved, and we need to help the tribal leaders develop clearer understandings of the importance of this kind of work and what good it can do. If we want to create change, we have to empower ourselves to do so. The people, the tribes, will be our most important sources of strength.

Gifted talent has always been abundant among Indian people, and it is certain that more talent will emerge in such projects as tribal theaters, music and dance workshops, creative writing projects, film programs, and cultural study groups. To nurture this new generation of communicators/artists, a complex support network must be established by all the tribes, which will assure the development of this vital resource. Public and private arts funding for American Indian communicators in terms of money per capita is far below what has been disbursed for non-Indian arts projects. It is imperative that the tribes find ways to allocate their own resources and funds to support their creative members.

With tribal support of their communicators/artists will come an expansion of the professional expertise base. Actors, directors, designers, writers, technical personnel, administrators, managers, and producers are all in positions which, when employed, generate both income and tax revenues, as well as prestige for the tribe.

In recent years, American Indian tribes have grown more confident and more experienced in meeting the challenges of a new world. They have grown more sophisticated in their appreciation and respect for their creative, artistic members. As the national American Indian community as a whole grows steadily stronger, so does the need for artistic innovation and sources for new traditions. The new responsibilities that the Media Age bestows on Indian communicators are cogently described by Richard La Course:

(Left to right) Chester Mahooty, an elder of the Zuni tribe of New Mexico, Morgan Tosee, of the Comanche tribe of Oklahoma, and Ramona Roach, a Navajo from New Mexico, are among the all-Native American dancers and musicians with the American Indian Dance Theatre.

Indian communicators, like their non-Indian counterparts, must be busy transcribing the first rough draft of the contemporary history of Indian people, and they must take this moment in Indian history with the utmost seriousness. From within the perspective of Indian concerns, they must have the willingness and the responsibility to hold up a mirror to their times, and to the occasionally troubled and murky matters of tribal times in flux. Indian communicators at this point in history must, as in the past, become the reflective, self-aware and trained eyes and ears of our Indian tribal societies. And they must participate in the strengthening of the tribe and the community through their commitment to handing on, and handing down, the tribal realities of the present and the past.

Indian people have endured in large part because of their extraordinary ability to adapt and to be innovative and creative when circumstances require them to be. As they proceed into the Media Age and learn to utilize its technologies for their varied needs and purposes, the American Indian cultural presence and heritage will likely grow stronger, richer, and more resilient.

Hanay Geiogamah
University of California, Los Angeles

INDIANS IN FILM AND THEATER ♦ ♦ ♦ ♦ ♦ ♦ ♦ ♦ ♦ ♦ ♦ ♦

In the history of film and theater, Indian culture and characters have usually been portrayed from the point of view of non-Indian history and culture. This portrayal tends to vary between the adulation of the "noble savage," in which Indians are seen as always proud, independent, and honorable people, and the more negative view that Indians are "bloodthirsty savages." In general, Indian people do not like the images by which they are portrayed in commercial films, largely because the usual film images stereotype Indian characters and do not give reasonable or well-grounded understandings of Indian cultures. Increasingly, however, independent Native playwrights and film producers are making their own plays and films, which offer audiences new perspectives on Indian culture and identity within works that arise from Indian experiences and understandings.

The Indian in Film   The popularity of Kevin Costner's *Dances with Wolves* (1990) brought the Indian-as-subject back to the American movie screen. During the 1970s and 1980s, the decline of the Western film resulted in fewer film portrayals of Indians. Indian actors and themes nearly vanished from movie theaters, although exceptions like *Windwalker* (1980) seemed to mourn the loss of Indian tradition. While *Dances with Wolves* is highly acclaimed for casting lead Indian actors, for providing sympathetic Indian portrayals, and for the use of authentic Indian language, filmmakers since the early 1900s have experimented with similar themes and images.

The initial depictions of American Indians in films were influenced, in part, by popular novels, circus-like wild west shows, and stage plays of the noble savage that were firmly embedded in American culture. The earliest films were silent, only several minutes in length, and lacked any significant type of story development. One of the first known films about American Indians was *The Sioux Ghost Dance* made in 1894 by the (Thomas) Edison Studios. Two sequences in the film portrayed five Sioux Indians, in full regalia of breechcloth and headfeathers, beating on drums and dancing on a stage.

Film narratives increasingly grew more sophisticated, however, as artists freely adapted popular literary works to the screen. In *Pocahontas* (1908), Edison Studios reenacted the story of John Rolfe of early Virginia Colony and his marriage in 1614 to Pocahontas, the daughter of Powhatan, leader of a powerful Indian confederacy. In *Hiawatha* (1907), the Independent Motion Picture Company filmed the well-known poem of the same title by Henry Wadsworth Longfellow, the nineteenth-century U.S. poet. Film pioneer, D. W. Griffith, in *Leather Stocking* (1909), reworked James Fenimore Cooper's *Leather Stocking Tales*, which were stories of frontier romance and adventure during the 1750s. Griffith also directed the first screen version of Helen Hunt Jackson's novel, *Ramona* (1910), a biographical story of a southern California Indian woman and her struggle to survive. Griffith made several dozen short Westerns that display a variety of Indian images. In *The Battle at Elderbush Gulch* (1914), a non-Indian kills the son of a Sioux leader and thereafter the Sioux terrorize a community of innocent settlers. In *The Redman and the Child* (1908), however, a more sympathetic view of Indians is portrayed when an Indian rescues a kidnapped non-Indian boy and avenges the death of the boy's grandfather by killing the offending outlaws. Other Griffith stories developed idyllic tales of Indian lovers; *The Mended Lute* (1909) and *A Squaw's Love* (1911) both told of Indian romances in the secluded wilderness.

Griffith's contemporary, Thomas Ince, occasionally explored the cultural aspects of Indian life. Ince transported a group of Sioux Indians from South Dakota to his ranch in Santa Ynez, California, where he regularly employed them in his Western-theme movies. In *The Indian Massacre* (1913, also known as *The Heart of an Indian*), an Indian kidnaps a non-Indian baby to replace the loss of an Indian woman's son who had died. Among many Indian nations, young children were sometimes captured to replace relatives who died. When the film's conclusion shows the Indian mother grieving her son's death, the imagery of maternal bonding is powerful.

The later films of 1910 to 1915 brought more serious portrayals of Indian life. Although initially drawing upon the noble versus savage stereotypes, these films later grappled with issues such as Indian and non-Indian intermarriage, discrimination, and estrangement from one's own or another culture. Based on Edwin Milton Royle's popular state play of the same name, *The Squaw Man* (1914, co-directed by Cecil B. DeMille and Oscar C. Apfel) shows the troubles of an Indian woman's marriage to a non-Indian. Not all intermarriages were doomed, however. In *The Red Woman* (1917), an educated Indian woman ultimately marries a non-Indian miner and they have a child.

The "marginal man" theme—that of an educated Indian who is scorned by both Indian people and U.S. society—can be found as early as 1910 in *Red Eagle's Love Affair* and, more prominently, in Alan Hale's *Braveheart* (1925, produced by Cecil B. DeMille and based on William DeMille's play, *Strongheart*). Typically in these films, the Indian returns to his tribe and his non-Indian love interest remains behind. Other, bolder films condemned federal Indian policies. While social reformers attacked government administration of Indian reservations and missionary efforts among the Indians, *The Vanishing American* (1925) delivered a sharp indictment of the country's reservation system.

The silent film era introduced many talented Indian actors to the screen. Although non-Indians, including Blacks and Japanese, frequently portrayed Indian characters, a few notable Native

Americans performed in key roles. William Eagleshirt (Sioux) regularly portrayed Indian leads in Thomas Ince's films. Dark Cloud, an actor of reported Native ancestry, portrayed Indian leads for Griffith, and Mona Darkfeather (Seminole) acted for the Florida-based Kalem studios. John Big Tree, a Seneca, began acting in silent features and later became a regular in the Westerns of the politically controversial, complex director John Ford, who cast Big Tree in *The Iron Horse* (1924), *Drums along the Mohawk* and *Stagecoach* (1939), and *She Wore a Yellow Ribbon* (1948). Charles Stevens, allegedly of Apache descent, appeared opposite the famous star Douglas Fairbanks in *Wild and Woolly* (1917). Stevens also played several roles with make-up changes in *The Thief of Bagdad* (1924). James Young Deer (Winnebago) served as a technical advisor to D. W. Griffith. In 1912, Young Deer was appointed by the French owned Pathé Frères studios to head up their southern California productions, where he directed dozens of short Westerns. Edwin Carewe, a quarter Chickasaw, is best noted for directing the third screen version of *Ramona* in 1928.

In the late 1920s, the advent of "talking" pictures did not immediately alter the Indian's screen image. Although Raoul Walsh's mega-budget *The Big Trail* (1930) failed at the box office and consequently buried the epic Western for several years, Hollywood movie makers took a closer look at Indian life. Several key films followed the method of Edwin Curtis's *In the Land of the War Canoes* (1914), a fictionalized semi-documentary of the Kwakiutl, who lived along the coast of British Columbia in Canada. Other films that employed Curtis's semi-documentary method were *The Silent Enemy* (1930), a story of Ojibway Indians before European arrival; Cecil B. DeMille's third version of *The Squaw Man* (1931); Metro-Goldwyn-Mayer's tribute to America's northern neighbors in *Eskimo* (1933, subtitled in English); and the screen adaptation of writer Oliver LaFarge's Pulitzer Prize-winning tale of *Laughing Boy* (1934), a story of romance between a Navajo boy and girl of the same clan. The subject of intermarriage again surfaced in *Behold My Wife!* (1934), a story of a wealthy easterner who marries an Apache woman in order to spite his parents. Intermarriage was also a theme in the Academy Award-winning *Cimarron* (1930), a story of the Oklahoma Land Rush, during which the hero's son

Plains Indians who played roles in Hollywood movies take a break on the rollercoaster ride, Long Beach, California, 1930s.

marries the family's Indian servant. Before his untimely death in 1935, the renowned Cherokee statesman, writer, and comedian, Will Rogers, starred as a non-Indian in several John Ford movies. Rogers thus came to represent the "successful" Indian in U.S. society.

In the 1930s, the rise of the "B-Western"—independent, low-budget cowboy pictures made for the second half of a theater's double bill—endlessly recycled the most simplistic plots and good versus bad characterizations. Costly scenes of Indian attacks or buffalo stampedes were reused in subsequent pictures, and non-Indians in Indian make-up served as inexpensive substitutes for Indian extras. Movie serials popularized the Indian-as-villain or -ally in titles such as *The Last of the Mohicans* (1932), *The Miracle Rider* (1935), and *The Lone Ranger* (1938), the latter featuring Thunder Cloud (Cherokee) as the screen's first Tonto, the Indian friend of the Lone Ranger. Jay Silverheels, a Mohawk Indian, portrayed Tonto in the 1950s television series, and Michael Horse, of Zuni, Yaqui, and Mescalero Apache descent, played Tonto in the more recent film, *Legend of the Lone Ranger* (1981).

By the mid-1930s, the Indians' screen image began to recede as studios reestablished the nineteenth-century belief in a Manifest Destiny—the idea of inevitable U.S. expansion across the North American continent. The cowboy became the benevolent hero, driving Indians from the plains and making the frontier safe for settlers. From Cecil B. DeMille's *The Plainsman* in 1936, which immortalized Western personalities such as Wild Bill Hickok and Buffalo Bill Cody, to John Ford's *Stagecoach* in 1939, in which the Apaches are mowed down like blades of grass, these Western pictures cast Indians as unwelcome aliens in their own land and left an indelible mark on the American mind.

The outbreak of World War II in Europe forced studios to re-examine their portrayal of interethnic relations. The War Department advised Hollywood not to condone domestic racial prejudice while America was fighting the racist dictators of Germany and Japan. Thus, overnight the Japanese and Germans became the

Urban Indian picketing Warner Brothers in the making of the movie They Died with Their Boots On.

screen's villains, while Indians became allies. In DeMille's *Northwest Mounted Police* (1940), Cree leader Big Bear aides Canadian troopers in central Western Canada during the 1885 Métis uprising of primarily French-Indian mixed blood people. In *They Died with Their Boots On* (1941), contrary to historical fact, Indian fighter and army officer George Armstrong Custer became the personal guardian of the Sioux people.

As government Indian policy changed in the 1950s with federal termination of Indian reservations and encouragement of Indian assimilation into U.S. society, Hollywood lost little time in advocating the postwar sentiment of racial, ethnic and cultural equality for all peoples. It was not uncommon for Westerns like *Broken Arrow* (1950)—the story of the friendship between Thomas Jeffords, a U.S. mail rider, and the Apache leader Cochise—to propose assimilation, the Indian acceptance of U.S. culture, as a solution for Indian poverty and political subjugation. Later Westerns, however, shed their idealism while becoming more skeptical of peaceful human relations. John Ford's *The Searchers* (1956) suggests that savagery is innate in both Indians and non-Indians, while Richard Brooks's *The Last Hunt* (1955) delivers a scathing indictment against the nineteenth-century U.S. slaughter of the buffalo on the Plains and the callous treatment of Indians.

According to these movies, assimilation for Indians was impossible within the culturally and politically hostile U.S. In the later fifties and early sixties, Westerns examined the struggles of Indian mixed-bloods, who found peace only outside society's boundaries. Don Siegel's *Flaming Star* (1960) replays the "marginal man" theme, in which a half-breed is torn between his Indian and European heritages. In Delbert Mann's *The Outsider* (1961), Pima Indian Ira Hayes finds himself unable to reconcile with celebrity status in U.S. society when he is celebrated as a war hero.

Meanwhile, Indian-theme movies were enjoying a surge of popularity in Europe. German author Karl Friedrich May (1842-1912) wrote a series of novels about the American West. May's books, featuring the adventures of Winnetou, an Apache, and his fair-haired companion, Old Shatterhand, influenced an entire generation of European readers. Beginning in 1962 with *Der Schatz Im Silbersee* (The Treasure of Silver Lake), West German studios filmed eleven of these early American tales, many of which featured U.S. actor Lex Barker as Old Shatterhand and French actor Pierre Brice as Winnetou.

By the 1970s, Westerns delivered their fiercest attacks ever against U.S. Indian policies. In a complete turnaround from the Manifest Destiny emphasis of the thirties, U.S. soldiers were now portrayed killing and maiming innocent Indians. Resentment against United States involvement in Vietnam, along with government distrust, dominated Arthur Penn's *Little Big Man* (1971), which featured Squamish actor Dan George, whose memorable performance earned him an Academy Award nomination as best supporting actor. Similarly, Ralph Nelson's *Soldier Blue* (1970) casts the U.S. Army as relentless murderers in its graphic recreation of the massacre of Cheyenne and Arapaho Indians at Sand Creek (Colorado) in 1864. In *Ulzana's Raid* (1972), director Robert Aldrich implies that the U.S. Army's policy to exterminate Indians drove the Apache to aggressive self-defense.

The 1970s saw a sharp decline in the popularity of Westerns, and Indians in movies began to appear "outside" society's boundaries. *One Flew over the Cuckoo's Nest* (1975) confines its characters, one of whom is played by Creek Indian Will Sampson, to a state mental hospital. *Harry and Tonto* (1974)

Will Sampson (Creek) and Jack Nicholson starred in the hit movie One Flew Over the Cuckoo's Nest *(1975).*

Copyright 1975 The Saul Zaentz Company. All rights reserved.

places an adventurous old man in the same jail cell with Indian actor Dan George. Occasionally, Hollywood mixed Indian mysticism with contemporary horror. Both *The Manitou* (1978) and *Nightwing* (1979) resort to Indian spiritualism to explain the unexplainable.

Television struggled to fill the gap with pro-Indian sagas that attempted to rewrite U.S. history in order to "balance" the record. "I Will Fight No More Forever" (ABC, 1975) was the story of Chief Joseph of the Nez Percé and boasted that "real" Indians played Indians. "Mystic Warrior" (ABC, 1984), based on Ruth Beebe Hill's novel *Hanta Yo* about Sioux life on the Plains, made a case for the viability of Indian culture and society. The miniseries "Roanoke" (PBS, 1986) claimed to use authentic Native American language with English subtitles.

Television's outcries against U.S. injustice toward Indians and demands for appreciating Indian cultures gave sympathetic support to the growing Indian self-determination movement. Many Native American activist groups protested against what they believed were media perpetuations of cultural distortions and historical inaccuracies. Particularly troublesome was the casting of British actor Trevor Howard as the Indian lead in *Windwalker* (1980), a story of the Cheyenne and their struggles against their traditional enemies, the Crow. Howard's presence seemed out of step with Hollywood's recent pro-Indian gestures, reminding Native Americans that the movie industry had little confidence in their talent.

Powwow Highway (1988), an independent film that received only limited distribution, cast Gary Farmer (Mohawk) in the lead role as Philbert, a good-natured fellow who teaches his cynical companion, played by A Martinez ("Santa Barbara" and "L. A. Law") to rediscover his Indian identity. Set against the post-activism of the 1970s, the film shows that Indian culture and spirituality are necessary for Indian self-determination and survival. Similarly, Michael Apted's *Thunderheart* (1992) sets its characters within the politically divided Oglala Sioux Nation. When a part-Indian Federal Bureau of Investigation (FBI) agent is sent to resolve a reservation murder, he confronts his own Native identity. In

Thunderheart, both Graham Greene (Oneida) and Sheila Tousey (Menominee, Stockbridge, and Munsee) give strong performances in supporting roles. Only on rare occasions have Indian women played pivotal roles in movies; major exceptions are Tousey's performance in *Thunderheart* and Cree-Métis actress Tantoo Cardinal in the Canadian film *Loyalties* (1985).

Kevin Costner's *Dances with Wolves* (1990) sparked a renewed interest in Indian-theme movies. *Dances with Wolves* is the story of Civil War Lieutenant John J. Dunbar and his life among the Lakota Sioux. Among the featured Indian actors in key roles, most notable was Graham Greene, who was nominated for an Academy Award as best supporting actor. The film, however, provides little understanding about Indian culture; rather it projects a European romantic image of the noble savage. In the romantic tradition, the movie's hero longs for the unspoiled wilderness, pursues his own "dream woman," and searches for life uncontaminated by urban society. Two previous films explored the theme of a heroic non-Indian man living among the Sioux. Sam Fuller's *Run of the Arrow* (1956) was a bleak account of a disillusioned Confederate volunteer who seeks refuge among the Lakota and marries a Lakota woman. Elliot Silverstein's *A Man Called Horse* (1970) told the story of an aristocratic Englishman who is captured and tortured by the Sioux. He eventually becomes their leader and continues his adventures in *Return of a Man Called Horse* (1976) and *Triumphs of a Man Called Horse* (1984).

Despite its enthusiastic reception, *Dances with Wolves* brought little change to Hollywood's portrayal of Indian life and people. Two years later, Michael Mann's *The Last of the Mohicans* (1992) simply reworked a century-old theme. Mann presents the story of how Hawkeye, a colonial backwoodsman, and his faithful Indian companions, Chingachgook and Uncas, defeat the Huron leader Magua. James Fenimore Cooper's novel *The Last of the Mohicans* has been filmed at least a dozen times and was the subject of a television series in 1957–58. The longevity of *Mohicans* suggests that Hollywood prefers to isolate its Indians safely within the romantic past, rather than take a close look at Native American issues in the contemporary world.

Since the early 1970s, Indians throughout North America have been creating alternative productions to Hollywood movies. Armed with cameras and microphones, independent Indian film-makers have mastered the techniques of directing and writing to produce their own unique cinematic perspective. Bob Hicks's amusing satire *Return of the Country* (1982) is a case in point. Hicks, a Creek-Seminole, turns the non-Indian perspective upside down. In his film, Indians discover America and promptly establish a Bureau of Caucasian Affairs, which mimics the real life Bureau of Indian Affairs. *Return of the Country* presents a world in which non-Indian children are forced to abandon the English language, shed their European-style dress, and disavow Christian religion. In a similar light, *Harold of Orange* (1983), screenplay by Gerald Vizenor (Chippewa), mocks the well-intentioned though paternalistic institutions that dominate Indian reservation communities. A reservation "trickster," played by Oneida comedian Charlie Hill, and his fellow "Warriors of Orange" disarm a non-Indian organization by ridiculing its so-called philanthropic motives. Through wry humor, *Harold of Orange* removes the thin veneer that often masks subtle forms of prejudice.

In *Itam Hakim, Hopiit* (1984), renowned Hopi photographer and filmmaker Victor Masayesva, Jr., creates his own cinematic language by dismantling the Western documentary style of talking heads and linear narration. The narrator's English translation is simultaneously played with the Hopi-speaking voice and, when blended with natural sounds and lyrical images, results in a mythical version of Hopi history. Masayesva's more recent *Pott Starr* (1990), a clever blend of real life and animation, pokes fun at commercial tourism and non-Indian fascination with Hopi artifacts.

Other Indian filmmakers bridge the gap of cross-cultural communication and provide their own perspectives of contemporary issues. In *The Great Spirit Within the Hole* (1983), Chris Spotted Eagle (Houma) reveals the struggles of Native Americans in prison to exercise religious freedom. Spotted Eagle, in *Our Sacred Land* (1984), captures the fierce tenacity of the Lakota Sioux to reclaim control over the Black Hills of South Dakota. As told by descendants of survivors, the poignant *Wiping the Tears of Seven Generations* (1991), by Gary Rhine and Fidel Moreno (Yaqui-Huichol), documents the events surrounding the 1890 massacre at Wounded Knee in present-day southern South Dakota. More recently, PBS aired a two-hour television special, "Surviving Columbus" (1992), which traces Pueblo history from European contact to the present. "Surviving Columbus" was produced in cooperation with KNME Television in Albuquerque, New Mexico, and the Institute of American Indian Arts in Santa Fe. Production included an all-Indian crew consisting of Edmund Ladd (Zuni), producer; George Burdeau (Blackfeet), co-executive producer; Diane Reyna (Taos Pueblo), director; and Simon Ortiz (Acoma Pueblo), writer.

For Canada's First Nations, the country's media resources have encouraged remarkable growth in independent filmmaking. Key Canadian government agencies, such as the National Film Board and Telefilm Canada, provide Native filmmakers with funding and distribution. In 1990, for example, the National Film Board inaugurated Studio One, which provides training and production assistance to Canada's Native filmmakers. Located in Edmonton, Alberta, Studio One counters the non-representation of Canadian Indians in mainstream media and places Native media images in control of the indigenous people themselves. Studio One's first producer, Carol Geddes (Tlingit) is a nationally acclaimed filmmaker and writer.

Today the National Film Board supports the talents of many documentary filmmakers, among them Alanis Obomsawin (Abenaki). For more than a decade, Obomsawin has tackled some of the most controversial issues facing Native Canadians. In *Richard Cardinal: Cry From a Diary of a Métis Child* (1986), she exposes Canada's woefully inadequate and inhuman child welfare system. Obomsawin confronts Quebec's minister of fisheries in *Incident at Restigouche* (1984) for ordering two police raids against the Micmac nation, whose members sought to exercise traditional fishing rights.

To the far north in the Canadian Arctic lies the home of the Inuit Broadcasting Corporation (IBC), a model for indigenous broadcasters throughout the world. Frustrated with the invasion of English-language television in their society, the region's Native people countered with their own satellite broadcasting center that produces documentary, drama, animation, and children's programs entirely in the Inuit language. The IBC's lively history is told in *Starting Fire with Gunpowder* (1991), directed by William Hansen and David Poisey (Inuit). For Canadian as well as U.S. Indians, the Inuit Broadcasting Corporation demonstrates that media control is a vital step toward creating a truly Native voice beyond commercial cinema.

Natives and the Theater

Just as it has taken a long time for North American Indian people to begin to control how they are represented in film, Indian involvement in theater is a recent phenomenon. Non-Indian playwrights and performers have created countless plays about Indian people, which often bear little resemblance to the people they claim to describe. As Native theater artists become prominent, their voices begin to challenge the common preconceptions that non-Indian audiences have about Native peoples.

Representation of North American Indians began with the first theatrical event performed in North America. Entitled *The Theatre of Neptune in New France,* the play was written in 1606 by Marc Lescarbot and performed on the shores of Port Royal (present-day Nova Scotia, Canada) to celebrate the return of the city's founders from an exploratory mission. The play's performance portrayed Indians in ways that marked Indian characterizations in plays over the next two hundred years. The speeches delivered by the "natives" (Frenchmen in Indian costume) were written in an artificially heightened and unnatural style and the main duty of the Native characters in the performance was to welcome settlers, who were portrayed as a much-needed "civilizing influence."

In *Native Americans as Shown on the Stage 1753–1916* (1988), Eugene Jones suggests that the representation of Indians during the colonial period was determined largely by the audience's need to feel comfortable displacing the Indians from their traditional lands. Between 1660 and 1800, where there was little westward settler expansion and therefore little Indian contact, Native people were seen as unreal and fantastic creatures. In the early 1800s, settlers increasingly felt the Indian presence, and playwrights satisfied their audience's desire to see on stage (and therefore somehow come to terms with) "real life" Natives by developing plays containing Indian figures who were both noble and unthreatening to colonial power. For example, Mordecai Manuel Noah's play *She Would Be a Soldier: or, the Plains of Chippewa* (1819) shows noble Natives who helped the United States fight the War of 1812. From 1830 to 1840, as settlers migrated westward, the necessity of dispossessing Native people from valuable land sparked anxiety, and the common belief that Native people were a "dying race" helped relieve the tension. As late as 1886, the Canadian play *Tecumseh: A Drama*, by Charles Mair, suggests that Indian nobility was transferred to the colonizing people.

After the removal of many Indians from the East between 1830 and 1870 and the suppression of Native resistance in the Plains Wars of the 1870s, relations between Natives and settlers had clearly deteriorated. Reflecting the dark mood were plays such as Louisa Medina's *Nick of the Woods; or, the Jibbenainosay* (1838), which depicted Indians as worthless savages fit for extermination by superior settlers. The blatant racism of this period is exemplified by popular melodramas such as V.J. Arlington's *The Red Right Hand* (1876), written with a part for U.S. Army scout and showman William Frederick ("Buffalo Bill") Cody (1846–1917), in which Cody tears off an Indian's scalp, presents it to the audience and shouts "The first scalp for Custer!"

During the latter part of the nineteenth century and into the twentieth, some plays began to portray Indians as people rather than in stereotypical savage or noble terms. Although these more sympathetic plays were marred with misunderstanding and inaccuracy, they make a hopeful contrast to the Indian caricatures usually seen on stage. Ina Dillaye's play *Ramona* (1887) showed Native people with recognizable human virtues such as honor and intelligence. Some playwrights wrote plays, such as Mary Austin's *The Arrow-Maker* (1911), featuring only Indian characters.

Theatrical images of Native people were still created and performed for non-Indians until 1932, when Lynn Riggs, an Oklahoman playwright who was part Cherokee, wrote *The Cherokee Night*. Riggs's landmark work discussed issues such as the failure of the U.S. assimilation policy and the loss of tribal and personal identity among Native people. Riggs's achievement, however, was not reinforced by other playwrights and, for the next thirty years, the public representation of Native people was largely determined by the motion picture industry.

In the 1960s, interest in Indians as theatrical subjects resurfaced. Arthur Kopit's *Indians* (1968) was a typical example of a play written by a non-Indian that expressed general discontent by using Indian characters as symbols of society's victims. The Indian people served to illustrate a general social problem, such as alienation from society or "non-Indian guilt," but the play did not address specific issues affecting Indians. By presenting Natives as doomed victims of social forces beyond their control, Canadian George Ryga's plays, *Indian* (1962) and *The Ecstasy of Rita Joe* (1970), updated the "dying race" idea prevalent in the 1800s.

In the 1970s, fueled in part by growing Indian activism and self-awareness, the Native American theater community markedly intensified its creative activity. In its portrayal of the intense misery and hopelessness of a Native alcoholic, *Body Indian* (1972), by Hanay Geiogamah (Kiowa and Delaware), is an early example of Indian realism. *Foghorn* (1973), Geiogamah's next play, is a free-form examination of Native and non-Native relations, while *49* (1975) mixes realistic and experimental techniques to produce a positive affirmation of renewed Indian cultures. Written by John Kaufman, a Nez Percé, and Wayne Johnson, *The Indian Experience* (1975) also stresses positive interpretations of Indian history and culture. In the 1970s, several Native theater companies, such as the Red Earth Performing Arts Company in Seattle and the Native American Theater Ensemble in Oklahoma, were formed and devoted to performing works by or about Native people.

During the 1980s, Native theater in Canada was especially active, with the formation of Native Earth Performing Arts Company (Toronto), 4 Winds Theatre (Hobbema), Awasikan Theatre (Winnipeg), Tununiq Theatre (Baffin Island) and De-Bah-Jeh-Mu-Jig Theatre (Manitoulin Island). Many troupes, such as the Inuit Company Tununiq Theatre, concentrate on performing community-based awareness plays targeting specific social problems such as wife beating or child abuse. What characterizes all Native plays is their fusion of traditional material with contemporary staging techniques. The plays of Tomson Highway (Cree) take place on the fictional Wasaychigan Hill Reservation. Highway's *The Rez Sisters* (1986) focuses on the humorous and sad exploits of Native women in the Wasaychigan Hill community, and *Dry Lips Oughta Move to Kapuskasing* (1989) explores the dark and troubling sexism of Native men on the fictional reservation. Daniel David Moses (Delaware) uses a Nez Percé coyote legend as a foundation for his play *Coyote City* (1988), in which a girl is contacted by her dead lover. *Almighty Voice and His Wife* (1991), another play by Moses, employs the clichés and stereotypes of a nineteenth-century melodrama to satirize non-Indian perceptions of Native people. Playwright Jim Morris (Cree) presents Native myths in their original language, in *Son of Ayash* (1990).

The 1980s also saw collaboration between non-Natives, who sought deeper understanding of Native cultures, and Natives, who wanted to control how their people and culture were presented on stage. In Canada, writer and performer Linda Griffiths and Métis writer Maria Campbell produced a collaborative play entitled *Jessica* (1986). Another collaborative Canadian project was *NO'ZYA* (Our Footprints, 1987) by David Diamond, in association with the Gitskan and Wet'suet'en peoples of the Canadian Northwest Coast. Both *Jessica* and *NO'ZYA* are distinguished by presentations of traditional Native spirituality and storytelling. The fact that a Gitskan elder toured with *NO'ZYA* as an advisor suggests a new commitment to presenting on stage authentic and responsible images of Native people and their culture.

Considering the strong role of women in numerous Native societies, it is not surprising that many Indian playwrights are women.

A scene from the play Dry Lips Oughta Move to Kapuskasing (1989) by Tomson Highway. Native Earth Performing Arts, Inc., Toronto, Ontario, Canada.

Early European playwrights were especially fascinated with Indian women, whom they perceived as sexually exciting and more open than Indian males to "civilizing" influence. In plays such as Lewis Deffebach's *Oolaita: or, the Indian Heroine* (1821), the Native female was presented as a spirited "gentle native," who was plagued by villainous circumstances and who died at the play's end. The woman's main role in these plays was to offer protection to non-Natives and, in the process, admit her inferiority. In their fight for equality, Native women playwrights have worked to dispel such harmful myths and, through the medium of theater, addressed real social concerns. Spiderwoman Theater (New York) is an innovative, all-female company whose plays often emphasize social issues that affect Native women. *Night of the Trickster* (1992), written by Métis writer Beatrice Culleton, examines the effect of rape on Native women in particular, but also as a universal problem. The play *Moonlodge* (1990), by Margo Kane (Saulteaux/ Cree/Blackfoot), advocates the rejection of female stereotypes and affirms the value of female Native communities. In order to develop a more respectful and honest identity for Native women, Monique Mojica (Kuna/Rappahannock), in *Princess Pocahontas and the Blue Spots* (1991), attacks the empty and sexist literary images of Indian women commonly found in literature.

Clearly, the development of the images of Natives on stage and in films has been progressive and hopeful. The trend away from artificial and stereotypical treatment of Indian people in favor of multicultural collaboration indicates a new willingness of non-Indian people to listen and learn. Now being heard are strong Native voices that offer alternative visions of Indian identity and critical reevaluations of our shared history.

Angela Aleiss
University of California, Los Angeles

Robert Appleford
University of Toronto

♦ ♦ ♦ ♦ ♦ ♦ ♦ ♦ ♦ ♦ ♦ ♦ ♦ ♦ ♦ ♦ ♦ ♦ **BIOGRAPHIES**

George Burdeau is a screenwriter and director of Blackfeet descent. He was born on November 16, 1944. He received a bachelor's degree in communications from the University of Washington and did graduate work at the Anthropology Film Center in Santa Fe, New Mexico. He also studied at the Institute of American Indian Arts in Santa Fe.

Burdeau has more than twenty film and television credits as a producer, director, or writer. The earliest of these include various documentaries on Native American subjects that were produced for the Public Broadcasting System, and since the mid-1980s Burdeau has become increasingly active as a producer and director for major network television programs. Among his more recent credits are "99 Ways to Find the Right Man" (1986), a one-

George Burdeau
1944–

Blackfeet producer, director, and screenwriter

hour comedy special broadcast on Valentine's Day over ABC-TV, and "Color Us California" (1986), a one-hour special on immigrants in the Los Angeles area.

Burdeau is currently director of the Communication Arts Department at the Institute of American Indian Arts.

Gil Cardinal

1950–

Cree/Métis filmmaker

A skilled director, producer, writer, and editor, Gil Cardinal has been working both in front of and behind the camera for twenty years. He graduated in 1973 from the Radio and TV Arts program at the Northern Alberta Institute of Technology in Edmonton, and in 1976 became the director and associate producer of "Come Alive," a daily, live magazine-format show in Alberta. Cardinal continued to produce and direct a variety of shows, including "Shadow Puppets," a series of seven programs (1978-80) adapting Cree and Blackfoot legends to electronic animation.

Cardinal began his association with Canada's National Film Board, a federally established organization devoted to the advancement of film, in 1980. His numerous projects include *Children of Alcohol* (1983), a documentary on the effects of parental alcoholism; *Discussions in Bioethics: The Courage of One's Convictions* (1985), an inquiry into medical/legal ethics; and *Fort McPherson* (1986), a look at a community's struggle with alcohol and suicide. *Foster Child* (1987), which traces Cardinal's search for his natural family and features him as a director, associate editor, and subject, has won nine film festival awards since its premier.

Cardinal's varied experience in Canadian media also includes a half-hour television drama, "Bordertown Cafe" (1988), and a one-hour documentary, *Tikinagan* (1991), for Tamarack Productions of Toronto, Ontario. His latest National Film Board documentary, *The Spirit Within* (1990), co-directed with Wil Campbell, focuses on the importance of Indian spirituality for Native inmates in Canada.

Tantoo Cardinal

1950–

Cree/Métis actress

Born in Fort McMurray and raised in Anzac, a small town 350 miles northeast of Edmonton, Alberta, Tantoo Cardinal is one of Canada's most renowned Native film actresses. Never formally trained as an actress, she began her career in the 1970s with a series of small roles in film, theater, and television. Her first feature film appearance occurred in *Marie Anne* in 1977, produced in Canada by Fraser Films and directed by Martin Walters. In 1985, Cardinal played the lead role in *Loyalties,* a feature film written, directed, and produced by Anne Wheeler, which tells the fictional story of a British man who moves to the Canadian plains to escape his past. For her stirring performance, Cardinal was nominated for the prestigious Canadian film award, the Genie, as best actress, and she received a best actress award at the American Indian Film Festival, as well as a number of other awards. Her performance served to expand Cardinal's audience beyond the Native community in which she was well known.

Cardinal is perhaps best known for her supporting role as the wife of a Lakota medicine man in *Dances with Wolves,* a 1990 Kevin Costner production. Other notable performances include a supporting role in *Black Robe,* a 1991 Canadian-Australian joint production directed by Bruce Beresford, detailing the story of a French missionary's quest to convert Native people to Christianity; and the title role in *Silent Tongue,* a 1993 film directed by Sam Shepard.

Cardinal has also enjoyed significant success in television and theater. Her numerous television credits include a lead role in *Gunsmoke,* a Movie of the Week remake, and guest star appearances on" The Campbells," "Street Legal," and "Wonderworks," as well as hosting a five-episode public television series entitled "As Long as the Rivers Flow" and a nine-episode series entitled "Native Indians: Images of Reality." Cardinal is married and lives in southern California.

Gary Dale Farmer
1953–

Cayuga actor, producer, and activist

Gary Dale Farmer is an actor and producer involved with Native American projects for film, TV, and radio. Born on the Six Nations Reserve in Ontario, Canada, on June 12, 1953, Farmer studied at Genesee Community College and Syracuse University (both in New York State). He also had theater training at various private studios in Toronto, Canada.

He co-starred in *Powwow Highway* (1988), which won best film at the American Indian Film Festival and for which he took the best actor award. His performance also won him a nomination for best actor from the Independent Feature Project West, in Los Angeles. Other films Farmer has appeared in are *The Believers* (1987), *Police Academy* (1984), *The Big Town* (1987), *Renegades* (1989), and *Blue City Slammers.* He appeared in the 1992 film *The Dark Wind,* based on the novel by Tony Hillerman, and co-executive produced by Robert Redford.

Farmer has many acting credits in television, theater, and radio dramas, and recently he has also been active as a producer of television and radio programs dealing with Native American subjects. He produced a series of television shows called *Our Native Land* for the Canadian Broadcasting Corporation, and in 1989 he produced and hosted a magazine-style radio program called *Prevailing Winds.* He also produced and hosted a series of eight thirty-minute programs called *Powwow* for Multilingual Television (MTV) in Canada.

Since 1989, Farmer has lectured on Native American issues and other related topics at Dartmouth College, Cornell University, and many other campuses in the United States and Canada. In these talks, he discusses Native media programming, the importance of literacy, protecting the environment, and the need for taking an active role in community affairs.

Carol Geddes
1945–

Tlingit filmmaker and writer

Born in the small Yukon village of Teslin, Carol Geddes received a B.A. in English and philosophy from Carleton University in Ottawa, Ontario, Canada's capital city. She later did post-graduate work in communications at Concordia University in Montreal, Quebec.

Beginning in 1983, Geddes has devoted herself to filmmaking and occasional writing. In her first documentary, *Place For Our People* (1983), Geddes introduced the successful Montreal Native Friendship Centre and called for the development of similar community institutions across the country. In 1986, Geddes wrote and compiled a report entitled *Community Profiles: The Native Community,* for the National Film Board of Canada, a federally funded organization devoted to the advancement of film. Geddes's report highlighted the needs of First Nations in Canada and evaluated existing films on Native people. From 1986 to 1990, Geddes produced twenty videos, many focusing on the traditions and art of Native people in Canada. Her first major film, *Doctor, Lawyer, And Indian Chief* (1986), documented the lives of five Native women in Canada and won an award at the 1988 National Educational Film and Video Festival in San Francisco. As a writer, Geddes received the National Magazine's Silver Foundation Award in 1991 for her article, "Growing Up Native," which appeared in *Homemaker's* magazine.

In 1990, Geddes was appointed the first producer of the National Film Board's Studio One, located in Edmonton, Alberta, and devoted entirely to the production of indigenous media. Although she has since returned to full-time filmmaking, Geddes continues to work actively with the National Film Board.

Hanay Geiogamah
1945–

Kiowa/Delaware playwright, director, and teacher

Hanay Geiogamah was artistic director of the Native American Theater Ensemble (NATE) in New York City from 1972 to 1976. He received a bachelor's degree in theater and drama in 1980 from Indiana University in Bloomington, where he worked also as freelance director, producer, and instructor-organizer for American Indian communications and arts projects. From 1980 to 1982, he was the artistic director of Native Americans in Arts in New York City. Then in 1983, he was visiting professor of theater and Native American Studies at Colorado College in Colorado Springs. He also has been artistic director of the Native American Theater Ensemble in Los Angeles and of the American Indian Dance Theatre, a national professional dance company.

Geiogamah served as director of communications and then executive director of the American Indian Registry for the Performing Arts in Los Angeles from 1984 to 1988, and in 1989, he worked as technical consultant advisor for *The Dark Wind*, a feature film produced by Wildwood Production, whose executive producer was Robert Redford. In the following years, he combined his professional career with teaching experiences, as well as with writing and producing plays. From spring 1988 through January 1989, he conducted tours of the American

Indian Dance Theatre in the United States and Europe, with a special eight-week engagement at the Casino de Paris Theater in Paris, France. In 1989, Geiogamah co-directed and helped produce the American Indian Dance Theatre's Special on "Great Performances, Dance in America Series," aired nationally on the Public Broadcasting System in 1990. Also in 1990, he wrote a teleplay based on N. Scott Momaday's 1969 book *The Way To Rainy Mountain*. From 1984 to 1992, Geiogamah taught in the theater department at the University of California, Los Angeles.

Geiogamah's plays have been written for productions by American Indian theaters and performing arts groups. Among them are *Body Indian* (1972), performed both in the United States and in Europe; *Foghorn* (1973), premiere production by the Native American Theater Ensemble Theater in Reichskabarrett, West Berlin, Germany; and *Coon Cons Coyote* (1976). He has received various honors and awards, such as the William Randolph Hearst National Writing Award from the University of Oklahoma in 1966–67 and the Charles MacMahon Foundation Scholarship in Journalism in 1963, and he was guest speaker at the American Theater Association's 46th National Convention in New York City in 1982. From 1972 to 1989, Geiogamah received numerous grants from a variety of institutions to develop and promote NATE, the American Indian Registry for Performing Arts, and for NAPAF, the American Indian Dance Theatre/Native American Performing Arts Foundation.

Dan George
1899–1981

Squamish actor

Dan George was an accomplished and acclaimed actor, perhaps best known for his portrayal of a Cheyenne elder named Old Lodge Skins in the film *Little Big Man*. For this role, he was awarded the New York Film Critics Award for best supporting actor in 1970. Popularly referred to as Chief Dan George, he was born on the Burrard Indian Reserve near Vancouver, British Columbia, and began acting only late in life. Until the age of sixty, he worked as a longshoreman, logger, and musician. He was chief of the Squamish band of Burrard Inlet, British Columbia, from 1951 to 1963.

Dan George was discovered as an actor in 1959, and he dedicated the rest of his life to improving the image of Indian people in film, theater, and television. He portrayed an Indian elder in Canadian television and theater, including the Canadian Broadcasting Corporation production of "Caribou Country" and the original production of "The Ecstasy of Rita Joe," a contemporary drama about Indian people. He had roles in at least eight feature films, including *Smith* (1969), *Harry and Tonto* (1974), and *The Outlaw Josey Wales* (1975), as well as his role in *Little Big Man*. He also was the author of two books of prose-poetry, *My Heart Soars* (1974) and *My Spirit Soars* (1982). Dan George refused to endorse Indian political causes, but throughout his career he sought to change dominant images of Indian people in the media. Dan George died in Vancouver at the age of eighty-two.

A film actor who has found success in both Canada and the United States, Graham Greene is a full-blood Oneida, born on the Six Nations Reserve in southwestern Ontario in 1950. He began his career in television, film, and radio in 1976. Before becoming an actor, Greene worked at a number of different jobs, including stints as a high steel worker, a civil technologist, and a draftsman. He also worked as an audio technician for rock and roll bands and owned his own recording studio in Hamilton, Ontario.

Graham Greene
1950–

Oneida actor

Greene also lived for a short time in Britain in the early 1980s, where he performed on stage. Upon his return to Canada, Greene was cast in the British film, *Revolution*, starring Al Pacino and directed by Hugh Hudson. Greene is perhaps best known for his performance in *Dances with Wolves*, a 1991 film produced and directed by Kevin Costner, which won several Academy Awards, including the award for best picture. Greene portrayed Kicking Bird, an elder who strove to protect his people from attacks by American authorities. In addition, Greene has been cast in a number of television series and is known for his work in "The Campbells," "Spirit Bay," "Captain Power," "Running Brave," "Adderley," "Night Heat," and

"Pow-Wow Highway." His performances are not restricted to film; Greene has been very active on the Toronto theater scene, recently winning a Dora Mavor Moore Award for best actor for his performance in the acclaimed *Dry Lips Oughta Move to Kapuskasing*, a hugely successful play written by Tomson Highway, a renowned Canadian Cree playwright. Graham Greene currently resides in Toronto, Canada.

Tomson Highway
1951–

Cree playwright

Tomson Highway was born in a tent along his father's trapline in northern Manitoba on December 6, 1951. His first language was Cree; he learned English when he was sent to a boarding school in The Pas, Manitoba, at the age of six. Highway remained at the Catholic-run school until he was fifteen, returning to his family for only two months each year. He went on to high school in Winnipeg, Manitoba, living in white foster homes and graduating in June 1970. At the University of Manitoba and later at the University of Western Ontario, Highway studied music, graduating with a bachelor of music honors in 1975. He then worked for seven years with several Native organizations, helping to develop cultural programs with Native inmates and children.

At the age of thirty, Highway decided to write his first play, hoping to bring life on "the rez" to a mainstream audience. The reaction to *The Rex Sisters* in December 1986 took Highway by surprise. It was a huge success, winning the prestigious Dora Mavor Moore award for best new play in Toronto's 1987-88 theater season; it was runner-up for the Floyd S. Chalmers award for outstanding Canadian play of 1986. *The Rex Sisters* toured to sold-out audiences across Canada and was one of two plays representing Canada on the mainstage of the Edinburgh International Festival, a festival that showcases international drama. Highway's next play, *Dry Lips Oughta Move to Kapuskasing*, won four Dora Mavor Moore awards, including best new play. Until June 1992, Highway was the artistic director of Native Earth Performing Arts, Inc., Toronto's only professional Native theater company. Highway has written five other plays and continues in his quest to celebrate Canada's Native people through his art.

Jane Lind was one of seven children born on her fathers's trapping grounds in Humpback Bay, near the village of Perryville on the Alaska Peninsula. She is of Aleut, Russian, and Swedish descent, and she was raised in the Russian Orthodox Church.

Lind began her professional career while a high school student at the Institute of American Indian Arts in Santa Fe, New Mexico. Her performances there led her to a variety of roles in famous theaters. In the early seventies, she helped found the Native American Theater Ensemble and performed in various productions, such as Hanay Geiogamah's *Body Indian,* John Vaccaro's *Night Club,* and Andrei Serban's *Fragments of a Greek Trilogy.* After appearing in *The Taming of the Shrew* at the Alaska Repertory Company in 1982, Lind helped teach drama in rural communities in Alaska, as a way to help children improve their educational skills and self-esteem.

During the ensuing years, she has sung, acted, and directed in various productions across the United States and Europe, including a stage performance with Robert Redford. In numerous off-Broadway productions, she has played in Peter Brook's *The Birds,* Ellen Stewart's *Another Phaedra Via Hercules,* Dave Hunsaker's *The Summer Face Woman,* and Jack Gelber's *The Independence of Eddi Rose.* Lind also has worked for television productions such as *Footprints in Blood, Days Of Our Lives,* and *Ryans Hope.*

In 1991, Lind appeared in the movie Salmonberries, directed by Percy Adlon, which won the first place in a Canadian film festival. She played the Eskimo wife opposite Chuck Connors. In 1992, Lind was the female lead and choreographer for Robert Jonanson's production of *Black Elk Speaks,* a new version of Christopher Sergel's play, originally presented at the Folger Theater in Washington, D.C., and based on the book *Black Elk Speaks.*

Phil Lucas is the owner of Phil Lucas Productions, Inc., an independent film production company that develops projects for motion picture and television productions. In 1970, he received a bachelor's degree in science and visual communication from Western Washington University in Bellingham, Washington. From 1979 to 1981, he was the co-producer, writer, and co-director of a five-part Public Broadcasting Corporation series, "Images of

Jane Lind
contemporary

Aleut actress, director, and choreographer

Phil Lucas
contemporary

Choctaw producer and director

Indians," which explored the problem of Indian stereotypes as portrayed and perpetuated by Hollywood Western movies. The series won a Special Achievement Award in Documentary Film in 1980 from the American Indian Film Institute and the Prix Italia Award in 1981.

His productions deal with accurate portraits of Indians, as in *Nez Percé: Portrait of People* (1982), a twenty-three-minute color film on the culture and history of the Nez Percé tribe. His commitment to spreading information about issues affecting the Indian community has been strengthened in recent years through the production of documentaries on the AIDS virus, and drug and alcohol prevention, such as *Circle of Warriors* (1989) and *Lookin' Good* (1988). Alcoholism is treated also in "Where We've Been And Where We're Going" (1983), a two-part series produced for the University of Lethbridge in Alberta, Canada. In *I'm Not Afraid of Me* (1990), Lucas presents the story of a Native woman and her daughter, both of whom have AIDS.

In 1989, Lucas completed a fifteen-part series that explores the reality of Indian lives, told from their point of view, called "Native Indians: Images of Reality." More recently, he has produced a one-hour documentary exploring the contributions of the Iroquois Confederacy to the U.S. Constitution and democracy, based on Bruce Johansen's book *Forgotten Founders* (1982).

Alanis Obomsawin

1932–

Abenaki filmmaker

Raised on the Odonak Reserve in Quebec, Obomsawin appeared in the 1970 Canadian film, *Eliza's Horoscope,* before becoming one of the country's leading documentary filmmakers. Her first film, *Christmas at Moose Factory* (1971), reveals Cree life-style as seen through the drawings and paintings of its children.

Obomsawin's early films celebrate the richness and diversity of Indian culture. *Mother of Many Children* (1977) highlights the language and storytelling of traditional women, and *Amisk* (1977) explores the beauty of Indian dance and music.

Later films reveal Obomsawin's deep commitment to Canada's struggling Native people. *Incident at Restigouche* (1984) documents the brutal Quebec Provincial Police raid on the Restigouche

Reserve over fishing rights, and *Richard Cardinal: Cry from a Diary of a Métis Child* (1986) is a heartbreaking story of a young Cree adolescent whose abuse and neglect by the child welfare system leads to his suicide. *Poundmaker's Lodge: A Healing Place* (1987) examines an Indian drug and alcohol center, and *No Address* (1988) focuses on Montreal's homeless aboriginal people. *Oka* (1993) is a forthcoming documentary about the crisis between Mohawk Indians and provincial and federal authorities in the summer of 1990.

Obomsawin's first solo record album, *Bush Lady*, includes her own songs in Abenaki, English, and French. In 1983, she was awarded the Canadian government's highest honor—the prestigious Order of Canada—for her dedication to the country's indigenous people.

**Gary Robinson
1950–**

Mississippi Choctaw and Cherokee writer, producer, and director

Gary Robinson is a writer, producer, director, cinematographer, and video editor of Choctaw and Cherokee Indian heritage. He has a master's degree in film and television production and over twenty years experience. Since 1980, his work has primarily focused on American Indian subject matter.

Early in his career, Robinson assisted in the production of educational media programs and trained teachers in the proper use of audiovisual and video equipment for the educational media section of the Tulsa (Oklahoma) public school system. Additionally, he coordinated daily programming on two city-wide educational cable television channels.

From 1981 to 1990, he worked for the Creek Nation of Oklahoma writing, producing, and directing video programs about the history, culture, and current affairs of the Creek tribe. He also wrote news articles and features for the Creek tribal newspaper, handled all the tribe's photographic needs, assisted in typesetting, paste up, and layout of the tribal newspaper, and helped develop promotional materials for the tribe.

During the same period, he produced video and audiovisual programs for Indian organizations and clients through Pathfinder

Communications, an independent production and consulting company that Robinson formed in 1981. The company also made presentations to educators on the effective use of instructional media technologies.

In 1990, he co-founded American Indian Media Services, Inc., an Oklahoma-based, nonprofit corporation dedicated to providing a variety of media services to Indian tribes, organizations, and businesses. He continues to work on projects with American Indian Media Services when called upon.

During the course of his career, Robinson has produced and directed over fifty film and video programs about Native American history, health, education, economic development in Native communities, and other issues affecting Native peoples.

Since 1990, Robinson has been an independent film and video maker working on projects concerning healing and recovery in native communities. In 1993, he served as director of photography on the Public Broadcasting System documentary *Dances for the New Generations*, which was nominated for an Emmy and won Best Documentary awards at both the American Indian Film Festival and the Red Earth Film Festival. He now lives in Santa Fe, New Mexico.

Will Sampson

1934–87

Creek actor

Will Sampson was a widely known American Indian actor when he died in 1987. He received high acclaim for his portrayal of an Indian chief feigning muteness in the film *One Flew over the Cuckoo's Nest* (1975).

Sampson was born and raised in Oklahoma. He came to acting late in life. After stints as a cowboy, forest ranger, and professional artist, he received an opportunity that would change his life. A friend of Sampson who was a rodeo announcer had been asked by a member of producer Michael Douglas's staff to keep his eye out for a "large" Indian. Sampson, who was six feet seven inches tall, was found and subsequently hired for the part in *One Flew over the Cuckoo's Nest*. The film, based on a novel by Ken Kesey, won five Academy Awards and critical praise for Sampson's portrayal of Chief Bromden. Sampson was nominated for an Academy Award as best supporting actor, and his acting career was launched.

Sampson went on to act in a number of other films, including *The Outlaw Josey Wales, White Buffalo, Buffalo Bill and the Indians, Old Fish Hawk* (in which he played the title role), *Orca,* and *Fighting Back.* In 1982, he was awarded best narration honors by the Alberta, Canada, film commission for his work on *Spirit of the Hunt,* a major Canadian film. Sampson also joined the American Indian Theater Company of Oklahoma and played the role of Red Cloud in the production of *Black Elk Speaks.*

Sampson said that he studied acting the way he prepared for his paintings of cowboys, Indians, and western landscapes. "I research thoroughly," said Sampson, who did not accept the *Cuckoo's Nest* role until he had read the book. "I've done paintings of all the great Indian chiefs and I studied everything about them." His art work has been featured in numerous shows, exhibitions, and galleries.

For years, Sampson suffered with scleroderma, a chronic degenerative disease. In 1987, Sampson died forty-three days after undergoing a heart-lung transplant.

Jay Silverheels is probably best known for his role as Tonto, the Indian partner of the Lone Ranger, in a popular television series of the 1950s.

Jay Silverheels
1912–80

Mohawk actor

Silverheels, whose real name was Harold J. Smith, was born in Canada and came to the United States as a member of Canada's national lacrosse team in 1938. A short time later he began acting in films. His first role was as the Indian prince in *The Captain from Castille.* In 1950, he portrayed Geronimo in the movie *Broken Arrow,* which has been hailed as the first film to portray Indians in a sympathetic light. Silverheels gained his greatest notoriety, however, playing Tonto. He was actually the second actor to play the role of the Lone Ranger's sage companion. The popular series ran for eight years. Two film features were also made based on the television series, and Silverheels appeared in both.

In the middle 1960s, Silverheels founded the Indian Actors Workshop in Hollywood. He was the original director of this organization. During the same period, he worked extensively with public service projects focusing on substance abuse and the elderly. In 1979, he became the first Native American awarded a star on Hollywood's Walk of Fame. He died the next year.

Chris Spotted Eagle
contemporary

Houma producer and
director

Chris Spotted Eagle is an independent film producer and director from Minneapolis, Minnesota. He has worked as a photojournalist, advertising photographer, and project manager and field producer at Twin Cities Public Television, KTCA, in Minneapolis. He has produced such films as *Our Sacred Land* (1984) and *The Great Spirit Within the Hole* (1983). His work emphasizes the expression of Indian views on land and legal issues that affect Indian peoples in the twentieth century. Spotted Eagle's major films are designed to give non-Indian audiences access to the thoughts and political positions that American Indians have on land issues and on world view, especially creation histories and views of the sacred found within various Indian nations. Spotted Eagle has served as a staff director for the American Indian Center in Minneapolis and as a board member of numerous civic and community organizations including the Minnesota Humanities Commission. His interests include cultural work, art, and social activism toward peace and justice. He is a veteran of the U.S. Army and Air Force. Spotted Eagle is a member of the Muskogean-speaking Houma people, some of whom still live in Louisiana. In Muskogean, *Houma* means red and, with the word okla (people), it is the root of the word *Oklahoma* or red people.

U.S. and Canada Press

NEWSPAPERS:

TRIBAL, CONFEDERATION, NATIVE NATION ◆ ◆ ◆ ◆ ◆ ◆ ◆ ◆

Tribal, confederation, and Native nation newspapers primarily publish news (political, social, educational, economic, health, sports) of and for their respective tribal communities and some national Indian news.

UNITED STATES ◆ ◆ ◆ ◆ ◆ ◆ ◆ ◆ ◆ ◆ ◆ ◆ ◆ ◆ ◆ ◆ ◆

Arizona

AK-CHIN O'ODHAM RUNNER
42507 Peters & Nall
Maricopa, AZ 85239
(602)568-2095
Ak-Chin Indian Community;
monthly

FORT APACHE SCOUT
P.O. Box 898
Whiteriver, AZ 85941-0898
(602)338-4813
White Mountain Apache;
biweekly

HOPI TUTU-VEH-NI
Office of Public Relations
P.O. Box 123
Kykotsmovi, AZ 86039
(602)734-2441
Hopi; biweekly

NAVAJO TIMES
P.O. Box 310
Window Rock,
Navajo Nation, AZ 86515-0310
(602)871-6641
Navajo; weekly

Florida

SEMINOLE TRIBUNE
6333 Northwest 30th St.
Hollywood, FL 33024
(305)964-1875
Seminole of Florida; biweekly

Idaho COEUR D'ALENE
COUNCIL FIRES
Tribal Headquarters
Plummer, ID 83851
(208)274-3101
Coeur d'Alene; monthly

SHO-BAN NEWS
P.O. Box 900
Fort Hall, ID 83203
(208)238-3888
Shoshone-Bannock, Idaho;
weekly

Minnesota DE-BAH-JI-MON
Rte. 3, P.O. Box 100
Cass Lake, MN 56633
Leech Lake Chippewa;
monthly

Mississippi CHOCTAW COMMUNITY
NEWS
Communications Program
P.O. Box 6010
Philadelphia, MS 39350
(601)656-5251
Mississippi Band of Choctaw;
monthly

Montana CHAR-KOOSTA NEWS
P.O. Box 278
51396 Highway 93 N.
Pablo, MT 59855
(406)675-3000
Flathead
(Salish and Kootenai);
weekly

New York INDIAN TIME
P.O. Box 196
Mohawk Nation
Rooseveltown, NY 13683-0196
(518)358-9531
Akwesasne/Six Nations;
weekly

CHEROKEE ONE FEATHER
P.O. Box 501
Cherokee, NC 28719
(704)497-5513
Eastern Band of Cherokee;
weekly

North Carolina

**MANDAN HIDATSA
ARIKARA TIMES**
Fort Berthold
Communications Enterprise
HCR3, P.O. Box 1
New Town, ND 58763
(701)627-3333
Mandan, Hidatsa, Arikara;
weekly

North Dakota

BISHINIK
Choctaw Nation of
Oklahoma
P.O. Box 1210
Durant, OK 74702-1210
(405)924-8280
Oklahoma Choctaw;
monthly

CHEROKEE ADVOCATE
P.O. Box 498
Tahlequah, OK 74465
(918)456-0671
Cherokee Nation of
Oklahoma; monthly

CHICKASAW TIMES
P.O. Box 1548
Ada, OK 74820
(405)436-2603
Chickasaw NaMuscogee
(Creek) Nation; monthly

HOW-NI-KAN
1901 Gordon Cooper Dr.
Shawnee, OK 74801
(405)275-3121
Citizen Band Potawatomi;
monthly

**MUSCOGEE NATION
NEWS**
P.O. Box 580
Okmulgee, OK 74447
(918)756-8700
Muscogee (Creek) Nation;
monthly

SAC AND FOX NEWS
Rte. 2, P.O. Box 246
Stroud, OK 74079
(918)968-3526
Sac and Fox; monthly

Oklahoma

Oregon	SPILYAY TYMOO P.O. Box 870 Warm Springs, OR 97761 (503)553-1644 Confederated Tribes of Warm Springs; biweekly
Washington	TRIBAL TRIBUNE P.O. Box 150 Nespelem, WA 99155 (509)634-4116 Colville Confederated Tribes; monthly
Wisconsin	HO-CHUNK WO-LDUK Wisconsin Winnebago Business Committee P.O. Box 667 Black River Falls, WI 54615 (715)284-9343 Wisconsin Winnebago; monthly
Wyoming	WIND RIVER NEWS P.O. Box 900 Lande, WY 82520 (307)332-2323 Shoshoni, Northern Arapaho; weekly

CANADA ✦ ✦ ✦ ✦ ✦ ✦ ✦ ✦ ✦ ✦ ✦ ✦ ✦ ✦ ✦ ✦ ✦ ✦

British Columbia	SECWEPEMC NEWS 345 Yellowhead Hwy. Kamloops, BC V2H 1H1 (604)828-9784 Shuswap Nation; monthly

◆ ◆ ◆ ◆ ◆ ◆ ◆ ◆ ◆ ◆ ◆ NEWSPAPERS: STATE, PROVINCIAL, REGIONAL, CORPORATION

State, provincial, regional, and corporation newspapers primarily publish news of and for their respective constituencies and some national news.

◆ ◆ ◆ ◆ ◆ ◆ ◆ ◆ ◆ ◆ ◆ ◆ ◆ ◆ ◆ ◆ ◆ ◆ ◆ UNITED STATES

THE COUNCIL
122 First Ave.
Fairbanks, AK 99701
(907)452-8251
Alaska Natives; monthly

Alaska

NEWS FROM NATIVE
CALIFORNIA
P.O. Box 9145
Berkeley, CA 94709
(510)549-3564
State; quarterly

California

OURSELVES: NI-MAH-MI-
KWA-ZOO-MIN
Minnesota Chippewa Tribe
Cass Lake, MN 56633
(218)335-8581
Minnesota reservations;
monthly

Minnesota

LAKOTA TIMES
P.O. Box 2180
Rapid City, SD 57709
(605)341-0011
Pine Ridge Sioux;
weekly

South Dakota

Wisconsin NEWS FROM INDIAN
COUNTRY
Indian Country
Communications
Rte. 2, Box 2900-A
Hayward, WI 54843
(715)634-5226
Great Lakes Region; semi-
monthly

CANADA ✦ ✦ ✦ ✦ ✦ ✦ ✦ ✦ ✦ ✦ ✦ ✦ ✦ ✦ ✦ ✦ ✦ ✦ ✦

Alberta TREATY SEVEN NEWS
P.O. Box 106
Standoff, AB T0L 1Y0
(403)737-2121
Formerly Kainai News;
monthly

British Columbia AWA'K'WIS
P.O. Box 2490
Port Hardy, BC V0N 2P0
(604)949-9433
Kwakiutl, Kwakwakwakw
Nations; monthly

HA-SHILTH-SA
P.O. Box 1383
Port Alberni, BC V9Y 7M2
(604)724-5757
Nuu-cha-nulth Tribes; monthly

KAHTOU
Kahtou Communications
Society of British Columbia
203 540 Burrard St.
Vancouver, BC V6C 2K1
Bimonthly

Northwest
Territories PRESS INDEPENDENT
Native Communications
Society of Western Northwest
Territories Media Center
5120 49th St.
Yellowknife, NT X1A 1P8
(403)873-2661
Dene and Métis; weekly

NEW BREED JOURNAL
Saskatchewan Native
Communications Corporation
Bay 202
173 Second Ave. S.
Saskatoon, SK S7K 1K6
(306)653-2253
Métis; monthly

Saskatchewan

◆ ◆ ◆ ◆ ◆ ◆ ◆ ◆ ◆ ◆ ◆ ◆ ◆ ◆ **NEWSPAPERS: NATIONAL**

AKWESASNE NOTES
Mohawk Nation
P.O. Box 196
Rooseveltown, NY 13683-0196
(518)358-9531
Occasional

TREATY COUNCIL NEWS
710 Clayton St., No. 1
San Francisco, CA 94117
(415)566-0251
Quarterly

WIND SPEAKER
Aboriginal Multi-Media
Society of Alberta
15001 112 Ave.
Edmonton, AB T5M 2V6
(403)455-2700
Biweekly

◆ ◆ ◆ ◆ ◆ ◆ ◆ ◆ ◆ ◆ ◆ ◆ ◆ ◆ **NEWSPAPERS: URBAN**

THE CIRCLE
Minnesota American
Indian Center
1530 East Franklin Ave.
Minneapolis, MN 55404
(612)871-4555
Monthly

MAGAZINES ✦

AMERICAN INDIAN ART MAGAZINE
7314 East Osborne Dr.
Scottsdale, AZ 85251
(602)994-5445
Quarterly

JOURNAL OF ALASKA NATIVE ARTS
Institute of Alaska Native Arts
P.O. Box 80583
Fairbanks, AK 99708
(907)456-7491 or
(907)456-7406
Quarterly

NATIVE NATIONS
Solidarity Foundation
P.O. Box 1201
Radio City Station, NY
10101-1201
(212)765-9731
Bimonthly

NATIVE PEOPLES
Media Concepts Group, Inc.
P.O. Box 36820
Phoenix, Az 85067-6820
(602)252-2236
Quarterly

TURTLE QUARTERLY
Native American Center for the Living Arts25 Rainbow Mall
Niagara Falls, NY 14303
(716)284-2427
Quarterly

WINDS OF CHANGE
AISES Publishing, Inc.
1630 30th St., Suite 301
Boulder, CO 80301
(303)444-9099
Quarterly

ACADEMIC JOURNALS: UNITED STATES ✦ ✦ ✦ ✦ ✦ ✦ ✦ ✦ ✦

AKWE: KON PRESS
American Indian Program
Cornell University
300 Caldwell Hall
Ithaca, NY 14853
(607)255-4308
Quarterly

AMERICAN INDIAN AND ALASKA NATIVE MENTAL HEALTH RESEARCH
Department of Psychiatry
University of Colorado
Health Sciences Center
4200 East Ninth Ave.
Campus Box C249-17
Denver, CO 80262
Three issues per year and one monograph

AMERICAN INDIAN
CULTURE AND RESEARCH
JOURNAL
American Indian Studies Center
University of California
3220 Campbell Hall
405 Hilgard Ave.
Los Angeles, CA 90024-1548
(310)206-7508
Quarterly

AMERICAN INDIAN LAW
REVIEW
College of Law
University of Oklahoma
300 Timberdale Rd., Room 335
Norman, OK 73019
(405)325-2840
Biannual

AMERICAN INDIAN
QUARTERLY
Department of Anthropology
University of Oklahoma
Norman, OK 73019
(405)325-3261
Quarterly

JOURNAL OF AMERICAN
INDIAN EDUCATION
Center for Indian Education
Arizona State University
College of Education
Tempe, AZ 85287-1311
(602)255-4308; Triannual

NARF LEGAL REVIEW
1506 Broadway
Boulder, CO 80302
(303)447-8760; Quarterly

STUDIES IN AMERICAN
INDIAN LITERATURE
Department of English
California State University,
Fullerton
Fullerton, CA 92634
(714)449-7039; Quarterly

WICAZO SA REVIEW
Indian Studies Department
Eastern Washington
University
Cheney, WA 99004
(509)359-2441; Quarterly

♦ ♦ ♦ ♦ ♦ ♦ ♦ ♦ ♦ ♦ ♦ ♦ **ACADEMIC JOURNALS: CANADA**

ABSTRACTS OF NATIVE
STUDIES
Bear Publishing
Department of Native Studies
Brandon University
1229 Lorne Ave.
Brandon, MB R7A 6A9
(204)727-9640
Irregular

CANADIAN JOURNAL OF
NATIVE EDUCATION
Publication Services
University of Alberta
4-116 Education North Bldg.
Edmonton, AB T6G 2G5
(403)492-4204
Biannual and occasional
supplements

CANADIAN JOURNAL OF
NATIVE STUDIES
Bear Publishing
Department of Native Studies
Brandon University
1229 Lorne Ave.
Brandon, MB R7A 6A9
Attn: Dr. Samuel Corrigan
(204)728-9520
Biannual

CANADIAN NATIVE LAW
REPORTER
Native Law Centre
University of Saskatchewan
141 Diefenbaker Centre
Saskatoon, SK S7N 0W0
(306)966-6189
Quarterly

EN'OWKIN JOURNAL OF
FIRST NORTH AMERICAN
PEOPLE
En'owkin Centre
257 Brunswick
Penticton, BC V2A 5P9
(604)493-7181
Annual

ÉTUDES/INUIT/STUDIES
Department D'anthropologie
Pavilion Jean Durand
Université Laval
Quebec, PQ G1K 7P4
(418)656-2353
Quarterly

INUIT ART QUARTERLY
2081 Merivale Rd.
Nepean, ON K2G 1G9
(613)224-8189
Quarterly

JOURNAL OF
INDIGENOUS STUDIES
Gabriel Dumont Institute of
Native Studies and Applied
Research
121 Broadway Ave. E.
Regina, SK S4N 0Z6
(306)934-4941
Biannual

NATIVE STUDIES REVIEW
Department of Native Studies
University of Saskatchewan
Saskatoon, SK S7N 0W0
(306)277-6178
Quarterly

RECHERCHES
AMERINDIENNES AU
QUEBEC
6742 rue Saint-Denis
Montreal, Quebec H2S 2S2
(514)277-6178

Radio, Television, and Theater Organizations

RADIO AND

TELEVISION MEDIA: UNITED STATES ◆ ◆ ◆ ◆ ◆ ◆ ◆ ◆ ◆ ◆

Alaska

ASRC
COMMUNICATIONS, INC.
P.O. Box 129
Barrow, AK 99723
(907)852-8633

NATIONAL NATIVE NEWS
Alaska Public Radio Network
810 East Ninth Ave.
Anchorage, AK 99501
(907)277-2776

Arizona

NAVAJO NATION OFFICE
OF BROADCAST SERVICES
P.O. Box 2310
Window Rock, AZ 86515
(602)871-6655

California

THE AMERICAN INDIAN
HOUR
American Indian All Tribes
Church
4009 South Halldale Ave.
Los Angeles, CA 90062
(213)299-1810

NATIVE AMERICAN MEDIA
ENTERPRISES, INC.
1762 Corning St.
Los Angeles, CA 90035
(310)841-0836

Minnesota

MIGIZI
COMMUNICATIONS, INC.
First Person Radio
3123 East Lake St., Suite 200
Minneapolis, MN 55406
(612)721-6631

RED LAKE CHIPPEWA
RADIO PROJECT
Red Lake, MN 56671
(218)679-334, ext. 44

Montana BLACKFEET MEDIA
c/o Blackfeet Community
College
P.O. Box 850
Browning, MT 59417

Nebraska NATIVE AMERICAN
PUBLIC BROADCASTING
CONSORTIUM
P.O. Box 83111
Lincoln, NE 68501
(402)472-3522

Oklahoma AMERICAN INDIAN
MEDIA SERVICES, INC.
P.O. Box 875
Beggs, OK 74421
(918)267-4940

Oregon CONFEDERATED TRIBES
TELECOMMUNICATION
PROJECT
P.O. Box C
Warm Springs, OR 97761
(503)553-1161

South Carolina NATIVE AMERICAN
INDIAN MEDIA
CORPORATION
P.O. Box 17341
Spartanburg, SC 29301
(803)576-8900

Tennesse NATIVE AMERICAN
INDIAN MEDIA
CORPORATION
P.O. Box 59
Strawberry Plains, TN 37871
(615)933-0606

CANADA

ABORIGINAL MULTI-MEDIA SOCIETY OF ALBERTA (AMMSA)
15001 112th Ave.
Edmonton, AB T5M 2V6
(403)455-2700

ABORIGINAL RADIO AND TELEVISION SOCIETY
P.O. Box 2250
Lac La Biche, AB T0A 2C0
(403)623-3333

BLACKFOOT RADIO NETWORK
Indian News Media
P.O. Box 120
Standoff, AB T0L 1Y0
(403)653-3301

NATIVE COMMUNICATIONS SOCIETY OF BRITISH COLUMBIA
1161 West Georgia St.
Vancouver, BC V6E 3H4
(604)684-7375

THE NATIVE VOICE
200-1755 E. Hastings St.
Vancouver, BC V5L 1T1
(604)255-3137

NATIVE COMMUNICATIONS INC.
76 Severn Crescent
Thompson, MB R8N 1M6
(204)778-8343

NATIONAL ABORIGINAL COMMUNICATION SOCIETY
P.O. Box 2250
10106 102nd Ave.
Lac La Biche, AB T0A 2C0
(403)623-3301

NATIVE PERSPECTIVE (a division of AMMSA)
10106 102nd St.
P.O. Box 2250
Lac La Biche, AB T0A 2C0
(403)623-3333

NORTHERN NATIVE BROADCASTING
P.O. Box 1090
202 4650 Lazelle Ave.
Terrace, BC V8G 4V1
(604)638-8137

NATIVE MEDIA NETWORK
P.O. Box 848
Portage La Prairie, MB R1N 3C3
(204)239-1920

Alberta

British Columbia

Manitoba

NATIVE MEDIA NETWORK
204 424 Logan Ave.
Winnipeg, MB R3A 0R4
(204)943-6475

Newfoundland OKALAKATIGET SOCIETY
P.O. Box 160
Nain, NF A0P 1L0
(709)922-2955

Northwest INUIT BROADCASTING
Territories CORPORATION
P.O. Box 700
Iqaluit, NT X0A 0H0
(403)979-6231

INUVIALUIT
COMMUNICATIONS SOCIETY
P.O. Box 1704, Semmler Bldg.
McKenzie Rd.
Inuvik, NT X0E 0T0
(403)979-2320

NATIVE
COMMUNICATIONS
SOCIETY OF THE
WESTERN
NORTHWEST TERRITORY
P.O. Box 1919, Aquarius Bldg.
Yellowknife, NT X1A 2P4
(403)873-2661

Nova Scotia NATIVE COMMUNICATIONS
SOCIETY OF NOVA SCOTIA
P.O. Box 344
Sydney, NS B1P 6H2
(902)539-0045

Ontario INUIT BROADCASTING
CORPORATION (IBC)
703 251 Laurier Ave.
Ottawa, ON K1P 5J6
(613)235-1892

NATIONAL ABORIGINAL
COMMUNICATIONS
SOCIETY (NACS)
105 298 Elgin St.
Ottawa, ON K2P 1M3
(613)230-6244

WAWATAY NATIVE
COMMUNICATIONS
SOCIETY
P.O. Box 1180, 16 Fifth Ave.
Sioux Lookout, ON P0V 2T0
(807)737-2951

JAMES BAY CREE
COMMUNICATIONS
SOCIETY
Directeur générale
1, Place Ville Marie, Suite 3434
Montreal, PQ H3B 3N9
(514)861-5837

SOCIETE DE
COMMUNICATIONS
ATIKAMEKW
MONTAGNAIS (SOCAM)
80 boul Bastien
Village des hurons
(Wendake), PQ G0A 4V0
(418)843-3873

SASKATCHEWAN NATIVE
COMMUNICATIONS
CORPORATION
202 173 Second Ave. S.
Saskatoon, SK S7K 1K6
(306)653-2253

NORTHERN NATIVE
BROADCASTING YUKON
(NNBY)
4228 A Fourth Ave.
Whitehorse, YK Y1K 1K1
(403)688-6629

TAQRAMIUT NIPINGAT,
INC. (TNI)
185 ave. Dorval, Suite 501
Dorval, PQ H9S 3G6
(514)631-1394

TEWEGAN
COMMUNICATION
SOCIETY
351 ave. Centrale
Val d'Or, PQ J9P 1P6
(819)825-5192

YE SA TO
COMMUNICATIONS
SOCIETY
22 Nisutlin Dr.
Whitehorse, YK Y1A 3S5
(403)667-2775

Quebec

Saskatchewan

Yukon

◆ ◆ ◆ ◆ ◆ ◆ ◆ ◆ ◆ ◆ ◆ ◆ ◆ ◆ **THEATER: UNITED STATES**

ATLATL
402 West Roosevelt
Phoenix, AZ 85003
(602)253-2731

Arizona

California

AMERICAN INDIAN
REGISTRY
1717 North Highland Ave.,
Suite 614
Hollywood, CA 90028
(213)962-6594

NATIVE AMERICAN
THEATRE ENSEMBLE
c/o Native American Media
Enterprises, Inc.
1762 Corning St.
Los Angeles, CA 90035
(310)841-0836

Minnesota

OGITCHIDAG
GIKINOOAMAAGAD
PLAYERS
Minneapolis American Indian
AIDS Task Force
1433 E. Franklin Ave., Suite 1
Minneapolis, MN 55404
(612)870-1723

New Mexico

INTER-TRIBAL INDIAN
CEREMONIAL ASSOCIATION
P.O. Box 1
Church Rock, NM 87311
(505)863-3896

New York

AMERICAN INDIAN
COMMUNITY HOUSE
THEATRE
404 Lafayette St.
New York, NY 10003
(212)598-0100

AMERICAN INDIAN
DANCE THEATRE
223 East 61st St.
New York, NY 10021
(212)308-9555

OFF THE BEATEN PATH
c/o American Indian
Community House Theatre
404 Lafayette St.
New York, NY 10003
(212)598-0100

SPIDERWOMAN THEATER
77 Seventh Ave., Apt. 85
New York, NY 10003
(212)243-6209

THUNDERBIRD
AMERICAN INDIAN
DANCERS
c/o American Indian
Community House Theatre
404 Lafayette St.
New York, NY 10003
(212)598-0100

**AMERICAN INDIAN
THEATER COMPANY**
P.O. Box 701926
Tulsa, OK 74170
(918)838-3875

**CHICKAHOMINY RED MEN
DANCERS**
Wayne B. Adkins, coordinator
2106 Seddergh Dr.
New Kent, VA 23124
(804)932-4406

Oklahoma

Virginia

♦ **CANADA**

FOUR WINDS THEATRE
P.O. Box 912
Hobbema, AB T0C 1N0
(403)585-3904

Alberta

**CEN'KLIP NATIVE
THEATRE**
c/o United Native Friendship
Centre
2902 29th St.
Vernon, BC V1T 1Y7
(604)542-1247

SPIRIT SONG
454-C West Broadway
Vancouver, BC V5Y 1R3
(604)877-1338

British Columbia

AWASIKAN THEATRE INC.
Portage Pl.
Y300 393 Portage Ave.
Winnipeg, MB R3B 3H6
(204)942-7291

Manitoba

**DE-BA-JEAH-MU-JIG
THEATRE GROUP**
Excelsior P.O.
West Bay, ON P0P 1G0
(705)377-5506

**DEBAJEHMUJIG THEATRE
GROUP**
Wikwemikong, ON P0P 2J0
(705)859-2317

Ontario

NATIVE EARTH
PERFORMING ARTS INC.
37 Spadina Rd.
Toronto, ON M5R 2S9
(416)922-7616

NATIVE THEATRE
SCHOOL
204 9 St. Joseph St.
Toronto, ON M4T 1J6
(416)972-0871

Quebec ONDINNOK INC.
705 1030 St. Alexandre
Montreal, PQ H2Z 1E3
(519)875-7175

Saskatchewan Saskatchewan Native
Theatre
919 Broadway Ave.
Saskatoon, SK S7N 1B8
(306)244-7779

SPIRIT BAY PRODUCTIONS
406 517 Wellington St. W.
Toronto, ON M5V 1E9
(416)596-8783

For the most current information on theaters across North America, contact:

ASSOCIATION FOR
NATIVE DEVELOPMENT
IN THE PERFORMING
AND VISUAL ARTS
204 9 St. Joseph St.
Toronto, ON M4Y 1J6
(416)972-0871

*I*ndex

A

ABC: Americans Before Columbus, 5
Abenaki, 58
Aboriginal Native Rights Committee of the Interior, 387
Activist Movements: Canadian Native, 20; U.S. Indian, 1
Adams, Hank, 29
Adams, John, 62
Adena Culture, 55
Ahenakew, Edward, 378
AKA Graffiti Man, 48
Akwesasne Notes, 5
Alaska Area Native Health Service, 226
Alaska Federated Natives (AFN), 226, 233, 235
Alaska National Lands Conservation Act, 228
Alaska Native: health, 227; population, 225; subsistence, 227; unemployment, 226
Alaska Native Brotherhood (ANB), 42
Alaska Native Claims Settlement Act, 233–35; corporations, 230; economic development, 229; land claims, 207; land rights, 16; land settlement, 224–25; self-government, 232
Alaska State Rural Affairs Commission, 233
Alaska Statehood Act, 222
Albany Plan of Union, 61
Alcatraz Island, 31; John Trudell, 47; occupation, 12, 13, 322; Richard Oakes, 41
Aleut: culture, 216; economy, 215; language, 397, 401, 410; loan words, 414; Modoc prisoners, 327; Russian alphabet, 436; Russian contact, 221

Alexander Band, 370
Alexian Brothers noviciary, 16
Alexie, Sherman, 682–99
Algonkian: loan words, 413
All Indian Pueblo Council, 144
Allen, Paula Gunn, 683–99
Allied Indian Tribes of British Columbia, 43
American Fur Company, 204
American Horse, 181–82
American Indian Culture and Research Journal, 321
American Indian Defense Association, 3–4
American Indian Historical Society, 5
American Indian Magazine, 184
American Indian Movement (AIM), 30–33, 38–40, 43–44, 47–48; founded, 4; protests, 14; Wounded Knee II, 15, 178
American Indian Policy Review Commission, 16
American Indian Quarterly, 321
American Indian Registry for the Performing Arts, 704
American Indian Stories, 184
American Revolution, 76–78, 88–89. See also American Revolutionary War
American Revolutionary War, 77, 122
American War for Independence. See American Revolutionary War
Anasazi, 19, 129
Apache, 151, 482; Chiricahua, 151, 155; culture, 131, 133; Jicarilla, 133; Kiowa, 133; Lipan, 133; migrations, 131, 133; Mimbreno, 151; raids, 133; survival, 134; White Mountain, 155
Apache Wars, 150

Apodaca, Paul, 609, 631
Appomattox Courthouse, 83
Aquash, Anna Mae, 30
Aquash, Nogeeshik, 30
Arapaho, 9, 165, 251
Arbuckle, General Matthew, 250
Arikara, 164
Art, 550, 556, 559
Arthur, President Chester A., 300
Assembly of First Nations, 350; Georges Erasmus, 384; leaders, 396; Ovide Mercredi, 389–96; political activity, 335; Status Indians, 20
Assiniboine, 165
Association on American Indian Affairs, 223
Athabascan, 219–20, 403
Atomic Energy Commission, 222
Aztec-Tanoan, 407
Aztecs, 129
Aztlán, 129

B

Bad Heart Bull, Wesley, 39
Badlands National Monument, 14
baidarka, 215
Banks, Dennis J., 31–33, 38–39, 44
Bannock War, 49
Banyacya, Thomas, Sr., 510
barabaras, 216
Barboncito, 149–50
Barnwell, Colonel John, 121
Battle for Los Angeles, 311
Battle of Beecher's Island, 268
Battle of Dull Knife, 185, 188
Battle of Fallen Timbers, 79
Battle of Horseshoe Bend, 107
Battle of Little Bighorn, 186, 192
Battle of Point Pleasant, 80
Battle of Prairie Dog Creek, 268
Battle of Slim Buttes, 182
Battle of the Little Big Horn, 165
Battle of the Little Bighorn, 182, 185, 382
Battle of the Platte Bridge, 267
Battle of the Rosebud, 185, 192, 300
Battle of the Thames, 91
Battle of the Washita, 251
Battle of Tippecanoe, 90, 521–23

Bear Flag Revolt, 311
Bellecourt, Clyde, 33
Beothuk, 335
Bering, Vitus, 221
Big Bear (Mistahimaskwa), 379
Big Foot, 48
Bighouse Religion, 513, 520
Bill C-31, 333
Black Bear,, 393–96
Black Hawk, 75–76, 78, 515, 522
Black Hawk's War, 75, 521
Black Hills, 18, 182–92
Black Kettle, 252, 262–64
Blackfeet, 165–67, 179
Blackfoot Confederacy, 383, 393–96; artists, 629–31
Blondin, Ethel, 379, 380
Blood, 382, 393
Blue Lake (Maxolo), 516
boarding schools, 210, 313–17, 345
Boldt Decision, 212–14
Boldt, George H., 11, 214
Bonnin, Gertrude Simmons, 182
Bonnin, Raymond Talesfase, 183
Bosque Redondo, 135, 150, 154
Boston Charlie, 326
Boudinot, Elias, 103
Bozeman, John, 182
Bozeman Trail, 181, 187–89, 267
Bozeman Trail War, 165
Brando, Marlon, 11, 29
Brant, Beth, 684–99
Brant, Joseph (Thayendanegea), 76–77, 88
Brant, Molly, 76
Bridger, Jim, 299
British Colonial Office, 336
British North America Act of 1867, 336
Brotherton, 82–83
Brown, Governor Edmund G., Jr., 323
Brown, Jerry, 31
Bruchac, Joseph, 684–99
Bruyere, Louis (Smokey), 33–34
Bull Bear, 189, 268
Burdeau, George, 727–29
Bureau of Indian Affairs (BIA): occupation of headquarters, 15; protests, 14–15; reform, 319; takeover, 31, 33, 44, 48; tribal protests, 8; Ute protest, 9. *See also* Office of Indian Affairs
Bury My Heart at Wounded Knee, 33

Bush, Barney, 685, 699
Bush, President George, 178

C

Cabot, John, 203
Caddo, 126
Cahuilla, 308, 310, 328
Calder, Frank Arthur, 34
Calder v. The Queen, 35, 373
California Indian treaties, 312, 316
California Indian Brotherhood, 316
California Indian Conference, 324
California Indian Legal Services, 321
California Mission Indians, 328
California Rural Indian Health Board, 321
California Trail, 297
Cameahwait, 191
Camp Brown, 300
Camp Grant, 156
Camp Stevens Treaty, 11
Camp Yellow Thunder, 40
Campbell, Ben Nighthorse, 294–95
Canadian Constitution, 208, 340, 361
Canadian Indian cultures, 335
Canadian Pacific Railroad, 392
Canby, General Edward, 153, 326
Cannon, T.C., 262
Canyon de Chelly, 129, 149–50, 615
Captain Jack, 153, 312, 323–27
Cardinal, Tantoo, 728-729
Carleton, General James H., 150
Carlisle Indian School, 141, 183
Carson, Colonel Kit, 150, 154–55, 297–99
Carter, President Jimmy, 69
Catawba, 100–102, 120
Catlin, George, 94, 521–23
Cayuga, 36, 71, 80
Chaco Canyon, 129
Charbonneau, Toussaint, 190
Charlottetown Accord, 365, 368, 372
Charter of Aboriginal Rights, 360
Chemakuan, 408
Cherokee, 45, 120; Act of Union, 270–71; constitu-
    tional government, 99, 250, 269; culture, 95–
    96; Eastern Band, 102, 105; Indian Territory,
    104; National party, 269; principal

chief, 264, 267–69; removal, 103, 246; songs,
    574; syllabary, 269, 436
Cherokee Foundation, 265
Cherokee Historical Association, 105
Cherokee Phoenix, 270
Cheyenne, 182, 185–87, 267; language, 410;
    migrations, 163; protest Canton Lake
    drainage, 9; removal, 240; resistance, 165;
    Treaty of Medicine Lodge, 251; Wolf Soldiers,
    250
Cheyenne and Arapaho War, 185, 262
Chiago, Michael, 611–31
Chickasaw, 45, 99, 115–17
Chickasaw Bluffs, 116
chiki, 108
Chingachgook, 40
Chinook Jargon, 409, 413
Chipewyan, 388–89
Chippewa, 86; migrations, 162; treaty rights, 59, 64,
    66. *See also* Ojibway
Chiricahua Apache, 616
Chirikof, Alexei, 220
Chivington, Col. John, 263–65
Choctaw, 45, 99, 111–13, 126, 245
Chota, 96
Chronicles of Oklahoma, 242
Chumash, 308
Cibecue, 155
Civil Rights Movement, 5, 10
Civil War, 46, 83, 124, 151, 240
Civilian Conservation Corps, 170
Clark, William, 190
Cleveland Indian Center, 39
Clinch, General Duncan, 125
Coast Guard lifeboat station, 14
Coast Miwok, 303–305
Coast Salish, 208
Cochise, 150–51, 155
Coler, Jack, 44
Collier, John, 3, 171, 146
Comanche, 37, 132, 240, 251, 266
Committee for Original People's Entitlement
    (COPE), 381
Community Action Program, 147, 177
Constitution (United States), 64
Constitution Act, 1867, 337, 341
Constitution Act, 1982, 331, 357
Constitutional Convention, 62

Cook-Lynn, Elizabeth, 686–99
Coon Come, Matthew, 380–81
Coosa, 121
Cornoyea, Nellie, 381–82
Cornplanter, 77–78, 88
Cornstalk, 80
Cotechney, 121
Council of 44 Chiefs, 295. See aslo Cheyenne
Council of Energy Resource Tribes (CERT), 6
County of Oneida v. Oneida Indian Nation, 72–73
Court of Claims, 18, 183
Coweta, 122
Cowichan Band, 387
Cowkeeper, 108
Coyote, 431, 614–31
Crazy Horse, 184–85
Crazy Snake Creek, 254
Cree, 46, 378–79; chief, 380; James Bay Project, 381;
      land claims, 26; language, 47; leaders, 391–96;
      reservation assignment, 165; self-government,
      370; syllabics, 378, 436
Creek, 45, 122–24; migrations, 108; politics, 96;
      removal, 108, 246; traditional government,
      99
Creek War, 269. See Red Stick War; 1836, 107;
      Choctaw, 113
Crook, General George, 182–85, 192, 271
Crooked Lance Society, 267
Crow, 188
Crowfoot (Isapo-Muxika), 382–83, 392–96
Curtis Act, 45, 104, 113, 241
Custer, Colonel George Armstrong, 165, 185–86,
      190–92 , 264

D

Dakota, 410
Dale, Edward E., 242
dance, 567
Dancing Rabbit Creek Treaty, 113
Dartmouth College, 82
Datsolalee, 612–31
Davidson, Isabel, 395–96
Davis, General Jefferson C., 326
Dawes Commission: allotment, 253, 259; Chickasaw,
      117; enrollment, 253; Five Civilized Tribes, 241
day schools, 317

Declaration of Independence, 64
Deer, Ada, 35
Deganawida, 60, 511–23
Deganawidah-Quetzecoatl (DQ) University, 32, 322
Delaware, 56–59, 86, 513
Delaware Prophet, 85, 512–23
Delgadito, 149
Deloria, Vine Jr., 506,
Dene Nation, 350, 356, 379, 384
Denedah, 349
Department of Indian and Northern Affairs, 34, 338
Deskahe. *See* General Deskahe
Determination of Rights and Unity for Menominee
      Shareholders (DRUMS), 67
Dog Soldiers, 268
Dominion Lands Act, 1879, 334
Dorris, Michael, 687–99
Drake, Sir Francis, 303–305
Dreamer Religion, 500, 518
Dull Knife, 185–87
Dumont, Gabriel, 22, 383
Dundy, Elmer, 271
Duwamish, 213

E

earth-divers, 445
Edensaw, Charles, 559
Edenshaw, Charlie, 613
Eisenhower, President Dwight D., 222
Emisteseguo, 122
Episcopalians, 478
Erasmus, Georges, 377, 384
Erdrich, Louise, 687–99
Eskimo, 233
Estanislao, 307
Eyak, 403

F

Farmer, Gary Dale, 729–40
Federal Bureau of Investigation (FBI), 39, 43–45, 48
Federal Subsistence Board, 229
festivals, 567
Fetterman, Captain William, 189
Fetterman Fight, 185

First Ministers' Conference, 360–62, 365
First Nations Congress, 396
First Seminole War, 124
Fish Eaters Band, 393
Fish-ins, 10
fishing rights, 11, 29, 48, 209, 214
Five Civilized Tribes, 45, 240
Five Nations. See Iroquois Confederacy
Five Tribes Act of 1906, 242
Fonseca, Harry, 325, 613–31
Forsyth, Major George, 268
Fort Alcatraz, 156
Fort Apache Reservation, 134
Fort Apache Timber Company, 134
Fort Berthold Reservation, 164
Fort Buford, 193
Fort Defiance, 150, 153, 155
Fort Detroit, 85
Fort Duquesne, 120
Fort Elliot Treaty, 213
Fort Esperance, 385
Fort Fauntleroy, 153
Fort Garry (Winnipeg), 385, 394–96
Fort Hall Indian Reservation, 298
Fort Jackson, 123
Fort Laramie, 189
Fort Laramie Treaty, 182; of 1868, 182–84, 187, 191, 271
Fort Larned Council, 268
Fort Lawton, 14
Fort Lewis, 14
Fort Lyon, 263
Fort Marion, 266
Fort McLane, 152
Fort Monroe, 76
Fort Peck Indian Reservation, 29, 179
Fort Phil Kearny, 188
Fort Prince of Wales, 388–89
Fort Rae, 384
Fort Robinson, 185–86
Fort Sill, 157, 266
Fort Sumner, 154–55
Fort Totten, 179
Fort Washakie, 300
Fort Wayne, 78–79
Fort Wingate, 153
Four Mothers Society, 46
freedmen, 117
French and Indian War, 77, 85, 120

Fritz Scholder, 629
fur trade, 97, 203

G

Gabrielino, 310, 325
Gaiwiio, 494, 513–23
Gall, 182, 185–86
Gall (Pizi), 186
gaming, 111
Ganado Mucho, 153–55
Gay Head, 71
Geddes, Carol, 730–40
Geiogamah, Hanay, 731–40
Gender, 98
General, Alexander (), 36
General Allotment Act, 10, 168, 210, 314–16, 319
General Federation of Women's Clubs, 145
George, Dan, 732–40
George III, 336
Geronimo, 134, 156–57
Ghost Dance: 1870, 312; 1890, 6–7, 187, 190, 522; beginning of, 6; First, 155; Wounded Knee Massacre, 7
Gitksan, 208, 370
Gladwin, Major Henry, 85
Gold Rush: California, 311
Gorman, Carl, 614–31
Gorman, R.C., 615–31
Graffiti Man Band, 48
Gran Apacheria, 133
Grand Council of the Cree, 380
Grant, Cuthbert, 384–85
Grant, President Ulysses S., 83, 154, 189, 300, 326
Great Jim Thorpe Run, 32
Great Law, 511
Great Sioux Reservation, 271
Great Smoky Mountains National Park, 105
Great Whale Project, 380
Greatest Horse Thief in History, 298
Green Corn Ceremony, 93
Greene, Graham, 733–40
Greenpeace, 384
Gregory, Dick, 11
Gros Ventre, 165
Guerin v. Regina, 338
Gwi'chin, 26, 356

H

Hagler, 120
Haida, 43; artists, 613; contemporary life, 207;
    culture, 218; language family, 403; sculpter,
    625–31
Hancock, 120–21
Hancock, General Winfield Scott, 268
Hancock, John, 61
Handsome Lake, 6, 62, 77, 513–14
Hano Pueblo, 623
Harjo, Joy, 688
Harmar, General Josiah, 79
Harper, Elijah, 362, 369, 385, 390
Harris, Fred, 37
Harris, LaDonna, 37
Harrison, William Henry, 520
Haskell Indian Junior College, 5
Haudenosaunee, 60. *See also* Iroquois, Six Nations
Hawthorn Inquiry, 25
Hayfield Fight, 189
Head Start Program, 178
Hearne, Samuel, 389–90
Hensley, William L., 233
Hiawatha, 60, 511
Hickory Ground, 122
Hidatsa, 164, 190
Highway, Tomson, 734
Hogan, Linda, 689
Hokan-Coahuiltecan, 405
Holy Being (Navajo), 448
Hopewell Culture, 55
Hopi: ancestors, 141–43; artists, 619–31; kivas, 129;
    migrations, 130; Snake Dance, 582; spiritual
    leaders, 510
Hopi-Navajo Land Dispute, 510–23
House Joint Resolution 1042, 13
Houser, Allan, 616–31
Howard, General Oliver O., 49, 155
Howe, Oscar, 617–31
Hudson's Bay Company, 389–96
Hudson, Charles, 93
Hudson's Bay Company: Métis, 204, 353, 385, 389–
    96
Hunt, Michael, 29
Hupa, 312
Huron, 86, 335, 511–23

I

iksa, 126
Illinois Confederacy, 56, 86
Incident at Oglala, 48
Indian Act, 20, 208, 332, 335, 338
Indian Activist Movements, 6
Indian Advocacy, 4
Indian Association of Alberta, 395
Indian Claims Commission, 18, 317
Indian Defense League, 7, 37
Indian Emergency Conservation Work, 170
Indian Financing Act, 17
Indian Gaming Regulatory Act, 2
Indian Intercourse Act, 73
Indian Leader, 5
Indian New Deal, 171
Indian Removal Act, 116, 124
Indian Reorganization Act, 8, 105, 171, 210
Indian Rights Association, 223, 314
Indian Rights Organizations, 2
Indian Self-Determination and Education Assistance
    Act, 17
Indian Shaker Church, 517
Indian Territory, 46, 263, 266; emigrant Indians, 164;
    established, 239; Ponca, 38; proposed, 238;
    Seminole, 125; U.S. settlers, 240
Indian Trade and Intercourse Act of 1790, 68–70, 73
Indians of All Tribes, 12
Indians of All Tribes, Inc., 47
Individual Indian Monies, 170
Indo-European, 399
Inter-American Indigenous Institute, 37
Interior Salish people, 386
Inuit, 233; Alaska, 215; constitutional recognition,
    331; constitutional rights, 333; culture, 346;
    economic change, 350; government services,
    347; land claims, 26; language, 397, 401;
    protest, 223; self-government, 372; subsis-
    tence, 217
Inuit Broadcasting Corporation, 351
Inuit Circumpolar Conference, 351
Inuit Committee on National Issues, 348
Inuit of Nunavut, 349
Inuit Tapirisat of Canada, 22, 347, 381
Inuktitut, 401
Inupiaq, 401
Inupiat, 234

Inupiat Paitot, 234
Inuvialuit, 26, 349, 381
Iroquoian language, 413
Iroquoian peoples, 60
Iroquois, 120; culture, 55; delegations to UN, 9; economy, 335; expansion, 161; fur trade, 59; land claims, 63; repatriation, 63. *See also* Iroquois Confederacy, Six Nations
Iroquois Confederacy, 36, 76–77, 83, 511; Kinzua Dam, 8; origin, 60; sovereignty, 64; Tuscarora, 121
Isaac Steven's Treaty, 295
Ishi, 327–28

J

Jackson, Andrew, 76
Jackson, General Andrew, 107, 123, 269
Jackson, Helen Hunt, 328
Jackson, President Andrew, 238, 246
James Bay and Northern Quebec Agreement in 1975, 347
James Bay II, 380
Jamestown Colony, 87–88
Jay Treaty, 7, 63
Jefferson, Thomas, 61, 80, 244
Jesup, General T.S., 125
Jim Thorpe Memorial Games, 32
Johnson, Ethel, 395
Johnson, Pauline, 689–99
Johnson, Sir William, 76
Jones, John, 49
Joseph, 295–96. *See also* Chief Joseph
Juaneño, 325

K

kachinas, 158
Kahnawake Mohawk, 370
Kalaallisut, 401
Kansas Territory, 239
Karankawa, 409
Karuk, 411
Kateri Tekakwitha, 519–23
Keeler, William W., 264
Keetoowah Society, 45, 46, 248

Kelly, Peter, 43
Kenekuk, 6, 514
Kennedy, John F., 29
Kennedy, Robert, 29
Keokuk, 78
Keresan, 409
Ketcher, John, 267
Kickapoo, 6, 86, 514
Kickapoo Prophet, 514
Kicking Bear, 187
Kicking Bird, 266
Killsright, Joe, 44
King, Charles Bird, 76, 88
King Philip, 81
King Philip's War, 58, 84
Kinzua Dam, 8
Kiowa, 266; Christian churches, 486; principal chief, 266; removal, 240; Treaty of Medicine Lodge, 251
Klamath, 211, 326
Kroeber, Alfred, 327
Kroeber, Theodora, 328
Kumeyaay, 308
Kupa, 312–14; war with San Diego, 312
Kutenai, 408
Kwawkgewlth, 395

L

La Flesche, Francis, 38
La Flesche, Joseph, 38
La Flesche, Susan, 38
La Flesche, Susette, 38
La Pena, Frank, 325
Lake Mohonk Conference of the Friends of the Indian, 3
Lakota, 436, 617. *See also* Sioux, Dakota
LaMarr, Jean, 325
Land Claims, 18, 233, 375
Laulewasika. *See* Shawnee Prophet
Le Clercq, Father Chrestien, 436
League of Indians of Canada, 47
Leech Lake Indian Reservation, 31
Left Hand (Nawat), 265
Lewis, Meriwether, 190
Life among the Paiutes, Their Wrongs and Claims, 50
Lincoln, President Abraham, 262, 266

Lind, Jane, 735–40
Little Bad Man (Ayimisis), 379
Little Crow, 188
Little Pomp, 191
Little Raven, 265
Little Shell, 165
Little Talisee, 121–22
Little Turtle (Michikinikwa), 78–79
Little Wolf, 185–88
Locke, Kevin, 617
Logan, John, 80
Loloma, Charles, 618
Lomahaftewa, Linda, 620
Lone Man, 188
Lone Wolf (Guipago), 266
Long Walk, 155
Longest Walk, 16
Lord Dunmore's War, 80
Los Angeles Arts Festival, 610
Louis Riel, 383, 393–96
Louisiana Colony, 126
Lubicon Cree, 341–43
Lucas, Phil, 735
Luiseño, 626–31
Luna, James, 325

M

MacDonald, Peter, 138, 152
Mackensie Valley Pipeline, 384
Macro-Algonkian, 403
Macro-Siouan, 399, 404
Maine Indians' Claims Case, 70
Maine Indian's Claims Settlement Act of 1980, 69
Major Ridge, 126
Malecite, 335
Malheur Reservation, 49
Malki Museum, 324
Mamanti, 266
Man Afraid of His Horses, 189
Mandans, 164
Mangas Coloradas, 150–51
Mangus, 152
Manitoba Act, 1870, 334, 353
Manitoba Legislative Assembly, 362
Mankiller, Wilma, 103–104, 267
Manriquez, L. Frank, 325

Manuel, George, 386
Manuelito, 149–50, 153–54
Marchand, Leonard Stephen, 387–88
Martinez, Maria, 562
Marufo, Annie, 41
Masau-u, 142
Masayesva, Victor, 707
Mashpee, 71–73
Massasoit, 81, 84
Matheson, Edward, 378
Matheson, Reverand John, 378
Matonabbee, 388–89
Matthiessen, Peter, 45
McCombs, Solomon, 620
McEachern, Chief Justice Allan, 374
McGhee, Lynn, 108
McGillivray, Alexander, 95, 116, 121–22
McIntosh, William, 122–23
McKay, Jean-Baptiste, 422
McKenna-McBride Commission, 43
McLaughlin, James, 187
Means, Russell, 38–40
Medicine Lodge Council, 268, 515
Medicine Lodge Treaty, 266–68
Meech Lake Accord: Native exclusion, 361; Native Oppositin, 386; Native opposition, 385; non-ratification, 362, 369; Ovide Mercredi, 390
Meeker, Nathan, 297
Menominee, 35, 66–67
Menominee Restoration Committee, 35
Menominee Warrior Society, 16
Mercredi, Ovide, 389–96
Mesa Verde, 129
Mescalero Reservation, 157
Métchi, 410
Métis, 33; Alberta, 355, 375; and Sioux, 385; classification, 333; constitutional rights, 331, 368; farms, 355; land losses, 355; nationalism, 384; Northwest Company, 385; politicians, 390–96; rebellion, 383; reservation assignment, 166; scrip, 354
Métis Association of the NWT, 356
Métis Betterment Act, 355
Métis National Council, 21, 333, 355
Mexican-American War, 129, 133
Miami, 78, 86
Miccosukee, 111
Micmac, 30, 335

Migratory Bird Treaty Act, 223
Miles, General Nelson A., 156, 188
Mingo, 80
Minniconjous. *See also* Sioux
Miskito Indians, 40
Mission Indian,, 308–309
Mission Indian Federation, 315
Mission La Purisima, 308
Mission Reserve, 43
Mission San Gabriel, 308
Mission San Miguel, 308
Mission Santa Barbara, 308
Mission Santa Cruz, 308
missionaries: Franciscan, 305; Morman, 101; Office of
    Indian Affairs, 314
missions: California, 306; Spanish Catholic, 143
Mississippi Choctaw, 114
Mississippi Culture, 55, 93
Mitchell, George, 33
Miwok, 310–11
Mobilian Jargon, 409
Modoc, 153, 325–26
Modoc War, 312, 325–27
Mohave, 310
Mohawk, 76; Akwesasne Notes, 5; land claims, 71,
    342; Oka, 336, 342; socioeconomic condi-
    tions, 343; sovereignty, 366; St. Lawrence
    Seaway project, 8; traditional government, 339
Mohawk Institute, 393–96
Mohawk Reservations, 62
Mohawk Workers, 37
Mohegan, 70
Momaday, N. Scott, 690
Montauk, 82
Montauk, Mary, 82
Montezuma, Carlos, 691
Mooney, James, 522
Moore, Colonel James, 121
Mormons, 298–99
Morongo Indian Reservation, 324
Morrisseau, Norval, 621–24
Mother Earth, 597
Mount Rushmore, 14
Mounties, 392
Mucho, Ganado, 154
Mulroney, Prime Minister Brian, 362
Murray, William H., 255
music, 567

Muskogean, 414
Musqueam Band, 338

N

Naches, 49
Naiche, 155–57
Nakai, R. Carlos, 622
Nampeyo, 623
Nanakonagos, Moses, 621
Nanay, 156
Nanticoke, 58
Narragansett, 72, 84, 89
Naskapi, 370
National Advisory Council on Indian Education, 101
National American Indian Brotherhood, 47
National Assembly of British Columbia, 34
National Committee to Save the Menominee People,
    35
National Congress of American Indians, 4
National Council of American Indians, 184
National Indian Brotherhood, 335, 359, 387
National Indian Education Association, 5
National Indian Youth Council, 4, 11
National Tribal Chairman's Association, 5
Native American Church: Plains, 181
Native American Coalition of Tulsa, 260
Native American Heritage Commission, 323
Native American Rights Fund, 5
Native Brotherhood of British Columbia, 396
Native Claims Office, 373
Native Council of Canada, 21, 33, 334, 336, 354
Native North American languages, 397
Native Women's Association of Canada: Status Indian
    women, 23
Natural Resources Transfer Act, 1930, 341
Navajo, 135–36, 149–55, 159; artists, 614–15; BIA
    livestock reduction, 8; code talkers, 152;
    constitutional convention, 136; court, 141;
    culture, 131; elections, 141; Fairchild assembly
    plant, 16; language, 398, 411; migration, 430;
    migrations, 131; Offico of Navajo Labor
    Relations, 139; pacification, 135; raids, 132–33;
    war ceremonials, 472
Navajo Business Council, 135
Navajo Community College, 5, 139
Navajo Fair, 508

Navajo Forest Products Industry, 137
Navajo Times, 5
Navajo-Hopi Land dispute, 8
Nevaquaya, Doc Tate, 586
New Deal, 8, 170
New France, 61
New Oraibi, 510
New Stockbridge, 83
New Tidings Religion, 498
Newfoundland Company, 89
News From Native California, 324
Nez Percé, 295–96. See also Joseph, Chief Joeseph
Niatum, Duane, 692
Nichol, Frederick, 40
Nicola Valley Indian Bands, 388
Nighthawk Keetoowah, 45, 46. See also Keetoowah
Nike Missile site, 14
Nipmuck, 84
Nisga'a, 34, 373
Nisqually, 213
Nixon, Presdent Richard M. M.: Indian Policy, 148
Nixon, President Richard M., 148, 178; Alaska
　　Natives, 224; Alcatraz Island, 13; Taos Blue
　　Lake, 516
Norquay, John, 390
North American Indian Brotherhood, 43, 387
North West Company, 384
Northern Arapaho. See also Arapaho
Northern Cheyenne, 189. See also Cheyenne;
　　cattle operations, 168; coal development,
　　178; con-temporary culture, 181; ranchers,
　　167; reser-vation assignment, 165; unem-
　　ployment, 180
Northwest Alaska Native Association, 234
Northwest Coast, 195, 199–201, 206
Northwest Passage, 203
Northwest Rebellion, 379, 383, 392–96
Norton, Richard, 388
Numaga, 49
Nunavut, 28, 349, 372
Nunna Hidihi. See Ridge, Major
Nuu-chah-nulth, 387

O

Oakes, Richard, 40–41
Oakes, Yvonne, 41

O'Bail, John, 77
Obomsawin, Alanis, 736–40
Occum, Samson, 82
Odjig, Daphne, 623
Office of Economic Opportunity: Plains, 177
Office of Indians Affairs: irrigation, 167
Office of Navajo Labor Relations, 139
Oglala. See also Sioux
Ojibway, 33
Ojibway, 33, 56, 621
Okanagan, 388
Oklahoma Constitutional Convention, 254
Oklahoma Enabling Act, 242
Oklahoma Indian Welfare Act, 243
Oklahoma Indians, 248–49, 255, 258, 262
Oklahoma Organic Act, 241
Oklahoma tribes, 238, 243, 247
Oklahomans for Indian Opportunity, 37
Oklahoma's Unassigned Lands, 246
Old Indian Legends, 183
Old Joseph, 518
Old Mokeen, 262
Old Northwest, 78, 85
Old Northwest Territory, 90
Old Piqua, 89
Old Settlers, 246, 270
Old Spanish Trail, 299
Old Tassel, 103
Omaha, 38, 167
Omaha Treaty, 168
Oneida, 36, 71, 82, 121
Onondaga, 19, 32, 63
Ontario Métis and Non-Status Indian Association,
　　33
O'Odham, 397
Oonoleh, 271
Opechancanough, 87
Opothleyoholo, 123–24
Oregon Trail, 189, 297, 299
Organic Act, 222
Ormsby, Major William, 49
Ortiz, Simon, 693
Osage,, 126, 245
Osceola, 124–25
Ottawa, 56, 85–86, 162
Ouray, 296–97
Owen, Robert L., 248

P

Pagan Party, 88
Paiute, 6, 49, 522–23
Paiute War, 49
Pala, 315
Pamunkey, 73
Pan-American Games, 294
Panton, Leslie & Company., 122
Parker, Cynthia, 515
Parker, Ely S., 83
Parker, Isaac C., 240
Parker, Quanah, 266, 515
Parrish, Samuel, 49
Passamaquoddy, 18, 58, 67
Path Killer, 269
Pauktuutit, 23
Paul, William Lewis, 41–42
Paull, Andrew, 43
Pawnee, 164, 188, 467
Payamataha, 115
Payepot (One Who Knows the Secrets of the Sioux), 391
Peace Policy, 313
Peltier, Leonard, 32, 38, 43–45, 48
Penobscot, 58, 68
Penutian, 405
Pequot, 58s, 70
Peta Nocona, 515
Peyote Religion, 516
Philip, 84–85
Piapot, 391
Pilgrims, 81, 89
Pima-Papago, 414
Pine Ridge Reservation, 30–32, 39, 44, 48, 186, 190
Piomingo, 115
Pit River, 322
Pit River Indian Movement, 41
Plains Chippewa, 165. *See also* Chippewa, Ojibway
Plains Sign Language, 415
Plains tribes, 181
Plenty Hoops, Winona, 605
Ploughed Under: The Story of an Indian Chief, 38
Plymouth, 81
Poarch Band of Creek, 108
Pocahontas, 87–88
Pocatello, 297–98

Pomo, 315, 322
Pomponio, 307
Ponca, 38, 164, 271–72
Pontiac, 59, 85–86, 512
Popé, 132, 144, 157
Port Madison Reservation, 213
Posey, Alexander, 694
Potawatomi, 56, 59, 86, 245
Poundmaker, 46, 383, 392
Poundmaker Reserve, 46, 379
Powell, J.W., 400
Powhatan, 87
Powhatan Confederacy, 58, 86–87
Proclamation of 1763, 80, 336
promishleniki, 221
Prophetstown, 90, 520
Public Law 280, 320
Public Law 93-531, 510
Pueblo: contemporary culture, 508; cultural survival, 149; culture, 131; Indian Reorganization Act, 143; kivas, 129; land losses, 145; languages, 144; Revolt, 132, 143–44; trade, 133; water rights, 146
Pueblo Lands Act, 145
Puritans, 81, 84
Pushmataha, 126
Puyallup, 16

Q

qargi, 218
Quakers, 3
Qualla Boundary, 102, 106
Quechan, 308
Queen Victoria, 382

R

Rachlin, Carol, 261
Radio Free Alcatraz, 47
Ramona, 328
Rampart Dam, 235
Rancheria Act of 1958, 320
rancherias, 319
Reagan, President Ronald, 178
Red Cloud, 181–84, 188–91

Red Cloud Reservation, 190
Red Cloud's War, 181, 182
Red Crow, (Mekaisto), 393–96
Red Earth Celebration, 255
Red Jacket, 77, 88
Red Paper, 357
Red Power, 5–6,10, 16
Red River Métis, 21
Red River War, 266
Red Stick Creek, 126
Red Stick War, 122–23. *See also* Creek War
Red Sucker Lake Band, 386
Redstar, Kevin, 624
Reid, Bill, 625
Relocation Program 138, 174–75
Removal Policy, 98
repatriation, 18, 63, 323
reservations, 319
residential boarding schools, 344
Revard, Carter, 695
revitalization movements, 7
Rhode Island Indian Claims Settlement Act, 17
Ridge, John, 103
Ridge, John Rollin, 695
Ridge, Major, 103, 126–27
Riel, Jr., Louis David, 394
Riel, Louis Jr., 22, 353–54, 379, 383, 394–96
Riel, Louis Sr., 394–96
Rinehart, William, 49
Robinson, Gary, 737
Robinson-Huron Treaty, 336
Robinson-Superior Treaty, 336
Rock, Howard, 234–35
Rocky Boy Reservation, 165
Rolfe, John, 87–88
Roman Nose, 267–68
Romero, Juan de Jesus, 516
Roosevelt, President Franklin D., 145
Rose, Wendy, 696
Ross, Elizabeth Ann, 386
Ross, John, 268
Royal Commission on Aboriginal Peoples, 377, 384
Royal Proclamation, 86
Royal Proclamation of 1763, 24
Russian American Company, 221

S

Sac and Fox, 78, 245
Sacajawea, 190–91
Sacred Run, 32
Sacred Soul, 32
Saddle Lake Indian Reserve, 395
Sainte-Marie, Buffy, 626
Salish, 43
Salishan, 408, 414
Salt Lake Road, 297
Sampson, Will, 738–40
San Carlos Reservation, 155–56
San Juan Pueblo, 158
Sand Creek Battle, 165
Sand Creek Massacre, 189, 262, 265
Sand Point Reserve, 621
Santa Clara Pueblo, 630–31
Santa Fe, 158
Santa Fe Trail, 262
Sapir, Edward, 400, 430
Satanta, 266
Satiacum, Robert, 11
Saukenuk, 78
Sawridge Band, 370
Scarfaced Charlie, 326
Schaghticoke, 70
Schochin, John, 312
Scholder, Fritz, 626
Schonchin John, 326
Scott, General Winfield, 75
Scott, Thomas, 353
Sealth. *See* Seattle
Sechelt Act, 370
Sechelt Band, 370
Second Seminole War, 124
Seminole, 45, 108–11,125
Seneca, 8, 77, 83, 86–88, 245
Sequoya League, 314
Sequoyah, 269–71, 436
Sequoyah Constitutional Convention, 255
Setter, Elizabeth, 390
Seventh Cavalry, 7, 264
Shahaptan, 6. *See also* Smohalla
Shamans, 218
Shawnee, 59, 80, 86, 89, 120, 245
Shawnee Prophet, 90, 514, 522. *See also* Tenskwatawa
Sheridan, Major General Philip, 263

Shoshoni, 49, 165, 190–91, 297, 299, 300
Shuswap, 386
Sign Language, 415
Siletz, 211
Silko, Leslie Marmon, 697–99
Silverheels, Jay, 739–40
Simon, Mary, 351
Siouan, 414
Sioux, 78, 181–82, 185–87, 190–92; artists, 617; beadworker, 601; Black Hills, 18; Brulé, 184; cattle operations, 168; farming, 167; Hunk-papa, 189–91; land leases, 168; migrations, 162; Oglala, 30, 189; pre-Plains culture, 163; resistance, 165; Teton, 184, 188; treaty with Métis, 383; warfare, 189; woman, 182; Wounded Knee Massacre, 38
Sitting Bull, 182, 185–87, 191–93, 382
Six Nations. *See* Iroquois Confederacy
Six Nations Reserve, 36
Six Towns, 126
slaves, 109, 311
Slocum, John, 517–23
Smith, Captain John, 411
Smith, Kathleen, 325
Smith, Redbird, 45–46
Smithsonian Institution, 19
Smohalla, 6, 518
Smoke, 188
Snake War, 49
Soap, Charley, 267
Social Security Act, 171
Society of American Indians, 3
Sohappy, Sr., David, 214
Sohappy v. Washington State, 214
Soto, Henando de, 96
Southeastern Peoples, 94–95
Southern Arapaho, 265. *See also* Arapaho
Southern Cheyenne, 188, 263–65. *See also* Cheyenne, Northern Cheyenne
Southern Yana, 327
Special Committee on Indian Self-Government, 369
Special Joint Committee on a Renewed Canada, 363
Speck, Frank, 36
Spotted Eagle, Chris, 740
Squamish Nation, 43
Squanto, 81
St. Clair, General Arthur, 79
St. Lawrence Seaway, 8

St. Marks, 124
St. Regis Reservation, 40
Standing Bear, 38, 271–72
Standing Rock Reservation, 187, 193
status Indian, 332
Steinhauer, Henry Bird, 395
Steinhauer, Ralph, 395
Steinhauer, Ralph Garvin, 395
Summers-Fitzgerald, Diosa, 628
Sun Dance, 44
Sunrise Park Ski Resort, 134
Survival of American Indians Association, 29
Sutter, John Agust, 310

T

Tachnechdorus. *See* Logan, John
Tailfeathers, Gerald, 628–31
Talisee, 123
Tall Bull, 268
TallMountain, Mary, 698–99
Taos Pueblo, , 147, 158, 516
Taskigi, 269
Tasquantum. *See* Squanto
Tecumseh, 59, 79, 89, 90, 126, 520–21
Tekakwitha, Kateri, 519
Tenskwatawa, 520–23. *See also* Shawnee Prophet. *See also* Shawnee Prophet; revitalization movement, 6
Termination Policy, 35, 320
Thanksgiving, 81
The Alaska Fisherman, 42
The Indian Historian, 5
The Last of the Mohicans, 32, 40
The Midwinter Rites of the Cayuga Longhouse, 36
The Tundra Times, 234–35
The Weekly Independent, 38
Third Colorado Volunteers, 263
Third Seminole War, 124–25
Thomas, William H., 103
Thompson, Wiley, 125
Thunderheart, 32, 48
Tibbles, Thomas H., 38, 271
Timberlake, Lt. Henry, 95
Tlingit, 41, 42; contemporary life, 207; culture, 218; language family, 403
Tohono O'Odham, 130, 611

Tonawanda, 63, 83
Tongass National Forest, 42
Tongue River Reservation, 165
Tootoosis, Jr., John Baptiste, 46–47
Toypurina, 308
Trail of Broken Treaties, 15, 31, 48
Trail of Tears: Cherokee, 127, 270; Five Civilized
    Tribes, 240, 246; Oklahoma Indians, 238
treaties 24, 208, 311
Treaty at Doak's Stand, 112
Treaty at Fort Hopewell: Chickasaw, 115
Treaty at Fort Smith, 251
Treaty at Medicine Lodge, 251
Treaty at Mount Dexter, 112
Treaty Number 3, 336
Treaty Number 6, 368, 379
Treaty Number 7, 368, 382
Treaty Number 11, 336
Treaty of 1832, 107
Treaty of Box Elder, 298
Treaty of Cession, 221
Treaty of Fort Adams, 112
Treaty of Fort Bridger, 299
Treaty of Fort Jackson, 107
Treaty of Fort Laramie: 1968, 189
Treaty of Ghent, 7
Treaty of Greenville, 79, 89
Treaty of Guadalupe Hidalgo, 135, 311
Treaty of Indian Springs, 123
Treaty of New Echota, 103, 127
Treaty of Oregon, 205
Treaty of Pontotoc Creek, 116
Treaty of San Lorenzo, 116
treaty rights, 16
Tribal Government Tax Status Act, 73
Tribal Self-Determination Rights, 19
Truckee, 49
Trudeau, Prime Minister Pierre, 25, 359
Trudell, John, 47–48
Trudell, Tina, 48
Truman, President Harry, 222
Tsabetsye, Roger, 629
Tschaddam. *See also* Indian Shaker Church
Tsimpshian, 42
Tsimshian, 218
Tuckabatchee, 123
Tullis, Eddie L., 108
Tungavik Federation of Nunavut, 22, 348

Turtle Mountain Reservation, 165, 179
Tuscarora, 8, 63, 120–21
Twin Cities Naval Air Station, 14

U

Uintah and Ouray Reservation, 183
umialik, 218
Union of British Columbia Indian Chiefs, 387, 396
Union of Saskatchewan Indians, 47
Union Pacific Railroad Company, 300
Unitah Reservation, 297
United Indian Councils of the Mississauga and Chip,
    370
United Indians of All Tribes Foundation, 211
United Native Nations, 396
United States v. Washington, 212
Unto These Hills, 105
Ute, 9, 132, 155, 296
Uto-Aztecan, 397, 407, 414

V

Velarde, Pablita, 630–31
Vishinski, Andrei Y., 9
visual arts, 593
Vizenor, Gerald, 699
Voegelin, C. F., 400
Voegelin, F. R., 400
Voight Decision, 65
Von Graffenried, Christoph, 120

W

Wabokieshek (White Cloud), 522. See Winnebago
    Prophet
Wagon Box Fight, 189
Wahpeton Indian School, 44
Wahunsonacock. See Powhatan
Wakashan, 408
Walkara (Walker), 298–99
Walker Lake Reservation, 522–23
Walker War, 299
Walks as She Thinks, 188
Wallace, Wayne, 260

Wampanoag, 56, 71, 81, 84
Wanapam, 518
Wandering Spirit (Kapapamahchakwew), 379
War for the Black Hills, 185, 188
War of 1812, 91, 204
War on Poverty, 177, 321
War Party, 32Washakie (Gambler's Gourd), 298–99
Washington, General George, 76
Washington, President George, 79, 89, 122
Washington Territory, 295
Washo, 612
Wassaja, 5
Wayne, General Anthony, 79
Weber, David, 306
Western Territory Bill of 1834, 238
Wet'suwet'en, 370
Wheaton, Lieutenant Colonel Frank, 326
Wheelock, Eleazor, 82
White Earth Reservation, 33
White Mountain Apache, 134
White Paper, 25, 357–59
Whorf, B. L., 429
Wikwemikong Indian Reserve, 623
Wild River Shoshoni, 298
William Cody's Wild West Show, 193
Williams, Roger, 81, 84
Williams, Ronald, 44
Wilson, Bill, 395
Wilson, Charles William, 395
Wilson, David, 522–23
Wilson, Dick, 40
Wilson, Jack. *See* Wovoka
Wilson, James, 62
Wilson, Richard, 15
Wind River Reservation, 299
Winnebago, 164, 167, 471
Winnebago Prophet, 521
Winnebago Uprising, 521
Winnemucca, Sarah, 49–50
Winters Doctrine, 146
Wintun: rancheria, 315

Wodziwob, 6
women: Aleut, 216; California Indian, 306; Cherokee, 102, 243; intermarriage, 352; language differences, 418; Métis, 23, 352
Women of the Métis Nation, 23
Women's National Advisory Council on Poverty, 37
Women's National Indian Association, 2
Woodland Cree Band, 342
World Council of Indigenous Peoples, 34, 387
Wounded Knee, 30–33, 38–39, 48
Wounded Knee Massacre, 7
Wovoka, 6, 522–23
Wright, Allen, 247

Y

Ya-Ka-Ama, 322
Yahi, 327, 328
Yakima Nation's Treaty, 214
Yakima Reservation, 49
Yakima War, 213
Yankton Sioux Agency, 182
Yaqui, 502, 508
Yellow Thunder Camp, 18
Yellow Thunder, Raymond, 39
Yellowstone Park, 300
Yokut, 311
Young, 299
Young, Brigham, 299
Yozcolo, 310
Yuchi, 399
Yukian, 408
Yupik, 215–17, 233, 401

Z

Zah, Peterson, 140, 158
Zarcillas Largas, 153
Zuni Pueblo 19,147–48, 629–31

*I*llustrations

Activism: *p. 3:* The Quaker City banquet of the Society of American Indians. Hotel Walton, February 14, 1914 (courtesy of the National Archives); *p. 8:* Tuscarora protest against the New York State Power Authority's condemnation of their lands for a reservoir, 1958 (courtesy of the Buffalo and Erie County Historical Society); *p. 10:* Tuscarora protesting reservoir (courtesy of the Buffalo and Erie County Historical Society); *p. 12:* Indian children playing on Alcatraz Island during the 1969–71 occupation. Note burnt out structure (previously warden's house) (photographer unknown); *p. 13:* During the 1969–71 Indian occupation of Alcatraz Island, Indian men and women learned beadwork and other cultural skills (photographer unknown); *p. 27:* Canadian Natives protesting before Parliament for land rights and aboriginal rights within the Canadian Constitution (courtesy of Canapress Photo Service); *p. 31:* Dennis J. Banks (photo by Alice Lambert); *p. 35:* Ada Deer; *p. 41:* Richard Oakes (courtesy of Stephen Lehmer); *p. 41:* William Lewis Paul, Sr. (courtesy of the Alaska Historical Library); *p. 47:* John Trudell (courtesy of Stephen Lehmer); *p. 49:* Sarah Winnemucca (courtesy of the Nevada State Historical Society).

Native Peoples of the Northeast: *p. 56:* Contemporary Indian tribes of the northeastern United States; *p. 57:* Key to Tribal Territories (courtesy of the Government Printing Office, Washington, D.C.); *p. 61:* On June 11, 1776, an Onondaga sachem gave John Hancock an Iroquois name at Independence Hall (drawing by

John Kahionhes Fadden); *p. 66:* Anishnabe man and woman gather wild rice from canoe in Minnesota (courtesy of the Minnesota Historical Society); *p. 78:* Keokuk (courtesy of Smithsonian Institution); *p. 83:* Ely S. Parker.

Native Peoples of the Southeast: *p.94:* Contemporary southeastern tribes; *p. 107:* Christy Godwin O'Barr, Poarch Creek Indian Princess in 1987, sings at a 1987 Thanksgiving powwow (courtesy of Elizabeth D. Purdum, used by permission from *Indians of the Southeastern United States in the Late 20th Century*, edited by J. Anthony Paredes, 1992, The University of Alabama); *p. 112:* Evajean Felihkatubbee, Choctaw Indian woman, cleaning a basket; *p. 119:* Dedication of new Poarch Creek Tribal Center, April 1987. Poarch Creek elder gives opening blessing at the ceremony (courtesy of Elizabeth D. Purdum, used by permission from *Indians of the Southeastern United States in the Late 20th Century,* edited by J. Anthony Paredes, 1992, The University of Alabama).

Native Peoples of the Southwest: *p. 130:* Contemporary southwestern tribes; *p. 131:* Hopi child clown (courtesy of Owen Seumptewa); *p. 137:* A middle-aged Navajo woman stands next to her traditional hogan in Tuba City, Arizona (courtesy of Paul Natonabah, *Navajo Times*); *p. 140:* Navajo medicine man Albert Yazzie chats with Navajo Education Center staff after performing a Navajo Protection Way ceremony for Navajo servicemen and women who were involved in the Persian Gulf war with Iraq (courtesy of Paul Natonabah, *Navajo Times*); *p. 142:* "Lynn," a Hopi woman (courtesy of Owen Seumptewa); *p.146:* Matachine dancers at San Juan Pueblo (courtesy of Mark Nohl, New Mexico Economics & Tourism Department, Joseph M. Montoya Building, 100 St. Francis Drive, Santa Fe, New Mexico 87503); *p. 148:* San Ildefonso Pueblo feast day (courtesy of Mark Nohl, New Mexico Economics & TourismDepartment., Joseph M. Montoya Building, 100 St. Francis Drive, Santa Fe, New Mexico 87503); *p. 153:* Manuelito (courtesy of the Colorado Historical Society); *p. 156:* Natchez (Naiche) (courtesy of the Colorado Historical Society); *p. 159:* Peterson Zah (courtesy of Paul Natonabah, *Navajo Times*).

Native Peoples of the Northern Plains: *p. 162:* Contemporary Plains Indian tribes; *p. 173:* Blackfeet residence with sweat lodge and canvas lodge in foreground, Blackfeet Reservation, Montana (courtesy of Ken Blackbird); *p. 177:* Kicking Women Singers at the North American Indian Days, Browning, Montana (courtesy of Ken Blackbird); *p. 179:* Mosquito Run, Milk River Indian Days, August 1986, Fort Belknap Agency, Montana (courtesy of Ken Blackbird); *p. 183:* Gertrude Simmons Bonnin (courtesy of Bruguier Collection); *p. 186:* Dull Knife; *p. 187:* Gall (courtesy of the Colorado Historical Society); *p. 189:* Red Cloud.

Native Peoples of the Northwest Coast: *p. 197:* Contemporary Northwest Coast Indian tribes; *p. 200:* The inside of a house at Nootka Sound, from the Cook Expedition, 1778 (courtesy of John Webber, artist. Special Collections Division, University of Washington Libraries, Negative N. NA 3918); *p. 204:* Cedar house, Dundas Island, British Columbia (courtesy of Chris Wooley); *p. 209:* Native fashion show, Prince George, British Columbia (courtesy of Chris Wooley).

Native Peoples of Alaska: *p. 216:* Chief Shake's House at Wrangell, about the turn of the twentieth century; *p. 217:* Contemporary Alaska Native tribes; *p. 218:* Major languages of Alaska Natives (courtesy of Alaska Native Language Center); *p. 223:* Inuit children, Barrow, Alaska (courtesy of Tessa Macintosh); *p. 233:* William L. Hensley.

Native Peoples of Oklahoma: *p. 239:* Contemporary Oklahoma Indian tribes. (courtesy of Duane Champagne); *p.241:* Indian Territory, removal to 1855. Reprinted from *Atlas of American Indian Affairs*, by Francis Paul Prucha, by permission of the University of Nebraska Press. Copyright 1990 by the University of Nebraska Press); *p. 242:* Indian Territory, 1855–66 Reprinted from *Atlas of American Indian Affairs*, by Francis Paul Prucha, by permission of the University of Nebraska Press. Copyright 1990 by the University of Nebraska Press); *p. 245:* Indian Territory, 1866–89. Reprinted from *Atlas of American Indian Affairs*, by Francis Paul Prucha, by permission of the University of Nebraska Press. Copyright 1990 by the University of Nebraska Press); *p.256:* Ponca Indian "Afternoon Dance" near Ponca City, Oklahoma (courtesy of Stephen Lehmer); *p. 263:* Black Kettle (courtesy of the Colorado Historical Society); *p. 264:* William W. Keeler (courtesy of Corprate Archives, Phillips Petroleum); *p. 266:* Lone Wolf (courtesy of Amon Carter Museum, Forth Worth, Texas); *p. 267:* Wilma P. Mankiller (courtesy of Cherokee Nation Communications); *p. 268:* Roman Nose (courtesy of the Kansas State Historical Society); *p. 269:* John Ross.

Native Peoples of the Plateau, Great Basin, and Rocky Mountains: *p. 274:* Contemporary Rocky Mountain Indian tribes; *p. 281:* The prophet Wovoka (seated) in his later years (courtesy of the Nevada State Historical Society); *p. 290:* Nii'eihii No'eiihi', or the Eagle Drum, is the official ceremonial and social drum group of the Arapaho tribe. Their presence is required at any large gathering. Seated front left is Helen Cedartree, a noted elder of the tribe. Taken at the annual Ethete (Wyoming) Celebration Pow-wow (courtesy of Sara Wiles); *p. 292:* Ben Goggles was in his 70s when he died in 1978. He was the father of ten daughters and the head of the Arapaho Sun Dance for many years. His Arapaho name was Hoonino' or Quill (courtesy of Sara Wiles); *p. 293:* Cleone Thunder was born in April 1903 and has lived most of her life in the Wyoming. Her Arapaho name, Hiisei Nouuceh, or Woman Running out of the Lodge, was given to her by her father. It commemorates a brave Crow woman who ran from her tipi holding a baby and faced attacking Arapaho warriors (courtesy of Sara Wiles); *p. 295:* Joseph; *p. 299:* Washakie (courtesy of the Smithsonian Institution).

Native Peoples of California: *p. 302:* Contemporary California Indian tribes; *p. 304:* The traditional tribal areas of the Indians of California; *p. 313:* Spring Rancheria (Cahuilla), c. 1886 (courtesy of Historic Resource Department, Riverside, California); *p. 315:* Sensioni Cibimoat, basket maker from Warner's Ranch, 1903 (courtesy of Los Angeles City Library); *p. 316:* Gabrielino traditional homes, Mission San Gabriel (courtesy of Los Angeles City Library); *p. 318:* Ramona Lugu, Cahuilla, at her home (courtesy of Los Angeles City Library); *p. 322:* Powwow singers, Alcatraz Island, 1969 (courtesy of Stephen Lehmer); *p. 323:* Sign pointing to Pit River Nation, 1973 (courtesy of Stephen Lehmer); *p. 326:* Captain Jack.

The Canadian Natives: *p. 337:* Indian treaty area in Canada. Maps by Brian McMillan from *Native Peoples and Cultures of Canada* by Alan D. McMillan, 1988, published by Douglas & McIntyre. Reprinted by permission; *p. 342:* Indians demonstrating in the early 1960s; *p. 344:* Dene school children, Northwest Territory; *p. 348:* Inuit hunting seals on the ice. The Inuit and their way of life, as observed by Frobisher's men on Baffin Island in 1576–78. Engravings, after drawings by Captain G.F. Lyon on Melville Peninsula in 1822, published in W.E. Parry, *Journal of a second voyage for the discovery of a North-west Passage*, London, 1824 (courtesy of the American Heritage Press); *p. 352:* Inuit meeting to discuss hamlet business, Cape Dorset, Northwest Territory (courtesy D. Mandin, NT government); *p. 358:* Chipewyan Indian houses, Smith Landing, Fort Smith; *p. 371:* Cree woman sewing; *p. 376:* Sally Karatak at museum in traditional Inuit beaded dress. Yellowknife, Northwest Territory (courtesy Tessa Macintosh, NT government); *p. 382:* Crowfoot; *p. 388:* Leonard Stephen Marchand; *p. 392:* Poundmaker.

Native North American Languages: *p. 402:* Map of Native North American Language, Families, and Phyla. From *International Encyclopedia of Linguistics,* volume 3, edited by William Bright. Copyright 1992 by Oxford University Press, Inc. Reprinted by permission; *p. 406:* Map of Athabaskan migrations from the sub-Arctic to the Southwest (courtesy of Oxford University Press); *p. 412:* Examples of Plains sign language; *p. 416:* Nootka text (courtesy of Yale University); *p.435:* Cherokee syllabary (mistakenly called "Alphabet"). From *Beginning Cherokee,* by Ruth Bradley Holmes and Betty Sharp Smith, 2d ed. Norman: University of Oklahoma Press, 1977; *p. 437:* Example of Cherokee in Sequoyah's syllabary, in phonetic transcription, and in translation. From *Beginning Cherokee,* by Ruth Bradley Holmes and Betty Sharp Smith, 2d ed. Norman: University of Oklahoma Press, 1977; *p. 438.* The Inuit people of the Arctic try to preserve their language by providing reading material in Inuit for their young people (courtesy of Inuit Broadcasting Corporation).

Religion: *p. 443:* Ceremonies at the death of a chief or of priests. Drawing by Le Moyne, engraving from T. de Bry, *America,* part II, 1591, plate XL (courtesy of American Heritage Press); *p. 450:* Native leaders often consulted shamans on important issues. Drawing by Le Moyne, engraving from T. de Bry, *America,* Part II, 1591, plate XI (courtesy of American Heritage Press); *p. 461:* The humpback flute player Kokopelli, with horned serpent (Utah) (courtesy of Linda Connor); *p. 467:* Arapaho Ghost Dance (courtesy of Smithsonian Institution); *p. 474:* A Sun Dance at Pine Ridge, a Sioux reservation in southern South Dakota (courtesy of Stephen Lehmer); *p. 477:* Apache Crown Dance, White Mountain Apache Reservation, Whiteriver, Arizona, 1971. This traditional puberty rite is performed to this day, blessing the participant with a prosperous future (courtesy of Stephen Lehmer); *p. 484:* Baptism of Paiute Indians (courtesy of Smithsonian Institution); *p. 486:* Native American revitalization movements; *p. 489:* John Wilson introduced many elements of Christianity into the peyote religion. His version is the generally recognized version of the religion today (courtesy of the Museum of the American Indian, Smithsonian Institution); *p. 490:* Quanah Parker, Comanche leader who greatly facilitated the spread of the peyote religion among the Plains Indians during the 1880s and 1890s ; *p. 498:* Revival of the Ghost Dance, May 1974 (courtesy of Richard Erdoes); *p. 507:* Reconstructed Iroquois longhouse in Brantford, Ontario. A False Face mask grimaces in the foreground; *p. 523:* Wovoka (courtesy of the Nevada State Historical Society.

Health: *p. 527: Mode of Treating the Sick.* Drawing by Le Moyne, engraving from T. de Bry, *America,* part II (courtesy of American Heritage Press.; *p. 803 :* Plains medicine lodge. The central figure, apparently the medicine man, holds a pipe in his right hand and the patient's wrist in the other, as if taking the pulse. From "Life of an Indian," *Harper's Illustrated Weekly,* June 20, 1868. From *American Indian Medicine,* by Virgil J. Vogel. Copyright © 1970,

University of Oklahoma Press; *p. 533:* Medicine man ministering to a patient. Notice the bowl and pestle for mixing medicines. The medicine man is shaking a gourd rattle and may be singing a medicine song. From *History, Condition and Prospect of the Indian Tribes,* by Henry R. Schoolcraft (courtesy of Chicago Historical Society); *p. 537:* May apple (Podophyllum peltatum L.) American Indian purgative. From *American Indian Medicine*, by Virgil J. Vogel. Copyright © 1970, University of Oklahoma Press.; *p. 542:* Flowering dogwood (**Cornus florida** L.). American Indian febrifuge (fever reducing agent). From *American Indian Medicine,* by Virgil J. Vogel. Copyright © 1970. University of Oklahoma Press.

Arts: *p. 551:* Petroglyph, Galisteo, New Mexico, 1991 (courtesy of Linda Connor); *p 552:* New Mexico petroglyph (courtesy of Linda Connor); *p. 555:* Carving of Hopi kachina (courtesy of Owen Seumptewa); *p. 557:* Decorative elements of Hopi architecture. Detail from photo by Owen Seumptewa; *p. 564:* Indian artist Norval Morrisseau at work; *p. 566:* Watercolor of Southwestern Indian children by Earl Sisto for 1992 UCLA Indian Child Welfare Conference; *p. 571:* Excerpt from Creek Gar Dance with leader-chorus responses and alternation of words and vocables (courtesy of Charlotte Heth); *p. 573:* Plains rawhide drum, played by several men simultaneously (courtesy of Charlotte Heth); *p. 574:* Peter Garcia, drummer, at San Juan Pueblo Yellow Corn Dance (courtesy of Charlotte Heth); *p. 576:* Cloud Dance, San Juan Pueblo. Men are playing gourd rattles (courtesy of Charlotte Heth); *p. 577:* Northern Plains Traditional dancer at Red Earth, Oklahoma City, Oklahoma (courtesy of Charlotte Heth); *p. 579:* Cheyenne children playing hand games at Red Earth, Oklahoma City, Oklahoma (courtesy of Charlotte Heth); *p. 592:* Excerpt from Forty-nine Dance song, "One-Eyed Ford," with English words and vocables (courtesy of Charlotte Heth); *p. 594:* Kwakiutl totem poles at Alert Bay (circa 1910); *p. 595:* Crow beaded mirror with case, Montana, circa 1880 (courtesy of the Philbrook Art Center, Tulsa, Oklahoma); *p. 598:* Navajo sandpainting rug woven by Altnabah. Early twentieth century. Museum of Northern Arizona, object number E3716 (courtesy of Museum of Northern Arizona, Route 4, Box 720, Flagstaff, Arizona 86001, photo by

Anthony Richardson); *p. 599:* Masked dancers participating in a Kwakiutl winter ceremonial; *p. 603:* Maria Martinez, potter of San Ildefonso Pueblo, New Mexico, and her blackware designs, 1940s (courtesy of the Museum of New Mexico—Palace of the Governors); *p. 604: Agents of Oppression.* Diego Romero, contemporary artist/potter. This bowl combines a blend of traditional Mimbres (A.D. 500–1100) pottery with a concern for contemporary Native American issues. Romero is a graduate of the Institute of American Indian Arts, Santa Fe, New Mexico, and received the Master of Fine Arts degree from the University of California, Los Angeles (courtesy of Diego Romero); *p. 608:* Nora Naranjo-Morse, *Pearlene Teaching Her Cousins Poker*, 1987. Mixed media (courtesy of Nora Naranjo-Morse); *p. 609:* Paul Apodaca; *p. 622:* R. Carlos Nakai (photo by John Running); *p. 624:* Kevin Redstar; *p. 628:* Bert D. Seabourn.

Native American Literature: *p. 667:* Early American Indians often recorded histories and stories on rocks and cliffs at sacred sites. The above petroglyphs were found in San Gabriel Canyon in Southern California (courtesy of the Los Angeles Public Library); *p. 669:* Stories and legends were often re-enacted through dances. Here the American Indian Dance Theatre performs an Eagle Dance (courtesy of Hanay Geiogamah); *p. 670:* Northwest Coast dancers embodied spiritual beings and re-enacted creation histories and traditional stories (courtesy of Hanay Geiogamah); *p. 682:* Sherman Alexie; *p. 683:* Paula Gunn Allen (photo by Tama Rothchild); *p. 684:* Joseph Bruchac (photo by Martin Benjamin); *p. 686:* Elizabeth Cook-Lynn (photo by Carolyn Forbes); *p. 688:* Joy Harjo (photo by Robyn Stoutenburg); *p. 696:* John Rollin Ridge; *p. 698:* Mary TallMountain.

Media: *p. 703:* Fancy Shawl Dance. A highlight of the American Indian Dance Theatre performance is the Women's Fancy Shawl Dance, in which female members of the company exhibit their grace and virtuousity as they spin around the stage, displaying intricate dance steps while twirling colorful shawls to the beat of the drum (courtesy of Hanay Geiogamah); *p. 704:* Southern Men's Traditional Dance. Morgan Tosee, a member of the Comanche tribe of Oklahoma, is a champion Southern Men's Traditional dancer with the American Indian Dance Theatre (courtesy of Hanay Geiogamah); *p. 709* (Left to right) Chester Mahooty, an elder of the Zuni tribe of New Mexico, Morgan Tosee, a member of the Comanche tribe of Oklahoma, and Ramona Roach, a Navajo tribe member from New Mexico, are part of the cast of all-Native American dancers and musicians with the American Indian Dance Theatre (courtesy of Hanay Geiogamah); *p. 714:* Plains Indians who played roles in Hollywood movies take a break on the rollercoaster ride, Long Beach, California, 1930s (courtesy of the Los Angeles Public Library); *p. 715:* Urban Indian picketing Warner Brothers in the making of the movie *They Died with Their Boots On* (courtesy of the Los Angeles Public Library); *p. 717:* Will Sampson (Creek) and Jack Nicholson starred in the hit movie *One Flew over the Cuckoo's Nest* (1975) Copyright 1975 The Saul Zaentz Company. All rights reserved; *p. 726:* A scene from the play *Dry Lips Oughta Move to Kapuskasing* (1989) by Tomson Highway. Native Earth Performing Arts, Inc., Toronto, Ontario, Canada; *p. 732:* Hanay Geiogamah; *p. 738:* Gary Robinson; *p. 739:* Will Sampson (courtesy of the Saul Zaentz Company. All rights reserved); *p. 740:* Chris Spotted Eagle (photo by Allen Beaulieu).

Afterword

Suzan Shown Harjo

For Native Peoples in America, this is a great time to be alive. We are the children of cultural magnificence; the parents of the visions and dreams of our ancestors. We are the modern evidence of our ancient continuums.

In these extraordinary times, even the most ordinary among us have exceptional opportunities within our reach. The best of us hold the key to healing our quarter of Mother Earth. The worst of us have the comfort of traditions and values that hold the key to personal healing.

An increasing number of those we choose to represent us or to follow embody those qualities most prized in the Indian world—courage, compassion, generosity, kindliness, humility, clarity, and joyousness.

More often than not, our own leaders are in control of decisions affecting our lives. We are returning to our time-tested models of functional leadership, developing good following skills, and inviting the reluctant to pony up and share the burden of being a ringleader.

We are becoming wise enough to know that government—anyone's government—is only one place to find leadership, and the last that should control our religions, philosophies, arts, or freedom.

Do we have bad men and women among us? Of course. It should neither surprise nor discourage us that we have people who have given up on our future, whose vision is clouded by convenience and measured in minutes, rather than generations. It is for those who lead nowhere and astray, who market our sovereignty as legal loopholes, who pimp our religions, who warm at the edges of foreign fires, that our grandmothers taught us to say, "poor, pitiful ones."

Are there still those who covet our countries and our very souls? Without doubt. The issues in 1492 were gold, real estate, and religion. They remain unchanged in today's culturally deprived, quick-fix society.

Prophesies revealed long ago are being realized, and non-Indians these days do not ignore or discount modern Indian predictions as readily as did their predecessors. There simply is an insufficient number of Americans who believe that we should be outlaws for the crimes of defending and worshipping on sacred ground to sustain the antiquated and mean-spirited laws that exist. The law of the land is changing to accord respect for this land and for those who know her best.

The ground is shifting because we have said, "Enough is enough." We, the people our ancestors made us—the ones they lived and died for and willed incalculable riches that we do not have the right to squander or dishonor—we are the ones who are shaping public opinion and new policies to resolve negative conditions.

When we articulate the problem, the solution, and our priorities, we often startle ourselves with our own ability to achieve our goals.

At this time, under new laws that we have crafted, our relatives and sacred objects are returning home from museums and educational institutions nationwide. We have the privilege of settling the spirits. For many of our ancestors of the not-so-distant past, commemorating and mourning ceremonies were a luxury in life on the run. We today are mourning for them and for ourselves, learning the mighty power of grief, using ceremonies that honor the dead and revitalize the living.

We today are celebrating the recovery of much of our history. We are greeting sacred, living beings who have been "museum pieces" during all our lifetimes, honored in our memories and customs, but never seen in their context by anyone living. With their return to the Native Peoples who have the collective knowledge and wisdom to feed and care for them properly comes information about yesterday and tomorrow—how to reconcile the past, prepare for the future, avoid the voices of distraction.

This is the spiritual and tangible equivalent of the buffalo coming back.

They bring strength over a long journey, confidence in the longer one ahead. They fill the heart with joy and give assurance as real as a healthy birth. We are so fortunate to be the ones here at this place and moment.

This is a good day to live.

Suzan Shown Harjo is president of the Morning Star Institute in Washington, D.C.

This piece first appeared in *Native Peoples*, Winter, 1994. Reprinted by permission of the publisher and the author.